THE RESPONSE TO ALLEN GINSBERG 1926–1994

Visit to Southern Folklore Center, Oxford, Miss.
April 19, 1987.

Allen Ginsberg

THE RESPONSE TO ALLEN GINSBERG 1926–1994

A Bibliography of Secondary Sources

BILL MORGAN

With a Foreword by Allen Ginsberg

Bibliographies and Indexes in American Literature,
Number 23

GREENWOOD PRESS
Westport, Connecticut • London

Library of Congress Cataloging–in–Publication Data

Morgan, Bill.
    The response to Allen Ginsberg, 1926–1994 : a bibliography of
secondary sources / Bill Morgan : with a foreword by Allen Ginsberg.
        p.   cm.—(Bibliographies and indexes in American literature,
    ISSN 0742–6860   ;   no. 23)
    Includes indexes.
    ISBN 0–313–29536–0 (alk. paper)
    1. Ginsberg, Allen, 1926–   —Criticism and interpretation—
Bibliography.   I. Title.   II. Series.
Z8342.5.M66   1996
[PS3513.I74]
811′.54—dc20   95–26449

British Library Cataloguing in Publication Data is available.

Library of Congress Catalog Card Number: 95–26449
ISBN: 0–313–29536–0
ISSN: 0742–6860

First published in 1996

Greenwood Press, 88 Post Road West, Westport, CT 06881
An imprint of Greenwood Publishing Group, Inc.

Printed in the United States of America

The paper used in this book complies with the
Permanent Paper Standard issued by the National
Information Standards Organization (Z39.48–1984).

10 9 8 7 6 5 4 3 2 1

For Judy

affezionato angelo

Contents

Foreword

Mr. Morgan has spent over a decade & half on my publications tracking down innumerable bibliographic items from encyclopedic Italian tomes to Chinese minutiae in 42 languages. Part of my own work the last four decades has been correspondence with translators on various continents answering textual questions, formulating footnotes so that American localisms be understood in say Albanian or Urdu. Mr. Morgan's also fashioned a chronological accounting of reviews & articles in USA & abroad. This has been a mountain of work for him, and I'm grateful for his devotion to the task & meticulous persistence for so long a time --

As I've transferred my Archives (which includes copies of most items cataloged here) to Stanford University I'm triply grateful for this catalogue of translations and critiques, as, thru Mr. Morgan's labors, the physical items are also catalogued and retrievable, which makes assemblage to forthcoming volumes of *Selected Literary Essays, Selected Interviews & Selected Letters* a rational task.

I hope scholars present & future will appreciate & enjoy the conscious effort that's been put into the enormity of this & Volume I of Morgan's descriptive Bibliography of my own work, and that it will be serviceable as well in exploring the literary-cultural renaissance currently known as the Beat Generation, a phenomenon which seems more significant even in these millennial 1990's than the mid-Century 40's & 50's of original appearance.

Allen Ginsberg
October 11, 1995

Acknowledgments

What could be more obvious than the need for a special note of thanks to Allen Ginsberg. Without unlimited access to his massive archive this bibliography could never have been completed. His fabled generosity is evident by these results. Only his penchant for saving each and every press clipping over the past half century has enabled the compiler to collate this volume. Attempting a secondary bibliography without access to this archive would have been futile. For that reason, Stanford University Library must be thanked for placing this archive in their permanent collection, thus enabling future students and scholars to locate many of the items listed here.

Special thanks are extended to my wife, who patiently suffered through years of visits to out-of-the-way bookshops and libraries and who never complained about the pile of newsprint chips left behind on the living room floor. Her enthusiasm and faith made all that follows possible.

Bob Rosenthal deserves grateful treatment in heaven for his steadfast loyalty to this fifteen-year project. His role as Allen Ginsberg's secretary gives him more knowledge about the origin of materials listed here than even Allen himself, and he never hesitated in sharing that knowledge with me. Jack Hagstrom, friend and bibliographer, helped with many problems of technique and description, a perfect foil for my questions. His efforts helped put order to the chaos.

Collective praise to Allen Ginsberg's staff over many years (Dave Breithaupt, Althea Crawford, Jacqueline Gens, David Greenberg, Peter Hale, Helena Hughes, Juanita Lieberman, Gina Pellicano, Ben Schafer, Rani Singh, Victoria Smart, Vicki Stanbury), the staff at Stanford University Libraries (Margaret Kimball, Linda Long, William McPheron, Steven Mandeville-Gamble, David Sullivan), and the staff at Columbia University Libraries (John Albrey, Jean Ashton, Mimi Bowling, Bernard Crystal, Rudolph Ellenbogen, Patrick Lawlor, Kenneth A. Lohf, Kevin O'Connor, Henry Rowen, Ellen Scaruffi, Allison Scott, Jane Siegel, Marvin Taylor, Brad Westbrook, Hugh Wilburn). Thanks to the Greenwood Press and editor, George F. Butler, for guidance along the way.

Since this bibliography is a companion and an extension of *The Works Of Allen Ginsberg 1941-1994: A Descriptive Bibliography* published in 1995 by Greenwood Press, I refer interested scholars to the complete list of acknowledgments listed there. To reproduce those five pages of names here would be a pleasure but unfortunately not within our paging allocation. Their help is doubly appreciated.

Frequent reference was made to George Dowden, *A Bibliography of Works by Allen Ginsberg,* published by City Lights, 1971, and to Michelle P. Kraus, *Allen Ginsberg: An Annotated Bibliography, 1969-1977,* published by Scarecrow Press, 1980. Both of these were very important checklists of Ginsberg's earlier works and made this researcher's work much easier.

In addition, many others have helped over the past year to put final touches on research here assembled. Heartfelt thanks to: Rod Anstee, Jewish National and University Library (Libby Kahane), Neal Neches, Ron Patterson, Stephen Ronan, Peterjon Skelt, and Ron Whitehead. And finally, thanks to all those thousands of people who have written about and reported on Allen Ginsberg over the past 50 years; their work is herein detailed.

Introduction

Allen Ginsberg once asked what is the use of a bibliography like this? Too long for brief classroom reports, too detailed for casual reference seekers, too comprehensive for all but the most scholarly purposes. One writer chronicling the 1960s was looking for a particular article on Allen's trip to India, another writer was looking for all references to Allen's relationship with his father, and still another researcher was looking for reviews of *Howl*. Allen, himself, finds the section on translations useful, helping him to keep track of the countless translations of his poems into 32 different languages. He is always happy to find a new one to add to the list. For each person, the bibliography was useful as a single source to begin the searches. It never replaced the articles they were looking for, but it did define and limit the field of needed articles. The section devoted to a bibliography of biographical and critical articles reads like a biography in itself. It provides readers with a way to examine the contemporary media reaction to the work and life of Allen Ginsberg. By just reading through the titles of the articles about Allen, you can begin to understand how powerful and far-reaching his influence has been. These articles chronicle the constantly changing public opinions of this celebrated poet, a folk hero and cultural icon for more than a generation. From article titles like "The Know-Nothing Bohemians" to "Playing Carnegie Hall With A 'Howl'" the list flows from shock to adulation, ebbing and resurging over the years with quite a few reminders that "The Beat Goes On."

The first section of this bibliography is a complete, comprehensive guide to the foreign language translations of the work of Allen Ginsberg. The second section is a comprehensive history of all writings about Allen Ginsberg. These writings may be biographical in content, may contain quotes by Ginsberg, may be entire interviews, book reviews of his works, or perhaps general literary criticism which mentions his contribution to the craft of poetry. I have excluded a few items that merely mention Ginsberg and have little scholarly value. Items omitted include such things as announcements of readings and calendar listings lacking additional background information about Ginsberg. Also excluded are most reviews of books by other authors which mention Ginsberg and reviews of anthologies which only enumerate Ginsberg's contributions. There are a few exceptions to this rule. For example, reviews of biographies about Allen Ginsberg commonly critique Ginsberg himself and therefore are included. Also excluded from this section are the introductions, biographical essays, and critical materials contained in Ginsberg's own books and translations. Many of these contain important writings about Ginsberg and should not be overlooked, but these books are listed in other sections of the bibliography and would be repetitious here. It must also be noted that all of Ginsberg's writings are in some way autobiographical in themselves, should be treated as primary resources, and are all listed in the earlier volume of this bibliography. Poems about Allen Ginsberg and works of fiction are generally excluded. This restriction includes the novels of Jack Kerouac and John Clellon Holmes containing characters modeled upon Ginsberg.

Translations are arranged by language. Within each language they are further divided into chronological sections of Books, Anthologies, Periodicals, and Miscellaneous Publications. Due to a lack of periodical indexes for many languages, this section relies heavily on material gathered by Ginsberg on his worldwide trips. Many national libraries helped with exhaustive searchers of their collections. For example, Romania and Japan responded to my queries with long lists of periodical appearances, many previously unknown to us. Some other countries, such as China, were unable to provide this help, and as a result those sections may not be as adequately documented. Many translations were published in pirated editions, especially in Eastern European countries. These have been difficult to track down, but are identified where known. The compiler has made every effort to be complete, but in some cases there will be missing entries, and we would welcome any information concerning such items. Transliterations were made from non-Roman alphabets in most cases following the ALA-LC Romanization Tables.

Section headings in this volume are labeled by the letters 'H' and 'J'. Thus these sections follow the 'A' through 'G' sections found in the earlier volume of this comprehensive bibliography, *The Works of Allen Ginsberg 1941-1994: A Descriptive Bibliography*. A section headed with the letter 'I' was intentionally omitted, this being standard practice in order to avoid any confusion with the numeral '1'.

The second section of this volume draws together all publications containing material written about Allen Ginsberg and his work. This section includes interviews, biographical works as well as book reviews and general literary criticism. All of these items are placed chronologically to form a bio-bibliography of the poet. Question-and-answer-formatted interviews are identified as "interview format" here, while articles that quote out of context from interviews are referred to by the amount of material quoted, i.e., "quoted briefly" or "quoted at length." Reprintings of articles are noted where known. Since wire service articles are frequently edited differently depending upon individual publisher's requirements, each item is placed chronologically. Chronological order always prevails. Each year is divided into a periodical section followed by a book section. Descriptions are based upon the compiler's examination of the items. Throughout the text "AG" refers to Allen Ginsberg. Notes are given after a citation where necessary.

Items not seen by the compiler are identified throughout the bibliography with an asterisk (*). In many cases the item was viewed only as a clipping in Ginsberg's archive, and we were at the mercy of the person who labeled the clipping. For example, a clipping may have come from the *Beaver County Times* and dated June 24, 1968 by the person sending the clipping to Ginsberg. Without a page number it was impossible to verify some of these citations using interlibrary loan resources. If the date were incorrect, it would stand as such here. Any citation without a page number means that the compiler has seen the clipping but has not located a copy of the entire newspaper. Occasionally the various editions of a newspaper have played havoc with research. A story which appears in the local edition of a New York newspaper may have been left out of the microfilmed national edition. Where positive identification of an edition has been found, a note will guide the reader to the correct source. Dates of publication and page numbers have been verified with publishers whenever possible.

Items with month-only or seasonal dates are listed as if published on the first day of the month or season unless the publisher could supply a more accurate or official publication date, (i.e., Winter [Dec. 1962] 1963). In those cases the dates are included within square brackets. Therefore a date of April 1985 is filed as if it appeared on April 1, 1985, and Fall 1970 is filed as if appeared on Sept. 22, 1970. Items with only a year designation are listed as if the publication date were after December 31 of that year. Where two periodicals have the same date, the order is alphabetical by periodical title. Publication dates which the compiler has found to be different from or more exact than the issue date on the periodical are given in square brackets and arranged according to that date.

In a very few instances items with assigned numbers were added or deleted between the time indexing was completed and the time the type was set. In the case of an added citation, the number of the previous entry was used with the addition of the letter 'x'. For example, if a citation was added between items numbered J923 and J924, the new citation would be assigned the number J923x. If an item has been deleted, a note beside that number stating that it has been "intentionally omitted" has been inserted.

Two indexes are included. The poem titles index lists the title of each poem as it appears in Ginsberg's *Collected Poems* followed by the list of translations of that poem. Poems are identified by first line only when they lack a title. When the articles *a, an,* or *the* appear as the first word of a title, they are ignored, as standard library practice dictates.

The general index includes authors, titles, and translators from both sections. Following a periodical's title is the place of publication to help distinguish one periodical from another. Reference is always to the item number within the bibliography.

Bill Morgan

New York City, September 12, 1995

BIBLIOGRAPHY

H

Translations of Writings by Allen Ginsberg

AFRIKAANS

Periodicals:

H1   [3 poems] *Tydskrif Vir Letterkunde,* vol. 3, no. 1 (Feb. 1965) pp. 85-88.
Translation, by Marié Blomérus: Lied [Song] — Agter Die Werklike [In Back Of
the Real] — Affodil [An Asphodel]

H2   [2 poems] *Tydskrif Vir Letterkunde,* vol. 4, no. 1 (Feb. 1966) pp. 11-12.
Translation, by Marié Blomérus: Blou Engel [Blue Angel] — Vreemde Nuwe
Huis In Berkeley [A Strange New Cottage In Berkeley]

ALBANIAN

Periodicals:

H3   [5 poems] *Jehona,* vol. 24, no. 3/4 (May 20, 1986) pp. 46-51.
Translation, by Resul Shabani: Lotë [Afternoon Seattle (excerpt)] — Për Veprat E
Barouzit [On Burroughs' Work] — Rrëmujë [A Desolation] — Kadish
[Kaddish (excerpt)] — Supermarketi Në Kaliforni [A Supermarket In
California]

H4*   [2 poems] *Hoto Ere* (Sept. 15, 1986) p. 20.
Translation of: Psalmi I [Psalm I] — Mandalla [Mandalla]

H5   [2 poems] *Fjala,* vol. 19, no. 18 (Oct. 15, 1986) pp. 8-9.
Translation by Fadil Bajraj: Ulurimë [Howl]
Translation by Abdullah Konushevci: Amerike [America]

H6   [11 poems] *Jehona,* vol. 24, no. 7 (Nov. 20, 1986) pp. 13-23.
Translation by Abdullah Konushevci: Kënga [Song] — Qofshin Bekuar Muzat
[Blessed Be the Muses] — Metafizika [Metaphysics] — Dridhërima E Perdes
[The Trembling Of the Veil] — Poezi Mbi Amerikën [A Poem On America] —
Lotët [Afternoon Seattle (excerpt)] — Ata Dy [Those Two] — Shkruar Në
Endrrën Time Nga V.C. Uuiljemsi [Written In My Dream By W.C. Williams]
— Ruhr-Gebiet [Ruhr-Gebiet] — Guru [Guru] — Evropë! Evropë! [Europe!
Europe!]

H7*   [poem] *Fjala,* vol. 20, no. 4 (Feb. 15, 1987)
Translation by Fadil Bajraj: [A Supermarket In California]

H8*   [poem] *Zeri I Rinisë,* no. 1241 (Feb. 20, 1988)
Translation by Fadil Bajraj: Kenga [Song]

H9*   [poem] *Bota E Re,* vol. 20, no. 9 (May 1, 1988)
Translation by Fadil Bajraj: Amerike [America]

H10*   [poem] *Zeri I Rinisë,* no. 1258-1259 (June 18-25, 1988)
Translation by Fadil Bajraj: Amerike [America]
Translation by Abdullah Konushevci: Amerike [America]

H11*   [poem]. *Zeri I Rinisë,* no. 1267-1268 (Aug. 8, 1988) p. 30.
Translation by Fadil Bajraj: Elegji Për Ce Gevarën [Elegy Ché Guévara]

H12   [4 poems] *Koha,* vol. 11, no. 1-2 (1989) pp. 106-108.
Translation by Fadil Bajraj: Kral Malajes [Kral Majales] — Kush [Who] — Duke
E Mbrojtur [Defending the Faith] — Elegji Për Çe Gevarën [Elegy Ché
Guévara]

H13*   [10 poems] *Jeta E Re,* vol. 62, no. 5 (1991)
Translation by Fadil Bajraj: [Cafe In Warsaw — It's All So Brief — Why I
Meditate — Maturity — Hadda Be Playing On the Jukebox — Why Is God
Love, Jack? — Malest Cornifici Tuo Catullo — Arguments — Prophecy —
Land O' Lakes, Wisc.]

H14*   [poem]. *Zeri I Rinisë* (Nov. 19, 1994) p. 39.
Translation by Fadil Bajraj: Hulumtimi [Research]

ARABIC

Anthologies:

H15   Sayegh, Tawfig (ed.). *[Fifty Poems From Contemporary American Poetry].*
Beirut, Lebanon: Dar El-Yaqza [in association with Franklin Publications, Inc.,
New York, NY], 1963.
Translation by Tawfig Sayegh: [Sunflower Sutra]

Periodicals:

H16   [poem] *UNESCO Courier* [Arabic edition] no. 11 (Nov. 1982) pp. 11-12.
Translation of: [Plutonian Ode (excerpt)]

H17*   [poem]. *Al-Karmel Magazine,* no. 43 (1992) pp. 134-144.
Translation of: [Howl]

ARMENIAN

Periodicals:

H18   [5 poems]. *Garun,* no. 176, no. 8 (1981) pp. 70-73.
Translation by Artem Harutc Yunyan: Sunflower Sutra ‖ Arevacalki Sutra — A
Supermarket In California ‖ Kaliforniayi Supermarkete — Scribble — After
Dead Souls — My Sad Self ‖ Im Txur Ese

BENGALI

Periodicals:

H19   [2 poems]. *Uttursuri,* year 10, vol. 1 (Oct.-Dec. 1963) pp. 115-130.
      Translation by Mihir Kumar Gupta: [Howl — Footnote To Howl]

H20   [poem]. *Chinha,* no. 1 (1963) pp. 44-46.
      Translation by Debi Roy: [Kaddish (excerpt)]

H21* [prose and 2 poems]. *Krittibas,* no. 16 (1963) pp. 90-106.
      Translation by Sunil Gangopadhya: [*Indian Journals* (excerpts in English only)
      — Mescaline — At Apollinaire's Grave]

H22* [poem]. *PA,* vol. 2 (Fall [1985]) pp. 144-173.
      Translation by Malay Roychoudhuri: [Kaddish]

H22X [poem]. *Desh Weekly* (July 11, 1992) pp. 32-34.
      Translation by Sunil Ganguley: [After Lalon]

BULGARIAN

Books:

H23   Ginsberg, Allen. *Krila Nad Chernata Shakhta [Selected Poems].* Sofia, Bulgaria:
      Narodna Kultura, 1983.
      Translation by Vladimir Levchev: Voi [Howl, parts 1 & 2] — Edin Supermarket
      V Kaliforniia [A Supermarket In California] — Poslanie [Message] — Siianie
      Ot Vratata Na Prosvetlenite [Sather Gate Illumination] — Slunchogledova Sutra
      [Sunflower Sutra] — Na Lindzi [To Lindsay] — Kadish [Kaddish, parts 1, 3
      and 5] — Poema Raketa [Poem Rocket] — Kum Koi Da Sum Dobup [Who Be
      Kind To] — Amneziakalna Zhazhda Za Slava [Amnesiac Thirst For Fame] —
      Krila Izdignati Nad Chernata Shakhta [Wings Lifted Over the Black Pit] —
      Septembri Po Dzhesorskia Put [September On Jessore Road]

Anthologies:

H24* Mileva, Leda and Popov, Nikolay. *Amerikanski Poeti.* Sofia, Bulgaria: Narodna
      Kultura, 1970, pp. 219-225.
      Translation by Nikolay Popov: Voi [Howl (excerpt)] — Supermarket V
      Kalifornia [A Supermarket In California] — Amerika [America]

Periodicals:

H25* [poem]. *Panorama,* no. 3 (1980) pp. 17-20.
      Translation by Vladimir Filipov: Slunchogledova Sutra [Sunflower Sutra]

H26   [poem]. *UNESCO Courier [Bulgarian edition],* vol. 35, no. 10 (Nov. 1982) pp.
      13-14.
      Translation of: [Plutonian Ode (excerpt)]

H27* [poem]. *Most,* no. 2-3 (1989) pp. 57-59.
      Translation by Liudmila Verikh and Rumen Shomov: Transkriptsia Na Organna
      Muzika [Transcription Of Organ Music]

H28*   [6 poems]. *Plamuk,* no. 7 (1990) pp. 197-202.
Translation by Georgi Gorov: Prorochestvo [Prophecy] — Zashto Krotuvam —
Tezi Dvamata [Those Two On Marine Street] — Sprikhav Chinovnik [Big
Eats] — Napisano V Sunia Mi [Written In My Dream By William Carlos
Williams] — Vsichko E Tolkova Kratko [It's All So Brief]

H29*   [poem]. *Lit. Vestnik,* no. 21 (May 31-June 5, 1993) p. 7.
Translation by Vladimir Levchev: Grafiti V 12-ta Kabinka Na Muzhkata Toaletna
V Letishteto Na Sirakiuz [Graffiti 12th Cubicle Men's Room Syracuse Airport]

H30*   [2 poems]. *Glas,* no. 11 (Spring 1994) pp. 38-40.
Translation by Vladimir Levchev: Esenni Lista [Autumn Leaves] — Po Leilun
[After Lalon]

CATALAN

Books:

H31   Ginsberg, Allen. *Kaddish I Altres Poemes.* Barcelona, Spain: Edicions del Mall,
1987.
Translation by Josep Costa: [Introduction (first appearance here)] — Kaddish ||
Kaddish — Poem Rocket || Poema Coet — Europe! Europe! || Europa! Europa!
— To Lindsay || A Lindsay — Message || Missatge — To Aunt Rose || A La Tia
Rose — At Apollinaire's Grave || Davant La Tomba D'Apollinaire — The Lion
For Real || Un Lleó De Debò — Ignu || Ignu — Death To Van Gogh's Ear! ||
Mori L'Orella De Van Gogh! — Laughing Gas || Gas Exhilarant — Mescaline ||
Mescalina — Lysergic Acid || Àcid Lisèrgic — Magic Psalm || Salm Màgic —
The Reply || La Resposta — The End || Fi

Periodicals:

H32   [poem]. *La Trinchera,* no. 1 (March 1966) p. 6.
Translation by Nicanor Ancoechea: Supermercado De California [A Supermarket
In California]

H33   [poem]. *UNESCO Courier [Catalan edition],* vol. 35, no. 10 (Nov. 1982) pp.
13-14.
Translation of: [Plutonian Ode (excerpt)]

H34*   [4 poems]. *Revista Atlantica,* no. 8 (1994)
Translation by Carlos Edmundo De Ory: Esfinter || Sphincter — La Quinta
Internacional || Fifth Internationale — Cuando La Luz Aparenzca || When the
Light Appears — Mensaje Personal || Personals Ad

CHINESE

Books:

H35   Ginsberg, Allen. *Allen Ginsberg.* Baoding, China: Hebei University Foreign
Language Dept., Feb. 1985. [Level 82]
Translation by Ding Juhua: [Footnote To Howl — Homework — Song — Love
Forgiven — Fourth Floor, Dawn — Spring Fashions — Don't Grow Old

H36   Ginsberg, Allen. *[Kaddish].* Guandong, Canton, China: Flower City Publishing
House, 1991.
Translation by Shaoxiong Zhang: [Improvisation In Beijing — Howl — Footnote
To Howl — A Strange New Cottage In Berkeley — A Supermarket In

California — Sunflower Sutra — Transcription Of Organ Music — Sather Gate Illumination — America — Afternoon Seattle — Tears — Psalm III — Ready To Roll — Kaddish — Magic Psalm — Television Was a Baby Crawling Toward That Deathchamber — Today — Café In Warsaw — Kral Majales — Beginning Of a Poem Of These States — Thoughts Sitting Breathing — What Would You Do If You Lost It? — Yes, And It's Hopeless — Ego Confession — Junk Mail]

Anthologies:

H37   Xiang Xiang (ed.). [*Contemporary American Poetry: A New Visage*]. Taiwan: 1972, pp. 52-68.
Translation, by Xiang Xiang: [Howl]

H38   [*Modern American Poetry, Vol. II*]. Peking, China: Foreign Literature Publishing House, 1985, pp. 511-527.
Translation, by Yihen H. Zhao: [Howl (excerpt) — A Supermarket In California — My Alba — My Sad Self — On Burroughs' Work — Sunset — Who Runs America? — The Warrior]

H39   Lu Yuan (ed.). [*The Neighbors' Flutes*]. China: 1986, pp. 179-184.
Translation by Lu Yuan: [A Supermarket In California — The End]

H40   [*Mok E Tzen Cho: Contemporary American Poetry*]. Kwong Tze, Hunan Province, China: Hunan Province People's Publishing House, 1987, pp. 81-92.
Translation by Zhao Qiong and Dao Zi: [Howl]

H41   Xiaolong, Qiu and others (eds.). [*Masterpieces Of Famous Foreign Poets*]. Shanghai: Shanghai Cultural Publishers, 1987, pp. 113-117.
Translation by Zheng Ming: [Howl (excerpt)]

Periodicals:

H42   [2 poems]. [*Contemporary Foreign Literature*], no. 3 (1981) pp. 153-156.
Translation by Yifan Zhao: [My Alba]
Translation by Yiheng Zhao: [Howl (excerpt)]

H43   [poem]. *UNESCO Courier* [Chinese edition], vol. 35, no. 10 (1983) pp. 13-14.
Translation: [Plutonian Ode (excerpt)]

H44   [2 poems]. [*World Literature*] (Jan. 1985) pp. 291-292.
Translation by Haixin Xu: [Returning To the Country For a Brief Visit — Don't Grow Old]

H45   [poem]. [*Su Que Bao: Poetry Press*] (Nov. 21, 1985) p. 4.
Translation by Zhao Qiong and Dao Zi: [Howl]

H46*   [poem]. *American Literature*, no. 1 (1986)
Translation by Chiao Qiong: [America]

H47   [2 poems]. *Front Line*, no. 1 (May 1987) p. 44.
Translation by Ai Wei Wei: [Surprise Mind — Maturity]

H48   [poem]. *First Line*, no. 4 (March [15], 1988) pp. 94-95.
Translation by Yan Li: [On Cremation Of Chögyam Trungpa]

H49   [poem and 2 drawings]. *First Line*, no. 5 (July 15, 1988)
Translation by Yan Li.

H50   [poem]. *First Line*, no. 13 (April 1991) p. 151.
Translation by Hao Yi Ming: [Maturity]

CZECH

Books:

H51   Ginsberg, Allen. *Vyber Z Basni*. Prague, Czechoslovakia: [a student project from the School of Graphic Arts], 1989.
Translation by Jan Zabrana: Kvileni [Howl] — Ameriko [America] — Tete Ruzene [To Aunt Rose] — Opravdu Lev [The Lion For Real] — Netypicky Pripad [An Atypical Affair] — Ignu [Ignu] — Jablko Noci [The Night-Apple] — Slunecnicova Sutra [Sunflower Sutra] — Kral Majales [Kral Majales]

H52   Ginsberg, Allen. *Allen Ginsberg*. Prague, Czechoslovakia: n.p., 1989.
Translation by Jan Zabrana: Kvileni [Howl] — Ameriko [America] — Slunecnicova Sutra [Sunflower Sutra] — Opravdu Lev [The Lion For Real] — Tete Ruzene [To Aunt Rose] — Ignu [Ignu] — Kral Majales [Kral Majales]

H53   Ginsberg, Allen. *Kvileni*. Prague, Czechoslovakia: Odeon, 1990.
Translation by Jan Zabrana: Divoky Sirotek [Wild Orphan] — Netypicky Pripad [An Atypical Affair] — Jablko Noci [The Night-Apple] — Pribeh Gregory Corsa [Gregory Corso's Story] — Dva Chlapci Sli Do Pohadkove Restaurace [Two Boys Went Into a Diner] — Asfodel [An Asphodel] — Pisen [Song] — Za Realitou [In Back Of the Real] — Milostna Basen Na Tema Z Whitmana [Love Poem On Theme By Whitman] — Kvileni [Howl] — Samoobsluha V Kalifornii [A Supermarket In California] — Transkripce Varhanni Hudby [Transcription Of Organ Music] — Slunecnicova Sutra [Sunflower Sutra] — Ameriko [America] — Ve Skladisti Zavazadel Autobusove Spolecnosti Greyhound [In the Baggage Room At Greyhound] — Osviceni U Satherovy Brany [Sather Gate Illumination] — Basen Raketa [Poem Rocket] — Evropo! Evropo! [Europe! Europe!] — Lindsaymu [To Lindsay] — Vzkaz [Message] — Tete Ruzene [To Aunt Rose] — U Apollinairova Hrobu [At Apollinaire's Grave] — Opravdu Lev [The Lion For Real] — Ignu [Ignu] — Smrt Van Goghovu Uchu! [Death To Van Gogh's Ear] — Kadis [Kaddish] — Kyselina Lysergova [Lysergic Acid] — Konec [The End] — Zmena: Rychlik Kjoto/Tokio [The Change: Kyoto-Tokyo Express] — Labuti Jezero [Swan Lake] — Kral Majales [Kral Majales]

H54   Ginsberg, Allen. *Vylizanej Mozek!* Prague, Czechoslovakia: Vokno, 1991.
Translation by Frantisek Vasek: Na Koho Byt Mily [Who Be Kind To] — Prvni Mejdan U Kena Keseyho S Hell's Angels [First Party At Ken Kesey's With Hell's Angels] — Navsteva Walesu [Wales Visitation] — Zari Na Jessore Road [September On Jessore Road] — Ayerska Skala / Pisen Uluru [Ayers Rock/Uluru Song] — Nemocny Blues [Sickness Blues] — Nestarni [Don't Grow Old] — Vylizanej Mozek! [Birdbrain!] — Blues O Ceste Letadlem [Airplane Blues]
Translation by Lubos Snizek: Pri Hovoru O I-Ting, Koureni Travy, Poslechu Fugs Hrajicich Blakea [Consulting I Ching Smoking Pot Listening To the Fugs Sing Blake] — Elegie Pro Neala Cassadyho [Elegy For Neal Cassady] — Jdi Do Prdele [Kiss Ass] — Na Nealuv Popel [On Neal's Ashes] — Milarepova Chut [Milarepa Taste] — Bitva Mezi Jahvem A Allahem [Jaweh And Allah Battle] — Plutonska Oda [Plutonian Ode] — Ruhr-Gebiet [Ruhr-Gebiet] — Oda Na Selhani [Ode To Failure] — Proc Medituji [Why I Meditate] — Verejna Poezie [A Public Poetry] — Tamty Dva [Those Two] — Dospelost [Maturity] — Improvizace V Pekingu [Improvisation In Beijing] — Napsano W. C. Williamsem V Mem Snu [Written In My Dream By W.C. Williams] — Cteni Basni Po Tu-Iho [Reading Bai Juyi] — Proroctvi [Prophecy]

Translation by Pavla Slaba and Lubos Brozek: Odpadky Pretekajici Popelnice Na Rozpalenem Asfaltu Smacenem Destem [Rain-Wet Asphalt Heat, Garbage Curbed Cans Overflowing] — Zahrady Pameti [Memory Gardens] — Vanocni Darecek [Xmas Gift] — Zpatky Na Venkove Na Kratkou Navstevu [Returning To the Country For a Brief Visit] — Nocni Zablesk [Night Gleam] — Dech Myslenky [Mind Breaths] — Domaci Ukol [Homework]

Translation by Nemo: Prosim Pane [Please Master]

Translation by Martin Machovec: Ano, A Je To Beznadejny [Yes And It's Hopeless] — Prepadeni [Mugging] — Bojujeme S Preludy, Bojujeme S Preludy [Fighting Phantoms Fighting Phantoms] — Svetova Karma [World Karma]

Translation by Jiri Josek: Gospel Vznesenych Pravd [Gospel Noble Truths] — Industrialni Vlny [Industrial Waves] — Bily Rubas [White Shroud] — Cerny Rubas [Black Shroud] — Kosmopolitni Pozdravy [Cosmopolitan Greetings] — Evropa Si Rika: Kdo Vi [Europe, Who Knows?] — Nanao Sakaki [Nanao Sakaki] — Navrat Krale Majales [Return Of Kral Majales]

Anthologies:

H55   *Svetova Literatura 10, 1956-1965.* Prague, Czechoslovakia: Odeon Nakladatelstvi Krasne Literatury A Umeni, 1966, pp. 206-209.
Translation by Jan Zabrana: Opravdu Lev [The Lion For Real] — Tete Ruzene [To Aunt Rose]

H56   Mares, Stanislav and Zabrana, Jan (eds.). *Novi Americti Basnici.* Prague, Czechoslovakia: Klub Pratel Poezi, 1967, pp. 86-98.
Translation by Jan Zabrana: Osviceni U Satherovy Brany [Sather Gate Illumination] — Tete Ruzene [To Aunt Rose] — Milostna Basen Na Tema Z Whitmana [Love Poem On a Theme By Whitman] — Netypicky Pripad [An Atypical Affair] — Jablko Noci [The Night-Apple] — Pribeh Gregoryho Corsa [Gregory Corso's Story] — Dva Chlapci Sli Do Pohadkove Restaurace [Two Boys Went Into a Dream Diner]

H57   Labáth, Jan. *Rozlucka S Vetrom.* Novy Sad, Yugoslavia: Obzor, 1981, pp. 141-148.
Translation by Jan Labath: Samoobsluha V Kalifornii [A Supermarket In California] — Prva Zabava U Kena Keseysa S Anjelmi Pekla [First Party At Ken Kesey's With Hell's Angels] — Opis: Dazd' Na Dasaswamedh [Describe: The Rain On Dasaswamedh Ghat] — Zaznam Sna: 8. Juna 1955 [Dream Record: June 8, 1955]

H58   Pridal, Antonin (ed.). *Horoskop Orloje.* Prague, Czechoslovakia: Odeon, 1987, pp. 205-226.
Translation by Jan Zabrana: Samoobsluh V Kalifornii [A Supermarket In California] — Transkripce Varhanni Hudby [Transcription Of Organ Music] — Ve Skladisti Zavazadel Autobusove Spolecnosti Greyhound [In the Baggage Room At Greyhound] — Pisen [Song] — Za Realitou [In Back Of the Real] — Basen Raketa [Poem Rocket] — Evropo! Evropo! [Europe! Europe!]

H59   Burroughs, William and Ginsberg, Allen. *Teplous / Dopisy O Yage.* Prague, Czechoslovakia: Vydavatelstvi X-Egem, 1991.
Translation by Josef Rauvolf: Dopisy O Yage [Yage Letters] — [blurb by AG about *Queer* on the back cover]

Periodicals:

H60   [poem]. *Literary Noviny,* vol. 14, no. 12 (March 20, 1965) p. 8.
Translation by Jan Zabrana: Labuti Jezero [Swan Lake]

H61   [poem]. *Mlada Fronta,* vol. 21, no. 117 (May 16, 1965) p. 5.
Translation by Jan Zabrana: Labuti Jezero [Swan Lake]

H62   [4 poems]. *Svetova Literatura,* no. 5/6 (1969) pp. 140-149.
Translation by Jan Zabrana: Transkripce Varhanni Hudby [Transcription Of
Organ Music] — Ve Skladisti Zavazadel Greyhoundu [In the Baggage Room
At Greyhound] — Basen Raketa [Poem Rocket] — Kyselina Lysergova
[Lysergic Acid]

H63   [poem]. *Sesity,* no. 30 (April 1969) pp. 9-13.
Translation by Jan Zabrana: Kvileni [Howl]

H64   [poem]. *Vokno Noviny,* no. 14 (April 13, 1990) front cover.
Translation by Frantisek Starek Cunas: Prvni Myslenka, Nejlepsi Myslenka ‖
First Thought, Best Thought

H65   [poem]. *Magazin Dnes + TV,* vol. 4, no. 1 (Oct. 21, 1993) p. 32.
Translation by Josef Rauvolf: Soukromy Inzerat [Personals Ad]

H66   [poem]. *Soho Revue,* vol. 3, no. 11 (Nov. 1993) pp. 22-23.
Translation by Jan Zabrana: Prosím, Pane [Please Master]

H67   [4 poems and 2 drawings]. *Zurnál UP,* no. 3 (Nov. 24, 1993) pp. 2-8.
Translation by Jan Zabrana: Song ‖ Písen — Howl (excerpt) ‖ Kvílení — The
Green Automobile (excerpt) ‖ Zeleny Automobil — Autumn Leaves — [2
drawings]

Miscellaneous:

H68   [program]. *Poesie Allena Ginsberga.* Prague, Czechoslovakia, Sept. 28, 1963.
Translation by Jan Zabrana: Vzkaz [Message] — Lindsaymu [To Lindsay]

DANISH

Books:

H69   Ginsberg, Allen. *Nyt Fra Jorden.* Århus, Denmark: Rhodos, 1969.
Translation by Erik Thygesen: Hyl [Howl] — Fodnote Til Hyl [Footnote To
Howl] — Et Supermarked I Californien [A Supermarket In California] —
Amerika [America] — Kaddish [Kaddish] — Digt Raket [Poem Rocket] —
Løven Virkelig [The Lion For Real] — Lysergsyre [Lysergic Acid] — Om
Burroughs' Vaerk [On Burroughs' Work] — Kaerlighedsdigt Over Tema Af
Whitman [Love Poem On Theme By Whitman] — Saelsomt Nyt Hus I
Berkeley [A Strange New Cottage In Berkeley] — Til En Gammel Digter I
Peru [To an Old Poet In Peru] — Midt I Et Langt Digt Om 'Disse Vore Stater'
[Kansas City To Saint Louis] — Kyoto-Tokio Ekspressen [The Change:
Kyoto-Tokyo Express] — Kral Majales [Kral Majales] — Wichita, Sutra
[Wichita Vortex Sutra]

Anthologies

H70   Thygesen, Erik (ed.). *San Francisco Renaissancen.* Odense, Denmark: Sirius
Forlagt, 1964, pp. 61-75.
Translation by Ib Ørnskov and Erik Thygesen: Hyl [Howl]
Translation by Per Vestergaard: Bag Den Virkelige [In Back Of the Real] —
Amerika [America]

H71* Burroughs, William S. *Junkie Og Uddrag Fra Yage-Brevene.* Copenhagen, Denmark: Stig Vendelkaer, 1966, p. 191.
Translation by Erik Thygesen: Om Burroughs' Vaerk [On Burroughs' Work]

H72 Boesen, Peter and Søndergaard, Vagn (eds.). *Til Maend.* Denmark: Lyrikbogklubben Borgen-Gyldendal, 1980, pp. 18-20.
Translation by Stefan George: Åh Herre [Please Master]

Periodicals:

H73 [poem]. *Vindrosen,* vol. 6, no. 4 (May 1959) pp. 249-257.
Translation by Poul Sørensen: Hylen [Howl]

H74 [poem]. *Politiken* (Jan. 14, 1983) section 2, p. 5.
Translation by Dan Turell: Fader Død [Father Death Blues]

DUTCH

Books:

H75 Ginsberg, Allen. *Proef M'N Tong In Je Oor.* Amsterdam, The Netherlands: De Bezige Bij, 1966. [Series: Literaire Reuzenpocket 188]
Translation by Simon Vinkenoog: Howl [Howl] — Voetnoot Bij Howl [Footnote To Howl] — Zonnebloem Soetra [Sunflower Sutra] — Amerika [America] — Kaddish [Kaddish] — Gedicht Raket [Poem Rocket] — Boodschap [Message] — Dood Aan Van Gogh's Oor! [Death To Van Gogh's Ear!] — Meskaline [Mescaline] — LSD [Lysergic Acid] — Magische Psalm [Magic Psalm] — Het Einde [The End] — Op Het Werk Van Burroughs [On Burroughs' Work] — Liefdesgedicht Op Een Thema Van Whitman [Love Poem On Theme By Whitman] — Een Vreemd Nieuw Buitenhuis In Berkeley [A Strange New Cottage In Berkeley] — Sather Gate Verlichting [Sather Gate Illumination] — Derde Psalm [Psalm III] — Tranen [Tears] — Aan Een Oude Dichter In Peru [To An Old Poet In Peru] — Aantekeningen Gemaakt Bij Het Opnemen Van Howl [liner notes from *Howl,* Fantasy recording] — Aantekeningen Over Jonge Dichters [Notes On Young Poets] — Abstraktie In Poëzie [letter to Emmanuel A. Navaretta] — David Widgery, Gesprekken Met Allen Ginsberg [interview with AG]

H76 Ginsberg, Allen. *De Verandering.* Rotterdam, The Netherlands: Cold Turkey Press, 1973.
Translation by Gerard Belart: TV Was Een Baby Die Naar Die Doodskamer Toekroop [Television Was a Baby Crawling Toward That Deathchamber] — De Verandering: Kyoto-Tokyo [The Change] — Wales Visitatie [Wales Visitation] — [interview excerpt in English only from *Mystery In the Universe*]

H77 Ginsberg, Allen. *Plutonische Ode/Plutonian Ode.* Heerlen, The Netherlands: Uitgeverij 261, 1980.
Translation by Simon Vinkenoog: Plutonian Ode || Plutonische Ode

H78 Ginsberg, Allen. *Howl.* The Netherlands: [Een Piraatjes-Uitgave!] 1984.
Translation by Simon Vinkenoog: Howl [Howl]
Note: This edition is a photocopy piracy of the poem *Howl* in Dutch only, copied from the translation in *Proef M'N Tong In Je Oor.* Bound by vocational education students in metal wrappers with 2 nails protruding through the binding that act as staples. Blind stamped on the cover. Passed out at Turnhout [Piester Cabaret] Belgium, May 16, 1984.

Anthologies:

H79   Leary, Timothy and Vinkenoog, Simon. *Het ABZ Van De Psychedelische Avant-Garde.* The Netherlands: A.W. Sijthoff's Uitgeversmaatschappij, N.V., 1972, p. 98.
Translation by Simon Vinkenoog: [letter to Simon Vinkenoog]

H80* *Tussen Hemel En Hema: Twaalf Liverpoolse Gedichten.* Amsterdam, The Neterlands: C.J. Aarts, 1972.
Translation by Willem Wilmink: [Liverpool Muse]

H81   Van Son, Jacques. *The Beat Generation/Bob Dylan.* [Utrecht, The Netherlands]: Spektakel/Walhalla, 1979, pp. 38-43, 45-46, 55.
Translation: [excerpt of Howl] — [prose] — [excerpts from an interview with Peter Chowka in Dutch only]

H82   Galloway, David and Sabisch, Christian (eds.). *Wij Twee Jongens.* Amsterdam, The Netherlands: Manteau, 1984, pp. 254-257.
Translation by Simon Vinkenoog: Een Supermarkt In Californie [A Supermarket In California] — Alstublieft Meester [Please Master] — Regennatte Asfalthitte, Stoeprand Vuilnisbakken Overvol [Rain-West Asphalt Heat, Garbage Curbed Cans Overflowing]

H83   Mollison, Elizabeth and Meijer, Henk Romijn (eds.). *Spiegel Van De Engelse Poëzie Uit De Gehele Wereld.* Amsterdam, The Netherlands: Meulenhoff, 1989, pp. 236-239.
Translation: Poem Rocket ‖ Gedicht Raket

H84   Ginsberg, Allen; Dieleman, Ko and Korlaar, Ed. *Howl/Auw.* Amsterdam, The Netherlands: Uitgeverij Kokadorus, 1992.
Translation by Simon Vinkenoog: Howl [Howl]

H85   Van Vliet, Eddy (ed.). *De Bezige Bij Bloemlezing: Poëzie.* Amsterdam, The Netherlands: Uitgeverij de Bezige Bij, 1994, p. 177.
Translation by Simon Vinkenoog: Het Einde [The End]

Periodicals:

H86   [letter]. *Randstad,* no. 1 (Autumn 1961) pp. 109-113.
Translation by Frits Onderdijk [pseudo. of Simon Vinkenoog]: Abstractie In Poëzie [letter to Emmanuel A. Navaretta]

H87   [poem]. *UNESCO Courier* [Dutch edition], vol. 35, no. 10 (Nov. 1982) pp. 13-14.
Translation: [Plutonian Ode (excerpt)]

Miscellaneous:

H88   [program]. *Poetry International Rotterdam.* Rotterdam, The Netherlands: Rotterdamse Kunststichting, June 19-23, 1973, pp. [100-120].
Translation by Simon Vinkenoog: Op Neal's As ‖ On Neal's Ashes — Proef Milarepa Taste ‖ Milarepa Taste — Hum Bom! ‖ Hum Bom! — Alstublieft Meester ‖ Please Master — Wat Zou Je Doen Als Je Het Kwijtraakte? ‖ What Would You Do If You Lost It? — Elegie Voor Neal Cassady ‖ Elegy For Neal Cassady

H89   [program]. *Poetry International 1979.* Rotterdam, The Netherlands: June 11-16, 1979, p. 29.
Translation by Simon Vinkenoog: Proef Milarepa [Milarepa Taste] — Op Neal's As [On Neal's Ashes]

ESTONIAN

Periodicals:

H90   [4 poems]. *Vikerkaar,* no. 6 (1990) pp. 1, 18-29.
Translation by Tonu Onnepalu: Järelmarküs Howl'Ile [Footnote To Howl] —
Ulg [Howl] — «Ära Saa Vanaks» [Don't Grow Old]
Translation by Joel Sang: Laul [Song]

FINNISH

Books:

H91   Ginsberg, Allen. *Huuto Ja Muita Runoja.* Turku, Finland: Kustannusliike Tajo,
1963.
Translation by Anselm Hollo: Huuto [Howl] — Ignu [Ignu] — Maaginen Psalmi
[Magic Psalm]
Translation by Matti Rossi: Meskaliini [Mescaline] — Loppu [The End]

H92   Ginsberg, Allen.   *Kuolema Van Goghin Korvalle.*   Turku, Finland:
Kustannusliike Tajo, 1963.
Translation by Pennti Saarikoski: Amerikka [America] — Kaddish [Kaddish]
Translation by Matti Rossi: Vachel Lindsaylle [To Lindsay] — Rose-Tädille [To
Aunt Rose] — Urkumusiikkia Sanoiksi [Transcription Of Organ Music] —
Vastaus [The Reply]
Translation by Anselm Hollo: Kuolema Van Goghin Korvalle! [Death To Van
Gogh's Ear!] — Apollinairen Haudalla [At Apollinaire's Grave] — Runoraketti
[Poem Rocket]
Translation: Eurooppa! Eurooppa! [Europe! Europe!] — Greyhound-Aseman
Matkatavarahuoneessa [In the Baggage Room At Greyhound] — Kalifornian
Ruokamarkkinat [A Supermarket In California] — Auringonkukan Sutra
[Sunflower Sutra] — Todellinen Leijona [The Lion For Real] — Viesti
[Message II] — Mandala [Mandala]

Periodicals:

H93   [poem]. *Parnasso,* vol. 59, no. 5 (1959) pp. 208-212.
Translation by Anselm Hollo: Amerikka [America]

H94   [poem]. *Parnasso,* vol. 61, no. 2 (1961) pp. 96-101.
Translation by Anselm Hollo: Huuto [Howl]

H95   [poem]. *Teekkari,* no. 3 (May 18, 1961) pp. 7-8.
Translation by Anselm Hollo: Kuolema Van Goghin Korvalle! [Death To Van
Gogh's Ear]

FLEMISH

Periodicals:

H96*   [poem]. *Vlaamse Gids,* vol. 49, no. 12 (Dec. 1965) pp. 800-804.
Translation by Willem M. Roggeman: America [America]

H97   Evtoesjenko, Evgeny; Ginsberg, Allen and Cardenal, Ernesto. [prose]. *De Rode
Vaan,* vol. 63, no. 23 (May 28-June 1, 1984) p. 22.
Translation: Verklaring Van Drie [Declaration Of Three]

FRENCH

Books:

H98   Ginsberg, Allen. *Kaddish Et Autres Poèmes 1958-1960.* Paris, France:
Christian Bougois, 1967.
Translation by Claude Pélieu: Kaddish [Kaddish] — Poem Rocket [Poem
Rocket] — Europe! Europe! [Europe! Europe!] — A Vachel Lindsay [To
Lindsay] — Message [Message] — Tante Rose [To Aunt Rose] — Au
Tombeau D'Apollinaire [At Apollinaire's Grave] — Ignu [Ignu] — A Mort
L'Oreille De Van Goh [Death To Van Gogh's Ear!] — Gaz Hilarant [Laughing
Gas] — Mescaline [Mescaline] —Psaume Magique [Magic Psalm] — Notes
Sur Kaddish — Aubade [My Alba] — Sakyamuni Sortant De La Montagne
[Sakyamuni Coming Out From the Mountain] — La Havane 1953 [Havana
1953] — Sieste A Xbalba Et Retour Aux Etats-Unis [Siesta In Xbalba And
Return To the States] — Sur Le Travail De Burroughs [On Burroughs' Work]
— Poeme D'Amour Sur Un Theme De Whitman [Love Poem On Theme By
Whitman] — Reve Enregistre: 8 Juin 1955 [Dream Record: June 8, 1955] —
Fragment 1956 [Fragment 1956] — Un Etrange Pavillon A Berkeley [A
Strange New Cottage In Berkeley] — Sather Gate Illumination [Sather Gate
Illumination] — Graffiti [Scribble] — Apres-Midi A Seattle [Afternoon Seattle]
— "De Retour A Times Square, Revant De Times Square" [Back On Times
Square, Dreaming Of Times Square] — Mon Moi Triste [My Sad Self] —
Revenez Je Vous En Supplie Et Soyez Gai [I Beg You Come Back & Be
Cheerful] — Notes Sur Reality Sandwiches

H99   Ginsberg, Allen. *Planet News.* Paris, France: Christian Bourgois, 1971.
Translation by Mary Beach and Claude Pélieu: Who Will Take Over The
Universe? ‖ Qui Va S'Emparer De L'Univers? — Journal Night Thoughts ‖
Pensées D'Un Journal Nocturne — Television Was A Baby Crawling Toward
That Deathchamber ‖ La Télévision Était Un Bébé Rampant Vers La Chambre
De La Mort — This Form Of Life Needs Sex ‖ Cette Forme De Vie A Besoin
De Sexe — Sunset *S. S. Azemour* ‖ Coucher De Soleil À Bord Du *SS
Azemour* — Seabattle Of Salamis Took Place Off Perama ‖ Bataille Navale De
Salamis S'Étant Passée Au Large De Perama — Galilee Shore ‖ Au Bord De La
Galilée — Stotras To Kali Destroyer Of Illusions ‖ Stotras À Kali Destructrice
Des Illusions — Describe: The Rain On Dasaswamedh ‖ Décrire: La Pluie À
Dasawamedh — Death News ‖ Death News — Vulture Peak: Gridhakuta Hill ‖
Gridhakuta Hill: Le Pic Du Vautour — Patna-Benares Express ‖ L'Express
Patna-Bénarès — Last Night In Calcutta ‖ La Dernière Nuit À Calcutta — The
Change: Kyoto-Tokyo Express ‖ La Transformation: Kyoto-Tokyo Express —
Why Is God Love, Jack? ‖ Pourquoi Dieu Est-Il Amour, Jack? — Morning ‖
Matinale — Waking In New York ‖ Réveil À New York — After Yeats ‖ Après
Yeats — I Am Victim Of Telephone ‖ Je Suis Victime Du Téléphone — Today ‖
Aujourd'Hui — Message II ‖ Message II — Big Beat ‖ Grand Rythme — Cafe
In Warsaw ‖ Un Café À Varsovie — The Moments Return ‖ Les Instants
Reviennent — Kral Majales ‖ Kral Majales — Guru ‖ Gouroue — Drowse
Murmurs ‖ Murmures Somnolents — Who Be Kind To ‖ Avec Qui Etre Gentil
— Studying The Signs ‖ Etudiant Les Enseignes — Portland Coloseum ‖
Portland Coloseum — First Party At Ken Kesey's With Hell's Angels ‖
Première Party Chez Ken Kesey Avec Les Hells' Angels — Carmel Valley ‖
Carmel Valley — A Methedrine Vision In Hollywood ‖ Une Vision À
Hollywood — Chances "R" ‖ Chances "R" — Wichita Vortex Sutra ‖ Wichita
Vortex Sutra — Uptown ‖ Uptown — To the Body ‖ Au Corps — City
Midnight Junk Strains ‖ Un Air De Camé Dans La Ville Minuit — Holy Ghost
On the Nod Over the Body Of Bliss ‖ Le Saint-Esprit Branché Sur Le Corps De
La Béatitude — Wales Visitation ‖ Wales Visitation — Pentagon Exorcism ‖
Pentagon Exorcism — Notes Et Notules

H100 Ginsberg, Allen. *Reality Sandwiches*. Paris, France: Christian Bourgois, 1972.
Translation by Mary Beach and Claude Pélieu: [blurb from back cover of City
Lights paperback edition in French only] — My Alba ‖ Aubade — Sakyamuni
Coming Out From the Mountain ‖ Sakyamuni Sortant De La Montagne —
Havana 1953 ‖ La Havane 1953 — Siesta In Xbalba And Return To the States ‖
Sieste À Xbalba Et Retour Aux Etats-Unis — On Burroughs' Work ‖ Sur Le
Travail De Burroughs — Love Poem On Theme By Whitman ‖ Poème
D'Amour Sur Un Thème De Whitman — Dream Record: June 8, 1955 ‖ Rêve
Enregistré: 8 Juin 1955 — Fragment 1956 ‖ Fragment 1956 — A Strange New
Cottage In Berkeley ‖ Un Étrange Pavillon À Berkeley — Sather Gate
Illumination ‖ Sather Gate Illumination — Scribble ‖ Graffiti — Afternoon
Seattle ‖ Après-Midi À Seattle — Back On Times Square, Dreaming Of Times
Square ‖ "De Retour À Times Square, Rêvant De Times Square" — My Sad
Self ‖ Mon Moi Triste — I Beg You Come Back & Be Cheerful ‖ Revenez Je
Vous En Supplie Et Soyez Gai — To an Old Poet In Peru ‖ A Un Vieux Poète
Au Pérou — Aether ‖ Ether — Notes Sur *Reality Sandwiches*

H101 Ginsberg, Allen. *Howl and Other Poems*. Paris, France: Christian Bourgois,
1977.
Translation by Robert Cordier and Jean-Jacques Lebel: Howl ‖ Howl — Footnote
To Howl ‖ Howl, Post-Scriptum — À Supermarket In California ‖ Un
Supermarche En Californie — Transcription Of Organ Music ‖ Transcription
De Musique D'Orgue — Sunflower Sutra ‖ Tournesol Soutra — America ‖
Amerique — In The Baggage Room At Greyhound ‖ Dans La Salle Des
Bagages Du Greyhound — Psalm III ‖ Psaume III — An Asphodel ‖ Un
Asphodele — The Green Automobile ‖ L'Automobile Verte — Song ‖ Song —
Wild Orphan ‖ Orphelin Sauvage — In Back Of The Real ‖ Au Revers Du Reel
— Notes Écrites Lorsqu' "Howl" Finit Par Être Gravé Sur Disque [liner notes
for *Howl* recording]

H102 Ginsberg, Allen. *Kaddish*. Paris, France: Christian Bourgois, 1977.
Translation by Mary Beach and Claude Pélieu: Kaddish ‖ Kaddish — Poem
Rocket ‖ Poem Rocket — Europe! Europe! ‖ Europe! Europe! — To Lindsay ‖
A Lindsay — Message ‖ Message — To Aunt Rose ‖ A Tante Rose — At
Apollinaire's Grave ‖ Au Tombeau D'Apollinaire — The Lion For Real ‖ Un
Lion Pour De Vrai — Ignu ‖ Ignu — Death To Van Gogh's Ear ‖ A Mort
L'Oreille De Van Gogh — Laughing Gas ‖ Gaz Hilarant — Mescaline ‖
Mescaline — Lysergic Acid ‖ Acide Lysergique — Magic Psalm ‖ Psaume
Magique — The Reply ‖ La Résponse — The End ‖ La Fin — Notes Sur
Kaddish

H103 Ginsberg, Allen. *Journaux Indiens, Mars 1962-Mai 1963*. Paris, France:
Christian Bourgois, 1977.
Translation by Philippe Mikriammos: Journaux Indiens [Indian Journals]

H104 Ginsberg, Allen. *La Bataille De Yahvé Et D'Allah*. Rome, Italy: Muro Torto,
1979.
Translation by Gérard-Georges Lemaire: La Bataille De Yahvé Et D'Allah [Jaweh
And Allah Battle]

H105 Ginsberg, Allen. *La Chute De L'Amerique*. Paris, France: Flammarion, 1979.
Translation by Gérard-George Lemaire and Anne-Christine Taylor:
Commencement D'Un Poème De Ces États [Beginning Of a Poem Of These
States] — Continuation D'Un Long Poème De Ces États, S.F. Et Plus Au Sud
[Continuation San Francisco Southward] — Ces États, En Arrivant A L.A.
[These States Into Los Angeles] — Poésie D'Autoroute L.A.-Albuquerque-
Texas-Wichita [Hiway Poesy L.A. To Wichita] — Auto Poésie: En Cavale De
Bloomington [Auto Poesy: On the Lam From Bloomington] — De Kansas City
A Saint Louis [Kansas City To St. Louis] — Bayonne En Entrant Dans

N.Y.C. [Bayonne Entering N.Y.C.] — Ailes Dressées Au-Dessus Du Puits
Noir [Wings Lifted Over the Black Pit] — Cleveland, Les Plaines [Cleveland,
The Flats] — Un Voeu [A Vow] — Or Automnal: Arrière-Saison En Nouvelle
Angleterre [Autumn Gold: New England Fall] — Fait, Achevé Avec La Plus
Grande Pine [Done, Finished With The Biggest Cock] — Autoroute A Péage
De Bayonne A Tuscarora [Bayonne Turnpike To Tuscarora] — Une Fenêtre
Ouverte Sur Chicago [An Open Window On Chicago] — De Retour Vers Le
Nord Du Vortex [Returning North Of Vortex] — Lécher Le Cul [Kiss Ass] —
Élégie Che Guevara [Elegy Che Guevara] — Litanie Des Bénéfices De Guerre
[War Profit Litany] — Élégie Pour Neal Cassady [Elegy For Neal Cassady] —
De Chicago A Salt Lake City Par Avion [Chicago To Salt Lake By Air] —
Flash Des Années 30 A Manhattan [Manhattan Thirties Flash] — S'Il Te Plaît
Maître [Please Master] — Une Prophétie [A Prophecy] — Bixby Canyon
[Bixby Canyon] — Traverser Le Pays [Crossing Nation] — Fumée Dévalant
La Rue [Smoke Rolling Down Street] — Pertussin [Pertussin] — Tourbillons
De Poussiére Noire Sur L'Avenue D [Swirls Of Black Dust On Avenue D] —
Violence [Violence] — Par Dela Durango Argenté Au-Dessus Des Craquelures
De La Sierra Du Mexic [Past Silver Durango Over Mexic Sierra Wrinkles] —
Sur Les Cendres De Neal [On Neal's Ashes] — En Route Pour Chicago
[Going To Chicago] — Grant Park: 28 Août 1968 [Grant Park: August 28,
1968] — Accident De Voiture [Car Crash] — De Nouveau Au-Dessus De
Denver [Over Denver Again] — S'Élevant Au-Dessus Des Rues De Detroit
Obscurcies Par La Nuit [Rising Over Night-Blackened Detroit Streets] —
Univers Imaginaire [Imaginary Universes] — A Poe: En Survolant La Planète,
Albany-Baltimore Par Les Airs [To Poe: Over The Planet, Air Albany-
Baltimore] — Dimanche De Pâques [Easter Sunday] — S'Endormir Aux États-
Unis [Falling Asleep In America] — Passage Du Nord-Ouest [Northwest
Passage] — Orée Du Désert De Sonora [Sonora Desert Edge] — Reflets Dans
Un Oeil Endormi [Reflections In Sleepy Eye] — Fête De L'Indépendance
[Independence Day] — Dans Une Cabane D'Ermite Au Clair De Lune [In a
Moonlit Hermit's Cabin] — Chaleur D'Asphalte Transie De Pluie,
Débordement De Poubelles Bosselées [Rain-Wet Asphalt Heat, Garbage
Curbed Cans] — La Mort Sur Tous Les Fronts [Death On All Fronts] —
Jardins De La Mémoire [Memory Gardens] — Flash Back [Flash Back] —
Graffiti 12e Cabine Des Pissotières Aéroport De Syracuse [Graffiti 12th
Cubicle Men's Room Syracuse] — Arrières-Pensées [After Thoughts] — G.S.
Lisant Des Poèmes A Princeton [G.S. Reading Poesy At Princeton] —
Vendredi Treize [Friday the Thirteenth] — Mobilisation À D.C. [D.C.
Mobilization] — Églogue [Ecologue] — Guru Om [Guru Om] — "Avez-Vous
Vu Ce Film?" [Have You Seen This Movie?] — Goût De Milarepa [Milarepa
Taste] — Survolant Laramie [Over Laramie] — Bixby Canyon Voie Océane
Brise Verbale [Bixby Canyon Ocean Path Word Breeze] — Hûm Bom [Hum
Bom!] — Septembre Sur La Route De Jessore [September On Jessore Road]
— Postface [Afterwords] — Notes

H106   Ginsberg, Allen. *Howl and Other Poems/Kaddish*. Paris, France: Christian
Bourgois, 1980.
Translation by Robert Cordier and Jean-Jacques Lebel: Howl ‖ Howl — Footnote
To Howl ‖ Howl, Post-Scriptum — A Supermarket In California ‖ Un
Supermarché En Californie — Transcription Of Organ Music ‖ Transcription
De Musique D'Orgue — Sunflower Sutra ‖ Tournesol Soutra — America ‖
Amérique — In the Baggage Room At Greyhound ‖ Dans La Salle Des
Bagages Du Greyhound — Psalm III ‖ Psaume III — An Asphodel ‖ Un
Asphodèle — The Green Automobile ‖ L'Automobile Verte — Song ‖ Song —
Wild Orphan ‖ Orphelin Sauvage — In Back Of The Real ‖ Au Revers Du Réel
— Notes Écrites Lorsque "Howl" Finit Par Être Gravé Sur Disque [liner notes
for *Howl* Fantasy recording].
Translation by Mary Beach and Claude Pélieu: Kaddish ‖ Kaddish — Poem
Rocket ‖ Poem Rocket — Europe! Europe! ‖ Europe! Europe! — To Lindsay ‖

A Lindsay — Message ‖ Message — To Aunt Rose ‖ A Tante Rose — At Apollinaire's Grave ‖ Au Tombeau D'Apollinaire — The Lion For Real ‖ Un Lion Pour De Vrai — Ignu ‖ Ignu — Death To Van Gogh's Ear ‖ A Mort L'Oreille De Van Gogh! — Laughing Gas ‖ Gaz Hilarant — Mescaline ‖ Mescaline — Lysergic Acid ‖ Acide Lysergique — Magic Psalm ‖ Psaume Magique — The Reply ‖ La Réponse — The End ‖ La Fin — Notes Sur *Kaddish*

H107   Ginsberg, Allen. *Venez Tous Vous Braves Garçons.* Paris, France: Artista, 1981. [broadside edition]
Translation by Gérard-Georges Lemaire: Venez Tous Vous Braves Garçons [Come All Ye Brave Boys]

H108   Ginsberg, Allen. *Miroir Vide.* Paris, France: Graphium, 1982.
Translation by Gérard-Georges Lemaire: J'Ai L'Impression D'Être Comme Dans Un Cul [I Feel As If I Am At a Dead] — C'Te Nuit Tout Va Bien...Quel Futur [Tonite All Is Well...What a] — Psaume I [Psalm I] — Ports De Cezanne [Cezanne's Ports] — Apres Tout, Qu'Y A-T-Il D'Autre A Dire Ici? [After All, What Else Is There To Say?] — Feodor [Fyodor] — Le Tremblement Du Voile [The Trembling Of the Veil] — Une Institution Depourvue De Signification [A Meaningless Institution] — Metaphysique [Metaphysics] — En Societe [In Society] — Dans La Mort, Ne Peux Atteindre Ce Qui Est Le Plus Proche [In Death, Cannot Reach What Is Most Near] — C'Est A Propos De La Mort [This Is About Death] — Vive La Toile D'Araignee [Long Live the Spiderweb] — J'Ai Tenté De Concentrer [I Attempted To Concentrate] — Notes De Marijuana [Marijuana Notation] — Un Spiritual Dingue [A Crazy Spiritual] — J'Ai Un Pouvoir Accru [I Have Increased Power] — Hymne [Hymn] — Crepuscule [Sunset] — Un Fantome Peut Venir [A Ghost May Come] — Une Desolation [A Desolation] — Les Termes Dans Lesquels Je Pense La Realite [The Terms In Which I Think Of Reality] — Un Poeme Sur L'Amerique [A Poem On America] — L'Heure Du Dejeuner D'Un Poseur De Briques [The Bricklayer's Lunch Hour] — Apres Les Ames Mortes [After Dead Souls] — La Pomme De Nuit [The Night-Apple] — Deux Garçons Sont Alles A Un Cafe De Reve [Two Boys Went Into a Dream Diner] — Comment Il A Ete Mis En Boite Dans L'Usine De Rubans [How Come He Got Canned At the Ribbon Factory] — Une Affaire Banale [A Typical Affair] — Une Affaire Pas Banale [An Atypical Affair] — Le Poeme Archetype [The Archtype Poem] — Paterson [Paterson] — L'Ange Bleu [The Blue Angel] — J'Ai Fait L'Amour Avec Moi-Même [I Made Love To Myself] — J'ai Appris Un Monde De Chacun [I Learned a World From Each] — Histoire De Gregory Corso [Gregory Corso's Story] — En Rentrant Chez Moi La Nuit [Walking Home At Night] — L'Etranger Au Suaire [The Shrouded Stranger]

H109   Ginsberg, Allen. *Journal 1952-1962.* Paris, France: Christian Bourgois, 1984.
Translation by Yves LePellec: Journal [*Journals Early 50s Early 60s*]

H110   Ginsberg, Allen. *Iron Horse.* Paris, France: Le Livre À Venir & Solin, 1985.
Translation by Catherine Bailly: Iron Horse ‖ Iron Horse [French]

H111   Ginsberg, Allen. *American Haiku: 1983-1992.* Toulouse, France: Les Petits Classiques Du Grand Pirate, 1992.
Translation by Yves LePellec: American Haiku ‖ Haiku Américains — [2 drawings]

H112   Ginsberg, Allen. *La Nouvelle Chute De L'Amerique.* Paris, France: Éditions Du Solstice, 1992.
Translation by Gerard-G. Lemaire and Anne-Christine Taylor: America ‖ Amérique — Auto Poesy: On the Lam From Bloomington ‖ Auto Poésie: En Cavale de Bloomington — Bayonne Entering NYC ‖ Bayonne En Entrant Dans

NYC — Autumn Gold: New England Fall || Or Autumnal: Arrière-Saison En Nouvelle Angleterre — An Open Window On Chicago || Une Fenêtre Ouverte Sur Chicago — Over Denver Again || De Nouveau Au-Dessus De Denver — Northwest Passage || Passage Du Nord-Ouest — Graffiti 12th Cubicle Men's Room Syracuse Airport || Graffiti 12ᵉ Cabine Des Pissotièrres-Aéroport De Syracuse — Friday the Thirteenth || Vendredi Treize.
Translation by Yves LePellec: Hum Bom! || Hüm Bom! — Denver To Montana || De Denver Su Montana, Départ 27 Mai 1972

H113 Ginsberg, Allen. *After the Party / Apres La Fete.* Caen, France: Cahiers De Nuit, Collection JeudiGris, 1994.
Translation by Mary Beach and Serge Féray: After the Party || Après La Fête — C'mon Pigs Of Western Civilization Eat More Grease || Allez Porcs De La Civilisation Occidentale Mangez Encore De La Graisse

H114 Ginsberg, Allen. *Linceul Blanc (White Shroud).* Paris, France: Christian Bourgois, 1994.
Translation by Yves LePellec and Françoise Bourbon: Porch Scribbles || Griffonné Sous La Véranda — Those Two || Ces Deux-Là — Homage Vajracarya || Hommage À Vajracarya — Why I Meditate || Pourquoi Je Médite — Old Love Story || Vieille Histoire D'Amour — Airplane Blues || Blues De L'Avion — What You Up To? || "Quoi De Neuf?" — Maturity || Maturité — Throw Out the Yellow Journalists Of Bad Grammar & Terrible Manner || "Dehors Les Journaistes Pourris, Bande De Goujats Illettrés" — Irritable Vegetable || Carotte Irritée — Thoughts Sitting Breathing II || Pensé En Méditant, No. II — What the Sea Throws Up At Vlissingen || Ce Que La Mer Rejette À Vlissingen — I Am Not || Je Ne Suis Pas — I'm a Prisoner Of Allen Ginsberg || Je Suis Prisonnier D'Allen Ginsberg — 221 Syllabes [sic] At Rocky Mountain Dharma Center || 221 Syllabes Au Centre Dharma Des Rocheuses — Arguments || Disputes — Sunday Prayer || Prière Du Dimanche — Brown Rice Quatrains || Quatrains Au Riz Complet — They're All Phantoms Of My Imagining || Fantômes Par Moi Imaginés — White Shroud || Linceul Blanc — Empire Air || Ciel D'Empire — Surprise Mind || Idée Surprise — Student Love || Amour Étudiant — In My Kitchen In New York || Dans Ma Cuisine À New York — It's All So Brief || Tout Est Si Bref — I Love Old Whitman So || J'Aime Tant Ce Vieux Witman — Written In My Dream By W.C. Williams || Écrit Dans Mon Rêve Par W.C. Williams — One Morning I Took a Walk In China || Un Matin Je Me Suis Promené En Chine — Reading Bai Juyi || En Lisant Bai Juyi — Black Shroud || Linceul Noir — World Karma || Karma Du Monde — Prophecy || Prophétie — Memory Cousins || Cousins Du Souvenir — Moral Majority || Majorité Morale — The Guest || L'Invité — After Antipater || D'Après Antipater — Cadillac Squawk || Couac De Cadillac — Things I Don't Know || Tout Ce Que Je Ne Sais Pas

H115 Ginsberg, Allen. *Souffles D'Esprit / Ode Plutonienne.* Paris, France: Christian Bourgois, 1994.
Translation by Yves LePellec and Françoise Bourbon: Ayers Rock Uluru Song || Chant D'Ayers Rock Uluru — Xmas Gift || Cadeau De Noël — Thoughts Sitting Breathing || Pensé En Méditant — What Would You Do If You Lost It? || «Que Ferais-Tu Si Tu La Perdais?» — Under the World There's a Lot of Ass, a Lot Of Cunt || Sous La Terre C'Est Plein De Culs, Plein De Cons — Returning To the Country For a Brief Visit || Retour À La Campagne Pour Une Courte Visite — What I'd Like To Do || Ce Que J'Aimerais Faire — On Neruda's Death || Mort De Neruda — Mind Breaths || Souffles D'Esprit — Flying Elegy || Élégie En Vol — Teton Village || Teton Village — Sweet Boy, Gimme Yr Ass || Joil Môme, Donne-Moi Ton Cul — Jaweh And Allah Battle || Bataille Entre Yahvé Et Allah — Manifesto || Manifeste — Sad Dust Glories || Tristes Poussières De Gloire — Ego Confession || Confession D'Ego — Mugging || Agression — We Rise On Sun Beams And Fall In the Night || Nous

Nous Élevons Sur Les Rayons Du Soleil Et Redescendons Dans La Nuit —
Written On Hotel Napkin: Chicago Futures ‖ Écrit Sur Une Nappe D'Hôtel:
Futur De Chicago — Hospital Window ‖ Fenêtre D'Hôpital — Hadda Be
Playing On the Jukebox ‖ Fallait Que Ça Passe Au Jukebox — Sickness Blues
‖ Blues De La Crève — Cabin In the Rockies ‖ Cabane Dans Les Rocheuses —
Rolling Thunder Stones ‖ Pierres Du Tonnerre Qui Roule — Don't Grow Old ‖
Ne Devenez Jamais Vieux — Drive All Blames Into One ‖ «N'Accuse Que Toi-
Même» — Haunting Poe's Baltimore ‖ Hanté Par Poe À Baltimore —
Plutonian Ode ‖ Ode Plutonienne — Stool Pigeon Blues ‖ Blues Du Cafteur —
Punk Rock Your My Big Crybaby ‖ Punk Rock T'Es Mon Gros Bébé
Grognon — What's Dead? ‖ Qu'Est-Ce Qui Est Mort? — Grim Skeleton ‖
Sinistre Squelette — Father Guru ‖ Père Gourou — Manhattan May Day
Midnight ‖ Manhattan Premier Mai Minuit — Nagasaki Days ‖ Rencontre
Nagasaki — Old Pond ‖ Vieille Mare — Don't Grow Old ‖ «Ne Devenez
Jamais Vieux» — December 31, 1978 ‖ Décembre 1978 — Brooklyn College
Brain ‖ Grosse Tête De Brooklyn College — Garden State ‖ L'État Des Jardins
— Spring Fashions ‖ Collection De Printemps — To the Punks Of Dawlish ‖
Aux Paunks De Dawlish — Some Love ‖ Quelque Amour — Ruhr-Gebiet ‖
Ruhr-Gebiet — Homework ‖ Devoirs À La Maison — After Whitman &
Reznikoff ‖ D'Après Whitman Et Reznikoff — Reflections At Lake Louise ‖
Réflexions Au Bord Du Lac Louise — Red Cheeked Boyfriends Tenderly Kiss
Me Sweet Mouthed ‖ Des Amis Aux Joues Roses M'Embrassent De Leurs
Bouches Tendres — Fourth Floor, Dawn, Up All Night Writing Letters ‖
Quatrième Étage, Aube, Nuit Passée À Écrire Des Lettres — Ode To Failure ‖
Ode À L'Échec — Birdbrain! ‖ Tête De Noeud — Eroica ‖ Symphonie
Héroïque — Defending the Faith ‖ «Défenseurs De La Foi»

Anthologies:

H116 Bosquet, Alain (ed.). *Trente-Cinq Jeunes Poètes Américains*. Paris, France:
Librairie Gallimard, 1960, pp. 384-391.
Translation by Alain Bosquet: America ‖ Amérique

H117 Lebel, Jean-Jacques. *La Poésie De La Beat Generation*. Paris, France: Denoël,
1965, pp. 89-132.
Translation by Jean-Jacques Lebel: Western Union Telegramme [telegram] —
Howl [Howl] — Kaddish [Kaddish] — The End [The End] — Poème
D'Amour Sur Un Thème De Walt Whitman [Love Poem On a Theme By Walt
Whitman] — Sur L'Oeuvre De Burroughs [On Burroughs' Work] — L.S.D.
[Lysergic Acid] — Mandala [Mandala] — La Transformation [The Change]

H118 Bellour, Raymond (ed.). *Les Cahiers De L'Herne: Henri Michaux*. Paris,
France: Cahiers De L'Herne, 1966, pp. 35-38.
Translation by Pierre Alien: Henri Michaux [prose]

H119 Bernard, Pierre (ed.). *Dossier LSD*. Paris, France: Le Soleil Noir, 1967, pp. 75-
76 and back cover.
Translation by Jean-Jacques Lebel: Réponse Au "Krapouillot" Communiquée À
Mandala Par Allen Ginsberg [Public Solitude] — LSD 25 (Fragment) &
Mandala [Lysergic Acid (excerpt)]

H120 Burroughs, William and Ginsberg, Allen. *Les Lettres Du Yage*. Paris, France:
Editions L'Herne, 1967. [Series: Les Livres Noirs]
Translation by Claude Pélieu and Mary Beach: Les Lettres Du Yage [*The Yage
Letters*]

H121   Burroughs, William; Pélieu, Claude and Kaufman, Bob. *Textes*. Paris, France: Editions De L'Herne, 1967, p. 132.
Translation by Jean-Jacques Lebel: Sur L'Oeuvre De Burroughs [On Burroughs' Work]

H122   Dommergues, Pierre. *Les U.S.A. À La Recherche De Leur Identité*. Paris, France: Editions Bernard Grasset, 1967, pp. 109-115, 322-326.
Translation: Poesie, Violence Et Tendresse [Poetry, Violence & the Trembling Lambs] — [Boston *Naked Lunch* Trial]

H123   Lowenfels, Walter and Braymer, Nan (eds.). *89 [i.e., Quatre-Vingt-Neuf] Poètes Américains Contre La Guerre Au Vietnam*. Paris, France: Éditions Albin Michel, 1967, pp. 60-64.
Translation: Extrait De: Soûtra À Wichita [Wichita Vortex Sutra (excerpt)]

H124*   Burroughs, William S. (ed.). *Jack Kerouac*. Paris, France: Editions De L'Herne, 1971, pp. 93-95.
Translation by Mary Beach: [Empty Skulled New] — Jack Kerouac Est Mort

H125*   Burroughs, William S. *Junkie*. Paris, France: Editions Pierre Belfond, 1972.
Translation by Catherine Cullaz and Jean-René Major: [Introduction]

H126   Kramer, Jane. *Allen Ginsberg En Situation*. Paris, France: Union Generale D' Editions, 1973.
Translation by Claude Gilbert: Allen Ginsberg En Situation [*Allen Ginsberg in America*]

H127   Tysh, Christine. *Allen Ginsberg*. Paris, France: Editions Seghers, 1974, pp. 123-179. [Series: Poètes D'Aujourd'Hui 221].
Translation by Claude Guillot: [letter to the readers of *Paris Review*].
Translation by Mary Beach and Claude Pélieu: Sakyamuni Sortant De La Montagne [Sakyamuni Coming Out From the Mountain] — Sather Gate Illumination [Sather Gate Illumination] — A Mort L'Oreille De Van Gogh! [Death To Van Gogh's Ear] — Kaddish [Kaddish] — La Transformation: Kyoto-Tokyo Express [The Change: Kyoto-Tokyo Express] — Avec Qui Être Gentil [Who Be Kind To].
Translation by Alain Bosquet: Amérique [America]

H128   *Wozu? A Quoi Bon? Why?* Paris, France: Le Soleil Noir, 1978.
Translation by Georges Louisy & Nidra Poller: [prose postcard in English and French] — The Rune ‖ Le Rune

H129*   Burroughs, William S. *Le Camé*. Paris, France: Editions Pierre Belfond, 1979.
Translation by Philippe Mikriammos: [Introduction to *Junkie*]

H130   Jaubert, Alain and Sacks, Susan (eds.). *Allen Ginsberg: Om..., Entretiens Et Témoignages (1963-1978)*. Paris, France: Éditions du Seuil, 1979, pp. 63-86.
Translation by Claude Portail and Joseph Gaines: Rencontres Avec Ezra Pound, Notes De Journal (1967) [Encounters With Ezra Pound, Journal Notes].
Translation by Alain Jaubert and Susan Sacks: Quelques Mantras (1969) [Some Mantras]

H131   *Art Contre/Against Apartheid*. Paris, France: Artists Of the World Against Apartheid, 1983, p. 36.
Translation by Gérard-Georges Lemaire: Far Away ‖ Loin

H132   *Christian Bourgois 1966-1986*. Paris, France: Christian Bourgois, 1986, pp. 126, 135.
Translation: [For Carl Solomon] — Gregory Corso (prose)

H133   Darras, Jacques (ed.). *Arpentage De La Poésie Contemporaine.* Amiens, France: Trois Cailloux, 1987, pp. 124-132.
Translation by Jacques Darras: Kaddish [Kaddish] — Quoi De Mort? [What's Dead?] — Ode À L'Échec [Ode To Failure] — Amérique [America]

H134   McShine, Kynaston (ed.). *Andy Warhol: A Retrospective* [French edition]. Paris, France: Centre Georges Pompidou, 1989.
Translation: [Despite the Coolness Of Warhol's Art (prose)]

H135   Michel, Albin. *Allen Ginsberg & La Beat Génération 89.* Paris, France: Question de Littérature, 1989, pp. 18-19, 42-45. [Series: Filigrane 3].
Translation by Françoise Bourbon: Dans Ma Cuisine À New York [In My Kitchen In New York] — En Lisant Bai Juyi [Reading Bai Juyi]

H136   Sakaki, Nanao. *Casse Le Miroir.* Bagnolet, France: Mai Hors Saison, 1990.
Translation by Patrice Repusseau: Cerveau Lavé Par De Nombreux Torrents [Brain Washed By Numerous Mountain Streams]

H137   Katz, Eliot. *Les Voleurs Au Travail.* Paris, France: Europe Poésie, 1992, pp. 7 and back cover.
Translation by Arielle Denis: Préface [preface] — [blurb]

H138   Pélieu, Claude. *23.* Herouville-St.-Clair, France: I.C.B.M. / Editions Cactus, 1992, pp. 27-29.
Translation by Mary Beach: Notes Sur Claude Pelieu || Notes On Claude Pelieu (prose)

Periodicals:

H139   [poem]. *L'Express,* no. 453 (Feb. 18, 1960) p. 32.
Translation by Alain Bosquet: Amerique [America]

H140   [poem]. *Les Lettres Nouvelles,* no. 4 (June 1960) pp. 43-48. [Nouvelle Série].
Translation by Roger Giroux: Death To Van Gogh's Ear [Death To Van Gogh's Ear]

H141   [poem]. *L'Arche,* no. 48 (Jan. 1961) pp. 26-29.
Translation by Colette Elstein: Kaddich || Kaddish (excerpt)

H142   [poem]. *Dire,* no. 6 (Autumn 1963) pp. 35-39.
Translation by F.J. Temple: A Supermarket In California || Un Supermarché En Californie

H143   [3 poems]. *Les Temps Modernes,* vol. 20, no. 223 (Dec. 1964) pp. 981-989.
Translation by Alain Jouffroy: Poeme D'Amour Sur Un Theme De Walt Whitman [Love Poem On a Theme By Walt Whitman] — LSD 25 [Lysergic Acid] — The End [The End]

H144   [poem]. *Identités,* no. 10 (Spring 1965) p. 2.
Translation by Jean-Jacques Lebel: Howl [Howl (excerpt)]

H145   [poem]. *Crapouillot,* no. 71 (1966) p. 47.
Translation by Claude Pelieu: Ginsberg Pourrissant [Mescaline]

H146   [poem]. *Le Monde,* supplement to no. 6990, vol. 24 (July 5, 1967) p. 5.
Translation by D'Andre Chassigneux: Soutra Du Vortex De Wichita [Wichita Vortex Sutra (excerpt)]

H147   [letter]. *Oeuf,* no. 5 (May 3, 1970) p. [3].
Translation by Claude Pélieu: [letter to David Kennedy]

H148*   [poem]. *Planète Plus* (April-May 1971)
Translation: Aubord De La Galilee [Galilee Shore] — Kral Majales [Kral Majales]

H149   [poem]. *Actuel,* no. 10-11 (July-Aug. 1971) pp. 16-19.
Translation by Jean-Jacques Lebel: Howl [Howl]

H150   [5 poems and prose]. *Ellipse,* no. 8-9 (1971) pp. 80-127.
Translation by Jean-Jacques Lebel: Howl || Howl.
Translation by Roch Carrier: A Supermarket In California || Un Super-Marché En Californie
Translation by Jean Basile: America || America
Translation by Monique Grandmangin: Sunflower Sutra || Tournesol Sutra
Translation by Joseph Bonenfant: At Apollinaire's Grave || Sur La Tombe D'Apollinaire
Translation by Marc Lebel: En Marge De Howl Et Autres Poêmes [Notes for *Howl And Other Poems*]

H151   [poem and drawing]. *Odradek,* vol. 14, no. 6 (1973) loose leaf. [Revue "L'Essai" no. 58]
Translation by Francine Réquilé; Francis Edeline and Jacques Izoard: What Would You Do If You Lost It? || Que Ferais-Tu Si Tu Le Perdais? — [drawing]

H152   [3 poems]. *Entretiens,* vol. 34 (1975) pp. 59-71, 236-245.
Translation by Jacqueline Starer: Spiritual Loufoque || A Crazy Spiritual — Tante Rose || To Aunt Rose
Translation by Mary Beach and Claude Pélieu: September On Jessore Road || Sur La Route De Jessore

H153   [poem]. *Les Temps Modernes,* vol. 32, no. 361-362 (Aug.-Sept. 1976) pp. 444-447.
Translation by Jean-Jacques Lebel: A Vendre A Vendre [For Sale For Sale]

H154   [prose]. *Art Press International,* no. 27 (April 1979) p. 12.
Translation by Claude Portail and Joseph Gaines: Rencontre Avec Ezra Pound [Encounters With Ezra Pound]

H155   [poem]. *Canal,* no. 29-31 (July-Sept. 1979) p. 21.
Translation by Philippe Mikriammos: Blanche Luminescence Sur Des Crânes En Sueur [D.C. Mobilization]

H156*   [3 poems]. *Sphinx,* no. 7-8 (Nov. 1979)
Translation by Lucien Suel: [For Creeley's Ear — Nagasaki Days — Old Pond]

H157   [poem]. *Magazine Littéraire,* no. 157 (Feb. 1980) pp. 26-27.
Translation by Gérard-Georges Lemaire: T.S. Eliot Est Entre [T.S. Eliot Entered My Dreams]

H158   [3 poems]. *Dirty,* vol. 1, no. 4-5 (Autumn 1980) pp. 90-93.
Translation by Gérard-Georges Lemaire: 23 Nov. 1963: Seul [Nov. 23, 1963: Alone] — Fragment: Les Noms [Fragment: The Names]
Translation by Eric Sarner: Ode Plutonienne || Plutonian Ode (excerpt)

H159   [poem]. *UNESCO Courier* [French edition], vol. 35, no. 10 (Nov. 1982) pp. 13-14.
Translation: Plutonian Ode [Plutonian Ode (excerpt)]
Note: This was also published in a Braille French edition.

H160 [poem]. *Temps Economie Litterature* (Dec. 9-15, 1982) p. 7.
Translation by Jean-Jacques Lebel: Ode Plutonienne [Plutonian Ode]

H161 [poem]. *Change,* vol. 42 (May 1983) pp. 83-85.
Translation by Jean-Jacques Lebel: Tête De Noeud! [Birdbrain]

H162 [8 poems]. *Tribu,* no. 6 ([April-June] 1984) pp. 38-48.
Translation by Yves LePellec: Maturity ‖ Jeune Homme Je Buvais De La Bière Et Vomissais De La Bile Verte — Collections De Printemps [Spring Fashions] — Ne Devenez Jamais Vieux [Don't Grow Old]
Translation by Francoise Bourbon: Retour A La Campagne Pour Une Courte Visite [Returning To the Country For a Brief Visit] — Blues De La Crève [Sickness Blues] — D'Après Whitman Et Reznikoff [Lower East Side] — Ode A L'Échec [Ode To Failure] — Agression [Mugging]

H163 [poem]. *L'Autre Journal,* no. 7 (Dec. 1990) pp. 84-85.
Translation by Yves LePellec and Françoise Bourbon: Improvisation In Beijing ‖ Improvisation À Beijing

H164 [prose and 2 doodles]. *Le Nouvel Observateur,* special no. 22-24 (Nov. 1994) p. 248.
Translation by Yves LePellec: De New York À Portland, ME [New York To Portland]

H165 [2 poems]. *Luvah: Revue Trimestrielle,* no. 23 (1994) pp. 67-73.
Translation by Claude Pelieu: Excrement ‖ Excrément — C'Mon Pigs Of Western Civilization Eat More Grease

Miscellaneous:

H166 [publisher's advertising flyer]. *Les Cahiers Noirs Du Soleil 1.* Paris, France: Le Soleil Noir, ca. 1978.
Translation by Jean-Jacques Lebel: Mandala [Mandala]

H167 [program]. *Guerra Alla Guerra.* Milan, Italy: Dec. 14-16, 1982, p. 12.
Translation by Jean-Jacques Lebel: Ode Plutonienne [Plutonian Ode]

H168 [flyer]. *Tare.* Liege, Belgium: Cirque Diverse, Feb. 19, 1983.
Translation by Roger Sweet and others: Tare [Birdbrain!]

H169 [publisher's advertising pamphlet]. *Casse Le Miroir, by Nanao Sakaki.* Bagnolet, France: Mai Hors Saison, ca. 1990.
Translation by Patrice Repusseau: Cerveau Lavé Par De Nombreux Torrents [Brain Washed By Numerous Mountain Streams]

GERMAN

Books:

H170 Ginsberg, Allen. *Das Geheul Und Andere Gedichte.* Wiesbaden, West Germany: Limes Verlag, 1959.
Translation by Wolfgang Fleischmann and Rudolf Wittkopf: Howl ‖ Das Geheul — Footnote To Howl ‖ Fussnote Zum Geheul — A Supermarket In California ‖ Ein Selbstbedienungsladen In Kalifornien — Transcription Of Organ Music ‖ Übertragung Von Orgelmusik — Sunflower Sutra ‖ Das Sonnenblumensutra — America ‖ Amerika — In the Baggage Room At Greyhound ‖ Im

Gepäckraum In Greyhound — Wild Orphan || Wilder Waise — At Apollinaire's Grave || An Apollinaires Grab

H171   Ginsberg, Allen. *Kaddisch*. Wiesbaden, West Germany: Limes Verlag, 1962.
Translation by Anselm Hollo: Psalm I || Psalm I — Over Kansas || Über Kansas — The Lion For Real || Der Löwe Wirklich — To Lindsay || An Lindsay — Cezanne's Ports || Die Häfen Des Cezanne — The Blue Angel || Der Blaue Engel — To Aunt Rose || An Tante Rose — Message || Botschaft — Europe! Europe! || Europa! Europa! — Lysergic Acid || Lysergische Säure — Mescaline || Meskalin — The Reply || Die Antwort — Kaddish || Kaddisch — Hymmnn || Hymmnnus

H172   Ginsberg, Allen. *Planet News, Gedichte*. Munich, West Germany: Carl Hanser, 1969.
Translation by Heiner Bastian: Wer Wird Das Universum Übernehmen? [Who Will Take Over the Universe?] — TagebuchNachtGedanken [Journal Night Thoughts] Fernsehen War Ein Baby Das Auf Jene Todeszelle Zukroch [Television Was a Baby Crawling Toward That Deathchamber] — Galiläa-Ufer [Galilee Shore] — Beschreibe: Der Regen Auf Dasaswamedh [Describe: The Rain On Dasaswamedh] — Todesnachricht [Death News] — Geier-Höhe: Gridhakuta Hügel [Vulture Peak: Gridhakuta Hill] — Patna-Benares Express [Patna-Benares Express] — Letzte Nacht In Kalkutta [Last Night In Calcutta] — Die Veränderung: Kyoto-Tokyo-Express [The Change: Kyoto-Tokyo Express] — Erwachen In New York [Waking In New York] — Nach Yeats [After Yeats] — Botschaft II [Message II] — Die Augenblicke Kehren Wieder [The Moments Return] — Kral Majales [Kral Majales] — Erste Party Bei Ken Kesey Mit The Hell's Angels [First Party At Ken Kesey's With Hell's Angels] — Guru [Guru] — Wichita Vortex Sutra [Wichita Vortex Sutra] — Uptown [Uptown] — StadtMitternachtRauschGedicht [City Midnight Junk Strains] — Pentagon Exorzismus [Pentagon Exorcism]

H173   Ginsberg, Allen. *Indisches Tagebuch*. Munich, West Germany: Carl Hanser, 1972.
Translation by Carl Weissner: Indisches Tagebuch [Indian Journals]

H174a   Ginsberg, Allen. *Iron Horse*. Göttingen, West Germany: Expanded Media Editions, 1973.
Translation by Carl Weissner: Iron Horse [Iron Horse]
H174b   Ginsberg, Allen. *Iron Horse*. Bonn, West Germany: Expanded Media Editions, 1978. [second printing]
Note: As the first printing.

H175   Ginsberg, Allen. *Der Untergang Amerikas Gedichte 1965-1971*. Munich, West Germany: Hanser Verlag, 1975.
Translation by Carl Weissner: Dem Andenken Walt Whitmans Gewidmet [Dedication] — Anfang Eines Gedichts Über Diese Staaten [Beginning Of a Poem Of These States] — Diese Staaten, Nach L.A. [These States, Into L.A.] — Autobahngedicht L.A.-Albuquerque-Texas-Wichita [Hiway Poesy LA-Albuquerque-Texas-Wichita] — Kansas City Nach Saint Louis [Kansas City To Saint Louis] — Ein Schwur [A Vow] — Schluss Mit Dem Grössten Schwanz [Done, Finished With the Biggest Cock] — Blick Aus Dem Offenen Fenster Auf Chicago [An Open Window On Chicago] — Rückkehr Nördlich Des Vortex [Returning North Of Vortex] — Flug Über Die Nation [Crossing Nation] — Gewalt [Violence] — Wieder Über Denver [Over Denver Again] — Für Poe: Überm Planeten, Flug Albany-Baltimore [To Poe: Over the Planet, Air Albany-Baltimore] — Nordwest-Route [Northwest Passage] — Einsiedlerhütte Im Mondschein [In a Moonlit Hermit's Cabin] — Regennasser Asphalt, Schwüle, Überquellende Mülltonnen Am Strassenrand [Rain-Wet Asphalt Heat, Garbage Curbed Cans Overflowing] — Tod An Allen Fronten

[Death On All Fronts] — Gärten Der Erinnerung [Memory Gardens] — Freitag Der Dreizehnte [Friday the Thirteenth] — D.C. Mobilization [D.C. Mobilization] — Ökolog [Ecologue] — "Habt Ihr Diesen Film Gesehen?" [Have You Seen This Movie?] — [blurb on back cover]

H176   Ginsberg, Allen. *Gärtender Erinnerung*. Munich, West Germany: Wilhelm Heyne Verlag, 1978.

Translation by Heiner Bastian: TagebuchNachtGedanken [Journal Night Thoughts] — Galiläa-Ufer [Galilee Shore] — Todesnachricht [Death News] — Geier-Höhe: Gridhakuta Hügel [Vulture Peak: Gridhakuta Hill] — Letzte Nacht In Kalkutta [Last Night In Calcutta] — Die Veränderung: Kyoto-Tokyo-Express [The Change: Kyoto-Tokyo Express] — Erwachen In New York [Waking In New York] — Die Augenblicke Kehren Wieder [The Moments Return] — Wichita Vortex Sutra [Wichita Vortex Sutra] — StadtMitternachtRauschGedicht [City Midnight Junk Strains]

Translation by Carl Weissner: Anfang Eines Gedichtes Über Diese Staaten [Beginning Of a Poem Of These States] — Autobahngedicht L.A.-Albuquerque-Texas-Wichita [Hiway Poesy LA-Albuquerque-Texas-Wichita] — Ein Schwur [A Vow] — Blick Aus Dem Offenen Fenster Auf Chicago [An Open Window On Chicago] — Flug Über Die Nation [Crossing Nation] — Gewalt [Violence] — Regennasser Asphalt, Schwüle, Überquellende Mülltonnen Am Strassenrand [Rain-Wet Asphalt Heat, Garbage Curbed Cans Overflowing] — Gärten Der Erinnerung [Memory Gardens] — Ökolog [Ecologue] — [blurb on back cover]

H177   Ginsberg, Allen. *Poesiealbum 127*. East Berlin, East Germany: Neues Leben, 1978.

Translation by Wolfgang Fleischmann and Rudolf Wittkopf: Ein Selbstbedienungsladen In Kalifornien [A Supermarket In California] — Übertragung Von Orgelmusik [Transcription Of Organ Music]

Translation by Heiner Bastian: Galiläa-Ufer [Galilee Shore] — Letzte Nacht In Kalkutta [Last Night In Calcutta] — Erwachen In New York [Waking In New York] — Nach Yeats [After Yeats] — Guru [Guru] — Erste Party Bei Ken Kesey Mit The Hell's Angels [First Party At Ken Kesey's With the Hell's Angels] — Uptown [Uptown]

Translation by Carl Weissner: Ein Schwur [A Vow] — Schluss Mit Dem Grössten Schwanz [Done, Finished With the Biggest Cock] — Flug Uber Die Nation [Crossing Nation] — Einsiedlerhütte Im Mondschein [In a Moonlit Hermit's Cabin] — Tod An Allen Fronten [Death On All Fronts] — Freitag Der Dreizehnte [Friday the Thirteenth]

H178   Ginsberg, Allen. *Das Geheul Und Andere Gedichte*. Wiesbaden, West Germany: Limes Verlag, 1979.

Translation by Carl Weissner: Howl ‖ Das Geheul — Footnote To Howl ‖ Fussnote Zum Geheul — A Supermarket In California ‖ Ein Supermarkt In Kalifornien — Transcription Of Organ Music ‖ Transkription Von Orgelmusik — Sunflower Sutra ‖ Sonnenblumen-Sutra — America ‖ Amerika — In the Baggage Room At Greyhound ‖ In Der Gepäckhalle Des Greyhound — Wild Orphan ‖ Wilder Waise — At Apollinaire's Grave ‖ An Apollinaires Grab

H179a   Ginsberg, Allen. *Notizbücher 1952-1962*. Munich, West Germany: Carl Hanser, 1980.

Translation by Bernd Samland: Notizbücher 1952-1962 [*Journals, Early 50s Early 60s*]

H179b   Ginsberg, Allen. *Notizbücher 1952-1962*. Reinbek Bei Hamburg, West Germany: Rowohlt, 1982.

Note: As first Carl Hanser edition.

H180   Ginsberg, Allen. *Herzgesänge*. Hamburg, West Germany: Loose Blätter Presse, 1981.
Translation by Michael Mundhenk: Jaweh And Allah Battle ‖ Jaweh Und Allah Kämpfen — Tübingen-Hamburg Schlafwagen ‖ Tübingen-Hamburg Schlafwagen — Ode To Failure ‖ Ode Auf Das Scheitern — Homework ‖ Hausarbeit — Relections At Lake Louise ‖ Reflexionen Am Lake Louise — Τεθυακην Δολιγω Πιδευβηω Ραινομαι [Tethauken D'Oligo 'Pideubeo Rainomai] ‖ Τεθυακην Δολιγω Πιδευβηω Ραινομαι
Translation by Eckhard Rhode: Wie T.S. Eliot Mir Im Traum Begegnete [T.S. Eliot Entered My Dreams]
Translation by Jürgen Schmidt: Nagasaki Days ‖ Nagasaki Tage — Ruhrgebiet ‖ Ruhr-Gebiet — Warrior ‖ Krieger — As I Sit Writing Here ‖ "Während Ich Hier Sitze Und Schreibe"
Translation by Michael Mundhenk and Klaus Feiten: Plutonian Ode ‖ Plutonische Ode

H181a   Ginsberg, Allen. *Jukebox Elegien*. Munich, West Germany: Carl Hanser, 1981.
Translation by Bernd Samland: Das Grüne Automobil [The Green Automobile] — Zu Burroughs' Werk [On Burroughs' Work] — Liebesgedicht Über Ein Thema Von Whitman [Love Poem On Theme By Whitman] — Malest Cornifici Tuo Catullo [Malest Cornifici Tuo Catullo] — Traumaufzeichnung: 8. Juni 1955 [Dream Record] — Ein Fremdes Neues Cottage In Berkeley [A Strange New Cottage In Berkeley] — Sather Gate Illumination [Sather Gate Illumination] — Amerikanisches Wechselgeld [American Change] — "Zurück Auf Dem Times Square, Vom Times Square Träumen" ['Back On Times Square, Dreaming Of Times Square'] — Mein Trauriges Ich [My Sad Self] — An Einen Alten Dichter In Peru [To an Old Poet In Peru] — Gedicht-Rakete [Poem Rocket] — Ignu [Ignu] — Tod Dem Ohr Van Goghs! [Death To Van Gogh's Ear!] — Magischer Psalm [Magic Psalm] — Diese Art Leben Braucht Sex [This Form Of Life Needs Sex] — Morgen [Morning] — Ich Bin Ein Opfer Des Telefons [I Am Victim Of Telephone] — Heute [Today] — Freundlich Zu Wem [Who Be Kind To] — Wales-Visitation [Wales Visitation] — Gold Fällt: Herbst In Neu-England [Autumn Gold: New England Fall] — Arschkuss [Kiss Ass] — Elegie Ché Guévara [Elegy Ché Guévara] — Elegie Für Neal Cassady [Elegy For Neal Cassady] —Bitte Herr [Please Master] — Über Neals Asche [On Neal's Ashes] — Unterwegs Nach Chicago [Going To Chicago] — Imaginäre Universen [Imaginary Universes] — September Auf Der Strasse Von Jessore [September On Jessore Road] — Ayers Rock Uluru Song [Ayers Rock Uluru Song] — Geistesatem [Mind Breaths] — Teton Village [Teton Village] — Schlacht Zwischen Jaweh Und Allah [Jaweh And Allah Battle] — Werd Nicht Alt (I-X) [Don't Grow Old] — Land O' Lakes, Wisc. [Land O' Lakes, Wisc.]
Translation by Carl Weissner: "Was Würdest Du Tun, Wenn Du Das Alles Verlierst?" [What Would You Do If You Lost It?] — Ego-Beichte [Ego Confession] — Es Musste Auch Noch Aus Der Jukebox Dröhnen [Hadda Be Playing On the Jukebox]
Translation by Michael Munkhenk and Klaus Feiten: Plutonische Ode [Plutonian Ode]

H181b   Ginsberg, Allen. *Jukebox Elegien*. Munich, West Germany: Wilhelm Heyne Verlag, 1983.
Note: As first Carl Hanser edition.

H182   Ginsberg, Allen. *Eroica Und Andere Gedichte*. Göttingen, West Germany: Verlag Altaquito, 1984. [Series: Altaquito Sonderblätter 33]
Translation by Jürgen Schmidt: Grimmiges Skelett [Grim Skeleton] — Manhattan May Day Midnight [Manhattan May Day Midnight] — 31. Dezember 1978 [Dec. 31, 1978] — Las Vegas: Improvisierte Verse Für El Dorado H.S. Newspaper [Las Vegas: Verses Improvised For El Dorado H.S. Newspaper] — Eroica [Eroica]

H183 Ginberg, Allen. *Beim Lesen Der Gedichte Von Bai Juyi.* Göttingen, West Germany: Verlag Altaquito, 1988. [Series: Altaquito Sonderblätter 75]
Translation by Jürgen Schmidt: Beim Lesen Von Bai Juyi [Reading Bai Juyi]

H184 Ginsberg, Allen. *Das Geheul Für Carl Solomon.* Offenbach/Main, Germany: Bernd Vatter (privately printed), 1991.
Translation by Carl Weissner: Das Geheul [Howl]
Notes: Printed as a student project in an edition of 50 copies.

H185 Ginsberg, Allen. *Viele Lieben / Many Loves.* Hannover, Germany: Apartment Edition, 1994. [Series: Apartment Edition 9]
Translation by Jürgen Schmidt: Lied ‖ Song — Viele Lieben ‖ Many Loves — Warum Ist Gott Liebe, Jack? ‖ Why Is God Love, Jack? — Nacht Glanz ‖ Night Gleam — Süsser Knabe, Gib Mir Deinen Arsch ‖ Sweet Boy, Gimme Yr Ass — Gedanken Während Eines Atemzuges ‖ Thoughts On a Breath — Alte Liebesgeschichte ‖ Old Love Story — In Meiner Küche In New York ‖ In My Kitchen In New York — Aufgeschrieben In Meinem Traum Von W.C.W. ‖ Written In My Dream By W.C. Williams — Schweigende Mehrheit ‖ Moral Majority — Du Weisst Es Nicht ‖ You Don't Know It — Schwere Arbeit ‖ Hard Labor — Sphinkter ‖ Sphincter — Ich Ging In Den Film Des Lebens ‖ I Went To the Movie Of Life — Über Die Verbrennung Chögyam Trungpas, Vidyadhara ‖ On Cremation Of Chögyam Trungpa, Vidyadhara
Note: The English-language versions of these poems are printed on a separate folded page inserted into this book.

Anthologies:

H186 Corso, Gregory and Höllerer, Walter (eds.). *Junge Amerikanische Lyrik.* Munich, West Germany: Carl Hanser Verlag, 1961, pp. 36-51.
Translation by Maria Sporleder, Rudolf Wittkopf and Walter Höllerer: Back On Times Square Dreaming Of Times Square ‖ Wieder Auf Times Square; Träumend Von Times Square — Squeal ‖ Gequiek — Wrote This Last Night ‖ Schrieb Dies Gestern Abend — Sunflower Sutra ‖ Sonnenblumensutra — Poem Rocket ‖ Raketen Gedicht
Note: Issued with a recording.

H187a Paetel, Karl O. (ed.). *Beat, Eine Anthologie.* Reinbek Bei Hamburg, West Germany: Rowohlt, 1962, pp. 60-73, 124-5, 238-245.
Translation by Willi Anders: Amerika [America] — Hinter Den Dingen [In Back Of the Real] — Kaddish [Kaddish] — Kurzzeilen-Improvisation [Short Line Improvisation] — Der Verhüllte Fremde [The Shrouded Stranger] — Tod Dem Ohr Van Goghs [Death To Van Gogh's Ear] — Zupf Mein Blümchen [Pull My Daisy (by AG, Jack Kerouac and Neal Cassady)] — Die Dharma-Bums [prose book review of *The Dharma Bums*] — Bemerkungen Zur Plattenaufnahme Von "Howl" [Notes for *Howl and Other Poems (Fantasy recording)*]
H187b Paetel, Karl O. (ed.). *Beat, Eine Anthologie.* Augsburg, West Germany: Maro Verlag, 1988, pp. 60-73, 124-5, 238-245.
Note: Contents as above.

H188 Corso, Gregory. *In Der Flüchtigen Hand Der Zeit.* Wiesbaden, West Germany: Limes Verlag, 1963.
Translation by Anselm Hollo: [prose blurb on inside back cover flap].

H189 Heise, Hans-Jürgen (ed.). *Das Bist Du Mensch.* Munich, West Germany: Hartfrid Voss Verlag, 1963, p. 35.
Translation by Rudolf Wittkopf: Aus "Übertragung Von Orgelmusik" [Transcription Of Organ Music]

H190   Burroughs, William and Ginsberg, Allen. *Auf Der Suche Nach Yage.*
Wiesbaden, West Germany: Limes Verlag, 1964, pp. 71-86, 93.
Translation by Katharina and Peter Behrens: [letter to William Burroughs] —
[prose footnote to letter] — [letter to whom it may concern]

H191   Link, Franz (ed.). *Amerikanische Lyrik.* Stuttgart, W. Germany, Philipp
Reclam, 1974, pp. 410-413.
Translation: A Supermarket In California ‖ Ein Supermarkt In Kalifornien

H192   Pelieu, Claude. *Amphetamin Cowboy.* Bonn, West Germany: Expanded Media
Editions, 1976, p. 5.
Translation by Carl Weissner: Vorwort [Foreword]

H193   Derschau, Christoph. *Die Ufer Der Salzlosen Karibik.* Kaufbeuren, West
Germany: Pohl 'N Mayer, 1977.
Translation by Christoph Derschau: [At Apollinaire's Grave (excerpt)]

H194   *Fiesta In Foresta, Poema La Siesta.* Göttingern, West Germany: Verlag
Altaquito, 1979, pp. 45-46, 49, 124-126.
Translation: In Back Of the Real ‖ Hintes Den Dingen — Don't Grow Old ‖ Werd
Nicht Alt

H195   Burroughs, William S. *Zwischen Mitternacht Und Morgen.* Basel, Switzerland:
Sphinx Verlag, 1980, pp. 41-46.
Translation by Udo Breger: Der Traum Von Tibet [The Dream Of Tibet]

H196   Derschau, Christoph. *Die Guten Wolken.* Erlangen, West Germany: Klaus G.
Renner, 1980, p. 93.
Translation: [prose blurb]

H197   Hartmann, Walter (ed.). *Zum Schutze Aller Lebewesen.* Linden, West Germany:
Volksverlag, 1980, pp. 22-34, 37-40.
Translation by Walter Hartmann: Weg Mit Plutonium! (by AG and Col. Sutton
Smith) [Nuts To Plutonium!] — Plutonische Ode [Plutonian Ode]

H198   Galloway, David and Sabisch, Christian (eds.). *Calamus.* Reinbek Bei
Hamburg, Germany: Rowalt Verlag, 1981, pp. 223-229.
Translation by Carl Weissner: Ein Supermarkt In Kalifornien [A Supermarket In
California] — Regennasser Asphalt, Schwüle, Überquellende Mülltonnen An
Strassenrand [Rain-Wet Asphalt Heat, Garbage Curbed Cans Overflowing].
Translation by Christian Sabisch: Bitte Herr [Please Master]

H199   Höllerer, Walter (ed.). *Autoren Im Haus.* Berlin, West Germany: Galerie
Wannsee Verlag, 1982, pp. 70-71.
Translation by Wolfgang Fleischmann: An Apollinaires Grab [At Apollinaire's
Grave]

H200   Schmiele, Walter (ed.). *Poesie Der Welt Nordamerika.* Frankfurt, West
Germany: Ullstein, 1984, pp. 332-335.
Translation by Wolfgang Fleischmann: Wild Orphan ‖ Wilder Waise

H201   Kurtz, Michael. *Stockhausen.* Basel, Switzerland: Bärenreiter Kassel, 1988, p.
178.
Translation: [letter to Michael Kurtz]

H202   Waldman, Anne. *Den Mond In Farbe Sehen.* Augsburg, West Germany: Maro
Verlag, 1988, pp. [6-7].
Translation: Introduction ‖ Introduction

H203   McShine, Kynaston (ed.). *Andy Warhol: A Retrospective* [German edition].
       Munich, Germany: Prestel Verlag, 1989.
       Translation: Despite the Coolness Of Warhol's Art [prose]

H204   Geist, Peter and others (eds.). *Lyrik Der Moderne.* Berlin, Germany: Volk und
       Wissen Verlag, 1992, pp. 82-85.
       Translation by Carl Weissner: Done, Finished With the Biggest Cock ‖ Schluss
       Mit Dem Grössten Schwanz

H205   Campe, Joachim (ed.). *Matrosen Sind Der Liebe Schwingen.* Frankfurt Am
       Main, Germany: Insel Verlag, 1994, pp. 151-155.
       Translation by Carl Weissner: Regennasser Asphalt, Schwüle Überquellende
       Mülltonnen Am Strassenrand [Rain-Wet Asphalt Heat, Garbarge Curbed Cans
       Overflowing]
       Translation by B. Samland: Über Neals Asche [On Neal's Ashes]
       Translation by Thomas Böhme: Jimmy Berman Rag [Jimmy Berman Rag]

H206   *Kellners Gästebuch.* Hamburg, Germany: Kellner, 1994, pp. 163-165.
       Translation by Michael Mundhenk, Klaus Feiten, and Jürgen Schmidt: Über Die
       Verbrennung Chögyam Trungpas, Vidyadhara [On Cremation of Chögyam
       Trungpa, Vidyadhara]

Periodicals:

H207* [poem]. *Blätter Und Bilder,* no. 2 (May-June 1959) pp. 25-26, 31.
       Translation by Wolfgang Fleishmann and Rudolf Wittkopf: Amerika [America]

H208   [poem]. *Neuen Presse* (Oct. 31, 1959)
       Translation: Amerika [America (excerpt)]

H209   [poem]. *Süddeutsche Zeitung,* no. 28/29 (Nov. 1959)
       Translation: Ein Selbstbedienungsladen In Kalifornien [A Supermarket In
       California]

H210   [poem]. *Neue Züricher Zeitung* (Dec. 13, 1959)
       Translation by Wolfgang Fleischmann and Rudolf Wittkopf: A Supermarket In
       California ‖ Ein Selbstbedienungsladen In Kalifornien

H211   [poem]. *Akzente,* no. 1 (1959) pp. 34-35.
       Translation by Walter Höllerer: Das Geheul [Howl (excerpt)]

H212* [prose]. *Blätter Und Bilder,* no. 10 (Sept.-Oct. 1960) pp. 28-30.
       Translation by Marguerite Schlüter: Auch Das Ist Amerika [Poetry, Violence,
       And the Trembling Lambs]

H213   [poem]. *Periskop,* no. 1 (Dec. 1961) pp. 25-26.
       Translation by Anselm Hollo: An Tante Rose [To Aunt Rose]

H214* [poem]. *Rhinozeros,* no. 5 (1961) pp. [20-21].
       Translation by Dieter E. Zimmer: The End ‖ Das Ende

H215* [3 poems]. *Periskop,* no. 3 (March 1962) p. 18.
       Translation by Anselm Hollo: Metaphysisch [Metaphysics] — Eine Welt Hab Ich
       Bei Jedem Geliebten Erlent [I Learned A World From Each] — Ich Umarmte
       Mich Selbst [I Made Love To Myself]

H216   [poem]. *Mahenjodaro,* vol. 2, no. 3-4 (Nov. 1963-April 1964) unpaged.
       Translation by Anselm Hollo: Whatever It May Be Whoever It May Be ‖ Was Es
       Auch Sein Mag Wer Es Auch Sein Mag

H217* [poem]. *Netz,* no. 2 (1963) pp. 6-11.
Translation: An Einen Alten Dichter in Peru ‖ To An Old Poet In Peru

H218* [poem]. *Rhinozeros,* no. 9 (1964) p. 14.
Translation by Anselm Hollo: Whatever It May Be Whoever It May Be ‖ Was Es Auch Sein Mag Wer Es Auch Sein Mag

H219 [poem]. *Akzente,* vol. 15, no. 3 (June 1968) pp. 200-202.
Translation by Heiner Bastian: Kral Majales [Kral Majales]

H220 [poem]. *Gasolin 23,* no. 2 (April 1973) p. 19.
Translation: Dillinger [Dillinger]

H221* [poem]. *Podium,* no. 11 (1974) p. 131.
Translation by Doris Müchringer: Liebesgedicht Nach Einem Thema Von Whitman [Love Poem On Theme By Whitman]

H222 [2 poems]. *National Zeitung* (April 12, 1975) NZ Am Wochenende section, p. 3.
Translation by Carl Weissner: Ein Schwur [A Vow] — Gewalt [Violence]

H223 [prose]. *Päng,* vol. 6, no. 11 (Summer 1976) p. 25.
Translation: Om Ah Um: 44 Vorläufige Fragen An Dr. Timothy Leary [44 Temporary Questions For Timothy Leary]

H224 [2 poems]. *Akzente,* vol. 23, no. 6 (Dec. 1976) pp. 551-555.
Translation by Carl Weissner: Ego-Beichte [Ego Confession] — "Was Würdest Du Tun, Wenn Du Das Da Alles Verlierst?" [What Would You Do If You Lost It?]

H225 [2 poems]. *Exempla,* vol. 3, no. 1 (1977) pp. 5-16, 19-23.
Translation by Jörg Ross: Das Geheul [Howl] — Jaweh & Allah Battle ‖ Die Schlacht Von Jahweh Und Allah

H226 [poem]. *Deutsch Heft,* vol. 6, no. 8 (June 1977) pp. [1, 3-5].
Translation by Carl Weissner: Es Musste Auch Noch Aus Der Jukebox Dröhnen [Hadda Be Playing On the Jukebox]

H227 [prose]. *Götter Dämmerung,* no. 1 (June 1977) p. [19]
Translation by T. Schroeder: Allen Ginsberg Über The Fugs [*The Fugs* (liner notes)].

H228 [poem]. *Inzwischen,* no. 3-4 (ca. 1979) [issue called *Frank O'Hara*] pp. 31-32.
Translation by Ulrich Gunreben: Stadt Mitternacht Rausch Gedicht [City Midnight Junk Strains]

H229 [poem]. *Alta Quito Zeitung,* no. 2 (May-June 1980) pp. 26-34.
Translation by Andreas Meyer and Reinhard Harbaum: Plutonium Ode [Plutonian Ode]

H230 [poem]. *Sprache Im Technischen Zeitalter,* vol. 74, no. 15 (June 1980) Literatur Im Technischen Zeitalter section, pp. 48-57.
Translation by Michael Mundhenk and Klaus Feiten: Plutonian Ode ‖ Plutonische Ode

H231 [poem]. *Berner Zeitung* (Nov. 29, 1980) p. 9.
Translation by Peter Schrang and Daniel Leutenegger: Ruhr [Ruhr-Gebeit]

H232 [prose]. *Alemantschen: Materialien Für Radikale Ökologie*, no. 1 (Dec. 1980) p. 110.
Translation by Ruedi Lüscher: Brief An Antler [letter to Antler]

H233 [prose]. *Sphinx Magazin*, no. 11 (Dec. 1980) pp. 28-29.
Translation: Der Traum Von Tibet [The Dream Of Tibet]

H234 [poem]. *Humus*, no. 4 (1980) pp. 54-55.
Translation: Plutonische Ode [Plutonian Ode]

H235 [prose]. *Die Tageszeitung*, no. 799/24 (June 16, 1982) pp. 14-15.
Translation by Gerlinde Mander: Rauchende Schreibmaschinen [Smoking Typewriters]

H236 [2 poems]. *Altaquito Sonderblätter*, no. 20-21 (Oct. 1982) [issue called *Lines Of Feeling*] pp. 32-38.
Translation by Jürgen Schmidt: Was Ist Tot? [What's Dead?] — Spatzenhirn [Birdbrain]

H237 [poem]. *UNESCO Kurier* [German edition], vol. 23, no. 11 (Nov. 1982)
Translation: [Plutonian Ode (excerpt)]

H238 [prose]. *Radar*, no. 1 (1982) pp. 46-47.
Translation: [introduction for *Letters To Allen Ginsberg* by William Burroughs]

H239 [prose and poems]. *Apartment*, no. 1 (Feb. 1983) [issue called *New York Poets: Allen Ginsberg*] ll. [1-31].
Translation by Jürgen Schmidt: Belgrader Rede [prose statement made in Belgrad Oct. 17, 1980 about poetics] — Hum Bomb [Hum Bom] — Punk Rock Du Mein Plärr Baby [Punk Rock Your My Big Crybaby] — Den Punks Von Dawlish [To the Punks Of Dawlish] — Capitol Air [Capitol Air] — Spatzenhirn! [Birdbrain!] — Airplane Blues [Airplane Blues] — Der Schwarze Mann [The Black Man] — "Worauf Hast Du Bock?" [What You Up To?] — Eine Öffentliche Poesie [A Public Poetry] — Schmäh Gedicht [Throw Out the Yellow Journalists Of Bad Grammar] — Diese Zwei [Those Two On Marine Street] — Warum Ich Meditiere [Why I Meditate] — Do the Meditation [Do the Meditation Rock] — Capitol Air [in English only with facsimile holograph notes and corrections]

H240 [prose]. *Apartment*, no. 2 (Feb. 1983) [issue called *New York Poets: Peter Orlovsky*] l. [3, 12-14].
Translation by Jürgen Schmidt: Peter Orlovsky [cover blurb from *Clean Asshole Poems*] — Kollaboration: Brief An Charlie Chaplin [letter to Charlie Chaplin by Peter Orlovsky and AG]

H241 [prose]. *Nana: Hannoversche Wochenschar*, no. 5 (Feb. 3, 1983)
Translation by H.C.J.: [Declaration Of Three (excerpt)]

H242 [prose]. *Radar*, no. 2 (1983) pp. 54-55.
Translation: [introduction for *Letters to Allen Ginsberg* by William S. Burroughs]

H243 [poem]. *Tages-Anzeiger Magazin* (April 27, 1985) p. 49.
Translation: Weisse Hülle [White Shroud]

H244 [3 poems]. *Bestände*, no. 19-20 (Spring [March] 1991) pp. 37, 49 and back cover.
Translation by Christian Loidl: In My Kitchen In New York ‖ In Meiner Küche In New York.

Translation by Heiner Bastian: First Party At Ken Kesey's With Hell's Angels ‖ Erste Party Bei Ken Kesey Mit the Hell's Angels — Guru [Guru]

H245   [poem]. *Lesezirkel,* no. 54 (Dec. 1991) p. 14.
Translation by Christian Loidl: American Haiku ‖ American Haiku [German]

H246   [prose]. *Sisyphus,* no. 13-15 (1992) [also called *Die Jack Kerouac School of Disembodied Poetics*] pp. 38-43, 56.
Translation by Christian Loidl: Meditation Und Poetik [Meditation And Poetics] — Verschiedene Anschauungen Zum Bewussten Arrangieren Offener Versformen Auf Einer Seite [prose list of recommended reading] — Dreizehn Schritte Zur Überarbeitung [prose list of writing procedures] — [notes for a Christian Loidl poem]

H247   [2 poems]. *Akzente,* vol. 41, no. 1 (Feb. 1994) pp. 41-42.
Translation by Adolf Endler: Frieden In Bosnien-Herzegowina [Peace In Bosnia-Herzegovina] — Yiddishe Kopf [Yiddishe Kopf]

H248   [3 poems]. *Litfass,* vol. 18, no. 60 (April 1994) pp. 15-17.
Translation by Adolf Endler: Frieden In Bosnien-Herzegowina [Peace In Bosnia-Herzegovina] — Rückkehr Des Kral Majales [Return Of Kral Majales] — Yiddishe Kopf [Yiddishe Kopf]

Miscellaneous:

H249*   [calendar]. *Ottersberger Abreiss.* Ottersberg, Germany: Schülerdruckerei Manufaktur, 1973.
Translation by Michael Kurtz: [Returning To the Country For a Brief Visit]
Note: Both German and English versions of this poem appear on the pages for the dates April 21-27, 1974.

H250   [program]. *Cosmopolitan Greetings: Jazz Opera.* By George Gruntz and Allen Ginsberg. Cologne, Germany: WDR, May 26, 1992.
Translation by Carsten G. Pfeiffer: Jumping the Gun On the Sun ‖ [Jumping the Gun On the Sun (German)] — Happening Now? ‖ [Happening Now? (German)] — Those Two ‖ [Those Two (German)] — Maturity ‖ [Maturity (German)] — Bop Lyrics ‖ [Bop Lyrics (German)] — 7th Avenue Express ‖ [7th Avenue Express (German)] — Funny Death ‖ [Funny Death (German)] — An Eastern Ballad ‖ [An Eastern Ballad (German)] — Song ‖ [Song (German)] — Prophecy ‖ [Prophecy (German)]

GREEK

Books:

H251   Ginsberg, Allen. *Συγχρονη Ποιηση [Eisagoge Poiese].* Athens, Greece: Boukoumanes, 1974.
Translation by Jennie Mastorski: Ουρλιαχτο [Howl] — Amepikh [America] — Kaddish [Kaddish] — Ποιημα Πυραυλοσ [Poem Rocket] — Στη Θεια Ροζα [To Aunt Rose] — Το Λιονταρι Στ' Αληθινα [The Lion For Real] — Θανατοσ Ετ' Αοτι Του Βαν Γκογκ [Death To Van Gogh's Ear] — Η Αποκριση [The Reply] — Ο Σακυαμουνι Βγαινει Απ' Το Βουνο [Sakyamuni Coming Out From the Mountain] — Στριγγλισμα [Squeal] — Πισω Στην Ταιμσ Σκουεαρ Να Ονειρευομαι Την Ταιμσ Σκουεαρ [Back On Times Square, Dreaming Of Times Square] — Επικαιρα Απο

Θωρηκτο [Battleship Newsreel] — Σε Παρακαλω Να Ξαναγυρισεισ Και Να 'Σαι Χαρουμενοσ [I Beg You Come Back And Be Cheerful] — Σ' Ενα Γερο Ποιητη Στο Περου [To an Old Poet In Peru] — Υμνοσ Στην Καλι Που Καταστρεφει Τισ Ψευδαισθησεισ [Stotras To Kali Destroyer Of Illusions] — Kral Majales [Kral Majales] — Αρχη Ενοσ Ποιηματοσ Τουτων Των Πολιτειων [Beginning Of a Poem Of These States] — To Tama [A Vow] — Φανταστικοι Κοσμοι [Imaginary Universes] — Θανατοσ Σ' Ολα Τα Μετωπα [Death On All Fronts]

H252a Ginsberg, Allen. *Ποιηματα [Poiemata].* Athens, Greece: Akmon, 1978.

Translation by Aris Berlis: Ουρλιαχτο [Howl] — Γποσημειωση Στο Ουρλιαχτο [Footnote To Howl] — Ενα Σουπερμαρκετ Στην Καλιφορνια [A Supermarket In California] — Το Διδαγμα Του Ηλιοτροπιου [Sunflower Sutra] — Amepikh [America] — Kantiz [Kaddish] — Ποιημα Ρουκεττα [Poem Rocket] — Ευρωπη! Ευρωπη! [Europe! Europe!] — Στη Θεια Ροζα [To Aunt Rose] — Στον Ταφο Του 'Απολλιναιρ [At Apollinaire's Grave] — Το Λιονταρι Στ' Αληθεια [The Lion For Real] — Αγνοοζ [Ignu] — Θανατοζ Στ Αυτι Του Βαν Γκογκ! [Death To Van Gogh's Ear!] — Μεσκαλινη [Mescaline] — Μαγικοζ Ψαλμοζ [Magic Psalm] — [liner notes for *Howl* Fantasy recording] — [*Paris Review* interview]

H252b Ginsberg, Allen. *ΠΟΙΗΜΑΤΑ [Poiemata].* Athens, Greece: Ekdoseis Sunecheia, 1990.
Notes: A new edition of the identical collection.

H253 Ginsberg, Allen. *Ποιηματα [Poiemata].* [Greece?]: Ekdoseis Paschale, ca. 1983.

Translation by Panos Panasses: Ο Δλιμμενοϖ Μου Εαυτοϖ [City Midnight Junk Strains] — Για Το Εργο Του Μπαρροουζ [On Burroughs' Work] — Ενα Σουπερμαρχετ Στην Καλιφορνια [A Supermarket In California] — Το Διδαγμα Του Ηλιοτροπιου [Sunflower Sutra] — Στη Θεια Ροζα [To Aunt Rose] — Υμνοϖ [Kaddish (Excerpt)] — Η Συνεχεια Ενοϖ Μεγαλου Ποιηματοϖ Απ Αυτεϖ Τιϖ Πολιτειεϖ [Continuation Of a Long Poem Of These States]

H254 Ginsberg, Allen. *Πλοψτωνια Ωδη [Ploutonia Ode].* Athens, Greece: Apopira Publications, 1985.

Translation by Tasos Samartzes: Πλοψτωνια Ωδη [Plutonian Ode] — Τομπλουζ Του Χαφιε [Stool Pigeon Blues] — Πανκ Ροκ Εισαι Το Αγαπημενο Μου Κλαψιαρικο Μωρο [Punk Rock Your My Big Crybaby] — Ποιοι Νεκροι [What's Dead?] — Ο Φοβεροσ Σκελετοσ [Grim Skeleton] — Μεσανυχτα Πρωτομαγιασ Στο Μανχαταν [Manhattan May Day Midnight] — Μερεσ Του Ναγκασακι [Nagasaki Days] — «Μη Γερασεισ» [Don't Grow Old] — 31 Δεκεμβριου 1978 [December 31, 1978]

— Το Σαινι Του Κολεγιου Του Μπρουκλιν [Brooklyn College Brain] — Η Πολιτεια Με Τουσ Κηπουσ [Garden State] — Ανοιξιατικη Μοδα [Spring Fashions] — Για Τουσ Πανκσ Του Ντοουλισ [To the Punks Of Dawlish] — Λιγη Αγαπη [Some Love] — Ρουρ Γκεμπιτ [Ruhr-Gebiet] — Στιχοι Γραμμενοι Για Τη Φοιτητικη Διαδηλωση Εναντια Στην Υποχρεωτικη Στρατολογηση 1980 [Verses Written For Student Antidraft Registration Rally 1980] — Οικιακα [Homework] — Στ' Αχναρια Του Ουιτμαν Και Του Ρεζνικοφ [After Whitman And Reznikoff] — Στοχασμοι Στη Λιμνη Λουιζ [Reflections At Lake Louise] — «Τεθνακην Δ' Ολιγω 'Πιδευης Φαινομαι» [Red-Cheeked Boyfriends] — Ωδη Στην Αποτυχια [Ode To Failure] — Ο Κουφιοκεφαλοσ [Birdbrain!] — Ηρωικη [Eroica] — Η Μελωδια Του Καπιτωλιου [Capitol Air]

H255 Ginsberg, Allen. *Το Ουρλιαχτο [To Oyrliachto].* Athens, Greece: Eleytheros Typos, 1987.

Translation by Giorgoz Mplanaz and Demetrez Poulikakoz: Ουρλιαχτο [Howl] — Amepikh [America] — Ενασ Ασφοδελοσ [An Asphodel] — Ψαλμοσ III [Psalm III] — Αστειοσ Θανατοσ [Funny Death] — Για Το Εργο Του Μπαροουζ [On Burroughs' Work] — Ποιημα Ερωτικο Πανω Σε Θεμα Του Ουιτμαν [Love Poem On Theme By Whitman] — Τραγουδι [Song] — Malest Cornifici Tuo Catullo [Malest Cornifici Tuo Catullo] — Γκραντ Παρκ [Grant Park: August 28, 1968] — Αγριο Ορφανο [Wild Orphan] — Πιεω Απο Το Πραγματικο [In Back Of the Real] — Wichita Vortex Sutra [Wichita Vortex Sutra]

H256 Ginsberg, Allen. *Ημερολογια [Emerologia].* Athens, Greece: I.D. Kollarov & Sias A.E., 1993.

Translation by Spyros Meimares: Ημερολογια [*Journals Early Fifties Early Sixties*]

Anthologies:

H257 Burroughs, William S. *Junky.* Athens, Greece: Apopira Publications, 1983, pp. 5-10.

Translation by Nikos Pratsines and Ntina Sotera: Eisauoue [Introduction]

Periodicals:

H258 [poem]. *Μαρτυριεσ [Martyrs],* vol. 9 (May 1964) pp. 21-23.

Translation by Kleitos Kyros: Amepikh [America]

H259* [poem]. *Παλι [Pali],* no. 2-3 (April 1965) pp. 45, 47-48.

Translation by Dimitri Poulikakos: Amepikh [America]

H260 [poem]. *Παλι [Pali],* no. 5 (Dec. 1965) pp. 35, 37-38.

Translation by Spyros Meimaris: Μαγικοσ Ψαλμοσ [Magic Psalm]

H261 [3 letters]. *Ζαλη [Zaln]* (Oct. 1985) pp. 96-99.
Translation: [letters from A G to Neal and Carolyn Cassady]

H262* [prose]. *Το Βημα [To Bema]* (Dec. 5, 1993)
Translation: [*Journals Early Fifties Early Sixties* (excerpt)]

H263 [prose]. *Κυριακατικη Αυγη [Kuriakatike Auvi]* (Dec. 12, 1993) p. 31.
Translation by Stavroula Papaspurou: [*Journals Early Fifties Early Sixties* (excerpt)]

Miscellaneous:

H264 [program]. *Βραδια Allen Ginsberg [Bradia Allen Ginsberg]*. Greece: Theatro Kotopoule-Rech, Dec. 20, 1993.
Translation by Dino Siotis: Μικρη Αυυελια [Personals Ad] — Κοσμοπολιτκοι Χαιρετιομοι [Cosmopolitan Greetings]
Translation by Spyros Meimaris: Σφιυκιηραρ [Sphincter] — Μιμουμενορ Τον Λαλον [After Lalon]

GUJARATI

H265* [poem]. *Aso,* no. 10-11 (Feb. 1965) pp. 154-155.
Translation by Arun Kolotkar: [Kaddish (excerpt)]

HEBREW

Books:

H266 Ginsberg, Allen. *[Kaddish and Other Poems]*. Tel Aviv, Israel: Am Oved Publishers Ltd., 1988.
Translation by Natan Zach: [Kaddish] ‖ Kaddish — [White Shroud] ‖ White Shroud — [Wild Orphan] ‖ Wild Orphan — [Transcription of Organ Music] ‖ Transcription of Organ Music — [A Supermarket in California] ‖ A Supermarket in California — [Guru] ‖ Guru — [Message II] ‖ Message II — [A Prophecy] ‖ A Prophecy — [Over Laramie] ‖ Over Laramie — [Galilee Shore] ‖ Galilee Shore — [Jahweh and Allah Battle] ‖ Jahweh and Allah Battle — [Cabin in the Rockies] ‖ Cabin in the Rockies — [Reading French Poetry] ‖ Reading French Poetry — [You Might Get In Trouble] ‖ You Might Get In Trouble — [Don't Grow Old] ‖ Don't Grow Old — [After Whitman & Reznikoff] ‖ After Whitman & Reznikoff — [Those Two] ‖ Those Two — [Why I Meditate] ‖ Why I Meditate — [Throw Out the Yellow Journalists of Bad Grammar And Terrible Manner] ‖ Throw Out the Yellow Journalists of Bad Grammar and Terrible Manner — [Irritable Vegetable] ‖ Irritable Vegetable — [I'm a Prisoner of Allen Ginsberg] ‖ I'm a Prisoner of Allen Ginsberg — [Transformation of Bai's "A Night in Xingyang"] ‖ Transformation of Bai's "A Night in Xingyang" — [Surprise Mind] ‖ Surprise Mind — [It's All So Brief] ‖ It's All So Brief

Anthologies:

H267   Omer, Dan (ed.). *[An Anthology of American Beat Poetry].* Jerusalem, Israel: I. Marcus, 1971, pp. 87-149.
Translation by Dan Omer: [Howl — A Supermarket In California — America — Kaddish — Poem Rocket

H268   Peled, Oded (ed.). *[I Hear America Singing].* Haifa, Israel: Yaron Golan Publishing House, 1989, pp. 54-63.
Translation by Oded Peled: [Guru — Tonite All Is Well — Memory Cousins — A Desolation — At Apollinaire's Grave]

H269   Zach, Natan (ed.). *IGRA: Almanac for Literature and Art.* Israel: n.p., 1990, pp. 338-345.
Translation: May Days 1988 || [May Days 1988]

Periodicals:

H270   [poem]. *Iked,* no. 2 (July 1960) pp. 37-38.
Translation by Isumor Yeiuz Kest: [Howl (excerpt)]

H271*   [poem]. *Ah'Shav,* no. 7-8 (Spring 1962) p. 127.
Translation by Tharon Shobtai: [A Supermarket in California]

H272*   [poem]. *Ah'Shav,* no. 31-32 (1975)
Translation by Oded Peled: [Guru]

H273   [poem]. *Proza,* no. 4-5 (May 6, 1976) pp. 10-23.
Translation by David Avidan: [Kaddish]

H274   [poem]. *UNESCO Courier [Hebrew edition],* vol. 35, no. 10 (Nov. 1982) pp. 13-14.
Translation: [Plutonian Ode (excerpt)]

H275*   [poem]. *Ah'Shav,* no. 47-48 (1983)
Translation by Oded Peled: [At Apollinaire's Grave]

H276   [2 poems]. *Hadoar,* vol. 66, no. 3 (Nov. 28, 1986) p. 19.
Translation by Hanita Brand: [White Shroud (excerpt) — Teton Village]

H277   [3 poems]. *Moznaim,* no. 7-8 (1987) pp. 2-4.
Translation by Natan Zach: [Jaweh and Allah Battle — I'm a Prisoner of Allen Ginsberg — Galilee Shore]

HINDI

H278   [poem]. *UNESCO Courier* [Hindi edition], vol. 35, no. 10 (1983) pp. 13-14.
Translation: [Plutonian Ode (excerpt)]

H279   Intentionally omitted.

H280   [excerpt from journals]. *Pravarshan* (1988) pp. 118-132.
Translation by Krishan Balder Vaid: [Journals Oct.-Nov. 1967]

H281   Intentionally omitted.

HUNGARIAN

Books:

H282   Ginsberg, Allen. *Nagyáruház Kaliforniában*. Budapest, Hungary: Európa
Könyvkiadó, 1973.
Translation by Ottó Orbán: A Leples Bitang [The Shrouded Stranger] —
Nagyáruház Kaliforniában [A Supermarket in California] — Napraforgó Szutra
[Sunflower Sutra] — Üvöltés [Howl] — Lindsayhez [To Lindsay] —
Apollinaire Sírjánál [At Apollinaire's Grave] — Meszkalin [Mescaline]
Translation by István Eörsi: Kaddis [Kaddish] — Róza Néninek [To Aunt Rose]
— Burroughs Müvéröl [On Burroughs' Work] — Feljegyzés Egy Álomról:
1955. Június 8-án 86 [Dream Record: June 8, 1955] — Szomorú Énem [My
Sad Self] — Az Isten Miért Szeretet, Jack? [Why Is God Love, Jack?] — Az
Elsö Buli Ken Keseyéknél A Pokol Angyalaival [First Party At Ken Kesey's
With Hell's Angels] — Amerika [America]

H283   Ginsberg, Allen. *A Leples Bitang*. Budapest, Hungary: Európa Könyvkiadó,
1984.
Translation by Ottó Orbán: A Leples Bitang [The Shrouded Stranger] — Üvöltés
[Howl] — Nagyáruház Kaliforniában [A Supermarket In California] —
Napraforgó Szutra [Sunflower Sutra] — Lindsayhez [To Lindsay] —
Apollinaire Sírjánál [At Apollinaire's Grave] — Meszkalin [Mescaline]
Translation by István Eörsi: Metafizika [Metaphysics] — Társaságban [In
Society] — "Szeretkeztem Magammal" [I Made Love To Myself] — Amerika
[America] — Kaddis Naomi Ginsbergért [Kaddish] — Üzenet [Message] —
Róza Néninek [To Aunt Rose] — A Valóságos Oroszlán [The Lion For Real]
— A Válasz [The Reply] — Burroughs Müvéröl [On Burroughs' Work] —
Szerelmes Vers Whitman Témájára [Love Poem On Theme By Whitman] —
Feljegyzés Egy Álomról [Dream Record] — Szomorú Énem [My Sad Self] —
Az Isten Miért Szeretet, Jack? [Why Is God Love, Jack?] — Kávéház
Varsóban [Cafe In Warsaw] — Guru [Guru] — Az Elsö Buli Ken Keseyéknél
A Pokol Angyalaival [First Party At Ken Kesey's With Hell's Angels] —
Elégia Neal Cassadyért [Elegy For Neal Cassady] — Neal Hamvairól [On
Neal's Ashes] — Szeptember A Jessore-i Úton [September On Jessore Road]
— Sok Szerelmem [Many Loves] — Blues Hajnali Négykor [4AM Blues] —
Jöjj Vissza, Karácsony [Come Back Christmas] — MacDougal-Utcai Blues
[MacDougal Street Blues] — Könnygáz Rag [Tear Gas Rag] — Ayers Rock
Uluru Ének [Ayers Rock Uluru Song] — Karácsonyi Ajándék [Xmas Gift] —
Vidékre Visszatérve Rövid Látogatásra [Returning To the Country For a Brief
Visit] — Éjszakai Derengés [Night Gleam] — Neruda Halálára [On Neruda's
Death] — Nemes Igazságok Evangéliuma [Gospel Noble Truths] — Ne Vénülj
Meg [Don't Grow Old] — Kenjetek Mindent Egyvalakire [Drive All Blames
Into One] — Nagaszaki-Napok [Nagasaki Days] — Vén Tó [Old Pond] —
Plutó(nium)i Óda [Plutonian Ode]
Translation by Györe Balázs: Ezüst Durangón Túl, A Mexikói Sierra Redöi Fölött
[Past Silver Durango Over Mexico Sierra Wrinkles] — Reflexiók
Álmosszemben [Reflections In Sleepy Eye] — Halál Mindenütt [Death On All
Fronts] — Laramie Fölött [Over Laramie]

H284   Ginsberg, Allen. *Május Királya*. Budapest, Hungary: Cserepfalvi Könyvkiado,
1990.
Translation by István Eörsi: Üvöltés [Howl] — Halál Van Gogh Fülére [Death
To Van Gogh's Ear] — Kral Majales [Kral Majales] — Seggcsok [Kiss Ass]
— Igenis Reménytelen [Yes And It's Hopeless] — Annyi A Segg A Világban,
Annyi A Pina [Under the World There's a Lot Of Ass, a Lot Of Cunt] — Jahve
És Allah Tusázik [Jaweh And Allah Battle] — Kiáltvány [Manifesto] —
Betegség-Blues [Sickness Blues] — Házimunka [Homework] — Seggfej!
[Birdbrain!] — Parlamenti Nóta [Capitol Air] — Azok Ketten [Those Two] —

Repülögép-Blues [Airplane Blues] — Érettség [Maturity] — Halotti Lepel [White Shroud] — Világ-Karma [World Karma] — A Vendég [The Guest] — Kozmopolita Üdvözlet [Cosmopolitan Greetings]

Anthologies:

H285   *Üvöltés.* Budapest, Hungary: Európa Könyvkiadó, 1967, pp. 73-95, 314-318.
Translation by Ottó Orbán: A Leples Bitang [Shrouded Stranger] — Nagyáruház Kaliforniában [A Supermarket In California] — Üvöltés [Howl]
Translation by István Eörsi: Kaddish [Kaddish (excerpt)]
Translation by István Geher: Az "Üvöltés És Más Versek" Elé [liner notes for *Howl* (Fantasy recording)]

H286*   Lowenfels, Walter (ed.). *Hol Van Vietnam?* Budapest, Hungary: Európa, ca. 1968.
Translation by Dezsö Tandori: Sutra Wichita Örvényéböl [Wichita Vortex Sutra]

H287*   *Kezek Dicsérete.* Hungary: Kozmosz Könyvek, 1969.
Translation: Uzenet [Message]

H288*   Somlyó, György (ed.). *Hármostükör: Válogatott Müforditások.* Budapest, Hungary: Szépirodalmi Kiadó, 1970.
Translation: Amerika [America]

H289*   Jánosy, István. *A Valóságos Oroszlán.* Budapest, Hungary: Magvetö, 1971.
Translation: Kaddish II [Kaddish (excerpt)] — Róza Néninek [To Aunt Rose] — A Valóságos Oroszlán [The Lion For Real]

H290*   *Emlékvirágzás: Amerikai Szerelmes Versek.* Hungary: Magyar Helikon, 1972.
Translation by Ottó Orbán: A Leples Bitang [The Shrouded Stranger]

H291*   Orbán, Ottó (ed.). *Aranygyapju: Válogatott Versforditások.* Budapest, Hungary: Európa, 1972.
Translation by Ottó Orbán: A Leples Bitang [The Shrouded Stranger] — Malest Cornfici Tuo Catullo [Malest Cornfici Tuo Catullo] — Nagyáruház Kaliforniában [A Supermarket In California] — Lindsayhez [To Lindsay] — Apollinaire Sirjánál [At Apollinaire's Grave]

H292*   Somlyó, György (ed.). *Szélrózsa: Összegyüjtött Versforditások.* Budapest, Hungary: Magvetö, 1973.
Translation: A Csuklyás Csavargó [The Shrouded Stranger] — Üvöltés [Howl] — Amerika [America] — Üzenet [Message] — Lindsay-Hez [To Lindsay]

H293*   Franyó, Zoltán (ed.). *Válogatott Müforditások.* Budapest, Hungary: Magvetö, 1974.
Translation: Vad Árva [Wild Orphan]

H294   Eörsi, István (ed.). *Ruhapróba.* Budapest, Hungary: Európa Könyvkiadó, 1975, pp. 261-302.
Translation by István Eörsi: Kaddis [Kaddish] — Üzenet [Message] — Szeptember A Jessore-i Úton [September On Jessore Road] — Róza Néninek [To Aunt Rose] — Az Isten Miért Szeretet, Jack? [Why Is God Love, Jack?] — Amerika [America] — Feljegyzés Egy Álomról [Dream Record: June 8, 1955]

H295*   Szilágyi, Domokos. *Válogatott Versek És Müforditások.* Budapest, Hungary: Magvetö, 1979.
Translation: Utolsó Éjszaka Kalkuttában [Last Night In Calcutta]

H296 Kodolányi, Gyula (ed.). *Szavak A Szélbe*. Budapest, Hungary: Európa Könyvkiadó, 1980, pp. 275-285.
Translation by Györe Balázs: Ezust Durangon Tul, A Mexikoi Sierra Redoi Folott [Past Silver Durango Over Mexic Sierra Wrinkles] — Reflexiok Almosszemben [Reflections In Sleepy Eye] — Halal Mindenutt [Death On All Fronts] — Laramie Folott [Over Laramie]

H297 Vas, István (ed.). *Hét Tenger Éneke, vol. 8.* Gyoma, Hungary: Szépirodalmi Könyvkiadó, 1982, pp. 426-431.
Translation by István Vas: Napraforgó Szutra [Sunflower Sutra] — Kaliforniai Szuperpiac [A Supermarket In California] — Versrakéta [Poem Rocket]

H298* Hárs, Ernö (ed.). *Arnyak A Barlang Falán*. Budapest, Hungary: Európa, 1983.

H299 *Lélegzet*. Budapest, Hungary: Magvetö Könyvkiadó, 1985, pp. 9-10. [Series: AK Füzetak 14]
Translation by Györe Balázs: A Költészet Ereje És Gyöngesége [Power And Weakness In Poetry]

H300* *Amerikai Költök Antológiája*. Budapest, Hungary: Európa, 1990.
Translation by Ottó Orbán: Üvöltés [Howl]
Translation by István Eörsi: Kaddis [Kaddish] — Róza Néninek [To Aunt Rose]
Translation by István Jánosy: A Valóságos Oroszlán [The Lion For Real]

Periodicals:

H301 [2 poems]. *Nagyvilág,* vol. 8, no. 6 (June 1963) pp. 898, 902-903.
Translation by György Somlyó: A Csuklyás Csavargó [The Shrouded Stranger] — Milyen Beton- És Aluminium-Szfinksz Verte Szét A Fejüket [Howl, pt. III]

H302 [poem]. *Nagyvilág,* vol. 10, no. 6 (June 1965) pp. 821-822.
Translation by István Vas: Napraforgó Szutra [Sunflower Sutra]

H303* [poem]. *Hid,* no. 3 (1968) p. 324.
Translation by Gy Gömöri: Vers-Rakéta [Poem Rocket]

H304* [poem]. *Nagyvilág,* vol. 14, no. 4 (April 1969) pp. 517-518.
Translation by Dezsö Tandori: Sutra Wichita Örvényéböl [Wichita Vortex Sutra]

H305 [2 poems]. *Nagyvilág,* vol. 14, no. 8 (Aug. 1969) pp. 1170-1172.
Translation by István Jánosy: A Valóságos Oroszlán [The Lion For Real] — Róza Néninek [To Aunt Rose]

H306* [poem]. *Kortárs,* no. 1 (1969) p. 114.
Translation by Márton Kalász: Ujra A Times Square-En A Times Squareról Álmodozva [Back On Times Square Dreaming Of Times Square]

H307 [5 poems]. *Nagyvilág,* vol. 16, no. 2 (Feb. 1971) pp. 189-196.
Translation by István Eörsi: Szomorú Énem [My Sad Self] — Feljegyzés Egy Álomról: 1955. Június 8-ÁN [Dream Record: June 8, 1955] — Az Isten Miért Szeretet, Jack? [Why Is God Love, Jack?] — Az Elsö Buli Ken Keseyéknél A Pokol Angyalaival [First Party At Ken Kesey's With Hell's Angels]
Translation by Ottó Orbán: Apollinaire Sirjánál [At Apollinaire's Grave]

H308* [poem]. *Utunk,* no. 48 (1973) p. 9.
Translation by Z. Márki: Egy Kaliforniai Áruházban [A Supermarket In California]

H309   [poem]. *Nagyvilág,* vol. 19, no. 1 (Jan. 1974) pp. 21-24.
Translation by István Eörsi: Szeptember A Jessore-i Úton [September On Jessore Road]

H310*   [poem]. *Utunk,* no. 28 (1976) p. 6.
Translation by Domokos Szilágyi: Utolsó Éjszaka Kalkuttában [Last Night In Calcutta]

H311*   [3 poems]. *Uj Symposion,* no. 149 (1977) p. 454.
Translation by Attila Balázs: A Vég [The End] — Lindsayhez [To Lindsay] — Az Elsö Buli Ken Keseyék-Nél A Pokol Angyalaival [First Party At Ken Kesey's With Hell's Angels]

H312   [5 poems]. *Nagyvilág,* vol. 23, no. 12 (Dec. 1978) pp. 1818-1822.
Translation by István Eörsi: Jehova És Allah Harcol [Jaweh And Allah Battle (excerpt)] — Karácsonyi Ajándék [Xmas Gift] — Betegség-Bú [Sickness Blues] — Nemes Igazságok Evangéliuma [Gospel Noble Truths] — Vidékre Visszatérve Rövid Látogatásra [Returning To the Country For a Brief Visit]

H313*   [3 poems]. *Uj Symposion,* no. 188 (1980) pp. 417-419.
Translation by Attila Balázs: Keressünk Bünbakot [Drive All Blames Into One] — Az Elme Lélegzete [Mind Breaths] — Punk Rock Te Vagy Az Én Nagy Nyafka Babucim [Punk Rock Your My Big Crybaby]

H314   [poem]. *Nagyvilág,* vol. 26, no. 8 (Aug. 1981) pp. 1151-1155.
Translation by István Eörsi: Ne Vénülj Meg [Don't Grow Old]

H315*   [poem]. *Magyar Szó* (Aug. 22, 1981) p. 12.
Translation by István Eörsi: Rezignáltam [Resigned]

H316   [poem]. *Nagyvilág,* vol. 26, no. 11 (Nov. 1981) pp. 1626-1630.
Translation by István Eörsi: Plutó(nium) I Óda [Plutonian Ode]

H317   [4 poems]. *Jelenlét,* no. 13 (1983) pp. 69-73.
Translation by István Eörsi: A Világ Külszine Alatt Annyi A Segg, A Pina [Under the World There's a Lot Of Ass, a Lot Of Cunt] — Halál Van Gogh Fülére [Death To Van Gogh's Ear!] — Kiáltvány [Manifesto] — Seggcsók [Kiss Ass]

H318   [4 poems]. *Nagyvilág,* vol. 28, no. 6 (June 1983) pp. 806-809.
Translation by István Eörsi: Metafizika [Metaphysics] — Szerelmes Vers Whitman Témájára [Love Poem On Theme By Whitman] — Kenjetek Mindent Egyvalakire [Drive All Blames Into One] — Elégia Neal Cassadyért [Elegy For Neal Cassady]

H319   [poem]. *Nagyvilág,* vol. 30, no. 1 (Jan. 1985) pp. 74-76.
Translation by István Eörsi: Halotti Lepel [White Shroud]

H320*   [2 poems]. *Magyar Szó* (Aug. 24, 1986) p. 14.
Translation by Béla Bede: Nagyáruház Kaliforniában [A Supermarket In California]
Translation by István Eörsi: Halotti Lepel [White Shroud]

H321*   [poem]. *Magyar Napló,* no. 17 (1990) p. 5.
Translation by Ottó Fenyvesi: A Balek [Birdbrain!]

H322*   [poem]. *Helikon,* no. 21 (1992) p. 9.
Translation by István Eörsi: Szomoru Énem Frank O'Harának [My Sad Self]

H323 [poem]. *Népszabadság* (Sept. 18, 1993) p. 26.
Translation by István Eörsi: Improvizáció Beijingben [Improvisation In Beijing]

H324 [poem]. *Magyar Narancs* (Sept. 23, 1993) p. 39.
Translation by István Eörsi: Béke Bosznia-Hercegovinában [Peace In Bosnia-Herzegovina]

H325 [poem]. *Népszabadság* (Sept. 25, 1993) p. 33.
Translation by István Eörsi: A Kutatás [Research]

H326 [poems]. *Szombat,* vol. 5, no. 9 (Nov. 1993) pp. 35-36.
Translation by István Eörsi: Kaddis [Kaddish (fragments)] — Jiddis Kopf [Yiddishe Kopf]
Translation by Ottó Orbán: A Leples Bitang [The Shrouded Stranger]

Miscellaneous:

H327 Hobo Blues Band. *Oly Sokáig Voltunk Lenn...* [recording]. Hungary: Pepita, SLPX 17694. Stereo, 33 1/3 rpm. 1983.
Translation by István Eörsi: Halál Apa Blues [Father Death Blues, recorded on side B, band 5]

ITALIAN

Books:

H328a Ginsberg, Allen. *Jukebox All'Idrogeno.* Milan, Italy: Arnoldo Mondadori Editore, 1965. [Series: Nuovi Scrittori Stranieri 9]
Translation by Fernanda Pivano: Howl ‖ Urlo — Footnote to Howl ‖ Nota A Urlo — A Supermarket In California ‖ Un Supermarket In California — Transcription Of Organ Music ‖ Trascrizione Di Musica Da Organo — Sunflower Sutra ‖ Sutra Del Girasole — America ‖ America — In the Baggage Room At Greyhound ‖ Nel Bagagliaio Di Greyhound — An Asphodel ‖ Un Asfodelo — Song ‖ Canzone — Wild Orphan ‖ Orfano Selvaggio — In Back Of the Real ‖ Dietro Al Reale — Kaddish ‖ Kaddish — Poem Rocket ‖ Poesia Razzo — Europe! Europe! ‖ Europa! Europa! — To Lindsay ‖ A Lindsay — Message ‖ Messaggio — To Aunt Rose ‖ Alla Zia Rosa — At Apollinaire's Grave ‖ Sulla Tomba Di Apollinaire — The Lion For Real ‖ Il Leone Sul Serio — Ignu ‖ Ignu — Death To Van Gogh's Ear! ‖ Morte All'Orecchio Di Van Gogh! — Laughing Gas ‖ Gas Esilarante — Mescaline ‖ Mescalina — Lysergic Acid ‖ Acido Lisergico — Magic Psalm ‖ Salmo Magico — The Reply ‖ La Risposta — The End ‖ Fine — The Change: Kyoto-Tokyo Express ‖ Il Mutamento: Rapido Kyoto-Tokyo — Notes [notes by Pivano with AG's help] — Note Scritte Quando Finalmente Venne Inciso "Urlo" [Notes for *Howl And Other Poems (recording)*] — Poesia, Violenza E Gli Agnelli Tremanti [Poetry, Violence And the Trembling Lambs] — Commento Alla Seconda Edizione Di "Kaddish" [comments from the blurb on the back cover of the second and later printings of city lights book *Kaddish*]
H328b Ginsberg, Allen. *Jukebox All'Idrogeno.* Milan, Italy: Arnoldo Mondadori, 1979. [Series: Poesia E Teatro 13]
Contents: As Mondadori edition above.
H328c Ginsberg, Allen. *Jukebox All'Idrogeno.* Parma, Italy: Ugo Guanda Editore, 1992.
Contents: As Mondadori edition above.

H329 Ginsberg, Allen. *Sutra Del Girasole.* Verona, Italy: Editiones Dominicae, 1969.
Translation by Fernanda Pivano: Sutra Del Girasole [Sunflower Sutra]

H330   Ginsberg, Allen. *Diario Indiano.* Rome, Italy: Arcana Editrice, 1973. [Series: Situazioni 6]
Translation by Fernanda Pivano: Diario Indiano [Indian Journals] — [Notes]

H331a   Ginsberg, Allen. *Mantra Del Re Di Maggio: Sandwiches Di Realtà 1953-1960, Notizie Del Pianeta 1961-1967.* Milan, Italy: Arnoldo Mondadori, 1973.
Translation by Fernanda Pivano: Conversazione Sulla Prosodia [Intervista Di Fernanda Pivano A Allen Ginsberg Registrata A New York Il 22 Novembre 1968 — The Green Automobile || L'Automobile Verde — On Burroughs' Work || Sul Lavoro Di Burroughs — Over Kansas || Sul Kansas — Malest Cornifici Tuo Catullo || Malest Cornifici Tuo Catullo — Dream Record: June 8, 1955 || Sogno: 8 Giugno 1955 — Blessed Be the Muses || Siano Benedette Le Muse — Fragment 1956 || Frammento 1956 — A Strange New Cottage In Berkeley || Una Strana Villa Nuova A Berkeley — Scribble || Scarabocchio — Psalm III || Salmo III — Tears || Lacrime — Ready To Roll || Pronto Ad Andare — Wrote This Last Night || Scritto Ieri Notte — American Change || Spiccioli Americani — Back On Times Square, Dreaming Of Times Square || "Di Ritorno A Times Square, Sognando Times Square" — My Sad Self || Il Mio Triste Io — Funny Death || Buffa Morte — Battleship Newsreel || Notiziario Nave Di Battaglia — I Beg You Come Back & Be Cheerful || Ti Prego Torna Indietro & Stai Allegro — Ringraziamenti [Acknowledgements] — Who Will Take Over the Universe? || Chi Si Impadronirà Dell'Universo? — Television Was a Baby Crawling Toward That Deathchamber || La Televisione Era Un Bimbo Che Si Strascicava Verso Quella Camera Della Morte — This Form Of Life Needs Sex || Questa Forma Di Vita Ha Bisogno Del Sesso — Sunset *S.S. Azemour* || Tramonto "S.S. Azemour" — Describe: The Rain On Dasaswamedh || Descrivete: La Pioggia Su Dasaswamedh — Death News || Notizia Di Morte — Patna-Benares Express || Rapido Patna-Benares — Why Is God Love, Jack? || Perché Dio È Amore, Jack? — I Am a Victim Of Telephone || Sono Una Vittima Del Telefono — Today || Oggi — Message II || Messaggio II — Café In Warsaw || Caffè A Varsavia — The Moments Return || Tornano I Momenti — Kral Majales || Kral Majales — Guru || Guru — Who Be Kind To || Con Chi Essere Gentile — Portland Coloseum || Portland Coloseum — First Party At Ken Kesey's With Hell's Angels || Primo Party Da Ken Kesey Con Gli Angeli Dell'Inferno — Carmel Valley || Valle Carmel — A Vision In Hollywood || Una Visione A Hollywood — Chances "R" || Chances "R" — Wichita Vortex Sutra || Wichita Vortex Sutra — Uptown || Uptown — To the Body || Al Corpo — City Midnight Junk Strains || Arie Di Droga In Città Mezzanotte — Holy Ghost On the Nod Over the Body Of Bliss || Spirito Santo Sonnecchiante Sul Corpo Della Beatitudine — Wales Visitation || Visitazione Al Galles — Pentagon Exorcism || Esorcismo Al Pentagono — Note A Sandwiches Di Realtà [Notes by Pivano with AG's help] — Note A Notizie Del Pianeta [notes by Pivano with AG's help] — Un'Autobiografia Concisa De Allen Ginsberg [Autobiographical Precis] — Presentazione A "Sandwiches Di Realta" [blurb for *Reality Sandwiches*] — Presentazione A "Notizie Del Pianeta" [blurb for *Planet News*] — Precisazione Di Allen Ginsberg All'Intervista Registrata Da Thomas Clark [includes letter by AG]

H331b   Ginsberg, Allen. *Mantra Del Re Di Maggio: Sandwiches Di Realtà 1953-1960, Notizie Del Pianeta 1961-1967.* Milan, Italy: Arnoldo Mondadori, 1976. [Series: Oscar Mondadori Poesia: Gli Oscar Poesia L229]
Contents: As first Mondadori edition above.

H332a   Ginsberg, Allen. *Primi Blues: Rags, Ballate E Canti Con L'Armonium 1971-1975.* Milan, Italy: Ugo Guanda, 1978. [Series: Quaderni Della Fenice, 35]
Translation by Carlo A. Corsi: Spiegazione Di "Primi Blues" [Explanation of *First Blues*] — Vomit Express || Espresso Del Vomito — Going To San Diego || Andando A San Diego — Jimmy Berman Rag || Rag Di Jimmy Berman — Many Loves || Molti Amori — 4 AM Blues [includes music notation] || Blues Delle Quattro Di Mattina — New York Blues [includes music notation] || Blues

Di New York — NY Youth Call Annunciation [includes music notation] ‖ Ai Giovani Di New York: Grido Annunciazione — Come Back Christmas [includes music notation] ‖ Torna Natale! — MacDougal Street Blues ‖ Blues Di MacDougal Street — CIA Dope Calypso [includes music notation] ‖ Calipso Della Droga CIA — Troost Street Blues ‖ Blues Di Troost Street — Put Down Yr Cigarette Rag [includes music notation] ‖ Rag: Mettete Giù Le Sigarette — Slack Key Guitar [includes music notation] ‖ Chitarra Scordata — Flying To Fiji ‖ In Volo Per Fiji — Postcard To D-- ‖ Cartolina A D-- — Reef Mantra ‖ Mantra Del Banco Corallino — Siratoka Beach Croon ‖ Brontolio A Siratoka Beach — Bus Ride Ballad Road To Suva [includes music notation] ‖ Ballata Di Un Viaggio In Autobus Verso Suva — Tear Gas Rag [includes music notation] ‖ Rag Dei Candelotti — Blue Gossip ‖ Maldicenza Blu — The House Of the Rising Sun ‖ La Casa Del Sole Nascente — Everybody Sing [includes music notation] ‖ Cantate Tutti Quanti — Prayer Blues [includes music notation] ‖ Blues Preghiera — Broken Bone Blues [includes music notation] ‖ Blues Delle Ossa Rotte — When I Woke Up This Morning ‖ "Quando Mi Sono Svegliato Stamattina" — On Reading Dylan's Writings ‖ Leggendo Bob Dylan — Stay Away From the White House [includes music notation] ‖ State Lontani Dalla Casa Bianca — 2 AM Dirty Jersey Blues ‖ Blues Dello Sporco Jersey Alle Due Di Notte — Hardon Blues ‖ Blues Dell'Arrapata — Dope Fiend Blues ‖ Blues Dello Sballato — End Vietnam War ‖ Basta Con La Guerra In Vietnam — Guru Blues [includes music notation] ‖ Blues Del Guru

H332b   Ginsberg, Allen. *Poesie Da Cantare: Primi Blues.* Rome, Italy: Lato Side, 1979.
[Series: Lato Side 14]
Contents: As first Ugo Guanda edition.

H333   Ginsberg, Allen. *Diario Beat.* Rome, Italy: Newton Compton Editori, 1979.
[Series: Newton Narratori #4]
Translation by Umberto Capra: Diario Beat [*Journals Early Fifties Early Sixties*]

H334   Ginsberg, Allen. *La Caduta Dell'America.* Milan, Italy: Arnoldo Mondadori, 1981.
Translation by Fernanda Pivano: Discorso Di Allen Ginsberg Letto Da Peter Orlovsky In Occasione Della Consegna Del National Book Award In Poetry, 18 Aprile 1974, Lincoln Center, NY [*The Fall of America* Wins a Prize] — Premessa [Preface] — Kansas City To Saint Louis ‖ Da Kansas City A Saint Louis — Bayonne Entering NYC ‖ Bayonne Entrando A New York City — Iron Horse ‖ Cavallo D'Acciaio — A Vow ‖ Un Voto — Autumn Gold: New England Fall ‖ Oro D'Autunno: Nuova Inghilterra — An Open Window On Chicago ‖ Una Finestra Aperta Su Chicago — Kiss Ass ‖ Leccaculo — Elegy Ché Guévara ‖ Elegia A Ché Guévara — War Profit Litany ‖ Litania Del Profitto Di Guerra — Elegy For Neal Cassady ‖ Elegia Per Neal Cassady — Manhattan Thirties Flash ‖ Flash Manhattan Anni Trenta — Please Master ‖ Prego Padrone — A Prophecy ‖ Una Profezia — On Neal's Ashes ‖ Sulle Ceneri Di Neal — Going To Chicago ‖ Andando A Chicago — Grant Park: August 28, 1968 ‖ Grant Park: 28 Agosto 1968 — Car Crash ‖ Incidente D'Auto — Over Denver Again ‖ Di Nuovo Su Denver — Imaginary Universes ‖ Universi Immaginari — Rising Over Night-Blackened Detroit Streets ‖ Alzandomi Sulle Strade Di Detroit Oscurate Dalla Notte — Easter Sunday ‖ Domenica Di Pasqua — Falling Asleep In America ‖ Addormentandomi In America — Northwest Passage ‖ Passaggio A Nordovest — Sonora Desert-Edge ‖ Orlo Deserto Di Sonora — Independence Day ‖ Giorno Dell'Indipendenza — Rain-Wet Asphalt Heat, Garbage Curbed Cans Overflowing ‖ Calore Di Asfalto Bagnato Di Pioggia, Pattumiere Al Marciapiede Straripanti — Death On All Fronts ‖ Morte Su Tutti I Fronti — Memory Gardens ‖ Giardini Della Memoria — Flash Back ‖ Flash Back — Graffiti 12th Cubicle Men's Room Syracuse Airport ‖ Graffiti Del 12° Gabinetto Per Uomini All'Aeroporto Di Syracuse — After Thoughts ‖ Ripensamenti — G.S. Reading Poesy At Princeton ‖ G.S. Legge Poesia A

Princeton — Friday the Thirteenth ‖ Venerdì Tredici — D.C. Mobilization ‖ Mobilitazione Nel D.C. — Ecologue ‖ Egloga — Guru Om ‖ Guru Om — Milarepa Taste ‖ Sapore Di Milarepa — Over Laramie ‖ Su Laramie — Bixby Canyon Ocean Path Word Breeze ‖ Bixby Canyon Oceano Sentiero Brezza Verbale — September On Jessore Road ‖ Settembre Su Jessore Road — After Words ‖ Postologo — Note Ai Testi [Notes by Pivano with AG's help] — Allen Ginsberg: Sommario Autobiografico [Autobiographical Precis]

Anthologies:

H335   Izzo, Carlo (ed.). *Poesia Americana Del '900.* Parma, Italy: Ugo Guanda, 1963, pp. 764-771.
Translation by Carlo Izzo: The Shrouded Stranger ‖ Lo Straniero Ammantato — A Supermarket In California ‖ Supermercato In California

H336a   Pivano, Fernanda (ed.). *Poesia Degli Ultimi Americani.* Milan, Italy: Feltrinelli Editore, 1964, pp. 144-191. [Series: Le Comete 35]
Translation by Giulio Saponaro: Aether ‖ Etere — Love Poem On Theme By Whitman ‖ Poesia D'Amore Su Un Tema Di Whitman — To an Old Poet In Peru ‖ A Un Vecchio Poeta Del Perú — Sather Gate Illumination ‖ L'Illuminazione Del Sather Gate

H336b   Pivano, Fernanda (ed.). *Poesia Degli Ultimi Americani.* Milan, Italy: Feltrinelli Editore, 1973, pp. 94-133. [Series: Universale Economica 694]
Contents: As first Feltrinelli edition above.

H337*   Williams, William Carlos. *Paterson.* Milan, Italy: Lerici Editore, 1966.
Translation by Alfredo Rizzardi: [3 letters to William Carlos Williams]

H338a   Burroughs, William and Ginsberg, Allen. *Le Lettere Dello Yage.* Milan, Italy: Sugar Editore, 1967. [Series: I Giorni 19]
Translation by Donatella Manganotti: Le Lettere Dello Yage [letters to William S. Burroughs from *The Yage Letters*]

H338b   Burroughs, William and Ginsberg, Allen. *Le Lettere Dello Yage.* Milan, Italy: SugarCo Edizioni, 1977.
Contents: As first Sugar Editore edition above.

H339   Corso, Gregory. *Benzina.* Parma, Italy: Guanda, 1969, pp. 11-14.
Translation by Gianni Menarini: [Introduction to *Gasoline*]

H340   Menarini, Gianni (ed.). *Poesia E Rabbia: Antologia Poetica.* Milan, Italy: Accademia-Sansoni, 1971, pp. 124-133.
Translation by Gianni Menarini: Wichita Vortex Sutra ‖ Wichita Vortex Sutra

H341   Menarini, Gianni (ed.). *Vietnam Poeti Americani.* Parma, Italy: Guanda Editore, 1972, pp. 94-103, 207-210.
Translation by Gianni Menarini: Wichita Vortex Sutra (excerpt) ‖ Da Wichita Vortex Sutra — [prose]

H342a   Pivano, Fernanda (ed.). *L'Altra America Negli Anni Sessanta, vol. 1.* Rome, Italy: Officina Edizioni, 1972, pp. 111-115.
Translation by Fernanda Pivano: Lettera A Neal [letter to Neal Cassady]

H342b   Pivano, Fernanda (ed.). *L'Altra America Negli Anni Sessanta, vol. 1.* Milan, Italy: Edizioni Il Formichiere, 1978.
Contents: As first Officina Edizioni edition above.

H342c   Pivano, Fernanda (ed.). *L'Altra America Negli Anni Sessanta, vol. 1.* Milan, Italy: Arcana Editrice, 1993, pp. 128-132.
Contents: As first Officina Edizioni edition above and vol. 2 below combined here into a single volume.

H343a Pivano, Fernanda (ed.). *L'Altra America Negli Anni Sessanta, vol. 2.* Rome, Italy: Officina Edizioni, 1972, pp. 17-20.
Translation by Fernanda Pivano: Proposte Per La Marcia Del 20 Novembre 1965 [Proposal For a March first printed in English in *Berkeley Barb*]

H343b Pivano, Fernanda (ed.). *L'Altra America Negli Anni Sessanta, vol. 2.* Milan, Italy: Edizioni Il Formichiere, 1979.
Contents: As first Officina Edizioni edition above.

H344a Pivano, Fernanda (ed.). *L'Altra America Negli Anni Sessanta, vol. 5.* Rome, Italy: Officina Edizioni, 1972, pp. 165-173, 178-186.
Translation by Fernanda Pivano: La Calma [The Diggers] — Solitudine Pubblica [Public Solitude]

H344b Pivano, Fernanda (ed.). *L'Altra.America Negli Anni Sessanta, vol. 5.* Milan, Italy: Edizioni Il Formichiere, 1979.
Contents: As first Officina Edizioni edition above.

H344c Pivano, Fernanda (ed.). *L'Altra America Negli Anni Sessanta, vol. 2.* Milan, Italy: Arcana Editrice, 1993, pp. 588-596, 603-611, 614-621.
Contents: As first Officina Edizioni edition volume 5 above with the addition of the music notation for Blake's "The Grey Monk" and "Nurse's Song" in AG's facsimile holograph notebook.

H345 Kerouac, Jack. *Visioni Di Cody.* Rome, Italy: Arcana Editrice, 1974, pp. v-xv.
Translation by Fernanda Pivano: Il Grande Ricordatore [The Great Rememberer]

H346 Pivano, Fernanda. *C'Era Una Volta Un Beat.* Rome, Italy: Arcana Editrice, 1976, pp. 33-34, 58-59.
Translation by Fernanda Pivano: [3 letters by AG]

H347 Corso, Gregory. *Poesie.* Milan, Italy: Bompiani, 1978, pp. 216-218.
Translation by Gianni Menarini: Prefazione A Gasoline [Introduction to *Gasoline*]

H348 Bacigalupo, Massimo (ed.). *Poesia In Pubblico.* Genova, Italy: Comune Di Genova, Assessorato Ai Beni Culturali, 1979, pp. 35-43.
Translation by Massimo Bacigalupo: Canto Uluru Di Ayers Rock [Ayers Rock Uluru Song] — Regalo Di Natale [Xmas Gift] — Capanna Nei Rockies [Cabin In the Rockies] — Non Invecchiare [Don't Grow Old] — Blues Di Malattia [Sickness Blues] — Ode Plutonia [Plutonian Ode]

H349* Cassady, Carolyn. *Cuore Di Beat.* Rome, Italy: Savelli Editori, 1980.
Translation: [letters to Neal and Carolyn Cassady]

H350 Schwartz, Arturo (ed.). *Anarchia E Creativita.* Milan, Italy: La Salamandra, 1981, pp. 87-90. [Series: Biblioteca Di An.Archos]
Translation by Fernanda Pivano: T.S. Eliot Entrò Nei Miei Sogni [T.S. Eliot Entered My Dreams]

H351 Urbani, Serena and Valenti, Cristina (eds.). *Dedicato A Julian Beck.* Pontedera, Italy: Santarcangelo Dei Teatri, 1986, pp. 33-35.
Translation by Serena Urbani: Il Living Theatre E I Suoi Critici USA [Living Theatre And Its U.S. Critics]

H352 McShine, Kynaston (ed.). *Andy Warhol: A Retrospective* [Italian edition]. Milan, Italy: Editions Fabbri/Bompiani, 1989.
Translation: Despite the Coolness Of Warhol's Art (prose)

Periodicals:

H353* [poem]. *Il Verri*, no. 1 (Feb. 1962) p. 73.
Translation by Glauco Cambon: Un Supermarket In California [A Supermarket In California]

H354 [poem]. *Questo E Altro*, no. 40 (July 1963) pp. 131-133.
Translation by Ariodante Marianni, Mary De Rachewiltz, Giovanni Giudici: Da Kaddish [Kaddish (excerpt)]

H355* [2 poems]. *Terzo Programma*, guaderni trimestrali, no. 1 (1963) pp. 109-184.
Translation by Claudio Gorlier: [America — Howl]

H356 [prose]. *Il Mondo* (Nov. 30, 1965) p. 10.
Translation by Fernanda Pivano: [letter to Fernanda Pivano]

H357 [2 poems]. *Prospetti*, no. 1 (March 1966) pp. [7-11].
Translation by Romeo Lucchese: Un Supermercato In California [A Supermarket In California] — Europa! Europa! [Europe! Europe!]

H358 [poem]. *Il Tarocco*, vol. 2, no. 3-4 (Oct. 1966) pp. 44-47.
Translation by Gianni Menarini: Wichita Vortex Sutra-Proemio [Proem To Wichita Vortex Sutra]

H359 [poem]. *Nuova Presenza*, vol. 10, no. 27-28 (1967-68) pp. 14-21.
Translation by Piero Sanavio: Wichita Vortex Sutra (excerpt) || Aforismi Del Vortice Di Wichita

H360 [prose and drawing]. *Che Fare*, no. 1 (May 29, 1967) pp. 43-49.
Translation by Isabella Leonetti: La Solitudine Pubblica [Public Solitude] — [drawing of skull within a star of David and three fish which share a common head]

H361 [poem]. *Che Fare*, no. 2 (Nov. 8, 1967) pp. 98-99.
Translation by Paolo Lionni: Kral Majales [Kral Majales]

H362 [poem]. *Ad Libitum*, no. 4 ([Feb. 10] 1968) pp. 16-29.
Translation by Rolando Bacchielli: Middle Of a Long Poem On 'These States' Kansas City To St. Louis || A Metà Di Un Lungo Poema Su "Questi Stati Uniti" Da Kansas City A St. Louis

H363 [letter and poem]. *Pianeta Fresco*, no. 2-3 (Winter 1968) pp. 6-9, 15-19.
Translation by Fernanda Pivano: [letter to Neal Cassady] — Centro Di Una Lunga Poesia Su "Questi Stati" [Beginning Of a Poem Of These States]

H364 [poem]. *Fuori!*, no. 0 (Dec. 1971) p. 20.
Translation by Fernanda Pivano: Rain-Wet Asphalt Heat, Garbage Curbed Cans Overflowing || Colore Di Asfalto Lucido Sulla Strada Bidoni Straboccanti Di Rifiuti

H365 [poem and prose]. *Paria*, no. 8 (ca. 1971) pp. 2, 11.
Translation: Hum Bom! || Hum Bomb! — [prose from Dylan's album liner notes]

H366 [poem]. *Fuori!*, no. 2 (July-Aug. 1972) p. 4.
Translation by Fernanda Pivano: Rain-Wet Asphalt Heat, Garbage Curbed Cans Overflowing || Colore Di Asfalto Lucido Sulla Strada Bidoni Straboccanti Di Rifiuti

H367   [poem]. *L'Espresso,* vol. 22, no. 15 (April 11, 1976) p. 53.
Translation by Gioia Zannino Angiolillo: Doveva Esser Suonato Sul Juke-Box [Hadda Be Playing On the Jukebox]

H368   [3 poems]. *La Città Futura,* no. 42 (Nov. 8, 1978) p. 9.
Translation by Patrizia Lalla: Cos' È Morto? [What's Dead?] — Il Giorno Di Nagasaky A Rocky Flats [Nagasaki Days] — Amore Nero [Lack Love]
Note: Mistake in the translation here the title "Lack Love" was translated as "Black Love".

H369   [poem]. *L'Espresso,* vol. 25, no. 21 (May 27, 1979) pp. 150-151.
Translation by Fernanda Pivano: All'Inferno Con Plutonio [Plutonian Ode]

H370   [prose]. *Masquerade,* no. 3 (Dec. 24, 1979) p. 18.
Translation: [prose concerning Burroughs]

H371   [poem]. *Il Diaframma,* no. 249 (April-May 1980) p. [14].
Translation by Fernanda Pivano: America [America]

H372   [2 poems]. *Percorsi,* vol. 2, no. 5-6 (Dec. 1981) pp. 5-10.
Translation by Fernanda Pirano [sic]: Vecchio Pieta, Il Soggetto Finale Della Poesia Balugina Mesi [Don't Grow Old] — Buddha Mori' Terra Di Laghi, Wisconsin [Land O' Lakes, Wisc.]

H373   [poem]. *UNESCO Courier* [Italian edition], vol. 35, no. 10 (Nov. 1982) pp. 13-14.
Translation: [Plutonian Ode (excerpt)]

H374   [prose]. *Mgur Poesia,* no. 2 (1994) pp. 2-15.
Translation by Rita Degli Esposti: Sutra Del Cuore [Kerouac's Ethic]

Miscellaneous:

H375   [flyer]. *Fried Shoes Cooked Diamonds.* Santhià, Italy: Carmina Cinematografica S.R.L., ca. 1979.
Translation: [letter]

H376   [program]. *Teatro Nuovo: Hydrogen Jukebox.* Spoleto, Italy: XXXIII Festival Dei Due Mondi, June 29-July 1, 1990.
Translation by Fernanda Pivano: Azzurra Luce Del Fulmine Riempie Le Pianure Dell'Oklahoma [Iron Horse (excerpt)] — Chi È Il Nemico, Anno Dopo Anno? [Iron Horse (excerpt)] — Geova Con Bomba Atomica [Jaweh And Allah Battle] — Consultando I Ching Fumando Erba Ascoltando I Fugs Che Cantano Blake [Consulting I Ching Smoking Pot Listening To the Fugs Sing Blake] — Come Sto Male! [Marijuana Notation] — La Stanza Imbiancata, Tetto [To P.O.] — Rapido Patna-Benares [Patna-Benares Express (excerpt)] — E Il Vasto Spazio Stellato [Last Night In Calcutta (excerpt)] — Sotto L'Ala D'Argento [Crossing Nation (excerpt)] — Di Nuovo Su Denver [Over Denver Again] — Andando A Chicago [Going To Chicago (excerpt)] — Explosioni Squarcio Grigio Giornale Pomeriggio Spire Aria Manhattan [To Poe: Over the Planet, Air Albany-Baltimore (excerpt)] — Sono Vecchio Adesso, E Solo Nel Kansas [Wichita Vortex Sutra (excerpt)] — Quale Sfinge Di Cemento E Alluminio Gli Ha Sfracellato Il Cra [Howl (excerpt)] — Lunghe Strade Di Pietra Inanimate, Ripetitivi Schianti Di Mac [Manhattan Thirties Flash] — 2,000,000 Uccisi In Vietnam [Nagasaki Days (excerpt)] — Seduto Su Un Tronco D'Albero Con Mezza Tazza Di Tè [Cabin In the Rockies] — Zia Rosa [To Aunt Rose] — Se Avessi Un'Automobile Verde [The Green Automobile (excerpt)] — Mexcity Tavola Di Drogheria, Gigantesco [Violence] — Richard Secord E Oliver North [CIA Dope Calypso (excerpt)] — Uscii & La Bomba

Aveva [Nagasaki Days (excerpt)] — Quando Il Lago Rosso Si Riempie Compaiono Pesci [Ayers Rock Uluru Song] — Fuori! Fuori! [White Shroud (excerpt)] — Ehi Padre Morte [Father Death Blues] — Numeri Nell'Archivio US [Addendum: Numbers In the File Cabinet] — CIA Dope Calypso [CIA Dope Calypso (excerpt)]

JAPANESE

Books:

H377   Ginsberg, Allen. *Hoko [Howl and Other Poems]*. Tokyo, Japan: Nasu Shobo, 1961.
Translation by Yasujiro Furusawa: [Howl — A Supermarket In California — A Transcription Of Organ Music — Sunflower Sutra — America — In the Baggage Room At Greyhound]

H378   Ginsberg, Allen. *Allen Ginsberg Shishu.* Tokyo, Japan: Shichosha, 1965.
Translation by Yu Suwa: [Howl — Footnote To Howl — A Supermarket In California — Transcription Of Organ Music — Fragment 1956 — The Shrouded Stranger — The Trembling Of the Veil — After Dead Souls — Gregory Corso's Story — Metaphysics — The Night-Apple — Sunset — Marijuana Notation — Paterson — Sakyamuni Coming Out From the Mountain — Ready To Roll — A Strange New Cottage In Berkeley — To Lindsay — To Aunt Rose — The Lion For Real — At Apollinaire's Grave — Death To Van Gogh's Ear — Kaddish (excerpt)]

H379   Ginsberg, Allen. *Allen Ginsberg Shishu.* Tokyo, Japan: Shichosha, 1968. [Second edition]
Translation by Yu Suwa: [Howl — Footnote To Howl — A Supermarket In California — Transcription Of Organ Music — Fragment 1956 — The Shrouded Stranger — The Trembling Of the Veil — After Dead Souls — Gregory Corso's Story — Metaphysics — The Night-Apple — Sunset — Marijuana Notation — Paterson — Sakyamuni Coming Out From the Mountain — Ready To Roll — A Strange New Cottage In Berkeley — To Lindsay — To Aunt Rose — The Lion For Real — At Apollinaire's Grave — Death To Van Gogh's Ear — Kaddish (excerpt) — (letter to Yu Suwa) — (drawing from *Yage Letters*)]

H380   Ginsberg, Allen. *Kaddisshu.* Tokyo, Japan: Shichosha, 1969.
Translation by Yu Suwa and Yukinori Tachibana: [Kaddish]

H381   Ginsberg, Allen. *Hametsu O Owaraseru Tameni.* Tokyo, Japan: Shichosha, 1971.
Translation by Yu Suwa: [First Manifesto To End the Bringdown]

H382   Ginsberg, Allen. *Uchu No Iki [Allen Verbatim].* Tokyo, Japan: Shobunsha, 1977.
Translation by Yu Suwa: Uchu No Iki [*Allen Verbatim* (abridged)]

H383   Ginsberg, Allen. *Kanashiki Kafun No Kagayaki [Sad Dust Glories].* Tokyo, Japan: Shoshinsha, 1978.
Translation by Yu Suwa: [Green Notebook — Writ In Moonbeam — Energy Vampire — Driving Volkswagon — Mr Sharpe the Carpenter From Marysville — Walking Uphill Woolen — The Moon Followed By Jupiter Thru Pinetrees — Sad Dust Glories — When I Sit — The Mood — Kenji Miyazawa — Could You Be Here? — Wind Makes Sound — For Sale For Sale]

H384   Ginsberg, Allen. *Indo Nikki [Indian Journals]*. Tokyo, Japan: Sanrio, 1980.
Translation by Yu Suwa: Indo Nika [Indian Journals]

H385   Ginsberg, Allen. *Allen Ginsberg Shishu [Selected Poems Of Allen Ginsberg]*.
Tokyo, Japan: Shichosha, 1983. [Third edition]
Translation by Yu Suwa: [Howl — Footnote To Howl — A Supermarket In
California — Transcription Of Organ Music — Fragment 1956 — The
Shrouded Stranger — The Trembling Of the Veil — After Dead Souls —
Gregory Corso's Story — Metaphysics — The Night-Apple — Sunset —
Marijuana Notation — Paterson — Sakyamuni Coming Out From the Mountain
— Ready To Roll — A Strange New Cottage In Berkeley — To Lindsay — To
Aunt Rose — The Lion For Real — At Apollinaire's Grave — Death To Van
Gogh's Ear — Kaddish (excerpt) — (drawing from *Yage Letters*)]

H386   Ginsberg, Allen. *Ginzubuga Shishu [Selected Poems of Allen Ginsberg]*.
Tokyo, Japan: Shichosha, 1986. [Fourth edition]
Translation by Yu Suwa: [Howl — Footnote To Howl — A Supermarket In
California — Transcription Of Organ Music — Fragment 1956 — The
Shrouded Stranger — The Trembling Of the Veil — After Dead Souls —
Gregory Corso's Story — Metaphysics — The Night-Apple — Sunset —
Marijuana Notation — Paterson — Sakyamuni Coming Out From the Mountain
— Ready To Roll — A Strange New Cottage In Berkeley — Kaddish (excerpt)
— The End — On Burroughs' Work — Dream Record: June 8, 1955 — 'Back
On Times Square, Dreaming Of Times Square' — Journals Jan. 1, 1960 —
Morning — Kral Majales — The Change: Kyoto-Tokyo Express — Pentagon
Exorcism — Genocide — Senate News — Portland Coliseum — First Party At
Ken Kesey's With Hell's Angels — Memory Gardens — (letter to Yu Suwa)
— (drawing from *Yage Letters*) — (drawing on cover) — (drawing of
apartment)]

H387   Ginsberg, Allen. *Howl: Forest, Water and People*. Kyoto, Japan: Kyoto
University, 1988.
Translation by Koun Iidaka: Cosmopolitan Greetings ‖ [Cosmopolitan Greetings]
Translation by Nanao Sakaki: Europe, Who Knows? ‖ [Europe, Who Knows?]
— [Plutonian Ode]
Translation by Sogyu Fukumura: Nanao: Brain Washed By Numerous Mountain
Streams ‖ [Nanao]
Translation by Hiki: Proclamation ‖ [Proclamation] — [A Crazy Spiritual] —
[The Shrouded Stranger] — [The Bricklayer's Lunch Hour] — [In Society]
Translation by Hiroaki Kirano: Sphincter ‖ [Sphincter]
Translation by Yo Makayama: On the Conduct Of the World Seeking Beauty
Against Government ‖ [On the Conduct of the World Seeking Beauty Against
Government] — Velocity of Money ‖ [Velocity of Money]
Translation by Yuzu Katagiri: Improvisation in Beijing ‖ [Improvisation in
Beijing] — [Howl]
Translation by Midori Hayashi: Going To the World of the Dead [includes music
notation] ‖ [Going To the World Of the Dead] — A Western Ballad [includes
music notation] ‖ [A Western Ballad]
Translation by Hidetoshi Tomiyama: [Rain-Wet Asphalt Heat, Garbage Curbed
Cans Overflowing]
AG; Snyder, Gary; McClure, Michael; Kyger, Joanne; and Sakaki, Nanao.
Message To Friends In Japan [collaboration] — Pull My Daisy

H388   Ginsberg, Allen. *Amerika No Botsuraku [The Fall of America]*. Tokyo, Japan:
Shichosha, 1989.
Translation by Hidetoshi Tomiyama: [Beginning Of a Poem To These States —
Continuation Of a Long Poem Of These States — These States — Hiway
Poesy LA-Albuquerque-Texas-Wichita — Auto Poesy — Kansas City To Saint
Louis — Bayonne Entering NYC — Wings Lifted Over the Black Pit —

Cleveland, the Flats — A Vow — Autumn Gold — Done, Finished With the
Biggest Cock — Bayonne Turnpike To Tuscarora — An Open Window On
Chicago — Returning North Of Vortex — Kiss Ass — Elegy Ché Guévara —
War Profit Litany — Elegy For Neal Cassady — Chicago To Salt Lake By Air
— Manhattan 'Thirties Flash — Please Master — A Prophecy — Bixby
Canyon — Crossing Nation — Smoke Rolling Down Street — Pertussin —
Swirls Of Black Dust On Avenue D — Violence — Past Silver Durango Over
Mexic Sierra Wrinkles — On Neal's Ashes — Going To Chicago — Grant
Park: August 28, 1968 — Car Crash — Over Denver Again — Imaginary
Universes — Rising Over Night-Blackened Detroit Streets — To Poe: Over the
Planet, Air Albany-Baltimore — Easter Sunday — Falling Asleep In America
— Northwest Passage — Sonora Desert-Edge — Reflections In Sleepy Eye —
Independence Day — In a Moonlit Hermit's Cabin — Rain-Wet Asphalt Heat,
Garbage Curbed Cans Overflowing — Death On All Fronts — Memory
Gardens — Flash Back — Graffiti 12th Cubicle Men's Room Syracuse Airport
— After Thoughts — G.S. Reading Poesy At Princeton — Friday the
Thirteenth — D.C. Mobilization — Ecologue — Guru Om — Have You Seen
This Movie? — Milarepa Taste — Over Laramie — Bixby Canyon Ocean Path
Word Breeze — Hum Bom! — September On Jessore Road — Airplane Blues
— Do the Meditation Rock — The Little Fish Devours the Big Fish —
Happening Now? — A Public Poetry — What You Up To? — Maturity —
Throw Out the Yellow Journalists Of Bad Grammar & Terrible Manner —
Going To the World Of the Dead — Irritable Vegetable — Thoughts Sitting
Breathing II — What the Sea Throws Up At Vlissingen — I Am Not — I'm A
Prisoner Of Allen Ginsberg — 221 Syllables At Rocky Mountain Dharma
Center — Fighting Phantoms Fighting Phantoms — Arguments — Sunday
Prayer — Brown Rice Quatrains — They're All Phantoms Of My Imagining —
White Shroud — Empire Air — Surprise Mind — Student Love — The
Question — In My Kitchen In New York — It's All So Brief — I Love Old
Whitman So — Written In My Dream By W.C. Williams — One Morning I
Took A Walk In China — Reading Bai Juyi — Black Shroud — World Karma
— Prophecy — Memory Cousins — Moral Majority — The Guest — After
Antipater — Jumping the Gun On the Sun — Cadillac Squawk — Things I
Don't Know]

H389   Ginsberg, Allen. *Shiroi Katabira: Allen Ginsberg Shishu [White Shroud]*.
Tokyo, Japan: Shichosha, 1991.
Translation by Makoto Takashima: [Porch Scribbles — Industrial Waves —
Those Two — Homage Vajracarya — Why I Meditate — Love Comes — Old
Love Story — Airplane Blues — Do the Mediation Rock — The Little Fish
Devours the Big Fish — Happening Now? — A Public Poetry — What You
Up To? — Maturity — Throw Out the Yellow Journalists Of Bad Grammar &
Terrible Manner — Going To the World Of the Dead — Irritable Vegetable —
Thoughts Sitting Breathing II — What the Sea Throws Up At Vlissingen — I
Am Not — I'm a Prisoner Of Allen Ginsberg — 221 Syllables At Rocky
Mountain Dharma Center — Fighting Phantoms Fighting Phantoms —
Arguments — Sunday Prayer — Brown Rice Quatrains — They're All
Phantoms Of My Imagining — White Shroud — Empire Air — Surprise Mind
— Student Love — The Question — In My Kitchen In New York — It's All
So Brief — I Love Old Whitman So — Written In My Dream By W. C.
Williams — One Morning I Took a Walk In China — Reading Bai Juyi —
Black Shroud — World Karma — Prophecy — Memory Cousins — Moral
Majority — The Guest — After Antipater — Jumping the Gun On the Sun —
Cadillac Squawk — Things I Don't Know]

Anthologies:

H390* *Bito Shishu*. Tokyo, Japan: Kokubunsha, 1962, pp. 48-75.
Translation by Yuzuru Katagiri: Hoeru [Howl]

H391* *Allen Ginsberg.* Tokyo, Japan: Doin No Kai, 1963, pp. 24-41.
Translation by Yu Suwa: Hoeru [Howl]

H392* *Sekai Shiron Taikei: Gendai America Shiron Taikei.* Tokyo, Japan: Shisosha, 1964.
Translation by Yu Suwa: Hoeru [Howl]

H393* Burroughs, William S. and Ginsberg, Allen. *Mayaku Shokan [The Yage Letters].* Tokyo, Japan: Shichosha, 1966. '
Translation by Ieda Takaaki and Yu Suwa: Mayaku Shokan [*The Yage Letters*]

H394* *Gendaisin No Shiso: Hankoteki Ningen.* Tokyo, Japan: Hebonsha, 1967, pp. 221-237.
Translation by Yu Suwa: Hoeru [Howl]

H395 DiPrima, Diane (ed.). *Amerika Hansen Shishu.* Tokyo, Japan: Akitsu Shoten, 1972, pp. 35-73.
Translation by Yuzuru Katagiri: [Wichita Vortex Sutra]
Translation by Yu Suwa: [Pentagon Exorcism] — [Genocide]

H396 Nikuri, Toshikuzu (ed.). *Amerika No Sekai.* Tokyo, Japan: Taishukan Publishing Co., 1981, pp. 253-255.
Translation by Toshikuzu Nikuri: A Supermarket In California || [A Supermarket In California]

H397 Suwa, Yu. *Alen Ginzubaga.* Tokyo, Japan: Yayoishbo, 1988.
Translation by Yu Suwa: [To Aunt Rose — Paterson — Transcription Of Organ Music — Sunflower Sutra — Howl — At Apollinaire's Grave — Death To Van Gogh's Ear — The Lion For Real — Kaddish — The Shrouded Stranger — After Dead Souls — Sunset — Metaphysics — A Strange New Cottage In Berkeley — 'Back On Times Square, Dreaming Of Times Square' — Reality Sandwiches — Marijuana Notation — Kral Majales — Mescaline — Wichita Vortex Sutra]

H398* McShine, Knyaston (ed.). *[Andy Warhol: A Retrospective].* Tokyo, Japan: Libroport Publishing, 1989.
Translation: Despite the Coolness Of Warhol's Art (prose)

H399 *On Paper Gallery: Communication For Peace.* Tokyo, Japan: Aqua Planet, 1989, postcard #15.
Translation: Homework || [Homework]
Note: A book of post cards which can be torn out and sent, AG is postcard #15.

Periodicals:

H400 [poem]. *Wasedabaigau Shimubun,* vol. 789 (Oct. 13, 1959) p. 4.
Translation by Yu Suwa: Apollinaire No Haka De [At Apollinaire's Grave (excerpt)]

H401 [poem]. *Gendai Shi Techo* (Jan. 1960) p. 31.
Translation by Yu Suwa: Hime [Howl]

H402 [poem]. *Goriika* (Feb. 1960) supplement.
Translation by Yu Suwa: Apollinaire No Haka De [At Apollinaire's Grave]

H403 [poem]. *Goriika,* vol. 8, no. 47 (Aug. 1960) pp. 7-21.
Translation by Yu Suwa: Hoeru [Howl]

H404* [poem]. *Shigaku* (Nov. 1963)
Translation: [Kaddish (excerpt)]

H405* [poem]. *Subterraneans,* extra issue (1963)
Translation: [To Lindsay]

H406* [poem]. *Ro* (Oct. 1964)
Translation: [Marijuana Notation]

H407* [poem]. *Ro* (Nov. 1964)
Translation: [Sakyamuni Coming Out From the Mountain]

H408 [poem]. *Mugen,* no. 17 (1964) pp. 120-121.
Translation by Yu Suwa: [To Aunt Rose]

H409* [2 poems]. *Gendai Shi Techo* (March 1966)
Translation by Yu Suwa: [2 poems]

H410 [2 poems]. *Ao* (April 1966), pp. 13-16.
Translation by Yukio Matsuda: Mashi Shihen [Magic Psalm]
Translation by Shozo Tokunaga: Himamari No Kyoten [Sunflower Sutra]

H411 [prose]. *Sekai Heima Undo Shiryo* (April 1966) pp. 10-11.
Translation: Hitomeni Tsuku Demono Yarikata-Kushin No Shirri To Soshiki
[How To Make a March/Spectacle]

H412 [poem]. *Gendai Shi Techo* (July 1966) pp. 106-110.
Translation by Yu Suwa: Gogatsu No Osama [Kral Majales]

H413 [poem]. *Gendai Shi Techo* (Jan. 1967) pp. 68-83.
Translation by Yuzuru Katagiri: [Wichita Vortex Sutra]

H414 [poem]. *Gendai Shi Techo* (Sept. 1967) pp. 94-100.
Translation by Yu Suwa: Henka: Kyoto-Tokyo Kyuko [The Change: Kyoto-
Tokyo Express]

H415* [prose]. *Psyche Journal* (1967)
Translation by Sansei Yamao: [Renaissance Or Death]

H416 [poem]. *Goro,* no. 4 (Feb. 24, 1977) pp. 46-51.
Translation by Yu Suwa.

H417 [poem]. *UNESCO Courier* [Japanese edition], vol. 35, no. 10 (Jan. 1983) pp.
13-14.
Translation: [Plutonian Ode (excerpt)]

H418 [poem]. *Subaru,* no. 7 (July 1983) pp. 68-72.
Translation by Yu Suwa: [Plutonian Ode]

H419 [prose]. *Subaru,* no. 9 (Sept. 1983) pp. 152-158.
Translation by Robert Cheshire: [Nuts To Plutonium]

H420 [2 poems]. *Edge II,* vol. 2, no. 2 (Spring 1984) pp. 22-29.
Translation by Yu Suwa: Memory Gardens ‖ [Memory Gardens] — Elegy For
Neal Cassady ‖ [Elegy For Neal Cassady]

H421 [7 poems]. *Gendai Shi Techo,* vol. 31, no. 2 [issue called *Beat Generation*] (Jan.
30, 1988) pp. 127-145.
Translation by Yu Suwa: [Airplane Blues]

Translation by Kazuko Shiraishi and John Salt: [Six Questions & Answers (questionnaire) — Cosmopolitan Greetings]
Translation by Hidetoshi Tomiyama: [A Methedrine Vision in Hollywood — Iron Horse — The Holy Ghost On the Nod Over the Body Of Bliss — To Poe: Over the Planet, Air Albany-Baltimore]

H422   Ginsberg, Allen; McClure, Michael; Kyger, Joanne; Sakaki, Nanao and Snyder, Gary. [prose]. *Nigen Kazoku,* no. 176 (Aug. 1, 1988) pp. 30-34.
Translation: [Eco Poetry Round Up]

H423   [poem]. *Nigen Kazoku,* no. 178 (Oct. 1, 1988) p. 30.
Translation by Tsuno Iidaka: [Europe, Who Knows?]

H424   [6 poems]. *Gendai Shi Techo,* vol. 32, no. 2 (Feb. 1989) pp. 7-15, 80-85.
Translation by Yuzuru Katagiri: [Sakyamuni Coming Out From the Mountain]
Translation by Hidetoshi Tomiyama: [Sunflower Sutra — Father Death Blues — Birdbrain — After Antipater — Why I Meditate]

H425   [poem]. *Sekai,* no. 528 (June 1989) pp. 1-8.
Translation by Kouun Iidaka: [Cosmopolitan Greetings]

H426   [poem]. *Nigen Kazoku,* no. 199 (Sept. 1, 1990) pp. 4-5.
Translation by Nanao Sakaki: [Europe, Who Knows?]

H427   [2 poems]. *Cool Resistance Press,* vol. 12 (Jan. 1992) pp. 3, 5, 7 and cover.
Translation by Kenichi Eguchi: Hum Bomb! — Just Say Yes Calypso || [Just Say Yes Calypso]

H428   [poem]. *Blue Beat Jacket,* no. 1 (Oct. 5, 1993) pp. 1-3.
Translation by Yushuke Keida: [For Carl Solomon (dated Feb. 26, 1993)]

H429   [prose]. *Blue Beat Jacket,* no. 2 (Dec. 15, 1993) pp. 10-15.
Translation by Yushuke Keida: [Introduction to Jack Kerouac's *Pomes All Sizes*]

H430   [prose]. *Blue Beat Jacket,* no. 3 (Feb. 1, 1994) p. 17.
Translation by Yushuke Keida: Homage To Hersch || [Homage To Hersch]

H431   [poem]. *GQ Japan,* no. 20 (Oct. 1994) pp. 38-43.
Translation by Kazuko Shiraishi: [The Charnel Ground]

Miscellaneous:

H432   [program]. *Alen Ginzubagu In Tokyo Yakushishu [Allen Ginsberg In Tokyo].* Oct. 21, 1988. One gathering of 32 leaves, English and Japanese dos-a-dos, 21.0 x 14.7 cm.
Translation by Yu Suwa: Howl (excerpt) || [Howl] — Sunflower Sutra || [Sunflower Sutra] — Kaddish (excerpt) || [Kaddish] — Ayers Rock Uluru Song || [Ayers Rock Uluru Song] — Father Death Blues (with music notation) || [Father Death Blues] — Birdbrain! || [Birdbrain!] — Airplane Blues || [Airplane Blues] — After Antipater || [After Antipater] — Why I Meditate || [Why I Meditate] — Little Planet [translation by Allen Ginsberg]

H433   [program]. *Fetus Of Nature: Koichi Tamano And Harupin-Ha World Survival Tour, 1989.* Berkeley, CA: privately printed, 1989.
Translation by Eric Selland: [prose blurb]

H434   [flyer]. *Mushimarudokugi.* Osaka, Japan: Feb. 7-9, 1992.
Translation: I Chanced Upon Mushimal (prose) || [I Chanced Upon Mushimal]
Note: Advertisement for dance program.

H435   [exhibition catalog]. *The Museum Inside the Telephone Network: InterCommunication '91.* Tokyo, Japan: Nippon Telegraph and Telephone Corporation, 1992.
Translation: American Haiku ‖ [American Haiku]

KOREAN

Anthologies:

H436   Ginsberg, Allen and Eun, Ko. *[Poetry].* Seoul, South Korea: 1990.
Translation by Ko Eun: [America — A Supermarket In California — Sunflower Sutra — Birdbrain! — Written In My Dream By W.C. Williams]

Periodicals:

H437   [poem]. *UNESCO Courier* [Korean edition], vol. 35, no. 10 (Nov. 1982) pp. 13-14.
Translation: [Plutonian Ode (excerpt)]

H438   [poem]. *[Literature, Art, Philosophy]*, no. 44 (May 1990) pp. 67-79.
Translation by Song Moon-Kun: [Howl]

H439   [8 poems and prose]. *Shimunhak,* no. 7 [issue no. 228] (July 1990) pp. 110-148.
Translation by Yeam Hong Choi: [Howl — A Supermarket In California — America — An Asphodel — Wild Orphan — In Back Of the Real]
Translation by Kim Yun Bok: [221 Syllables At Rocky Mountain Dharma Center — White Shroud (excerpt) — Written In My Dream By W.C. Williams — Meditation And Poetics (prose)]

Miscellaneous:

H440   [program]. *[Allen Ginsberg / Ko Eun].* Seoul, South Korea: Aug. 28, 1990, pp. 4-33.
Translation by Suh Kyunghee: America ‖ [America]
Translation by Kim Myong-Hwan: A Supermarket In California ‖ [A Supermarket In California] — Sunflower Sutra ‖ [Sunflower Sutra] — Birdbrain! ‖ [Birdbrain!] — Written In My Dream By W.C. Williams ‖ [Written In My Dream By W.C. Williams]

LITHUANIAN

Periodicals:

H441   [2 poems]. *Tiesa* (Nov. 22, 1985) p. 3.
Translation by Antanas Danielius: Supermarket As Kalifornijoj [A Supermarket In California] — Kauksmas [Howl (excerpt)]

H442   [2 poems]. *Literatura Ir Menas,* no. 48 [issune 2035] (Nov. 30, 1985) p. 3.
Translation by Antanas Drilinga: Europa! Europa! [Europe! Europe!] — Malda Uz Mirusius [Kaddish (excerpt)]

MACEDONIAN

Books:

H443   Ginsberg, Allen. *Poetry /Poezija.* Skopje, Yugoslavia: Makedonska Kniga, 1986.
Translation by Savo Tsvetanovski: The Eye Altering Alters All ‖ Okoto Menuvajki Se Menuva Se — The Trembling Of the Veil ‖ Treperenje Na Prevezot — A Meaningless Institution ‖ Zaludna Institucija — Psalm I ‖ Psalm I — After All, What Else Is There To Say? ‖ Po Se, Sto Da Se Kaze? — Tonite All Is Well ‖ Vecerva Se E Dobro — Fyodor ‖ Fjodor — Epigram On a Painting Of Golgotha ‖ Epigram Na Edna Slika Na Golgota — I Attempted To Concentrate ‖ Se Obidov Da Gi Zberam — Metaphysics ‖ Metafizka — Sunset ‖ Zajdisonce — Paterson ‖ Paterson — The Shrouded Stranger ‖ Tuginec So Nametka — Cezanne's Ports ‖ Pristanistata Na Sezan — A Desolation ‖ Samotija — A Poem On America ‖ Pecna Na Amerika — After Dead Souls ‖ Po Mrtvite Dusi — Walking Home At Night ‖ Vrakajki Se Doma Noke — A Ghost May Come ‖ Mozebi Ke Naide Duh — I Feel As If I Am At a Dead ‖ Uvstvuvam Kako Da Sum Vo Kor — My Alba ‖ Mojata Alba — Song ‖ Pesna — In Back Of the Real ‖ Zad Realnoto — On Burroughs' Work ‖ Za Delata Na Barouz — Blessed Be the Muses ‖ Blagosloveni Da Se Muzite — Howl ‖ Rev — A Supermarket In California ‖ Supermarket Vo Kalifornija — Sunflower Sutra ‖ Soncogledova Sutra — America ‖ Amerika — Tears ‖ Colzi — In the Baggage Room At Greyhound ‖ Vo Garderobata Na Grejhaund — Poem Rocket ‖ Pesna Raketa — Death To Van Gogh's Ear! ‖ Smrt Na Uvoto Na Van Gog! — Europe! Europe! ‖ Evropa! Evropa! — Laughing Gas ‖ Gas Za Smeenje — My Sad Self ‖ Moeto Tazno Jas — Kaddish ‖ Kadis — Lysergic Acid ‖ Lisergicna Kiselina — I Beg You Come Back & Be Cheerful ‖ Ve Molam Vratete Se I Bidete Veseli — Guru ‖ Guru — Wichita Vortex Sutra (excerpt) ‖ Vicita Vorteks Sutra — A Prophecy ‖ Prorostvo — Who ‖ Koj — On Neruda's Death ‖ Za Smrtta Na Neruda — Manifesto ‖ Manifest — Written On Hotel Napkin: Chicago Futures ‖ Napisano Na Hotelska Salveta: Cikaskite Idnini — Plutonian Ode ‖ Plutoniumska Oda — Ruhr-Gebiet ‖ Ruhr-Gebiet — Tübingen-Hamburg Schlafwagen ‖ Vo Vagonot Za Spienj E Megu Tibingen-Hamburg — After Whitman & Reznikoff ‖ Spored Vitmen I Reznikov — Ode To Failure ‖ Oda Na Neuspehot — Defending the Faith ‖ „Branejki Ja Verata" — The Black Man ‖ Crnec — Those Two ‖ Tie Dve — Happening Now? ‖ Toa Li Se Slucuva Sega? — Going To the World Of the Dead ‖ Odejki Vo Svetot Na Mrtvite — Far Away ‖ Daleku — It's All So Brief ‖ Se E Tolku Kratkotrajno — I Love Old Whitman So ‖ Go Sakam Vitmen Mnogu — Written In My Dream By W.C. Williams ‖ Napisana Od V.K. Vilijams Vo Mojot Son — Prophecy ‖ Prorostvo — I Am Not ‖ Jas Ne Sum — Things I Don't Know ‖ Nestata Sto Ne Gi Znam

Anthologies:

H444   Ilin, Dusica (ed.). *Zlaten Venets / Zlatni Venac / The Golden Garland.* Novi Sad, Yugoslavia: Knjizevna Zajednica Novog Sada, 1986, pp. 375-394.
Translation by Savo Tsvetanovski: In Back Of the Real ‖ Zad Stvarnoto — On Burroughs' Work ‖ Za Delata Na Barouz — America (excerpt) ‖ Amerika — Kaddish (excerpt) ‖ Kadish — Manifesto ‖ Manifest

Periodicals:

H445   [poem]. *Jehona,* vol. 17, no. 7 (1979) pp. 801-805.
Translation by A. Gajtani: Amerika [America]

H446   [poem]. *UNESCO Courier* [Macedonian edition], vol. 35, no. 10 (Nov. 1982) pp. 13-14.
Translation: [Plutonian Ode (excerpt)]

H447   [6 poems]. *Stremez,* vol. 30, no. 6 (1986) pp. 429-436.
Translation by Savo Tsvetanovski: Toa Li Se Slucuva Sega? [Happening Now?] — Tie Dve [Those Two] — Daleku [Far Away] — Se E Tolku Kratkotrajno [It's All So Brief] — Prorostvo [Prophecy] — Nestata Sto Ne Gi Znam [Things I Don't Know]

H448   [poem and prose]. *Nova Makedonija* (March 29, 1986) p. 6.
Translation by Savo Tsvetanovski: Pustos [A Desolation] — [prose speech]

H449   [poem and prose]. *Vecher* (March 29, 1986) p. 10.
Translation by Save Tsvetanovski: Okoto Menuvajki Se Menuva Se [The Eye Altering Alters All] — [prose speech]

H450   [poem]. *Studentski Zbor* (April 8, 1986)
Translation by Savo Tsvetanovski: Pesna [Song]

H451   [2 poems]. *Nova Makedonija,* vol. 42, no. 14156 (June 21, 1986) p. 6.
Translation by Savo Tsvetanovski: Pristanistata Na Sezan [Cezanne's Ports] — Tie Dve [Those Two]

H452   [poem]. *Nova Makedonija* (Aug. 16, 1986)
Translation by Savo Tsvetanovski: Crnec [The Black Man]

MALAYSIAN

Periodicals:

H453   [poem]. *UNESCO Courier* [Malaysian edition], vol. 35, no. 10 (Nov. 1982) pp. 13-14.
Translation: [Plutonian Ode (excerpt)]

NORWEGIAN

Books:

H454a   Ginsberg, Allen. *Hyl.* Oslo, Norway: Pax Forlag, 1968.
Translation by Olav Angell: Hyl [Howl] — Et Supermarked I California [A Supermarket In California] — Transkripsjon Av Orgelmusikk [Transcription Of Organ Music] — Solsikke Sutra [Sunflower Sutra] — Amerika [America] — I Bagasjeoppbevaringen På Greyhound [In the Baggage Room At Greyhound] — En Aspodell [An Asphodel] — Sang [Song] — Faderløs [Wild Orphan] — Bak Den Virkelige [In Back Of the Real]

H454b   Ginsberg, Allen. *Hyl Og Andre Dikt.* Oslo, Norway: Pax Forlag AS, 1983.
Translation by Olav Angell: Hyl [Howl] — Fotnote Til Hyl [Footnote To Howl] — Et Supermarked I California [A Supermarket In California] — Transkripsjon Av Orgelmusikk [Transcription Of Organ Music] — Solsikke Sutra [Sunflower Sutra] — Amerika [America] — I Bagasjeoppbevaringen På Greyhound [In the Baggage Room At Greyhound] — En Aspodell [An Asphodel] — Sang [Song] — Farløs [Wild Orphan] — Bak Den Virkelige [In Back Of the Real]

H455 Ginsberg, Allen. *I Hjertet Av Malstrømmen.* Oslo, Norway: J.W. Cappelens
Forlag, 1992.
Translation by Jòn Sveinbjørn Jònsson: Den Liksvøpte Fremmede [The
Shrouded Stranger] — Ved Apollinaires Grav [At Apollinaire's Grave] —
«Tilbake På Times Square, Drømmer Om Times Square» ['Back On Times
Square, Dreaming Of Times Square'] — Wichita Malstrøm Sutra [Wichita
Vortex Sutra] — Minnenes Hager [Memory Gardens] — Triste Støvminner
[Sad Dust Glories] — Ikke Bli Gammal [Don't Grow Old] — Plutonium Ode
[Plutonian Ode] — Leser Bai Juyi [Reading Bai Juyi]
Translation by Olav Angell: Farløs [Wild Orphan] — En Aspodell [An Asphodel]
— Sang [Song] — Bak Den Virkelige [In Back Of the Real] — Hyl [Howl] —
Fotnote Til Hyl [Footnote To Howl] — Et Supermarked I California [A
Supermarket In California] — Solsikke Sutra [Sunflower Sutra] —
Transkripsjon Av Orgelmusikk [Transcription Of Organ Music] — Amerika
[America] — I Bagasjeoppbevaringen På Greyhound [In the Baggage Room At
Greyhound] — Kaddish [Kaddish]

Anthologies:

H456 Angell, Olav (ed.). *USA Express.* Oslo, Norway: Bokklubbens Lyrikkvenner,
1983, pp. 13-31.
Translation by Olav Angell: Kaddish [Kaddish]

H457 Naess, Kate. *Gjendiktninger.* Oslo, Norway: Dreyer, 1989, pp. 70-71.
Translation: Til Tante Rose [To Aunt Rose]

H458 Jónsson, Jón Sveinbjørn (ed.). *Beat.* Oslo, Norway: Den Norske Lyrikklubben,
1994, pp. 10-11, 32-55.
Translation: Forward || Forord [prose]
Translation by Olav Angell: Hyl [Howl] — Fotnot Til Hyl [Footnote To Howl]
— Amerika [America]
Translation by Jan Erik Vold: Kontinentet På Tvers [Crossing Nation] — Over
Neals Aske [On Neal's Ashes]
Translation by Jón Sveinbjørn Jónsson: Etter Lalon [After Lalon] — Høstløv
[Autumn Leaves] — Etter Olav H. Hauge [After Olav H. Hauge]

Periodicals:

H459 [poem]. *Vinduet,* vol. 15, no. 3 (1961) pp. 216-219.
Translation by Yngvar Ustvedt: Dod Over Van Goghs Ore [Death To Van Gogh's
Ear]

H460 [5 poems]. *Vinduet,* vol. 28, no. 3 (1974) pp. 23-24.
Translation by Jan Erik Vold: Kontinentet På Tvers [Crossing Nation] — Over
Neals Aske [On Neal's Ashes] — Fantasiverdner [Imaginary Universes] —
Inskripsjoner Pa Veggen, Tolvte Bas, Herretoalettet, Syracuse Flyplass
[Graffiti 12th Cubicle Men's Room Syracuse Airport] — Hum Bom! [Hum
Bom!]

H461 [poem]. *Klassekampen,* vol. 15, no. 22 (Jan. 27, 1983) p. 5.
Translation by Jón Sveinbjørn Jónsson: Krigeren Er Redd [Verses Written For
Student Antidraft Registration Rally 1980]

H462 [poem]. *Basta!,* vol. 3, no. 5 (1992) p. 13.
Translation by Olav Angell: Amerika [America]

H463 [3 poems]. *Lyrikk Magasin,* no. 3 (1994) pp. 38-41.
Translation by Jón Sveinbjørn Jónsson: Høstløv [Autumn Leaves] —
Ringmuskel [Sphincter] — Etter Olav H. Hauge [After Olav H. Hauge]

PERSIAN

Periodicals:

H464 [poem]. *UNESCO Courier* [Persian edition], vol. 35, no. 10 (Nov. 1982) pp. 13-14.
Translation: [Plutonian Ode (excerpt)]

POLISH

Books:

H465 Ginsberg, Allen. *Skowyt I Inne Wiersze.* Bydgoszcz, Poland: Pomorze, 1984.
Translation by Grzegorz Musial: Howl II Skowyt — Footnote To Howl II Przypis Do Skowytu — A Supermarket In California II Supermarket W Kalifornii — Transcription Of Organ Music II Transkrypcja Organowa — Sunflower Sutra II Sutra O Sloneczniku — America II Ameryka — In the Baggage Room At Greyhound II W Przechowalni Bagazu Greyhounda — An Asphodel II Zlotoglow — Song II Piosenka — Wild Orphan II Dziki Sierota — In Back Of the Real II Na Tylach Rzeczy

H466 Ginberg, Allen. *Utwory Poetyckie.* Krakow, Poland: Wydawnictwo Literackie, 1984.
Translation by Bogdan Baran: Howl II Skowyt — America II Ameryko — A Supermarket In California II Supermarket W Kalifornii — In the Baggage Room At Greyhound II Przechowalnia Bagazu U Greyhounda — Transcription Of Organ Music II Transkrypcja Muzyki Organowej — Sunflower Sutra II Sutra Slonecznikowa — An Asphodel II Zlotoglow — In Back Of the Real II Na Zapleczu Rzeczywistosci — Kaddish II Kaddysz — Mescaline II Meskalina — Lysergic Acid II LSD — The Reply II Odpowiedz — The End II Koniec — To Lindsay II Do Lindsaya — Dream Record: June 8, 1955 II Zapis Snu: 8 Czerwca 1955 — On Neal's Ashes II Nad Popiolami Neala — Psalm III II Psalm III — Funny Death II Zabawna Smierc — At Apollinaire's Grave II Na Grobie Apollinaire'a — Europe! Europe! II Europa! Europa! — On Burroughs' Work II O Dziele Burroughsa — My Sad Self II Moje Smutne Ja — American Change II Amerykanskie Drobne — A Vow II Slubowanie — September On Jessore Road II Wrzesien Na Jessore Road — Uptown II Na Przedmiesciach — Big Beat II Big-Beat — To An Old Poet In Peru II Staremu Poecie Z Peru — Sunset S.S. Azemour II Zachod Slonca: S.S. Azemour — Stotras To Kali Destroyer Of Illusions II Stotry Do Kali, Niszczycielki Zludzen — Last Night In Calcutta II Ostatnia Noc W Kalkucie — The Change: Kyoto-Tokyo Express II Prezemiana: Ekspres Kioto-Tokio — Who Be Kind To II Dla Kogo Byc Milym — To the Body II Do Ciala — Today II Dzisiaj — Carmel Valley II Dolina Karmel — Galilee Shore II Wybrzeze W Galilei — Wales Visitation II Zwiedzanie Walii — A Prophecy II Proroctwo — Falling Asleep In America II Zasypianie W Ameryce

H467 Ginsberg, Allen. *Wiersze.* Poland: Miniatura, 1990.
Translation by Jacek Sieradzan: Kosmopolityczne Pozdrowienia [Cosmopolitan Greetings] — Siakjamuni Schodzi Z Gor [Sakyamuni Coming Out From the Mountain] — Koloseum W Portland [Portland Coliseum] — Duch Swiety Drzemiacy Nad Cialem Szczesliwosci [Holy Ghost On the Nod Over the Body Of Bliss] — Zrobione, Skonczone Z Najwiekszym Chujem [Done, Finished With the Biggest Cock] — Egzorcyzmowanie Pentagonu [Pentagon Exorcism] — Pocaluj Tylek [Kiss Ass] — Guru Om [Guru Om] — Smak Milarepy [Milarepa Taste] — Kto [Who] — Kraina O'Lakes, Wisc. [Land O'Lakes, Wisc.] — Mysli Oddychania Na Siedzaco [Thoughts Sitting Breathing] — „Co Zrobisz Jesli To Stracisz?" [What Would You Do If You Lost It?] — Tak I To

Jest Beznadziejne [Yes And It's Hopeless] — Co Chcialbym Zrobic [What I'd Like To Do] — Bitwa Allacha Z Jahwe [Jaweh And Allah Battle] — Manifesto [Manifesto] — Wyznanie Ego [Ego Confession] — Mysli Na Oddechu [Thoughts On a Breath] — Wspanialosc Smutnego Kurzu [Sad Dust Glories] — Nie Starzej Sie [Don't Grow Old] — Kraina O'Lakes, Wisconsin, Seminarium Wadzrajany [Land O'Lakes, Wisconsin: Vajrayana Seminary] — Dla Uszu Creeleya [For Creeley's Ear] — Co Jest Martwe? [What's Dead?] — Oda Plutonu [Plutonian Ode] — Refleksje Nad Jeziorem Louise [Reflections At Lake Louise] — Ptasi Mozdzek [Birdbrain!] — Dlaczego Medytuje? [Why I Meditate] — Karma Swiata [World Karma] — Piata Niedzynarodowka [Fifth Internationale] — Zauwazylem Morze, Zauwazylem Muzyke Chcialem Tanczyc [On Cremation Of Chögyam Trungpa, Vidyandra]

H468   Ginsberg, Allen. *Znajomi Z Tego Swiata.* Krakow, Poland: Wydawnictwo, 1993.
Translation by Piotr Sommer and Andrzej Szuba: Miedzy Ludzimi [In Society]
Translation by Piotr Sommer: Przerwa Na Obiad [The Bricklayer's Lunch Hour] — Drzaca Zaslona [The Trembling Of the Veil] — W Smierci, Nie Sposob Dotknac Tego Co Najblizej [In Death, Cannot Reach What Is Most Near] — Porty Cezanne'a [Cezanne's Ports] — Dwaj Chlopcy Poszli Do Knajpki Swoich Marzen [Two Boys Went Into a Dream Diner] — Zapis Po Marihuanie [Marijuana Notation] — Opowiadanie Gregory'ego Corso [Gregory Corso's Story] — Na Tylach Rzeczywistosci [In Back Of the Real] — O Utworach Burroughsa [On Burroughs' Work] — Zapis Snu: 8 Czerwca 1955 [Dream Record: June 8, 1955] — Blogoslawione Niechaj Beda Muzy [Blessed Be the Muses] — Supermarket W Kalifornii [A Supermarket In California] — Lzy [Tears] — Zapisek [Scribble] — Do Lindsaya [To Lindsay] — Do Ciotki Rose [To Aunt Rose] — Pierwszy Bankiet U Kena Keseya Z Aniolami Piekla [First Party At Ken Kesey's With Hell's Angels] — Uptown [Uptown] — Prezent Gwiazdkowy [Xmas Gift] — Nocny Blask [Night Gleam] — Wioska W Teton [Teton Village] — Szalas W Gorach Skalistych [Cabin In the Rockies] — Do Szesciu Narodow W Rezerwacie Tuscarora [Rolling Thunder Stones] — Moda Wiosenna [Spring Fashions] — Trzecie Pietro, Swit, Cala Noc Pisalem Listy [Fourth Floor, Dawn, Up All Night Writing Letters] — "Obroncy Wiary" [Defending the Faith] — Napisane W Moim Snie Przez W.C. Williamsa [Written In My Dream By W.C. Williams] — Proroctwo [Prophecy]
Translation by Andrzej Szuba: Oko Zmieniajac Sie Zmienia Wszystako [The Eye Altering Alters All] — Instytucja Bez Sensu [A Meaningless Institution] — Prosze Cie, Otworz Okno I Wpusc Mnie Do Srodka [Please Open the Window And Let Me In] — Metafizyka [Metaphysics] — Jablko Nocy [The Night-Apple] — Asfodel [An Asphodel] — Psalm III [Psalm III] — Przeslanie [Message] — Koniec [The End] — Zachod Slonca: S.S. Azemour [Sunset S.S. Azemour] — Warszawska Kawiarnia [Café in Warsaw] — Dolina Carmel [Carmel Valley] — Na Popioly Neala [On Neal's Ashes] — Niedziela Wielkanocna [Easter Sunday] — Unosimy Sie Z Promieniami Slonca I Opadamy Noca [We Rise On Sun Beams And Fall In the Night] — Praca Domowa [Homework] — Ja Tak Kocham Starego Whitmana [I Love Old Whitman So] — Kiedys Rano W Chinach Wybralem Sie Na Spacer [One Morning I Took a Walk In China] — Moralna Wiekszosc [Moral Majority]
Translation by Julia Hartwig: Zachod Slonca [Sunset] — Moze Przyjsc Widmo [A Ghost May Come] — Niezwykly Nowy Domek W Berkeley [A Strange New Cottage In Berkeley] — Transkrypcja Muzyki Organowej [Transcription Of Organ Music] — W Bagazowni Greyhounda [In the Baggage Room At Greyhound] — 269 Sylab Z Osrodka Dharmy W Gorach Skalistych [221 Syllables At Rocky Mountain Dharma Center] — Czarny Calun [Black Shroud]
Translation by Artur Miedzyrzecki: Wiersz O Ameryce [A Poem On America] — Wedlug Martwych Dusz [After Dead Souls] — Nad Grobem Apollinaire'a [At Apollinaire's Grave] — Wedlug Yeatsa [After Yeats] — Duch Brooklynskiego College'u [Brooklyn College Brain]

H469   Ginsberg, Allen. *Kadysz I Inne Wiersze 1958-1960.* Bydgoszcz, Poland: Pomorze, 1992.
Translation by Grzegorz Musial: Kaddish || Kadysz — Poem Rocket || Wiersz Rakieta — Europe! Europe! || Europa! Europa! — To Lindsay || Do Lindsay'a — Message || Wiadomosc — To Aunt Rose || Do Ciotki Rozy — At Apollinaire's Grave || Nad Grobem Apollinaire'a — The Lion For Real || Lew Na Zywo — Ignu || Ignu — Death To Van Gogh's Ear || Smierc Dla Ucha Van Gogha! — Laughing Gas || Gaz Rozweselajacy — Mescaline || Meskalina — Lysergic Acid || Kwas Lizergowy — Magic Psalm || Psalm Magiczny — The Reply || Odpowidez — The End || Koniec

Anthologies:

H470   Truszkowska, Teresa (ed.). *Wizjonerzy I Buntownicy.* Krakow, Poland: Wydawnictwo Literackie, 1976, pp. 97-1943.
Translation by Teresa Truszkowska: Howl (excerpt) || Skowyt — Footnote To Howl || Przypisek Do "Skowytu" — Sunflower Sutra || Sutra O Sloneczniku — Transcription Of Organ Music || Transkrypcja Na Muzyke Organowa — In the Baggage Room At Greyhound || W Przechowalni Bagazu Linii Greyhound — Kaddish (excerpt) || Kaddish — To Aunt Rose || Do Ciotki Rozy — Poem Rocket || Wiersz Rakieta — Wrote This Last Night || Pisane Ostatniej Nocy — Café In Warsaw || Warszawska Kawiarnia

H471   Rybowski, Tadeusz (ed.). *Wsrod Amerykanskich Poetow.* Wroclaw [and Warsaw], Poland: Zaklad Narodowy Im. Ossolinskich, 1979, pp. 26-30.
Translation by Tadeusz Rybowski: Ameryka [America] — Przeslanie [Message] — Dziennik: 22 Listopada 1963 [Wrote This Last Night]

H472   Boczkowski, Krzysztof. *Biale Usta.* Warsaw, Poland: Mlodziezowa Agencja Wydawnicza, 1989, pp. 118-122, 125-126.
Translation by Krzysztof Boczkowski: Ameryko [America] — Nocne Jablko [The Night-Apple] — Na Popioly Neala [On Neal's Ashes]

H473   Hartwig, Julia and Miedzyrzecki, Artur (eds.). *Opiewam Nowoczesnego Czlowieka: Antologia Poezji Amerykanskiej.* Warsaw, Poland: RePrint, 1992, pp. 299-308.
Translation by Julia Hartwig: Supermarket W Kalifornii [A Supermarket In California] — W Bagazowni Greyhounda [In the Baggage Room At Greyhound]
Translation by Artur Miedzyrzecki: Nad Grobem Apollinaire'a [At Apollinaire's Grave]
Translation by Piotr Sommer: Zapis Snu: 8 Czerwca 1955 [Dream Record: June 8, 1955] — Lzy [Tears] — Do Lindsaya [To Lindsay]

H474   Sieradzan, Jacek (ed.). *Drogi Karmy I Sciezka Dharmy.* Katowice, Poland: Verbum Marek Gorny, 1993, pp. 27-79.
Translation by Jacek Sieradzan: Sakjamuni Schodzi Z Gor [Sakyamuni Coming Out From the Mountain] — Bitwa Allacha Z Jahwe [Jaweh And Allah Battle] — Kraiina O'Lakes, Wisc. [Land O'Lakes, Wisc.] — Kraina O'Lakes, Wisconsin, Seminarium Wadzrajany [Land O'Lakes, Wisconsin: Vajrayana Seminary] — Dla Uszu Creeleya [For Creeley's Ear] — Refleksje Nad Jeziorem Louise [Reflections At Lake Louise] — Ptasi Mozdzek [Birdbrain!] — Dlaczego Medytuje? [Why I Meditate?] — Karma Swiata [World Karma] — Antywojenne Gry Wiosna 1971 [Anti-War Games] — Kosmopolityczne Przemowienia [Cosmopolitan Greetings] — Piata Miedzynarodowka [Fifth Internationale] — Na Kremacje Vidjadhary Chögyama Trungpy [On Cremation Of Chögyam Trungpa, Vidyadhara] — Prosba Blagalna O Odrodzenie Sie Vidjadhary Chögyama Trungpy Rinpocze [Supplication For the Rebirth Of the Vidyadhara Chögyam Trungpa, Rinpoche]— Ksiezyc W Kropli Rosy [The

Moon In the Dewdrop Is the Real Moon]
Translation by Jacek Sieradzan and Pawel Kolasa: Egzorcyzmowanie Pentagonu
[Pentagon Exorcism] — Mysli siedzenie Oddychanie [Thoughts Sitting
Breathing] — Co Zrobisz Jesli To Stracisz? [What Would You Do If You Lost
It?] — Kto [Who] — Te Stany: Do Konwencji Prezydenckiej W Miami [These
States: To Miami Presidential Convention] — Tak I To Jest Beznadziejne [Yes
And It's Hopeless] — Co Chcialbym Zrobic [What I'd Like To Do] —
Manifest [Manifesto] — Smutne Zakurzone Chwaly [Sad Dust Glories] —
Wyznania Ego [Ego Confession] — Mysli Na Oddechu [Thoughts On a
Breath] — Co Jest Martwe? [What's Dead?] — Oda Plutonu [Plutonian Ode]
Translation by Pawel Kolasa: Smak Milarepy [Milarepa Taste] — Slon W
Medytacyjnej Sali [Elephant In the Meditation Hall]

Periodicals:

H475 [poem]. *Odglosy,* no. 14 (1963) p. 7.
Translation by Roman Gorzelski: Mandala [Mandala]

H476 [poem]. *Tematy,* no. 9 (Winter [Jan.] 1964) pp. 160-171.
Translation by Waclaw Iwaniuk: Skowyt [Howl]

H477 [poem]. *Jazz,* vol. 9, no. 7-8 (Aug. 1964) pp. 24-25.
Translation by Waclaw Iwaniuk: Skowyt [Howl]

H478 [2 poems]. *Tematy,* vol. 8, no. 29-30 (Spring-Summer 1969) pp. 159-166.
Translation by Jerzy Niemojowski: Ameryka [America] — Ignu [Ignu]

H479 [poem]. *Zycie Literackie,* vol. 19, no. 33 [issue 916] (Sept. 1969) p. 4.
Translation by Teresa Truszkowska: Smierc Dla Ucha Van Gogha [Death To Van
Gogh's Ear (excerpt)]

H480 [poem]. *Poezja,* no. 7 (July 1973) pp. 53-54.
Translation by Tadeusz Slawek: Kalifornijski Supermarket [A Supermarket In
California]

H481 [poem]. *Nowy Wyraz,* no. 9 (Sept. 1974) p. 41.
Translation by Roman Pytel: Pierwsze Przyjecie U Kena Keseya Z Aniolami Z
Piekla [First Party At Ken Kesey's With Hell's Angels]

H482 [poem]. *Literatura Na Swiecie,* vol. 42, no. 10 (Oct. 1974) pp. 141-151.
Translation by Teresa Truszkowska: Skowyt [Howl (excerpt)]
Translation by Leszek Elektorowicz: Skowyt [Howl (excerpt)]

H483 [poem]. *Magazyn Kulturalny,* no. 3 (1974) p. 19-20.
Translation by Teresa Truszkowska: Do Ciotki Rozy [To Aunt Rose] — Pisane
Tej Ostatniej Nocy [Wrote This Last Night] — Pisk [Squeal]

H484 [poem]. *Nowy Wyraz,* vol. 4, no. 7-8 [issue 38-39] (July-Aug. 1975) p. 58.
Translation by Krzysztof Boczkowski: Nocne Jablko [The Night-Apple]

H485 [5 poems]. *Literatura Na Swiecie,* vol. 62, no. 6 (June 1976) pp. 184-187.
Translation by Piotr Sommer: O Utworach Burroughsa [On Burroughs' Work]
— Zapis Snu: 8 Czerwca 1955 [Dream Record: June 8, 1955] — Lzy [Tears]
— Zapisek [Scribble] — Do Lindsay'a [To Lindsay]

H486* [poem]. *Puls,* no. 1 (Oct. 1977)
Translation: Kral Majales [Kral Majales]

H487   [poem]. *Literatura Na Swiecie,* vol. 71, no. 3 (1977) pp. 124-131, 192-203.
Translation by Krzysztof Boczkowski: Ameryko [America]

H488   [4 poems]. *Litteraria,* no. 10 (1977) pp. 192-203.
Translation by Grzegorz Musial: Ekspres Kioto-Tokio [The Change: Kyoto-Tokyo Express] — Do Lindsaya [To Lindsay] — Ostatnia Noc W Kalkucie [Last Night In Calcutta] — Psalm Magiczny [Magic Psalm]

H489   [poem]. *Okolice,* no. 3 (1977) pp. 93-98.
Translation by Miroslaw Peczak: Europo! Europo! [Europe! Europe!]

H490   [poem]. *Tygodnik Kulturalny,* no. 8 (1977) p. 6.
Translation by Roman Gorzelski: Smierc Dla Ucha Van Gogha [Death To Van Gogh's Ear]

H491   [poem]. *Puls,* no. 4-5 (Fall-Winter [ca. April 1979] 1978-1979) pp. 66-73.
Translation by Piotr Allen [pseud. of Piotr Bikont]: Skowyt [Howl]

H492   [poem]. *Integracje,* no. 4 (1979) p. 55.
Translation by Tadeusz Slawek: Sutra Slonecznika [Sunflower Sutra]

H493   [3 poems and prose]. *Student,* no. 17 (1979) p. 5-13.
Translation by Bogdan Baran: Moje Smutne Ja [My Sad Self] — Zapis Snu: 8 Czerwca 1955 [Dream Record: June 8, 1955] — Amerykanskie Drobne [American Change] — Rozum Oslepiajacy [Mind Breaths] — Umieraj Godnie W Twej Samotnosci [A Public Solitude]

H494   [poem]. *Nowy Wyraz,* vol. 9, no. 12 (Dec. 1980) pp. 5-21.
Translation by Bogdan Baran: Kaddysz [Kaddish]

H495   [poem]. *Zdanie,* no. 3 (1982) p. 45.
Translation by Teresa Truszkowska: Poslanie II [Psalm III]

H496   [3 poems]. *Zdanie,* vol. 12, no. 3 (March 1983) pp. 21-23, inside front cover.
Translation by Teresa Truszkowska: Warszawska Kawiarnia [Cafe In Warsaw (excerpt)] — Do Ciala [To the Body] — Big Beat [Big Beat] — Smierc Na Wszystkich Frontach [Death On All Fronts]

H497   [poem]. *Pismo,* vol. 3, no. 7-9 (July-Sept. 1984) pp. 188-192.
Translation by Teresa Truszkowski: LSD [Lysergic Acid]

H498   [poem]. *Zdanie,* vol. 13, no. 3 (March 1984) p. 59.
Translation by Krzysztof W. Krzeszowski: W Bagazowni Dworca Autobusowego [In the Baggage Room At Greyhound]

H499   [poem]. *Literatura Na Swiecie,* no. 8-9 [issue 169-170] (Aug.-Sept. 1985) pp. 151-174.
Translation by Grzegorz Musial: Kadysz [Kaddish]

H500   [poem]. *Poezja,* no. 10 (Oct. 1985) pp. 6-8, 67-70.
Translation by Jerzy Niemojowski: Ameryka [America] — Ignu [Ignu]

H501   [poem]. *Rzeczywistosc,* no. 11 (1985) p. 3.
Translation by Jerzy Niemojowski: Ameryka [America]

H502   [prose]. *Pismo,* vol. 5, no. 2 (Feb. 1986) pp. 51-69.
Translation by Teresa Truszkowska: Chinska Palarnia Opium [*Indian Journals* (excerpt)]

H503 [poem]. *Literatura,* no. 6 [issue 69] (1988)
Translation by Anna and Piotr Maleccy: Zlowieszczy Kosciotrup [Grim Skeleton]

H504 [poem]. *Dekada Literacka,* no. 33 (Nov. 1-15, 1991) p. 3.
Translation by Anna Maleccy and Piotr Maleccy: Sygnal Z Manhattanu Nadany O Polnocy W Maju [Manhattan May Day Midnight]

H505 [poem]. *Tworczosc,* no. 10 (1991) pp. 3-7.
Translation by Artur Miedzyrzecki: Nad Grobem Apollinaire'a [At Apollinaire's Grave]

H506 [poem]. *Literatura Na Swiecie,* no. 8-9 (1992) pp. 215-233.
Translation by Piotr Sommer and Andrzej Szuba: Miedzy Ludzmi [In Society]
Translation by Piotr Sommer: Przerwa Na Obiad [The Bricklayer's Lunch Hour] — Szalas W Gorach Skalistych [Cabin In the Rockies] — Proroctwo [Prophecy] — Do Ciotki Rose [To Aunt Rose] — Do Szesciu Narodow W Rezerwacie Tuscarora [Rolling Thunder Stones] — Prezent Gwiazdkowy [Xmas Gift]
Translation by Andrzej Szuba: Praca Domowa [Homework] — Ja Tak Kocham Starego Whitmana [I Love Old Whitman So] — Moralna Wiekszosc [Moral Majority] — Na Popioly Neala [On Neal's Ashes] — Kiedys Rano W Chinach Wybralem Sie Na Spacer [One Morning I Took a Walk In China]
Translation by Julia Hartwig: Czarny Calun [Black Shroud] — Niezwykly Maly Domek W Berkeley [A Strange New Cottage In Berkeley] — Zachod Slonca [Sunset] — Transkrypcja Muzyki Organowej [Transcription Of Organ Music]
Translation by Artur Miedzyrzecki: Nocny Blask [Night Gleam] — Wiersz O Ameryce [A Poem On America]

H507 [poem]. *Odra,* no. 7-8 (1992) p. 31.
Translation by Piotr Sommer: Supermarket W Kalifornii [A Supermarket In California] — Lzy [Tears] — Do Lindsaya [To Lindsay]

H508 [poem]. *Res Publica Nowa,* no. 2 (1992) p. 72.
Translation by Piotr Sommer: Na Tylach Rzeczywistosci [In Back Of the Real] — W Smierci, Nie Sposob Dotknac Tego Co Najblizej [In Death, Cannot Reach What Is Most Near]

H509 [5 poems]. *Tytulu,* vol. 5, no. 1 (1992) pp. 40-44.
Translation by Grzegorz Musial: Pierwaze Przyjecie U Kena Kesey'a Z Hell's Angels [First Party At Ken Kesey's With Hell's Angels] — Zapis Snu: 8 Czerwca 1955 [Dream Record: June 8, 1955] — Malest Cornifici Tuo Catullo [Malest Cornifici Tuo Catullo] — O Prochach Neal'a [On Neal's Ashes] — Profesorek Z Brooklynu [Brooklyn College Brain]

H510 [10 poems]. *Naglos,* no. 9-10 [issue 34-35] (Feb.-March 1993) pp. 32-37.
Translation by Piotr Sommer: Opowiadanie Gregory'Ego Corso [Gregory Corso's Story] — O Utworach Burroughsa [On Burroughs' Work] — Zapis Snu: 8 Czerwca 1955 [Dream Record: June 8, 1955] — Zapisek [Scribble] — Pierwszy Bankiet U Kena Keseya Z Aniolami Piekla [First Party At Ken Kesey's With Hell's Angels] — Uptown [Uptown] — Wioska W Teton [Teton Village] — Moda Wiosenna [Spring Fashions] — Trzecie Pietro, Swit, Cala Noc Pisalem Listy [Fourth Floor, Dawn, Up All Night Writing Letters] — Proroctwo [Prophecy]

Miscellaneous:

H511 [music setting]. Schäffer, Boguslaw. *Howl.* Warsaw, Poland: Polskie Wydawnictwo Muzyczne, 1974.
Translation by Leszek Elektorowicz: Howl (excerpt) || Howl

PORTUGUESE

Books:

H512   Ginsberg, Allen. *Uivo*. Lisbon, Portugal: Publicações Dom Quixote, 1973.
[Series: Cadernos De Poesia #26]
Translation by José Palla E Carmo: Uivo [Howl] — Nota De Rodapé Ao Poema
"Uivo" [Footnote To Howl] — Canção [Song] — Na Parte De Trás Do Real
[In Back Of the Real] — Acerca Da Obra De Burroughs [On Burroughs' Work]
— Salmo 3° [Psalm III] — O Meu Triste Eu [My Sad Self] — Foguetão Poema
[Poem Rocket] — Na Sepultura De Apollinaire [At Apollinaire's Grave] —
Morte À Orelha De Van Gogh! [Death To Van Gogh's Ear] — Primeira Festa
Em Casa Do Ken Kesey, Com Os "Hell's Angels" [First Party At Ken Kesey's
With Hell's Angels] — Na Parte Elegante Da Cidade [Uptown] — Exorcismo
Do Pentágono [Pentagon Exorcism] — Litania Dos Lucros De Guerra [War
Profit Litany] — Universos Imaginários [Imaginary Universes] — Morte Em
Todas As Frentes [Death On All Fronts] — Mobilização Em Washington [D.C.
Mobilization]

H513   Ginsberg, Allen. *Uivo: Kaddish E Outros Poemas*. Porto Alegre, Brazil: L&PM,
1984.
Translation by Cláudio Willer: Uivo [Howl] — Nota De Pé De Página Para Uivo
[Footnote To Howl] — Um Supermarcado Na Califórnia [A Supermarket In
California] — Transcrição De Música De Órgão [Transcription Of Organ
Music] — Sutra Do Girassol [Sunflower Sutra] — América [America] —
Canção [Song] — Kaddish [Kaddish] — Europa! Europa! [Europe! Europe!]
— Para Lindsay [To Lindsay] — Mensagem [Message] — Para Tia Rose [To
Aunt Rose] — No Túmulo De Apollinaire [At Apollinaire's Grave] — Morte à
Orelha De Van Gogh! [Death To Van Gogh's Ear!] — Mescalina [Mescaline]
— Ácido Lisérgico [Lysergic Acid] — Salmo Mágico [Magic Psalm] — A
Resposta [The Reply] — O Fim [The End] — O Automóvel Verde [The Green
Automobile] — Sobre A Obra De Burroughs [On Burroughs' Work] — Poema
De Amor Sobre Um Tema De Whitman [Love Poem On Theme By Whitman]
— Malest Cornifici Tuo Catullo [Malest Cornifici Tuo Catullo] — Registro De
Um Sonho: 8 De Junho, 1955 [Dream Record: June 8, 1955] — Fragmento
1956 [Fragment 1956] — Um Estranho Chalé Novo Em Berkely [A Strange
New Cottage In Berkeley] — Iluminação De Sather Gate [Sather Gate
Illumination] — Garatuja [Scribble] — Meu Triste Eu [My Sad Self] — Peço-
Lhe Que Volte & Fique Contente [I Beg You Come Back And Be Cheerful] —
Para Um Velho Poeta No Peru [To an Old Poet In Peru]

H514   Ginsberg, Allen. *A Queda Da América*. Porto Alegre, Brazil: L&PM, 1987.
Translation by Paulo Henriques Britto: Princípio De Um Poema Destes Estados
[Beginning Of a Poem Of These States] — Continuação De Um Longo Poema
Destes Estados: De São Francisco Pro Sul [Continuation San Francisco
Southward] — Estes Estados, Chegando A Los Angeles [These States Into L.
A.] — Poesia Estradeira Los Angeles-Albuquerque-Texas-Wichita [Hiway
Poesy L.A.-Albuquerque-Texas-Wichita] — Autopoesia: Fugindo De
Bloomington [Auto Poesy: On the Lam From Bloomington] — De Kansas City
A Saint Louis [Kansas City To St. Louis] — De Bayonne A Nova Iorque
[Bayonne Entering N.Y.C.] — Asas Sobre O Buraco Negro [Wings Lifted
Over the Black Pit] — Cleveland, A Baixada [Cleveland, the Flats] — Um
Juramento [A Vow] — Ouro Outonal: Outono Na Nova Inglaterra [Autumn
Gold: New England Fall] — Pronto, Terminei Com A Maior Pica [Done,
Finished With the Biggest Cock] — Estrada De Bayonne A Tuscarora
[Bayonne Turnpike To Tuscarora] — Janela Aberta Sobre Chicago [An Open
Window On Chicago] — Voltando A Norte Do Vórtice [Returning North Of
Vortex] — Lambe Saco [Kiss Ass] — Elegia Che Guevara [Elegy Che
Guevara] — Ladainha Dos Lucros Da Guerra [War Profit Litany] — Elegia

Para Neal Cassady [Elegy For Neal Cassady] — De Chicago A Salt Lake De Avião [Chicago To Salt Lake By Air] — Cena De Manhattan Central [Manhattan 'Thirties Flash] — Por Favor Meu Amo [Please Master] — Uma Profecia [A Prophecy] — Bixby Canyon [Bixby Canyon] — Atravessando A Nação [Crossing Nation] — Fumaça Fluindo Rua Abaixo [Smoke Rolling Down Street] — Pertussin [Pertussin] — Torvelinhos De Poeira Preta Na Avenida D [Swirls Of Black Dust On Avenue D] — Violência [Violence] — Passando Por Silver Durango Sobrevoando Rugas Da Serra Mexicana [Past Silver Durango Over Mexico Sierra Wrinkles] — As Cinzas De Neal [On Neal's Ashes] — Rumo A Chicago [Going To Chicago] — Grant Park, 28 De Agosto De 1968 [Grant Park: August 28, 1968] — Desastre De Carro [Car Crash] — Sobrevoando Denver Outra Vez [Over Denver Again] — Subindo Sobre Ruas De Detroit Negras De Noite [Rising Over Night-Blackened Detroit Streets] — Universos Imaginários [Imaginary Universes] — Para Poe: Sobrevoando Planeta, Ar Albany-Baltimore [To Poe: Over the Planet, Air Albany-Baltimore] — Domingo De Páscoa [Easter Sunday] — Adormecendo Na América [Falling Asleep In America] — Passagem Do Noroeste [Northwest Passage] — Orla Do Deserto De Sonora [Sonora Desert Edge] — Reflexões Em Sleepy Eye [Reflections In Sleepy Eye] — Dia Da Independência [Independence Day] — Numa Cabana De Eremita Enluarada [In a Moonlit Hermit's Cabin] — Calor De Asfalto Molhado De Chuva, Latas De Lixo Em Meio-Fio Transbordando [Rain-Wet Asphalt Heat, Garbage Curbed Cans] — Morte De Todos Os Lados [Death On All Fronts] — Jardins Da Memória [Memory Gardens] — Flashback [Flash Back] — Graffiti 12a Privada Banheiro Dos Homens Aeroporto De Syracuse [Graffiti 12th Cubicle Men's Room Syracuse Airport] — Depois Do Ato [After Thoughts] — G.S. Lendo Poesia Em Princeton [G.S. Reading Poesy At Princeton] — Sexta-Feira Treze [Friday the Thirteenth] — Mobilização De Washington [D.C. Mobilization] — Ecologa [Ecologue] — Guru Om [Guru Om] — "Você Já Viu Esse Filme?" [Have You Seen This Movie?] — Um Gosto De Milarepa [Milarepa Taste] — Sobrevoando Laramie [Over Laramie] — Brisa Verbal Caminho Oceânico Bixby Canyon [Bixby Canyon Ocean Path Word Breeze] — Bomba Bum [Hum Bom] — Setembro Na Estrada De Jessore [September On Jessore Road]

Anthologies:

H515   De Seabra, Manuel (ed.). *Antologia Da Novíssima Poesia Norte-Americana.* Lisbon, Portugal: Editorial Futura, 1973, pp. 17-40.
Translation: Na Campa De Apollinaire [At Apollinaire's Grave] — Um Supermercado Na California [A Supermarket In California] — Alvejado A Tiro Nas Costas Por Uma Folha Caida [Shot In the Back By a Fallen Leaf] — O Espirito Santo Na Reveréncia Sobre O Corpo Do Éxtase [Holy Ghost On the Nod Over the Body Of Bliss] — Registo De Um Sonho: 8 De Junho De 1955 [Dream Record: June 8, 1955] — America [America] — Para Quem Ser Bondoso [Who Be Kind To]

H516   Keys, Kerry Shawn (ed.). *Quingumbo, Nova Poesia Norte-Americana.* São Paulo, Brazil: Escrita, 1980, pp. 103-117.
Translation by Leonardo Fróes: Sunflower Sutra ‖ Sutra Do Girassol — Wales Visitation ‖ Presença Em Gales
Translation by Flávio Moreira Da Costa: A Supermarket In California ‖ Um Supermercado Na Califórnia
Translation by Maria Amélia Mello: First Party At Ken Kesey's With Hell's Angels ‖ Primeira Festa Na Casa De Ken Kesey Com Os Hell's Angels

Periodicals:

H517   [poem]. *Ultramar,* vol. 1, no. 3 (1960) p. 2.
Translation by Raquel Señoret & J.T.: Kaddish [Kaddish (excerpt)]

H518   [poem]. *UNESCO Courier* [Portuguese edition], vol. 35, no. 10 (Nov. 1982) pp. 13-14.
Translation: [Plutonian Ode (excerpt)]

H519   [poem]. *Dimensão,* vol. 6, no. 11 (Spring 1985) pp. 34-36.
Translation by Flávio Moreira Da Costa: A Supermarket In California || Um Supermercado Na Califórnia

H520   [poem]. *Folha De S. Paulo* (May 22, 1988) p. A47.
Translation by Antonio Invar: All Through the Sixties the Dope Flew Free || Nos Anos Sessenta A Droga Voava Livre

ROMANIAN

Anthologies:

H521   Sterian, Margareta (ed.). *Aud Cantand America: Antologie De Poezie Moderna Americana.* Bucharest, Romania: Editura Dacia, 1973, pp. 245-248.
Translation by Margareta Sterian: Cantec [Song]

H522   Levitchi, Leon and Dorin, Tudor (eds.). *Antologie De Poezie Americana De La Inceputuri Pina Azi.* Bucuresti, Romania: Editura Minerva, 1978, pp. 298-300.
Translation by Petre Solomon: America [America (excerpt)]
Translation by Virgil Teodorescu and Petronela Negosanu: Un Magazin Cu Autoservire In California [A Supermarket In California]

H523   Caraion, Ion (ed.). *Antologia Poeziei Americane.* Bucharest, Romania: Editura "Univers", 1979, pp. 520-525.
Translation by Petre Solomon: Un "Supermarket" In California [A Supermarket In California]
Translation by Ion Caraion: Cintec [Song] — Urlet De Minie [Howl (excerpt)] — Indaratul Realitatii [In Back Of the Real]

H524   Teodorescu, Virgil & Negosanu, Petronela (eds.). *Lirica Americana Contemporana.* Bucharest, Romania: Editura Albatros, 1980, pp. 146-152.
Translation by Virgil Teodorescu and Petronela Negosanu: Floarea-Soarelui Sutra [Sunflower Sutra] — Un Magazin Cu Autoservire In California [A Supermarket In California]

H525   Sorescu, Marin. *Tratat De Inspiratie.* Craiova, Romania: Scrisul Romanesc, 1985, pp. 260-266.
Translation by Marin Sorescu: Satul Teton [Teton Village] — Maretia Tristei Tarine [Sad Dust Glories] — Brate Rupte, Genunchi Moi [Don't Grow Old] — O Sa Patesc Si Eu La Fel? [Don't Grow Old] — Poem [Don't Grow Old] — Tribunal Auriu [Nagasaki Days] — Dar De Craciun [Xmas Gift] — Cintec Uluru Al Stincii Ayers [Ayers Rock/Uluru Song] — Blues Al Tatalui Moarte [Father Death Blues] — Declaratie [Manifesto] — Coliba In Muntii Stincosi [Cabin In the Rockies] — Nobile Adevaruri [Gospel Noble Truths]

Periodicals:

H526*   [poem]. *Tribuna,* vol. 9, no. 5 (Feb. 4, 1965) p. 12.
Translation by Al Caprariu: Mandala [Mandala]

H527*   [poem]. *Caiet,* no. 5 (May 1968) p. xix.
Translation: America [America]

H528* [poem]. *Tribuna,* vol. 13, no. 28, (July 10, 1969) p. 8.
Translation by Vasile Grunea: Sutra Wichita [Wichita Vortex Sutra (excerpt)]

H529* [poem]. *Tribuna,* vol. 13, no. 52 (Dec. 25, 1969) p. 8.
Translation by Sylvia Aron and Petru M. Has: In Spatele Realului [In Back Of the Real]

H530* [poem]. *Ramuri,* vol. 7, no. 1 (Jan. 15, 1970) p. 24.
Translation by Marcel Pop-Cornis: In Dosul Realitatii [In Back Of the Real]

H531* [poem]. *Tomis,* vol. 5, no. 2 (Feb. 1970) p. 12.
Translation by Nicolae Motoc and Metodiu Radulescu: Un Magazin Cu Autoservire In California [A Supermarket In California] — Sutra Florii-Soarelui [Sunflower Sutra]

H532* [poem]. *Steaua,* vol. 21, no. 6 (June 1970) pp. 71-72.
Translation by Marcel Pop-Cornis: Ghiocel [Genocide]

H533* [poem]. *Tomis,* vol. 6, no. 5 (May 1971) p. 12.
Translation by Nicolae Motoc: Malest Cornifici Tuo Catullo [Malest Cornifici Tuo Catullo]

H534 [poem]. *Steaua,* vol. 24, no. 4 (Feb. 16-28, 1973) pp. 16-17.
Translation by Mircea Zaciu: Supermarket In California [Supermarket In California]

H535* [poem]. *Utunk,* vol. 28, no. 49 (Dec. 1973) p. 9.
Translation by Marki Zoltan: Egy Kaliforniai Aruhazban [A Supermarket In California]

H536* [poem]. *Igaz Szo,* vol. 24, no. 4 (April 1976) pp. 376-377.
Translation: Arucsarnok Kaliforniaban [A Supermarket In California]

H537 [poem]. *Secolul 20,* vol. 185, no. 6 (June 1976) pp. 32-48.
Translation by Virgil Teodorescu and Petronela Negosanu: Un Magazin Cu Autoservire In California [A Supermarket In California]

H538* [poem]. *Utunk,* vol. 31, no. 28 (July 1976) p. 6.
Translation by Domokos Jorditasai: Utolso Ejszaka Kalkuttaban [Last Night In Calcutta]

H539* [poem]. *Luceafarul,* vol. 19, no. 27 (July 3, 1976) p. 7.
Translation: Strigat [Howl (excerpt)]

H540* [poem]. *Steaua,* vol. 27, no. 10 (Oct. 1976) pp. 29-30.
Translation by Mircea Zaciu: La Mormantul Lui Apollinaire [At Apollinaire's Grave]

H541* [poem]. *Vatra,* vol. 7, no. 1 (Jan. 20, 1977) p. 14.
Translation by Virgil Stanciu: Lui Lindsay [To Lindsay]

H542* [poem]. *Luceafarul,* vol. 20, no. 15 (April 9, 1977) p. 8.
Translation by C. Dumitrescu: America [America (excerpt)]

H543* [poem]. *Vatra,* vol. 10, no. 7 (July 20, 1980) p. 13.
Translation by Petru Iliesu and Marcel Pop-Cornis: Ignu [Ignu]

H544   [poem]. *Orizont,* vol. 31, no. 41 [issue 655] (Oct. 9, 1980) p. 8.
Translation by Marcel Pop-Cornis: In Depozitul De Bagaje Al Ogarului Cenusiu
[In the Baggage Room At Greyhound]

H545*   [poem]. *Orizont,* vol. 32, no. 26 (July 2, 1981) p. 8.
Translation by Ion Iuga and Traian Gardut: Marile Magazine In California [A
Supermarket In California]

H546*   [poem]. *Steaua,* vol. 32, no. 10 (Oct. 1981) pp. 20-21.
Translation by Ioana Ieronim and Horia Popescu: Urlet [Howl]

H547   [4 poems]. *Steaua,* vol. 37, no. 10 (Oct. 1986) pp. 19-20.
Translation by Aurel Roul: Cine [Who] — Cei Doi [Those Two] — Profetii
[Prophecy]
Translation by A. Zarnescu: Salutari Cosmopolite [Cosmopolitan Greetings]

H548*   [poem]. *Luceafarul,* vol. 31, no. 7 (Feb. 13, 1988) p. 8.
Translation by Diana Ionita and Traian T. Cosovei: Mesaj [Message] — Lui
Lindsay [To Lindsay]

H549   [poems]. *Orizont,* no. 30 (July 29, 1988) p. 16.
Translation by Anghel Dumbraveanu and Mircea Mihaies: Tremurul Valului [The
Trembling Of the Veil] — De Fapt. Ce-Ar Mai Fi De Spus? [After All What
Else Is There To Say?] — Porturile Lui Cezanne [Cezanne's Ports] — Am
Invatat Cite O Lume [I Learned a World From Each] — Lacrimi [Tears] —
Unui Batrin Poet Peruan [To an Old Poet In Peru] — Guru [Guru] — Dupa
Yeats [After Yeats] — Psalm I [Psalm I]

H550*   [poem]. *Contrapunct,* vol. 2, no. 15 [issue 67] (April 12, 1991) p. 16.
Translation by Magda Carneci: Psalm Magic [Magic Psalm]

H551*   [3 poems]. *Contrapunct,* vol. 2, no. 26 (June 28, 1991) p. 16.
Translation by Magda Carneci: Sfirisit — Psalm [Psalm] — Metafizica
[Metaphysics]

H552*   [poems]. *Poesis,* no. 4-5 (April-May 1993) pp. 20-21.
Translation by Virginia Stanescu and Gabriel Stanescu: Kral Majales [Kral
Majales] — Profetie [Prophecy] — Totul E Asa De Scurt [It's All So Brief] —
Omagiu Lui Vajracarya [Homage Vajrachara] — Sa Se Intemple Acum?
[Happening Now?] — Nu Sint [I Am Not] — Vegetal Iritabil [Irritable
Vegetable] — Argumente [Arguments] — De Ce Meditez [Why I Meditate] —
Surpriza Memoriei [Surprise Mind] — Cele Doua [Those Two] — Maturitate
[Maturity] — Dupa Antipater [After Antipater]

RUSSIAN

Books:

H553   Ginsberg, Allen. *Kaddish / Kaddish.* St. Petersburg, Russia: Nikolai
Yakumchuk, 1993.
Translation by Vukmora Sosnory: Kaddish [Kaddish]

Anthologies:

H554   *Sovremennaia Amerikanskaia Pozziia.* Moscow, USSR: Progress, 1975, pp.
359-372.
Translation by Andrei Sergeiev: Supermarket V Kalifornii [A Supermarket In
California] — Obedennyi Perery V Kamenshchikov [The Bricklayer's Lunch

Hour] — Uedinenie [A Desolation] — Posle Chteniia "Mertvykh Dush" [After Dead Souls] — Sutra Podsolnukha [Sunflower Sutra] — Moia Utrenniaia Pesnia [My Alba] — Moe Pechalnoe Ia [My Sad Self] — Nabrosok [Scribble] — Amerikanskie Dengi [American Change] — Probuzhdenie V Niu-Iorke [Waking In New York]

H555 Zverev, A. (ed.). *Pozziia Ssha.* Moscow, USSR: Khudozhestvennaya Literatura, 1982, pp. 725-733.
Translation by G. Sumanobcha: Amerika [America]
Translation by A. Sergeiev: Supermarket V Kalifornii [Supermarket In California] — Sutra Podsolnukha [Sunflower Sutra] — Moe Pechalnoe Ya [My Sad Self]
Translation by R. Dubrokuia: Poslednyaya Noch V Kalkutte [Last Night In Calcutta]

H556 Dzhimbinov, S.B. (ed.). *Amerikanskaya Poeziya.* Moscow, USSR: Raduga Publishers, 1983, pp. 462-469.
Translation by A. Sergeiev: A Supermarket In California ‖ Supermarket V Kalifornii — Sunflower Sutra ‖ Sutra Podsolnukha

H557 Voznesenski, A. *Proraby Dukha.* Moscow, USSR: Sovetskii Pisatel, 1984, pp. 466-467.
Translation: Dzhessorskaya Doroga [September On Jessore Road (excerpt)]

H558 Akchurin, Marat (ed.). *A Double Rainbow.* Moscow, USSR: Moldaya Gvardiya, 1988, pp. 117, 118.
Translation by Ilya Kutik: The Blue Angel ‖ Ilia Kutik
Note: Book bound dos-a-dos with Russian translation.

Periodicals:

H559 [poem]. *Inostrannaya Literatura,* no. 8 (1961) p. 174.
Translation by Andrei Sergeiev: Rynok V Kalifornii [A Supermarket In California]

H560 [2 poems]. *Inostrannaya Literatura,* no. 9 (1966) pp. 182-183.
Translation by Andrei Sergeiev: Moya Utrennyaya Pesnya [My Alba] — Sutra Podsolnukha [Sunflower Sutra]

H561 [poem]. *Sovetskaya Molodezh* (Dec. 4, 1971)
Translation by Valery Minushin: [After Dead Souls]

H562 [poem]. *Literaturnaya Gazeta,* no. 15 (Dec. 9, 1971)
Translation by Andrei Voznesensky: Azhessorskaya Doroga [September On Jessore Road (excerpt)]

H563 [poem]. *Pamir,* no. 1 (1974)
Translation by Valery Minushin: [Bricklayer's Lunch Hour]

H564 [poem]. *Kurer Yunesko [UNESCO Courier]* [Russian edition], vol. 35, no. 10 (Dec. 1982) pp. 13-14.
Translation by A. Ibragimov: [Plutonian Ode (excerpt)]

H565 [6 poems]. *Inostrannaya Literatura,* vol. 15, no. 10 (1986) pp. 108-115.
Translation by Andrei Sergeiev: Bruklunskts Akademucheskts Um [Brooklyn College Brain] — Chemvermyts Zmakh, Rassvem, Vsiu Noch Pusal Pus'ma [Fourth Floor, Dawn, Up All Night Writing Letters] — Shpana [Mugging] — Kmo Upravliaem Amerikoi [Who Runs America] — Uedtshehutse V

Skalusmykh Iuorakh [R.M.D.C.] — Iz Utskla "Ne Smarets" [Don't Grow Old]

H566 [poem]. [*Slobo/Word*], no. 15 (Winter 1993) pp. 128-131.
Translation by Alexander Mejirov: [After Lalon] ‖ After Lalon

H567 [2 poems]. [*Inostrannaya Literatura*], no. 3 (March 1994) pp. 5-8.
Translation by Andrei Sergeiev: Nad Shmamamy [Crossing Nation] — Avariia [Car Crash]

SERBO-CROAT

Books:

H568 Ginsberg, Allen. *Hidrogenski Dzuboks*. Belgrad, Yugoslavia: Narodna Knjiga, 1983.
Translation by Zoran Petkovic and Mihailo Ristic: Jugoslovenskim Citaocima [prose introduction] — Zalazak Sunca [Sunset] — Naici Ce Mozda Duh [A Ghost May Come] — U Drustvu [In Society] — Zapis O Marihuani [Marijuana Notation] — Paterson [Paterson] — Luda Duhovna Pesma [A Crazy Spiritual] — Iza Stvarnog [In Back Of the Real] — Moja Alba [My Alba] — Zeleni Automobil [The Green Automobile] — Pesma [Song] — O Barouzovom Radu [On Burroughs' Work] — Supermarket U Kaliforniji [A Supermarket In California] — Suncokretova Sutra [Sunflower Sutra] — Zapis Sna: 8. Jun 1955 [Dream Record: June 8, 1955] — Malest Cornifici Tuo Catullo [Malest Cornifici Tuo Catullo] — Pogledao Sam Preko Ramena [Looking Over My Shoulder] — Zimska Haiku [Winter Haiku] — Prosla Je Jos Jedna [Another Year] — Prestao Sam Da Se Brijem [I Quit Shaving] — Lezim na Boku [Lying On My Side] — Na Petnaestom Spratu [On the Fifteenth Floor] — Na Tremu [On the Porch] — Urlik [Howl] — Beleska Uz Urlik [Footnote To Howl] — Amerika [America] — Prosvetljenje Na Sejder Gejtu [Sather Gate Illumination] — U Garderobi Grejhaunda [In the Baggage Room At Greyhound] — Spreman Za Pokret [Ready To Roll] — Evropa! Evropa! [Europe! Europe!] — Smrt Van Gogovom Uhu! [Death To Van Gogh's Ear!] — Zaista Lav [The Lion For Real] — Kadis [Kaddish] — Himmnna [Hymmnn From Kaddish] — Kraj [The End] — Opisati: Kisu Nad Dasasvamedom [Describe: The Rain On Dasaswamedh] — Poslednja Noc U Kalkuti [Last Night In Calcutta] — Zrtva Sam Telefona [I Am a Victim Of Telephone] — Trenuci Se Vracaju [The Moments Return] — Kral Majales [Kral Majales] — Guru [Guru] — Vicita Vorteks Sutra [Wichita Vortex Sutra (excerpt)] — Zavet [A Vow] — Jesenje Zlato: Novoengleska Jesen [Autumn Gold: New England Fall] — Elegija Za Nila Kesidija [Elegy For Neal Cassady — Smrt Na Svim Frontovima [Death On All Fronts] — Ekolog [Ecologue (excerpt)] — Mnoge Ljubavi [Many Loves] — Uluru-Pesma Ejerove Stene [Ayers Rock Uluru Song] — KO [Who] — Da I Beznadezno Je [Yes And It's Hopeless] — Ispod Sveta Je Mnogo Dupeta, Mnogo Picaka [Under the World There's a Lot Of Ass, a Lot Of Cunt] — Dasi Uma [Mind Breaths] — Bas-Je-Moralo Da Se Odsvira Na Dzuboksu [Hadda Be Playing On the Jukebox] — Nemoj Nikada Ostareti [Don't Grow Old] — Rur-Gebajt [Ruhr-Gebiet] — "Branili Su Veru" [Defending the Faith] — Kapitolska Pesmica [Capitol Air] — Zasto Meditiram [Why I Meditate]

H569 Ginsberg, Allen. *Urlik Uma*. Beograd, Yugoslavia: DOB, 1983.
Translation by Vojo Sindolic: U Drustvu [In Society] — Zidarski Rucak [Bricklayer's Lunch Hour] — Zeleni Automobil [Green Automobile] — Ljubavna Pesma Na Vitmenovu Temu [Love Poem On a Theme By Whitman] — Urlik [Howl] — Evropa, Evropa! [Europe! Europe!] — Poruka [Message] — Za Tetku Rouz [To Aunt Rose] — Na Apolinerovom Grobu [At

Apollinaire's Grave] — Kadis [Kaddish (excerpt)] — Ovaj Oblik Zivljenja
Zahteva Seks [This Form Of Life Needs Sex] — Patna-Benares Ekspres
[Patna-Benares Express] — Poslednja Noc U Kalkuti [Last Night In Calcutta]
— Promena: Kjoto-Tokio Ekspres [Change: Kyoto-Tokyo Express] — Zasto
Je Bog Ljubav, Dzek? [Why Is God Love, Jack?] — Danas [Today] — Kafana
U Varsavi [Cafe In Warsaw] — Prema Kome Biti Dobar [Who Be Kind To] —
Prva Zabava Kod Kena Kizija Sa Andelima Pakla [First Party At Ken Kesey's
With Hell's Angels] — Poseta Velsu [Wales Visitation] — Elegija Za Nila
Kesidija [Elegy For Neal Cassady] — Molim Te Gospodaru [Please Master] —
Nad Nilovim Pepelom [On Neal's Ashes] — Ponovo Nad Denverom [Over
Denver Again] — Iznad Laramija [Over Laramie] — Izdasi Uma [Mind
Breaths] — Nemojte Stariti [Don't Grow Old] — Pank Rok Ti Si Moj Veliki
Placljivko [Punk Rock Your My Big Crybaby] — Oda Plutonijumu [Plutonian
Ode] — Pankerima Iz Dolisa [To the Punks Of Dawlish] — Oda Neuspehu
[Ode To Failure] — Pticji Mozak [Birdbrain] — Eroica [Eroica]

Anthologies:

H570 *Antologija Moderne Americke Poezije*. Beograd, Yugoslavia: Prosveta, 1972,
pp. 264-267.
Translation by Ivan V. Lalic: Samoposluga U Kaliforniji [A Supermarket In
California] — Urlik [Howl (excerpt)]

H571 Bajac, Vladislav and Sindolic, Vojo (eds.). *Pesnici Bit Generacije*. Beograd,
Yugoslavia: Sveske, 1979, pp. 28-38.
Translation by Vojo Sindolic: Setna Prasnjava Blazenstva [Sad Dust Glories
(excerpt)] — Pogled Unazad [Flash Back] — Prva Zabava Kod Kena Keseya
Sa Andelima Pakla [First Party At Ken Kesey's With Hell's Angels] — Sta Bih
Voleo Da Radim [What I'd Like To Do] — Ispod Sveta Mnogo Je Guza,
Mnogo Pizde [Under the World There's a Lot Of Ass, a Lot Of Cunt] —
Koliba Na Stenjaku [Cabin In the Rockies] — Selo Teton [Teton Village] —
Zemlja Jezera, Wisconsin [Land O' Lakes, Wisc.] — Milarepa Ukus [Milarepa
Taste]

H572 Soljan, Antun. *Zlatna Knjiga Americke Poezije*. Zagreb, Yugoslavia: Nakladni
Zavod Matice Hrvatske, 1980.
Translation by Antun Soljan: Velika Samoposluga U Kaliforniji [A Supermarket
In California] — Ljubavna Pjesma Na Whitmanovu Temu [Love Poem On
Theme By Whitman]
Translation by Giga Gracan: Suncokretova Sutra [Sunflower Sutra]

H573 Bajac, Vladislav and Kopicl, Vladimir (eds.). *Trip*. Belgrad: Yugoslavia:
Narodna Knjiga, 1983, pp. 49-57.
Translation by Vladislav Bajac: Ameriko [America] — Kral Majales [Kral
Majales] — Zasto Je Bog Ljubav, Dzek? [Why Is God Love, Jack?] — Pank
Rok, Ti Si Moj Veliki Placljivko [Punk Rock Your My Big Crybaby]

H574 Ivanisevic, Katica. *Suvremena Americka Knjizevnost I*. Pula, Yugoslavia:
Istarska Naklada, 1984, pp. 33-36.
Translation by Vojo Sindolic: Urlik [Howl]

H575 Djurovic, Radmilo (ed.). *17 Gay Pesama*. Beograd: Yugoslavia: privately
printed, 1986, pp. 13-16.
Translation by Vojo Sindolic: Molim Te Gospodaru [Please Master]

H576 Ilin, Dusica (ed.). *Zlaten Venets / Zlatni Venac / The Golden Garland*. Novi Sad,
Yugoslavia: Knjizevna Zajednica Novog Sada, 1986, pp. 375-394.
Translation by Zoran Petkovic and Mihailo Ristic: In Back Of the Real || Iza

Stvarnog — On Burroughs' Work || O Barouzovom Radu — America (excerpt)
|| Amerika — Kaddish (excerpt) || Kadis — Manifesto || Manifest

H577* Sindolic, Vojo (ed.). *Too Beat To Split.* Dubrovnik, Yugoslavia: Libar, 1988,
pp. 6-7.
Translation: Citajuci Bai Juyia [Reading Bai Juyi (excerpt)]

Periodicals:

H578 [poem]. *Nin,* vol. 10 (March 6, 1960) p. 478.
Translation: Ameriko [America]

H579 [poem]. *Knjizevne Novine,* vol. 11 (April 8, 1960) p. 116.
Translation by Nikola Preradovic: Smrt Za Van Gogovo Uvo [Death To Van
Gogh's Ear]

H580 [poem]. *Knjizevne Novine,* vol. 11 (July 22, 1960) p. 126.
Translation by Cedomir Minderovic: Urlik [Howl]

H581 [poem]. *Polja,* vol. 8 (Nov. 31, 1962) p. 59.
Translation by Bogomil Duzel: Apollinai Recvom Grobu [At Apollinaire's Grave]

H582 [poems]. *Delo,* vol. 8, no. 8 (1962) pp. 207-216.
Translation by Srda Popovic: Amerka [America] — Sjupermarkit U Kaliforniji [A
Supermarket In California] — U Garderobi U Grejhaundu [In the Baggage
Room At Greyhound] — Transkripci Ja Muzike Za Orgulje [Transcription Of
Organ Music]

H583 [poem]. *Razlog,* vol. 2, no. 9 (1962) pp. 788-797.
Translation by Zvonimir Mrkonjic: Urlanje [Howl]

H584 [poem]. *Polet,* vol. 2, no. 6 (1967) p. 6.
Translation: Molitva Za Novog Covjeka

H585* [3 poems]. *Republika,* vol. 23, no. 6 (1967) pp. 270-271.
Translation by Vladimir F. Reinhofer: Fusnota Ka Urlanju [Footnote To Howl]
— Supermarket U Kaliforniji [A Supermarket In California] — Amerika
[America]

H586* [poem]. *Republika,* vol. 24, no. 1 (1968) p. 57.
Translation by Vladimir Reinhofer: S Onu Stranu Stvarnosti [In Back Of the
Real]

H587 [poem]. *Omladinski Tjednik,* vol. 3 (Oct. 1, 1969) p. 62.
Translation by Vladimir F. Reinhofer: Divlje Siroce

H588 [poem]. *Gdje* (Nov. 4, 1969) p. 4.
Translation by Nikola Djordjevic: U Garderobi Greyhounda [In the Baggage
Room At Greyhound]

H589 [5 poems]. *Studentski List,* vol. 24 (Dec. 16, 1969) p. 26.
Translation by Marin Caric: Prvi Tulum Kod Ken Keseyevih S Paklenim
Andjelima [First Party At Ken Kesey's With Hell's Angels] — Portland
Coloseum [Portland Coloseum] — Predgradje — Televizija Bijase Djecje
Puzanje Prema Toj Komori Smrti [Television Was That Baby Crawling
Towards That Deathchamber] — Duh Sveti Nagnut Nad Tijelom Blazenstva [I
Am a Victim Of Telephone]

H590 [poem]. *Student,* vol. 33 (Dec. 23, 1969) pp. 27-28.
Translation by Ljubisa Ristic: Kral Majales [Kral Majales]

H591 [poem]. *Bagdaia,* Vol. 11, no. 122 (1969) p. 10.
Translation by Tihomir Vuckovic: Zlatoglav [Autumn Gold]

H592 [poem]. *Ovdje,* vol. 1, no. 5 (1969) p. 21.
Translation by Tihomir Vuckovic: Amerika [America]

H593 [poem]. *Ovdje,* vol. 2, no. 8 (1970) p. 23.
Translation by Tihomir Vuckovic: Zlatoglav [Autumn Gold]

H594 [poem]. *Polja,* vol. 15, no. 140-141 (1970) p. 31.

H595 [poem]. *Gradina,* vol. 6, no. 1 (1971) p. 35.
Translation by Vlada Stojiljkovic: Kadis [Kaddish]

H596 [poem]. *Trag,* vol. 6 (April 2, 1972) p. 10.
Translation by D.V.: Amerika [America]

H597 [4 poems]. *Lica,* vol. 6, no. 8 (1976) pp. 51-55.
Translation by Dzenan Ekic: Divlji Orfej — Za Lindzi [To Lindsay] — Pjesma [Song] — Suncokret Sutra [Sunflower Sutra]

H598 [4 poems]. *Haiku, Casopis Za Haiku Poeziju,* vol. 2, no. 4 [issue 8] (Winter 1978) pp. 235-237.
Translation by Vojo Sindolic: Koliba Na Stenjaku [Cabin In the Rockies] — Selo Teton [Teton Village] — Zemlja, Jezera, Viskonsin [Land O' Lakes, Wisc.] — Milarepa Ukus [Milarepa Taste]

H599 [poem and letter]. *Vidici,* vol. 24, no. 5-6 (Sept.-Oct. 1978) pp. 10-11, 22-23.
Translation by Ljiljana Kojic-Bogdanovic and Branko Aleksic: Urlik [Howl (excerpt)]
Translation by Ivana Bogdanovic: Beat Poetike. Ginsberg O Poeziji I Stvaranuju [excerpt from a letter to Howard Schumann]

H600 [3 poems]. *Ibor,* vol. 26, no. 4-5 (Aug. 1979) pp. 37-39.
Translation by Dean Herenda: Tko Ce Zavladati Univerzumom [Who Will Take Over the Universe?] — Egzorcizam U Pentagonu [Pentagon Exorcism] — Molim Te Ucitelju [Please Master]

H601 [6 poems]. *Student,* vol. 43, no. 24-25 (Dec. 26, 1979) p. 14.
Translation by Dejan D. Markovic: Urlik [Howl (excerpt)] — Supermarket U Kaliforniji [A Supermarket In California (excerpt)] — Sutra O Suncokretu [Sunflower Sutra (excerpt)] — Poseta Velsu [Wales Visitation (excerpt)] — Nemojte Stariti [Don't Grow Old (excerpt)] — Toliko Je Bulja, Toliko Picaka Na Ovome Svetu [Under the World There's a Lot Of Ass, a Lot Of Cunt]

H602* [poem]. *Halo,* no. 3 (March 1980) pp. 22-23.
Translation by Vojo Sindolic: Sta Bih Voleo Da Radim [What I'd Like To Do]

H603 [poem]. *Rukovet,* vol. 26, no. 4 (July-Aug. 1980) pp. 369-371.
Translation by Robert G. Tili: Ameriko [America]

H604 [poem]. *Mladost,* vol. 61, no. 1210 (Oct. 31, 1980) p. 9.
Translation by Vojo Sindolic: Patna-Benares Expres [Patna-Benares Express]

H605   [poem]. *Dzuboks,* no. 102 (Nov. 21, 1980) p. 71.
Translation by Vojo Sindolic: Punk Rock Ti Si Moj Veliki Placljivko [Punk Rock Your My Big Crybaby]

H606   [poem]. *Knjizevne Novine,* vol. 32 (Dec. 11, 1980) p. 616.
Translation by Robert G. Tili: Bolesljivi Bluz [Sickness Blues]

H607   [poem]. *Mladost,* vol. 63, no. 1287 (May 31, 1982) Mlada Literatura supplement, no. 14, p. 7.
Translation by Ivana Milankovic; Zoran Petkovic and Mihailo Ristic: Jesenje Zlato: Novoengleska Jesen [Autumn Gold: New England Fall]

H608   [poem]. *Student,* vol. 46, no. 14 (May 12, 1982) p. 15.
Translation by Zoran Petkovic and Mihajlo Ristic: Da I Beznadezno Je [Yes And It's Hopeless]

H609   [poem]. *UNESCO Courier* [Serbo-Croat edition], vol. 35, no. 10 (Nov. 1982) pp. 13-14.
Translation: [Plutonian Ode (excerpt)]

H610   [5 poems and prose]. *Knjizevnost,* vol. 32-74, no. 9 (1982) pp. 1344-1361.
Translation by Zoran Petkovic and Mihailo Ristic: Paterson [Paterson] — Suncokretova Sutra [Sunflower Sutra] — Evropa! Evropa! [Europe! Europe!] — Zavet [A Vow] — Dasi Uma [Mind Breaths] — Bas-Je-Moralo Da Se Odsvira Na Dzuboksu [Hadda Be Playing On the Jukebox]
Translation by Ivana Milankov: Jedan Od Mojih Nacina Pristupa Literaturi je Pogledati Van Sebe I Odreci Se I Odreci Se Ideja Sta Bi Poezija Trebola Da Bude

H611   [poem]. *Lica,* vol. 10, no. 9-10 (1982) pp. 30-35.
Translation by Sead Sadic: Urlik [Howl]
Translation by Dean Herenda: Egzorcizam U Pentagonu [Pentagon Exorcism]

H612   [poem]. *Delo,* vol. 29, no. 1 (Jan. 1983) pp. 6-16.
Translation by Zoran Petkovic and Mihailo Ristic: Urlik [Howl]

H613   [poem]. *Gradina,* vol. 18, no. 3 (1983) pp. 122-124.
Translation by Dragana R. Masovic: Amerika [America]

H614   [3 poems]. *Quorum,* vol. 2, no. 1 ([Feb.] 1986) pp. 278-299.
Translation by Borivoj Radakovic: Wichita Vortex Sutra [Wichita Vortex Sutra] — Portland Coloseum [Portland Coliseum] — Prva Zabava Kod Kenna Kesseya S Andelima Pakla [First Party At Ken Kesey's With Hell's Angels]

H615   [poem]. *Reporter,* no. 964 (April 1986) p. 63.
Translation by Vojo Sindolic: Bluz Oceve Smrti [Father Death Blues]

H616   [poem]. *Oslobodenji* (April 2, 1986)
Translation by Vojo Sindolic: Prva Zabava Kod Kena Kesseya Sa Andelima Pakla [First Party At Ken Kesey's With Hell's Angels]

H617   [4 poems and 2 letters]. *Polja,* vol. 32, no. 327 (May 1986) pp. 234-237.
Translation by Zoran Petkovic: Lisergicna Kiselina [Lysergic Acid] — Elegija Za Ce Gevaru [Elegy Che Guevara]
Translation by Mihailo Ristic: Poseta Velsu [Wales Visitation] — Pismo Gregori Korsou [letter to Gregory Corso]
Translation by Dubravka Prendic: Slusajuci „Leonoru" Citanu Naglas U Amity Street 203 [Haunting Poe's Baltimore]

Translation by Mihailo Ristic and Zoran Petkovic: O Sudionicima Bit Pokreta [letter to Peter Orlovsky]

H618 [12 poems]. *Ars,* vol. 1, no. 1 (June 1986) pp. 13-21.
Translation by Vojo Sindolic: O Borouzovom Radu [On Burroughs' Work] — Psalm III [Psalm III] — Suze [Tears] — „Vrativsi Se Na Tajms Skver, Sanjajuci Tajms Skver" ['Back On Times Square, Dreaming Of Times Square'] — Moje Tuzno Ja [My Sad Self] — Sumrak Na M.B. „Azemur" [Sunset S.S. Azemour] — Vijesti O Smrti [Death News] — Poruka II [Message II] — Trenuci Se Vracaju [The Moments Return] — Dolina Karmel [Carmel Valley] — Tijelu [To the Body] — Egzorcizam U Pentagonu [Pentagon Exorcism]

H619 [prose]. *Gradina,* vol. 21, no. 6 (June 1986) pp. 78-92.
Translation by Vojo Sindolic: Susreti Sa Ezrom Paundom [Encounters With Ezra Pound]

H620 [[poem]. *Oko,* vol. 13, no. 371 (June 5, 1986)
Translation by Vojislav Despotov and Borivoj Radakovic: Pjesni Dubrovacke

H621 [poem]. *Knjizevna Rec,* vol. 15, no. 282-283 (July 14, 1986) p. 41.
Translation by Vojo Sindolic: Suncokresova Susra [Sunflower Sutra]

H622 [prose]. *Oko,* vol. 13, no. 374 (July 17-31, 1986) p. 9.
Translation by Borivoj Radakovic: Moc I Nemoc Poezije [Speech Written After Winning "Golden Wreath"]

H623 [letter]. *Struga,* no. 5 (Aug. 1986) p. 1.
Translation: [letter to Struga]

H624 [poem]. *Pobjeda* (Aug. 23, 1986)
Translation by Vojo Sindolic: Trenudzi Se Vracaju [The Moments Return]

H625 [poem]. *Politika,* vol. 83, no. 26180 (Aug. 23, 1986) p. 9.
Translation by Zoran Petkovic and Mihailo Ristic: Zalazak Sunca [Sunset]

H626 [2 poems]. *Non,* no. 577 (Aug. 24, 1986) pp. 22-23.
Translation by Mihailo Ristic: Prema Antipateru [After Antipater] — Dzrni Pokrov [Black Shroud]

H627 [poem]. *Putevi,* vol. 32, no. 5 (Sept.-Oct. 1986) pp. 39-43.
Translation by Borivoja Radakovica: Plutonijska Oda [Plutonian Ode]

H628 [poem]. *Svijet,* no. 1475 (Sept. 5, 1986) p. 31.
Translation by Vojo Sindolic: Kadis [Kaddish (fragment)]

H629 [2 poems]. *Lira,* no. 1 (Oct. 5, 1986) p. 3.
Translation by Zoran Petkovic and Mihailo Ristic: Zasto Meditiram [Why I Meditate] — Blues Oceve Smrti [Father Death Blues]

H630 [prose]. *Gradina,* vol. 21, no. 12 (Dec. 1986) pp. 94-100.
Translation by Dragana Masovic: Poezija, Nasilje I Ustreptale Ovcice [Poetry, Violence And Trembling Lambs] — Beleske O Zavrsnoj Veriziji Urlika [Notes Written On Finally Recording Howl]

H631 [poem]. *Americka Knjizevnost,* vol. 162, no. 2 [issue 437] (1986) pp. 273-278.
Translation by Vladislavom Bajcom: Letopis Matice Srpske [Kaddish]

H632 [poem]. *Dialogi,* vol. 22, no. 6-7 (1986) pp. 67-77.
Translation by Boris Cizej: Krik — Kalifornijska Samopostreznica [A Supermarket In California] — Zapisi Orgelske Glasbe [A Transcription Of Organ Music]

H633 [5 poems]. *Jehona,* vol. 24, no. 3-4 (1986) pp. 46-51.
Translation by R. Shabani: Lotë [Tears] — Për Veprat E Barouzit [On Burroughs' Work] — Rrëmujë [A Desolation] — Kadish [Kaddish (excerpt)] — Supermarketi Në Kaliforni [A Supermarket In California]

H634 [poem]. *Odjek,* vol. 39, no. 18 (1986) p. 7.
Translation by Vojo Sindolic: Suncokretova Sutra [Sunflower Sutra]

H635 [poem]. *Razgledi,* vol. 28, no. 5-6 (1986) pp. 457-465.
Translation by Dragi Mihajlovski: Supermarket Vo Kalifornija [A Supermarket In California]

H636 [poem]. *Zivot,* vol. 35, no. 5-6 [issue 69] (1986) p. 471.
Translation by Slobodan Blagojevic: Zrtva Sam Telefona [I Am A Victim Of Telephone]

H637 [2 poems]. *Summer Times,* no. 2 (Aug. 1987) p. 2.
Translation by Vojo Sindolic: Slavenima [To Slavs] — Na Prodaju Na Prodaju [For Sale, For Sale]

H638 [5 poems]. *Pismo,* vol. 3, no. 11 (Fall 1987) pp. 47-54.
Translation by Nina Zivancevic: Citajuci Bai-Dzuija [Reading Bai Juyi (excerpt)] — Dzrni Pokrov [Black Shroud] — Napisano U Mom Snu Od Strane Vilijama K. Vilijamsa [Written In My Dream By W.C. Williams] — Ja Nisam [I Am Not] — Nervozno Povrce [Irritable Vegetable]

H639 [poem]. *Non* (April 1988) p. 33.
Translation by Dejan D. Mannovic: Toliko Je Bulja, Toliko Picaka Na Ovome Svetu [Under the World]

H640 [poem]. *Omladinska ISKRA,* no. 64 (Nov. 11, 1988) p. 17.
Translation by Vojo Sindolic: Bijeli Pokrov [White Shroud]

H641 [poem]. *Knjizevna Revija,* no. 27 (March 1989) p. 14.
Translation by Z. Petkovic and M. Ristic: Mnoge Ljubavi [Many Loves]

H642 [poem]. *Delo,* vol. 35, no. 8 (1989) pp. 209-215.
Translation by Zoran Petkovic: Citajuci Bai Dzuija [Reading Bai Juyi]

H643 [poem]. *Knjilevna Rec,* no. 400 (Sept. 10, 1992) p. 13.
Translation by Vojo Sindolic: Stihovi Napisani Za Studetski Skup Protiv Pegrutovanja [Verses Written For Student Antidraft Registration Rally]

H644 [poems]. *Kepes Ifjusag,* vol. 47, no. 2039 (Oct. 29, 1992) pp. 14-15.
Translation: Üvöltés [Howl (excerpt)] — Seggcsók [Kiss Ass] — Betegség-Blues [Sickness Blues]

H645 [2 poems]. *Bagdala,* vol. 35, no. 404-405 (Aug.-Oct. 1993) pp. 13-14.
Translation by Vojo Despotov: Lopovi Ukradose Ovu Pesmu [A Thief Stole This Poem] —Jesenje Lisce [Autumn Leaves]

SLOVENE

Books:

H646   Ginsberg, Allen. *Vytie*. Bratislava, Czechoslovakia: Slovensky Spisovatel, 1991.
Translation by Ján Buzássy And Zuzana Hegedüsová: Amerika [America] — Supermarket V Kalifornii [A Supermarket In California] — Slnecnicová Sutra [Sunflower Sutra] — Skutocne Lev [The Lion For Real] — Ignu [Ignu] — Vytie [Howl] — Poznámka Pod Ciarou K Vytiu [Footnote To Howl] — Pri Apollinairovom Hrobe [At Apollinaire's Grave] — Smrt Van Goghovmu Uchu! [Death To Van Gogh's Ear!] — Kadis [Kaddish] — Moje Smutné Ja [My Sad Self] — Slzy [Tears] — Osvietenie Sather Gate [Sather Gate Illumination]

Perioodicals:

H647   [poem]. *UNESCO Courier* [Slovene edition], vol. 35, no. 10 (Nov. 1982) pp. 13-14.
Translation: [Plutonian Ode (excerpt)]

SPANISH

Books:

H648   Ginsberg, Allen. *Aullido*. Santiago, Chile: Editorial Del Pacífico, 1957. [Series: Revista Literaria De La SECH, 1]
Translation by Fernando Alegriá: Aullido ‖ Howl

H649   Ginsberg, Allen. *América*. Lima, Peru: Taller De Artes Graficas, 1961. [Series: La Rama Florida, 5]
Translation by José Maria Oviedo: América [America]

H650   Ginsberg, Allen. *Antología Poética*. Buenos Aires, Argentina: Ediciones Del Mediodía, 1969.
Translation by Marcelo Covian: Siento Como Si Estuviera En Un Callejón [I Feel As If I Am At a Dead] — Esta Noche Todo Está Bien...Qué [Tonite All Is Well] — Salmo Primero [Psalm I] — Aullido [Howl] — Un Supermercado En California [A Supermarket In California] — Girasol Sutra [Sunflower Sutra] — América [America] — Una Flor [An Asphodel] — Kaddish [Kaddish] — En La Tumba De Apollinaire [At Apollinaire's Grave] — El Leon De Verdad [The Lion For Real] — Muerta A La Oreja De Van Gogh [Death To Van Gogh's Ear] — Mescalina [Mescaline] — Mi Alba [My Alba] — El Automovil Verde [The Green Automobile] — Sobre El Trabajo De Burroughs [On Burroughs' Work] — Malest Cornifici Tuo Catullo [Malest Cornifici Tuo Catullo] — Notas De Un Sueño [Dream Record] — Benditas Sean Las Musas [Blessed Be the Muses] — A Un Viejo Poeta En El Peru [To an Old Poet In Peru] — Eter [Aether] — ¿Quien Se Apoderara Del Universo? [Who Will Take Over the Universe?] — Noticias De Muerte [Death News] — Mensaje II [Message II] — Kral Majales [Kral Majales]

H651   Ginsberg, Allen. *Aullido Y Otros Poemas*. Montevideo, Uruguay: Los Huevos Del Plata, 1969.
Translation by Andres Boulton Figueira De Mello: Aullido [Howl] — Apéndice Para Aullido [Footnote To Howl] — Poema Cohete [Poem Rocket] — Salmo Magico [Magic Psalm]

H652   Ginsberg, Allen. *Aullido, Seleccion De Poemas*. Barcelona, Spain: Star
Books/Producciones Editoriales, ca. 1976.
Translation by Sebastian Martinez; Jaime Rosal and Luis Vigil: I Feel As If I Am
At a Dead || Me Siento — Tonite All Is Well...What a || Esta Noche — Psalm I ||
Salmo I — Metaphysics || Metafisicos — Marijuana Notation || Notas Sobre La
Marihuana — Howl || Aullido — Footnote To Howl || Nota A Aullido —
America || América — Kaddish || Kaddish — The Green Automobile || El
Automóvil Verde — On Burroughs' Work || Acerca Del Trabajo De Burroughs
— Who Will Take Over the Universe? || ¿Quién Se Apodera Del Universo? —
Kral Majales || Kral Majales

H653   Ginsberg, Allen. *La Caida De America*. Madrid, Spain: Visor, 1977.
Translation by Antonio Resines: Comienzo De Un Poema De Estos Estados
[Beginning Of a Poem Of These States] — Continuación De Un Largo Poema
De Estos Estados [Continuation Of a Long Poem Of These States] — Estos
Estados, Entrando En L.A. [These States, Into L.A.] — Poesía De Autopista
LA-Albuquerque-Texas-Wichita [Hiway Poesy LA-Albuquerque-Texas-
Wichita] — Auto Poesía. Huyendo De Bloomington [Auto Poesy: On the Lam
From Bloomington] — De Kansas City A San Luis [Kansas City To Saint
Louis] — Bayonne Entrando A N.Y.C. [Bayonne Entering NYC] — Alas
Alzadas Sobre La Negra Sima [Wings Lifted Over the Black Pit] — Cleveland,
Las Planicies [Cleveland, The Flats] — Un Juramento [A Vow] — Oro De
Otoño: Otoño En Nueva Inglaterra [Autumn Gold: New England Fall] — Se
Acabó Se Terminó Todo Con El Más Grande Pene Que Jamás Hayan Visto
[Done, Finished With the Biggest Cock] — Autopista De Peaje Hasta
Tuscarora [Bayonne Turnpike To Tuscarora] — Una Ventana Abierta Sobre
Chicago [An Open Window On Chicago] — Vuelta Por El Norte Del Vortex
[Returning North Of Vortex] — Lamer El Culo [Kiss Ass] — Elegía Che
Guevara [Elegy Che Guevara] — Letanía De Las Gsanancias De Guerra [War
Profit Litany] — Elegía Para Neal Cassady [Elegy For Neal Cassady] — De
Chicago A Salt Lake Por Aire [Chicago To Salt Lake By Air] — Flash De Los
Años Treinta En Manhattan [Manhattan Thirties Flash] — Por Favor Maestro
[Please Master] — Una Profecía [A Prophecy] — El Cañón De Bixby [Bixby
Canyon] — Cruzando La Nación [Crossing Nation] — Humo Rodando Calle
Abajo [Smoke Rolling Down Street] — Pertussin [Pertussin] — Remolinos De
Polvo Negro En La Avenida D [Swirls Of Black Dust On Avenue D] —
Violencia [Violence] — Más Allá De Durango De Plata Sobre Las Arrugas De
Mexic Sierra [Past Silver Durango Over Mexic Sierra Wrinkles] — Sobre Las
Cenizas De Neal [On Neal's Ashes] — En Camino A Chicago [Going To
Chicago] — Parque Grant: "28 De Agosto De 1968" [Grant Park: August 28,
1968] — Choque De Automóviles [Car Crash] — De Nuevo Sobre Denver
[Over Denver Again] — Universos Imaginarios [Imaginary Universes] —
Elevándose Sobre Las Calles Oscurecidas Por La Noche De Detroit [Rising
Over Night-Blackened Detroit Streets] — A Poe: Sobre El Planeta, Air Albany-
Baltimore [To Poe: Over the Planet, Air Albany-Baltimore] — Domingo De
Pascua [Easter Sunday] — Quedarse Dormido En América [Falling Asleep In
America] — Paso Del Noroeste [Northwest Passage] — Al Borde Del Desierto
De Sonora [Sonora Desert-Edge] — Reflejos En Un Ojo Adormilado
[Reflections In Sleepy Eye] — Día De La Independencia [Independence Day]
— En Un Choza De Ermitaño Iluminada Por La Luna [In a Moonlit Hermit's
Cabin] — Calor Húmedo De Lluvia En El Asfalto, Latas Desbordadas De
Basura En El Bordillo [Rain-Wet Asphalt Heat, Garbage Curbed Cans
Overflowing] — Muerte En Todos Los Frentes [Death On All Fronts] —
Jardines De La Memoria [Memory Gardens] — Flash Back [Flash Back] —
Graffiti En El Cubículo Núm. 12 Del Servicio De Caballeros Aeropuerto De
Syracuse [Graffiti 12th Cubicle Men's Room Syracuse Airport] —
Pensamientos A Posteriori [After Thoughts] — G.S. Leyendo Poesía En
Princeton [G.S. Reading Poesy At Princeton] — Viernes Trece [Friday the
Thirteenth] — Movilización En D.C. [D.C. Mobilization] — Ecólogue

[Ecologue] — Guru Om [Guru Om] — ¿Han Visto Esta Película? [Have You Seen This Movie?] — Sabor A Milarepa [Milarepa Taste] — Sobre Laramie [Over Laramie] — La Brisa De Palabras Del Sendero Del Océano De Bixby Canyon [Bixby Canyon Ocean Path Word Breeze] — Hum Bom! [Hum Bom!] — Septiembre En La Carretera De Jessore [September On Jessore Road]

H654 Ginsberg, Allen. *Sandwiches De Realidad*. Madrid, Spain: Visor, 1978.
Translation by Antonio Resines: Mi Alba [My Alba] — Sakyamuni Saliendo De La Montaña [Sakyamuni Coming Out From the Mountain] — El Automóvil Verde [The Green Automobile] — La Habana 1953 [Havana 1953] — Siesta En Xbalba Y Vuelta A Los Estados Unidos [Siesta In Xbalba] — Sobre Los Trabajos De Burroughs [On Burroughs' Work] — Poema De Amor Basado En Un Tema De Whitman [Love Poem On Theme By Whitman] — Sobre Kansas [Over Kansas] — Malest Cornifici Tuo Catullo [Malest Cornifici Tuo Catullo] — Registro De Un Sueño: 8 Junio 1955 [Dream Record] — Benditas Sean Las Musas [Blessed Be The Muses] — Fragmento 1956 [Fragment 1956] — Una Extraña Casita De Campo Nueva En Berkeley [A Strange New Cottage In Berkeley] — Iluminación De Sather Gate [Sather Gate Illumination] — Garrapato [Scribble] — Seattle Al Atardecer [Afternoon Seattle] — Salmo III [Psalm III] — Lágrimas [Tears] — Preparado Para Echar A Rodar [Ready To Roll] — Escribí Esto La Noche Pasada [Wrote This Last Night] — Chillido [Squeal] — Calderilla Americana [American Change] — "De Vuelta A Times Square, Soñando Con Times Square" ['Back On Times Square, Dreaming Of Time Square'] — Mi Triste Yo [My Sad Self] — Funny Death [Funny Death] — Noticiario De Buque De Guerra [Battleship Newsreel] — Te Ruego Que Vuelvas Y Estés Alegre [I Beg You Come Back & Be Cheerful] — Un Viejo Poeta En Perú [To An Old Poet In Peru] — Eter [Aether]

H655 Ginsberg, Allen. *Aullido, Kaddish Y Otros Poemas*. Toluca, México: Universidad Autónoma Del Estado De México, 1981. [Series: La Abeja En La Colmena, 5]
Translation by José Vicente Anaya: Aullido [Howl] — Kaddish [Kaddish] — America [America] — ¡Muerte A La Oreja De Van Gogh! [Death To Van Gogh's Ear!] — ¡Europa! ¡Europa! [Europe! Europe!]

H656 Ginsberg, Allen. *Aullido Y Otros Poemas*. Madrid, Spain: Visor, 1981.
Translation by Katy Gallego: Howl ‖ Aullido — Footnote To Howl ‖ Nota A Pie De Página A Aullido — A Supermarket In California ‖ Un Supermercado En California — Transcription Of Organ Music ‖ Transcripción De Música De Órgano — Sunflower Sutra ‖ Sutra Del Girasol — America ‖ América — In the Baggage Room At Greyhound ‖ En La Consigna De La Greyhound — An Asphodel ‖ Un Asfódelo — Song ‖ Canción — Wild Orphan ‖ Huérfano Salvaje — In Back Of the Real ‖ En El Reverso De Lo Real

H657 Ginsberg, Allen. *Oda Plutoniana Y Otros Poemas (1977-1980)*. Madrid, Spain: Visor, 1984.
Translation by Antonio Resines: Oda Plutoniana [Plutonian Ode] — Blues Del Chivato [Stool Pigeon Blues] — Punk Rock Eres Tú Mi Gran Llorón [Punk Rock Your My Big Crybaby] — ¿Qué Ha Muerto? [What's Dead?] — Adusto Esqueleto [Grim Skeleton] — Desamor [Lack Love] — Padre Guru [Father Guru] — Medianoche Del 1.° De Mayo En Manhattan [Manhattan May Day Midnight] — Adaptado De "Que Despierte El Leñador", De Neruda [Adapted From Neruda's "Que Dispierte El Lenador"] — Días De Nagasaki [Nagasaki Days] — Viejo Estanque [Old Pond] — Culpar Al Pensamiento, Aferrarse A Lo Falso [Blame the Thought, Cling To the Bummer] — "No Envejezcas" [Don't Grow Old] — El Amor Volvió [Love Returned] — 31 De Diciembre 1978 [December 31, 1978] — Cerebro De Brooklin College [Brooklyn College Brain] — Estado Jardín [Garden State] — Modas De Primavera [Spring Fashions] — Las Vegas: Versos Improvisados Para El Periódico De La Escuela

Secundaria De El Dorado [Las Vegas: Verses Improvised For El Dorado H.S. Newspaper] — A Los Punks De Dawlish [To the Punks Of Dawlish] — Algo De Amor [Some Love] — Tal Vez El Amor [Maybe Love] — Ruhr-Gebiet [Ruhr-Gebiet] — Tubingen-Hamburg Schlafwagen [Tubingen-Hamburg Schlafwagen] — Amor Perdonado [Love Forgiven] — Versos Escritos Para La Reunión Estudiantil En Contra Del Alistamiento 1980 [Verses Written For Student Antidraft Registration Rally 1980] — Tareas Domésticas [Homework] — Qué Alivio [What Relief] — Bajo East Side [Lower East Side] — Yo Estaba En La Universidad A Los Diecinueve Años [I Was In College Age Nineteen] — Reflexiones En El Lago Louise [Reflections At Lake Louise] — Amigos De Sonrojadas Mejillas Me Besan Tiernamente Con Dulces Bocas [Red Cheeked Boyfriends Tenderly Kiss Me Sweet Mouthed] — Cuarto Piso, Amanecer, Toda La Noche En Vela Escribiendo Cartas [Fourth Floor, Dawn, Up All Night Writing Letters] — Oda Al Fracaso [Ode To Failure] — ¡Cabezachorlito! [Birdbrain!] — Heroica [Eroica] — "Defendiendo La Fe" [Defending the Faith] — Aire Del Capitolio [Capitol Air]

H658   Ginsberg, Allen. *Aullido Y Otros Poemas.* Buenos Aires, Argentina: Los Grandes Poetas, 1988.
Translation by Jorge Ariel Madrazo: Primos De La Memoria [Memory Cousins] — Escrito En Mi Sueño Por W.C. Williams [Written In My Dream By W.C. Williams] — Aullido [Howl (excerpt)] — Un Supermercado En California [A Supermarket In California] — América [America (excerpt)] — Sutra Del Girasol [Sunflower Sutra] — Kaddish [Kaddish (excerpt)] — El León De Verdad [The Lion For Real] — Calor Húmedo De Lluvia En El Asfalto, Latas Desbordadas De Basura En El Bordillo [Rain-Wet Asphalt Heat, Garbage Curbed Cans Overflowing] — Egloga [Ecologue (excerpt)]

H659   Ginsberg, Allen. *Material De Lectura.* Mexico City, Mexico: Universidad Nacional Autónoma De México, ca. 1988. [Series: Poesia Moderna, 94]
Translation by Alberto Blanco: Puesta De Sol S.S. Azemour [Sunset S.S. Azemour] — ¿Quién Se Hará Cargo Del Universo? [Who Will Take Over the Universe?] — Esta Forma De Vida Necesita Sexo [This Form Of Life Needs Sex] — A La Manera De Yeats [After Yeats] — Guru [Guru] — Valle De Carmel [Carmel Valley] — Primera Fiesta En La Casa De Ken Kesey Con Los Hell's Angels [First Party At Ken Kesey's With Hell's Angels] — En Lo Alto De La Ciudad [Uptown] — Al Cuerpo [To the Body] — ¿Por Qué Dios Es Amor, Jack? [Why Is God Love, Jack?] — Canción Uluru De La Roca Ayers [Ayers Rock Uluru Song] — Así Es Y No Hay Esperanza [Yes And It's Hopeless] — En La Muerte De Neruda [On Neruda's Death] — Respiraciones Mentales [Mind Breaths] — Tenían Que Estarla Tocando En La Rocola [Hadda Be Playing On the Jukebox] — No Te Vuelvas Viejo [Don't Grow Old] — Tierra De Lagos, Wisc. [Land O'Lakes, Wisc.] — Medianoche De Mayo En Manhattan [Manhattan May Day Midnight] — Tarea [Homework] — Oda Al Fracaso [Ode To Failure]

Anthologies:

H660   Urtecho, José Coronel and Cardenal, Ernesto (eds.). *Antologia De La Poesía Norteamericana.* Madrid, Spain: Aguilar, 1963, p. 465.
Translation: A Lindsay [To Lindsay]

H661*   Shand, William and Girri, Alberto (ed.). *Poesia Norteamericana Contemporanea.* Buenos Aires, Argentina: Bibliográfica Omega, 1966, pp. 220-221. [Series: Colección América En Letras, 39]
Translation by William Shand and Alberto Girri: Un Supermercado En California ‖ A Supermarket In California

H662*   Girri, Alberto (ed.). *15 Poetas Norteamericanos.* Buenos Aires, Argentina: Bibliográfica Omega, 1966, pp. 236-247. [Series: Colección América En Letras, 42]
Translation by Alberto Girri: Love Poem On Theme By Whitman ‖ Poema De Amor Sobre Un Tema De Whitman — A Supermarket In California ‖ Un Supermercado En California — America (excerpt) ‖ América — To an Old Poet In Peru (excerpt) ‖ A Un Viejo Poeta Del Perú

H663   Barnatán, Marcos Ricardo (ed.). *Antología De La "Beat Generation".* Barcelona, Spain: Plaza and Janes, 1970, pp. 69-127.
Translation by Marcos Ricardo Barnatán: Howl (excerpt) ‖ Aullido — Song ‖ Canción — Kaddish (excerpt) ‖ Kaddish — To Lindsay ‖ A Lindsay — Message ‖ Mensaje

H664*   Covián, Marcelo (ed.). *Nueva Poesía U.S.A., De Ezra Pund A Bob Dylan.* Ediciones De La Flor, 1970.
Translation by Marcelo Covián.

H665a   Burroughs, William and Ginsberg, Allen. *Cartas Del Yage.* Buenos Aires, Argentina: Ediciónes Signos, 1971, pp. 61-75, 81.
Translation by M. Lasserre: [letters to W.S. Burroughs]
H665b   Burroughs, William and Ginsberg, Allen. *Cartas Del Yage.* Barcelona, Spain: Producciones Editoriales, 1977, pp. 81-95, 99.
Contents: Translation by Alberto Estival: [letters to W.S. Burroughs]

H666   Randall, Margaret (ed.). *Poesia Beat.* Madrid, Spain: Visor, 1977, pp. 11-34.
Translation by Jeronimo-Pablo Gonzalez Martin: Una Institución Sin Sentido [A Meaningless Institution] — Supermercado En California [A Supermarket In California] — América [America] — [letter to W.S. Burroughs] — Mescalina [Mescaline] — Exorcismo Del Pentágono [Pentagon Exorcism]

H667   Aridjis, Homero (ed.). *Antología Del Primer Festival Internacional De Poesía.* Mexico City, México: Joaquín Mortiz, 1982, pp. 89-97.
Translation by Margarita González Arredondo: ¡Cabeza De Chorlito! [Birdbrain!] — Aires Del Capitolio [Capitol Air]
Translation by Miguel Grinberg: Kaddish [Kaddish (excerpt)]
Translation by Alberto Blanco: Evangelio De Las Verdades Nobles [Gospel Noble Truths] — Canción Uluru De La Roca Ayers [Ayers Rock Uluru Song] — En La Muerte De Neruda [On Neruda's Death] — Blues Del Padre Muerte [Father Death Blues]

H668   Grinberg, Miguel. *La Generacion De La Paz.* Buenos Aires, Argentina: Editorial Galerna, 1984, pp. 5-6, 107-109, 176-177.
Translation: Introduccion — Pichicata Mata [Let's Issue A General Declaration] — Oda Plutoniana [Plutonian Ode (excerpt)]

H669   Ginsberg, Allen and Cassady, Neal. *Cartas De Amor Ambiguo.* Barcelona, Spain: Laertes S.A. De Ediciones, 1985.
Translation by Marta Pérez: Cartas De Amor Ambiquo [letters to Neal Cassady from *As Ever*]

H670   Fagundo, Ana María (ed.). *Antología Bilingüe De Poesíe Norteamericana Contemporánea: 1950-1980.* Madrid, Spain: Ediciones Jose Porrua Turanzas, 1988, pp. 69-72.
Translation by Ana María Fagundo: A Supermarket In California ‖ Un Supermercado En California

H671   Tejada, Roberto (ed.). *El Algún Otro Lado.* Mexico City, Mexico: Vuelta, 1992, pp. 170-201.

Translation by Juan Almela: Siesta In Xbalba And Return To the States || Siesta En Xbalbá Y Regreso A Estados Unidos

H672   Abrams, D. Sam (ed.).   *Poesia Anglesa I Nord-Americana Contemporània.*
Barcelona, Spain: Edicions 62, 1994, pp. 363-365.
Translation by Teresa Sàrries: Udol [Howl (excerpt)]

Periodicals:

H673   [poem]. *Revista Literaria De La Sociedad De Escritores De Chile,* vol. 1, no. 3
(Nov. 1957) [new series] pp. 184-197.
Translation by Fernando Alegriá: Aullido || Howl

H674   [2 poems]. *Boletin Cultural Peruano,* vol. 3, no. 6 (April-June 1960) pp. 16-17.
Translation by C.E. Zavaleta: Kaddish [Kaddish (excerpt)] — Cancion [Song]

H675   [poem]. *El Comercio* (May 15, 1960) p. 8.
Translation by José Miguel Oviedo and Carlos Zavaleta: Moloch [Howl (excerpt)]

H676* [poem]. *El Escarabajo De Oro* [later *El Grillo De Papel*], vol. 2, no. 6 (Oct.-Nov.
1960) p. 16.
Translation: America [America (excerpt)]

H677   [poem]. *Airón,* vol. 1, no. 3-4 (May 1961) pp. 14-17.
Translation by Madela Ezcurra and Leandro Katz: Aullido [Howl]

H678   [poem]. *Revista De La Universidad De Mexico,* vol. 15, no. 11 (July 1961) p. 7.
Translation by Ernesto Cardenal: A Lindsay [To Lindsay]

H679   [poem]. *Eco Contemporaneo,* vol. 1, no. 1 (Nov.-Dec. 1961) pp. 34-37.
Translation by Miguel Grinberg: America [America]

H680* [poem]. *Esquirla* [ca. 1961]
Translation by Leandro Katz and Madela Ezcurra: Aullido [Howl]

H681   [poem]. *Vanguardia,* vol. 2, no. 14 [ca. 1961]
Translation by Ernesto Cardenal: A Lindsay [To Lindsay]

H682* [poem]. *Palabra,* no. 2 (1962) pp. 4-5.
Translation: Kaddish [Kaddish (excerpt)]

H683   [4 poems]. *El Corno Emplumado/Plumed Horn,* no. 2 (April 1962) pp. 53-57.
Translation by Margaret Randall and Sergio Mondragón: Un Supermercado En
California [A Supermarket In California] — Mensaje [Message] — El Fin [The
End]
Translation by Agustí Bartra: Aullido [Howl (excerpt)]

H684   [poem]. *Eco Contemporaneo,* vol. 1, no. 3 (May-July 1962) p. 22.
Translation by Miguel Grinberg: Mensaje [Message]

H685   [poem]. *Ventana,* vol. 3, no. 14 [series 3] (Aug. 1962) pp. 1-13.
Translation by Roberto Cuadra: Aullido [Howl]

H686* [poem]. *Eco Contemporaneo,* vol. 1, no. 4 (Dec. 1962) pp. 73-75.
Translation by Miguel Grinberg: Cancion [Song]

[letter]. *Eco Contemporaneo,* vol. 1, no. 4 (Dec. 1962) p. 128.
Translation by Miguel Grinberg: [letter to Miguel Grinberg]

H687   Intentionally omitted.

H688*   [poem]. *Eco Contemporaneo,* vol. 2, no. 5 (Winter 1963) pp. 83-90.
Translation by Miguel Grinberg: Contribucion En Prosa A La Revolución Cubana
[Prose Contribution To Cuban Revolution]

H689*   [poem]. *Syrma,* no. 3 (April 1964) p. 16.
Translation by Miguel Grinberg: Mensaje [Message]

H690   [poem]. *CAL [Critica. Arte. Literatura],* no. 31 (June 20, 1964) unpaged.
Translation by Rosa Del Olmo: Fragmento [I Beg You Come Back And Be
Cheerful (excerpt)]

H691*   [poem]. *Opium,* no. 3 1/2 (Nov. 1965) p. 21.
Translation by Julio Valmaggia and Reynaldo Mariani: Chillido [Squeal]

H692*   [letter]. *Eco Contemporaneo,* vol. 2, no. 8-9 (Winter 1965) pp. 118-123.
Translation by Miguel Grinberg: [letter to Miguel Grinberg]

H693*   [poem]. *Nuestro Cine,* no. 38 (1965) pp. 34-37, 39-43, 47-49.
Translation by Carol Moeller and Pedro C. Muste: [Death To Van Gogh's Ear —
Sunflower Sutra — The Fall Of America]
Note: This is a translation of the full script of the film *Guns of the Trees* by Jonas
Mekas which itself contains the above poetry by AG.

H694   [poem]. *El Corno Emplumado,* no. 17 (Jan. 1966) pp. 135-158.
Translation by Ernesto De La Peña: Kaddish [Kaddish]

H695*   [2 poems]. *Boletin Cultural Peruano,* vol. 3, no. 6 (April-June 1966) pp. 15-17.
Translation by C.E. Zavaleta: Kaddish [Kaddish (excerpt)] — Cancion [Song]

H696   [poem]. *El Corno Emplumado,* nol. 19 (July 1966) pp. 63-65.
Translation by Arnold Belkin: America [America]

H697*   [poem]. *Setecientos Monos,* no. 8 (Aug. 1966) pp. 12-14.
Translation by Luis María Castellanos: En La Tumba De Apollinaire [At
Apollinaire's Grave]

H698*   [poem]. *Orfeo,* no. 21-22 (1966) pp. 61-63.
Translation by Rosamel Del Valle: En La Tumba De Apollinaire [At Apollinaire's
Grave]

H699*   [2 poems]. *El Angel Del Altillo,* no. 1 (1967) pp. 15-18.
Translation by Miguel Grinberg: Sutra Del Girasol [Sunflower Sutra]
Translation by Bobby Curto: Kaddish [Kaddish (excerpt)]

H700   [prose and 4 poems]. *Haoma,* vol. 1, no. 3 (April 1968) pp. 48-61.
Translation by Andres Boulton Figueira De Mello: Renacimiento O Morir [Public
Solitude] — Aullido [Howl] — Apendice Para Aullido [Footnote To Howl] —
Poema Cohete [Poem Rocket] — Salmo Magico [Magic Psalm]

H701   [poem]. *Barrilete,* vol. 5, no. 1 (Oct. 1968) pp. 12-14.
Translation by Miguel Grinberg: A Quien Dar Bondad [Who Be Kind To]

H702*   [poem]. *Papeles: Revista Del Aleneo De Caracas,* no. 10 (Feb. 1970) pp. 31-34.
Translation: Wichita Vortex Sutra [Wichita Vortex Sutra (excerpt)]

H703   [poem]. *Planete,* no. 21 (April-May 1971)
Translation by Enrique Ivaldi: Al Borde De Galielea [Galilee Shore]

H704   [prose]. *Contracultura,* vol. 2, no. 1 (Aug. 1971) p. 16.
Translation: Pichicata Mata [Let's Issue A General Declaration]

H705   [poem]. *Nosferatu,* vol. 2, no. 4-5 (Jan. 1974) pp. 29-31.
Translation by Enrique Ivaldi: Al Borde De Galilea [Galilee Shore]

H706   [poem]. *La Cultura En México,* no. 666 (Nov. 13, 1974) Suplemento de
Siempre!, p. viii.
Translation by Carlos Monsivais: Muerte A La Oreja De Van Gogh! [Death To
Van Gogh's Ear!]

H707   [3 poems]. *Revista De La Universidad De Mexico,* vol. 30, no. 2 (Oct. 1975) pp.
18-20.
Translation by Mauricio Schoijet: A Poe: Sobre El Planeta Por Aire Entre Albany
Y Baltimore [To Poe: Over The Planet, Air Albany-Baltimore] — Letania De
Las Ganacias De Guerra [War Profit Litany] — Bayonne Entrando A LA
Ciudad De Nueva York [Bayonne Entering NYC]

H708* [poem]. *El Nacional* (Feb. 15, 1976)
Translation by Antonia Arráiz Parra: Yahve Y Ala Combaten [Jaweh And Allah
Battle]

H709   [8 poems]. *El Zaguan,* no. 5 (Jan. 28, 1977) pp. 46-56.
Translation by Alberto Blanco: Sunset S.S. Azemour ‖ Puesta De Sol S.S.
Azemour — After Yeats ‖ A La Manera De Yeats — Why Is God Love, Jack? ‖
¿Por Que Dios Es Amor, Jack? — First Party At Ken Kesey's With Hell's
Angels ‖ Primera Fiesta En La Casa De Ken Kesey Con Los Hell's Angels —
Guru ‖ Guru — Carmel Valley ‖ Valle De Carmel — Uptown ‖ Uptown — To
The Body ‖ Al Cuerpo

H710   [poem]. *Vigencia,* vol. 2, no. 20 (Dec. 1978) p. 29.
Translation by Miguel Grinberg: Oda Plutoniana [Plutonian Ode]

H711   [prose]. *Siempre!,* no. 885 (Feb. 21, 1979) La Cultura En Mexico supplement,
pp. 3-7.
Translation by Antonio Saborit: Paso Por Yucatan [*Journals Early Fifties Early
Sixties* (excerpt)]

H712* [poem]. *La Palabra Y El Hombre,* no. 31 [Nueva Epoca] (July-Sept. 1979) pp.
27-30.
Translation by José Vincente Anaya: Europa! Europa! [Europe! Europe!]

H713   [poem]. *Mutantia,* vol. 1, no. 1 (June-July 1980) pp. 84-87.
Translation by Miguel Grinberg: Oda Plutoniana [Plutonian Ode]

H714   [2 poems]. *Casa Del Tiempo,* vol. 1, no. 9 (May 1981) pp. xxi-xxii.
Translation by Sandro Cohen: Un Supermercado En California [A Supermarket
In California] — Reporte De Sueño: 8 De Junio De 1955 [Dream Record: June
8, 1955]

H715   Yevtushenko, Yevgeny; Ginsberg, Allen and Cardenal, Ernesto. [prose]. *El
Nuevo Diario* (Jan. 26, 1982) p. 12.
Translation by Ernesto Cardenal: [Declaration Of Three]

H716   [poem]. *El Correo De La UNESCO,* vol. 35, no. 11 (Nov. 1982) pp. 13-14.
Translation: [Plutonian Ode (excerpt)]
Note: There was also a Braille Spanish edition of this periodical.

H717   [3 poems]. *Poesia Libre,* vol. 4, no. 11 (June 1984) pp. 3-8.
Translation by Ernesto Cardenal: Continuacion De Un Largo Poema De Estos Estados [Continuation Of a Long Poem Of These States] — En La Bodega De Equipajes De La Greyhound [In the Baggage Room At Greyhound] — Letania De Las Ganancias De Guerra [War Profit Litany]

H718   [poem]. *Plural,* vol. 14-16, no. 162 (March 1985) pp. 2-6.
Translation by Mauricio Shoijet: Wichita Vortex Sutra [Wichita Vortex Sutra]

H719   [poem]. *Dimensão,* vol. 6, no. 11 (Spring 1985) pp. 34-36.
Translation by Manuel De Seabra: A Supermarket In California ‖ Um Supermercado Na Califórnia

H720   [poem]. *Diario De Poesía,* no. 1 (June 1986) p. 4.
Translation by Eduardo Stupía: Sudario Blanco [White Shroud]

H721   [poem]. *Equivalencias/Equivalences,* no. 14 (Jan. 1987) pp. 64-78.
Translation by Louis Bourne and Justo Jorge Padrón: Notas De Un Diario De China ‖ Notes From a Chinese Journal

H722* [3 poems]. *Hueso Húmero,* no. 22 (July 1987) pp. 103-105.
Translation: Expulsen A Los Periodistas Amarillos De La Mala Gramatica Y Los Horrendos Modales [Throw Out the Yellow Journalists Of Bad Grammar] — No Soy [I Am Not] — Amor De Estudiante [Student Love]

H723   [2 poems]. *Plural,* vol. xvi-x, no. 190 (July 1987) pp. 16-18.
Translation by Jorge Mouriño: Sutra Del Girasol [Sunflower Sutra] — Supermercado Californiano [A Supermarket In California]

H724   [poem]. *Diario 16* (Nov. 21, 1987) Culturas supplement, p. xii.
Translation by Carlos Edmundo De Ory: A Carlos Edmundo De Ory En El Gas Station [Proclamation]

H725   [poem]. *Culturas,* no. 140 (Dec. 12, 1987) Rafael Alberti supplement, p. 5.
Translation: El Manjar Del Poeta

H726   [poem]. *Portable Lower East Side,* vol. 6, no. 1 ([June] 1989) pp. 74-75.
Translation by Carlos Edmundo De Ory: Proclamation ‖ Proclamacion

H727   [poem]. *El Caimán Barbudo,* no. 10 (1990) Literario supplement.
Translation: Poema De Amor Sobre Un Tema De Walt Whitman [Love Poem On a Theme By Whitman]

H728   [poem]. *Underground Forest / La Selva Subterranea,* no. 10 (Oct. 12, 1991) pp. 36-37.
Translation by Jorge Madrazo: Written In My Dream By W.C. Williams ‖ Escrito En Mi Sueño Por W.C. Williams

H729   [poem]. *Culturas,* vol. 16, no. 364 (Oct. 3, 1992) p. 6.
Translation by Carlos Edmundo De Ory: Proclamación [Proclamation]

H730   [poem]. *El Pais,* vol. 12, no. 573 (Nov. 4, 1993) p. 2.
Translation by Carlos Edmundo De Ory: Esfínter [Sphincter]

H731   [poem]. *El Mundo* (Dec. 14, 1993)
Translation by Antolin Rato: Padre Muerte Blues [Father Death Blues]

H732   [poem]. *Istmica,* vol. 1, no. 1 (Spring 1994) pp. 158-159.
Translation by Jorge Madrazo: Escrito En Mi Sueño Por W.C. Williams [Written
In My Dream By W.C. Williams]

H733   [poem]. *Ancora,* vol. 23, no. 31 (Aug. 7, 1994) pp. 2D-3D.
Translation: A Frank O'Hara [My Sad Self]

Miscellaneous:

H734   [program]. *Noche De Poesia Internacional.* Morelia, Mexico: Aug. 16-23, 1981,
p. [5].
Translation by José Coronel Urtecho and Ernesto Cardenal: A Lindsay [To
Lindsay]

H735   [flyer]. Evtushenko, Eugenio; Ginsberg, Allen and Cardenal, Ernesto.
Declaración De Los Tres. Managua, Nicaragua: Ministry of Culture, Jan. 28,
1982. Two sheets, 27.6 x 21.4 cm. 50 copies printed.
Translation by Ernesto Cardenal: Declaración De Los Tres ‖ Declaration Of Three.
Note: Reprinted a few days later in an unknown quantity for distribution to
various publications. The reprinted version lacks the heading *Declaración de
los tres* on page two.

SWAHILI

Periodicals:

H736   [poem]. *UNESCO Courier* [Swahili edition], vol. 35, no. 10 (Nov. 1982) pp.
13-14.
Translation: [Plutonian Ode (excerpt)]

SWEDISH

Books:

H737   Ginsberg, Allen. *Tårgas & Solrosor.* Stockholm, Sweden: FIBs Lyrikklubb,
1971.
Translation by Gösta Friberg and Gunnar Harding: Howl [Howl] — Fotnot Till
Howl [Footnote To Howl] — Supermarket I Kalifornien [A Supermarket In
California] — Solrossutra [Sunflower Sutra] — Amerika [America] —
Sakyamuni Kommer Ut Från Berget [Sakyamuni Coming Out From the
Mountain] — Underlig Ny Sommarkåk I Berkeley [Strange New Cottage In
Berkeley] — Psalm III [Psalm III] — Till Faster Rose [To Aunt Rose] —
Kaddish [Kaddish] — Mandala [Lysergic Acid (excerpt)] — Jag Ber Dig Kom
Tillbaka & Var Glad Igen [I Beg You Come Back And Be Cheerful] — Till En
Gammal Poet I Peru [To An Old Poet In Peru] — Eter [Aether] — Strand I
Galileen [Galilee Shore] — Patna-Benares Expressen [Patna-Benares Express]
— Idag [Today] — Ögonblicken Återvänder [The Moments Return] — Kral
Majales [Kral Majales] — Guru [Guru] — Wales Visitation [Wales Visitation]
— Memory Gardens [Memory Gardens]

H738   Ginsberg, Allen. *Sorgsna Hyllningar Av Damm.* Mölndal, Sweden: Fri Press,
1976.
Translation by Mikael Ejdemyr: Grön Anteckningsbok [Green Notebook] —
Skrivet I Månljus [Writ In Moonbeam] — Energivampyr [Energy Vampire] —
Kör Folkvagn [Driving Volkswagon] — Mr Sharpe Byggnadssnickaren Från
Marysville [Mr Sharpe the Carpenter From Marysville] — Uppför Kullen Vävd
[Walking Uphill Woolen] — På Tal Om Féer [Talking About Fairies] —

Ekollonfolk [Acorn People] — Månen Åtföljd Av Jupiter Genom Tallar [The Moon Followed By Jupiter Thru Pinetrees] — Till De Döda [Sad Dust Glories] — Till Salu Till Salu [For Sale For Sale]

Anthologies:

H739   Ekner, Reider (ed.). *Helgon Och Hetsporrear, Poesi Från Beat Generation Och San Franciscorenäissansen.* Stockholm, Sweden: Rabén & Sjögren, 1960, pp. 41-56.
Translation by Lars Kleberg: Tjutet [Howl]
Translation by Reidar Ekner: Solrossutra [Sunflower Sutra] — Vid Apollinaires Grav [At Apollinaire's Grave]

H740   Harding, Gunnar (ed.). *4 Poeter.* Malung, Sweden: Bok Och Bild, 1966, pp. 21-31.
Translation by Gunnar Harding: Kaddish [Kaddish]

H741   Harding, Gunnar (ed.). *Amerikansk Undergroundpoesi.* Stockholm, Sweden: Wahlström & Widstrand, 1969, pp. 49-66.
Translation by Gunnar Harding: Wichita Vortex Sutra [Wichita Vortex Sutra]

H742   *Poesi Fran USA.* Stockholm, Sweden: FIBs Lyrikklubb, 1972, pp. 52-63.
Translation by Gunnar Harding: Ur En Dikt Om Dessa Stater [Beginning Of a Poem Of These States] — Pa Väg Mot Wichita, Kansas [Wichita Vortex Sutra]

H743   Rydén, Hugo and others (eds.). *Från Dickens Till Delblanc.* Stockholm, Sweden: Natur Och Kultur, 1979, pp. 195-197.
Translation by Gunnar Harding: Wichita Vortex Sutra [Wichita Vortex Sutra]

H744   Jarl, Stefan. *Ett Anständigt Liv.* Stockholm, Sweden: Panorstedt & Söners Förlag, 1980.
Translation: [Howl (excerpt)]

H745   Burroughs, William and Ginsberg, Allen. *Yagebreven.* Lund, Sweden: Bakhåll, 1983.
Translation by Peter Stewart: Yagebreven [letters to William Burroughs from *Yage Letters*]

H746*   *USA-Poesi.* Stockholm, Sweden: Café Existens, 1984, pp. 465, 473-474.
Translation by Gunnar Harding: Till Lindsay [To Lindsay] — En Profetia [A Prophecy] — Ayers Rock Uluru Song [Ayers Rock Uluru Song]

Periodicals:

H747*   [poem]. *BLM, Bonniers Litterära Magasin,* vol. 29, no. 7 (Sept. 1960) pp. 568-569.
Translation by Reidar Ekner: Solrossutra [Sunflower Sutra]
Note: This article was offprinted and appeared in 1960 under the cover title *Särtryck Ur BLM, Liten Beat-Antologi.*

H748   [poem]. *Lyrikvännen,* vol. 7, no. 2 (1960) p. 7.
Translation by Lars Kleberg: Ett Snabbköp I Kalifornien [A Supermarket In California] — Bakom Den Verkliga [In Back Of the Real]

H749*   [poem]. *Ord & Bild,* vol. 74, no. 4 (1965) pp. 355-358.
Translation by Gunnar Harding: Till Faster Rose [To Aunt Rose]
Note: This article was offprinted and appeared under the cover title *Särtryck.*

H750 [poem]. *Svenska Dagbladet* (Feb. 13, 1966) section 2, p. 1.
Translation by Gunnar Harding: Jag Ber Dig Kom Tillbaka & Var Glad [I Beg
You Come Back And Be Cheerful]

H751* [poem]. *Ord & Bild,* vol. 78, no. 3 (1969) pp. 181-183.
Translation by Gunnar Harding: Ur Wichita Vortex Sutra [Wichita Vortex Sutra
(excerpt)]

H752* [3 poems]. *Scen O. Salong,* vol. 56, no. 11-12 (1972) p. 17.
Translation by Gösta Friberg and Gunnar Harding: Psalm III [Psalm III] —
Patna-Benares Expressen [Patna-Benares Express] — Mandala [Mandala]

H753* [poem]. *Guru Papers,* no. 9-10 (1975) pp. 8-11.
Translation by Gunnar Harding: City Midnight Junk Strains [City Midnight Junk
Strains]

H754* [2 poems]. *Tidskrift,* vol. 9, no. 2 (1978) pp. 51-52.
Translation by Olov Henricson: [We Rise On Sun Beams And Fall In the Night
— Cabin In the Rockies]

H755 [poem & note]. *Expressen* (April 4, 1979) pp. 4-5.
Translation by Gunnar Harding: Plutoniskt Ode [Plutonian Ode] — [prose note]

H756* [2 poems]. *Lyrikvännen,* vol. 26, no. 6 (1979) pp. 28-31.
Translation by Gunnar Harding: Plutoniskt Ode [Plutonian Ode] — A terresa Norr
Om Malströmmen [Returning North Of Vortex]

H757 [poem]. *Dagens Nyheter* (Feb. 3, 1983) p. 4.
Translation by Otto Mannheimer: Ode Till Förlorarna [Ode To Failure]

H758 [poem]. *Aftonbladet* (Feb. 9, 1983)
Translation by Reidar Ekner: Farskalle! [Birdbrain!]

H759* [2 poems]. *Rip,* no. 4 (1983) unpaged.
Translation by Peter Luthersson: Första Festen Hos Ken Keseys Med Hell's
Angels [First Party At Ken Kesey's With Hell's Angels] — Supermarket I
Californien [A Supermarket In California]

H760 [poem]. *Sheherazade,* no. 1 (1990) pp. 15-16.
Translation by Per Planhammar: Jag Är Resande I Ett Frammande Land [Reading
Bai Juyi]

H761 [poem]. *Montage,* no. 24-25 (1991) pp. 4-10.
Translation by Eva Houltzén: I Oanständighetens Namm [The Names]

H762 [poem and prose]. *Artes,* no. 1 (1992) pp. 89, 92-101.
Translation by Gunnar Harding: Varför Jag Mediterar [Why I Meditate]
Translation by Sture Pyk: Meditation Och Diktning [Meditation And Poetics]

TAMIL

Periodicals:

H763 [poem]. *UNESCO Courier* [Tamil edition], vol. 35, no. 10 (Nov. 1982) pp. 13-
14.
Translation: [Plutonian Ode (excerpt)]

TURKISH

Books:

H764 Ginsberg, Allen and Ferlinghetti, Lawrence. *Amerika.* Istanbul, Turkey: Ada Yayinlari, 1976, pp. 34-45.
Translation by Orhan Duru and Ferit Edgü: Siir Sanati [Ars Poetica] — Amerika [America] — LSD 25 [Lysergic Acid] — Bildiri [Message] — Malest Cornifici Tuo Catullo [Malest Cornifici Tuo Catullo] — Uluma [Howl]

Periodicals:

H765 [poem]. *UNESCO Courier* [Turkish edition], vol. 35, no. 10 (Nov. 1982) pp. 13-14.
Translation: [Plutonian Ode (excerpt)]

H766 [2 poems]. *Sanat Dergisi,* vol. 70, no. 430 (April 15, 1983) p. 19.
Translation by Orhan Duru and Ferit Edgü: Bildiri [Message] — Siir Sanati [Ars Poetica]

H767 [4 poems]. *Imge,* third series (1985) pp. 14-16.
Translation by Özgül Uysal: Kalküta'da Son Gece [Last Night In Calcutta] — Guru [Guru] — Sarki [Song] — Cirisotu [An Asphodel]

H768 [poem]. *Cumhuriyet* (June 21, 1990) p. 8.
Translation by Sezer Duru: Ruhr Havzasi [Ruhr-Gebiet]

UKRANIAN

Anthologies:

H769 Drach, Ivan (ed.). *Do Dzherel.* Kiev, USSR: Dnipro Publishers, 1972, pp. 263-264.
Translation by Ivan Drach: Supermagazin U Kalifornii [A Supermarket In California]

URDU

Periodicals:

H770 [poem]. *UNESCO Courier* [Urdu edition], vol. 35, no. 10 (Nov. 1982) pp. 13-14.
Translation: [Plutonian Ode (excerpt)]

J

Biography and
General Criticism

1926

J1 [birth announcement]. *Newark Star Ledger* (June 7, 1926) p. 2.

1938

J2 Simons, John (ed.). *Who's Who In American Jewry, vol. 3, 1938-39*. New York, NY: National News Association, 1938, p. 329.
Note: AG mentioned in entry about Louis Ginsberg.

1943

J3 *Senior Mirror*. Paterson, NJ: Eastside High School, June 1943, pp. 25, 61.
Note: AG pictured in his high school yearbook.

1945

J4 *The Columbian Of 1945*. New York, NY: Columbia College, 1945, pp. 30-31, 77.
Note: AG mentioned and pictured in his college yearbook.

1946

J5* Pokress, Jack. [letter to the editor]. *Passaic Valley Examiner* ([after Sept. 14] 1946)
Note: Letter criticizes AG's review of Wm. Carlos Williams' *Paterson (Book 1)* which was in the Sept. 14, 1946 issue of this newspaper.

1947

J6 *The Columbian Of 1947*. New York, NY: Columbia College, 1947, p. 54.
Note: AG mentioned in his college yearbook.

J7 L., J. The Reading Glass. *Newark Sunday News* (Aug. 10, 1947) section 4, p. 8.
Note: Very short mention concerning AG's winning of the Woodberry Prize.

1948

J8 *The Columbian Of 1948*. New York, NY: Columbia College, 1948, p. 71.
Note: AG mentioned in his college yearbook.

1949

J9   Car Spill Leads To $10,000 Loot. *New York Sun* (April 22, 1949) pp. 1,13.
Note: AG is involved in a burglary ring.

J10   Wrong-Way Auto Tips Off Police To Narcotics-Ruled Burglary Gang. *New York World-Telegram* (April 22, 1949) p. 1.

J11   'Cinderella's Shoe' Traps 4 In Thefts. *Daily Mirror* (April 23, 1949)

J12   Woman, 3 Men Held In Thefts Of Gems, Furs. *New York Daily News* (April 23, 1949)

J13   One-Way Street Violation Traps Four As Robbers. *New York Herald Tribune* (April 23, 1949) p. 11.

J14   Car Spill Leads To $10,000 Loot. *New York Sun* (April 23, 1949) p. 7.
Note: Includes a photograph of AG.

J15   Wrong-Way Turn Clears Up Robbery. *New York Times* (April 23, 1949) p. 30.

J16   *The Columbian Of 1949.* New York, NY: Columbia College, 1949, p. 258.
Note: AG mentioned in his college yearbook.

1955

J17   Schneiderman, Harry and Karpman, Itzhak J. Carmin (eds.). *Who's Who In World Jewry, 1955.* New York, NY: Who's Who In World Jewry, 1955, p. 249.
Note: AG mentioned in the listing for Louis Ginsberg.

1956

J18   Eberhart, Richard. West Coast Rhythms. *New York Times Book Review* (Sept. 2, 1956) pp. 7, 18.

J19   Fletcher, Angus Stewart. [review of *Howl And Other Poems*]. *i.e.: The Cambridge Review,* no. 6 (Dec. 1, 1956) pp. 136-139, 141.

J20   Lipton, Lawrence. America's Literary Underground. *Coastlines,* vol. 2, no. 2 [issue 6] (Winter 1956) pp. 3-7.

J21   Intentionally omitted.

1957

J22   Dorn, Norman K. [review of *Howl And Other Poems*]. *San Francisco Chronicle* (Jan. 6, 1957) This World section, p. 19.

J23   Poet Ginsberg's Son 'Chip Off Old Block'. *Paterson Morning Call* (Jan. 7, 1957)

J24   Breit, Harvey. [column]. *New York Times Book Review* (Jan. 20, 1957) p. 8.
Note: AG quoted briefly about lifestyle.

J25   Grieg, Michael. The Lively Arts In San Francisco. *Mademoiselle,* vol. 44, no. 4 (Feb. 1957) pp. 142-143, 190-191.
Note: Includes photograph of AG.

J26   Balaban, Dan. 3 'Witless Madcaps' Come Home To Roost. *Village Voice* (Feb. 13, 1957) p. 3.
Note: AG quoted briefly about the scene.

J27   Rexroth, Kenneth. San Francisco's Mature Bohemians. *Nation,* vol. 184, no. 8 (Feb. 23, 1957) pp. 159-162.

Rosenthal, M.L. Poet Of the New Violence [review of *Howl And Other Poems*]. *Nation,* vol. 184, no. 8 (Feb. 23, 1957) p. 162.

J28   Klausner, Howard B. Paterson Man's Poems Draw Attention Of Major Critics. *Herald-News* (Feb. 25, 1957).
Note: AG quoted briefly about freedom.

J29   Hollander, John. [review of *Howl And Other Poems*]. *Partisan Review,* vol. 24, no. 2 (Spring 1957) pp. 296-298.

J30   Customs Officer Seizes Ginsberg Poetry Book. *Golden Gater* (March 29, 1957) p. 2.

J31   The Red-Eyed Censors. *Nation,* vol. 184, no. 16 (April 20, 1957) p. 335.

J32   City Lights Books, ACLU Fight Customs' Book Seizure. *Publishers Weekly,* vol. 171, no. 17 (April 29, 1957) p. 29.

J33   Gleason, Ralph J. Perspectives. *Down Beat,* vol. 24, no. 9 (May 2, 1957) p. 32.

J34   Stock, Robert. Letter From San Francisco. *Poetry Broadsides,* vol. 1, no. 2 (June 1957) p. 3+.

J35   Cops Arrest Seller Of Book, Magazine. *San Francisco Chronicle* (June 4, 1957) p. 3.

J36   Police Widen Search For 'Lewd' Books. *San Francisco Chronicle* (June 6, 1957) pp. 1, 4.

Making a Clown Of San Francisco. *San Francisco Chronicle* (June 6, 1957) p. 22.

Hogan, William. Orwell's 'Big Brother' Is Watching Over Us. *San Francisco Chronicle* (June 6, 1957) p. 23.

J37   Bookshop Owner Surrenders. *San Francisco Chronicle* (June 7, 1957) p. 2.

J38   Davies, Elton M.; Sandford, Leigh; Dagan, Diane; Scott, Jack; Jensen, J.N.; and Merritt, Leroy Charles. [letters to the editor]. *San Francisco Chronicle* (June 10, 1957) p. 20.

J39   Gleason, Ralph J. A Bindle Of Ginsberg Sets Up a Real Howl. *San Francisco Chronicle* (June 11, 1957) p. 21.

J40   State's Law On 'Obscene' Books Hit. *San Francisco Chronicle* (June 12, 1957) p. 5.

J41   Lawyer Raps Book Charge. *San Francisco Examiner* (June 12, 1957) p. 8.

J42   Tauber, Judith; Sheehan, Hugh; Gress, E.; Arnold, Ed; Beckerman, Merritt; Buss, William G.; Frederick, Winifred S.; and Davidson, Lucas. [letters to the editor]. *San Francisco Chronicle* (June 13, 1957) p. 24.

J43   A Course In World Literature — A La Captain Hanrahan. *People's World* (June 15, 1957) pp. 3, 14.

J44   Booksellers' Trial Today; Police Censors Assailed. *San Francisco Chronicle* (June 17, 1957) p. 14.

J45   Booksellers' Dismissal Plea Fails. *San Francisco Chronicle* (June 18, 1957) p. 18.

Parkinson, Thomas; Rafael, Richard V.; Prince, Lourie Q.; Reichert, Cathe G.; Leonard, C.; Wolf, Guy W.; and Minton, Mary Cain. [letters to the editor]. *San Francisco Chronicle* (June 18, 1957) p. 20.

J46   Rexroth, Kenneth. San Francisco Letter. *Evergreen Review,* vol. 1, no. 2 (Summer 1957) pp. 5-14.

J47   Dickey, James. [review of *Howl And Other Poems*]. *Sewanee Review,* vol. 65 (Summer 1957) pp. 509-530.

J48   Provoo, George K.; Hoffman, A.P.; Vance, Charles P.; Castor, Henry; Shields, A.M.; Tucker, Arlene; Beckerman, Merritt T.; and Sales, Grover. [letters to the editor]. *San Francisco Chronicle* (June 24, 1957) p. 18.

J49   'Dirty' Book Trial Set For July 8. *San Francisco Chronicle* (June 26, 1957) p. 5.

J50   Moss, Pete. [letter to the editor]. *San Francisco Chronicle* (June 27, 1957) p. 20.

J51   Cops Arrest 2 For Selling 'Obscene' Books. *American Civil Liberties Union News,* vol. 22, no. 7 (July 1957) p. 1.

J52   Glinn, Burt. New York's Spreading Upper Bohemia. *Esquire,* vol. 48, no. 1 [issue 284] (July 1957) pp. 46-52.

J53   Censorship And Cloistered Virtue. *Argonaut,* vol. 136, no. 4166 (July 5, 1957) pp. 3-4.

J54   Baker, George. Avante Garde At the Golden Gate. *Saturday Review,* vol. 40 (Aug. 3, 1957) p. 10.

J55   Roberts, John G. Juvenile Police Head Raids Bookshop In San Francisco. *National Guardian* (Aug. 5, 1957) p. 6.

J56   Murphy, George. Is 'Howl' a Dirty Word? Cops' Book Ban Nears Court. *San Francisco News* (Aug. 6, 1957)

J57   'Howl' Book Trial Opens Tomorrow. *San Francisco Chronicle* (Aug. 7, 1957) p. 24.

J58   Murphy, George. A Best-Seller Across the Country, S.F. Poet's Book Is Banned Here. *San Francisco News* (Aug. 7, 1957) p. 4.

Murphy, George. Cops Don't Allow No Renaissance Here. *San Francisco News* (Aug. 7, 1957) p. 24.

J59   Defense Will Seek Delay In 'Howl" Trial. *San Francisco Chronicle* (Aug. 8, 1957) p. 3.

J60   Trial For 'Howl' Delayed Until Next Friday. *San Francisco Chronicle* (Aug. 9, 1957) p. 3.

J61   The American Way. *Times Literary Supplement* (Aug. 16, 1957) p. iii.

J62   Crawford, Mary. Trial Recessed As Judge Curls Up With 'Howl'. *San Francisco News* (Aug. 16, 1957) p. 3.

J63   Anspacher, Carolyn. 'Howl' Trial Starts — Big Crowd. *San Francisco Chronicle* (Aug. 17, 1957) pp. 1, 6.

J64   Judge Delays 'Howl' Trial To Read Book Exhibits. *San Francisco Examiner* (Aug. 17, 1957) p. 3.

J65   Anspacher, Carolyn. Dismissal For 'Howl' Clerk Indicated. *San Francisco Chronicle* (Aug. 23, 1957) p. 4.

J66   Davidsohn, Harleigh. A Poem On Trial. *Bay Window,* vol. 1, no. 2 (Aug. 28, 1957) pp. 1, 9.

J67   Final Hearing Sept. 5; Partial Victory Scored. *American Civil Liberties Union News,* vol. 22, no. 8 (Sept. 1957) pp. 1-2.

J68   Eckman, Frederick. [review of *Howl And Other Poems*]. *Poetry,* vol. 90, no. 6 (Sept. 1957) pp. 386-397.

J69   'Howl' Not Dirty Book Say Experts, It's Art. *San Francisco News* (Sept. 5, 1957)

J70   Perlman, David. Critics Say 'Howl' Is Art As Prosecutor Seeks Dirt. *San Francisco Chronicle* (Sept. 6, 1957) p. 3.

J71   Big Day For Bards At Bay. *Life,* vol. 43, no. 11 (Sept. 9, 1957) pp. 105-108.
Note: AG photographed on p. 108.

J72   Roberts, John G. West Coast Censorship Trial Draws Big Audiences In Support Of Poem. *National Guardian* (Sept. 9, 1957)

J73   Popper, George A. Howl Trial Goes On. *Bay Window,* vol. 1, no. 4 (Sept. 11, 1957) pp. 1, 3.

J74   Podhoretz, Norman. A Howl Of Protest In San Francisco. *New Republic,* vol. 137 (Sept. 16, 1957) p. 20.

J75   [letters to the editor]. *Life,* vol. 43, no. 13 (Sept. 21, 1957)
Note: In response to article "Big Day For Bards At Bay" (Sept. 9, 1957).

J76   Rumaker, Michael. [review of *Howl And Other Poems*]. *Black Mountain Review,* no. 7 (Autumn 1957) pp. 228-237.

Williams, William Carlos. [Preface to] Empty Mirror. *Black Mountain Review,* no. 7 (Autumn 1957) pp. 238-240.
Note: This precedes the publication of *Empty Mirror.*

J77   Ferlinghetti, Lawrence. [review of *Howl And Other Poems*]. *Coastlines,* no. 8 [also called vol. 2, no. 4] (Autumn 1957) pp. 34-35.

J78   Margolis, William J. Editorial: Censorship Is Their Kind Of Hate. *Miscellaneous Man,* no. 13 (Autumn 1957) pp. 1-3.

J79   Popper, George A. Howl Trial Is Near Conclusion. *Bay Window,* vol. 1, no. 6 (Sept. 25, 1957) pp. 1, 5.

J80   Lask, Thomas. An Angry Poet's Call To Arms. *New York Times* (Sept. 29, 1957) section 2, p. 15.

J81   A.M.B. 'Howl' Trial Ends, Verdict Oct. 3. *American Civil Liberties Union News,* vol. 22, no. 9 (Oct. 1957) pp. 1-2.

J82   Court Holds 'Howl' Is Not Obscene. *Oakland Tribune* (Oct. 4, 1957) section B, p. 1.

J83   Perlman, David. 'Howl' Not Obscene, Judge Rules. *San Francisco Chronicle* (Oct. 4, 1957) pp. 1-2.

J84   O'Gara, Francis B. 'Howl' Ruled Not Obscene; 2 Acquitted. *San Francisco Examiner* (Oct. 4, 1957) pp. 1, 16.

J85   Crawford, Mary. Judge Horn Rules 'Howl' Is Not Obscene; Decision Sets Up Yard Stick For U.S. Courts. *San Francisco News* (Oct. 4, 1957) p. 3.

J86   Fuller, John G. Tradewinds. *Saturday Review,* vol. 40, no. 40 (Oct. 5, 1957) pp. 5-7.

J87   The Word On 'Howl'. *San Francisco Chronicle* (Oct. 6, 1957) This World section, p. 5.

J88   'Howl' Decision Landmark Of Law. *San Francisco Chronicle* (Oct. 7, 1957) p. 18.

J89   'Howl' Ruled Not Obscene; Frisco Bookseller Cleared. *Publishers Weekly,* vol. 172, no. 17 (Oct. 21, 1957) pp. 30-32.

J90   'Howl' Ruled Not Obscene; Two Acquitted. *American Civil Liberties Union News,* vol. 22, no. 10 (Nov. 1957) p. 1.

J91   SF Hails 'Howl' Acquittal. *Antiquarian Bookman,* vol. 20, no. 19 (Nov. 4, 1957) p. 1435.

J92   New Test For Obscenity. *Nation,* vol. 185, no. 15 (Nov. 9, 1957) p. 314.

J93   Gold, Herbert. Hip, Cool, Beat, ... And Frantic. *Nation,* vol. 185, no. 16 (Nov. 16, 1957) pp. 349-355.

J94   Andrews, Lyman, Jr. Ranting, Negativism Characterize New Writing. *Justice* (Nov. 19, 1957) p. 4.

J95   Ciardi, John. [review of *San Francisco Poets* (Evergreen recording)]. *Saturday Review,* vol. 40, no. 47 (Nov. 23, 1957) p. 32.
Note: Very critical of AG's reading and poetry.

J96   Jacobson, Dan. America's 'Angry Young Men'; How Rebellious Are the San Francisco Rebels? *Commentary,* vol. 24, no. 6 (Dec. 1957) pp. 475-479.

J97   Perlman, David. How Captain Hanrahan Made 'Howl' a Best-Seller. *Reporter,* vol. 17, no. 10 (Dec. 12, 1957) pp. 37-39.

J98   Blau, Herbert. [review of *Howl And Other Poems*]. *Evergreen Review,* vol. 1, no. 4 (Winter 1957) pp. 154-155.

J99   Pope, Richard L. [review of *Howl And Other Poems*]. *Poetry Broadsides,* vol. 1, no. 3 (Winter 1957-1958) p. 6.

J100*   Rexroth, Kenneth. Disengagement: The Art Of the Beat Generation. *New World Writing,* no. 11 (1957).

Books:

J101   San Francisco. Municipal Court. *In The Municipal Court Of The City And County Of San Francisco, State Of California, Honorable Clayton W. Horn, Judge; The People Of The State Of California, Plaintiff, Vs. Shigeyoshi Murao (And) Lawrence Ferlinghetti, Defendants. Opinion Of The Court.* (San Francisco, 1957)

1958

J102   Wain, John. Revolting Attitudes. *Observer* (Jan. 12, 1958)

J103   Tucker, Dan. Square's Beat — Verse Up In Hair. *Chicago American* (Jan. 30, 1958)

J104   Holmes, John Clellon. The Philosophy Of the Beat Generation. *Esquire,* vol. 49, no. 2 [issue 291] (Feb. 1958) pp. 35-38.
Note: AG quoted briefly about 'Howl'.

J105   Meister, Dick. How 'Howl' Became a Bestseller. *Progressive,* vol. 22, no. 2 (Feb. 1958) pp. 36-37.

J106   Podhoretz, Norman. The Know-Nothing Bohemians. *Partisan Review,* vol. 25, no. 2 (Spring 1958) pp. 305-318.

J107   Justice, Donald. [review of *Howl And Other Poems*]. *Western Review,* vol. 22, no. 3 (Spring 1958) pp. 231-234.

J108   Beatniks Corso, Ginsberg Howl before New Lec Crowd. *Harvard Crimson* (March 25-26, 1958)
Note: AG quoted briefly about beatniks.

J109   Corso, Gregory. Dichter Und Gesellschaft In Amerika. *Akzente,* no. 2 (April 1958) pp. 101-112.

J110   Burdick, Eugene. The Innocent Nihilists Adrift In Squaresville. *Reporter,* vol. 18, no. 7 (April 3, 1958) pp. 30-33.

J111   [review of *The Beat Generation & the Angry Young Men*]. *Time,* vol. 71, no. 23 (June 9, 1958) pp. 98, 100, 102.

J112   Ross, Basil. California's Young Writers, Angry And Otherwise. *Library Journal,* vol. 83, no. 12 (June 15, 1958) pp. 1850-1854.

J113   [letters to the editor]. *Partisan Review,* vol. 25, no. 3 (Summer 1958) pp. 472-479.

J114   Buchwald, Art. Two Poets In Paris. *New York Herald Tribune* (June 26, 1958)
Note: AG quoted briefly about poetry.

J115   Pryce-Jones, Alan. [article]. *Listener* (July 3, 1958) pp. 15-16.

J116   Merisse, Marc. Trois Représentants De La "Beat Generation" À Paris. *Rendus* (July 9-15, 1958)
Note: AG interview format in French only.

J117   Brustein, Robert. The Cult Of Unthink. *Horizon,* vol. 1, no. 1 (Sept. 1958) pp. 38-45, 134-135.

J118   Pritchett, V.S. The Beat Generation. *New Statesman,* vol. 56, no. 1434 (Sept. 6, 1958) pp. 292, 294, 296.

J119   Hyams, Joe. Good-By To the Beatniks! *San Francisco Chronicle* (Sept. 28, 1958) This Week section, pp. 4-6, 33-34.
Note: The *This Week* section also appears as a supplement in many other newspapers.

J120   Nichols, Luther. Kerouac As the Savant Of the Religious Beat. *San Francisco Examiner* (Oct. 5, 1958) Highlight section, p. 17.

On the Road Back. *San Francisco Examiner* (Oct. 5, 1958) Highlight section, p. 18.
Note: AG mentioned in this interview with Kerouac.

J121   Schleifer, Marc D. Here To Save Us, But Not Sure From What. *Village Voice* (Oct. 15, 1958) pp. 3, 9.
Note: AG quoted at length.

J122   Moore, Rosalie. The Beat And the Unbeat. *Poetry,* vol. 93, no. 2 (Nov. 1958) pp. 104-107.

J123   Allen Ginsberg Invited To Read Poetry Here. *Hunter Arrow* (Nov. 13, 1958) p. 3.

J124   Schleifer, Marc D. The Beat Debated — Is It Or Is It Not? *Village Voice* (Nov. 19, 1958) pp. 1, 3.

J125   Advisor Resigns After Ginsberg Reads Poetry. *Hunter Arrow* (Nov. 24, 1958) p. 3.
Note: AG quoted briefly about poetry reading.

J126   Borgzinner, Jon. Allen Ginsberg Reads Poetry. *Yale Daily News* (Nov. 25, 1958) p. 1.
Note: AG quoted briefly about writing.

J126x Podhoretz, Norman. Where Is the Beat Generation Going? *Esquire,* vol. 50, no. 6 [issue 301] (Dec. 1958) pp. 147-150.

J127* Brulez, Raymond. De Schrijver En De Huidige Samlenleving. *Nieuw Vlaams Tijdschrift,* vol. 12, no. 7 (ca. 1958) pp. 1121-1125.

Books:

J128   Feldman, Gene and Gartenberg, Max (eds.). *The Beat Generation And the Angry Young Men.* New York, NY: Dell, 1958.
Note: AG mentioned throughout.

J129   Schock, Jim. *Life Is a Lousy Drag.* San Francisco, CA: Unicorn, 1958, p. 14.
Note: AG mentioned in this condemnation of beat life.

1959

J130   Engelsing, Inge. Beatniks In San Francisco Tanzen Nicht Ums Goldene Kalb. *Europa-Ausgabe,* no. 2 (Jan. 9, 1959) p. 1.

J131   Stegner, Bentley. Those Beatniks Dig Madmadmad Soiree. *Chicago Daily Sun-Times* (Jan. 29, 1959) p. 1.
Note: AG quoted briefly about poetry scene.

J132   Tucker, Dan. Square's Beat — Verse Up In Hair. *Chicago American* (Jan. 30, 1959) pp. 1, 6.

J133   Leonard, William. Beatniks Shock, Amuse 700—at $1.50 a Head. *Chicago Daily Tribune* (Jan. 30, 1959) part 2, p. 5.
Note: AG quoted briefly about poetry reading with photograph of AG.

J134   Poetry With a Down-Beatnik. *Chicago Sun-Times* (Jan. 30, 1959) p. 3.

Kupcinet, Irv. Kup's Column. *Chicago Sun-Times* (Jan. 30, 1959) p. 52.
Note: AG quoted briefly about money.

J135   Shavians Meet the Beatniks. *Shaw Society Newsletter,* vol. 2, no. 1 (Feb. 1959) p. 1.

News And Noise. *Shaw Society Newsletter,* vol. 2, no. 1 (Feb. 1959) pp. 3-4.

J136   Lyon, Herb. Tower Ticker. *Chicago Daily Tribune* (Feb. 3, 1959) section 2, p. 2.
Note: AG quoted briefly.

J137   Manners And Morals. *Time,* vol. 73, no. 6 (Feb. 9, 1959) p. 16.
Note: AG quoted briefly.

J138   Gould, Gordon. Happy Poets—Some Poetry. *Shaw Society Newsletter,* vol. 2, no. 2 (March 1959) pp. 1, 4.
Note: AG quoted briefly.

J139   Stearn, Jess. Coffee Brews Up Some Rare Beans. *Daily News* (March 8, 1959) p. 64.

J140   Aronowitz, Alfred G. The Beat Generation, Part I. *New York Post* (March 9, 1959) pp. 4, 40.
Note: AG quoted at length throughout this series of articles.

J141   Aronowitz, Alfred G. The Beat Generation, Part 2. *New York Post* (March 10, 1959) pp. 4, 64.

J142   Aronowitz, Alfred G. The Beat Generation, Part 3. *New York Post* (March 11, 1959) pp. 4, 86.

J143   Aronowitz, Alfred G. The Beat Generation, Article IV. *New York Post* (March 12, 1959) pp. 4, 22.

J144   Aronowitz, Alfred G. The Beat Generation, Article V. *New York Post* (March 13, 1959) pp. 4, 32.

J145   Goldstein, Al. Bard Ginsberg Stuns Paceites. *Pace College Press,* vol. 22, no. 6 (March 13, 1959) pp. 1, 3.
Note: AG quoted briefly.

J146   Aronowitz, Alfred G. The Beat Generation, Part VI. *New York Post* (March 15, 1959) pp. M-4, 5.

J147   Aronowitz, Alfred G. The Beat Generation, Article VII. *New York Post* (March 16, 1959) p. 72.

J148   Aronowitz, Alfred G. The Beat Generation, Article IX. *New York Post* (March 18, 1959) p. 64.

J149   Schleifer, Marc D. Kenneth Patchen On the 'Brat' Generation. *Village Voice* (March 18, 1959) pp. 1, 7.

J150   Aronowitz, Alfred G. The Beat Generation, Part X. *New York Post* (March 19, 1959) p. 22.

J151   Aronowitz, Alfred G. The Beat Generation, Article XI. *New York Post* (March 20, 1959) p. 70.

J152   Fuller, John. Trade Winds. *Saturday Review,* vol. 42, no. 12 (March 21, 1959) pp. 12-14.
Note: AG quoted.

J153   Aronowitz, Alfred G. The Beat Generation, Article XII. *New York Post* (March 22, 1959) p. M5.

J154   Trilling, Diana. The Other Night At Columbia, a Report From the Academy. *Partisan Review,* vol. 26, no. 2 (Spring 1959) pp. 214-230.
Note: Review of a reading by AG at Columbia.

J155   Van Ghent, Dorothy. Comment. *Wagner Literary Magazine* (Spring 1959) pp. 27-28.

J156   Sisk, John P. Beatniks And Tradition. *Commonweal,* vol. 70, no. 3 (April 17, 1959) pp. 75-77.

J157   Elliott, George P. Who Is We. *Nation,* vol. 138, no. 17 (April 25, 1959) pp. 374-378.

J158   Aronowitz, Alfred. [article]. *L'Express,* no. 414 (May 21, 1959) pp. 28-31.
Note: AG quoted in this French translation of the *New York Post* series.

J159*   Rivers, Paula. In Defense Of the Beat Generation. *Realist* (June-July 1959) pp. 14-15.

J160   The Kerouac And Allen Record: They Weren't Beat—They Won. *New York Post* (June 3, 1959) p. 75.
Note: AG quoted briefly about a recording by Jack Kerouac and Steve Allen.

J161   Ansen, Alan. Anyone Who Can Pick Up a Frying Pan Owns Death. *Big Table,* vol. 1, no. 2 (Summer 1959) pp. 32-41.

        Bowles, Paul. Burroughs In Tangier. *Big Table,* vol. 1, no. 2 (Summer 1959) pp. 42-43.

J162   Ginsberg, Louis. To Allen Ginsberg. *Prairie Schooner,* vol. 33 (Summer 1959) pp. 172-173.

J163   Golffing, Francis and Gibbs, Barbara. The Public Voice: Remarks On Poetry Today. *Commentary,* vol. 28, no. 1 (July 1959) pp. 63-69.

J164   Nessor, Gregg. This Beatnik De-Generation! *New York Mirror Magazine* (July 12, 1959) pp. 4-5.

J165   Jones, LeRoi. Putdown Of the Whore Of Babylon. *Yugen,* no. 5 ([Aug. 20] 1959) pp. 4-5.

J166   Logue, Christopher. [review of *Zen And Japanese Culture* by D.T. Suzuki]. *New Statesman* (Aug. 29, 1959) pp. 251-252.
Note: AG quoted briefly.

J167   Bang Bong Bing. *Time,* vol. 74, no. 10 (Sept. 7, 1959) p. 80.

J168   McFadden, J.P. Howling In the Wilderness. *National Review,* vol. 7, no. 22 (Sept. 12, 1959) pp. 338-339.

J169   Richards, Steve. Beatniks Beat a Path To TV. *Sunday News* (Sept. 13, 1959) pp. 8, 14.

J170   Weiner, Harold. [letter to the editor]. *Village Voice* (Sept. 16, 1959) pp. 4, 16.

J171   Frumkin, Gene. The Great Promoter. *Coastlines,* no. 13 (Autumn 1959) pp. 3-10.
Note: AG quoted briefly.

J172   Tilling, Diana. [pseudo. for Robert Bly]. The Other Night In Heaven. *The Fifties,* no. 3 ([Fall] 1959) pp. 54-56.
Note: Parody of Diana Trilling article.

J173   Bremser, Ray. [letter to the editor]. *Village Voice* (Sept. 23, 1959) p. 4.

J174   Menninger, Karl. [letter to the editor]. *Mattachine Review,* vol. 5, no. 10 (Oct. 1959) p. 24.

J175   Barry, Joseph. Exiles At Home. *New York Post* (Nov. 18, 1959) p. 50.

J176   Kinter, W[illiam]. [letter to the editor]. *Muhlenberg Weekly* (Nov. 19, 1959) pp. 3, 6.

J177   O'Neil, Paul. The Only Rebellion Around. *Life,* vol. 47, no. 22 (Nov. 30, 1959) pp. 114-6, 119-20, 123-4, 126, 129-30.
Note: AG quoted briefly.

J178   Intentionally omitted.

J179   Tynan, Kenneth. Bearding the Beats. *Mattachine Review,* vol. 5, no. 12 (Dec. 1959) pp. 30-33.

J180   Endsville. *Time,* vol. 74, no. 24 (Dec. 14, 1959) p. 66.
Note: Review of *Pull My Daisy* (film).

J181   Editorial: Ginsberg Revisited. *Odyssey,* vol. 1, no. 4 (1959) pp. 4-10.

Books:

J182   Lipton, Lawrence. *The Holy Barbarians.* New York, NY: Julian Messner, 1959.

J183   Rexroth, Kenneth. *Bird In the Bush.* New York, NY: New Directions, 1959.

1960

J184* Suwa, Yu and Fukuda, Rikutaro. The Beat Generation And the Angry Young Men. *Gendaishi Techo* (Jan. 1960) p. 31.

J185 R., M. Beatitudes... *L.A.,* vol. 1, no. 10 (Jan. 1960) pp. 16-18.

J186 Ginsberg, Corso, Ferlinghetti. *WFMT Chicago Fine Arts Guide* (Jan. 1960) p. 18.

J187 Gartenberg, Max. The Jewishness Of Allen Ginsberg. *Reconstructionist,* vol. 25, no. 18 (Jan. 8, 1960) pp. 7-13.

J188 Allen Gineberg [sic] Dio A Conocer A Poetas De La "Beat Generation". *Cronica* (Jan. 21, 1960) p. 7.

J189 Se Pidio Que Universidad Propicie Formacion De Editorial Americana. *Cronica* (Jan. 22, 1960) p. 7.

J190 En Dialogo Abierto Poetas Yanquis Cantaron Al Sexo Y A La Rebeldia. *Cronica* (Jan. 23, 1960) p. 8.

J191 Carmona, Dário. Vivo Encuentro De Escritores. *Ercilla* (Jan. 27, 1960) pp. 6-7. *Note:* AG quoted briefly in Spanish only.

J192 Famoso Vate Norteamericano Busca Hierbas Medicinales. *El Diario Austral* (Jan. 29, 1960)

J193 Melnechuk, Theodore. Class Of 1948 Beats Ginsberg To Last Howl. *[Columbia College] Class Of 1948 Newsletter,* vol. 12, no. 2 (Feb. 1960) pp. 1, 3-4.

J194 Simon, John J. Alfred Kreymborg And the Beat Generation. *Promethean Review,* vol. 2, no. 1 (Feb.-March 1960) pp. 3-7.

J195 Russell, Ray. [review of *Howl And Other Poems* (recording)]. *Shaw Society Newsletter* (Feb. 1960)

J196 Martinez Moreno, Carlos. Escritores De America En Concepcion. *Marcha* (Feb. 6, 1960)

J197 Ciardi, John. Epitaph For the Dead Beats. *Saturday Review,* vol. 43, no. 6 (Feb. 6, 1960) pp. 11-13, 42.

J198 Krolow, Karl. [review of *Das Geheul Und Andere Gedichte* (Limes Verlag)]. *Westfalenpost* (Feb. 6, 1960).

J199 Bondy, Sebastian Salazar. La Torre De Marfil Derribada. *El Comercio* (Feb. 7, 1960) Suplemento Dominical, pp. 4-5.

J200 Sitwell, Edith. [letter to the editor]. *Life,* vol. 48, no. 5 (Feb. 8, 1960) p. 25.

J201 Alegriá, Fernando. Chileans Shouted 'Bravo' When the Beats Read Poetry. *San Francisco Chronicle* (Feb. 14, 1960) This World section, p. 16.

J202* Simon, John. Slight Of Foot. *Audit,* vol. 1, no. 1 (Feb. 22, 1960) pp. 3-9.

J203 Sabato, Ernesto. Los Escritores De Latinoamerica Frente Al Drama De Su Continente. *Cultura Peruana,* vol. 20, no. 141 (March 1960) unpaged.

J204   [review of *Das Geheul Und Andere Gedichte* (Limes Verlag)]. *Konkret* (March 1, 1960) p. 10.

J205   Schmied, Wieland. [review of *Das Geheul Und Andere Gedichte* (Limes Verlag)]. *Neue Deutsche Heft* (March 1960) pp. 1153-1154.

J206   Martinez Moreno, Carlos. Escritores De America En Concepcion. *Revista De La Universidad De Mexico* (March 1960) pp. 19-20.
        Note: First printed in *Marcha* (Feb. 6, 1960).

J207   El Barbudo A. Ginsberg Dio Seria Conferencia Sobre Poesia "Vapuleada". *La Nacion* (March 12, 1960)
        Note: AG quoted briefly in Spanish only.

J208   Poesia, Humor Y Macartismo. *Vistazo* (March 14, 1960)

J209   Blackburn, Paul. Writing For the Ear [review of *Howl And Other Poems* (recording)]. *Big Table,* vol. 1, no. 4 (Spring 1960) pp. 127-132.

        Carroll, Paul. Five Poets In Their Skins. *Big Table,* vol. 1, no. 4 (Spring 1960) pp. 133-138.
        Note: AG quoted briefly concerning his Chicago visit.

J210   Paetel, Karl O. [review of *Das Geheul Und Andere Gedichte* (Limes Verlag)]. *Deutsche Jugend* (April 1960) pp. 186-187.

J211   Pivano, Fernanda. Gli Americani Bruciati. *Successo,* vol. 2, no. 4 (April 1960) pp. 38-43.

J212   [article]. *Américas,* vol. 12, no. 5 (May 1960) pp. 11-12.

J213   Montgomery, John. To Be Beat Is To Be Outside. *Best Articles & Stories* (May 1960) pp. 55-56.

J214   Bloomquist, Edward R. Let's Think Twice About 'Free' Narcotics. *GP,* vol. 21, no. 5-6 (May-June 1960) pp. 149-162.

J215   Sokolsky, George E. They Do Their Best To Blacken the U.S. *New York Journal American* (May 5, 1960) p. 28.
        Note: AG quoted briefly.

J216   Llego A. Ginsberg El Poeta De La "Beat Generation". *El Comercio* (May 6, 1960)
        Note: AG quoted briefly in Spanish only.

J217   Un Elogio De Machu Picchu Hace Poeta Allen Ginsberg. *La Prensa* (May 6, 1960)
        Note: AG quoted briefly in Spanish only.

J218   Machu-Pichu No Es Para Los Pobres, Cuesta Nucho Dinero Subir Para Contemplarla. *El Comercio* (May 9, 1960) p. 1.
        Note: AG quoted briefly in Spanish only.

J219   Aronowitz, Alfred G. [review of *The Beats* by Seymour Krim]. *Village Voice* (May 18, 1960) pp. 1, 7, 10.

J220   New Wavelet. *Time,* vol. 75, no. 21 (May 23, 1960) p. 69.
        Note: Review of *Pull My Daisy* (film).

J221   Hoehl, Egbert. Literarische Orgien [review of *Das Geheul Und Andere Gedichte* (Limes Verlag)]. *Panorama München,* vol. 4, no. 6 (June 1960).

J222   Moore, Marianne. [review of *The New American Poetry,* edited by Donald M. Allen]. *New York Herald Tribune* (June 26, 1960) Book Review section, pp. 1, 11.

J223   La Torres, Alfonso. Allen Ginsberg: "Las Sucias Manos De La Sociedad No Pueden Tocar Mi Alma". *Cultura Peruana,* vol. 20, no. 143 (July 1960) unpaged.
        Note: AG quoted briefly in Spanish only.

J224   Wilson, Robert Anton. Ezra Pound At Seventy-Five. *Realist* (July-Aug. 1960) pp. 7-10.

J225   Kersten, Hans-Hermann. [review of *Das Geheul Und Andere Gedichte* (Limes Verlag)]. *Buchanzeiger Für Öffenbliche Bücherein,* vol. 13, no. 150-151 (Aug.-Sept. 1960).

J226   Hoehl, Egbert. Die Selbstgerechten [review of *Das Geheul Und Andere Gedichte* (Limes Verlag)]. *Kultur In Unserer Zeit,* no. 33 (Aug. 1960) p. 11.

J227   McDarrah, Fred W. The Anatomy Of a Beatnik. *Saga* (Aug. 1960) pp. 34-37, 87-88.
        Note: AG quoted briefly.

J228   The Hipster And the Beat. *Haagse Post,* no. 2387 (Sept. 10, 1960) pp. 13-15.

J229   Aronowitz, Alfred G. Portrait Of a Beat. *Nugget,* vol. 5, no. 5 (Oct. 1960) pp. 15-18, 24.
        Note: AG quoted briefly.

J230   Strawn, Bill. Duke Anthropologist Takes Look At Beatniks. *News And Observer* (Nov. 15, 1960) p. 7.

J231   Vinkenoog, Simon. Barbaren Van Het Leidseplein. *Twen* (Nov. 15, 1960) pp. 38-43.

J232   Chicago's Sacred And Profane "Little" Magazines. *Scene* (Nov. 26-30, 1960) pp. 4-5.

J233   Lyons, Leonard. [column]. *New York Post* (Dec. 21, 1960) p. 33.
        Note: AG quoted briefly.

J234   Rowan, John. Simplicity Under the Bomb. *And,* no. 2 (ca. 1960) pp. 9-11.

J235   [review of *Das Geheul Und Andere Gedichte* (Limes Verlag)]. *Geist Und Zeit,* no. 4 (1960).

J236   Gacki, S.K. The Beat Generation. *Nowy Swiat [Polish Morning World],* no. 1 (1960) p. 5.

J237   Ginsey Report: Correspondence On the Beats. *Wagner Literary Magazine* (1960-61) pp. 104-109.

Books:

J238   Goodman, Paul. *Growing Up Absurd.* New York, NY: Random House, 1960.
        Note: AG mentioned p. 280.

J239   Miller, James E., Jr.; Shapiro, Karl and Slote, Bernice. *Start With the Sun: Studies In Cosmic Poetry.* Lincoln, NE: University Of Nebraska Press, 1960.
Contents:
Miller, James E., Jr. Walt Whitman And the Secret Of History, pp. 15-28
Shapiro, Karl. The True Contemporary, pp. 206-225

1961

J240   Gartenberg, Max. Allen Ginsberg Et La "Beat Generation". *L'Arche,* no. 48 (Jan. 1961) pp. 20-25.

J241   Gutman, Walter K. Should Allen Ginsberg Be Invited To the White House? *Gutman Letter* (Jan. 24, 1961) pp. 1-3.

J242   Lafourcade, Enrique. Desayuno Con Los Beatniks. *La Nacion* (Jan. 29, 1961) p. 5.
Note: AG quoted briefly in Spanish only.

J243   Henson, Robert. "Howl" In the Classroom. *CEA [College English Association] Critic,* vol. 23, no. 2 (Feb. 1961) pp. 1, 8-9.

J244   Mailer, Norman. [letter to the editor]. *Village Voice* (Feb. 2, 1961)
Note: In support of AG poem.

J245   Rexroth, Kenneth. Bearded Barbarians Or Real Bards? *New York Times Book Review* (Feb. 12, 1961) pp. 1, 44-45.

J246   Fles, John. The Great Chicago Poetry Reading. *Swank* (March 1961) pp. 65-68, 70.
Note: AG quoted briefly.

J247   Buchwald, Art. Buchwald: Frost On Sandburg's Hair. *New York Herald Tribune* (March 19, 1961)
Note: Brief quote by Robert Frost concerning AG.

J248   Interview With Allen Ginsberg. *Monmouth Letters,* vol. 5, no. 1 (Spring 1961) pp. 10-12.
Note: AG interview format.

J249   Jouffroy, Alain. Allen Ginsberg À Paris. *Combat* (April 13, 1961)
Note: AG quoted briefly in French only.

J250   Gutman, Walter K. The American Was Not the First To Look Down On the Earth's Beauty. *Gutman Letter* (April 18, 1961)

J251   Grieg, Michael. [review of *Kaddish And Other Poems*]. *San Francisco Examiner* (May 4, 1961) p. 31.

J252   Wiseman, Thomas. Encounter. *Evening Standard* (May 12, 1961) p. 10.
Note: AG interview format.

J253   Meyerzove, Lee. [review of *Kaddish And Other Poems*]. *San Francisco State Gator* (May 12, 1961)

J254   Alvarez, A. [review of *Kaddish And Other Poems*]. *Observer,* no. 8863 (May 14, 1961) p. 30.

J255   McTruitt, James. [review of *Kaddish And Other Poems*]. *Washington Post* (June 18, 1961) p. E7.

J256   Alvarez, A. [review of *Kaddish And Other Poems*]. *San Francisco Examiner* (June 19, 1961) p. 29.

J257   Keown, Don. [review of *Kaddish And Other Poems*]. *Independent Journal* ([Summer] 1961).

J258   Angoff, Charles. [review of *Kaddish And Other Poems*]. *Jewish Exponent* (June 23, 1961).

J259   [review of *Kaddish And Other Poems*]. *Times Literary Supplement,* no. 3097 (June 30, 1961) p. 404.

J260   Carroll, Paul. [review of *Kaddish And Other Poems*]. *Evergreen Review,* vol. 5, no. 19 (July-Aug. 1961) pp. 114-116.

J261   Nelson, Ray. How To Be a Beatnik. *Habakkuk,* no. 6 (July 1961) pp. 28-36.

J262   Snyder, Gary. [letters to Ginsberg]. *Origin,* no. 2 (July 1961) pp. 63-64.

J263   Mekas, Jonas. The Honest Art Of Hollywood. *Swank,* vol. 8, no. 3 (July 1961) p. 41.

J264*   Bode, Carl. The Mixed Romantics. *John O'London's,* no. 4 (July 6, 1961) pp. 8-9.

J265   Dickey, James. [review of *Kaddish And Other Poems*]. *New York Times Book Review* (July 9, 1961) p. 14.

J266   Marowitz, Charles. Literature In a Strait-Jacket. *San Francisco Examiner* (July 16, 1961) p. 2.

J267   Nash, Ogden. Eh? [poem]. *New Yorker*, vol. 37, no. 24 (July 29, 1961) p. 20.
Note: AG mentioned briefly in a poem.

J268   Ignatow, David. [review of *Kaddish And Other Poems*]. *New Leader,* vol. 44, no. 30 (July 31-Aug. 7, 1961) pp. 24-25.

J269   Lundkvist, Artur. Profetpoesi På Amerikanska. *Stockholms Tidningen* (Aug. 8, 1961) p. 4.

J270   Gill, John J. and Rodman, Selden. [letters to the editor]. *New York Times Book Review* (Aug. 13, 1961)
Note: In response to the review of *Kaddish And Other Poems*.

J271   McHugh, Vincent. [review of *Kaddish And Other Poems*]. *San Francisco Chronicle* (Aug. 27, 1961) This World section, p. 26.

J272   Hall, Donald. The Battle Of the Bards. *Horizon,* vol. 4, no. 1 (Sept. 1961) pp. 116-121.

J273   Adib. Life And Letters. *Times Of India* (Sept. 15, 1961)
Note: Review of *The New American Poetry* edited by Donald M. Allen, discusses AG's work.

J274   Shapiro, Harvey. [review of *Kaddish And Other Poems*]. *Midstream,* vol. 7, no. 4 (Autumn 1961) pp. 95-98.

J275   Hornick, Lita. New Trends In American Poetry. *John O'London's* (Sept. 28, 1961)

J276   Rosenberg, Harold. [review of *Kaddish And Other Poems*]. *Commentary,* vol. 31, no. 1 (Oct. 1961) pp. 349-353.

J277   Scott, N. [review of *Kaddish And Other Poems*]. *People's World,* vol. 24, no. 42 (Oct. 21, 1961) pp. 6-7.

J278   Newberry, Mike. [review of *Kaddish And Other Poems*]. *Worker,* vol. 26, no. 49 (Oct. 31, 1961) p. 5.
Note: The page that this review appears on is incorrectly labeled Nov. 7, 1961.

J279   Kinter, William. Visio Pacis: The Literature Of the Beat Generation. *Frontiers,* vol. 13, no. 3 (Nov. 1961) pp. 11-18.

J280   Bowering, George. [review of *Empty Mirror*]. *Ubyssey* (Nov. 9, 1961).

J281   Cohen, Mortimer J. [review of *Kaddish And Other Poems*]. *Jewish Exponent* (Nov. 10, 1961) p. 21.

J282   Hazel, Robert. [review of *Empty Mirror*]. *Nation,* vol. 193, no. 16 (Nov. 11, 1961) pp. 381-2.

J283   Ronnen, Meir. 'Beat' Poets Dig the Holy Land. *Jerusalem Post* (Nov. 17, 1961) p. 6.
Note: AG quoted briefly.

J284   Evron, Boaz. Leaving the Battle. *Ha-aretz* (Nov. 24, 1961) p. 3.
Note: AG quoted briefly in Hebrew only.

J285   Beatniks Visit Israel, Laud Arabs For Smoking Hashish. *Jerusalem Post And Observer* (Dec. 8, 1961)
Note: This article is based on the Nov. 17, 1961 *Jerusalem Post* article with the same quotes as printed there.

J286*   Esty, J. and Lett, P. A Mutiny Alert. *Mutiny,* vol. 4, no. 1 (Winter 1961-62) pp. 3-8.

J287*   Haselmayer, Louis A. Beat Prophet And Beat Wit. *Iowa English Yearbook,* no. 6 (1961) pp. 9-13.

J288   Corso, Gregory. Interview With Allen Ginsberg. *Journal For the Protection Of All Beings,* no. 1 (1961) pp. 21-29.
Note: AG interview format.

Corso, Gregory and Ginsberg, Allen. Interview With William Burroughs. *Journal For the Protection Of All Beings,* no. 1 (1961) pp. 79-83.
Note: AG and Corso conduct an interview with William Burroughs in an interview format.

J289   Boheme Mit Bart. *Der Spiegel,* no. 4 (1961) pp. 59-61.

Books:

J290   Ebin, David. *The Drug Experience.* New York, NY: Orion Press, 1961.
Note: AG mentioned throughout.

J291   Ehrlich, J.W. (ed.). *Howl Of the Censor.* San Carlos, CA: Nourse Publishing Co., 1961.
Note: The complete story of the 'Howl' censorship trial.

J292 Parkinson, Thomas (ed.). *A Casebook On the Beat.* New York, NY: Crowell, 1961.
Contents:
Rexroth, Kenneth. Disengagement: The Art Of the Beat Generation, pp. 179-193.
Sisk, John P. Beatniks And Tradition, pp. 194-200.
Podhoretz, Norman. The Know-Nothing Bohemians, pp. 201-212.
Van Ghent, Dorothy. Comment, pp. 213-214.
O'Neil, Paul. The Only Rebellion Around, pp. 232-246.
Ciardi, John. Epitaph For the Dead Beats, pp. 257-265.
Gaiser, Carolyn. Gregory Corso: A Poet, The Beat Way, pp. 266-275.
Parkinson, Thomas. Phenomenon Or Generation, pp. 276-290.

J293 Pivano, Fernanda. *La Balena Bianca E Altri Miti.* Italy: Mondadori, 1961.
Note: AG mentioned throughout.

J294 Rexroth, Kenneth. *Assays.* New York, NY: New Directions, 1961.

J295 Rigney, Francis J. and Smith, L. Douglas. *The Real Bohemia.* New York, NY: Basic Books, 1961.
Note: AG mentioned throughout.

1962

J296 Gold, Michael. Soviet Readers' Interests Include Lenin, Salinger. *Worker* (Feb. 18, 1962) p. 7.

J297* Katagiri, Yuzuru. Ginsberg No Katarogu No Uta/Ginsberg No Shuhen. *Subterraneans* (March 1962).

Suwa, Yu. Ginsberg O Shonon. *Subterraneans* (March 1962)

J298 Poetry In English: 1945-1962. *Time,* vol. 79, no. 10 (March 9, 1962) pp. 92-95.

J299 Crunk. The Work Of Gary Snyder. *The Sixties,* no. 6 (Spring 1962) pp. 25-42.

J300 Parthasarathy, R. Meeting Allen Ginsberg. *Writers Workshop* (May-Aug. 1962) pp. 65-66.
Note: AG quoted.

J301 R., A.S. Chiaroscuro. *Illustrated Weekly Of India* (May 6, 1962) p. 17.

J302 Vasudev, S.V. The Holy Barbarians. *Illustrated Weekly Of India* (May 27, 1962) pp. 44-45.
Note: AG quoted.

J303 Rexroth, Kenneth. S.F.: The Cool Frontier. *Nugget,* vol. 7, no. 3 (June 1962) pp. 35, 44, 50.

J304 Hollo, Anselm. Sisäisen Avaruuden Puolesta? *Suomen Sosiali Demokraatti* (July 27, 1962)
Note: AG quoted in Finnish only.

J305 Wiskari, Werner. Soviet Poet Told His Work Is Weak. *New York Times* (July 29, 1962) p. 3.

J306 Wakefield, Dan. The Prodigal Powers Of Pot. *Playboy,* vol. 9, no. 8 (Aug. 1962) pp. 51-2, 58, 103-5.
Note: AG quoted briefly about drugs.

J307   Oppen, George. [review of *Kaddish And Other Poems*]. *Poetry,* vol. 100, no. 5 (Aug. 1962) pp. 329-333.

J308   Peregrine. The Odd American. *Sunday Amrita Bazar Patrika* (Aug. 5, 1962) p. 6.
Note: AG quoted briefly about drugs.

J309   Grossman, Allen R. Allen Ginsberg: The Jew As an American Poet [review of *Kaddish And Other Poems*]. *Judaism,* vol. 11, no. 4 (Fall 1962) pp. 303-308.

J310   [review of *Kaddish And Other Poems*]. *Jewish Spectator* (Oct. 1962) p. 28.

J311   Wilson, Robert Anton. [review of *Kaddish And Other Poems*]. *Liberation,* vol. 7, no. 9 (Nov. 1962) pp. 25-26.

J312   *Three Beat Poets: Gregory Corso; Allen Ginsberg; Lawrence Ferlinghetti. An Exhibition Of Books And Manuscripts Largely From the Harris Collection Of American Poetry And Plays In Brown University Library, Nov. 1962.* Providence, RI: Brown University Library, Nov. 1962.

J313   Burnham, Geoffrey. 'The Beats' Who Are These Guys? *Brown Daily Herald,* vol. 7, no. 5 (Nov. 12, 1962) supplement, pp. 3-6.

J314   [review of *Naked Lunch* by William Burroughs]. *Time,* vol. 80, no. 22 (Nov. 30, 1962) pp. 96-7.
Note: AG is mentioned and pictured.

J315   Mottram, Eric. Beat. *Ark,* no. 33 (1962) pp. 1-7.

Books:

J316   Untermeyer, Louis (ed.). *Modern American Poetry.* New York, NY: Harcourt, Brace & World, 1962. [new and enlarged edition]
Note: AG mentioned on p. 31.

J317   Wolf, Daniel and Fancher, Edwin (eds.). *The Village Voice Reader.* Garden City, NY: Doubleday & Co., 1962.
Contents: Schleifer, Marc D. Allen Ginsberg: Here To Save Us, But Not Sure From What, pp. 43-46.
Note: AG quoted at length, first printed in *Village Voice* (Oct. 15, 1958).

1963

J318   Rosenthal, M.L. [review of *Kaddish And Other Poems*]. *Reporter,* vol. 28, no. 1 (Jan. 3, 1963) pp. 46-49.

J319   Gervis, Stephanie. William Carlos Williams (1883-1963). *Village Voice* (March 7, 1963) pp. 1, 19.

J320   Buddhists Find a Beatnik 'Spy'. *New York Times* (June 6, 1963) p. 10.

J321   Glaser, Alice. Back On the Open Road For Boys. *Esquire,* vol. 60, no. 1 [issue 356] (July 1963) pp. 48-9, 115.
Note: AG quoted briefly about Benares, India.

J322   MacCraig, Norman. [review of *Reality Sandwiches*]. *New Statesman,* vol. 66, no. 1687 (July 5, 1963) p. 20.

J323   Buddhists Find a Beatnik 'Spy'. *[Columbia College] Class Of 1948 Newsletter,*
        vol. 15, no. 2 (Aug. 1963) p. 3.
        Note: Reprinted from the *New York Times* (June 6, 1963).

J324   Burt, Douglas. [review of *Howl And Other Poems*]. *Imola News,* vol. 20, no. 8
        (Aug. 1963) p. 17.

J325   White, C. [review of *Reality Sandwiches*]. *Manchester Guardian Weekly* (Aug.
        1, 1963) p. 11.

J326   Whalen, Philip. [review of *Reality Sandwiches*]. *San Francisco Chronicle*
        (Aug. 4, 1963) This World section, p. 29.
        Note: AG quoted briefly.

J327   Pinkus, Ruth. Ginsberg Finds Rhyme To Living. *Providence* (Aug. 5, 1963)
        Note: AG quoted.

J328   Levi, Peter. [review of *Reality Sandwiches*]. *Spectator,* vol. 211, no. 7050
        (Aug. 9, 1963) pp. 179-180.

J329   Olson/Creeley/Levertov/Duncan/Ginsberg/Whalen/Avison. *Tish,* no. 21 (Sept.
        1963) pp. 1-8.
        Note: AG quoted briefly.

J330   [review of *Reality Sandwiches*]. *Times Literary Supplement,* no. 3212 (Sept. 20,
        1963) p. 706.

J331   Skelton, Robin. [review of *Reality Sandwiches*]. *Critical Survey* (Autumn
        1963) pp. 164-168.

J332   Brooks, Eugene. To Allen Ginsberg [poem]. *University Review,* vol. 30, no. 1
        (Autumn [Oct.] 1963) p. 46.

J333   Friedenberg, Walter D. Czechs Avid For Fun — Made In USA. *New York
        World Telegram And Sun* (Oct. 17, 1963)

J334   Underwood, Paul. Poets Of Prague Challenge Party. *New York Times* (Oct. 20,
        1963) p. 10.

J335   Literary Lion. *San Francisco Examiner* (Oct. 24, 1963) p. 6.
        Note: AG quoted briefly.

J336   Caen, Herb. These Foolish Things. *San Francisco Chronicle* (Oct. 29, 1963) p.
        23.
        Note: AG quoted briefly.

J337   Kobler, John. The Dangerous Magic Of LSD. *Saturday Evening Post,* vol. 236
        (Nov. 2, 1963) pp. 30-2, 35-6, 39-40.

J338   Stanley, David. A Literary Confrontation. *San Francisco Examiner* (Nov. 13,
        1963) p. 3.
        Note: AG quoted briefly.

J339   Morse, Carl. [review of *Reality Sandwiches*]. *Village Voice* (Nov. 14, 1963)
        Voice Books supplement, pp. 11, 14.

J340   Scully, James. [review of *Reality Sandwiches*]. *Nation,* vol. 197, no. 16 (Nov.
        16, 1963) pp. 329-330.

J341   Harrity, Richard. Bohemia On the Bay. *Cosmopolitan,* vol. 155, no. 6 (Dec. 1963) pp. 22-27.

J342   Fiedler, Leslie A. A Kind Of Solution: the Situation Of Poetry Now. *Kenyon Review,* vol. 26, no. 1 [issue 100] (Winter [Dec. 22, 1963] 1964) pp. 54-79.

Books:

J343   Hazo, Samuel. *Hart Crane: An Introduction And Interpretation.* New York, NY: Barnes and Noble, 1963, pp. 133-4.

J344   Jones, LeRoi. *Blues People.* New York, NY: William Morrow & Co., 1963, p. 234.

J345   Ossman, David. *The Sullen Art.* New York, NY: Corinth, 1963, pp. 87-95.
            Note: AG interview format.

1964

J346   Ignatow, David. Williams' Influence: Some Social Aspects. *Chelsea,* no. 14 (Jan. 1964) pp. 154-161.

J347   Doss, Margot Patterson. Treat Your Feet To the Beat Beat. *San Francisco Chronicle* (Jan. 26, 1964) Bonaza section, pp. 16-17.
            Note: AG quoted

J348   [review of *The Lager Letters* by William Burros and Allen Ginsberg]. *Open Space,* no. 1 (Jan. 30, 1964) p. 43.
            Note: A spoof review.

J349   Aldrich, Michael R. Footprints In the Snow. *Nassau Literary Magazine* (Feb. 1964) pp. 4-32.

J350   [photograph of AG and Paul Blackburn]. *Poetry Society Of America Bulletin* (Feb. 1964) p. 39.

J351   Spector, R.D. [review of *Reality Sandwiches*]. *Saturday Review,* vol. 48, no. 5 (Feb. 1, 1964) p. 37.

J352   Jones, Landon Y. Ginsberg Reads Beat Poetry. *Daily Princetonian* (Feb. 14, 1964) p. 1.

J353   Bishop, Gordon B. Ginsberg, Beatnik Poet, Not a Great Deal Like Other Men. *Herald-News* (Feb. 26, 1964) p. 12.
            Note: AG quoted briefly.

J354   Crawford, John F. The Beats Return. *Columbia Daily Spectator* (Feb. 27, 1964) p. 2.

J355   Brenner, Michael. Ginsberg Among the Hindus. *Graduate Student Journal,* no. 3 (Spring 1964) pp. 5-18.
            Note: AG quoted briefly.

J356   Ginsberg Bugging NYC Council To Waive License Fee For "Beat" Poetry Readers. *Paterson Evening News* (March 24, 1964)
            Note: AG quoted briefly.

J357   Harrington, Stephanie Gervis. City Puts Bomb Under Off-Beat Culture Scene. *Village Voice* (March 26, 1964) pp. 1, 14.

J358   Ginsberg, Allen and Orlovsky, Peter. Thank God .... I Wasn't a Whore Boy. *Fuck You,* no. 5, vol. 6 (April 1964) ll. [17-19].
Note: AG interview format, conversation transcription.

J359   City Softens Approach To Poets In Cafes. *Village Voice* (April 2, 1964) p. 2.

J360   Harrington, Stephanie Gervis. Lenny Bruce's Fear: He Will Run Out Of Fare To the Supreme Court. *Village Voice* (April 9, 1964) p. 6.

J361   To Get Lobbying Scratch Man, Beats Sure Howl Loud. *Square Journal* (April 9, 1964) p. 1.

J362   Smith, Michael. Drizzle Does Not Dim Ardor Of Arts Marchers. *Village Voice* (April 30, 1964) pp. 1, 11.

J363   Capp, Al. Li'l Abner [comic strip]. *Daily News* (May 1964)
Note: Several times during the month a character called the Ginzbird appears "the most irritable unidentified flying object on earth".

J364   DiPrima, Diane. Fuzz's Progress. *Nation,* vol. 198, no. 19 (May 4, 1964) pp. 463-465.
Note: Concerns the origin of the Committee On Poetry.

J365   Constable, Rosalind. New York's Avante Garde, And How It Got There. *New York Herald Tribune* (May 17, 1964) New York Magazine section, pp. 6-22.

J366   Freedland, Nat. Allen Ginsberg And the Law. *New York Herald Tribune* (May 24, 1964) New York Magazine section, pp. 14-16.
Note: Concerns the debate over poetry readings in coffee houses.

J367   Barry, Ernie. A Conversation With Allen Ginsberg. *City Lights Journal,* no. 2 ([June-Oct.] 1964) pp. 131-138.
Note: AG interview format.

J368   Random Notes. *Kauri,* no. 1 (June-July 1964) p. 5.

J369   Ammons, A.R. [review of *Reality Sandwiches*]. *Poetry,* vol. 104, no. 3 (June 1964) pp. 186-187.

J370   Buckley, Thomas. 100 Fight Arrest Of Lenny Bruce. *New York Times* (June 14, 1964) p. 75.

J371   Gleason, Ralph J. Literati Defend Lenny Bruce. *San Francisco Chronicle* (June 16, 1964) p. 41.

J372   Shapiro, Karl. A Malebolge Of 1400 Books. *Carleton Miscellany,* vol. 5, no. 3 (Summer 1964) pp. 53-55.

J373   Eckman, Fern Marja. The New Moral Climate, Article 2. *New York Post* (June 23, 1964) p. 25.
Note: AG quoted briefly.

J374   Walsh, Chad. The War Between Iambs And Ids. *Book Week* (July 26, 1964) p. 2, 9.

J375   Lubasch, Arnold H. 'Villagers' Hold a Town Meeting. *New York Times* (July 29, 1964) P. 35.
Note: AG quoted briefly.

J376   Goodman, Susan. South Villagers Cheer Koch Move On McD. St. *Village Voice* (July 30, 1964) pp. 1, 9.
Note: AG quoted briefly.

J377   Prial, Frank. 'Originale' a Wacky Show With Frenzied Story Line. *New York World-Telegram And Sun* (Aug. 9, 1964)

J378   Meyerzove, Leland S. Allen Ginsberg: Poet Of Hebraic Mysticism [review of *Howl And Other Poems; Kaddish And Other Poems; Empty Mirror, Reality Sandwiches, Yage Letters* and *Howl* (Fantasy recording)]. *Burning Bush,* no. 2 (Sept. 1964) pp. 41-56.

J379   Originale. *New York Times* (Sept. 6, 1964) p. X7.

J380   Schonberg, Harold C. Music: Stockhausen's 'Originale' Given At Judson. *New York Times* (Sept. 9, 1964) p. 46.

J381   Erotic Lives And Loves Of 'Hungry Generation'. *Blitz* (Sept. 19, 1964).

J382   Birds, Beasts, And Bach. *Newsweek,* vol. 64, no. 12 (Sept. 21, 1964) p. 80.
Note: AG mentioned and pictured in this review of the play "Originale".

J383   Dundy, Elaine. Crane, Masters, Wolfe, Etc. Slept Here. *Esquire,* vol. 62, no. 4 [issue 371] (Oct. 1964) pp. 101-2, 165-7.
Note: AG quoted briefly.

J384   Baker, Russell. Art And the Alarming Philistine Shortage. *New York Times* (Oct. 8, 1964) p. 42.

J385   Harap, Louis. Literary Breakthrough—to What? *Jewish Currents,* vol. 18, no. 10 (Nov. 1964) pp. 16-22.

J386   Brackman, Jacob R. Hipster Phantasmagoria Stuns Lowell. *Harvard Crimson,* vol. 142, no. 133 (Nov. 13, 1964) p. 1.
Note: AG quoted briefly.

J387   India: The Hungry Generation. *Time,* vol. 84, no. 21 (Nov. 20, 1964) p. 44.

J388   Brackman, Jacob R. Allen Ginsberg. *Harvard Crimson,* vol. 142, no. 142 (Nov. 24, 1964) p. 2.
Note: AG quoted briefly.

J389   Allen Ginsberg, Peter Orlovsky To Give Poetry Reading Tonight. *Justice,* vol. 17, no. 8 (Nov. 24, 1964) p. 1.

J390   Gruen, John. The New Bohemia. *New York Herald Tribune* (Nov. 29, 1964) New York Magazine section, pp. 8-13, 17, 22, 24.
Note: AG quoted.

J391   [Currier, Barbara and Mr. Keller]. Four Who Swim Through the Desert. *Columbia College Today,* vol. 12, no. 2 (Winter 1964) pp. 58-67.
Note: AG quoted.

J392   LeRoi Jones Interview. *Monmouth Letters,* vol. 7, no. 2 (Winter 1964) pp. 7-15.

J393   American Poetry After the Second World War. *Mugen* (Winter 1964).

J394   Fiedler, Leslie A. Death Of the Novel. *Ramparts,* vol. 2, no. 4 (Winter 1964) pp. 2-14.

J395*   Taylor, William. The New Poetics Or Who Shot Tennyson's Eagle? *Trace,* no. 55 (Winter 1964) pp. 109-114.

J396   Hunsberger, Bruce. Kit Smart's Howl. *Wisconsin Studies In Contemporary Literature,* vol. 6, no. 1 (Winter [Dec. 22, 1964]-Spring 1965) pp. 34-44.

J397   Whitworth, Bill. With Cymbals And Symbols. *New York Herald Tribune* (Dec. 28, 1964) p. 13.
     Note: AG quoted briefly.

J398   Demonstration Held To Protest Laws Against Marijuana. *New York Times* (Dec. 28, 1964) p. 23.

J399   Caldwell, William A. Simeon Stylites. *Bergen Evening Record* (Dec. 30, 1964).
     Note: AG quoted briefly, quotes are identical to those published in the *New York Herald Tribune* (Dec. 28, 1964).

J400   Dowden, George. Some Information On How To Write the Poem. *Iconolatre,* no. 11 (ca. 1964) pp. 5-10.

J401   Manganotti, Donatella. Aspetti Della Poesia De Allen Ginsberg. *Studi Americani,* no. 10 (1964) pp. 395-427.

J402   Jouffroy, Alain. Introduction A La "Beat Generation". *Les Temps Modernes,* vol. 20, no. 223 (1964) pp. 961-983.

Books:

J403*   Berge, Carol. *The Vancouver Report.* New York, NY: Fuck You Press, 1964.
     Note: Report on the University Of British Columbia Poetry Seminar.

J404   Dickey, James. *The Suspect In Poetry.* Madison, MN: Sixties Press, 1964, pp. 16-19.

J405   Fiedler, Leslie A. *Waiting For the End.* New York, NY: Stein & Day, 1964.
     Note: AG mentioned throughout.

J406   Pivano, Fernanda. *America Rossa E Nera.* Florence, Italy: Vallecchi Editore, 1964, pp. 278-85, 287-90, 306.

J407   Trilling, Diana. *Claremont Essays.* New York, NY: Harcourt Brace Jovanovich, 1964.
     Note: Reprint of "The Other Night At Columbia" from *Partisan Review* (Spring 1959).

J408   *Who's Who In America, 1964-1965,* vol. 33. Chicago, IL: Marquis Who's Who Inc., 1964, p. 742.
     Note: AG appears here for the first time and then in all later editions.

1965

J409   Vinkenoog, Simon. Dertig Actualiteiten. *Ratio* (Jan.-Feb. 1965) p. 32.

J410   Sorrentino, Gilbert. [review of *The Yage Letters*]. *San Francisco Chronicle* (Jan. 3, 1965) Book Week section, p. 10.

J411   People. *Time,* vol. 85, no. 2 (Jan. 8, 1965) p. 26.

J412 [photograph of AG]. *Paterson Morning Call* (Jan. 11, 1965)
Note: Often reproduced photograph of AG with poster "Pot Is a Reality Kick".

J413 Ungar, Sanford J. State Moves To Ban 'Naked Lunch'; Mailer And Ginsberg Defend Novel. *Harvard Crimson* (Jan. 14, 1965) pp. 1, 3.
Note: AG quoted briefly.

J414 Two Give Praise To 'Naked Lunch'. *Boston Herald* (Jan. 14, 1965)
Note: AG quoted briefly.

J415 Augier, Angel. Presencia De Ginsberg. *El Mundo* (Jan. 24, 1965) p. 4.

J416 Richards, Margaret. Parnassus Has Been Dissolved. *Broadside,* vol. 2, no. 5 (Jan. 26, 1965) p. 1.

Brilliant, Ashleigh E. [letter to the editor]. *Broadside,* vol. 2, no. 5 (Jan. 26, 1965) p. 2.

Editorials: Looking At Parnassus And Academic Standards. *Broadside,* vol. 2, no. 5 (Jan. 26, 1965) p. 2.

J417 Pilat, Oliver. The Marijuana Story. *New York Post* (Feb. 14, 1965) p. 24.

J418 Goldhurst, Richard. Allen Ginsberg: Poet Of Hebraic Mysticism [review of *Howl And Other Poems; Kaddish And Other Poems* and *Reality Sandwiches*]. *Carolina Israelite,* vol. 23, no. 2 (March-April 1965) pp. 1-2, 30-31.

J419 Massachusetts Moves To Ban 'Naked Lunch'. *Newsletter On Intellectual Freedom,* vol. 14, no. 2 (March 1965) p. 15.
Note: AG quoted briefly, identical to quotes in *Harvard Crimson* (Jan. 14, 1965).

J420 Na Besedes Allenem Ginsbergem. *Rude Pravo* (March 3, 1965)

J421 [photograph of AG and legend]. *Vecernik* (March 5, 1965)

J422 B., L. Wir Sprachen Mit: Allen Ginsberg. *Aufbau Und Frieden* (March 6, 1965) p. 1.
Note: AG quoted briefly in German only.

J423 Hadrabova, Olga. Vecer S Allenom Ginsbergom. *Kulturny Zivot* (March 12, 1965) p. 8.
Note: AG quoted briefly in Czech only.

J424 Allen Ginsberg In Prague. *Prague News Letter,* vol. 21, no. 8 (March 20, 1965) p. 2.
Note: AG quoted briefly.

J425 Hajek, Igor. Z Bradburyovského Sveta. *Literary Noviny,* vol. 14, no. 12 (March 20, 1965) p. 8.
Note: AG quoted briefly in Czech only.

J426 Blackman, M.C. A Guggenheim Record. *New York Herald Tribune* (March 29, 1965)

J427 Jones, Ginsberg Win Guggenheims. *New York Post* (March 29, 1965) p. 23.

J428   Vackar, Pavel. "Proc" Ginsbergo Va Smutku. *Divadelni A Filmové Noviny* (March 31, 1965) p. 8.
Note: AG interview format in Czech only.

J429   Chari, V.K. Whitman And the Beat Poets. *Emerson Society Quarterly,* no. 39 ([April-June] 1965) pp. 34-37.

J430   Meeske, Marilyn. Memoirs Of a Female Pornographer. *Esquire,* vol. 63, no. 4 (April 1965) pp. 112-115.

J431   Cistin, Jan. Skoncil Majales, At Zije Majales! *Svobodne Slovo* (May 2, 1965)

J432   Allan [sic] Ginsberg Named King Of Prague's May Day Revel. *New York Times* (May 4, 1965) p. 50.

J433   Crown For Ginsberg. *New York Times* (May 9, 1965) section IV, p. 7.

J434   F., M. Allen Ginsberg A Morálka. *Mladá Fronta,* vol. 21, no. 117 (May 16, 1965) p. 5.
Note: AG quoted briefly in Czech only.

J435   Czechs Oust Ginsberg, 'Village' Poet. *New York Times* (May 17, 1965) p. 4.

J436   Kocovinci S Ginsbergem. *Rude Pravo* (May 17, 1965)

J437   Beatnik Poet Expelled. *Times* (May 18, 1965) p. 10.

J438   Allen Ginsberg Sai Lahtea Prahasta. *Uusi Suomi* (May 18, 1965)

J439   Endrst, Jeff. How a Beat Bard Was Beaten By the Reds As Undesirable. *Paterson Morning Call* (May 20, 1965)

J440   Polish Parties. *Times Literary Supplement* (May 20, 1965)

J441   Armstrong, Allen. Cross-Legged ... With Cymbals. *Sunday Sun* (May 23, 1965) p. 1.
Note: AG quoted briefly.

J442   McGrath, Tom. Ginsberg In London. *Peace News* (May 28, 1965) pp. 6-7.
Note: AG quoted briefly.

J443   The Boston Trail Of 'Naked Lunch'. *Evergreen Review,* vol. 9, no. 36 (June 1965) pp. 40-49, 87-88.
Note: AG quoted in trial testimony.

J444   Rexroth, Kenneth. The New American Poets. *Harper's Magazine,* vol. 230, no. 1381 (June 1965) pp. 65-71.

J445   Geller, Allen. An Interview With Allen Ginsberg. *Rogue,* vol. 10, no. 3 (June 1965) pp. 35-6, 72, 80.
Note: AG interview format.

J446   Endrst, Jeff. Diary Of Ex-Paterson Beat Poet Gives Czech Press Rare Excitement. *Paterson Morning Call* (June 2, 1965) pp. 1, 12.

J447   Klingenberg, Eberhard. Allen Ginsbergs Prager Eskapaden. *Feuilleton* (June 4, 1965) pp. 19-20.

J448   The Happening. *Time,* vol. 85, no. 23 (June 4, 1965) p. 26.

J449 Poets Summon the Souls. *Manchester Guardian Weekly* (June 5, 1965).
Note: AG quoted briefly.

J450 K., M. Allen Ginsberg I Moralnosc. *ITD,* no. 23 (June 6, 1965) p. 11.
Note: AG quoted briefly in Polish only.

J451 When Ginsberg... *Observer Weekend Review* (June 6, 1965) p. 36.

J452 Bearded Beat Poet Goes Howling To the Geordies. *Telegraph* (June 6, 1965) p.
5.
Note: AG quoted briefly.

J453 Lucie-Smith, Edward. The King Of the May. *Times* (June 6, 1965) p. 43.
Note: AG quoted at length.

J454 Gathering Of the Beat Men. *Daily Express* (June 10, 1965)
Note: AG quoted briefly.

J455 Beat Poets Talking, Shakespeare Listening. *Daily Mail* (June 10, 1965)

J456 Smith, Ken. Unshy Poets Meet Press. *London Daily Worker* (June 10, 1965)
Note: AG quoted briefly.

J457 Ginsberg For Albert Hall. *Peace News,* no. 1511 (June 11, 1965) p. 12.

J458 Off Off Beat. *Sun* (June 11, 1965)
Note: AG quoted briefly.

J459 Poets, But You Wouldn't Know It. *Daily Express* (June 12, 1965)
Note: AG quoted briefly.

J460 Passingham, Kenneth. Man, Just Dig These Crazy Couplets. *Daily Sketch* (June
12, 1965) p. 7.

J461 London Listens In On the Beat Poets. *New York Post* (June 12, 1965)

J462 Poetry 'Convention' Packs London Hall. *New York Times* (June 12, 1965) p. 21.

J463 Big Audience For Beat Poets. *Times* (June 12, 1965) p. 8.

J464 Quotesmanship. *London Tribune* (June 14, 1965)
Note: AG quoted briefly.

J465 Strange Sounds And Profanity, London Meets the Beats. *San Francisco
Chronicle* (June 14, 1965) p. 6.

J466 Deppa, Joan. "Fr-r-r, Ow, Ow" Poet Ginsberg a Wow At London Convention
Of Poets. *Paterson Evening News* (June 15, 1965)

J467 Fawcett, Jo; Lawson, Andrew; Halliday, Fred and Wyatt, Ian. Beat Night At the
Albert Hall. *Isis* (June 16, 1965) pp. 30-31.

J468 Stirring Times. *Times Literary Supplement* (June 17, 1965) p. 519.

J469 McGrath, Tom. Revolutions, Flowers And Poetry. *Peace News,* no. 1512 (June
18, 1965) p. 10.
Note: AG quoted briefly.

J470   Klingenberg, E. Ginsberg's Czech Expulsion. *Censorship,* no. 3 (Summer 1965) pp. 31-33.
Note: AG quoted briefly.

J471   Pascal, Jean-Marc. Moi Bob Dylan. *Sommaire,* no. 36 (July 1965) pp. 22-5, 120.

J472   Kostelanetz, Richard. Ginsberg Makes the World Scene. *New York Times Magazine* (July 11, 1965) pp. 22-3, 27-8, 30, 32-3.
Note: AG quoted at length.

J473   After the Beat Generation. *Touchstone,* no. 1 (July 26, 1965) pp. 4-8.

J474   Fischler, Stan. East Europe Goes East Village. *Village Voice* (July 29, 1965) pp. 5, 10.

J475   Wegars, Don. UC Rallies Protest Sit-In Sentences. *San Francisco Chronicle* (July 30, 1965) p. 2.
Note: AG quoted briefly.

J476   Meyerzove, Leland. The Wandering Jew. *Idiot,* no. 1 (Aug. 1965) pp. 2, 9.

J477   Williams, Hugo. Poetry, Sold Out. *London Magazine,* vol. 5, no. 5 (Aug. 1965) pp. 95-102.

J478   Sullivan, James W. Feds Vs. Villagers. *New York Herald Tribune* (Aug. 12, 1965) pp. 1+.

J479   Allen Ginsberg. *El Mundo* (Aug. 15, 1965) p. 39.

J480   Harrington, Michael. The New Activists. *New York Herald Tribune* (Aug. 29, 1965)

J481   Horovitz, Michael. [letter to the editor]. *Times Literary Supplement* (Sept. 2, 1965) p. 761.

J482   Where Have All the Poets Gone? *Daily Mail* (Sept. 7, 1965) p. 4.

J483   Smaridge, Regina. ...Childless, Lonely Old Gruffer... *Paterson Morning Call* (Sept. 18, 1965) Home Magazine section, pp. 2-3.
Note: Interview with AG's parents.

J484   Fiedler, Leslie A. The New Mutants. *Partisan Review,* vol. 32, no. 4 (Fall 1965) pp. 505-525.

J485   Berger, Art. Walt's Sons Speak. *American Dialog,* vol. 2, no. 3 (Oct.-Nov. 1965) pp. 6-8.

Katzman, Allen. Walt Whitman And the Common Man. *American Dialog,* vol. 2, no. 3 (Oct.-Nov. 1965) pp. 9-10.

J486   Widgery, David. Conversation With... *U,* vol. 3, no. 7 (Oct. 1965) pp. 7-13.
Note: AG interview format.

J487   Robinson, Douglas. Vietnam Protest Called a Success. *New York Times* (Oct. 18, 1965) p. 7.

J488   Robertson, Bob. S. F.'s Peaceful March Against the Viet War. *San Francisco Chronicle* (Oct. 18, 1965) pp. 1, 7.

J489   Allen Ginsberg Arrested For Topless Act. *Ditto,* vol. 1, no. 1 (Oct. 19, 1965) p. 1.
Note: This is a spoof article.

J490   [letters to the editor]. *Paterson Evening News* (Oct. 28, 1965)

J491   Weston, Ronald. Wm. Burroughs. *Fact,* vol. 2, no. 6 (Nov.-Dec. 1965) p. 14.

J492   Wesling, Donald. Berkeley: Free Speech And Free Verse. *Nation,* vol. 201, no. 15 (Nov. 8, 1965) pp. 338-340.

J493   The Hell's Angels Debating Debut. *San Francisco Chronicle* (Nov. 13, 1965) p. 6.
Note: AG quoted briefly.

J494   O'Brien, William. Hell's Angels Warn VDC Against Oakland March. *San Francisco Examiner* (Nov. 13, 1965) p. 5.

J495   Oakland 'State Of Emergency'. *San Francisco Chronicle* (Nov. 19, 1965) pp. 1, 18.
Note: AG quoted briefly.

J496   Vackar, Pavel. USA Avantgarda. *Film A Doba,* no. 11 (Nov. 20, 1965) pp. 12-21.
Note: AG quoted briefly in Czech.

J497   Brier, Royce. Mr. Ginsberg Was Sparkling. *San Francisco Chronicle* (Nov. 23, 1965) p. 40.

J498   Pivano, Fernanda. La Favola Di Ginsberg. *Il Mondo* (Nov. 30, 1965) p. 10.

J499   Junker, Howard. Résumé Of the Young Man As a Non-Generation. *Esquire,* vol. 64, no. 6 [issue 385] (Dec. 1965) p. 169.

J500*   Roggeman, Willem M. Allen Ginsberg. *Vlaamse Gids,* vol. 49, no. 12 (Dec. 1965) pp. 800-804.

J501   Corville, Carol. Poet Ginsberg's Day At College Heights. *San Matean,* vol. 86, no. 9 (Dec. 3, 1965) p. 3.
Note: AG quoted briefly.

J502   Hobbs, Lisa. Bob Dylan's Idea For a Symphony. *San Francisco Examiner* (Dec. 4, 1965) p. 9.

J503   Hallgren, Dick. Portrait Of the Artists As Old Men. *San Francisco Chronicle* (Dec. 6, 1965) p. 7.

Caen, Herb. Item, Item, Hoosegotta Item? *San Francisco Chronicle* (Dec. 6, 1965) p. 31.

J504   Meehan, Thomas. Public Writers No. 1? *New York Times Magazine* (Dec. 12, 1965) pp. 44-5, 130, 132-6.

J505   Rexroth, Kenneth. The New Poetry In Fine Voice. *San Francisco Chronicle* (Dec. 12, 1965) section 2, p. 4.

J506   Gleason, Ralph J. Lenny Bruce—Funny, Sad, Sharp. *San Francisco Chronicle* (Dec. 15, 1965) p. 47.

J507* How Crazy Can You Get? Department. *Stormtrooper* (Winter 1965)
Note: This is the newsletter of the American Nazi Party.

J508 Swardson, H.R. On the Poetical. *Ohio University Review,* vol. 7 (1965) pp. 5-20.

J509 Weimann, Robert. Allen Ginsberg Das Geschlagene Glück Amerikas: Beat-Lyrik Zwischen Anarchie Engagement. *Sinn Und Form,* vol. 17, no. 3-4 (1965) pp. 718-732.

J510 Theroux, Paul. Christopher Okigbo. *Transition,* vol. 5, no. 22 (1965) pp. 18-20.

Books:

J511 *Checklists Of Separate Publications Of Poets At the First Berkeley Poetry Conference, 1965.* Berkeley, CA: Cody's Books, 1965.
Note: Early bibliography of AG titles.

J512 Dommergues, Pierre. *Les Écrivains Américains D'Aujourd'Hui.* Paris, France: Presses Universitaires De France, 1965
Note: AG mentioned throughout.

J513 Lipton, Lawrence. *The Erotic Revolution.* Los Angeles, CA: Sherbourne Press, 1965, pp. 181, 251, 291-2.

J514 Lucie-Smith, Edward. *Mystery In the Universe, Notes On an Interview With Allen Ginsberg.* London, England: Turret Books, 1965.
Note: Extensive AG quotes.

J515 Rosenthal, M.L. *The Modern Poets: A Critical Introduction.* New York, NY: Oxford University Press, 1965.

J516 Schneiderman, Harry and Karpman, Itzhak J. Carmin (eds.). *Who's Who In World Jewry, 1965.* New York, NY: Who's Who In World Jewry, 1965, p. 310.

J517 Stepanchev, Stephen. *American Poetry Since 1945.* New York, NY: Harper & Row, 1965, pp. 133, 166-174, 207.

1966

J518 [photograph of AG]. *Chicago Tribune* (Jan. 2, 1966)
Note: Unusual photograph of AG with a fashion model.

J519 Kunkin, Art. Allen Ginsberg On Everything. *Los Angeles Free Press* (Jan. 21, 1966) pp. 6-8, 10.
Note: AG conversation quotes.

J520 [note]. *Los Angeles Free Press* (Jan. 28, 1966) p. 8.
Note: Correction of interview published in Jan. 21, 1966 issue.

J521 Siciliano, Enzo. L'Urlo Del Poeta Blasfemo [review of *Jukebox All'Idrogeno*]. *L'Espresso* (Jan. 30, 1966) p. 18.

J522 Pivano, Fernanda. Il Poeta Errante. *Il Mondo* (Feb. 1, 1966) pp. 9-10.

J523 Ginsberg, Il Beat [review of *Jukebox All'Idrogeno*]. *Successo,* no. 2 (Feb. 1966)

J524   Gigli, Lorenzo. Non Scandalizza Piu Il Grido Di Ginsberg. *Gazzetta Del Popolo* (Feb. 2, 1966)

J525   Mengeling, Marvin E. Two Poetic Approaches To Freudian Materials. *English Record,* vol. 16, no. 3 (Feb. 6, 1966) pp. 19-21.

J526   Whereatt, Robert. Poet Says City Trains, Then Stifles Its Talent. *Wichita Sunday Eagle And the Wichita Beacon* (Feb. 6, 1966) pp. 1A, 5A.
Note: AG quoted briefly.

J527   Mauro, Walter. L'America Di Allen Ginsberg [review of *Jukebox All'Idrogeno*]. *Il Mattino* (Feb. 10, 1966) p. 3.

J528   Steele, Mike. Mystery Poet Puzzles Crowd. *Topeka Daily Capital* (Feb. 12, 1966) pp. 1-2.
Note: AG quoted briefly.

J529   Everett, Bart. Poet Blasts Mid-West Culture Lag. *Kansas City Star* (Feb. 13, 1966) p. 12A.
Note: AG quoted.

J530   Sells, Steve. Poet, His Audience Let Hair Down In Recital. *Wichita Eagle* (Feb. 15, 1966)
Note: AG quoted briefly.

J531   Pestelli, Leo. [review of *Jukebox All'Idrogeno*]. *La Stampa* (Feb. 16, 1966)

J532   Vigorelli, Giancarlo. Il Rimbaud D'America [review of *Jukebox All'Idrogeno*]. *Il Tempo* (Feb. 16, 1966)

J533   Britt, Kent. Police, Poets In Standoff. *Wichita Beacon* (Feb. 17, 1966) p. 4A.
Note: AG quoted.

J534   Baker, Kelley. Poet Denies 'Beat' Reputation. *Daily Nebraskan* (Feb. 18, 1966) p. 1.
Note: AG quoted.

J535   Ferrari, Luciano. [review of *Jukebox All'Idrogeno*]. *La Notte* (Feb. 18, 1966) p. 4.

J536   Morris, Julie. Beat 'Poet Laureate' Jams Union Ballroom. *Daily Nebraskan* (Feb. 19, 1966) p. 4.
Note: AG quoted briefly.

Poet Impresses English Faculty. *Daily Nebraskan* (Feb. 19, 1966) p. 4.

J537   3,000 Listen To Beat Poet. *Lincoln Journal* (Feb. 19, 1966)

J538   Groetzinger, Deanna. 'I Am What I Am' Is View Of Beatniks' Poet Laureate. *Omaha World Herald* (Feb. 19, 1966)
Note: AG quoted briefly.

J539   Philosophy Club To Sponsor Beat Poet, Allen Ginsberg. *Wichita State Sunflower* (Feb. 21, 1966)
Note: AG quoted briefly.

J540   Garrity, Can. A Poet's Pilgrimage... *Wichita State Sunflower* (Feb. 22, 1966) p. 5.
Note: AG quoted at length.

J541   Kozicharow, Eugene. His Poetry Loud And Clear. *Kansas City Times* (Feb. 24, 1966)

J542   Meocci, Antonio. [review of *Jukebox All'Idrogeno*]. *La Piera Letterarice* (Feb. 24, 1966) p. 15.

J543   Martini, Carlo. Un Poeta Che Protesta Per I Giovani Scontenti. *L'Unione Sarda* (Feb. 24, 1966) p. 3.

J544   Baldacci, Luigi. Ginsberg Vuole Convertire Il Mondo Alla Poesia [review of *Jukebox All'Idrogeno*]. *Epoca* (Feb. 27, 1966)

J545   Rexroth, Kenneth. A Hope For Poetry. *Holiday,* vol. 39, no. 3 (March 1966) pp. 147-151.

J546   Pivano, Fernanda. La Libreria Della Pace. *Il Mondo* (March 1, 1966) p. 5.

J547   McNelly, Jane. 'Gospel Of Ginsberg' Heard By Audience In Ballantine. *Indiana Daily Student* (March 2, 1966)
Note: AG quoted briefly.

J548   Who Is To Blame? *Indiana Daily Student* (March 3, 1966) p. 4.

J549   Mitchell, Pam and Shafer, Sheldon. Bodine: No 'Witch Hunt'. *Indiana Daily Student* (March 4, 1966)

J550   B., L. I "Beatniks" D'America Nelle Poesie Di Ginsberg. *L'Unita* (March 6, 1966) p. 8.

J551   Kelly, Denis. Ginsberg, Poetic Prophecy Or Pornography? *Spectator,* vol. 1, no. 5 (March 7, 1966) pp. 1, 12.
Note: AG quoted briefly.

Warden, Jon. Ginsberg, Poetic Prophecy Or Pornography? *Spectator,* vol. 1, no. 5 (March 7, 1966) pp. 1, 12.
Note: Grouped under the same title as the previous article, this article does not quote AG.

J552   Sala, Alberico. Ribelle Con Borsa Di Studio [review of *Jukebox All'Idrogeno*]. *Corriere D'Informazione* (March 11-12, 1966)

J553   Ginsberg & Hawkins Featured In Final Two Days Of Festival. *Spectrum* (March 11, 1966) p. 1.

The Bard Of the Ganges To Visit Campus By Night. *Spectrum* (March 11, 1966)

J554   Kriegel, Martin D. Roundabout. *Spectrum* (March 15, 1966) p. 7.

J555   Knief, William D. Ginsberg, pt. 1. *Cottonwood Review,* vol. 1, no. 2 (Spring 1966) pp. 3-10.
Note: AG interview format.

J556   Pacini, Marcello. Jukebox All'Idrogeno [review of *Jukebox All'Idrogeno*]. *La Nazione* (March 22, 1966)

J557   Clark, Thomas. Allen Ginsberg, an Interview. *Paris Review,* vol. 10, no. 37 (Spring 1966) pp. 12-55.
Note: AG interview format.

J558 Fishman, Gail R. The Ginsbergs (Father, Son), Poetry Aces, To Duel With Poems At 30 Paces. *Paterson Evening News* (March 25, 1966) p. 2.

J559 Levin, Jay. The Ginsbergs Will Battle It Out In Verse. *New York Post* (March 30, 1966)

J560 [photograph with legend]. *East Village Other,* vol. 1, no. 9 (April 1-15, 1966) p. 1.
Note: AG quoted briefly.

J561 Dommergues, Pierre. Les Intellectuels Dans La Societe Americaine. *Le Monde* (April 1966)

J562 Gilroy, Harry. Poetry Society Hears Ginsbergs. *New York Times* (April 1, 1966) p. 27.
Note: AG quoted briefly.

J563 McTernan, William. Father And Pun! *Newark Evening News* (April 1, 1966) p. 25.

J564 The March 31st Meeting. *Poetry Society Of America Bulletin* (April 1966) pp. 3-10.

J565 Canaday, John. Art: Like the Stumpy Crocus, Rather Encouraging. *New York Times* (April 2, 1966)

J566 Deale, Ellen Vonden. Ginsbergs Draw In Poetry Battle. *Paterson Evening News* (April 2, 1966)

J567 Fishman, Gail R. The Ginsbergs May Do It Again. *Paterson Evening News* (April 5, 1966)

J568 Graziosi, Giancarlo. La Nuova America Canta Nei Versi Di Allen Ginsberg [review of *Jukebox All'Idrogeno*]. *Il Gazzettino* (April 6, 1966) p. 3.

J569 Porter, G. Bruce. LSD Booster Presents His Side. *New York World-Telegram And Sun* (April 6, 1966)

J570 Ginsberg And Son. *Newsweek,* vol. 67, no. 15 (April 11, 1966) p. 63.

J571 U.S. Plot To 'Set Up' Ginsberg For Arrest Is Described To Jury. *New York Times* (April 14, 1966) p. 35.
Note: AG quoted briefly.

J572 Levin, Jay. Jazzman Who Accused Feds Is Convicted. *New York Post* (April 15, 1966)
Note: AG quoted briefly.

J573 Yuncker, Barbara. LSD: Who Takes It And Why? Is It Really a Menace? *New York Post* (April 17, 1966) p. 29.
Note: AG quoted briefly.

J574 Kastner, Susan. The Avant Garde Organizes To Fight City Hall. *New York Post* (April 19, 1966) p. 19.
Note: AG quoted briefly.

J575 Zion, Sidney E. Avant Garde Group Charges Harassment By City. *New York Times* (April 19, 1966) p. 32.
Note: AG quoted briefly.

J576   Orlando, Ruggero. I Paradisi Scientifici. *L'Europeo,* vol. 22, no. 17 (April 21, 1966)

J577   MacAdams, Lewis. Allen Ginsberg/John Wieners. *Response* (April 22-23, 1966) p. 20.

J578   Pellaton, Jacqueline. 'Response' Panel Rambles Through Night Of Effluvia. *Sunday Times Advertiser* (April 24, 1966)
Note: AG quoted.

J579   Sullivan, Dan. Ivy Leaguers Ask What's Happening. *New York Times* (April 25, 1966) p. 34.

J580   Graeff, Ron. Ginsberg Stirs Overflow Crowd. *Daily Orange,* vol. 63, no. 108 (April 27, 1966) p. 1.

J581   Zion, Sidney E. Lindsay Placates Coffeehouse Set. *New York Times* (May 3, 1966) p. 49.
Note: AG quoted briefly.

J582   Aarons, Leroy F. Poet Allen Ginsberg Hies To the Capitol To Sing the Glory Of Legalized Weed. *Washington Post* (May 8, 1966) section A, pp. A1, A9.
Note: AG quoted.

J583   George, Gerald. Why Sparks Fly Over Mind-Altering Drug. *National Observer* (May 9, 1966) p. 26.

J584   Morrison, Michael. 16 Writers And Poets Stage Read-In For Viet Nam Peace. *Philadelphia Evening Bulletin* (May 9, 1966)

J585   Klimcke, Alfred P. Poets Employ Vivid Imagery At Penn To Denounce Vietnam War. *Philadelphia Inquirer* (May 9, 1966) p. 5.

J586   Jones, Landon Y., Jr. 'Response' 1966. *Princeton Alumni Weekly,* vol. 66, no. 26 (May 17, 1966) pp. 6-9.
Note: AG quoted briefly.

J587   Nadle, Marlene. Allen Ginsberg: Hustler For Life. *Village Voice* (May 26, 1966) pp. 1, 13-14.
Note: AG quoted at length.

J588   Farrell, Barry. The Guru Comes To Kansas. *Life,* vol. 60, no. 21 (May 27, 1966) pp. 78-80, 83-6, 89-90.
Note: AG quoted briefly.

J589   Prusnek, Judy. Poet-Idol Of Hip Set Reads For 650 At WRU. *Cleveland Press* (June 9, 1966)
Note: AG quoted briefly.

J590   Fried, Philip. Ginsberg Chants Mantras, Reads Poems To Full House. *Antioch College Record,* vol. 21, no. 45 (June 10, 1966) p. 1.

J591   Simons, Jeannie. Hark! Ginsberg Calls All Beards. *Cleveland Plain Dealer* (June 10, 1966) p. 17.

J592   'An Echo Of Silence' Is Noted. *San Francisco Chronicle* (June 14, 1966) p. 17.

J593   Marine On Pills Shot Viet Allies. *Cleveland Plain Dealer* (June 15, 1966)

J594 Healy, Paul. Vows 10,000 GIs Are Addicts. *Daily News* (June 15, 1966) p. 5.
Note: AG quoted briefly. The same article is printed in another edition of this newspaper under the title "Narcotics Expert At Ouiz Calls 10,000 GIs Addicts".

J595 Shuster, Alvin. Addict Says He Shot 2 South Vietnamese While 'High'. *New York Times* (June 15, 1966) pp. 1, 28.
Note: AG quoted briefly.

J596 Ginsberg's LSD Lecture To Senators. *San Francisco Chronicle* (June 15, 1966) pp. 1, 13.
Note: AG quoted.

Poet Claims LSD Tamed the Angels. *San Francisco Chronicle* (June 15, 1966) p. 13.
Note: AG quoted briefly.

J597 White, Jean M. Senators Hear Ginsberg, Poet Of Pot, But Indicate They Agree With Him Not. *Washington Post* (June 15, 1966) pp. A1, A7.
Note: AG quoted briefly.

J598 Troops Shot By Viet Vet On Pep Pills. *Wichita Eagle* (June 15, 1966) pp. 1, 12A.
Note: AG quoted briefly.

J599 Pallottelli, Duilio. Ci Salverà La Marijuana. *L'Europeo,* vol. 22, no. 25 (June 16, 1966) pp. 76-79.
Note: AG interview format in Italian only.

J600 Sylvester, Robert. Dream Street. *Daily News* (June 17, 1966) p. 72.

J601 Kastner, Susan. Arthur Miller On the Power Of the P.E.N. *New York Post* (June 17, 1966) p. 23.

J602 McNeill, Don. Ginsberg In Washington: Lobbying For Tenderness. *Village Voice* (June 23, 1966) pp. 13, 33.
Note: AG quoted at length.

J603 Bowart, Walter H. LSD Crosses Delaware. *East Village Other,* vol. 1, no. 15 (July 1-15, 1966) pp. 1, 7.
Note: AG quoted briefly.

J604 Gleason, Ralph J. New Front Opened By the Artists. *San Francisco Chronicle* (July 15, 1966) p. 45.

J605 Hallgren, Dick. Arthur Fiedler Sets a Welcome. *San Francisco Chronicle* (July 16, 1966) p. 2.

J606 Everett, Bart. LSD: Insight Into Depths Of the Mind. *Kansas City Star* (July 20, 1966) p. 10A.
Note: AG quoted briefly.

J607 Gleason, Ralph J. An Old Joint That's Really Jumpin'. *San Francisco Chronicle* (July 20, 1966) p. 39.

J608 Everett, Bart. Users Of Psychedelic Drugs Defend Mystic Cult. *Kansas City Star* (July 21, 1966) p. 6.
Note: AG quoted.

J609   LeRoi Jones Freed In Bail In Assault; Ginsberg Puts It Up. *New York Times* (July 31, 1966) p. 55.

J610   LeRoi Jones Denies His Bail Was Paid By Allen Ginsberg. *New York Times* (Aug. 1, 1966) p. 24.

J611   Tallmer, Jerry. Rebellion In the Arts, Part 5, Mixed Media. *New York Post* (Aug. 5, 1966) p. 33.
Note: AG quoted at length.

J612   Tallmer, Jerry. Rebellion In the Arts, Part 6, Toward a New Odets? *New York Post* (Aug. 6, 1966) p. 25.
Note: AG quoted at length.

J613   Prial, Frank. 'Originale' A Wacky Show With Frenzied Story Line. *New York World-Telegram And Sun* (Aug. 9, 1966)

J614   Tallmer, Jerry. Village Salutes Lenny Bruce. *New York Post* (Aug. 13, 1966) p. 3.

J615   Rosenthal, M.L. Poet And Public Figure. *New York Times Book Review* (Aug. 14, 1966) section VII, pp. 4-5, 28, 30.

J616   Grady, John. Ginsberg's Poetic Plea In LSD Issue Cheered. *Champaign-Urbana Courier* (Aug. 25, 1966) p. 3.
Note: AG quoted briefly.

J617   Ginsberg. *Congress Conservative,* vol. 3, no. 4 (Aug. 25, 1966) p. 1.

J618   Semas, Phil. Allan [sic] Ginsberg, Spokesman For Pot. *Congress News,* vol. 4, no. 3 (Aug. 25, 1966) p. 3.
Note: AG quoted briefly.

J619   Randal, Jonathan. Poet And U.S. Aide Back Drug Study. *New York Times* (Aug. 25, 1966) p. 31.
Note: AG quoted briefly.

J620   Cassidy, Joe. Poet Proves Park Is a 4-Letter Word. *Daily News* (Aug. 29, 1966) pp. 3, 18.
Note: There are 3 different versions of this article in 3 different editions of the newspaper, the second was changed after AG telephoned a complaint.

J621   Krim, Seymour. Beat Poets' Verse Is Blankety-Blank. *New York Post* (Aug. 29, 1966) p. 11.

J622   Pardi, Francesca. L'Urlo De Allen Ginsberg. *Nuova Antologia,* vol. 498 (Sept.-Oct. 1966) pp. 200-219.

J623   Jerome, Judson. Poetry How And Why. *Writer's Digest* (Sept. 1966) pp. 16-23, 94.
Note: AG quoted briefly.

J624   Wagner, David F. [review of *Allen Ginsberg Reads Kaddish* (recording)]. *Sunday Post-Crescent* (Sept. 4, 1966) p. S-22.

J625   Square Deal. *Newsweek,* vol. 68, no. 11 (Sept. 12, 1966) p. 53.
Note: AG quoted briefly.

J626   Ginsberg Sings, Recites Poetry To Another Bearded Alan. *Paterson Evening News* (Sept. 13, 1966) p. 36.
            Note: AG quoted.

J627   Liston, Carol. Unitarians To Ask Arts And Business Focus On Religion. *Boston Globe* (Sept. 29, 1966)

J628   Bowart, Walter. Provocation Politics. *East Village Other,* vol. 1, no. 21 (Oct. 1-15, 1966) p. 14.
            Note: AG interview format.

J629   Kotlowitz, Robert. [review of *Allen Ginsberg Reads Kaddish* (recording)]. *Harper's Magazine,* vol. 233, no. 1397 (Oct. 1966) pp. 134-135.

J630   Kostelanetz, Richard. Portrait Of Allen Ginsberg. *Jewish Digest,* vol. 11, no. 1 (Oct. 1966) pp. 32-36.
            Note: AG quoted briefly in this condensation of an article appearing in *New York Times Magazine* (July 11, 1965).

J631   A Pair Of Poets. *Rutgers Alumni Monthly* (Oct. 1966) p. 6.

J632   Menarini, Gianni. Intervista Con Allen Ginsberg. *Il Tarocco,* vol. 2, no. 3-4 (Oct. 1966) pp. 31-43.
            Note: AG interview format in Italian only.

J633   Sikes, James R. Swami's Flock Chants In Park To Find Ecstasy. *New York Times* (Oct. 10, 1966) p. 24.
            Note: AG quoted briefly.

J634   Carr, Mary F. and Kennelly, Judy. Ginsburg [sic] Con Expressioso. *Gothic Times,* vol. 1, no. 2 (Oct. 14, 1966) p. 3.
            Note: AG interview format.

J635   Pearl, Mike. The Mystery Of Folk Singer Bob Dylan. *World Journal Tribune* (Oct. 14, 1966) p. 3.
            Note: AG quoted briefly.

J636   Wade, David. Rabkin On Ginsberg Packs Hillel. *Spectator* (Oct. 17, 1966) pp. 1, 13.

J637   Haupt, Arthur. Allen Ginsberg Recites And Discusses Life In the Environs Of Spaulding And Thayer. *Dartmouth,* vol. 126, no. 18 (Oct. 18, 1966) pp. 1, 3.
            Note: AG quoted briefly.

J638   Leopold, Evelyn. A Homecoming For Allen. *Paterson Morning Call* (Oct. 24, 1966) p. 5.
            Note: AG quoted briefly.

J639   Weglein, Walter. The Poets Ginsberg Share Stage Here To SRO Audience. *Paterson Evening News* (Oct. 24, 1966)
            Note: AG quoted briefly.

J640   Ginsberg's Life With Father Goes To Pot. *Daily News* (Oct. 25, 1966) p. 38.
            Note: AG quoted briefly.

J641   Paterson Threatens To Arrest Ginsberg Over 'Marijuana'. *New York Times* (Oct. 25, 1966) p. 47C.
            Note: AG quoted briefly, the Late City Edition of the newspaper has different text.

J642   Bishop, Gordon. Police Want Ginsberg For Smoking Marijuana. *Passaic Herald-News* (Oct. 25, 1966) pp. 1-2.
Note: AG quoted briefly.

J643   Allen Ginsberg Hopes That City Will Go Back To Sleep. *Paterson Evening News* (Oct. 25, 1966) pp. 1, 18.
Note: AG quoted briefly.

The Strange World Of Allen G. *Paterson Evening News* (Oct. 25, 1966)

J644   Sotnick, Barton. Paterson Charges Poet With Smoking Marijuana. *Paterson Morning Call* (Oct. 25, 1966) pp. 1, 12.
Note: AG quoted briefly.

J645   Ginsberg Not Only Beard Wearer, Paterson Discovers. *Passaic Herald-News* (Oct. 26, 1966)
Note: AG quoted briefly.

J646   Sotnick, Barton. Cops Do Ginsberg Double-Take. *Paterson Morning Call* (Oct. 26, 1966) pp. 1, 28.

J647   Schwartz, Eugene. A Talk With Ginsberg. *Columbia Daily Spectator* (Oct. 27, 1966) Supplement, p. S-4.
Note: AG interview format.

J648   Voice Of the People: Brickbat And Bouquets For Ginsberg. *Paterson Evening News* (Oct. 28, 1966)

J649   Knief, William D. Ginsberg, Pt. II. *Cottonwood Review,* vol. 1, no. 3 (Nov. 1966) pp. 3-11.
Note: AG interview format.

J650   Moyano, Maricla. Life Delights In Life: The Beat Generation. *Vassar Review* (Nov. 1966) pp. 10-13.

J651   Callahan, John P. 25,000 War Critics Stage Rally Here. *New York Times* (Nov. 6, 1966) p. 42.
Note: AG quoted briefly.

J652   Ray Bremser: Jazz Poet. *In New York,* vol. 1, no. 14 (Nov. 7, 1966) pp. 24-28.

J653   Falls From On High. *Newsweek,* vol. 68, no. 19 (Nov. 7, 1966) p. 64.
Note: AG quoted briefly.

J654   McNeill, Don. Skates, Banners, Bells In Weekend Peace March. *Village Voice* (Nov. 10, 1966) pp. 13, 18.

J655   Ginsberg Haverford Sutra. *Haverford News* (Nov. 11, 1966) pp. 7-10.
Note: AG interview format.

J656   Morse, Jim. 'Poet Of Pot' Urges Orgies On Common. *Boston Herald* (Nov. 13, 1966) p. 52.
Note: AG quoted.

J657   Miles. Fulcrum. *International Times,* no. 3 (Nov. 14-27, 1966) p. 3.

J658   Kelly, Kevin. Ginsburg [sic] As a Guru. *Boston Globe* (Nov. 15, 1966)
Note: AG quoted briefly.

J659   Berg, Paul. Poet Of the "Improper": Poet Ginsberg And His Pad. *St. Louis Post-Dispatch* (Nov. 20, 1966) Pictures section, pp. 1-5.
Note: AG quoted briefly.

J660   Monsanto, Mendes [pseudo. of Lawrence Ferlinghetti]. The Little Presses — Courageous Discoverers. *San Francisco Chronicle* (Nov. 20, 1966) This World section, p. 49.

J661   Hicklin, Ralph. Ginsberg Asks LSD For All. *Globe And Mail* (Nov. 21, 1966) p. 14.
Note: AG quoted at length.

J662   Schwartz, Eugene. Notes On a Reading. *Columbia Daily Spectator* (Nov. 23-25, 1966)
Note: AG quoted briefly.

J663   Orgy On the Common. *Manchester Union Leader* (Nov. 26, 1966)
Note: AG is mentioned here, but not by name.

J664   The Everywhere Generation. *Newsweek,* vol. 68, no. 22 (Nov. 28, 1966) p. 43-48.

J665   Ginsberg, Allen and Corso, Gregory. La Douce Machine À Écrire. *Apparatus* (Dec. 1966) pp. 21-24.
Note: Translation by Jean-Jacques Lebel into French of an interview with William Burroughs that appeared first in *Journal For the Protection Of All Beings* (1961).

J666   Arrivals And Departures. *Boston Magazine,* vol. 58, no. 12 (Dec. 1966) pp. 27-29.
Note: AG quoted briefly.

J667   Patterson, Pat. Underground Uprising. *In New York,* vol. 1, no. 18 (Dec. 1966-Jan. 1967) pp. 10-14, 18.

J668   What Allen Ginsberg Said To Dr. Fox. *Innerspace,* vol. 1, no. 3 (Dec. 1966) pp. [5-7].
Note: AG quoted at length.

J669   Kremer, Robert. Interview With Ginsberg. *Notes From the Garage Door,* vol. 3, no. 1 (Dec. 1966) pp. 12-15.
Note: AG interview format.

J670   Jackson, Nancy Beth. Poet's Day: 'From Bed To Verse'. *Miami Herald* (Dec. 2, 1966)

J671   Bellingham, Bruce. Poet Allen Ginsberg Expresses His Ideas In Exclusive Northern Star Interview. *Northern Star,* vol. 12, no. 3 [issue also identified as vol. 13] (Dec. 9, 1966) p. 3.
Note: AG interview format.

J672   Ginsberg [Louis] Elected To Top Board Of Poetry Society. *Paterson Evening News* (Dec. 16, 1966)

J673   Shelton, Robert. Indian Raga Music Gains In Popularity Across U.S. *New York Times* (Dec. 20, 1966) p. 57.

J674   Loriga, Vincenzo. Il Caso Ginsberg: Origgonti Della Nuova Poesia. *Elsinore,* vol. 3, no. 21-22 (1966) pp. 72-79.

J675   Holt, John. On AG At Kansas And Related Topics. *Grist,* no. 6 (ca. 1966) unpaged.

Books:

J676*   Alvarez, A. Introduction: The New Poetry Or Beyond the Gentility Principle (in) Alvarez, A. (ed.). *The New Poetry.* London, England: Penguin, 1966, pp. 21-32.

J677   Burroughs, William. *Naked Lunch.* New York, NY: Grove Press [First Evergreen Black Cat Edition], 1966, pp. xviii-xxxiv.
    Note: Includes excerpts from AG's testimony at the Boston obscenity trial.

J678   Dembo, Lawrence S. *Conceptions Of Reality In Modern American Poetry.* Berkeley, CA: University Of California Press, 1966, pp. 80, 217-8.

J679   Gruen, John. *The New Bohemia.* New York, NY: Shorecrest, 1966, pp. 52, 54.
    Note: AG quoted briefly in this reprint from *New York Herald Tribune* (Nov. 29, 1964).

J680   *The Narcotic Rehabilitation Act Of 1966.* Hearings before a Special Subcommittee of the Committee on the Judiciary. United States Senate. 89th Congress. Second Session. Pursuant To S. Res. 199 Eighty-Ninth Congress on S. 2113, S. 2114, S. 2152 and LSD And Marihuana Use on College Campuses. Jan. 25, 26, and 27, May 12, 13, 19, 23, and 25, June 14, and 15, July 19, 1966. Printed for the use of the Committee on the Judiciary. Washington, DC: U.S. Government Printing Office, 1966.
    Note: Statement Of Allen Ginsberg, Poet, New York City, pp. 487-509. Tuesday, June 14, 1966, Afternoon Session. Questioned by Senators Javits and Burdick.

J681   Rahv, Philip (ed.). *Modern Occasions.* New York, NY: Farrar, Straus and Giroux, 1966.
    Contents: Donadio, Stephen. Some Younger Poets In America, pp. 226-246.

J682   Roy, Gregor. *Beat Literature.* New York, NY: Monarch Press, 1966.
    Note: AG mentioned throughout.

J683   Solomon, David (ed.). *The Marihuana Papers.* Indianapolis, IN: Bobbs-Merrill, 1966.
    Note: AG mentioned throughout.

J684   Wakefield, Dan. *Between the Lines.* Boston, MA: Little, Brown & Co., 1966, p. 214.
    Note: AG quoted briefly.

J685   Widgery, David. Gesprekken Met Allen Ginsberg (in) Ginsberg, Allen. *Proef M'n Tong In Je Oor.* Amsterdam, Holland: De Bezige Bij, 1966.
    Note: AG interview format translated by Simon Vinkenoog in Dutch only.

1967

J686   Rader, Jack. [letter to Allen Ginsberg]. *East Village Other,* vol. 2, no. 3 (Jan. 1-15, 1967) p. 2.

J687   Brandon, Henry. The New Left And the 'Hippies' Are Motivated. *Sunday Times* (Jan. 29, 1967)

J688   Changes. *City Of San Francisco Oracle,* vol. 1, no. 7 (Feb. 1967) pp. 2-3, 6-17, 29-34, 40-41.
Note: Interview format with Alan Watts, Timothy Leary, Gary Snyder and AG.

J689   Ginzap Raps. *Berkeley Barb,* vol. 4, no. 5 [issue 77] (Feb. 3, 1967) p. 3.

J690   Dropouts With a Mission. *Newsweek,* vol. 69, no. 6 (Feb. 6, 1967) pp. 92-95.

J691   Dunford, Gary. The Fugs Turned 'em All On... *Toronto Daily Star* (Feb. 13, 1967) pp. 1, 4.
Note: AG quoted briefly.

Thomas, Ralph. Sex (Psychedelic Or Otherwise) Was the Message. *Toronto Daily Star* (Feb. 13, 1967) p. 18.

J692   Cobb, David. The Fugs And Ginsberg. *Toronto Telegram* (Feb. 13, 1967).

J693   Marquette Bars Ginsberg From Fine Arts Festival. *New York Times* (Feb. 15, 1967) p. 32.

J694   Gold, Herbert. Where the Action Is. *New York Times Book Review* (Feb. 19, 1967) pp. 1, 50-52.

J695   McNeill, Don. An Opening To the West: Ashram On Hudson St. *Village Voice* (Feb. 23, 1967) pp. 1, 12.
Note: AG quoted briefly.

J696   James, George. The Poet And the Law: The Way It Was. *Paterson Morning Call* (Feb. 25, 1967) pp. 4-5.
Note: AG quoted briefly.

J697   Editorial. *Chicago Maroon,* vol. 76, no. 42 (Feb. 28, 1967) p. 5.

Star, Leanne. Ginsberg: Poetry Or Bull? *Chicago Maroon,* vol. 76, no. 42 (Feb. 28, 1967) p. 7.
Note: AG quoted briefly.

J698   Gilbert, Richard. London's Other Underground. *Town,* vol. 8, no. 3 (March 1967) pp. 28-33.

J699   Bishop, Gordon. Louis, Allen Ginsberg Hail Poetry With Puns And Chants. *Passaic Herald-News* (March 20, 1967)
Note: AG quoted briefly.

J700   Nowlan, Alden. They Came To Hear the Cat Blow. *Evening Times-Globe* (March 27, 1967) p. 1.

Nowlan, Alden. Ginsberg: 'Truth Is a Five-Letter Word'. *Evening Times-Globe* (March 27, 1967) p. 5.
Note: AG quoted at length.

J701   Nowlan, Alden. They Came To Hear the Cat Blow. *Telegraph-Journal* (March 27, 1967) p. 1.
Note: An identical article to the *Evening Times-Globe* (March 27, 1967).

Nowlan, Alden. Ginsberg: 'Truth Is a Five-Letter Word'. *Telegraph-Journal* (March 27, 1967) p. 5.
Note: AG quoted briefly in an identical article to the *Evening Times-Globe* (March 27, 1967).

J702   Micklin. Howls On the High Road To Nirvana. *Newsday* (March 28, 1967) p. 3A.

J703   Allen Ginsberg. *Impact,* no. 4 (April 1967) p. 28.

J704   Drug Committee Sponsors Evening Talk In Theater. *Heights Daily News,* vol. 36, no. 83 (April 4, 1967) p. 1.

J705   Lewando, Isabel. News Of Ogunquit. *York County Coast Star* (April 5, 1967)

J706   Ginsberg Due For Hopkins Reading. *Baltimore Sun* (April 6, 1967)

J707   Sabel, Brad. IMPACT To Probe Individual's Dilemma. *Vanderbilt Hustler* (April 7, 1967) p. 1.

J708   Goodhue, Huntly. Ginsberg Address Pending. *Vanguard,* vol. 22, no. 23 (April 7, 1967) pp. 1-2.

Faculty Say 'Yeh! Yeh!'. *Vanguard,* vol. 22, no. 23 (April 7, 1967) p. 1.

J709   Kushner, Trucia D. Banana Fad Splits Seer, Psychiatrist. *Patriot Ledger* (April 8, 1967) p. 3.
Note: AG quoted.

J710   Clark, Margie. At ETSU Monday: The 'Poet Of Pot'. *Kingsport Times News* (April 9, 1967) pp. 1, 12.

J711   Sutherland, Frank. Impact Hears 'Power' Call. *Nashville Tennessean* (April 9, 1967) pp. 1-2.
Note: AG quoted briefly.

Sutherland, Frank and Haile, John. Black Power Need Told. *Nashville Tennessean* (April 9, 1967) pp. 1, 6.
Note: AG quoted briefly.

J712   ETSU Students Call Off Ginsberg Plans. *Kingsport Times News* (April 10, 1967) p. 1.

J713   Linville, Jack. Controversial Figure Speaks In Johnson City. *Johnson City Press-Chronicle* (April 11, 1967) p. 12.
Note: AG quoted briefly.

J714   Graves Incidents Raciaux. *Le Monde* (April 11, 1967) p. 24.

J715   Porche, Verandah. Now Is the Time For Prophecy. *Boston University News,* vol. 51, no. 24 (April 12, 1967) pp. 3-4.
Note: AG quoted briefly.

J716   Poet Ginsberg Plans To Rescue Poet Levy. *Cleveland Press* (April 12, 1967) p. A6.
Note: AG quoted briefly.

J717   Zaremba, Chuck. Ginsberg To Read Today. *Daily Trojan* (April 13, 1967) p. 1.

J718   Ginsberg's Poetry Indicts Acquiescence To War. *Evening Sun* (April 13, 1967)
Note: AG quoted briefly.

J719   Ewegen, Bob. Ginsberg To Read Poetry In Macky. *Colorado Daily* (April 14, 1967) p. 3.

J720   Dicke, Bill. Ginsberg Worship: Poet In Alumni Park. *Daily Trojan* (April 14, 1967) p. 1.
Note: AG quoted briefly.

J721   Allen Ginsberg To Give Reading. *Daily Texan* (April 15, 1967)

J722   Ginsberg Entrances Incense Burners. *Colorado Daily* (April 17, 1967) p. 1.

J723   Ginsberg To Be Here Tuesday. *Daily Texan* (April 18, 1967)

J724   Zinsser, William K. The Love Hippies. *Look,* vol. 31, no. 8 (April 18, 1967) p. 4.

J725   Bullard, Paula. Ginsberg Entertains, Enchants Varied Spectators In Theater. *Daily Texan* (April 19, 1967)

J726   Cox, Harvey. An Open Letter To Allen Ginsberg. *Commonweal,* vol. 86, no. 5 (April 21, 1967) pp. 147-149.
Note: AG quoted briefly.

J727   Taylor, Mary Ross. I Dated Ginsberg. *Dirty We'Jun* (April 24, 1967) pp. 25-32.
Note: AG quoted briefly.

J728   Poison Pen Pals. *Writer's Forum,* vol. 3, no. 4 (Spring [April 24] 1967) p. 37.
Note: AG quoted briefly.

J729   Vinkenoog, Simon. Chappaqua [review of film]. *International Times,* no. 12 (April 28-May 12, 1967) pp. 5, 9.

   Beat Teachers. *International Times,* no. 12 (April 28-May 12, 1967) p. 11.

J730   Johnson, Pat. Destiny Of Dissent. *Vanderbilt Hustler,* vol. 78, no. 31 (April 28, 1967) p. 1.

J731   Il Fermo Di Ginsberg. *L'Espresso* (ca. May 1967)
Note: AG quoted briefly in Italian only.

J732   Bernard, Sidney. An Interview With Leroi Jones. *Literary Times,* vol. 4, no. 6 (Spring [May-June] 1967) p. 19.

J733   Prophet-King To Reign On Kenyon Scene. *Kenyon Collegian,* vol. 93, no. 21 (May 5, 1967) pp. 1, 6.

J734   Ginsberg Packs 'em In. *Long Island Press* (May 5, 1967) p. 7.
Note: AG quoted briefly.

J735   Ginsberg Discusses Open City Concept. *Open City,* vol. 2, no. 1 (May 5-11, 1967) p. 2.
Note: AG quoted.

J736   Controversy At Case. *Case Tech,* vol. 62, no. 26 (May 12, 1967) p. 2.

J737   Gould, Whitney. Allen Ginsberg, the Fugs Have Fun Being Disgusted. *Capital Times* (May 13, 1967) p. 11.

J738   Changes. *Paper,* vol. 2, no. 25 (May 16, 1967) pp. 7, 12.
Note: AG interview format, reprinted from *City Of San Francisco Oracle* (Feb. 1967).

J739   Waggoner, Karen. Poet Ginsberg Holds Court. *Eugene Register-Guard* (May 18, 1967)
Note: AG quoted briefly.

J740   Parchman, Frank. Appearance Scheduled Here Tonight By World-Noted Poet Allen Ginsberg. *Oregon State Daily Barometer* (May 18, 1967)

J741   Parchman, Frank. Allen Ginsberg Claims His Sex Madness Attracts His Followers. *Oregon State Daily Barometer* (May 19, 1967) p. 1.
Note: AG quoted briefly.

J742   Smith, Larry. Ginsberg Vows 'Propriety'. *Vanguard,* vol. 22, no. 34 (May 19, 1967)

J743   Hedges, Gerri Lent. Ginsberg Removes Coat; Labels War 'Fraud'. *Vanguard,* vol. 22, no. 35 (May 24, 1967) p. 2.
Note: AG quoted briefly.

Ginsberg Navel Named Public Enemy Number 1. *Vanguard,* vol. 22, no. 35 (May 24, 1967) p. 5.

J744   Nude Photo Upsets PSC. *Oregonian* (May 25, 1967)

J745   Bus Turns On Campus In Ginsberg Entrance. *Western Washington State College Collegian* (May 26, 1967) p. 1.

J746   Menarini, Gianni. Lettura Di Poeti Nel Greenwich Village. *Il Tarocco,* vol. 2, no. 5 (June 1967) pp. 12-17.

J747   Gregory, Elizabeth C. [letter to the editor]. *Oregonian* (June 13, 1967) p. 24.

J748   Thompson, Thomas. The New Far-Out Beatles. *Life,* vol. 62, no. 24 (June 16, 1967) pp. 100-2, 104-6.

J749   Hamill, Pete. The Crisis: A Time For Poets. *New York Post* (June 20, 1967) pp. 3, 30.
Note: AG quoted briefly.

J750   Fiedler, Leslie A. Master Of Dreams. *Partisan Review,* vol. 34, no. 3 (Summer 1967) pp. 339-356.

J751   McNeill, Don. Making Peace At the Peace Eye Bookstore. *Village Voice* (July 6, 1967) pp. 1, 3.
Note: AG quoted briefly.

J752   Il Poeta Ginsberg Nei Guai Per Una Poesia. *La Nazione* (July 9, 1967) p. 7.

J753   Italian Police Take Interest In Ginsberg Poetry Reading. *New York Times* (July 9, 1967) p. 15.

J754   S., R. Arrestato A Spoleto Il Poeta Ginsberg Che Legge In Pubblico Versi "Osceni". *La Stampa* (July 9, 1967) p. 5.

J755   Piersanti, Umberto. A Proposito De Ginsberg. *Ad Libitum: Rivista Trimestrale Di Cultura Contemporanea,* no. 3 (July 10, 1967) pp. 34-39.

J756   Successo A Spoleto Balletto Di Stoccarda. *Corriere Della Sera* (July 10, 1967) p. 6.

J757   People. *International Herald Tribune* (July 10, 1967)

J758   G., G. Il Poeta Allen Ginsberg Denunciato Per Oscenità. *Il Messagero* (July 10, 1967) p. 10.

J759   Magi, Piero. Ginsberg Offre Fiori All'Agente Che Lo Portò Al Commissariato. *La Nazione* (July 10, 1967) p. 13.

J760   Allen Ginsberg Is Charged With Obscenity In Spoleto. *New York Times* (July 10, 1967) p. 5.

J761   S., R. Il Poeta Ginsberg Denunciato Per "Oscenità" Al Festival Di Spoleto. *La Stampa* (July 10, 1967) p. 6.

J762   Ginsberg A Spoleto Denunciato Per Oscenità. *Il Tempo* (July 10, 1967)

J763   Mosca. Un Poeta In Questura. *Corriere D'Informazione* (July 11-12, 1967) p. 3.

J764   Smith, Jones. 'Happening' At Speakers Corner. *Times* (July 13, 1967) p. 2.

Howard, Philip. By the Seven Beards Of the Prophet Ginsberg. *Times* (July 13, 1967) p. 10.
Note: AG quoted briefly.

J765   H., B. U.S. Poet Sings His Verse To Cymbal Accompaniment. *Daily Telegraph* (July 17, 1967)

Riley, Norman. Rally To Legalize 'Pot' Attracts 5,000. *Daily Telegraph* (July 17, 1967) p. 13.

J766   Fiddick, Peter. Simple Message From All the Lovely People. *Guardian* (July 17, 1967) p. 14.
Note: AG quoted briefly.

J767   Schmidt, Dana Adams. British 'Smoke-In' Puffs Marijuana. *New York Times* (July 17, 1967) p. 9.
Note: AG quoted briefly.

J768   Jessel, Stephen. Drugs Call By 'Flower Children'. *Times* (July 17, 1967)

J769   Trois Mille "Hippies" Manifestemt Pour La Libre Consommation De La Marijuana. *Le Monde* (July 18, 1967) p. 18.

J770   Performing Poets. *Times Literary Supplement* (July 20, 1967)

J771   Rosenfeld, Albert. Marijuana: Millions Of Turned-On Users. *Life,* vol. 43, no. 2 (July 24, 1967) pp. 14-22.

J772   Skir, Leo. Elise Cowen: A Brief Memoir Of the Fifties. *Evergreen Review,* vol. 11, no. 48 (Aug. 1967) pp. 70-72, 103-105.
Note: AG quoted briefly.

J773   Playmen Intervista: Allen Ginsberg. *Playmen* (Aug. 1967) pp. 13-16.
Note: AG interview format in Italian only.

J774*   Vené, Gian Franco. Dal Village Alla Casa Bianca. *La Fiera Litteraria* (Aug. 3, 1967) pp. 5-7.

J775   Mossman, James. Love, Love, Love. *Listener,* vol. 78, no. 2001 (Aug. 3, 1967) pp. 133-134.
Note: AG quoted briefly.

J776   Ginsberg Family Recital. *Times* (Aug. 9, 1967) p. 6.

J777   Singalong With Ginsberg. *Sunday Times* (Aug. 13, 1967)
Note: AG quoted.

J778   S., P.H. Ginsberg's Father Here. *Times* (Aug. 23, 1967) p. 6.

J779   Ronse, Henri. [review of *Dossier LSD Mandala*]. *La Quinzaine Litteraire* (Sept. 1-15, 1967) p. 17+.

J780   Allen Ginsberg Fermato Con Altri 16 Capelloni. *Il Messagero* (Sept. 5, 1967) p. 5.
Note: AG quoted briefly in Italian only.

J781   Per 3 Ore «In Guardina» Il Poeta Allen Ginsberg. *Paese Sera* (Sept. 5, 1967) p. 5.
Note: AG quoted briefly in Italian only.

J782   Ginsberg Per Tre Ore Al Commissariato Colpevole Di Passeggiare Con I Beats! *L'Unita* (Sept. 5, 1967)
Note: AG quoted briefly in Italian only.

J783   Sanavio, Piero. Breakfast With the Buddha Of the Beats. *International Herald Tribune* (Sept. 6, 1967) p. 14.
Note: AG quoted.

J784   Rome Police Pick Up Ginsberg. *New York Times* (Sept. 6, 1967) p. 18.

J785   Beat Poet Arrested In Swoop On Spanish Steps. *Rome Daily American* (Sept. 6, 1967)
Note: AG quoted briefly.

J786   [article]. *L'Espresso* (Sept. 10, 1967)

J787   Borelli, Sauro. Allen Ginsberg La "Bestia Nera" Dei Benpensanti. *L'Unita* (Sept. 13, 1967) p. 8.

J788   Nabokov, Peter. Old Seton Castle Becomes Hindu Temple To Krishna. *New Mexican* (Sept. 17, 1967) pp. D1-2.

J789   Gladfelter, David. Ginsberg, Censorship, Milwaukee. *Arts In Society,* vol. 4, no. 3 (Fall-Winter 1967) pp. 548-552.
Note: AG quoted briefly.

J790   Bingham, June. The Intelligent Square's Guide To Hippieland. *New York Times Magazine* (Sept. 24, 1967) pp. 25, 68, 70, 73, 76, 81, 83-4.

J791   Candito, Mimmo. Allen Ginsberg La Struggente "Libertà" Dell'Uomo. *Il Lavoro* (Sept. 26, 1967) p. 3.
Note: AG interview format in Italian only.

Il Profeta Della "Beat Generation". *Il Lavoro* (Sept. 26, 1967) p. 3.
Note: AG quoted briefly.

[review of *Jukebox All'Idrogeno*]. *Il Lavoro* (Sept. 26, 1967) p. 3.
Note: Review of Nanda Pivano's translation.

Nel Cuore Vortice Dove L'Angoscia Risuona. *Il Lavoro* (Sept. 26, 1967) p. 3.

J792   [anonymous]. A Speech: Dialectics Of Liberation. *Digger Papers* (ca. Oct. 1967) pp. 4-7.
Note: AG quoted briefly but not attributed to him.

J793   Ginsbergs At ICA. *ICA Bulletin,* no. 174 (Oct. 1967) p. 15.

J794   Angelini, Claudio. Il Poeta Allen Ginsberg Ha Parlato Ieri A Napoli. *Il Mattino* (Oct. 1, 1967) p. 13.
Note: AG interview format in Italian only.

J795   Connolly, Cyril. [review of *TV Baby Poems*]. *Sunday Times* (Oct. 15, 1967) p. 32.

J796   Dodsworth, Martin. [review of *TV Baby Poems*]. *Listener,* vol. 78, no. 2012 (Oct. 19, 1967) pp. 506-507.

J797   Quasimodo, Salvatore. Un Nobel Incontra Un "Beat". *Il Tempo,* vol. 29, no. 43 (Oct. 24, 1967) pp. 33-34.

J798   Il Sacramento Dell' LSD. *ABC Milan*, vol. 8, no. 44 (Oct. 29, 1967) pp. 26-27.
Note: AG interview format in Italian only.

J799   Re, Ermanno G. Allen Ginsberg Ci Ha Detto. *Il Canguro,* vol. 1, no. 2 (Nov.-Dec. 1967) pp. 1-2.
Note: AG interview format in Italian only.

J800   Calligarich, Gianfranco. Io Sono Il Re Di Maggio. *Kent,* vol. 1, no. 9 (Nov. 1967) pp. 21-4, 125, 128.
Note: AG interview format in Italian only.

J801   Geller, Andrew. New Sexual Morality Killing Sex — Ginsberg. *Montreal Gazette* (Nov. 1, 1967)
Note: AG quoted briefly.

J802   Kypreos, Chris. Penthouse Interview, Allen Ginsberg. *Penthouse,* vol. 2, no. 12 (Nov. 1967) pp. 42-4, 46, 70.
Note: AG interview format.

J803   Symons, Julian. [review of *TV Baby Poems*]. *New Statesman,* vol. 74, no. 1912 (Nov. 3, 1967) p. 595.

J804   Williams, H.L. [review of *TV Baby Poems*]. *Western Mail* (Nov. 4, 1967) p. 8.

J805   Farren, Mick. Angels And Violence. *International Times,* no. 21 (Nov. 17-30, 1967) p. 13.

J806   Herres, David. How We Dumped the War. *Win,* vol. 3, no. 21 (Dec. 1967) p. 19.
Note: AG quoted briefly.

J807   Bishop, Gordon. On European Tour: Ginsbergs. *Herald-News* (Dec. 2, 1967) p. 24.
Note: AG quoted briefly.

J808   Bigart, Homer. 264 Seized Here In Draft Protest. *New York Times* (Dec. 6, 1967) pp. 1, 8.

J809   Benes, Edward and Meskil, Paul. All Cops Alerted For Today's Protest On Draft. *Daily News* (Dec. 6, 1967) p. 5.
Note: AG quoted briefly.

J810   Draft Protests. *Facts On File,* vol. 27, no. 1415 (Dec. 7-13, 1967) p. 517.

J811   Borelli, Sauro. Ginsberg Risponde Su Sesso E Altro Ancora. *Vie Nuove,* vol. 22, no. 49 (Dec. 7, 1967) pp. 10-12.
Note: AG interview format in Italian only.

J812   England Unsafe For Poets? *International Times,* no. 22 (Dec. 15-28, 1967) p. 3.

J813   Menkin, Edward Z. Allen Ginsberg: A Bibliography And Biographical Sketch. *Thoth,* vol. 8, no. 1 (Winter 1967) pp. 35-44.

J814   Van Oortmerssen, Hans. Ginsberg: Love, Love, Baby. *Depapierentijger,* no. 5 (ca. 1967) p. [6].
Note: AG interview format in Dutch only.

J815   Elliott, Bob. Interview With Allen Ginsberg. *Free Lance,* vol. 6, no. 1 (1967) pp. 15-21.
Note: AG interview format.

J816   [review of *Prose Contribution To Cuban Revolution*]. *Marrahwannah Quarterly,* vol. 3, no. 3 (1967) l. 34.

J817   Katz, Nathan. After Ginsberg. *Psychedelphia Period,* no. 4 (ca. 1967) p. 38.

Books:

J818   Andrews, George and Vinkenoog, Simon (eds.). *The Book Of Grass.* New York, NY: Grove Press, 1967.
Note: AG mentioned throughout.

J819   Barbeau, C.C. 'Beat' Writing (in) *New Catholic Encyclopedia, vol. 2.* New York, NY: McGraw-Hill, 1967, pp. 184-185.

J820   Brown, Joe David (ed.). *The Hippies.* New York, NY: Time Life Books, 1967.

J821   Dommergues, Pierre. *Les U.S.A. À La Recherche De Leur Identité.* Paris, France: Editions Bernard Grasset, 1967, pp. 322-326+.
Note: AG quoted briefly from testimony for Boston's *Naked Lunch* trial in French only.

J822   Ethridge, James M. and Kopala, Barbara (eds.). *Contemporary Authors, vol. 1-4 [first revision].* Detroit, MI: Gale Research Co., 1967, p. 370-1.
Note: AG quoted briefly.

J823   Hahn, Emily. *Romantic Rebels: An Informal History Of Bohemianism In America.* Boston, MA: Houghton Mifflin, 1967.
Note: AG mentioned throughout.

J824   Harold, Preston. *The Shining Stranger.* New York, NY: Wayfarer Press, 1967, pp. 274, 280.

J825   Hollander, Charles (ed.). *Background Papers On Student Drug Involvement.* Washington, DC: United States National Student Assn., 1967.
Note: Contains "Seminar On Marihuana And LSD Controls" which is a transcript of a debate between AG and James H. Fox, pp. 15-35.

J826   Holmes, John Clellon. *Nothing More To Declare.* New York, NY: Dutton, 1967, pp. 56-7, 59, 67.
Note: AG quoted briefly.

J827   La France, Marston (ed.). *Patterns Of Commitment In American Literature.* Toronto, Canada: University Of Toronto Press, 1967.
Contents: Hoffman, Frederick J. Contemporary American Poetry, pp. 193-207.

J828   Plimpton, George (ed.). *Writers At Work: The Paris Review Interviews* [Third Series]. New York, NY: Viking Press, 1967.
Contents: Clark, Thomas. Allen Ginsberg, pp. 279-320.
Note: AG interview format first printed in *The Paris Review* (Spring 1966).

J829   Podhoretz, Norman. *Making It.* New York, NY: Random House, 1967, pp. 39, 215, 253.

J830   Rosenthal, M.L. *The New Poets: American And British Poetry Since World War II.* New York, NY: Oxford University Press, 1967.

J831   Thompson, Hunter S. *Hell's Angels.* New York, NY: Random House, 1967.
Note: AG mentioned throughout.

J832   Tobias, Allen. *'Mind Is Shapely, Art Is Shapely': The World's a Beautiful Flower. A Critical Biography Of the American Poet Allen Ginsberg.* Unpublished Dissertation, State University Of NY At Stony Brook, 1967.

J833   Weatherhead, A. Kingsley. *The Edge Of the Image: Marianne Moore, William Carlos Williams And Some Other Poets.* Seattle, WA: University Of Washington Press, 1967.

1968

J834   Haroldson, Thomas. The White Negro—Ten Years Later. *Fifth Estate* (Jan. 1-15, 1968) p. 12.

J835   Bahrenburg, Bruce. Dissent Defended. *Newark Evening News* (Jan. 16, 1968) p. 48.
Note: AG quoted briefly.

J836   Aronowitz, Alfred G. An Anthology Of Ginsbergs. *New York Post* (Jan. 18, 1968) p. 4.
Note: AG quoted briefly.

J837   Lask, Thomas. Pair Of Ginsbergs Read Poetry Here. *New York Times* (Jan. 18, 1968) p. 49.

J838   Poet Allen Ginsberg Willing To Go To Jail For War Stand. *Paterson Evening News* (Jan. 18, 1968) p. 4.
Note: AG quoted briefly.

J839   Kempton, Sally. Viet Critics: They Put Themselves On the Line. *Village Voice* (Jan. 18, 1968) p. 1.

J840   [Bishop, Gordon]. Louis And Allen Ginsberg Read Poetry At Rutgers. *Passaic Herald-News* (Jan. 20, 1968) p. 11.
Note: AG quoted briefly.

J841   Berliner, David C. No Poetic License. *Newark Evening News* (Jan. 20, 1968)
Note: AG quoted briefly.

J842   Aronowitz, Alfred G. The Yogi Dusts Off His Cosmic Truths. *New York Post* (Jan. 22, 1968) p. 2.
Note: AG quoted briefly.

J843   Norton, Edward. A Family Of Poets. *Paterson Morning Call* (Jan. 27, 1968)

J844   Weiss, Burton Ira. [letter to the editor]. *Liberation,* vol. 12, no. 11 (Feb. 1968) p. 38.

J845   Eaton, William J. Yipes, Yippies Are Coming! *Chicago Daily News* (Feb. 2, 1968) p. 20.

J846   Donovan, Joe. Ginsberg Intones Chants, Poetry At Penn. *Philadelphia Daily News* (Feb. 9, 1968) p. 5.
Note: AG quoted briefly.

J847   Cooney, John E. Ginsberg Explains Pot And Politics. *Philadelphia Inquirer* (Feb. 9, 1968)

J848   End Of the Road. *Berkeley Barb* (Feb. 9, 1968)

J849   Ginsberg, Fugs Set For Gig At Appleton. *Post-Crescent* (Feb. 11, 1968) Showtime supplement, pp. 1, 9.

J850   Ginsberg To Present Works; Anti-Authoritarian Advocate. *Campus-Times* (Feb. 13, 1968) pp. 1, 5.

J851   Bryan, John. The Death Of Neal Cassady. *Open City,* no. 42 (Feb. 16-22, 1968) pp. 5, 8.

J852   Bergmanis, Talis. Ginsberg — Great Or Foul? *Rochester Democrat And Chronicle* (Feb. 16, 1968)

J853   Wagner, David F. Poetry? I Haven't the Fuggiest. *Post-Crescent* (Feb. 20, 1968) pp. B1, B3.

J854   Allen Ginsberg To Speak In Honor Lecture Series. *Northern Iowan* (Feb. 20, 1968) p. 1.

J855   Poet, Students Dance At McCarthy Grave. *Milwaukee Journal* (Feb. 21, 1968) p. 19.

J856   Hippie Rite For Senator Isn't Grave. *Milwaukee Sentinel* (Feb. 21, 1968)

J857   Hazard, James. Underground Emerges Noisily To Hear Guru Allen Ginsberg. *Paper For Central Wisconsin* (Feb. 21, 1968) p. B3.
Note: AG quoted briefly.

J858   Strange Things Are Happening At McCarthy's Grave. *Post-Crescent* (Feb. 21, 1968) p. B2.

J859   Walde, Jim. 1,000 Hear Poet's Stream Of Thought. *Daily Record* (Feb. 22, 1968)

J860   Wagner, David F. Controversy Boils Over Ginsberg 'Exorcism' Rites. *Post-Crescent* (Feb. 22, 1968) pp. B1, B4.

J861   Vonier, Richard S. Ginsberg Has Few Choice Words For MU. *Milwaukee Journal* (Feb. 23, 1968)
Note: AG quoted briefly.

J862   Gladfelter, David D. Poet Leads Parade To UWM. *Milwaukee Sentinel* (Feb. 23, 1968) pp. 1, 2.
Note: AG quoted briefly.

J863   So We Print Poster Yet! *Paper For Central Wisconsin* (Feb. 23, 1968) pp. 1, B7.

J864   Severin, Bill. Warns Of Mind Destroyers. *Waterloo Daily Courier* (Feb. 23, 1968) p. 1.

J865   We Are Visited By a Poet. *Post-Crescent* (Feb. 24, 1968)

J866   Kennedy, Bill. Gurus: A New Kind Of Big Daddy. *Albany Times-Union* (Feb. 25, 1968) pp. G1, 10.
Note: AG quoted.

J867   Carlson, Barbara. U Of H Students Dig 'Beat' Poet. *Hartford Courant* (Feb. 27, 1968) pp. 1, 14.
Note: AG quoted at length.

J868   Lindberg, John; Colas, Ralph G.; De Long, James E. and Haberer, Frederick M. [letters to the editor]. *Waterloo Daily Courier* (Feb. 28, 1968) p. 4.

J869   Severin, Bill. Ginsberg Simply 'Obscene'. *Waterloo Daily Courier* (Feb. 29, 1968) p. 1.

J870   Beasley, Marjorie. Hiding Reality Under Box Doesn't Prevent Its Existence. *Northern Iowan* (March 1, 1968) p. 4.

[letters to the editor]. *Northern Iowan* (March 1, 1968)

J871   Kyria, Pierre. Regards Sur La Littérature Américaine. *La Revue De Paris,* vol. 75, no. 3 (March 1968) pp. 117-122.

J872   GU Students Enchanted By 'Beat' Poet. *Washington Post* (March 1, 1968) p. B4.

J873   Foster, Susan and Thompson, Tracy. Allen Ginsberg. *RPM,* no. 1 (ca. March 3, 1968) pp. [20-27].
Note: AG interview format.

J874   This Time He Wore Clothes. *Harvard Crimson* (March 4, 1968) p. 1.

J875   [letter to the editor]. *Northern Iowan* (March 5, 1968)

J876   [letters to the editor]. *Post-Crescent* (March 5, 1968)

J877   Lask, Thomas. Poets Are United Against Editors. *New York Times* (March 6, 1968) p. 44.

J878   Beker, Marilyn. Ginsberg's Delivery Makes Ugliness Vanish. *Globe And Mail* (March 7, 1968)
Note: AG quoted briefly.

J879   Forman, Freda. Allen Ginsberg Meets University Community. *Statesman,* vol. 11, no. 24 (March 8, 1968) pp. 1, 2.
Note: AG quoted briefly.

J880   Rogers, Jerry. Hippie Poet Gets Cool Reception. *Hamilton Spectator* (March 9, 1968) p. 8.

J881   Italians Clear Ginsberg. *New York Times* (March 10, 1968) p. 20.

J882   Ginsberg Cleared. *Times* (March 11, 1968) p. 11.

J883   Leo, John. Antiwar Boycott Set At Columbia. *New York Times* (March 12, 1968)

J884   Ireland, Corydon. An Evening With Allen Ginsberg: A Change Of Pace? Oh Wow! *Spectrum* (March 12, 1968) p. 8.

J885   DeMagny, Olivier. [review of *Kaddish Et Autres Poèmes* (Christian Bourgois)]. *Le Magazine Littéraire* (March 16, 1968)

J886   All About Books...And Stuff. *Trenton Times Advertiser* (March 17, 1968)
Note: AG quoted briefly.

J887   Poets And Critics Debate "Poetry Now". *Publishers Weekly,* vol. 193, no. 12 (March 18, 1968)

J888   Groer, Anne. My Country Tis Of Thee. *Washington Free Press* (March 19, 1968) pp. 7-8.
Note: AG interview format.

Heyman, Barton. Ginsberg Raps At GU. *Washington Free Press* (March 19, 1968) p. 7.
Note: AG quoted briefly.

J889   Lowenfels, Walter. Black Renaissance. *American Dialog,* vol. 5, no. 1 (Spring 1968) pp. 30-31.

J890   Creeley, Robert. Contexts Of Poetry. *Audit,* vol. 5, no. 1 (Spring 1968) [issue called *Contexts Of Poetry*] pp. 1-18.
Note: AG quoted from transcript of discussion with Creeley.

J891   Ashley, Leonard. The Rules Of the Game. *Concerning Poetry,* vol. 1, no. 1 (Spring 1968) p. 1.

J892   Hart, Lawrence. The New Face Of Conformity. *Works,* vol. 1, no. 3 (Spring 1968) pp. 106-113.

J893   Stern, Michael. Political Activism New Hippie 'Thing'. *New York Times* (March 24, 1968) pp. 1, 72.
Note: AG quoted briefly.

J894   Dagnino, Antonio Eduardo and Guerrero, Jose Manuel Briceno. Allllen Ginnnnsberg. *Haoma,* vol. 1, no. 3 (April 1968) pp. 44-47.
Note: AG interview format.

J895   Bowering, George. [review of *T.V. Baby Poems*]. *Globe And Mail* (April 6, 1968) Globe Magazine section, p. 14.

J896   Bryan, John. Allen Ginsberg On Everything. *Open City,* no. 50 (April 12-18, 1968) p. 10.
Note: AG interview format.

J897   Peyton, Dave. Ginsberg, Gregory Rap U.S. *Herald-Advertiser,* vol. 68, no. 17 (April 28, 1968) pp. 1, 4.
Note: AG quoted briefly.

Lilly, Russ. Controversial Figures Attract Throng At Marshall U. *Herald-Advertiser,* vol. 68, no. 17 (April 28, 1968) p. 11.

J898   Grant, Sandra. Poetic. *Sunday Gazette-Mail* (April 28, 1968) p. 16A.
Note: AG quoted briefly.

J899   Allen Ginsberg Talk Barred At St. Bonaventure College. *New York Times* (May 3, 1968) p. 12.

J900   Compromise On Ginsberg Ends St. Bonaventure Sit-In. *New York Times* (May 5, 1968) p. 76.

J901   Mockridge, Norton. Ginsbergs: Like Father, Unlike Son. *Paterson Evening News* (May 6, 1968)

J902   Shaw, Jim. Krassner, Ginsberg Speak To Students. *Columbia Daily Spectator,* vol. 112, no. 113 (May 8, 1968) pp. 1, 4.

J903   Lewis, Dan. Ginsberg At Eastside Reunion. *Paterson Morning Call* (May 14, 1968)
Note: AG quoted briefly.

J904   Sherman, Jake. Ginsberg, Zevin Protest War In Talks At Albany State. *Albany Times-Union* (May 17, 1968)

J905   Blando, Bill. Student Protests 'Real Thing', Poet Allen Ginsberg Declares. *Knickerbocker News* (May 17, 1968) p. 5C.
Note: AG quoted.

J906   Lucie-Smith, Edward. Ovid, Where Are You? *New Statesman,* vol. 75, no. 1941 (May 24, 1968) p. 691.

J907   Reck, Michael. A Conversation Between Ezra Pound And Allen Ginsberg. *Evergreen Review,* vol. 12, no. 55 (June 1968) pp. 27-29, 84-86.
Note: AG quoted.

J908   Gleason, Ralph J. A Day Of Love, Hurt And Sorrow. *San Francisco Chronicle* (June 10, 1968) p. 49.

J909   Ginsberg On Cleaver. *San Francisco Express Times* (June 17, 1968) p. 3.
Note: AG quoted.

J910   Dudek, Louis. Poetry As a Way Of Life. *English Quarterly,* vol. 1, no. 1 (Summer 1968) pp. 7-17.

J911   Potter, Tully. [review of *TV Baby Poems*]. *Poetry Review,* vol. 59, no. 2 (Summer 1968) pp. 116-120.

J912   Ginsberg, Acid, Speed, Junk, Ecology, Birth, Psyche. *Los Angeles Free Press,* vol. 5, no. 26 [issue 206] (June 28, 1968) pp. 18-19, 22.
Note: AG interview format.

J913   Leary, Timothy. In the Beginning Leary Turned On Ginsberg And Saw That It Was Good. *Esquire,* vol. 70, no. 1 (July 1968) pp. 83-7, 116-7.

J914   Hedley, Leslie Woolf. Ginsberg Meets the Master. *Minority Of One* (July-Aug. 1968) p. 22.
Note: A parody of a conversation between AG and Ezra Pound.

J915   A Day In the Life, With Ginsberg. *Willamette Bridge* (July 19-Aug. 2, 1968) p. 5.

J916   Collier, Peter. Lawrence Ferlinghetti: Doing His Own Thing. *New York Times Book Review* (July 21, 1968) pp. 4-5+.

J917   Walsh, Chad. [review of *TV Baby Poems*]. *Washington Post* (July 28, 1968) Book World section, p. 4.

J918   Sterba, James. The Politics Of Pot. *Esquire,* vol. 70, no. 2 [issue 417] (Aug. 1968) pp. 58-61+.

J919   Katz, Bill. [review of *TV Baby Poems*]. *Library Journal,* vol. 93, no. 14 (Aug. 1968) p. 2882.

J920   The Digger Papers. *Realist,* no. 81 (Aug. 1968) p. 1.

J921   [review of *Airplane Dreams*]. *Toronto Life,* vol. 2, no. 10 (Aug. 1968) p. 23.

J922   Lewis, Dan. Did Ginsberg Stir Czech Unrest? *Paterson Morning Call* (Aug. 6, 1968) pp. 1, 6.
Note: AG quoted briefly.

J923   Hirschman, Jack. Ginsberg's Friends. *Open City,* no. 64 (Aug. 9-15, 1968) p. 4.

J923x   Donald M'Neill, 23, Reporter, Drowns. *New York Times* (Aug. 11, 1968) p. 35.

J924   Kramer, Jane. Profiles, Paterfamilias—1. *New Yorker*, vol. 44, no. 26 (Aug. 17, 1968) pp. 32-73.
Note: AG quoted at length.

J925   Kramer, Jane. Profiles, Paterfamilias—2. *New Yorker*, vol. 44, no. 27 (Aug. 24, 1968) pp. 38-91.
Note: AG quoted at length.

J926   Boyer, Brian. Yippies Invite a UN Observer To Chicago. *Chicago Sun-Times* (Aug. 27, 1968) p. 6.
Note: AG quoted briefly.

J927   The 'Politics Of Joy'. *Chicago Tribune* (Aug. 27, 1968) p. 14.

J928   Mabley, Jack. Radicals Wait For McCarthy Kids To Crack. *Chicago's American* (Aug. 27, 1968) p. 3.
Note: AG quoted briefly.

J929   Fox, Sylvan. 300 Police Use Tear Gas To Breach Young Militants' Barricade In Chicago Park. *New York Times* (Aug. 27, 1968) p. 29.

J930   Fox, Sylvan. Gas Is Used Again To Quell Protest. *New York Times* (Aug. 28, 1968) p. 36.
        Note: AG quoted briefly.

J931   Police Battle Youths. *Facts On File,* vol. 28, no. 1453 (Aug. 29-Sept. 4, 1968) p. 362.

J932   Lukas, J. Anthony. Police Battle Demonstrators In Street. *New York Times* (Aug. 29, 1968) p. 1, 23.
        Note: AG quoted briefly.

J933   Bowering, George. [review of *Airplane Dreams*]. *Globe And Mail* (Aug. 31, 1968) Globe Magazine section.

J934   Reck, Michael. Ein Gesprach Zwischen Ezra Pound Allen Ginsberg. *Das Wort,* vol. 9, no. 9 (Sept. 1968) pp. 689-690.
        Note: AG quoted briefly in German translation by Hanne Gabriele Reck.

J935   Cheshire, Maxine. Chicago Gets Lesson In Poetic License. *New York Post* (Sept. 3, 1968)

J936   Goldberg, Art. The Convention From Outside. *New York Free Press,* vol. 1, no. 35 (Sept. 5-12, 1968) pp. 3-4, 13.

J937   [photo]. *Time,* vol. 92, no. 10 (Sept. 6, 1968) p. 15.

J938   Davis, Douglas M. [review of *TV Baby Poems*]. *National Observer,* vol. 7, no. 37 (Sept. 9, 1968) p. B4.

J939   Smith, A.J.M. The Canadian Poet: Part II, After Confederation. *Canadian Literature,* no. 38 (Autumn 1968) pp. 41-49.

J940   Lyon, Thomas J. Gary Snyder, a Western Poet. *Western American Literature,* vol. 3, no. 3 (Fall 1968) pp. 207-216.

J941   Mann. Poet Ginsberg Receives Chilly SUCO Reception. *Oneonta Star* (Sept. 27, 1968) p. 5.
        Note: AG quoted briefly.

J942   Davie, David. On Sincerity: From Wordsworth To Ginsberg. *Encounter,* vol. 31, no. 4 (Oct. 1968) pp. 61-66.

J943   Pélieu, Claude. Les Impasses Autoritaires: Conversation Claude Pélieu Allen Ginsberg. *Opus International,* no. 8 (Oct. 1968) pp. 56-60.
        Note: AG interview format in French only.

J944   Mitchell, Adrian. Beatles. *Listener* (Oct. 3, 1968) p. 447.

J945   Lipton, Lawrence. The High Priest Of LSD. *Los Angeles Free Press,* vol. 5, no. 40 (Oct. 4-10, 1968) pp. 25-28.
        Note: AG interview format.

J946   Callaghan, Barry. [review of *Airplane Dreams*]. *Toronto Telegram* (ca. Oct. 13, 1968)

J947   Keyes, Mary. [review of *Airplane Dreams* and *TV Baby Poems*]. *Canadian Forum,* vol. 48, no. 574 (Nov. 1968) pp. 182-183.

J948 Schultz, John. Pigs, Prague, Chicago, Other Democrats, And the Sleeper In the Park. *Evergreen Review,* vol. 12, no. 60 (Nov. 1968) pp. 26-35, 78-80, 82.

J949 Ledbetter, Jack Tracy. Poets, Society And Religion. *Lutheran Witness,* vol. 87, no. 11 (Nov. 1968) pp. 20-22.
Note: AG quoted briefly.

J950 GIs Shun Hippies' Love-In At Dix. *Daily News* (Nov. 4, 1968) p. 30.

J951 Hip Groups' 'Love In' At Ft. Dix Proves Dud. *Paterson Evening News* (Nov. 4, 1968)

J952 ...The Bliss Of Your Own Kindness Will Flood the Police Tomorrow... *Observation Post,* vol. 44, no. 9 (Nov. 15, 1968) p. 2.
Note: AG quoted.

J953 Harrington, Stephanie. TV. *Village Voice* (Nov. 28, 1968) pp. 28-29.

J954 11 Students And Instructor End Fast Protesting Hunger. *New York Times* (Nov. 29, 1968) p. 46.

J955 'Guru' Ginsberg, Beat Poet, Injured In Albany Accident. *Knickerbocker News* (Nov. 30, 1968) p. 4A.

J956 Car Collision Hurts Poet Ginsberg And 4. *New York Times* (Nov. 30, 1968) p. 77.

J957 Beat Poet Ginsberg Injured In Crash. *Oakland Tribune* (Nov. 30, 1968)

J958 Allen Ginsberg Injured In Accident Near Albany. *Star* (Nov. 30, 1968)

J959 Elliott, George P. Destroyers, Defilers, And Confusers Of Men. *Atlantic Monthly,* vol. 222, no. 6 (Dec. 1968) pp. 74-80.

J960 Poet Injured. *Chicago Tribune* (Dec. 1, 1968)

J961 Allen Ginsberg Hurt In Crash. *Santa Barbara News-Press* (Dec. 1, 1968) p. A-11.

J962 Allen Ginsberg Resting After Crash Injuries. *Paterson Morning Call* (Dec. 2, 1968)

J963 Hare Krishna. *San Francisco Chronicle* (Dec. 5, 1968) p. 7.

J964 Kennedy, Bill. Life, Death, a Bodystump—Ginsberg In Demerol. *Albany Times-Union* (Dec. 5, 1968) p. 3.
Note: AG quoted.

J965 Cook, Bruce. Scruffy Vagabonds Who Shook Up America. *National Observer* (Dec. 9, 1968) p. 20.

J966 Lipton, Lawrence. Ginsberg Recovering. *Los Angeles Free Press* (Dec. 20, 1968) p. 8.
Note: AG quoted briefly.

Williams, Liza. For A.G. *Los Angeles Free Press* (Dec. 20, 1968) p. 8.
Note: Article about AG but he is never mentioned by name.

J967 Mottram, Eric. Intervista Con Allen Ginsberg Tenuta L'8/6/1965. *Pianeta Fresco,* no. 2-3 (Winter 1968) pp. 77-73.
Note: Printed upside down, hence the inverted pagination, AG interview format in Italian only.

Dialogo. *Pianeta Fresco,* no. 2-3 (Winter 1968) pp. 159-150.
Note: Printed upside down, hence the inverted pagination, AG interview format in Italian only translated by Miro Silvera and reprinted from the original English interview in *The City Of San Francisco Oracle* (Feb. 1967).

J968 Kennedy, Bill. Ginsberg's Albany Pain, Jordan Pain... *Albany Times-Union* (Dec. 22, 1968) p. F-1.
Note: AG quoted.

J969 Adhikary, Das. A.C. Bhaktivedanta Swami & Allen Ginsberg: A Conversation. *Back To Godhead,* vol. 2, no. 2 (1968) pp. 26-28.
Note: AG interview format.

J970 Mungo, Ray. [letter to the editor]. *Occasional Drop,* no. 1 (ca. 1968) p. 3.

Books:

J971 Berman, Ronald. *America In the Sixties: An Intellectual History.* New York, NY: The Free Press, 1968.

J972 Carroll, Paul. *The Poem In Its Skin.* Chicago, IL: Follett, 1968.
Note: AG mentioned throughout.

J973 Dickey, James. *Babel To Byzantium: Poets And Poetry Now.* New York, NY: Farrar, Straus and Giroux, 1968, pp. 52-55.

J974 *Grand Larousse Encyclopedique, Supplement.* Paris, France: Librairie Larousse, 1968, p. 419.

J975 Guimond, James. *The Art Of William Carlos Williams.* Urbana, IL: University Of Illinois Press, 1968, pp. 164, 195.

J976 Haning, Peter (ed.). *Midnight Penthouse.* London, England: Bernard Geiss, 1968, pp. 187-198.
Note: AG interview format, first printed in *Penthouse* (Nov. 1967).

J977 Harding, Gunnar. *Den Svenske Cyklistens Sång.* Malmo, Sweden: Wahlström & Widstrand, 1968, pp. 33-46.

J978 Kornbluth, Jesse (ed.). *Notes From the New Underground.* New York, NY: Viking Press, 1968, pp. 121-183.
Note: AG interview format, first printed in *City Of San Francisco Oracle* (Feb. 1967).

J979 Leary, Timothy. *High Priest.* New York, NY: World Publishing, 1968.
Note: AG mentioned throughout.

J980 Leary, Timothy. *The Politics Of Ecstasy.* New York, NY: College Notes & Texts, 1968.

J981 *Literarische Messe 1968.* Frankfurt Am Main, W. Germany: Metopen Verlag, 1968, pp. 13-33.
Note: AG interview format, first printed in City *Of San Francisco Oracle* (Feb. 1967) translated into German by Eva Bornemann.

J982   Metzner, Ralph (ed.). *The Ecstatic Adventure.* New York, NY: Macmillan, 1968.
Note: AG mentioned throughout.

J983   Nuttal, Jeff. *Bomb Culture.* New York, NY: Delta Book, 1968, 1970, pp. 213-214, 252.

J984   Rimanelli, Giose. *Tragica America.* Genova, Italy: Immordino Editore, 1968.

1969

J985   [article]. *Superlove,* no. 15 (Jan. 1969) p. 15.

J986   Garcia, Bob. How Braden Delivers. *Open City,* no. 85 (Jan. 3-9, 1969) p. 5.

J987   Brownjohn, Alan. Fblup! [review of *Planet News* and *Ankor Wat*]. *New Statesman,* vol. 77, no. 1974 (Jan. 10, 1969) p. 52.

J988   Walton, Bev. Bakken Collage Topic: Ginsberg Year-That-Was. *Vanguard* (Jan. 10, 1969)

J989   Ginsberg, Louis. The Kids Love Him...He Is the Voice Of Their Secret Dreams And Desires. *Chicago Sun-Times* (Jan. 12, 1969) Book Week, pp. 2-3.
Note: AG quoted briefly.

J990   Hamilton, Ian. [review of *Ankor Wat*]. *Observer,* no. 9262 (Jan. 19, 1969) p. 29.

J991   Holmes, Richard. [review of *Planet News*]. *Times* (Jan. 25, 1969) p. 22.

J992   [review of *Ankor Wat*]. *Times Literary Supplement,* no. 3492 (Jan. 30, 1969) p. 107.

J993   Weiler, A.H. Screen: 'Me And My Brother' Opens. *New York Times* (Feb. 3, 1969) p. 31.

J994   Mahoney, Larry. Poet Ginsberg Is a Hit At UM. *Miami Herald* (Feb. 5, 1969) p. 2-B.

J995   Overflow Crowd Hears Ginsberg Chant, Recite. *Observer,* vol. 3, no. 74 (Feb. 6, 1969) p. 2.
Note: AG quoted briefly.

J996   Lipton, Lawrence. [review of *Planet News*]. *Los Angeles Free Press* (Feb. 7, 1969) pp. 26-7.

J997   Art Show, Film Cancellation Brings Legal Issues. *Observer,* vol. 3, no. 75 (Feb. 7, 1969) pp. 2, 11.

J998   Warmington, Ella. Poet Sees Future Garden Of Eden. *St. Paul Dispatch* (Feb. 8, 1969) p. 11.
Note: AG quoted at length.

J999   Wascoe, Dan, Jr. Ginsberg Reads Poetry...And the Young Listen. *Minneapolis Tribune* (Feb. 9, 1969) p. 1B.
Note: AG quoted.

J1000   Literature And Revolution. *Spectator* (Feb. 11, 1969) p. 14.

J1001 Hillson, Jon. Ginsberg! *Colorado Daily,* vol. 17, no. 82 (Feb. 17, 1969) pp. 1, 3.

J1002 Stein, Charles. [review of *TV Baby Poems*]. *Nation,* vol. 208, no. 7 (Feb. 17, 1969) p. 217.

J1003 Morrison, Laurance. Pot's Flame Is High Enough: Ginsberg. *Newsday* (Feb. 27, 1969) p. 2B.
Note: AG quoted briefly.

Aronson, Harvey. An Old Beatnik Spoke Of Pot, Poetry. *Newsday* (Feb. 27, 1969) p. 2B.
Note: AG quoted briefly.

J1004 Lipton, Lawrence. [review of *Planet News*]. *Georgia Straight,* vol. 3, no. 47 (Feb. 28-March 6, 1969) pp. 11, 14.
Note: AG quoted briefly.

J1005 Blakeslee, Sandra. Students See Rise In Drug Arrests. *New York Times* (Feb. 28, 1969) p. 18.

J1006 Bannon, Anthony. Dissidents Break Up UB Drug Seminar. *Buffalo Evening News* (March 1, 1969) p. A-5.
Note: AG quoted briefly.

J1007 Yip Founders. *Kaleidoscope,* vol. 1, no. 9 (March 1-14, 1969) p. 12.

J1008 Jennings, C. Robert. Cultsville, U.S.A. *Playboy,* vol. 16, no. 3 (March 1969) pp. 86-8, 151-4, 156-7.

J1009 Nejgebauer, Aleksandar. Poezija I Omladina U Sad. *Polja,* vol. 15, no. 125-126 (March 1969) pp. 22-3.

J1010 Visitors To the Center. *Zen Bow,* vol. 2, no. 2 (March-April 1969) p. 7.

J1011 Blakeslee, Sandra. 'World Of Drugs' Engulfs Buffalo. *New York Times* (March 2, 1969) p. 62.
Note: AG quoted briefly.

J1012 Allen Ginsberg; The Man And His Beliefs. *Ecco Ergon,* vol. 5, no. 8 (March 4, 1969) p. 3.
Note: AG quoted briefly.

J1013 Persky, Stan. The Other World. *Georgia Straight,* vol. 3, no. 48 (March 7-13, 1969) pp. 12-13.

J1014 Persky, Stan. ...And Ginsberg. *Ubyssey* (March 7, 1969) pp. 2, 4.
Note: AG quoted.

J1015 Hazlett, Peter N. Ginsberg Puts Low-Key Blast On Establishment. *Maine Sunday Telegram* (March 9, 1969)
Note: AG quoted briefly.

J1016 Zweig, Paul. [review of *Planet News*]. *Nation,* vol. 208, no. 10 (March 10, 1969) pp. 311-313.

J1017 But For Ginsberg, Reality Is a Crutch. *Vancouver Sun* (March 10, 1969)
Note: AG quoted briefly.

J1018 Crowd Awestruck As Ginsberg Reads. *Vancouver Sun* (March 12, 1969) p. 39.
Note: AG quoted briefly.

J1019 Lamont, Corliss. [letter to the editor]. *New York Times* (March 13, 1969) p. 46.

J1020 Kohn, Jaakov. I Saw the Best Minds Of My Generation, pt. 1. *East Village Other,* vol. 4, no. 15 (March 14, 1969) pp. 6-7, 19.
Note: AG interview format.

J1021 Ginsberg Arts 1. *Georgia Straight,* vol. 3, no. 49 (March 14-20, 1969) pp. 10-11.
Note: AG transcript of speech.

J1022 Kleinhaus, Charles. Allen Ginsberg, part 1. *Spectator,* vol. 8, no. 7 (March 18, 1969) pp. 14-16.
Note: AG quoted briefly.

J1023 Kohn, Jaakov. I Saw the Best Minds Of My Generation, pt. 2. *East Village Other,* vol. 4, no. 16 (March 19, 1969) pp. 4, 12.
Note: AG interview format.

J1024 [article]. *Georgia Straight,* vol. 3, no. 50 (March 21-27, 1969) p. 3.

J1025 Parkinson, Thomas. Reflections On Allen Ginsberg As Poet [review of *Planet News*]. *Concerning Poetry,* vol. 2, no. 1 (Spring 1969) pp. 21-24.

J1026 Lawson, Todd S.J. Plaintiff Interview. *Plaintiff,* vol. 5, no. 3 (Spring-Summer 1969) pp. 25-32.
Note: AG interview format.

J1027 Robinson, Bill. [review of *Planet News*]. *Great Speckled Bird,* vol. 2, no. 2 (March 24, 1969) pp. 8-10.

J1028 Kleinhaus, Charles. Allen Ginsberg, part 2. *Spectator,* vol. 8, no. 8 (March 25, 1969) pp. 14-17.
Note: AG quoted briefly.

J1029 [review of *Planet News*]. *Cambridge News* (March 28, 1969)

J1030 Anderson, Tom. Say, Mr. Anderson—What About Impact? *Impact,* no. 6 (Spring [April] 1969) pp. 6-7, 30-31.
Note: AG quoted briefly.

J1031 W., J. [review of *Planet News*]. *Kliatt Paperback Book Guide,* vol. 3, no. 2 (April 1969) unpaged.

J1032 Mario, Jose. Allen Ginsberg En La Habana. *Mundo Nuevo,* no. 34 (April 1969) pp. 48-54.

J1033 Mendelson, Chaim. [review of *TV Baby Poems*]. *New:,* no. 9 (April 1969) pp. 33-35.

J1034 Carroll, Paul. Playboy Interview: Allen Ginsberg. *Playboy,* vol. 16, no. 4 (April 1969) pp. 81-92, 236-244.
Note: AG interview format.

J1035 Symposium On Drugs Is Mixed-Up Event. *UB Alumni News,* vol. 4, no. 1 (April 1969) pp. 4-5.
Note: AG quoted briefly.

J1036   Sabel, Brad. Ginsberg Invitation Decided On Today. *Vanderbilt Hustler,* vol. 80, no. 43 (April 1, 1969) pp. 1, 7.

J1037   Webster, Jack. Ginsberg And Webster. *Georgia Straight,* vol. 3, no. 52 (April 4-10, 1969) pp. 9-12.
Note: AG interview format.

J1038   VSAA Invites Ginsberg To Read Poetry May 7. *Vanderbilt Hustler,* vol. 80, no. 44 (April 4, 1969) p. 1.

J1039   6 Writers Named To Share $34,000 Worth Of Grants. *New York Times* (April 10, 1969) p. 15.

J1040   Waters, Geoff. The Chancellor's Difficult Role. *Versus* (April 10, 1969) p. 3.

J1041   Ogar, Richard A. [review of *Planet News*]. *San Francisco Sunday Examiner & Chronicle* (April 13, 1969) This World section, p. 36.

J1042   Palmer, Don. Ginsberg's World. *Sunday Review,* vol. 1, no. 8 (April 13, 1969) p. 1.

J1043   Kohn, Jaakov. Allen Ginsberg. *Ann Arbor Argus,* vol. 1, no. 5 (April 14-28, 1969) pp. 12-13.
Note: AG interview format.

J1044   Dean, Jerry. How Allen Ginsberg Performed At Harpur. *Sun-Bulletin* (April 15, 1969) p. 3.

J1045   Ginsberg To Hit Portland. *Vanguard,* vol. 24, no. 25 (April 18, 1969) p. 1.

J1046   Boyd, Gordon. Hill Trip. *Utica Daily Press* (April 22, 1969) p. 11.

J1047   Onley, Betty. Ginsberg To Kick Off Nat'l Affairs Week. *Gonzaga Bulletin,* vol. 59, no. 17 (April 25, 1969) pp. 1, 3.

J1048   A Czech Reject. *Tucson Citizen* (April 25, 1969)

J1049   Mathiason, David. Dressed In Corduroy Jacket, Ginsberg Digs Tape Recorder. *WSU Daily Evergreen,* vol. 75, no. 74 (April 25, 1969) p. 1.

J1050   Poet Allen Ginsberg Reads Works Tonight. *Arizona Daily Wildcat,* vol. 60, no. 133 (April 30, 1969) p. 1.

J1051* Zabrana, Jan. Uvodem Ke Ginsbergovu Kvileni. *Sesity* (April 30, 1969) p. 7.

Williams, William Carlos. Kvileni Pro Carla Solomona. *Sesity* (April 30, 1969) p. 8.
Note: Translation of the introduction to *Howl And Other Poems.*

J1052   Williams, Shirley. A Ginsberg Evening. *Albany Times-Union* (April 30, 1969) p. 3F.
Note: AG quoted briefly.

J1053   Burton, Ken. Reporter Hits Ginsberg In Row Over Sex Ideas. *Arizona Daily Star* (May 1, 1969)
Note: AG quoted briefly.

J1054 Ginsberg Lips Off, Struck In the Mouth. *Los Angeles Times* (May 1, 1969)
Note: A G quoted briefly.

J1055 DeTurk, David. Allen Ginsberg In Maine. *Word,* vol. 1, no. 1 (May 1969) pp. 1, 10.
Note: A G quoted briefly.

Dyroff, Jan Michael. [review of *Planet News*]. *Word,* vol. 1, no. 1 (May 1969) p. 10.

J1056 Buttenhuis, Peter. Canadian Literary Letter. *New York Times Book Review* (May 4, 1969) pp. 41-43.

J1057 Ginsberg To Try New Shot At VU. *Nashville Tennessean* (May 6, 1969)

J1058 Lipscomb, Joe. Poet Turns 'em On. *Nashville Tennessean* (May 7, 1969) p. 4.
Note: A G quoted briefly.

J1059 Ginsberg Visits UA, Reads His Poetry, Warns Doom Looms. *Arkansas Gazette* (May 8, 1969) p. 15A.
Note: A G quoted at length.

J1060 Schwager, Jane. Guru Reads Poems, Does Hindu Chants. *Mankato Free Press* (May 8, 1969)
Note: A G quoted briefly.

J1061 Ginsberg Visits U-A And Dedicates a Poem To Student Protester. *Pine Bluff Commercial* (May 8, 1969) p. 7.
Note: A G quoted at length.

J1062 Silberhorn, Ed. Ginsberg Sings To Blake And Buddha. *Versus* (May 8, 1969) p. 1.
Note: A G quoted at length.

J1063 Kodet, Rose. Ginsberg Sheds Topic Of Drugs, Reads Poetry. *Mankato State Reporter,* vol. 42, no. 83 (May 9, 1969) p. 1.
Note: A G quoted briefly.

J1064 Zyn. Ginsberg At G.U. *Spokane Natural,* vol. 3, no. 10 (May 9-23, 1969) p. 5.

J1065 People. *Time,* vol. 93, no. 19 (May 9, 1969) p. 50.
Note: A G quoted briefly.

J1066 Turner, David. Ginsberg Reads Poems Written On Plane, LSD Trips. *Vanderbilt Hustler* (May 9, 1969) p. 2.
Note: A G quoted briefly.

J1067 Rexroth, Kenneth. [review of *Allen Ginsberg In America* by Jane Kramer]. *New York Times Book Review* (May 11, 1969) pp. 8, 41.

J1068 Newsmakers. *Newsweek,* vol. 73, no. 19 (May 12, 1969) p. 58.
Note: A G quoted briefly.

J1069 Lucas, Jeffrey. Guru Appears At OSU; Message Causes Exit. *Columbus Dispatch* (May 13, 1969) p. 20A.

J1070 [editorial]. *Arkansas Gazette* (May 14, 1969) p. 6A.
Note: A G quoted briefly.

J1071 Lambert, Roger. Ginsberg Joins Swami In Indian Chant, Dance. *O.S.U.*
Lantern (May 14, 1969)
Note: AG quoted briefly.

J1072 Poet Ginsberg, Once Banned, Will Appear At Bona Friday. *Olean Times Herald*
(May 15, 1969) p. 5.

J1073 Lask, Thomas. [review of *Ankor Wat, Planet News* and *TV Baby Poems*]. *New*
York Times (May 17, 1969) p. 31.

J1074 Grissim, John, Jr. [review of *Planet News*]. *Rolling Stone,* no. 33 (May 17,
1969) insert p. 18.

J1075 Greenya, John. [review of *Allen Ginsberg In America* by Jane Kramer].
Washington Post (May 18, 1969) Book World section

J1076 Shapiro, Karl. [review of *Ankor Wat* and *Allen Ginsberg In America* by Jane
Kramer]. *Washington Post* (May 25, 1969) Book World section, p. 6.

J1077 Gold, Barbara. Om Om Om Om Om Om Om Om [review of *Allen Ginsberg In*
America by Jane Kramer]. *Baltimore Sun* (June 1, 1969)

J1078 Ginsberg, Louis. When Words Stopped School Bully He Felt Their Power.
Paterson Evening News (June 2, 1969) p. 4.
Note: AG quoted briefly, first printed in *Chicago Sun-Times* (Jan. 12, 1969).

J1079 Lipton, Lawrence. [review of *Allen Ginsberg In America* by Jane Kramer]. *Los*
Angeles Free Press (June 13-20, 1969) pp. 50, 68-69.

J1080 Volz, Joseph. The Poets Ginsberg. *Newark Sunday News* (June 15, 1969)
Magazine section, pp. 23-4, 26, 29-30.
Note: AG quoted briefly.

J1081 B., A. [review of *Planet News*]. *Ambience,* no. 3 (Summer 1969) p. 24.

J1082 Flood, Charles Bracelen. So Much More Than Cocktail Parties. *American PEN,*
vol. 1, no. 1 (Summer 1969) pp. 4-8.

J1083 Robinson, Jay T. Authors And Editors. *Publishers Weekly,* vol. 195, no. 25
(June 23, 1969) p. 18.
Note: AG quoted briefly.

J1084 Wirick, Richard. [review of *Planet News*]. *Damascus Free Press,* vol. 1, no. 6
(July 1969) p. 2.

J1085 Ginsberg, Louis. [letter to the editor]. *Playboy,* vol. 16, no. 7 (July 1969) pp.
9-10.

J1086 Berkson, Bill. [review of *Planet News*]. *Poetry,* vol. 114, no. 4 (July 1969) pp.
251-265.

J1087 Acid Return. *Good Times,* vol. 2, no. 25 (July 3, 1969) pp. 5-7.

J1088 Aronowitz, Alfred G. The Poet Packs 'em In At NYU. *New York Post* (July 29,
1969) p. 60.
Note: AG quoted briefly.

J1089 Allen Ginsberg. *Newsletter On the State Of the Culture* (July 30, 1969) p. 2.

J1090 [Gross, Amy]. We Talk To... *Mademoiselle,* vol. 69, no. 4 (Aug. 1969) p. 343.
Note: AG interview format.

J1091 Says Pentagon "Is Run On Benzedrine". *Springfield Herald* (Aug. 3, 1969) pp.
1, 4.
Note: AG quoted.

J1092 [review of *Allen Ginsberg In America* by Jane Kramer]. *Time,* vol. 94, no. 6
(Aug. 8, 1969) pp. 75-76.

J1093 Intentionally omitted.

J1094 Wallace, George. Poet Allen Ginsberg Casts Spell At Lehigh. *Allentown
Morning Call* (Aug. 21, 1969) pp. 5, 7.

J1095 Vendler, Helen. [review of *Planet News*]. *New York Times Book Review* (Aug.
31, 1969) p. 8.

J1096 Lehman, David. [review of *Ankor Wat*]. *Poetry,* vol. 114, no. 6 (Sept. 1969)
pp. 401-409.

J1097 Norton, Edward C. Louis Ginsberg & Sons, Poets. *Ave Maria* (Sept. 6, 1969)
pp. 23-27.

J1098 History Of the Movement. *Inquisition,* vol. 3, no. 4 (Sept. 17, 1969) p. 6.

J1099 Bukowski, Charles. The Night Nobody Believed I Was Allen Ginsberg.
Berkeley Tribe, vol. 1, no. 11 [issue 11] (Sept. 19-25, 1969) p. 12.

J1100 Another Party Ruled Off Ballot. *New York Times* (Sept. 19, 1969) p. 39.

J1101 Leibowitz, Herbert. [review of *Planet News*]. *Hudson Review,* vol. 22, no. 3
(Autumn 1969) pp. 500-501.

J1102 Messing, Gordon M. The Linguistic Analysis Of Some Contemporary
Nonformal Poetry. *Language And Style,* vol. 2, no. 4 (Fall 1969) pp. 323-
329.

J1103 Howard, Philip. £2,000 Deposit On an Irish Island. *Times* (Sept. 30, 1969) p.
2.

J1104 Wolff, R. [review of *Planet News*]. *Common Sense,* vol. 1, no. 14 (Oct. 1,
1969) p. 8.

J1105 Kajava, Jukka. Huuto Sanoin Ja Savelin. *Helsingin Sanomat* (Oct. 2, 1969) p.
37.

J1106 McClintock, Jack. Jack Kerouac Is On the Road No More. *St. Petersburg Times*
(Oct. 12, 1969) Floridian section, pp. 4, 6-10.

J1107 Aronowitz, Alfred G. Prose (Taxman) Dogs Poetry (Ginsberg). *New York Post*
(Oct. 14, 1969) pp. 2, 96.
Note: AG quoted.

J1108 Lichtenstein, Arthur. Allen Ginsberg Read In Detroit. *South End* (ca. Oct. 16,
1969)

J1109 Katzman, Allen. [review of *Planet News*]. *Los Angeles Free Press* (Oct. 17,
1969) p. 33.

J1110   Obituary [for Jack Kerouac]. *Daily News* (Oct. 22, 1969)

J1111   'Beat Generation' Father, Jack Kerouac, Is Dead At 47. *Detroit Free Press* (Oct. 22, 1969) p. 1B.

J1112   Lelyveld, Joseph. Jack Kerouac, Novelist, Dead; Father Of the Beat Generation. *New York Times* (Oct. 22, 1969) p. 47.
Note: AG quoted briefly.

J1113   'Beat' Writer Jack Kerouac Dies In Florida. *Rocky Mountain News* (Oct. 22, 1969) p. 42.

J1114   La Vigne, Sharon. Allen Ginsberg To Speak Here. *Independent,* vol. 10, no. 7 (Oct. 23, 1969) p. 1.
Note: AG quoted briefly.

J1115   Charney, Marc. Jack Kerouac Remembered By Beat, Hip Generations. *Lowell Sun* (Oct. 23, 1969) p. 3.
Note: AG quoted.

J1116   Landers, Robert K. Ginsberg Gives Forth On 'Politics Of Love'. *New Haven Journal-Courier* (Oct. 23, 1969) p. 4.
Note: AG quoted briefly.

J1117   Poet Praises Kerouac. *New Haven Register* (Oct. 23, 1969) p. 62.
Note: AG quoted briefly.

J1118   Luce, H. Christopher. Ginsberg Chants, Reads At PU; Author Kerouac Memorialized. *Yale Daily News,* vol. 91, no. 30 (Oct. 23, 1969) p. 1.
Note: AG quoted briefly.

J1119   Changes [part 1]. *Hotcha!,* no. 33 (Oct. 25-Nov. 8, 1969)
Note: AG interview format, first printed in *City Of San Francisco Oracle* (Feb. 1967).

J1120   Turner, Jean-Rae. Poet Ginsberg Bombs Out. *Daily Journal* (Oct. 29, 1969) p. 28.
Note: AG quoted briefly.

J1121   Werbin, Stuart. The Death, the Wake, And the Funeral Of Jack Kerouac. *Cambridge Phoenix,* vol. 1, no. 4 (Oct. 30-Nov. 5, 1969) pp. 1, 8-9.

J1122   Fraser, David. Ginsberg, The Trees Are Our Allies. *Fifth Estate,* vol. 4, no. 13 (Oct. 30-Nov. 12, 1969) pp. 8-9.
Note: AG interview format.

J1123   Gornick, Vivian. Jack Kerouac: 'The Night And What It Does To You'. *Village Voice* (Oct. 30, 1969) pp. 1, 27.
Note: AG quoted briefly.

J1124   The Flophouse Bard. *Daily Journal* (Oct. 31, 1969) p. 8.

J1125   Lovell, John M. Poet Ginsberg Finds 'Howl' Sounds Well 14 Years Later. *Portland Press Herald,* vol. 106, no. 115 (Oct. 31, 1969) p. 1.
Note: AG quoted.

J1126   Wetzler, Betty. Ginsberg Reads To 1000 In TPA. *Daily Journal* (ca. Nov. 1, 1969) pp. 1, 6.
Note: AG quoted briefly.

J1127   Eduskuntakin Herää?! *Ilkka* (Nov. 1, 1969)

J1128   Epäsiveellinen Julkaisu. *Kansan Uutiset* (Nov. 1, 1969)

J1129   Gregg, Paul and Gregg, Liz. Interview In a Hotel Room With Allen Ginsberg. *Strobe*, vol. 3, no. 1 ([Nov.] 1969) pp. 59-68.
   Note: AG interview format.

J1130   Richmond, John. Ginsberg Preaches Here And Now Philosophy. *Montreal Star* (Nov. 3, 1969) p. 38.
   Note: AG quoted at length.

J1131   Ginsberg Due Here Tonight. *Saratogian* (Nov. 5, 1969) p. 3A.

J1132   Benjamin, Judi and Dorio, Jo-Ann. [letters to the editor]. *Daily Journal* (Nov. 5, 1969) p. 6.

J1133   Huuto Yleisradiossa. *Kaleva* (Nov. 6, 1969)

J1134   Nummi, Lassi. Huuto, Kaiku, Äänten Sorinaa. *Uusi Suomi* (Nov. 6, 1969)

J1135   Shea, Eileen. In Praise Of Allan [sic] Ginsberg. *Agape* (Nov. 7, 1969) p. 3.
   Note: AG quoted briefly.

J1136   Cohan, Zara. [letter to the editor]. *Daily Journal* (Nov. 7, 1969) p. 6.

J1137   Todella Aihetta. *Karjalainen* (Nov. 7, 1969)

J1138   Yleisradio, Ginsberg, Syytteet Ja Vaalit. *Kansan Uutiset* (Nov. 8, 1969)

J1139   Olämplig, Sa Förlaget Om Ginsburgs Skriet. *Nasabladet* (Nov. 8, 1969)

J1140   Brousseau, Jean-Paul. Guru Ginsberg Parmi Nous. *La Presse* (Nov. 8, 1969)
   Note: AG quoted briefly in French only.

J1141   S., A. Lähetetyt Kirjoitukset. *Uusi Suomi* (Nov. 8, 1969)

J1142   Changes [part 2]. *Hotcha!*, no. 34 (Nov. 9-30, 1969) pp. 3-6.
   Note: AG interview format in German only, first printed in *City Of San Francisco Oracle* (Feb. 1967).

J1143   Gronow, Pekka. Mistä Rumat Sanat Tulevat? *Savon Sanomat* (Nov. 13, 1969)

J1144   Southwick, Tom. Like a Homosexual Capitalist, Afraid Of the Masses. *Skidmore News* (Nov. 13, 1969) pp. 1, 6.
   Note: AG quoted briefly.

J1145   Radiojohtajat Puivat "Huutoa". *Ilta-Sanomat* (Nov. 17, 1969)

J1146   Rickert, Angus. Ginsberg: Vivid, Ribald. *Ottawa Citizen* (ca. Nov. 17, 1969)
   Note: AG quoted briefly.

J1147   Työryhmä Pui "Huutoa". *Uusi Suomi* (Nov. 18, 1969)

J1148   Bruchac, Joe. The Gentlest Prophet: Ginsberg Reads At Skidmore. *Nickel Review*, vol. 4, no. 12 (Nov. 21, 1969) p. 5.
   Note: AG quoted briefly.

J1149   Ginsberg For AID. *Octopus*, vol. 2, no. 15 (Nov. 21, 1969) p. 1.

J1150 'Huuto' Oli Rikkomus Toimilupaa Vastaan. *Aanulehti* (Nov. 22, 1969)

J1151 Radion 'Huuto' Toimiluvan Vastainen. *Sruaa* (Nov. 22, 1969)

J1152 Seligsohn, Leo. Two Ginsbergs, a Study In Contrast. *Newsday* (Nov. 24, 1969)

J1153 Fraser, David. Trees Are Our Allies. *Good Times,* vol. 2, no. 46 (Nov. 27, 1969) pp. 10-11.
       Note: AG interview format, first printed in *Fifth Estate* (Oct. 30, 1969).

J1154 Hoffman Rejects Defense Witness. *New York Times* (Nov. 27, 1969) p. 30.

J1155 Ehrmann, Eric and Davis, Stephen. There Is Really Nothing Inside. *Rolling Stone* (Nov. 29, 1969) p. 34.
       Note: AG quoted briefly.

       Bangs, Lester. Elegy For a Desolation Angel. *Rolling Stone* (Nov. 29, 1969) p. 36.

J1156 Revell, Peter. [review of *TV Baby Poems*]. *Alphabet,* no. 17 (Dec. 1969) pp. 69-70.

J1157 Mark, J. The New Humor. *Esquire,* vol. 72, no. 6 (Dec. 1969) pp. 218-220, 329-330.

J1158 Radion Hallintoneuvosto Tuomitsi "Huuto" — Runon. *Helsingin Sanomat* (Dec. 1969) p. 16.

J1159 Changes. *Hotcha!,* no. 36 (Dec. 1969) pp. 6-7.
       Note: AG interview format in German only, first printed in *City Of San Francisco Oracle* (Feb. 1967).

J1160 Krown, Johnny. Journey To the East. *View From the Bottom,* vol. 1, no. 10 (Dec. 4, 1969) p. 10.
       Note: AG quoted briefly, cover incorrectly states no. 3 (Nov. 27, 1969).

J1161 Ram Das, Nee Richard Alpert, On the Road Past Acid To Yoga. *Los Angeles Free Press* (Dec. 5, 1969) pp. 46-47.

J1162 Rinne, Matti. Aitio Tuomitsee Kuulematta. *Ilta Sanomat* (Dec. 9, 1969) p. 8.

J1163 Huuto Huudosta Kumma Maanjäristys Suomessa. *Savon Sanomat* (Dec. 10, 1969)

J1164 Lounelalle Muistutus "Huudosta". *Turun Sanomat* (Dec. 10, 1969)

J1165 Huutoon Ei Vielä Vastausta. *Kansan Uutiset* (Dec. 11, 1969)

J1166 Ginsberg... *Octopus,* vol. 2, no. 16 (Dec. 11, 1969) pp. 4, 15.
       Note: AG quoted.

J1167 Ginsberg's 'Om Om' Rattles Judge. *Paterson Evening News* (Dec. 11, 1969) pp. 1, 4.

J1168 Newman, M.W. 'Om'-inous Day At '7' Trial As Ginsberg Does Encore. *Chicago Daily News* (Dec. 12, 1969) p. 6.

J1169 Coakley, Michael and Adelman, Sy. '7' Trial Erupts, Poet Hums. *Chicago Today* (Dec. 12, 1969) p. 7.

J1170 Chicago Trial Hears Poet's Hindu Chant. *Evening Bulletin* (Dec. 12, 1969) p. 19.
Note: AG quoted briefly.

J1171 Sirno, Mauri. Kulttuuririntama. *Hämeen Yhteistyo* (Dec. 12, 1969)

J1172 Huuto-Ohjelman Pallo Siirtyi Hallintoneuvostolle. *Kansan Uutiset* (Dec. 12, 1969)

J1173 Ciccone, F. Richard. Chicago Trial Gets a Touch Of the Poet. *New York Post* (Dec. 12, 1969) p. 26.
Note: AG quoted briefly.

J1174 Lukas, J. Anthony. Allen Ginsberg Meets a Judge And Is Clearly Misunderstood. *New York Times* (Dec. 12, 1969) pp. 33, 43.
Note: AG quoted briefly.

J1175 Judge Cuts Off Ginsberg's "Hare". *Paterson Evening News* (Dec. 12, 1969) pp. 1, 6.
Note: AG quoted briefly.

J1176 Aitio Vastasi "Huutoon". *Pohjolan Sanomat* (Dec. 12, 1969)

J1177 Jazz-Runo Huuto Aiheuttaa Kurinpalautuksia Radiossa. *Savon Sanomat* (Dec. 12, 1969)

J1178 'Huuto' Toimiluvan Vastainen. *Sruaa* (Dec. 12, 1969)

J1179 Enstad, Robert and Davis, Robert. Poet's Chants Incite Laughs At Riot Trial. *Chicago Tribune* (Dec. 13, 1969) section 1, p. 7.
Note: AG quoted briefly.

J1180 Fuller, Tony. Om Chanting Fails To Quiet Lawyers In Chicago Trial. *Evening Bulletin* (Dec. 13, 1969) p. 3.

J1181 Kärpäsiä Ia Härkäsiä. *Karjalainen* (Dec. 13, 1969)

J1182 Lukas, J. Anthony. A Chant By Ginsberg Fails To Charm Chicago Judge. *New York Times* (Dec. 13, 1969) p. 19.
Note: AG quoted briefly, another edition of this date and page give the article the title "'Om,' Ginsberg's Hindu Chant, Fails To Charm a Judge In Chicago".

J1183 Leapman, Michael. Sanskrit Prayer At US Trial. *Times* (Dec. 13, 1969) p. 4.
Note: AG quoted briefly.

J1184 [political cartoon featuring AG]. *Albany Times-Union* (Dec. 13, 1969) p. 14.

J1185 Intentionally omitted.

J1186 Kurinpalautusta Yleisradiolle. *Helsingin Sanomat* (Dec. 15, 1969)

J1187 The Judge: 'I Do Not Understand It'. *National Observer*, vol. 8, no. 50 (Dec. 15, 1969) p. 6.
Note: AG interview format from Chicago conspiracy trial testimony.

J1188 Radiossa Esitetysta Jazzrunosta Seuraa Kurinpitotoimenpiteita. *Savon Sanomat* (Dec. 15, 1969)

Kirjailijaliitto Aitiolle Huudosta. *Savon Sanomat* (Dec. 15, 1969)

J1189 Peck, Abe. Eco-Notes. *Seed,* vol. 4, no. 10 ([Dec. 15] 1969) pp. 4-5, 23, 25.
Note: AG interview format from Chicago conspiracy trial testimony.

J1190 Fraser, David. Trees Are Our Allies. *Extra,* vol. 2, no. 3 (Dec. 16, 1969) p. 10.
Note: AG interview format, first printed in *Fifth Estate* (Oct. 30, 1969).

J1191 Peck, Abe. The Defense Goes On the Offensive In the Chicago Conspiracy Trial.
Georgia Straight, vol. 3, no. 88 (Dec. 17-24, 1969) pp. 5-6.
Note: AG quoted briefly.

J1192 Berner, Arne. "Huudon" Kaikuja. *Turun Sanomat* (Dec. 17, 1969)

J1193 Hiltusen Kantelu "Huudosta" Viela Poliisin Pohdittavana. *Uusi Suomi* (Dec. 17,
1969)

J1194 Hallintoneuvoston Varoitus. *Aanulehti* (Dec. 19, 1969)

J1195 Glusman, Paul. Beauty Vs. Beast. *Berkeley Tribe,* vol. 1, no. 24 [issue 24]
(Dec. 19-26, 1969) p. 7.
Note: AG quoted briefly.

Peck, Abe. And If the Law Is Absurd...What Then? *Berkeley Tribe,* vol. 1, no.
24 [issue 24] (Dec. 19-26, 1969) pp. 14-15.
Note: AG interview format from Chicago conspiracy trial testimony.

J1196 Toimiluvan Noudattaminen Ei Ehdonvallan Alainen Asia. *Uusi Suomi* (Dec. 19,
1969) p. 2.

J1197 People. *Time,* vol. 94, no. 25 (Dec. 19, 1969) p. 37.

J1198 Froines, John. Con Spire: To Breathe Together. *Willamette Bridge,* vol. 2, no.
28 (Dec. 19, 1969—Jan. 1, 1970) pp. 20-1.
Note: AG quoted briefly.

J1199 Papa Ginsberg Chides Upstart Son, 41, On LSD. *Denver Post* (Dec. 22, 1969)
p. 1.
Note: AG quoted briefly.

J1200 Moraes, Dom. Somewhere With Allen And Gregory. *Horizon,* vol. 11, no. 1
(Winter 1969) pp. 66-67.
Note: AG quoted briefly.

J1201 Lyon, George W., Jr. Allen Ginsberg, Angel Headed Hipster. *Journal Of
Popular Culture,* vol. 3, no. 3 (Winter 1969) pp. 391-403.

J1202 Fabricio, Robert. The Ginsberg Generation Gap. *Miami Herald* (Dec. 22, 1969)
p. C-1.
Note: AG quoted briefly.

J1203 Loud, Profane Vie In Miami Stadium. *Denver Post* (Dec. 23, 1969) p. 12.

J1204 Pop Puts Down That Ginsberg Boy. *Detroit Free Press* (Dec. 23, 1969)

J1205 Wright, Carolyn Jay. Lights Up, Sound Off, Ginsberg Is Tuned Out. *Miami
Herald* (Dec. 23, 1969) pp. 1B-2B.

J1206 Peck, Abe. Allen Ginsberg Meets Julius Hoffman. *Georgia Straight,* vol. 3, no.
89 (Dec. 24-31, 1969) pp. 6-9.
Note: AG interview format from Chicago conspiracy trial testimony.

J1207   Music Drives Hippy Poet Off Stage. *Times* (Dec. 24, 1969) p. 3.

J1208   Peck, Abe. Allen Ginsberg Meets Julius Hoffman. *Distant Drummer,* no. 65 (Dec. 25, 1969-Jan. 1, 1970) pp. 3-4.
Note: AG interview format from Chicago conspiracy trial testimony.

J1209   Wright, Carolyn Jay. Ginsberg Will Ask U.S. To Order His Poetry Concert Rescheduled. *Miami Herald* (Dec. 25, 1969)

J1210   Frishman, Mel. Ginsbergs Try To Tune In To One Another. *Miami News* (Dec. 25, 1969) p. 8-C.
Note: AG quoted.

J1211   [Peck, Abe]. Eco-Notes. *Earth Read-Out,* no. 17 (Dec. 26, 1969) pp. 3-4.
Note: AG interview format, first printed in *Seed* (Dec. 15, 1969).

J1212   Peck, Abe. While Moloch Reigns In Chicago; Ochs, Ginsberg Speak. *Los Angeles Free Press* (Dec. 26, 1969) p. 4.

J1213   Simpson, Louis. Poetry In the Sixties—Long Live Blake! Down With Donne! *New York Times Book Review* (Dec. 28, 1969) pp. 1-2, 18.

J1214   Speaking Of People. *National Observer,* vol. 8, no. 52 (Dec. 29, 1969) p. 9.

J1215   Poet Sues For Stadium Use. *New York Times* (Dec. 31, 1969) p. 18.

J1216   Allen Ginsberg, Louis Ginsberg, Young Entertainers, Inc., and Harry Richman, Plaintiffs, v. The City Of Miami, Melvin Reese, Paul Andrews, and Manny Costa, Defendants. No. 69-1527-Civ-CA. United States District Court, S.D. Florida, Miami Division. Dec. 31, 1969.

J1217   *Federal Supplement* (307 Federal Supplement 675 [1969]) Ginsberg v. City Of Miami. Dec. 31, 1969, pp. 675-677.

J1218   [review of *Ankor Wat* and *Planet News*]. *Books & Writers* (ca. 1969-70) pp. 89-90.

J1219   Zverev, Alexei. [review of *TV Baby Poems*]. *Contemporary Literature Abroad,* no. 3 (1969)

J1220   Fox, Hugo. Mistica Norteamericana Del Siglo XX. *Eco Contemporaneo,* no. 12 (1969) pp. 10-15.

J1221   Howard, Richard. Allen Ginsberg: 'O Brother Of the Laurel, Is the World Real? Is the Laurel a Joke Or a Crown Of Thorns?'. *Minnesota Review,* vol. 9, no. 1 (1969) pp. 50-56.

J1222   Allen Ginsberg I Vidneskranken. *Politiken* (1969)
Note: AG interview format from Chicago conspiracy trial testimony in Danish only.

J1223   Pivano, Fernanda. Vodikova Hraci Skrin. *Svetova Literatura,* no. 5-6 (1969) pp. 117-139.

Books:

J1224   Allen, Walter. *The Urgent West: The American Dream And Modern Man.* New York, NY: Dutton, 1969, pp. 220-221.

J1225   Babcox, Peter; Babcox, Deborah and Abel, Bob. *The Conspiracy.* New York, NY: Dell, 1969.

J1226   Berke, Joseph (ed.). *Counter Culture.* London, England: Peter Owen, 1969.
Note: AG mentioned throughout.

J1227   Bowering, George. *How I Hear Howl.* Montreal, Canada: Beaver Kosmos, 1969.

J1228   *Brockhaus Enzyklopadia, vol. 7.* Wiesbaden, Germany: F.A. Brockhaus, 1969, p. 337.

J1229   DiPrima, Diane. *Memoirs Of a Beatnik.* New York, NY: Olympia Press, 1969, pp. 126-7, 130-3.

J1230   Faderman, Lillian and Bradshaw, Barbara (eds.). *Speaking For Ourselves.* Glenview, IL: Scott, Foresman & Co., 1969, p. 154.

J1231   Gumbo, Judy (ed.). *No Chanting In the Court.* Chicago, IL: The Conspiracy, 1969.
Note: AG interview format from Chicago conspiracy trial testimony, presented here as a play.

J1232   Horovitz, Michael (ed.). *The Children Of Albion: Poetry Of the Underground In Britain.* London, England: Penguin Books, 1969.

J1233   Howard, Richard. *Alone With America.* New York, NY: Atheneum, 1969, pp. 145-152.

J1234   Kostelanetz, Richard. *Master Minds.* New York, NY: Macmillan, 1969.
Note: AG quoted briefly and mentioned throughout.

J1235   Kramer, Jane. *Allen Ginsberg In America.* New York, NY: Vintage Books, 1970.
Note: AG quoted at length throughout.
[Published in England as] Kramer, Jane. *Paterfamilias, Allen Ginsberg In America.* London, England: Victor Gollancz, 1970.

J1236   Merrill, Thomas F. *Allen Ginsberg.* New York, NY: Twayne Publishers, 1969.
Note: AG mentioned throughout.

J1237   Roszak, Theodore. *The Making Of a Counter Culture.* Garden City, NY: Doubleday, 1969.
[Published in England by Faber and Faber, 1970]

J1238   Schneir, Walter (ed.). *Telling It Like It Was: The Chicago Riots.* New York, NY: Signet/New American Library, 1969, p. 107.
Note: AG interview format from the Chicago conspiracy trial testimony.

J1239   Spender, Stephen. *The Year Of the Young Rebels.* London, England: Weidenfeld & Nicolson, 1969.

1970

J1240   Om. *Ann Arbor Argus,* vol. 1, no. 16 [Jan. 1970] pp. 7, 9, 16-18.
Note: AG interview format from the Chicago conspiracy trial testimony.

J1241 Father-Son Rap On Drug Generation Gap. *Attack On Narcotic Addiction And Drug Abuse,* vol. 4, no. 1 (Winter [Jan.] 1970) p. 11.
Note: AG quoted briefly.

J1242 Dickstein, Morris. Allen Ginsberg And the 60's [review of *Planet News*]. *Commentary,* vol. 49, no. 1 (Jan. 1970) pp. 64, 66-70.

J1243 Allen Ginsberg And Bethlehem Asylum In Concert At Miami Marine Stadium. *Daily Planet,* vol. 1, no. 6 (Jan. 1, 1970) pp. 1, 8.

J1244 Amram, David. In Memory Of Jack Kerouac. *Evergreen Review,* vol. 14, no. 74 (Jan. 1970) pp. 40-41, 76-78.

J1245 Aldrich, Mike. [review of *Allen Ginsberg/William Blake* (recording)]. *Marijuana Review,* vol. 1, no. 5 (Jan.-June 1970) pp. [22-23].

J1246 Carroll, Margaret and Wright, Carolyn Jay. Judge OKs Ginsberg's Recital. *Miami Herald* (Jan. 1, 1970) pp. 1-2.

J1247 Peck, Abe. Ginsberg—A Co-Conspirator? *Nite Of the Hunter,* vol. 1, no. 2 (Jan. 1970) pp. 12-13.
Note: AG interview format from the Chicago conspiracy trial testimony.

J1248 Peck, Abe. I Don't Understand It. *Helix,* vol. 2, no. 1 (Jan. 2, 1970) pp. 6-7.
Note: AG interview from the Chicago conspiracy trial testimony.

J1249 Ginsberg Resets Poetry Reading. *Miami Herald* (Jan. 2, 1970) section B, p. 1.

J1250 Court Rules In Favour Of US Poet. *Times* (Jan. 2, 1970) p. 5.

J1251 Nelson, David. Ginsberg Reads, Lights Stay On. *Miami Herald* (Jan. 3, 1970) p. B-1.
Note: AG quoted briefly.

J1252 Glass, Ian. Poet Finally Does His Thing: %?&;3/4&. *Miami News* (Jan. 3, 1970) p. 4-A.
Note: AG quoted briefly.

J1253 Mahoney, Larry. Poet Ginsberg Is a Hit At UM. *Miami Herald* (Jan. 5, 1970)

J1254 Keasler, John. Ginsberg's Recital Better Than Counting Sheep. *Miami News* (Jan. 5, 1970) p. 8-B.

Roberts, Jack. Double Standard In Ginsberg Case. *Miami News* (Jan. 5, 1970)

J1255 Beat Poet Ginsberg Speaks Wednesday On BSC Campus. *Birmingham News* (Jan. 6, 1970)
Note: AG quoted briefly.

J1256 Besancon, Mike. Ginsberg Will Discuss His Works, Philosophy. *Duke Chronicle* (Jan. 6, 1970) pp. 1, 9.

J1257 Lewis, Mike. U.S. Choking On Fumes. *Birmingham Post-Herald* (Jan. 7, 1970) p. 23.
Note: AG quoted briefly.

J1258 Ginsberg In Court. *Protean Radish,* vol. 4, no. 14 (Jan. 7-13, 1970) pp. 1, 11-12.
Note: AG interview format from the Chicago conspiracy trial testimony.

J1259   Waddle, Chris. Sun Rises Despite Ginsberg Speech. *Birmingham Post-Herald* (Jan. 8, 1970)
Note: AG quoted briefly.

J1260   Emerson, Steve. Ginsberg: Political Poetry. *Duke Chronicle* (Jan. 8, 1970) p. 15.

J1261   Ginsberg Warns Of Efforts To Poison Earth With Fumes. *Durham Morning Herald* (Jan. 9, 1970)
Note: AG quoted.

J1262   Ginsberg Blasts U.S. At Duke. *Durham News & Observer* (Jan. 9, 1970)
Note: AG quoted briefly.

J1263   Froines, John. Chicago And Conspiracy, Conspiracy And Chicago. *Los Angeles Free Press,* vol. 7, no. 2 [issue 286] (Jan. 9-15, 1970) pp. 5, 20.
Note: AG quoted briefly, reprinted from *Willamette Bridge* (Dec. 19, 1969).

J1264   Mabry, Brenda. Ginsberg Enchants Huge Crowd With Poems, Mantras, Songs. *Duke Chronicle,* vol. 65, no. 67 (Jan. 10, 1970) pp. 1, 6.

J1265   Gwertzman, Bernard. The Backstage McCarthy. *San Francisco Chronicle* (Jan. 12, 1970) p. 7.

J1266   Burke, John C. Gloucester Poet Charlie Olson Buried. *Boston Globe* (Jan. 14, 1970) p. 3.

J1267   Kenyon, Paul B. Olson Rites Held. *Gloucester Daily Times* (Jan. 14, 1970) pp. 1, 12.

J1268   B'ham Southern Host To Ginsberg. *Alabama Independent,* vol. 7, no. 10 (Jan. 15, 1970) pp. 1, 5.

J1269   Huudon Tutkimukset Edelleenkin Kesken. *Uusi Suomi* (Jan. 16, 1970)

J1270   Watson, Penny. Allen Ginsberg / We Need a Lot Less Stone And a Lot More Tree Tenderness. *North Carolina Anvil,* vol. 3, no. 138 (Jan. 17, 1970) pp. 6-7.
Note: AG quoted briefly.

J1271   Blom, Carita. Raatikainen Vill Inte Svara Radioredaktörer Om 'Skriet'. *NYA Pressen* (Jan. 20, 1970)

J1272   Swindle, M.D. Business As Usual. *Kaleidoscope* (Jan. 21, 1970) p. 5.

J1273   Wells, Michael. The Second Coming. *Daily Planet,* vol. 1, no. 8 (Jan. 24, 1970) pp. 1, 3-5, 7, 19.
Note: AG quoted briefly.

Charbeneau, Mrs. Leslie. [letter to the editor]. *Daily Planet,* vol. 1, no. 8 (Jan. 24, 1970) p. 2.

J1274   Kenyon, Paul and Smith, Donna. Death Of a Poet. *North Shore Seventy,* vol. 5, no. 4 (Jan. 24, 1970) pp. 3-7.
Note: AG quoted briefly; this appears as a supplement in the following newspapers: *Beverly Times, Gloucester Daily Times, Newburyport Daily News, Peabody Times.*

J1275   Loquidis, John. Concave. *Chinook,* vol. 2, no. 4 (Jan. 29, 1970) p. 8.

J1276   "The Trees Are Our Allies..."   An Interview Allen Ginsberg. *Los Angeles Free Press,* vol. 7, no. 5 [issue 289] (Jan. 30, 1970) part 2, pp. 33, 35.
Note: AG interview format, reprinted from *Fifth Estate* (Oct. 30, 1969).

J1277   Hayman, Ronald. [review of *Ankor Wat* and *Planet News*]. *Encounter,* vol. 34, no. 2 (Feb. 1970) pp. 84-91.

J1278   Bishop, Gordon.   The Poets Ginsberg. *Sunday Star-Ledger* (Feb. 1, 1970) section 3, p. 1.

J1279   Dick, Kay. [review of *Paterfamilias* by Jane Kramer]. *Times* (Feb. 7, 1970) p. iv.

J1280   Muggeridge, Malcolm. [review of *Paterfamilias* by Jane Kramer]. *Observer Weekend Review* (Feb. 8, 1970)

J1281   St. Peter's Refuses Aid To Its Magazine. *New York Times* (Feb. 8, 1970) p. 70.

J1282   Trial Of Chicago 7. *Facts On File,* vol. 30, no. 1529 (Feb. 12-18, 1970) p. 91.

J1283   Epstein, Jason.   The Chicago Conspiracy Trial: Allen Ginsberg On the Stand. *New York Review Of Books,* vol. 14, no. 3 (Feb. 12, 1970) pp. 25-28.

J1284   Ginsberg To Speak To TU Students. *Trinitonian* (Feb. 13, 1970) p. 3.

J1285   Wolf, Robert.   Withholding Taxes. *Manhattan Tribune* (Feb. 14, 1970) p. 10.

J1286   Clurman, Harold.   100 Poets Tell Of Sorrow, Fear, Anger, Death. *New York Times* (Feb. 15, 1970) p. 32.

J1287   Fraser, David.   The Trees Are Our Allies. *Chinook,* vol. 2, no. 7 ([Feb. 19] 1970) p. 5.
Note: AG interview format, reprinted from *Fifth Estate* (Oct. 30, 1969).

J1288   Ginsberg. *Logos,* vol. 3, no. 1 (March 1, 1970) unpaged.
Note: AG quoted briefly, reprinted from *Strobe* (Nov. 1969).

J1289   Allen Ginsberg, the Trees Are Our Allies. *Win,* vol. 6, no. 4 (March 1, 1970) pp. 20-21.
Note: AG interview format.

J1290   Williams, Chris.   Pacifist War On the IRS. *New York Post* (March 3, 1970) p. 9.
Note: AG quoted briefly.

J1291   Kevään Kuluessa Päätetään Mahdollisista Syytteistä. *Ilta Sanomat* (March 5, 1970) p. 7.

J1292   The Talk Of the Town [column]. *New Yorker,* vol. 46, no. 3 (March 7, 1970) pp. 29-31.

J1293   Kopkind, Andrew.   In a Contemptible Court. *Great Speckled Bird,* vol. 3, no. 10 (March 9, 1970) pp. 8-9.

J1294   Knight, Jerry.   Ginsberg Leads I.S.U. Protesters. *Des Moines Register* (March 18, 1970) p. 3.
Note: AG quoted briefly.

J1295   [photograph]. *Herald-Whig* (March 18, 1970) p. 2A.

J1296 'Closed' Sign Doesn't Deter Draft System Protesters. *San Antonio Express* (March 20, 1970) p. 15-D.

Luna, Cy. 1,000 Hear Ginsberg's Chants. *San Antonio Express* (March 20, 1970)

J1297 Crowd Braves Chill. *San Antonio Light* (March 20, 1970) p. 8.

J1298 Allen Ginsberg. *Current Biography,* vol. 31, no. 4 (April 1970) pp. 13-16. *Note:* Reprinted in the annual cumulation on pp. 151-154.

J1299 Dennison, George. The Writer's Situation. *New American Review,* no. 9 (April 1970) pp. 93-99.

J1300 Butterick, George. On Maximus IV, V, VI. *West Coast Review,* vol. 4, no. 4 (April 1970) pp. 3-6. *Note:* AG quoted briefly.

J1301 Chicago: The Ginsberg Testimony. *Rolling Stone,* no. 55 (April 2, 1970) pp. 52-53. *Note:* AG interview format, from the Chicago conspiracy trial testimony.

J1302 Glazer, Fred. New Canyon Road Gallery Opens; Allen Ginsberg Reads Here. *New Mexican* (April 5, 1970) p. D7.

J1303 Loquidis, John. Concave. *Chinook,* vol. 2, no. 13 (April 9, 1970) p. 9.

J1304 Leary. *Helix,* vol. 2, no. 15 (April 9, 1970) p. 8. *Note:* AG quoted at length.

J1305 Peltonen, Heikki. [review of *Huuto Ja Meteli*]. *Savon Sanomat* (April 12, 1970) *Note:* Review of the book about the radio broadcast controversy of *Howl.*

J1306 Adhikary, Das. A.C. Bhaktivedanta Swami & Allen Ginsberg, pt. 1. *Chinook,* vol. 2, no. 15 ([April 16] 1970) *Note:* AG interview format reprinted from *Back To Godhead* (1968).

J1307 Boats, Mother. Cruising North Beach. *Berkeley Barb* (April 17-23, 1970) p. 4. *Note:* AG quoted.

J1308 20,000 In Park For Earth Day. *Evening Bulletin* (April 23, 1970) pp. 1, 10. *Note:* AG quoted briefly.

J1309 Haskin, Don and Donovan, Joe. It's All Over But the Wheezing. *Philadelphia Daily News* (April 23, 1970) p. 5.

J1310 Gillen, Beth and Young, James C. 30,000 Attend 'Earth Day' In Park. *Philadelphia Inquirer* (April 23, 1970) pp. 1, 3.

J1311 'Beat' Generation Poet Talks To BCC Students. *Fall River Herald News* (April 27, 1970) p. 18.

J1312 Adhikary, Das. [interview, pt. 1]. *Chinook,* vol. 2, no. 16 (April 30, 1970) pp. 6-7. *Note:* AG interview format, reprinted from *Back To Godhead* (1968).

J1313 Dvorchik Named Winner Of 1970 Stevens Poetry Award. *Connecticut Daily Campus* (April 30, 1970) p. 1.

J1314   Golden, Gerald A. Earth Digs... *Distant Drummer,* no. 83 (April 30, 1970) p. 3.

J1315   Aldrich, Mike. A Sigh Is a Sword. *Spectrum* (May 1, 1970) p. 5.

J1316   James, George. At Yale, the Torch Is Passed. *Sunday Record* (May 3, 1970) pp. 1, 18.
Note: AG quoted briefly.

J1317   Adhikary, Das. [interview] pt. 2. *Chinook,* vol. 2, no. 17 (May 7, 1970) pp. 6-7.
Note: AG interview format, reprinted from *Back To Godhead* (1968).

J1318   Mones, Leon. [review of *Morning In Spring* by Louis Ginsberg]. *Jewish News* (May 8, 1970) pp. 12, 59.

J1319   Katzman, Allen. Poor Paranoid's Almanac. *East Village Other,* vol. 5, no. 25 (May 19, 1970) pp. 4, 11.

J1320   Barnes, Clive. Stage: 'Chicago 70' At the Martinique. *New York Times* (May 26, 1970) p. 33.

J1321   Hiljainen Hautaus "Huudolle". *Turun Sanomat* (May 29, 1970)

J1322   Oh, Your Honor, I Object. *Countdown,* no. 3 (June 1970) pp. 128-103.
Note: AG interview format from Chicago conspiracy trial testimony, page numbering is intentionally backwards.

J1323   Farrell, Barry. Coming Together. *Hard Times,* no. 80 (June 1-8, 1970) pp. 3-4.
Note: AG quoted briefly.

J1324   Van Hoffman, Nicholas. The Chicago Conspiracy Circus. *Playboy,* vol. 17, no. 6 (June 1970) pp. 87-88, 94, 177-180, 182, 184, 186.
Note: AG interview format, from the Chicago conspiracy trial testimony.

J1325   Alexander, Floyce. Allen Ginsberg's Metapolitics: From Moloch To the Millennium. *Research Studies/Washington State University,* vol. 38, no. 2 (June 1970) pp. 157-173.

J1326   Bangs, Lester. [review of *Songs Of Innocence And Experience* (recording)]. *Rolling Stone,* no. 60 (June 11, 1970) p. 44.

J1327   Bradley, John and Goldstein, Joel. Journalism Shaping the World. *Ethos,* vol. 4, no. 2 (June 20, 1970) p. 3.
Note: AG quoted briefly.

J1328   Stafford, Peter. The Contriving Of a Religion, pt. 1. *Crawdaddy,* vol. 4, no. 9 (June 22, 1970) pp. 29-31.
Note: AG interview format.

J1329   Radicals Give Demands For July 4 Fete. *New York Times* (June 26, 1970) p. 16.

J1330   July 4 Group Bars Radicals' Demands. *New York Times* (June 27, 1970) p. 29.

J1331   Van Der Leun, Gerard. "Whatever Happens To Tim Leary Will Happen To America." A Conversation With Allen Ginsberg. *Organ,* vol. 1, no. 1 (July 1970) pp. 4-9.
Note: AG interview format.

J1332   Kamstra, Jerry. [review of *Indian Journals*]. *San Francisco Chronicle* (July 5, 1970) This World section, p. 37.

J1333   Stafford, Peter. The Contrivance Of Religion, pt. 2. *Crawdaddy,* vol. 4, no. 10 (July 6, 1970) pp. 26-28.
        Note: AG interview format.

J1334   News. *Chinook,* vol. 2, no. 26 (July 16, 1970) p. 3.

J1335   Wanderer a Problem For Police. *Newark Evening News* (July 19, 1970)

J1336   Whittemore, Reed. [review of *Indian Journals*]. *New Republic,* vol. 163, no. 4 [issue no. 2900] (July 25, 1970) pp. 17-18.

J1337   [review of *Indian Journals*]. *Independent Journal* (July 30, 1970)

J1338   P., R.A. [review of *Indian Journals*]. *Michigan Daily* (July 31, 1970) p. 9.

J1339   Wilentz, Joan. Life Among the Littles. *COSMEP Newsletter,* vol. 1, no. 12 (Aug. 1970) p. 1.

J1340   Pelieu, Claude. He Answers From His New Home. *Nola Express,* no. 61 (Aug. 7-20, 1970) p. 17.

J1341   [review of *Paterfamilias* by Jane Kramer]. *Times Of India,* vol. 10 (Aug. 16, 1970) pp. 4-6.

J1342   Shea, Joe. Telling It Again In the Southwest. *Village Voice* (Aug. 27, 1970) p. 3.
        Note: AG quoted briefly.

J1343   Jacobson, Robert. Spoleto Sampler, Minus Schippers. *Saturday Review,* vol. 53, no. 35 (Aug. 29, 1970) p. 44.

J1344   Simon, John A. [review of *Songs Of Innocence And Experience* (recording)]. *Harvard Crimson* ([Sept.] 1970) [1970 Registration issue] pp. 35-37.

J1345   Cushman, Jerome. [review of *Indian Journals*]. *Library Journal,* vol. 95, no. 15 (Sept. 1, 1970) p. 2801.

J1346   Kamstra, Jerry. [review of *Indian Journals*]. *Scanlan's Monthly,* vol. 1, no. 7 (Sept. 1970) pp. 72-73.

J1347   Ginsberg, Louis. [review of *Indian Journals*]. *Win,* vol. 6, no. 14 (Sept. 1, 1970) pp. 28-29.

J1348   Van Gelder, Lindsy. Oppressed? Dial 956-7032. *New York Post* (Sept. 2, 1970) p. 2.

J1349   Ginsberg Takes Tour Of City. *Spectator* (Sept. 11, 1970)
        Note: AG quoted briefly.

J1350   McFadden, Dave. Ginsberg Reveals 'Real Dope Pushers'. *Spectator* (Sept. 12, 1970) p. 7.
        Note: AG quoted.

J1351   Poet Says CODA Covers Up Abuses By Drug Industry. *Niagara Falls Review* (Sept. 14, 1970)
        Note: AG quoted briefly.

J1352 U.S. Poet So Intrigued Extends Rochdale Visit. *Toronto Star* (Sept. 14, 1970)

J1353 Ungaretti, Giuseppe. Presentation Of Allen Ginsberg's Poems. *Books Abroad,* vol. 44, no. 4 (Autumn 1970) pp. 559-563.

J1354 Poulin, A., Jr. Contemporary American Poetry: The Radical Tradition. *Concerning Poetry,* vol. 3, no. 2 (Fall 1970) pp. 5-21.

J1355 Raker, Gerry. Ginsberg Defends Leary In Millbrook Reading. *Poughkeepsie Journal* (Sept. 30, 1970) p. 11.
Note: AG quoted briefly.

J1356 Ginsberg Finds Millbrook Historic. *Millbrook Round Table* (Oct. 1, 1970) p. 1.
Note: AG quoted briefly.

J1357 Rosselli, John. [review of *Indian Journals*]. *Guardian Weekly,* vol. 103, no. 13 (Oct. 3, 1970) p. 18.

J1358 Blain, Margaret. Poets Ginsberg And Everson: A Freak And a Triple Virgo. *Tulane Hullabaloo* (Oct. 23, 1970) p. 2.
Note: AG quoted briefly.

J1359 Shearouse, Chris. Poet Sees 'Planet In Danger'. *States-Item* (Oct. 27, 1970) p. 27.
Note: AG quoted briefly.

J1360 Scharfman, Michael; Mandel, Howard and Hemingway, Sam. Louis And Allen. *Daily Orange,* vol. 69, no. 25 (Oct. 30, 1970) pp. 1, 6-7.
Note: AG interview format.

J1361 Head, Robert. Interview w/Allen Ginsberg, pt. 1. *Nola Express,* no. 67 (Oct. 30-Nov. 12, 1970) pp. 4-5.
Note: AG interview format.

J1362 Pivano, Fernanda. [interview with Fernanda Pivano]. *I Quaderni,* no. 11 (Nov. 1970) pp. 5-15.

J1363 Head, Robert. An Interview/Allen Ginsberg, pt. 1. *Chinook,* vol. 2, no. 42 (Nov. 12, 1970) pp. 6-7.
Note: AG interview format, reprinted from *Nola Express* (Oct. 30, 1970).

J1364 Head, Robert. An Interview w/Allen Ginsberg. *Berkeley Barb,* vol. 11, no. 19 [issue 274] (Nov. 13-19, 1970) pp. 10-11.
Note: AG interview format, reprinted from *Nola Express* (Oct. 30, 1970).

J1365 Writers In Prison. *Newsletter On the State Of the Culture* (Nov. 17, 1970) p. 4.

J1366 Ginsberg Alive. *Ethos,* vol. 4, no. 17 (Nov. 19, 1970) p. 12.

J1367 Arnson, Curtis. [review of *Indian Journals*]. *Jerusalem Post* (Nov. 20, 1970) p. 15.

J1368 Burke, Tim. Melodious Mantras Magnify Magic Of Musical Metaphors. *Spectrum,* vol. 21, no. 34 (Nov. 20, 1970) pp. 5, 12.

J1369 Brady, Charles A. [review of *Indian Journals*]. *Buffalo Evening News* (Nov. 21, 1970) p. B-8.

J1370 Radicals Gather To 'Fuse Culture'. *New York Times* (Nov. 22, 1970) p. 53.

J1371 Head, Robert. Allen Ginsberg, pt. 2. *Nola Express,* no. 69 (Nov. 27-Dec. 10, 1970) pp. 10-11.
Note: AG interview format.

J1372 Allen Ginsberg At Library Poetry Festival Sunday. *Paterson News* (Nov. 30, 1970)

J1373 Head, Robert. Allen Ginsberg, pt. 2. *Chinook,* vol. 2, no. 45 (Dec. 3, 1970) pp. 6-7.
Note: AG interview format, reprinted from *Nola Express* (Nov. 27, 1970).

J1374 Tuttle, Peter. Ginsberg Links Drug Addiction To 'Law And Order' Factions. *Columbia Daily Spectator,* vol. 115, no. 38 (Dec. 3, 1970) p. 3.
Note: AG quoted briefly.

J1375 Goldberg, M.F. Louis And Allen Ginsberg: A Visit With Father & Son. *Congress Bi-Weekly,* vol. 37 (Dec. 4, 1970) pp. 16-19.

J1376 Maruszcak, O.M. 500 Jam Library For Poetry Reading By Allen Ginsberg, Beats' Spokesman. *Paterson News* (Dec. 8, 1970)

J1377 'Fly By Night' Florists Attacked By Alderman. *Paterson News* (Dec. 9, 1970)

J1378 Willis, Ellen. [review of *Songs Of Innocence And Experience* (recording)]. *New Yorker,* vol. 46, no. 43 (Dec. 12, 1970) p. 187.

J1379 Aronowitz, Alfred G. The Poet. *New York Post* (Dec. 16, 1970) p. 74.

J1380 Ginsberg, Allen. Self-Interview. *Intrepid,* no. 18-19 (Winter [Dec. 22, 1970] 1971) pp. 52-61.
Note: AG interview format.

J1381 Durgnat, Raymond. [review of *Airplane Dreams*]. *Poetry Review,* vol. 61, no. 4 (Winter 1970-71) pp. 366-369.

J1382 Christ, You Know It Ain't Easy... *Venture,* no. 5 (Winter 1970) pp. 23-25.
Note: AG interview format, reprinted from the Chicago conspiracy trial testimony.

J1383 Gross, Kenneth. Allen Ginsberg, 'The Hindu Rabbi'. *Newsday* (Dec. 30, 1970) pp. 4-5.
Note: AG quoted.

J1384 Kaplan, Jonathan. A Talk With Allen Ginsberg. *Bard College Community Magazine,* no. 1 (1970) pp. 1-30.
Note: AG interview format.

J1385 The Lion For Real: Reflections On an Interview With Allen Ginsberg. *Helen Review,* vol. 1, no. 3 (1970) pp. 50-52.
Note: AG quoted at length.

Books:

J1386 Charters, Ann. *Scenes Along the Road: Photographs Of the Desolation Angels 1944-1960.* New York, NY: Portents/Gotham Book Mart, 1970.
Note: AG mentioned throughout.

J1387   Clavir, Judy and Spitzer, John (eds.). *The Conspiracy Trial.* Indianapolis, IN: Bobbs-Merrill, 1970, pp. 294-306, 328-9.
Note: AG interview format, from the Chicago conspiracy trial testimony.

J1388   Crews, Frederick and Schell, Orville (eds.). *Starting Over: A College Reader.* New York, NY: Random House, 1970, pp. 242-258.
Note: AG interview format, "Senate Testimony On Drugs".

J1389   French, Warren (ed.). *The Fifties: Fiction, Poetry, Drama.* Deland, FL: Everett/Edwards, 1970.
Contents: Widmer, Kingsley. The Beat In the Rise Of the Populist Culture, pp. 155-173.

J1390   Goodman, Mitchell (ed.). *The Movement Toward a New America.* Philadelphia, PA: Pilgrim Press, 1970.
Contents: Fraser, David. Ginsberg—Trees Are Our Allies, pp. 522-523.
Note: Interview format first printed in *Fifth Estate* (Oct. 30, 1969).
& If the Law Is Absurd...What Then?, pp. 566-567.
Note: Interview format from the Chicago conspiracy trial testimony.

J1391   Gross, Theodore L. (ed.). *Representative Men: Cult Heroes Of Our Time.* New York, NY: Free Press, 1970.
Contents: Kostelanetz, Richard. Allen Ginsberg: Artist As Apostle, Poet As Preacher, pp. 255-275.
Note: AG quoted briefly.

J1392* Hansen, Joseph. *Fadeout.* New York, NY: Harper & Row, 1970, p. 87.

J1393   Levine, Mark L.; McNamee, George C. and Greenberg, Daniel (eds.). *The Tales Of Hoffman.* New York, NY: Bantam Books, 1970, pp. 114-121.
Note: AG interview format from the Chicago conspiracy trial testimony.

J1394   McNeill, Don. *Moving Through Here.* New York, NY: Knopf, 1970.
Note: AG quoted throughout.

J1395   Murphy, Rosalie (ed.). *Contemporary Poets Of the English Language.* Chicago, St. James Press, 1970, pp. 419-421.

J1396   Rexroth, Kenneth. *The Alternative Society.* New York, NY: Herder & Herder, 1970.
Note: AG mentioned throughout.

J1397   Rodman, Selden. *South America Of the Poets.* New York, NY: Hawthorn Books, 1970, p. 20.

J1398   Roth, Cecil and Wigoder, Geoffrey (ed.). *The New Standard Jewish Encyclopedia,* 40th edition. Garden City, NY: Doubleday & Co., 1970, p. 758.

J1399   *Selected Transcripts From the Trial Of the Conspiracy.* Washington, DC: New Mobilization Committee To End the War In Vietnam, 1970, unpaged.
Note: AG interview format from the Chicago conspiracy trial conspiracy.

J1400   Spears, Monroe K. *Dionysus And the City: Modernism In Twentieth Century Poetry.* New York, NY: Oxford University Press, 1970.

J1401   Stein, Jean. *American Journey.* New York, NY: Harcourt Brace Jovanovich, 1970, pp. 186-189.
Note: AG interview format.

J1402 *Who's Who In America 1970-1971,* 36th edition. Chicago, IL: Marquis Who's Who, 1970, p. 830.

J1403 Zeh, John (ed.). *Earth Week '70.* Philadelphia, PA: Earthweek Committee Of Philadelphia, 1970, pp. 16-17.
Note: AG interview format, first printed in *Win* (March 1, 1970).

1971

J1404 Vostro Onore Mi Oppongo. *Ubu,* vol. 2, no. 1 (Jan. 1971) pp. 18-19.
Note: AG interview format, from the Chicago conspiracy trial testimony translated by F. Pivano in Italian only.

J1405 Scharfman, Michael and Mandel, Howard. Interview With Allen Ginsberg And His Father. *College Press Service,* no. 46 (Jan. 15, 1971) p. 1.
Note: AG quoted briefly, reprinted from *Daily Orange* (Oct. 30, 1970).

J1406 Hadden, Jeffrey. 'Beat' Poet Testifies In CIA Case. *Detroit News* (Jan. 15, 1971) p. 12-A.
Note: AG quoted briefly. Another edition of this paper gives the title as "Ginsberg Gets Court's 'Right On'.

J1407 Winfrey, Lee. Defense Seeks 18-Year-Olds For White Panther Jury. *Detroit Free Press* (Jan. 16, 1971) pp. 3A, 12A.
Note: AG quoted briefly.

J1408 Salpukas, Agis. Detroit Radicals Face Bomb Trial. *New York Times* (Jan. 17, 1971) p. 49.
Note: AG quoted briefly.

J1409 Rissover, Fredric. Beat Poetry, the American Dream And the Alienation Effect. *Speech Teacher,* vol. 20, no. 1 (Jan. 20, 1971) pp. 36-43.

J1410 Lipton, Lawrence. Radio Free America. *Los Angeles Free Press,* vol. 8, no. 4 [issue 340] (Jan. 22-28, 1971) p. 4.

J1411 Sprague, Bob. Local Poet Linked To Literary 'Culture Bums'. *Bethlehem Globe-Times* (Jan. 23, 1971) pp. 7, 12.

J1412 Raymont, Henry. Judges Of Book Awards Revolt On Use Of Nationwide Polling. *New York Times* (Jan. 26, 1971) p. 22.

J1413 Pleasants, Ben. [review of *Indian Journals*]. *Los Angeles Times* (Jan. 31, 1971) Calendar section, p. 46.

J1414 Beat Poetry. *Britannica Extension Service,* no. 107 (Feb. 1971) pp. 1-12.

J1415 [quotation]. *I.L.G.W.U. Locals 220-251 Newsletter,* vol. 5, no. 106 (Feb. 1971) p. 2.
Note: AG quoted briefly in English and Spanish.

J1416 Kelley, Ken. Judge Raps Tap. *Fifth Estate,* vol. 5, no. 20 (Feb. 4-17, 1971) p. 5.

J1417 Zwerlin, Michael. Tim's Letter, Interview w/ Eldridge. *Berkeley Tribe,* vol. 3, no. 3 (Feb. 5-12, 1971) pp. 13, 18-19.

J1418 Bass, Liz. Ginsburg [sic] To Read. *Cornell Daily Sun* (Feb. 5, 1971) pp. 1, 12.

J1419   Intentionally omitted.

J1420   Ginsberg Criticizes Poet Prize Award. *Newark Evening News* (March 3, 1971)

J1421   Gent, George. Bellow Wins 3d National Book Award. *New York Times* (March 3, 1971) p. 34.

J1422   McPherson, William. Mr. Bellow's 3d Award. *Washington Post* (March 3, 1971) pp. C1, C6.
Note: AG quoted briefly.

J1423   Tribble, Edwin. Book Awards Highlighted By Judging Controversy. *Washington Star* (ca. March 3, 1971)

J1424   Poetry Winner Ends Up At Heart Of the Matter. *New York Times* (March 5, 1971) p. 31.

J1425   Casey, Phil. Poets Ginsberg, Father And Son. *Washington Post* (March 5, 1971) pp. BB1, B13.
Note: AG quoted briefly.

J1426   Poetess Mona Van Duyn Rebuts Ginsberg's Attack On Her Award. *Paterson News* (March 6, 1971) p. 6.

J1427   Poet Ginsberg Here Tonight. *Diamondback,* vol. 63, no. 97 (March 8, 1971) p. 1.

J1428   Lehmann-Haupt, Christopher. Appraisal Of the Book Awards. *New York Times* (March 9, 1971) p. 35.

J1429   National Book Awards. *Facts On File,* vol. 31, no. 1585 (March 11-17, 1971) p. 199.

J1430   B., E.B.P. Blakean Ginsberg. *Hoya* (March 11, 1971)

J1431   Molineux, Will. Williamsburg 'Talks' Heard By 2,500 Youths. *Daily Press* (March 12, 1971) pp. 1, 10.

J1432   Graham, Fred P. President Urges 'Genuine Reform' Of Court System. *New York Times* (March 12, 1971) pp. 1, 18.

J1433   Bruckner, D.J.R. The Fads Of Art Make It Popular: The Art In the Fads Makes Them Last. *Los Angeles Times* (March 17, 1971) part 2, p. 8.

J1434   Starbuck, Jeff. Ginsberg: In Tune With Being Human. *Eagle,* vol. 45, no. 20 (March 19, 1971)

J1435   Untermeyer, Louis. The Law Of Order, the Promise Of Poetry. *Saturday Review,* vol. 54, no. 12 (March 20, 1971) pp. 18-20, 60.

J1436   We Came To Confer, Not To Confront. *Virginia-Pilot Action Magazine* (March 20, 1971) pp. 6-7.
Note: AG quoted briefly.

J1437   Craft Interview With Allen Ginsberg. *New York Quarterly,* no. 6 (Spring 1971) pp. 12-40.
Note: AG interview format.

J1438   Anderson, Jack. [column]. *Paterson News* (March 22, 1971) p. 22.

J1439   Kimball, G. Ginsberg At Harvard. *Phoenix,* vol. 3, no. 13 (March 30, 1971) p. 27.

J1440   Kundus, Bob. Electric Kool. *Ann Arbor Argus,* no. 39 [April 1971] pp. 20-21.
Note: AG quoted briefly.

J1441   Goddam the Pusherman! Opium War In Laos. *Spark,* vol. 4, no. 3 (April 1971) pp. 1, 7.

J1442   Schenker, Jon. Have a Meeting With Nixon, Rennie Davis. *Daily Kent Stater* (April 8, 1971) p. 10.
Note: AG quoted briefly.

J1443   Rosenbaum, Connie. Iowa Woman, Honored Poet. *Des Moines Register* (April 11, 1971) pp. 1, 3.

J1444   Peery, Richard M. Beat Poet-Spokesman Ginsberg Urges 'Psychedelic Studies'. *Cleveland Plain Dealer* (April 12, 1971)
Note: AG quoted briefly.

J1445   [article]. *Outlaw,* vol. 2, no. 1 (April 14-May 6, 1971) p. 13.
Note: AG quoted briefly.

J1446   Allen Ginsberg, Author Of 'Howl' Will Appear On Campus Tonight. *Branding Iron,* vol. 78, no. 24 (April 16, 1971) p. 1.

J1447   Missett, Kate. Ginsberg Mixes Poetry With Politics, Humor. *Casper Star-Tribune* (April 19, 1971) p. 2.
Note: AG quoted briefly.

J1448   Ginsberg Raps On Quad. *California Aggie* (April 27, 1971) p. 1.
Note: AG quoted briefly.

J1449   Ginsberg Raps On Quad. *California Aggie* (April 28, 1971) p. 1.
Note: AG quoted briefly.

J1450   Abramson, Hilary. Ginsberg Chants And 'Muckrakes'. *Daily Democrat* (April 28, 1971) pp. 1, 2.
Note: AG quoted at length.

J1451   B., A.L. Words About the Man With No Words. *Willamette Bridge,* vol. 4, no. 17 (April 29, 1971) pp. 12-13.

J1452   Papolos, Demitri. May Day And After... *Indications,* vol. 1, no. 1 (May 1971) pp. 20-23.
Note: AG interview format.

J1453   Hansen, Clifford P. [letter to the editor]. *Branding Iron* (May 14, 1971) p. 5.

J1454   S., P.H. Love And Peace. *Times* (May 22, 1971) p. 12.

J1455   Kepner, J. Ginsberg Blows Sacramento Minds. *Advocate,* no. 60 (May 26, 1971) p. 15.

J1456   Mauriac, Claude. [review of *Planet News* (Christian Bourgois)]. *Le Figaro* (May 28, 1971)

J1457 Tedesco, Frank. If You See Anything Horrible Don't Cling To It. *Berkeley Barb,* vol. 12, no. 21 [issue 303] (June 4-10, 1971) pp. 2-3, 11.
Note: AG interview format.

J1458 Levine, Steve. All Of Us Have a Stake In Allen Ginsberg's Bet. *Denver Post* (June 6, 1971)

J1459 Effeministrike. *Berkeley Barb,* vol. 12, no. 22 [issue 304] (June 11-17, 1971) p. 2.

J1460 Aaron. Two Eyes On Ginsberg. *Berkeley Tribe,* vol. 5, no. 19 [issue 99] (June 11-18, 1971) p. 12.
Note: AG quoted briefly.

J1461 Tedesco, Frank. If You See Anything Horrible Don't Cling To It. *Georgia Straight,* vol. 5, no. 175 (June 15-18, 1971) pp. 12-13.
Note: AG interview format, reprinted from *Berkeley Barb* (June 4-10, 1971).

J1462 Turner, Wallace. Coast Governor And Chief Hit Legal Marijuana Plea. *New York Times* (June 15, 1971) p. 27.
Note: AG quoted briefly.

J1463 Champion, Dale. S.F. Hearing On Marijuana Opens. *San Francisco Chronicle* (June 15, 1971) p. 4.
Note: AG quoted briefly.

J1464 CIA Aids Drug Fight, Hansen Says. *Cheyenne State Tribune* (June 17, 1971)

J1465 People. *Time,* vol. 97, no. 25 (June 21, 1971) p. 34.
Note: AG quoted briefly.

J1466 Mishra, Ajit Kumar. The Beatnik Vision Of Life. *Literary Criterion,* vol. 9, no. 4 (Summer 1971) pp. 51-58.

J1467 Nathan, Leonard. The Private 'I' In Contemporary Poetry. *Shenandoah,* vol. 22, no. 4 (Summer 1971) pp. 80-99.

J1468 Boats, Mother and Jail, John. Hasslin Willie Minzey. *Berkeley Barb,* vol. 12, no. 24 [issue 306] (June 25-July 1, 1971) pp. 2, 8.
Note: AG quoted briefly.

J1469 Stone Drag. *San Francisco Good Times,* vol. 4, no. 22 (June 25-July 9, 1971) p. 7.

J1470 Joris, Pierre. Allen Ginsberg Tel Qu'en Liu-Même Enfin. *Actuel,* no. 10-11 (July-Aug. 1971) pp. 20-22.
Note: AG interview format in French only.

J1471 Open Mind. *Berkeley Barb,* vol. 12, no. 25 [issue 307] (July 2-8, 1971) p. 2.

J1472 Wasserman, John L. Fillmore West—Final Moments. *San Francisco Chronicle* (July 7, 1971) p. 62.

J1473 Gefen, Pearl Sheffy. My Son the Guru, My Father the Poet. *Jerusalem Post Magazine* (July 9, 1971) p. 8.
Note: AG quoted briefly.

J1474 Baker, A.T. Poetry Today: Low Profile, Flatted Voice. *Time,* vol. 98, no. 2 (July 12, 1971) pp. 61, 65, E5, E7, 68.

J1475 Bess, Donovan. Writers Petition Swiss To Give Asylum To Leary. *San Francisco Chronicle* (July 15, 1971) p. 4.

J1476 Italy To Try Ginsberg—Obscenity. *San Francisco Examiner* (July 18, 1971)

J1477 Krebs, Albin. When In Peking... *New York Times* (July 20, 1971) p. 38.

J1478 Skits, March Staged For Jailed Group. *San Francisco Chronicle* (July 31, 1971) p. 10.
Note: AG quoted briefly.

J1479 Adler, Harold. Free Our Theater! *Berkeley Barb,* vol. 13, no. 4 [issue 312] (Aug. 6-13, 1971) pp. 1, 8.
Note: AG quoted briefly.

J1480 Living Poorly. *Good Times,* vol. 4, no. 25 (Aug. 6, 1971) p. 2.

J1481 Ehrmann, Eric. Angels Free Cabaret. *Berkeley Barb,* vol. 13, no. 5 [issue 313] (Aug. 13-19, 1971) p. 9.

J1482 Living Theatre's Day In Court. *Berkeley Barb,* vol. 13, no. 6 [issue 314] (Aug. 20-26, 1971) p. 7.

J1483 Crescent. Interrogation Of a Businessman By the Interior Police. *Kaliflower,* vol. 3, no. 17 (Aug. 26, 1971) pp. 7-12.
Note: AG interview format in which AG is identified as "Star" and interviewed by "Crescent" (Irving Rosenthal).

J1484 Harris, James T. Beard, Beer, Moon: An Interview With Allen Ginsberg. *Alternative Features Service,* vol. 1, no. 13 (Sept. 10, 1971) loose leaf.
Note: AG interview format.

J1485 A Gathering Of Ginsbergs. *Sunday Record* (Sept. 12, 1971) p. C17.

J1486 Harris, James T. Allen Ginsberg On Leary. *Chinook,* vol. 3, no. 34 (Sept. 16, 1971) p. 5.
Note: AG interview format, reprinted from *Alternative Features Service* (Sept. 10, 1971).

J1487 Harris, James T. Just Call Me Allen. *San Francisco Good Times,* vol. 4, no. 28 (Sept. 17-30, 1971) pp. 14-15.
Note: AG interview format, reprinted from *Alternative Features Service* (Sept. 10, 1971).

J1488 Harris, James T. Allen Ginsberg. *Staff* (Sept. 17-23, 1971) pp. 5, 8.
Note: AG interview format, reprinted from *Alternative Features Service* (Sept. 10, 1971).

J1489 Harris, James T. Allen Ginsberg. *Space City,* vol. 3, no. 16 (Sept. 21-27, 1971) pp. 8-9.
Note: AG interview format, reprinted from *Alternative Features Service* (Sept. 10, 1971).

J1490 Bowering, George. Ce Hurlement Que J'Entends. *Ellipse,* no. 8-9 ([Fall] 1971) pp. 128-140.

J1491 Colbert, Alison. A Talk With Allen Ginsberg. *Partisan Review,* vol. 38, no. 3 ([Fall] 1971) pp. 289-309.
Note: AG interview format.

J1492   Thomas, Mitchell. A Vigil For Everything. *San Francisco Chronicle* (Sept. 24, 1971) p. 9.

J1493   Marks, Howard. Discussions Highlight Poetry Symposium. *Tulane Hullabaloo,* vol. 72, no. 5 (Oct. 1, 1971) p. 1.

J1494   Ginsberg On Horror Of Bangla Desh. *Berkeley Barb,* vol. 13, no. 12 [issue 320] (Oct. 1-7, 1971) p. 6.
Note: AG quoted briefly.

J1495   Moss, Elli. Ginsberg: King Poet Of Beat Generation To Recite, Chant At UF Today. *Florida Alligator* (Oct. 1, 1971) p. 4.
Note: AG quoted.

J1496   Roberts, John. Ginsberg Chants Shantra To Begin TU Symposium. *Times Picayune* (Oct. 6, 1971) p. 3.

J1497   Harris, James T. Ginsberg And the Drunken Guru Or Drooling In Your Beard. *Harry,* vol. 2, no. 21 [issue 46] (Oct. 12, 1971) pp. 3, 15.
Note: AG interview format, reprinted from *Alternative Features Service* (Sept. 10, 1971).

J1498   Ginsberg's Coming—4 Years Late. *Marquette Tribune,* vol. 56, no. 12 (Oct. 13, 1971) pp. 1, 8.

J1499   Harris, James T. Ginsberg: Beard, Beer, Moon. *Great Speckled Bird,* vol. 4, no. 42 (Oct. 18, 1971) pp. 10-11.
Note: AG interview format, reprinted from *Alternative Features Service* (Sept. 10, 1971).

J1500   Tarnoff, Larry. Ginsberg's Images Too Fast To Savor. *Milwaukee Sentinel* (Oct. 18, 1971) p. 16.

J1501   Lask, Thomas. Voznesensky: 'A Poet Poses Questions'. *New York Times* (Oct. 21, 1971) p. 54.

J1502   Ginsberg Highlight Of Blake Festival Finale. *Vidette,* vol. 84, no. 15 (Oct. 21, 1971) p. 1.

J1503   Yaros, Kathryn. Ginsberg To Address Assembly. *Caellian,* vol. 33, no. 7 (Oct. 22, 1971)

J1504   Poet Allen Ginsberg To Speak. *Home Planet News* (ca. Oct. 22, 1971)

J1505   Ginsberg Chants. *Vidette,* vol. 84, no. 16 (Oct. 22, 1971) p. 1.

J1506   Cathedral's Sharp 'Pagan' Response. *San Francisco Chronicle* (Oct. 23, 1971) p. 2.

J1507   Johnston, David and Fries, Janet. Dr. Hip Revisited. *Berkeley Barb,* vol. 20, no. 15 [issue 480] (Oct. 25-31, 1971) p. 15.

J1508   Intentionally omitted.

J1509   Caen, Herb. [column]. *San Francisco Chronicle* (Oct. 25, 1971) p. 27.

J1510   Seiler, Michael. Ginsberg a 2-Part Phenomenon. *Dayton Journal Herald* (Oct. 26, 1971)

J1511 Spengler, David. Father's Hope Counters Son's Gloom. *Bergen Record* (Oct. 27, 1971)
Note: AG quoted briefly.

J1512 Savasana [pseud. of Julie Gibson]. The Difficulty Is Really Compassion. *Kaleidoscope,* vol. 5, no. 22 (Oct. 28-Nov. 11, 1971) p. 9.
Note: AG quoted briefly.

J1513 Lukas, J. Anthony. Bobby Seale's Birthday Cake (Oh, Far Out!). *New York Times Magazine* (Oct. 31, 1971) pp. 42, 44-46.

J1514 Harris, James T. Beard, Beer, Moon: An Interview With Allen Ginsberg. *Great Swamp Erie Da Da Boom,* vol. 1, no. 21 (Nov. 2-16, 1971) pp. 6, 19.
Note: AG interview format, reprinted from *Alternative Features Service* (Sept. 10, 1971).

J1515 Weidenthal, Bud. Press Reporter Beards Ginsberg In JCU Den. *Cleveland Press* (Nov. 5, 1971) p. C-6.
Note: AG quoted.

J1516 Kilman, Buzz. Allen Ginsberg. *Daily Planet,* vol. 1, no. 38 (Nov. 10, 1971) p. 8.
Note: AG quoted briefly.

J1517 Tallmer, Jerry. Soviet Poet Wows Town Hall. *New York Post* (Nov. 11, 1971)

J1518 Poets Read Here For Bengali Relief. *New York Times* (Nov. 21, 1971) p. 55.

J1519 Parrilla, Efrain. Ginsberg Says Counterculture Dead. *San Juan Star* (Nov. 24, 1971) p. 6.
Note: AG quoted briefly.

J1520 AHAS Raps With Allen Ginsberg. *All Hands Abandon Ship!,* vol. 2, no. 6 [issue no. 13] (Dec. 1971) pp. 1-2, 6.
Note: AG interview format.

J1521 Sinclair, Iain. Ginsberg: The Kodak Mantra Diaries. *Second Aeon,* no. 14 [Dec. 1971] pp. 85-93.
Note: AG interview format.

J1522 Spengler, David. Poets Shape Rehabilitation Into Lyrics Of Love. *Bergen Record* (Dec. 3, 1971)

J1523 Skir, Leo. Listening To Allen Ginsberg. *Gay,* vol. 3, no. 65 (Dec. 6, 1971) pp. 1, 4.
Note: AG quoted briefly.

J1524* Voznesensky, Andrei. Foreword To Translation Of Ginsberg's 'Jessore Road'. *Literature Gazeta,* no. 15 (Dec. 9, 1971)

J1525 Kilman, Buzz. Allen Ginsberg. *Daily Planet,* vol. 2, no. 1 (Dec. 10, 1971)
Note: AG quoted briefly, reprinted from *Daily Planet* (Nov. 10, 1971).

J1526 Sinclair Rally Draws 15,000. *Underground Press Syndicate,* vol. 2 (Dec. 10, 1971) pp. [1-2].

J1527 Reynolds, Roy. 15,000 Attend Sinclair Rally. *Ann Arbor News* (Dec. 11, 1971) p. 10.

J1528 Gray, Bill. 15,000 At Ann Arbor Rally To Aid John Sinclair. *Detroit News* (Dec. 11, 1971) p. 3-A.
Note: AG quoted briefly.

J1529 Schutt, David. 15,000 Youths At Ann Arbor Rally. *Toledo Blade* (Dec. 11, 1971)

J1530 Schwartz, Francis. Allen Ginsberg. *San Juan Star* (Dec. 12, 1971) Magazine section, pp. 10-11.
Note: AG quoted briefly.

J1531 Covington, Dick. Salve Regina Hears Allen Ginsberg. *Newport Daily News* (Dec. 15, 1971) p. 2.
Note: AG quoted briefly.

J1532 Fenton, David and Collins, John. John Sinclair Freedom Rally. *Ann Arbor Sun,* no. 22 (Dec. 17-30, 1971) p. 11.

Fleming, Thomas J. [letter to the editor]. *Ann Arbor Sun,* no. 22 (Dec. 17-30, 1971) Free John Now! supplement, p. 11.

J1533 Tripper, T. Radical Poet John Sinclair Gets Out Of Jail After Massive Michigan Youth Rally. *Liberation News Service,* no. 400 (Dec. 18, 1971) pp. 15-16.

J1534 Eaves, Morris. [review of *Allen Ginsberg/William Blake* (recording)]. *Blake Newsletter,* vol. 4, no. 3 [issue 15] (Winter 1971) pp. 90-97.

J1535 De Loach, Allen. Little Mags/Small Presses And the Cultural Revolution. *Intrepid,* no. 21-22 (Winter-Spring 1971-72) pp. 106-139.
Note: AG interview format.

J1536 Dullea, Gerard J. Ginsberg And Corso: Image And Imagination. *Thoth,* vol. 2, no. 2 (Winter 1971) pp. 17-27.

J1537 Colbert, Alison and Box, Anita. The West End Excerpts Of an Interview With Allen Ginsberg. *West End,* vol. 1, no. 1 (Winter 1971) pp. 2, 32-43.
Note: AG interview format.

J1538* Rubin, Jerry. The Freeing Of John Sinclair. *Underground Press Syndicate,* vol. 2, no. 26 (Dec. 24, 1971) pp. 9-12.

J1539 Miller, Allan W. [letter to the editor]. *New York Times* (Dec. 28, 1971) p. 28.

J1540 Harding, Gunnar. Allen Ginsberg. *Lyrikvännen,* vol. 18, no. 5 (1971) pp. 27-28.

J1541 Anderson, Jack. Unhappy Hippie Turns Muckraker. *Overseas Weekly,* vol. 26, no. 15 (1971) p. 3.

J1542 Robert Creeley. *Unmuzzled Ox,* [vol. 1, no. 1] (1971) pp. 23-45.

Books:

J1543 Bloom, Harold (ed.). *The Ringers In the Tower: Studies In Romantic Tradition.* Chicago, IL: University Of Chicago Press, 1971.
Contents: Bloom, Harold. On Ginsberg's *Kaddish* [review of *Kaddish And Other Poems*] pp. 213-215.

J1544 Buckner, H. Taylor. *Deviance, Reality And Change.* New York, NY: Random House, 1971, pp. 295, 354, 425.

J1545 Charters, Samuel. *Some Poems/Poets.* Berkeley, CA: Oyez, 1971, pp. 71-76.

J1546 Cook, Bruce. *The Beat Generation.* New York, NY: Charles Scribner's Sons, 1971.
Note: AG quoted throughout.

J1547 Dowden, George. *A Bibliography Of Works By Allen Ginsberg.* San Francisco, CA: City Lights Books, 1971.
Note: AG mentioned throughout.

J1548 *Encyclopedia Judaica,* vol. 7. New York, NY: Macmillan, 1971.
Contents: I., D. Allen Ginsberg.

J1549 Esler, Anthony. *Bombs, Beards And Barricades.* New York, NY: Stein & Day, 1971, pp. 214, 221, 227, 274.

J1550 Feder, Lillian. *Ancient Myth In Modern Poetry.* Princeton, NJ: Princeton University Press, 1971, pp. 411-412.

J1551 Fiedler, Leslie. *The Collected Essays Of Leslie Fiedler, vol. 1.* New York, NY: Stein and Day, 1971, pp. 394, 491-2.

Fiedler, Leslie. *The Collected Essays Of Leslie Fiedler, vol. 2.* New York, NY: Stein and Day, 1971.
Note: AG mentioned throughout.

J1552 Ginsberg, Allen. *Improvised Poetics.* San Francisco, CA: Anonym Press, 1971.
Note: AG interview format with Michael Aldrich, Edward Kissam and Nancy Blecker.

J1553 Grinspoon, Lester. *Marihuana Reconsidered.* Cambridge, MA: Harvard University Press, 1971, pp. 103-9, 147, 156-8, 274.

J1554 Hassan, Ihab. *The Dismemberment Of Orpheus.* New York, NY: Oxford University Press, 1971, p. 252.

J1555 Huebel, Harry R. *A Study Of the Beat Generation And Its Effect On American Culture.* Unpublished Doctoral Dissertation. Pullman, WA: Washington State University, 1971.

J1556 Krim, Seymour. *Shake It For the World.* New York, NY: Delta-Dell, 1971.
Note: AG mentioned throughout, also published in England by Allison & Busby in 1971.

J1557 Moritz, Charles (ed.). *Current Biography Yearbook 1970.* New York, NY: H.W. Wilson, 1971, pp. 151-154.

J1558 Mottram, Eric. *William Burroughs: The Algebra Of Need.* Buffalo, NY: Intrepid Press, 1971.

J1559 *New York Times Almanac.* New York, NY: New York Times, 1971.
Contents: Lask, Thomas. Poetry In Our Day, pp. 467-468.

J1560 P.E.N. American Center (ed.). *The World Of Translation.* New York, NY: P.E.N. American Center, 1971.

Contents: Pivano, Fernanda Sottsass. Modern Translation Into Italian, pp. 321-333.

J1561 Pélieu, Claude. *Embruns D'Exil Traduits Du Silence.* Paris, France: Christian Bourgois, 1971, pp. 207-215.
Note: AG quoted in French only, translated by Claude Pélieu from *Opus International* (Oct. 1968).

J1562 Pélieu, Claude. *Jack Kerouac.* Paris, France: L'Herne, 1971.

J1563 Poulin, A., Jr. (ed.). *Contemporary American Poetry.* New York, NY: Houghton Mifflin, 1971.

J1564 Raban, Jonathan. *The Society Of the Poem.* London, England: Harrap, 1971, pp. 37-38, 79-80.

J1565 Rexroth, Kenneth. *American Poetry In the Twentieth Century.* New York, NY: Herder & Herder, 1971.
Note: AG mentioned throughout.

J1566 Scaduto, Anthony. *Bob Dylan.* New York, NY: Grosset & Dunlap, 1971, pp. 201-202, 224.
Note: AG quoted briefly.

J1567 Sinclair, Iain. *The Kodak Mantra Diaries.* London, England: Albion Village Press, 1971.
Note: AG interview format throughout.

J1568 Weber, Alfred and Haack, Dietmar (eds.). *Amerikanische Literatur Im 20. Jahrhundert.* Göttingen, Germany: Vandernhoek And Ruprecht, 1971.
Contents: Vance, Thomas H. American Poetry Of Protest, From World War II To the Present, pp. 249-270.

1972

J1569 Allen, Henry. What the Seers Didn't See. *Washington Post* (Jan. 1, 1972) section D, pp. D1-D2.

J1570 Sheed, Wilfrid. The Good Word: Beat Down And Beatific. *New York Times Book Review* (Jan. 2, 1972) pp. 2, 21.

J1571 Tripper, T. Free John Sinclair Rally—Political And Cultural Energy Come Together. *Great Speckled Bird,* vol. 5, no. 1 (Jan. 10, 1972) pp. 12-13.

J1572 Ginsberg's Poem Adapted For Stage. *New York Post* (Jan. 20, 1972)

J1573 Shepard, Richard F. Yevtushenko Criticizes Journalists In Talk Here. *New York Times* (Jan. 22, 1972) p. 27.
Note: AG quoted briefly.

J1574 Simpson, Louis. The California Poets. *London Magazine,* vol. 11, no. 6 (Feb.-March 1972) pp. 56-63.

J1575 The Happy Homosexual. *New York Mattachine Times* (Feb.-March 1972) p. 12.

J1576 Lester, Elenore. Allen Ginsberg Remembers Mama. *New York Times* (Feb. 6, 1972) section 2, pp. 1, 5.
Note: AG quoted at length.

J1577   Horton, A.M. Ginsberg's Poetry Sways Big Crowd. *Kansas City Times* (Feb. 10, 1972) p. 3A.

J1578   [caption]. *University News,* vol. 9, no. 19 (Feb. 10, 1972) p. 2.
Note: AG quoted briefly.

J1579   Tallmer, Jerry. Lament For Naomi. *New York Post* (Feb. 11, 1972) p. 26.

J1580   Barnes, Clive. The Theater: 'Kaddish'. *New York Times* (Feb. 11, 1972) p. 27.

J1581   Wallach, Allan. Prosaic Poetry. *Newsday* (Feb. 11, 1972)

J1582   Lewis, Emory. 'Kaddish' Turns Private Grief Into Major Theater. *Bergen Record* (Feb. 11, 1972) p. D-9.

J1583   Bishop, Gordon. Allen Ginsberg Stages a Most Un-Traditional Play. *Star-Ledger* (Feb. 11, 1972) p. 35.

J1584   Barnes, Clive. The Theater: 'Kaddish'. *New York Times* (Feb. 12, 1972) p. 34.

A Correction. *New York Times* (Feb. 12, 1972) p. 36.

J1585   Shenker, Israel. The Life And Rhymes Of Ginsberg the Elder. *New York Times* (Feb. 13, 1972) p. 86.

J1586   Genia's Party. *San Francisco Chronicle* (Feb. 16, 1972) p. 23.

J1587   Spengler, David. Poet Provides a Touch Of Mystery. *Bergen Record* (Feb. 16, 1972) p. B10.

J1588   Lahr, John. On-Stage. *Village Voice* (Feb. 17, 1972) pp. 48, 50.

Smith, Michael. Theatre Journal. *Village Voice* (Feb. 17, 1972) pp. 49-50.

J1589   Fulton, Ashby. Poet Tsongas Hears Yevtushenko Read. *Berkeley Barb,* vol. 14, no. 7 [issue 340] (Feb. 18-24, 1972) p. 11.

J1590   Oliver, Edith. [theatre review of *Kaddish*]. *New Yorker,* vol. 47, no. 53 (Feb. 19, 1972) p. 82.

J1591   Krim, Seymour. We Were the Early Band Of the Insane. *Crawdaddy* (Feb. 20, 1972) section 2, pp. 34-35.

Montgomery, George. The Tourists Were Too Much With Their Fingers Snapping, Instead... *Crawdaddy* (Feb. 20, 1972) p. 37.

Solomon, Carl W. 'Howl' Written In Parting Gesture To Me. *Crawdaddy* (Feb. 20, 1972) p. 38.

J1592   Novick, Julius. After 'Kaddish's' Poetry Goes, What Is Left? *New York Times* (Feb. 20, 1972) Section 2, pp. 1, 3.

J1593   Skir, Leo. Sing Along With Ginsberg. *Gay,* vol. 3, no. 70 (Feb. 21, 1972) pp. 4-5.
Note: AG quoted briefly.

J1594   Bernard, Sidney. [theatre review of *Kaddish*]. *Newsletter On the State Of the Culture* (Feb. 21, 1972) pp. 2-3.

J1595   Kroll, Jack. The Song Of Naomi. *Newsweek,* vol. 79, no. 8 (Feb. 21, 1972) pp. 98-99.

J1596   Obenzinger, Hilton. La Huegla Poetry. *Sunday Paper,* no. 3 (Feb. 24-March 1, 1972) p. 11-B.

J1597   Cook, Bruce. Ginsberg's Painful Elegy Is Reborn. *National Observer,* vol. 11, no. 9 (Feb. 26, 1972) p. 23.

J1598   Clurman, Harold. Theatre. *Nation,* vol. 214, no. 9 (Feb. 28, 1972) pp. 285-286.

J1599   Alton, Lawrence. Sometimes a Great Commotion. *Westport Trucker,* vol. 2, no. 21 [issue 45] (Feb. 29-March 7, 1972) pp. 3, 9.

   Mackeral, Wholly. *Symposium News* Confiscated. *Westport Trucker,* vol. 2, no. 21 [issue 45] (Feb. 29-March 7, 1972) p. 5.

J1600   Hughes, Catharine. A 'Kaddish' For Us All. *America,* vol. 126, no. 9 (March 4, 1972) pp. 239-240.

J1601   O'Connor, John. Television: A Night With the Video Freaks. *New York Times* (March 5, 1972) section 2, p. 17.

J1602   Filho, Ibanez. Allen Ginsberg Vive Lutando Contra A Intransigencia. *Folha De S. Paulo* (March 6, 1972) p. 19.
   Note: AG quoted briefly in Portuguese only.

J1603   City Must Keep Enthusiasm Of the Festival. *Adelaide News* (March 8, 1972)

J1604   Adelaide Is Poets' Corner. *Advertiser* (March 8, 1972) p. 1.
   Note: AG quoted briefly.

J1605   An Interview With Allen Ginsberg. *Westport Trucker,* vol. 2, no. 22 [issue 46] (March 8-15, 1972) pp. 8-9.
   Note: AG interview format.

J1606   Groves, Don. [column]. *Adelaide News* (March 9, 1972) p. 16.
   Note: AG quoted briefly.

J1607   Hawley, Janet. Russian Poets Get a Dollar a Line For Their Poetry! *Australian* (March 9, 1972) p. 3.

J1608   Campbell, Mary. Ginsberg's 'Kaddish' Shifts Run. *Denver Post* (March 9, 1972) p. 73.

J1609   Atkins, Dennis. Vanguard Of Poets. *News* (March 9, 1972)

J1610   Fatchen, Max. Talking To Ginsberg Can Be Almost Spiritual. *Advertiser* (March 10, 1972)
   Note: AG quoted at length.

J1611   Lowensohn, Ron. The Breathing Center Of Poetry And Politics: Allen Ginsberg. *Daily Californian Arts Magazine* (March 10, 1972) pp. 6-7.
   Note: AG interview format.

J1612   Notes On People. *New York Times* (March 10, 1972) p. 48.

J1613 Taylor, Andrew. No Sound Of Silence But Some Zesty Outpourings [review of *Open Head*]. *Advertiser* (March 11, 1972) p. 20.
Note: AG quoted briefly.

J1614 Hawley, Janet. Adelaide, Adelaide, Ever-Grooving Adelaide. *Australian* (March 11, 1972) p. 13.
Note: AG quoted briefly.

J1615 B., A. Premature Obituary [review of *Open Head*]. *Mail* (March 11, 1972) p. 95.

J1616 Lester, Elenore. Cheers For 'Kaddish'. *New York Times* (March 12, 1972) pp. 6, 12.

J1617 Edmunds, Michael. Allen Ginsberg. *Tharunka,* vol. 18, no. 2 (March 14, 1972) p. 13.

J1618 Modules Vibrate In Park. *Advertiser* (March 15, 1972)

J1619 Premier Protests. *Advertiser* (March 16, 1972)

J1620 [photograph]. *Honi Soit,* vol. 45, no. 3 (March 16, 1972) front cover.

J1621 Dancing Ginsberg. *Advertiser* (March 17, 1972)
Note: AG quoted briefly.

J1622 Lewis, David. A Yankee Poet In Dreamtime. *News* (March 17, 1972) pp. 1, 39.
Note: AG quoted briefly.

J1623 Shmith, Michael. Ginsberg Turns To Music. *Melbourne Herald* (March 18, 1972)
Note: AG quoted.

J1624 Prior, Tom. A Prayer From America's Beat King. *Sun* (March 18, 1972) p. 4.
Note: AG quoted.

J1625 Faces Of the Festival. *Australian* (March 19, 1972) p. 24.

J1626 Veitch, Jock. Hippies' Poet Mr. Ginsberg Quieter Now. *Daily Telegraph* (March 20, 1972) p. 7.
Note: AG quoted briefly.

J1627 McLean, Frances. Avant Garde Poet's Plea For the Dreamtime. *Sydney Morning Herald* (March 20, 1972) p. 2.
Note: AG quoted at length.

J1628 Artist Remanded Following Upset At Recital. *Daily Mirror* (March 21, 1972) p. 5.

J1629 Impromptu Poetry. *Daily Telegraph* (March 21, 1972) p. 29.

J1630 Concert Brawl — 3 Police Hurt. *Daily Telegraph And Daily News* (March 21, 1972) p. 1.

J1631 Artist 'Disrobed' Police Tell Court. *Sun* (March 21, 1972)

J1632 5 Arrests At Poetry Recital. *Sydney Morning Herald* (March 21, 1972) p. 1.

J1633   Gerald, Gregory Fitz and Ferguson, Paul. The Frost Tradition: A Conversation With William Meredith. *Southwest Review,* vol. 57, no. 2 (Spring 1972) pp. 108-116.

J1634   Intellectual Woodstock. *Bulletin* (March 25, 1972) p. 15.

Anderson, Don. [review of *Open Head*]. *Bulletin* (March 25, 1972) p. 49.

J1635   Talbot, Colin. Ginsberg Ferlinghetti. *National U* (March 27, 1972) pp. 10-11.
Note: AG interview format.

J1636   Aboriginals 'Best Poets' — Ginsberg. *Northern Territory News* (March 27, 1972) p. 5.
Note: AG quoted.

J1637   Lupoff, Dick. Interview: Allen Ginsberg. *Changes,* no. 72 (April 1, 1972) pp. 1-2.
Note: AG quoted briefly.

Lebowitz, Fran. On Stage: Allen Ginsberg's Kaddish. *Changes,* no. 72 (April 1, 1972) p. 7.

J1638   "Urrr...rrr" In Tibetan. *Courier-Mail* (April 1, 1972) p. 3.
Note: AG quoted.

J1639   Hughes, Catharine. New York. *Plays And Players,* vol. 19, no. 7 [issue 223] (April 1972) pp. 52-53.

J1640   An Interview With Allen Ginsberg, pt. 2. *Westport Trucker,* vol. 2, no. 23 [issue 47] (April 1972) pp. 9-10.
Note: AG interview format.

J1641   Barnes, Clive. Stage: Moving Appeal Of 'Kaddish'. *New York Times* (April 2, 1972) p. 47.

J1642   Bachmann, Marcy. The Yevtushenko Method. *San Francisco Sunday Examiner And Chronicle* (April 2, 1972) California Living section, pp. 26-7, 29-30, 32-3.

J1643   S., P.H. Ginsberg Leaps. *Times* (April 3, 1972) p. 6.
Note: AG quoted briefly.

J1644   Notes On People. *New York Times* (April 12, 1972) p. 40.

J1645   Aronowitz, Alfred G. Time Out For 'Kaddish'. *New York Post* (April 14, 1972) p. 50.

J1646   Nolan, Frank. Allen Ginsberg: Poet-Musician, Shaman And Bard. *Polar Star,* vol. 29, no. 24 (April 14, 1972) p. 8.
Note: AG interview format.

J1647   Aronowitz, Alfred G. Items. *New York Post* (April 15, 1972) p. 26.

J1648   Bauman, Michael. Police Block 2,000 Capitol Protesters. *Wisconsin State Journal* (April 20, 1972) pp. 1-2.

J1649   Weiss, Carol. Ginsberg Protests the War. *Observer* (April 21, 1972)

J1650 Hewes, Henry. The Theater. *Saturday Review,* vol. 55, no. 17 (April 22, 1972) pp. 22-24.

J1651 Yevtushenko, Yevgeny. [letter to the editor]. *New York Times* (April 23, 1972) p. 14.

J1652 Liming, Robert G. Antiwar Protestors Rally In City. *State* (April 23, 1972) section D, pp. 1, 3.

J1653 Manglaviti, Leo. Ginsberg Among the Magnolias. *Paper* (April 27, 1972) p. 10.

J1654 Manglaviti, Leo. Hopkins' Vernal Days Filled With Literati. *Johns Hopkins News-Letter,* vol. 76, no. 47 (April 28, 1972)

J1655 Darnton, John. Columbia Students Press Efforts To Get Campus Back To Normal. *New York Times* (April 29, 1972) pp. 1, 14.
Note: AG quoted briefly.

J1656 Edelson, Morris. Allen Ginsberg In Madison. *Wisconsin Patriot,* vol. 2, no. 4 (May 1972) pp. 8-9.
Note: AG quoted briefly.

J1657 Müller, Fred. [review of *Indisches Tagebuch* (Carl Hanser)]. *Baseler Nachrichten* (May 4, 1972) p. 15.

J1658 Rinviato Il Processo Di Allen Ginsberg. *La Nazione* (May 6, 1972)

J1659 'Mutation Show' Awarded Top Obie. *New York Times* (May 9, 1972) p. 36.

J1660 Poet Ginsberg Leads Chants At Intersection. *Daily Camera* (May 10, 1972) p. 5.

J1661 Olsen, Jack and Pearce, Ken. War Protesters Conduct Peaceful Rally. *Denver Post* (May 14, 1972) p. 3.

J1662 Hipp, Edward S. Drama By Ginsberg Splendid. *Newark Evening News* (May 14, 1972)

J1663 Knight, Al. Small Crowd Turns Out For 'Major' Antiwar Rally At Capitol. *Rocky Mountain News* (May 14, 1972) p. 8.
Note: AG quoted briefly.

J1664 Ashton, John. Dylan Biographer Completes Tough Assignment. *Denver Post* (May 16, 1972) p. 32.

J1665 Foehr, Stephen and Lutz, Richard. American Mantra: An Interview With Allen Ginsberg. *Straight Creek,* vol. 1, no. 15 (May 18, 1972) pp. 1, 10.
Note: AG quoted at length.

J1666 Stevenson, Charlie. And All the Hills Echoed...! *Dragonseed,* vol. 1, no. 3 (June 1972) p. 6.

J1667 Ivanceanu, Vintila. [review of *Indisches Tagebuch* (Carl Hanser)]. *Die Welt* (June 1, 1972)

J1668 Brechbuhl, Beat. [review of *Indisches Tagebuch* (Carl Hanser)]. *Weldwocke* (June 7, 1972)

J1669 Muariac, Claude. [review of *Reality Sandwiches* (Christian Bourgois)]. *Le Figaro* (June 8, 1972)

J1670   Lewis, Flora. CIA Smack Smuggling. *Daily Planet,* vol. 1, no. 45 (June 10, 1972) pp. 3, 23.
Note: AG quoted briefly.

Rubin, Ginsberg, Hoffman, Back McGovern. *Daily Planet,* vol. 1, no. 45 (June 10, 1972) p. 6.
Note: AG quoted briefly.

J1671   Yost, George. The Romantic Movement Of Today And Earlier. *Forum,* vol. 10, no. 2 (Summer-Fall 1972) pp. 16-21.

J1672   Veatch, Henry B. The What And the Why Of the Humanities. *Key Reporter,* vol. 37, no. 4 (Summer 1972) pp. 2-4, 8.

J1673   Andre, Michael. A Talk With W.H. Auden. *Unmuzzled Ox,* vol. 1, no. 3 (Summer 1972) pp. 5-11.

J1674   Clarity, James F. Allen Ginsberg. *New York Times* (June 23, 1972) p. 38.

J1675   He Walks It Like He Talks It (Usually). *Creem* (July 1972) p. 59.

J1676   [review of *Indisches Tagebuch* (Carl Hanser)]. *Leseu* (July 1972)

J1677   [photograph with caption]. *Daily Sun Reporter* (July 7, 1972) p. 3.
Note: AG quoted briefly in caption.

J1678   Amlong, William R. and Pollard, Gayle. Convention Trouble Warned Unless 750 Poor Get Seats. *Miami Herald* (July 7, 1972) section C, p. 1.

J1679   S., A. [review of *Indisches Tagebuch* (Carl Hanser)]. *National Zeitung* (July 8, 1972)

J1680   Winfrey, Lee. Say 'Ah'. *Detroit Free Press* (July 11, 1972)
Note: AG quoted briefly.

J1681   Ginsberg's Saying 'Ah!' But Not 'Om' Or 'Hum'. *Miami Herald* (July 12, 1972) p. 29-A.
Note: AG quoted briefly.

J1682   Berlet, Chip. Final Act Closes On Miami. *Straight Creek,* vol. 1, no. 23 (July 13, 1972) pp. 5-6.
Note: AG quoted briefly.

J1683   Whited, Charles. Convention Notebook. *Miami Herald* (July 14, 1972) p. 1.

J1684   Lerner, Max. Agony And Ecstasy. *New York Post* (July 14, 1972)

J1685   No Violence Seen For G.O.P. Parley. *Chicago Tribune* (July 16, 1972) section 1, p. 5.
Note: AG quoted briefly.

J1686   The Battle For the Democratic Party. *Time,* vol. 100, no. 3 (July 17, 1972) p. 16.

J1687   Weiner, Rex. Trepidations And Disgust In Miami. *Georgia Straight,* vol. 6, no. 252 (July 27-Aug. 3, 1972) pp. 12-13.

J1688   Laemmle, Peter. [review of *Indisches Tagebuch* (Carl Hanser)]. *Frankfurter Rundschau* (July 29, 1972)

J1689   [review of *Indisches Tagebuch* (Carl Hanser)]. *Der Kleine Bund* (Aug. 13, 1972)

J1690   Kronholz, June and Werne, Jo. Famous, Non-Famous Caught In Sweeping Arrests In Beach. *Miami Herald* (Aug. 24, 1972) section D, p. 1.

Baxter, Mike. More Than 700 Are Arrested After Spreading Street Chaos. *Miami Herald* (Aug. 24, 1972) pp. 1, 28.

J1691   Berlet, Chip and Doering, Henry. The Other Miami Story. *Straight Creek,* vol. 1, no. 30 (Aug. 31, 1972) pp. 1, 7.

J1692   [review of *Indisches Tagebuch* (Carl Hanser)]. *Ruhr-Nachsichden* (Sept. 18, 1972)

J1693   Antin, David. Modernism And Post Modernism: Approaching the Present American Poetry. *Boundary 2,* vol. 1, no. 1 (Fall 1972) pp. 98-146.

J1694   Luster, Helen. Allen Ginsberg: The Green Man Is Alive & Thrives. *St. Andrews Review,* vol. 2, no. 1 (Fall-Winter 1972-73) pp. 35-41.

J1695   Denley, Susan. Against the War—In Poetry. *Tampa Times* (Oct. 3, 1972) section B, pp. 1, 2.
Note: AG quoted.

J1696   Smith, Lisa. Ginsberg Chants, Sings, Reads. *Oracle,* vol. 7, no. 58 (Oct. 4, 1972) p. 6.
Note: AG quoted briefly.

J1697   Caffery, Bethia. Ginsberg Sing-Chants a Personal Happening. *St. Petersburg Evening Independent* (Oct. 4, 1972) section B, p. 1.
Note: AG quoted briefly.

J1698   Prescott, J. Oliver. Ginsberg: A Man Very Much Alive. *St. Petersburg Times* (Oct. 4, 1972) p. D1.
Note: AG quoted.

J1699   2,000 March Here In War Protest. *New York Times* (Oct. 15, 1972) p. 16.

J1700   Grossman, Karl. Barefoot Ginsberg Wins 'em With Poetry Of 'War Statistics'. *Long Island Press* (Oct. 17, 1972) p. 6.
Note: AG quoted briefly.

J1701   Doar, Harriet. Poet Suggests Basic Sound. *Charlotte Observer* (Oct. 24, 1972) section C, pp. 1, 3.
Note: AG quoted briefly.

J1702   Jones, Dick. Nobody Asked Me—But... *Sentinel* (Oct. 28, 1972)
Note: AG quoted briefly.

J1703   Seligson, Tom. Abbie Hoffman: A Sympathetic Portrait. *Crawdaddy* (Nov. 1972)

J1704   Allen Ginsberg At the Smithsonian. *Smithsonian Associate,* vol. 1, no. 3 (Nov. 1972) p. 1.

J1705   Wylie, Hal. The Ginsberg Trip. *Gar,* vol. 2, no. 4 [issue 15] ([Nov. 3] 1972) pp. 1-2, 23, 25.
Note: AG quoted.

J1706 Lee, Michael and Fine, Steve. Webster Welcomes Ginsberg. *Broadside,* vol. 3, no. 3 (Nov. 6, 1972) p. 1.
Note: AG quoted briefly.

J1707 Standish, Myles. Allen Ginsberg—Wizard Of OM. *St. Louis Post-Dispatch* (Nov. 7, 1972) p. 3D.
Note: AG quoted.

J1708 Herkens, Ernst. [review of *Indisches Tagebuch* (Carl Hanser)]. *Aachener Volkszeitung* (Nov. 11, 1972)

J1709 Brand, Ginsberg To Speak. *New Mexico Daily Lobo* (Nov. 14, 1972) p. 1.

J1710 Castro, M. 'A Noble Poet Nobly Elegized' & Alan [sic] Ginsberg At Webster College. *St. Louis Outlaw,* vol. 3, no. 11 (Nov. 17-Dec. 14, 1972) pp. 13, 23.
Note: AG quoted.

J1711 Maxa, Kathleen. Mantras In the Smithsonian. *Evening Star And Daily News* (Nov. 20, 1972) p. E-7.
Note: AG quoted.

J1712 Leogrande, Ernest. To Sit In Judgment. *Daily News* (Nov. 22, 1972) p. 6.

J1713 This Week. *Drummer,* no. 219 (Nov. 30, 1972) p. 16.

J1714 Raddatz, Fritz J. Poetischer Materialist: Zum Tode Ezra Pounds. *Merkur,* vol. 26, no. 12 [issue 296] (Dec. 1972) pp. 1224-1232.
Note: AG interview format in German only.

J1715 Bakken, Dick. Allen Ginsberg At Portland State, May 22, 1967. *Portland Review Magazine,* vol. 19, no. 1 (Dec. 1972) pp. 90-91.
Note: AG interview format.

J1716 Writers Protest Grant. *Los Angeles Free Press,* vol. 9, no. 50 [issue 439] (Dec. 15-25, 1972) p. 8.

J1717 Auchinclose, Eve. The Social Critic Takes a Bow. *Washington Post* (Dec. 15, 1972)

J1718 Barnes, Harper. Ed Sanders And Ritual Violence In America. *Real Paper* (Dec. 20, 1972) p. 16.

J1719 Sienicka, Marta. William Carlos Williams, And Some Younger Poets. *Studia Anglica Posnaniensia,* vol. 4, no. 1-2 (1972) pp. 183-193.

Books:

J1720 Acton, Jay et al. *Mug Shots: Who's Who In the New Earth.* New York, NY: World, 1972, pp. 75-77.

J1721 Beaulieu, Victor-Lévy. *Jack Kérouac Essai-Poulet.* Montréal, Canada: Éditions Du Jour, 1972.
Note: AG mentioned throughout.

J1722 Biner, Pierre. *The Living Theatre.* New York, NY: Horizon Press, 1972, pp. 56, 58, 197, 232.
Note: AG quoted briefly.

J1723   Bowles, Paul. *Without Stopping.* New York, NY: Putnam's Sons, 1972, pp.
         339, 343, 349, 351.
         Note: AG quoted briefly.

J1724   Cargas, Harry J. *Daniel Berrigan And Contemporary Protest Poetry.* New
         Haven, CT: College & University Press, 1972.
         Note: AG mentioned throughout.

J1725   Cargas, Harry J. *Daniel Berrigan And the Ideas Found In Contemporary Anti-
         Establishment Poetry.* Unpublished Doctoral Dissertation, St. Louis
         University, [1972].

J1726   Ginsberg, Allen. *Testimonianza A Chicago.* Torino, Italy: Einaudi, 1972.
         [Series: Saggi 491]
         Note: AG quoted throughout in this Italian translation of the Chicago conspiracy
         trial testimony by Fernanda Pivano.

J1727   Grogan, Emmett. *Ringolevio: A Life Played For Keeps.* Boston, MA: Little,
         Brown and Co., 1972. [also London: Heinemann, 1972]
         Note: AG mentioned throughout.

J1728   Hoffman, Abbie; Rubin, Jerry and Sanders, Ed. *Vote!* New York, NY: Warner,
         1972.

J1729   Howard, Mel and Forcade, Tom (eds.). *The Underground Reader.* New York,
         NY: NAL, 1972.

J1730   Katzman, Allen (ed.). *Our Time.* New York, NY: Dial Press, 1972, pp. 115-
         127.
         Note: AG interview format, reprinted from the *East Village Other* (March 12,
         1969).

J1731   Kawin, Bruce F. *Telling It Again And Again.* Ithaca, NY: Cornell University,
         1972, p. 5.

J1732   Labin, Suzanne. *Hippies, Drugs And Promiscuity.* New Rochelle, NY:
         Arlington House, 1972.
         Note: AG mentioned throughout.

J1733   Malina, Judith. *The Enormous Despair.* New York, NY: Random House, 1972.
         Note: AG quoted briefly throughout.

J1734   [phonotape]. Merrill, Thomas F. *Allen Ginsberg.* Deland, FL: Everett/Edwards
         [1972], #825. 1 cassette (Modern American Poetry Criticism: Series). 84 min.

J1735   Mottram, Eric. *Allen Ginsberg In the Sixties.* Brighton, England: Unicorn
         Bookshop, 1972.
         Note: AG quoted and mentioned throughout.

J1736   Pivano, Fernanda (ed.). *L'Altra America Negli Anni Sessanta, vol. 1.* Rome,
         Italy: Officina Edizioni, 1972.
         Contents: Falzoni, G. *Allen Ginsberg E Gregory Corso Intervista A William
         Burroughs,* pp. 51-55.
            Note: AG interview format in Italian only.
         Redazionale: Complotto USA Per "Sistemare" Ginsberg, pp. 180-182.
            Note: Translation by G. Niccolai of article first appearing in *New York Times*
            (April 14, 1966).

Silvera, M. and Pivano, Fernanda. Allen Ginsberg, Gary Snyder, Alan Watts, Timothy Leary; Dialogo A Sausalito, pp. 48-108.
Note: AG interview format in Italian only first printed in *San Francisco Oracle* (Feb. 1967).

J1737 Pivano, Fernanda. *Beat Hippie Yippie.* Rome, Italy: Arcana Editrice, 1972.
Note: AG mentioned throughout.

J1738 Stafford, Peter. *Psychedelic Baby Reaches Puberty.* New York, NY: Delta Books, 1972, pp. 100-106, 111-117.
Note: AG interview format.

J1739 Watts, Alan. *In My Own Way.* New York, NY: Pantheon, 1972, pp. 309, 358.

1973

J1740 Young, Allen. Ginsberg. *Gay Sunshine,* no. 16 (Jan.-Feb. 1973) pp. 1, 4-10.
Note: AG interview format.

J1741 Conversation Between Allen Ginsberg And Peter Orlovsky. *Starscrewer,* no. 1 (Jan. 1973)
Note: AG quoted.

J1742 [photograph]. *Village Voice* (Jan. 12-18, 1973) p. 1.
Note: This is the first publication of the often reproduced photograph of AG wearing a stars and stripes hat.

J1743 Moon, Byron. [review of *The Fall Of America*]. *Minnesota Daily,* vol. 74, no. 89 (Jan. 29, 1973) pp. 13, 16.

J1744 Young, Allen. Ginsberg. *Georgia Straight,* vol. 7, no. 278 (Feb. 1-8, 1973) pp. 9, 16.
Note: AG interview format, reprinted from *Gay Sunshine* (Jan.-Feb. 1973).

J1745 Combecher, Hans. Allen Ginsbergs "In Back Of the Real": Ein Stück Beat Poetry. *Neueren Sprachen,* vol. 72, no. 2 (Feb. 1973) pp. 74-76.

J1746 Holmes, John Clellon. Gone In October. *Playboy,* vol. 20, no. 2 (Feb. 1973) pp. 96-8, 140, 158-160, 162-6.
Note: AG quoted at length.

J1747 Allen Ginsberg, Baba Ram Dass Give Concert. *El Prado Eagle,* vol. 1, no. 4 (Feb.-April 1973) p. 2.
Note: AG quoted briefly.

J1748 Craig, Paul. [review of *The Fall Of America*]. *Sacramento Bee* (Feb. 4, 1973) Leisure section, p. 13.

J1749 Arts Institute Elects Eight. *New York Times* (Feb. 10, 1973) p. 22.

J1750 Zaciu, Mircea. Seară Cu Tigri Si Allen Ginsberg. *Steaua,* vol. 24, no. 4 (Feb. 16-28, 1973) pp. 16-17.

J1751 Young, Allen. Ginsberg. *Georgia Straight,* vol. 7, no. 281 (Feb. 22-March 1, 1973) pp. 12-13, 21.
Note: AG interview format, reprinted from *Gay Sunshine* (Jan.-Feb. 1973).

J1752   Young, Allen. Allen Ginsberg 'Your Own Hurt Is Your Guru'— An Interview. *International Times,* no. 148 (Feb. 23-March 8, 1973) pp. 17-20.
Note: AG interview format, reprinted from *Gay Sunshine* (Jan.-Feb. 1973).

J1753   McGrath, Rick. [review of *The Fall Of America*]. *Richmond Review* (Feb. 28, 1973)

J1754   Gosciak, Joseph. Ginsbergs' Poetry Captures Listeners. *Today's Spirit* (Feb. 28, 1973)
Note: AG quoted briefly.

J1755   Kinnell, Galway. Whitman's Indicative Words. *American Poetry Review,* vol. 2, no. 2 (March-April 1973) pp. 9-12.

J1756   DeLaney, William. 2 Ginsberg—Father, Son—Unlike, Yet... *Daily Intelligencer* (March 1, 1973)
Note: AG quoted briefly.

J1757   Parkinson, Thomas. [review of *The Fall Of America*]. *Freedom News* (March 1973) p. 26.

J1758   Young, Allen. Ginsberg/Russia. *Gay Sunshine,* no. 17 (March-April 1973) p. 18.
Note: AG interview format, a section not included in *Gay Sunshine* (Jan.-Feb. 1973).

J1759   Young, Allen. Ginsberg. *Georgia Straight,* vol. 7, no. 282 (March 1-8, 1973) pp. 12-14, 16.
Note: AG interview format, reprinted from *Gay Sunshine* (March-April 1973).

J1760   Robbins, Al. Allen Ginsberg: Off To the Boneyard. *Drummer,* no. 233 (March 6, 1973) p. 9.
Note: AG interview format.

J1761   Epstein, Jules. Miles-Ginsberg: Out Of Rhythms. *Pennsylvania Voice* (March 7, 1973) p. 6.

J1762   Ginsberg At Hillel Tonight. *Rutgers Daily Targum,* vol. 104, no. 103 (March 9, 1973) p. 1.

J1763   McGrath, Rick. [review of *The Fall Of America*]. *Terminal City Express* (March 9, 1973) p. 19.

J1764   Gabel, Stephen. [review of *The Fall Of America*]. *Chicago Daily News* (March 10-11, 1973) Panorama section, p. 8.

J1765   Gaines, Jacob. [review of *The Fall Of America*]. *Independent Journal* (March 10, 1973) p. M31.

J1766   Young, Allen. Interberg With Ginsview. *Northwest Passage,* vol. 8, no. 11 (March 19-April 1, 1973) pp. 12-13, 22.
Note: AG interview format, reprinted from *Gay Sunshine* (March-April 1973).

J1767   Tytell, John. The Beat Generation And the Continuing American Revolution. *American Scholar,* vol. 42, no. 2 (Spring 1973) pp. 308-317.

J1768   Martin, Sam. [review of *The Fall Of America*]. *Door,* vol. 4, no. 18 (March 22-April 12, 1973) p. 14.

J1769* Jahn, Penelope. On Eating Dinner With Allen Ginsberg. *Is,* no. 15 (Spring 1973) p. 43.

J1770 Zweig, Paul. The New Surrealism. *Salmagundi,* no. 22-23 (Spring-Summer 1973) pp. 269-284.

J1771 Young, Allen. The Life & Loves Of Allen Ginsberg. *Real Paper,* vol. 2, no. 13 (March 28, 1973) pp. 8-12, 14.
Note: AG interview format, a different version of the interview from *Gay Sunshine* (Jan.-Feb. 1973).

J1772 Charters, Ann. Jack & Neal & Allen & Luanne & Carolyn. *Rolling Stone,* no. 131 (March 29, 1973) pp. 30-32, 34.

J1773 Peterson, John. Where's Timothy Leary? He's 'Moved Beyond Drugs'. *National Observer* (week ending March 31, 1973) p. 6.
Note: AG quoted briefly.

J1774 Detro, Gene. Poetry Notes: Book Views Ginsberg Visit. *Oregon Journal* (March 31, 1973) Weekend Living section, p. 4.

J1775 Clarke, Gerald. Checking In With Allen Ginsberg. *Esquire,* vol. 79, no. 4 (April 1973) pp. 92-95, 168, 170.
Note: AG quoted.

J1776 Huebel, Harry Russell. The 'Holy Goof': Neal Cassady And the Post-War American Counter Culture. *Illinois Quarterly,* vol. 35, no. 4 (April 1973) pp. 52-61.

J1777 W., H.C. [review of *The Fall Of America*]. *Kliatt Paperback Book Guide* (April 1973) p. 113.

J1778 Stew, Albert. [review of *The Fall Of America*]. *University Review,* no. 28 (April 1973) p. 4.

J1779 Young, Allen. 'Your Own Heart Is Your Guru'—An Interview. *Berkeley Barb,* vol. 17, no. 14 [issue no. 399] (April 6-12, 1973) pp. 19-21. [pt. 1 of 4]
Note: AG interview format, reprinted from *Gay Sunshine* (Jan.-Feb. 1973).

J1780 Conroy, S. Crip. Ginsberg Speaks On Poetry And War. *Good 5¢ Cigar,* vol. 3, no. 41 (April 6, 1973) p. 4.
Note: AG quoted at length.

J1781 Young, Allen. Ginsberg II: Peter, Cuba And Bright Empty Hearts. *Real Paper,* vol. 2, no. 15 (April 11, 1973) pp. 14-18.
Note: AG interview format.

J1782 Rogers, Michael. [review of *The Fall Of America*]. *Rolling Stone,* no. 132 (April 12, 1973) p. 68.

J1783 Smilow, David. Ginsberg Dialogue Compelling: Chapel Poetry Reading Mediocre. *Wellesley News,* vol. 67, no. 8 (April 12, 1973) pp. 1, 4.
Note: AG quoted.

J1784 Young, Allen. Allen Ginsberg. *Berkeley Barb,* vol. 17, no. 15 [issue 400] (April 13-19, 1973) pp. 10-11. [pt. 2 of 4]
Note: AG interview format, reprinted from *Gay Sunshine* (Jan.-Feb. 1973).

J1785   Vendler, Helen. [review of *The Fall Of America*]. *New York Times Book Review* (April 15, 1973) pp. 1, 14, 16, 18.

J1786   Andrews, Lyman. [review of *The Fall Of America*]. *Sunday Times* (April 15, 1973) p. 38.

J1787   Young, Allen. Allen Ginsberg. *Berkeley Barb,* vol. 17, no. 16 [issue 401] (April 20-26, 1973) pp. 15-17. [pt. 3 of 4]*
Note: AG interview format, reprinted from *Gay Sunshine* (Jan.-Feb. 1973).
*Part 4 was never printed.

J1788   Gent, George. Van Doren's Friends Bestow Laurel. *New York Times* (April 27, 1973)

J1789   [review of *The Fall Of America*]. *Times Literary Supplement,* no. 3712 (April 27, 1973) p. 474.

J1790   Gay Laureate For Poetry Festival. *Gay News,* no. 24 (May 1973) p. 4.

J1791   Leogrande, Ernest. The Road And the Riders. *Daily News* (May 1, 1973) p. 50.

J1792   Niederman, Fred. [review of *The Fall Of America*]. *Daily Nexus,* vol. 53, no. 119 (May 3, 1973) pp. 3-4.

J1793   Washam, Veronica. Establishment Honors Go To Anti-Establishment Poet. *Villager,* vol. 41, no. 5 (May 10, 1973) p. 5.
Note: AG quoted briefly.

J1794   Healy, Kathleen. Ginsberg: Free Spirit In Banged-Up Body. *Los Angeles Times* (May 13, 1973) section 4, pp. 10-13.
Note: AG quoted.

J1795   Chibeau, Edmond. Ferlinghetti, Ginsberg To Honor Rexroth. *Santa Barbara News & Review,* vol. 2, no. 10 [issue 34] (May 18, 1973) p. 18.

J1796   Hardin, R.F. [letter to the editor]. *Times Literary Supplement,* no. 3715 (May 18, 1973) p. 557.

J1797   Miles. Allen Ginsberg: Full Circle. *Berkeley Barb,* vol. 17, no. 21 [issue 406] (May 25-31, 1973) p. 18.

J1798   Detro, Gene. [column]. *Oregon Journal* (May 29, 1973) p. 11.

J1799   [review of *The Fall Of America*]. *Choice,* vol. 10, no. 4 (June 1973) p. 618.

J1800   Shively, Charles. [review of *Bixby Canyon Ocean Path Word Breeze, The Fall Of America, The Gates Of Wrath* and *Iron Horse*]. *Gay Sunshine,* no. 18 (June-July 1973) pp. 14-15.

J1801   Warner, Jon M. [review of *The Fall Of America*]. *Library Journal,* vol. 98, no. 11 (June 1, 1973) p. 1823.

J1802   Waugh, Dexter. Ginsberg Sings the Blues. *San Francisco Examiner* (June 4, 1973) p. 32.
Note: AG quoted briefly.

J1803   Barber, James. Allen Enjoyed It All — And So Did Audience. *Vancouver Provence* (June 4, 1973)

J1804   Hunter, Bob. [column]. *Vancouver Sun* (June 4, 1973) p. 32.
Note: AG quoted at length.

Rossiter, Sean. Crippled Poet Ginsberg Bruised But Still Vital. *Vancouver Sun* (June 4, 1973) p. 33.
Note: AG quoted briefly.

J1805   ...And the Deepest Om In the East. *Grape,* vol. 2, no. 11 (June 6-19, 1973) pp. 16-17.
Note: AG quoted.

J1806   Watergate Apocatastasis, pt. 1. *Georgia Straight,* vol. 7, no. 296 (June 7-14, 1973) pp. 12-13.
Note: AG quoted at length from lecture.

J1807   Cotter, James Finn. [review of *The Fall Of America*]. *America,* vol. 128, no. 22 [issue 3309] (June 9, 1973) pp. 533-535.

J1808   Murray, Michele. [review of *The Fall Of America*]. *National Observer,* vol. 12, no. 23 (June 9, 1973) p. 23.

J1809   [review of *The Fall Of America*]. *New York Times Book Review* (June 10, 1973) p. 41.

J1810   Watergate Apocatastasis, pt. 2. *Georgia Straight,* vol. 7, no. 297 (June 14-21, 1973) pp. 12-13.
Note: AG quoted at length from lecture.

J1811   Norris, Ruth. [review of *The Fall Of America*]. *Daily World* (June 15, 1973) p. 8.

J1812   *Knipselkrant,* no. 35 (ca. June 20, 1973)]
Note: AG mentioned throughout and quoted briefly, this is composed of newspaper clippings from other sources and assembled here, nothing original.

J1813   Allen Ginsberg...Rennie Davis And the Underground Press. *Georgia Straight,* vol. 7, no. 298 (June 21-28, 1973) p. 11.
Note: AG interview format.

J1814   Slater, George Dillon. [review of *The Fall Of America*]. *San Francisco Chronicle* (June 24, 1973) p. 39.

J1815   Watergate Apocatastasis G. Gordon Liddy — From Millbrook To Vancouver Airport. *Berkeley Barb,* vol. 17, no. 26 (June 29-July 5, 1973) pp. 10-11.
Note: AG quoted at length from lecture, first printed in *Georgia Straight* (June 7, 1973).

J1816   McNay, Michael. Verse Circus. *Guardian* (June 29, 1973) p. 13.

J1817   [article]. *San Francisco Phoenix,* vol. 1, no. 21 (June 29, 1973) p. 2.

J1818   The Times Diary. *Times* (June 29, 1973) p. 18.
Note: AG quoted briefly.

J1819   Hall, Donald. [review of *The Fall Of America*]. *American Poetry Review,* vol. 2, no. 4 (July-Aug. 1973) p. 37.

J1820   Brodey, Jim. [review of *The Gates Of Wrath*]. *City,* vol. 2, no. 10 (July-Aug. 1973) p. 41.

Yenne, Bill. [review of *The Fall Of America*]. *City,* vol. 2, no. 10 (July-Aug. 1973) p. 41.

J1821   Aldrich, Michael. R. Ginsberg pt. 1. *Grass Roots Gazette,* no. 3 (July 1973) pp. 1, 4-5.
        Note: AG interview format.

J1822   Jebb, Julien. Poetry International. *Times* (July 3, 1973) p. 9.

J1823   Reinhold, Robert. Captain Bly And the Good Ship Lollipop. *Smith,* no. 22-23 [issue called: *Nada i e,* vol. 0, no. 0] (July 4, 1973) pp. 60-73.

J1824   Commentary. *Times Literary Supplement,* no. 3722 (July 6, 1973) p. 778.

J1825   Lemon, Denis. 'Turn On, Tune In, And Drop Up'. *Gay News,* no. 27 (July 12-25, 1973) pp. 10-12.
        Note: AG interview format.

J1826   Rose, Frank. The School Of Hard Narcs. *Village Voice* (July 19, 1973) p. 20.

J1827   Gay Poetry, Sing Out—Come Out. *Gay News,* no. 28 (July 26-Aug. 8, 1973) p. 8.

J1828   Elliott, Gerald A. A Pride Of Poets. *Grand Rapids Press* (July 29, 1973) Wonderland Magazine section, pp. 3-7.
        Note: AG quoted briefly.

J1829   Allen Ginsberg Interview. *Glasgow Review* (Aug. 1973)
        Note: AG interview format.

J1830   Aldrich, Michael R. Ginsberg pt. 2. *Grass Roots Gazette,* no. 4 (Aug. 1973)
        Note: AG interview format.

J1831   Izoard, Jacques. J'ai Rencontré Allen Ginsberg À Rotterdam. *Le Journal Des Poétes,* vol. 43, no. 6 (Aug. 1973) p. 4.

J1832   Mortimer, Peter. Rare Reading. *Newcastle Journal* (Aug. 3, 1973)

J1833   Mortimer, Peter. Ginsberg—Master Of the Universe. *Newcastle Journal* (Aug. 7, 1973) p. 8.
        Note: AG quoted.

J1834   Fried, Jerome. [review of *The Fall Of America*]. *San Francisco Phoenix,* vol. 1, no. 24 (Aug. 10, 1973) p. 25.

J1835   [review of *The Gates Of Wrath*]. *Choice,* vol. 10, no. 7 (Sept. 1973) pp. 975-976.

J1836   Ginsberg In Glasgow. *Nuspeak,* no. 6 (ca. Sept. 1973)
        Note: AG quoted briefly.

J1837   First Thought Is Best Thought. *Scottish International,* vol. 6, no. 7 (Sept. 1973) pp. 18-23.
        Note: AG interview format, an earlier part of this interview appears in *Glasgow Review* (Aug. 1973).

J1838   Clancy, Laurie; Bramwell, Murray and Altman, Dennis. Notes On the Counter Culture. *Southern Review,* vol. 6, no. 3 (Sept. 1973) pp. 239-251.

J1839 Abramson, Neal. [review of *The Fall Of America*]. *Footnotes,* vol. 4, no. 1 (ca. Fall 1973) pp. 7-10.

J1840 Pritchard, William H. [review of *The Fall Of America*]. *Hudson Review,* vol. 26, no. 3 (Autumn 1973) pp. 592-594.

J1841 Peters, Robert. [review of *The Fall Of America*]. *New:,* no. 22-23 (Fall-Winter 1973-74) pp. 69-75.

J1842 Gruber, Ruth. An Interview With George Oppen And Ted Berrigan. *Chicago,* no. 1 [European Edition] (Oct. 1973) ll. 38-56.

J1843 Thornton, Gene. Photography. *New York Times* (Oct. 14, 1973) p. 17.

J1844 Allen Ginsberg. *Stylus,* vol. 47, no. 7 (Oct. 18, 1973) p. 11.

J1845 Henderson, Randi. Ginsberg Wonders Why It's Worse. *Evening Sun* (Oct. 19, 1973) p. B1.
Note: AG quoted.

J1846 Lindh, Howard. Allen Ginsberg, Noted Poet To Speak At Cortland. *Press,* vol. 31, no. 7 (Oct. 19, 1973) p. 4.

J1847 Weissner, Carl. Nach Vietnam Und Watergate. *National Zeitung* (Oct. 20, 1973) NZ Am Wochenende, pp. 3-4.
Note: AG interview format in German only.

J1848 Biro, Eileen. Ginsberg At the Hopkins... *News American* (Oct. 21, 1973) p. 3-B.
Note: AG quoted briefly.

J1849 Czarnecki, John. Allen Ginsberg Is Really All You Thought, And More. *Democrat And Chronicle* (Oct. 25, 1973) pp. C1-2.
Note: AG quoted.

J1850 Sadowski, Sally. The Second Coming Of Allen Ginsberg. *Stylus,* vol. 47, no. 8 (Oct. 25, 1973) p. 13.
Note: AG quoted briefly.

J1851 Chalker, Russell. East: Ginsberg. *Performance* (Oct. 26-Nov. 1, 1973) p. 5.
Note: AG quoted briefly.

J1852 McQuay, Dave. Celebrating Life With Ginsberg. *Towerlight,* vol. 27, no. 8 (Oct. 26, 1973) p. 13.
Note: AG quoted.

J1853 Bly, Robert. Developing the Underneath. *American Poetry Review,* vol. 2, no. 6 (Nov.-Dec. 1973) pp. 44-45.

J1854 Lerrigo, Charley. The Dharma Festival: Nirvana Next Exit...! *Boston Phoenix* (Nov. 6, 1973) p. 24.

J1855 Ribble, Mike. 'New Vision' Of Beat Poets Discussed By Ginsberg. *Central Michigan Life,* vol. 55, no. 34 (Nov. 14, 1973) p. 1.
Note: AG quoted briefly.

Wittebols, Jim. Etc. Discusses 'Beat Poets'. *Central Michigan Life,* vol. 55, no. 34 (Nov. 14, 1973) p. 5.

J1856 Westlund, Dick. Radical Ideas Adopted. *Daily Times-News* (Nov. 14, 1973) p. 1.
Note: AG quoted briefly.

J1857 Lipsky, Jon. Meeting Of the Masters: Allen Ginsberg, Baba Ram Dass & Rinpoche. *Free Paper,* vol. 1, no. 8 (Nov. 14, 1973) pp. 1, 24-25.
Note: AG interview format.

J1858 [review of *The Fall Of America*]. *New York Times Book Review* (Dec. 2, 1973) p. 79.

J1859 Vitka, Bill. Assasination Low Ball: Conversation With Ed Sanders.. *Drummer,* no. 273 (Dec. 11, 1973) p. 3.

J1860 Pete Brown. *Melody Maker* (Dec. 15, 1973)

J1861 Knief, William. Interview With Allen Ginsberg [part 1]. *Cottonwood Review* (Winter 1973-74)
Note: AG interview format, reprinted from *Cottonwood Review* (Spring 1966).

J1862 Lewis, Harry. [review of *The Fall Of America*]. *Mulch,* vol. 2, no. 2 [issue 4] (Winter 1973-74) pp. 145-147.

J1863 Rader, Dotson. Yevgeny Yevtushenko: The Cold Warrior As Poet. *Evergreen Review,* vol. 17, no. 96 (1973) pp. 124-136.
Note: AG quoted briefly.

J1864 Tibor, Kun. Vázlatok A Beat Irodalom Fejlödésrajzához. *Különlenyomat A Filológia Közlöny* (1973)

Books:

J1865 Anastas, Peter. *Glooskap's Children.* Boston, MA: Beacon Press, 1973.
Note: Although this appears to be an introduction in the form of a poem, it is in fact a quotation from a conversation with AG rearranged to look like a poem by Peter Anastas. The quotes are originally found in *North Shore Seventy* (Jan. 24, 1970).

J1866 Betting, Richard A. *The Reconciliation Of Spirit And Flesh In Allen Ginsberg's Poetry.* Unpublished Doctoral Dissertation, University Of Northern Colorado, 1973.

J1867 Buell, Lawrence. *Literary Transcendentalism.* Ithaca, NY: Cornell University Press, 1973, pp. 8n, 167, 179, 329.

J1868 Charters, Ann. *Kerouac: A Biography.* San Francisco, CA: Straight Arrow Books, 1973.
Note: AG mentioned throughout.

J1869 Christadler, Martin (ed.). *Amerikanische Literatur Der Gegenwart.* Stuttgart, Germany: Kröner, 1973.
Contents: Vietta, Susanne. Allen Ginsberg, pp. 581-601.

J1870 Crabtree, Lee. *An Unfinished Memoir.* New York, NY: Adventures In Poetry, ca. 1973.
Note: AG mentioned throughout.

J1871   Creeley, Robert. *Contexts Of Poetry: Interviews 1961-1971.* Bolinas, CA: Four
Seasons Foundation, 1973, pp. 29-43.
Note: AG interview format, reprinted from *Audit* (Spring 1968).

J1872   Gifford, Barry. *Kerouac's Town.* Santa Barbara, CA: Capra Press, 1973.
Note: AG mentioned throughout.

J1873   Ginsberg, Allen. *Manta Del Re Di Maggio.* Milan, Italy: Mondadori, 1973.
Contents: Pivano, Fernanda. Conversazione Sulla Prosodia, pp. 9-43.
Note: AG interview format in Italian only.
Contents: Clark, Thomas. Precisazione Di Allen Ginsberg All'Intervista
Registrata Da Thomas Clark, pp. 417-419.
Note: AG interview format in Italian only translated by Fernanda Pivano.

J1874   Hassan, Ihab. *Contemporary American Literature: 1945-1972.* New York, NY:
Frederick Ungar, 1973.
Note: AG mentioned throughout.

J1875   Hawkins, Gerald S. *Beyond Stonehenge.* New York, NY: Harper & Row,
1973, p. 263.

J1876   Hudson, Lee. *Beat Generation Poetics And the Oral Tradition Of Literature.*
Unpublished Doctoral Dissertation. University Of Texas At Austin, 1973.

J1877   Hudson, Theodore R. *From LeRoi Jones To Amiri Baraka: The Literary Works.*
Durham, NC: Duke University Press, 1973.
Note: AG mentioned throughout.

J1878   Kirsch, Hans-Christian. *Dies Land Ist Unser.* Munich, Germany: List Verlag,
1973.
Note: AG mentioned throughout.

J1879   Lin, Maurice Y. *Children Of Adam: Ginsberg, Ferlinghetti And Snyder In the
Emerson-Whitman Tradition.* Unpublished Doctoral Dissertation. University
Of Minnesota At Minneapolis, 1973.

J1880   *McGraw-Hill Encyclopedia Of World Biography, vol. 4.* New York, NY:
McGraw-Hill, 1973.
Contents: Gold, Robert S. Ginsberg, pp. 401-402.

J1881   Malkoff, Karl. *Crowell's Handbook Of Contemporary American Poetry.* New
York, NY: Thomas Y. Crowell, 1973, pp. 127-133.

J1882   Nahas, Gabriel G. *Marihuana—Deceptive Weed.* New York, NY: Raven Press,
1973, pp. 10, 278.

J1883   Phillips, Robert. *The Confessional Poets.* Carbondale, IL: Southern Illinois
University Press, 1973.
Note: AG mentioned throughout.

J1884   Richmond, Len and Noguera, Gary (eds.). *The Gay Liberation Book.* San
Francisco, CA: Ramparts Press, 1973, pp. 200-202.
Note: AG interview format, excerpts from the Chicago conspiracy trial testimony.

J1885   Shaw, Robert B. (ed.). *American Poetry Since 1960: Some Critical Perspectives.*
Cheadle Hulme, England: Carcanet Press, 1973.
Note: AG mentioned throughout. Published in the US in Chester Springs, PA by
Dufour Editions in 1974.

J1886   Sutton, Walter. *American Free Verse*. New York, NY: New Directions, 1973, pp. 142, 182-184, 208.

J1887   Welch, Lew. *How I Work As a Poet And Other Essays / Plays / Stories*. Bolinas, CA: Grey Fox Press, 1973, p. 29.
Note: AG quoted briefly.

1974

J1888   Leyland, Winston. Gerard Malanga: An Interview. *Gay Sunshine,* no. 20 (Jan.-Feb. 1974) pp. 4-8.

J1889   Russell, Peter. Ezra Pound: The Last Years. *Malahat Review,* no. 29 (Jan. 1974) pp. 11-44.

J1890   Goodman, Richard, Jr. An Evening With William Burroughs. *Michigan Quarterly Review,* vol. 13, no. 1 (Winter [Jan.] 1974) pp. 18-24.

J1891   Hartman, Rose. Abbie. *Soho Weekly News,* vol. 1, no. 13 (Jan. 3, 1974) pp. 1-2.

J1892   Gustaitis, Rasa. Alchemist, Astronomer, Guru, And Most Of All, Timothy Leary. *Washington Post* (Jan. 6, 1974) p. E7.

J1893   Carlson, Peter. 'Haiku My Eyes!': A Night Of Kerouac. *News,* vol. 6, no. 15 (Jan. 17, 1974) pp. 6-7.
Note: AG quoted briefly.

J1894   Goldstein, Richard. Growing Up With Bob Dylan. *New York,* vol. 7, no. 4 (Jan. 28, 1974) pp. 47-50.

J1895   Howl!!! *Bates College Student,* vol. 101, no. 2 (Jan. 31, 1974) p. 4.

J1896   Mancini, Anthony. Bob Dylan Comes Home. *New York Post* (Jan. 31, 1974) p. 26.

J1897   Moser, Norm. [review of *The Fall Of America*]. *Gar,* vol. 3, no. 3 [issue 22] (Feb.-March 1974) pp. 26-27.

J1898   Freeman, Deborah. Ginsberg. *Green Revolution,* vol. 12, no. 3 (Feb.-March 1974) pp. 11-14.
Note: AG interview format.

J1899   Bockris-Wylie. Allen Ginsberg On Heroes. *Drummer,* no. 282 (Feb. 12, 1974) pp. 3-4.
Note: AG interview format.

Bockris-Wylie. 20 Questions For Allen Ginsberg And Peter Orlovsky. *Drummer,* no. 282 (Feb. 12, 1974) pp. 4, 7.
Note: AG interview format.

J1900   Bristol, Bobbie. Magical Mystery Tour Of England In the Sixties. *Drummer,* no. 283 (Feb. 19, 1974) pp. 9-11.
Note: AG quoted briefly.

J1901   Patterson, Pat. Collegians Dig Ginsberg Duo. *Paterson News* (Feb. 22, 1974)

J1902 Little, John (ed.). *City Lights In North Dakota: The Poet Looks At Industry And Ecology.* Grand Forks, ND: University Of North Dakota English Department, March 1974.
Note: AG interview format.

J1903 Fallows, James. The Most Famous Journalist In America. *Washington Monthly,* vol. 7, no. 1 (March 1974) pp. 21-22.

J1904 Dilemma Draws Deep Breath In 10-Minute Silence. *Commercial Appeal* (March 3, 1974) section 1, p. 19.
Note: AG quoted briefly.

J1905 Kohn, Jaakov. A Phone Call From Jail. *Soho Weekly News* (March 6, 1974) p. 4.

J1906 McGuire, Mike. Allen Ginsberg—March 12. *Load,* vol. 2, no. 14 (March 12, 1974) p. 8.

J1907 [photograph]. *Meridian,* vol. 11, no. 21 (March 13, 1974) p. 7.

J1908 McClure, Michael. The Poet's Poet. *Rolling Stone,* no. 156 (March 14, 1974) pp. 33-34.

J1909 Vadnie, Michael. 7 'Beat' Poets Appear At 'City Lights In N.D.'. *Grand Forks Herald* (March 19, 1974) p. 20.

J1910 Smith, Stuart. 'Beat Generation' Poets Lash Out Against Dehumanization. *Grand Forks Herald* (March 20, 1974) p. 34.
Note: AG quoted briefly.

J1911 Kurtz. Reading, Breathing, & Biting—Ginsberg Absorbing & Profound. *Meridian,* vol. 11, no. 22 (March 20, 1974) p. 2.
Note: AG quoted briefly.

J1912 Vadnie, Michael. 'Beat Generation' Poets Reminisce About 'Frisco Renaissance'. *Grand Forks Herald* (March 21, 1974) p. 8.
Note: AG quoted briefly.

J1913 Slaughter, William. Eating Poetry. *Chicago Review,* vol. 25, no. 4 (Spring 1974) pp. 124-128.

J1914 Wm. Burroughs: An Interview. *Gay Sunshine,* no. 21 (Spring 1974) pp. 1-3.

J1915 Middlebrook, Diane. [review of *The Fall Of America* and *The Gates Of Wrath*]. *Parnassus,* vol. 2, no. 2 (Spring-Summer 1974) pp. 128-135.

J1916 Anderson, Jack. Poet's New Quest. *Paterson News* (March 22, 1974)

J1917 Vadnie, Michael and Smith, Stuart. Poet Recalls Movement At Conference. *Grand Forks Herald* (March 23, 1974) p. 4.

J1918 Smith, Stuart and Vadnie, Michael. Writers Conference Ends With Reading Of Classic Poem. *Grand Forks Herald* (March 24, 1974) pp. 33, 44.
Note: AG quoted.

J1919 Hill, Tracey. 'Prophet-Poet' Ginsberg To Read Works. *Denisonian,* vol. 108, no. 17 (March 27, 1974) pp. 3-4.

J1920 Ginsberg Coming! *Downtowner,* vol. 14, no. 17 (March 27, 1974)

J1921   Rockwell, John. Guru Brings Composers New Voice. *New York Times* (March 27, 1974) p. 32.

J1922   Allen Ginsberg Pulpit Speaker At Unitarian. *Montclair Times* (March 28, 1974)

J1923   Reprise. *Newsletter On the State Of the Culture* (March 30, 1974) p. 4.
Note: AG quoted briefly.

J1924   Bockris-Wylie. W.C. Williams Anecdote Meeting T.S. Eliot By Allen Ginsberg As Told To Bockris-Wylie. *World,* no. 29 (April 1974) p. 7.
Note: AG interview format, reprinted from *Drummer* (Feb. 12, 1974).

J1925   Cook, Bonnie L. Celebration: Allen Ginsberg — Bhagavan Das. *Drummer,* no. 289 (April 2, 1974) p. 5.
Note: AG quoted.

J1926   Ginsberg Show Hits SI Campus. *Downtowner,* vol. 14, no. 18 (April 3, 1974) p. 1.

J1927   Schourup, Larry. Ginsberg In A^2. *Ann Arbor Sun,* vol. 2, no. 7 (April 5-19, 1974) p. 7.

J1928   Ouroussoff, Alessandro. Rattling Radical Bones. *Daily Californian* (April 9, 1974) p. 11.

J1929   Foxworth, Andrea R. Ginsberg: Walt Whitman Of Our Time At RUCCAS. *Gleaner,* vol. 40, no. 23 (April 10, 1974) p. 1.

J1930   Sweeney, Patrick J. Ginsberg Returns. *Lanthorn,* vol. 6, no. 17 (April 11, 1974) p. 4.

J1931   [column]. *McGraw-Hill News,* vol. 15, no. 8 (April 11, 1974) p. 4.

J1932   Berman, Laura. 'Beat' Poet Ginsberg Still Playing the Circuit. *Michigan Daily* (April 13, 1974) pp. 1, 3.
Note: AG quoted.

J1933   Pynchon, Singer Share Fiction Prize. *New York Times* (April 17, 1974) p. 37.

J1934   Sanders, Ed. [review of *The Fall Of America*]. *Village Voice* (April 18, 1974) pp. 27-28.

J1935   Burroughs. *Anchor,* vol. 66, no. 21 (April 19, 1974)

J1936   Jones, Lauren E. Ginsberg: The Materialism Of Spirituality. *Ann Arbor Sun,* vol. 2, no. 8 (April 19-May 3, 1974) pp. 4-5.

J1937   Library Presents Poets Ginsberg And Reed In April 29 Reading. *Library Of Congress Information Bulletin,* vol. 33, no. 16 (April 19, 1974) pp. 128-129.

J1938   Weisman, Steven R. World Of Books Presents Its Oscars. *New York Times* (April 19, 1974) p. 24.

J1939   Two Authors Share Fiction Book Award. *Louisville Courier-Journal* (April 21, 1974)

J1940   O., C.E. The National Book Award 'Show'. *St. Louis Post-Dispatch* (April 21, 1974) p. 4B.

J1941 Crandall, Ellen. Ginsberg B'ham "74. *Northwest Passage,* vol. 10, no. 10 (April 22-May 6, 1974) p. 24.
Note: AG quoted briefly.

J1942 Poet Allen Ginsberg Slates Evening Talk. *Oklahoma Daily* (April 23, 1974) p. 18.

J1943 Smyth, Robert. A Day With Allen Ginsberg. *Denisonian,* vol. 108, no. 19 (April 24, 1974) pp. 2, 8.
Note: AG quoted briefly.

J1944 Ahern, Steven Dale; Bartz, Anne; Haves, Hyman H.; Jacoby, Jonathan; Reisner, Neil and Turner, Elizabeth Carey. [letters to the editor]. *Los Angeles Times* (April 24, 1974) part 2, p. 6.

J1945 Detro, Gene. Feminist Poet Draws 500 Here. *Oregon Journal* (April 24, 1974)

J1946 Hogan, William. The Book Awards As Bad Vaudeville. *San Francisco Chronicle* (April 24, 1974)

J1947 Smith, R.T. [review of *The Fall Of America*]. *Appalachian* (April 25, 1974) p. 9.

J1948 Brandenburg, John. Ginsberg Packs 'em In To Hear His Dark View Of America. *Oklahoma City Times* (April 25, 1974) p. 10.
Note: AG quoted.

J1949 Opens Poetry Series. *New York Times* (April 26, 1974) p. 41.

J1950 Upjohn, Marshall. Poet Blasts Nixon, Military, FBI. *Oklahoma Daily* (April 26, 1974) p. 16.
Note: AG quoted.

J1951 Lovell, John. Breath Is What Concerns Poet Ginsberg, He Explains. *Press Herald* (April 27, 1974) p. 26.
Note: AG quoted briefly.

J1952 National Book Award Winners. *Los Angeles Times* (April 28, 1974) Calendar section, p. 63.

J1953 Gildea, William. Voices Of Freedom Protesting. *Washington Post* (April 30, 1974) pp. B1, B9.
Note: AG quoted briefly.

J1954 Trescott, Jacqueline. Poets Among Poets, Just Like Ordinary Folks. *Washington Star-News* (April 30, 1974) section C, pp. C1, C2.
Note: AG quoted briefly.

J1955 Ball, Gordon. Ginsberg & Duncan. *American Poetry Review,* vol. 3, no. 3 (May-June 1974) pp. 52-58.
Note: AG interview format.

J1956 [Killeen, Mary]. Discussion Following Poetry Reading April 1973, Salem State College. *Gone Soft,* vol. 1, no. 3 (Spring [May] 1974) pp. 19-32.
Note: AG interview format.

J1957 Bockris-Wylie. Ginsberg On Heroes. *Georgia Straight,* vol. 8, no. 342 (May 2-9, 1974) pp. 12-13.
Note: AG interview format, reprinted from *Drummer* (Feb. 12, 1974).

J1958 Detro, Gene. Poet Ginsberg Shares Spotlight With Music. *Oregon Journal* (May 4, 1974)

J1959 Wallace, Kevin. Louis And Allen—The Filial Poetry Show. *San Francisco Chronicle* (May 10, 1974) p. 5.
Note: AG quoted briefly.

J1960 Lomax, Michele. The Ginsberg Generations Reveal Their Poetic Gap. *San Francisco Examiner* (May 10, 1974) p. 25.

J1961 Nemo, Fred and Poliat, Frank. Boogaloo II. *Portland Scribe* (May 11-17, 1974) pp. 6, 19.

J1962 Abramson, Neal. Rapping With Ginsberg. *Footnotes,* vol. 4, no. 2 (Spring [May 15] 1974) pp. 18-21.
Note: AG interview format.

J1963 Ouroussoff, Sandro. The Ginsberg Family's Poetry And Puns. *Daily Californian* (May 16, 1974) p. 18.
Note: AG quoted briefly.

J1964 Desruisseaux, Paul. Are We Ready For Two Ginsbergs? *Pacific Sun,* vol. 12, no. 20 (May 16-22, 1974) pp. 12-14.
Note: AG quoted briefly.

J1965 Jones, Lauren; Weinberg, Barbara and Fenton, David. Allen Ginsberg. *Ann Arbor Sun,* vol. 2, no. 10 (May 17-31, 1974) pp. 14-15, 22.
Note: AG interview format.

J1966 Bockris-Wylie. Ginsberg On Heroes. *Berkeley Barb* (May 17-23, 1974) pp. 12-13.
Note: AG transcription of conversation, reprinted from *Drummer* (Feb. 12, 1974).

J1967 Knight, Hans. The Howl Of Allen Ginsberg. *Sunday Bulletin* (May 19, 1974) Discover section, pp. 9, 11, 18-19.
Note: AG quoted briefly.

J1968 Braitman, Stephen M.H. 'Slice Of Reality Life' Interview With Allen & Louis Ginsberg. *Zenger's* (May 22, 1974) pp. 8-9.
Note: AG interview format.

J1969 Hammond, John. Tax Resistance In Kansas City. *Win,* vol. 10, no. 18 (May 23, 1974) pp. 16-17.

J1970 Cook, Bonnie L. Happy Birthday, Walt—Love, Allen. *Drummer,* no. 297 (May 28, 1974) p. 5.
Note: AG quoted briefly.

J1971 National Book Awards. *Facts On File,* vol. 34, no. 1751 (June 1, 1974) p. 448.

J1972 Moser, Norm. Watching As the Poets Break Outa the Corral. *Gar,* vol. 3, no. 5 [issue 24] (June-July 1974) pp. 26-29.

J1973 Löfström, Tomas. Amerika, När Kommer Du Att Bli En Ängel? *Studiekamraten,* vol. 56, no. 4-5 (June 1974) pp. 67-69.

J1974 Scott, Andrew. [review of *Gay Sunshine Interviews*]. *Georgia Straight,* vol. 8, no. 347 (June 6-13, 1974) p. 11.

J1975   Grant, Barry. [review of *The Fall Of America*]. *Ethos,* vol. 8, no. 2 (June 6, 1974) pp. 15-17.

J1976   Braitman, Stephen M.H. ...Violets Are Blue: On Father's Day, the Ginsbergs 2. *New York Times* (June 16, 1974) section 4, p. 21.
Note: AG interview format, first printed in *Zenger's* (May 22, 1974).

J1977   Knief, William. Interview With Allen Ginsberg, part 2. *Cottonwood Review* (Summer 1974) pp. 51-54.
Note: AG interview format, reprinted from *Cottonwood Review* (Nov. 1966).

J1978   Bernard, Sidney. Did NBA Know What It Was Doing When It Gave Allen the Laurel? *New York Smith* (Summer 1974) p. 10.

J1979   Tytell, John. A Conversation With Allen Ginsberg. *Partisan Review,* vol. 41, no. 2 ([Summer] 1974) pp. 253-262.
Note: AG interview format.

J1980   [review of *Allen Verbatim*]. *Kirkus Reviews,* vol. 42, no. 13 (July 1, 1974) p. 716.

J1981   Grant, Barry. [review of *Iron Horse*]. *Ethos,* vol. 8, no. 6 (July 18, 1974) pp. 9-10.

J1982   Jones, Lauren; Weinberg, Barbara and Fenton, David. Ginsberg Raps. *Georgia Straight,* vol. 8, no. 353 (July 18-25, 1974) pp. 13, 20.
Note: AG interview format, reprinted from *Ann Arbor Sun* (May 17, 1974).

J1983   Rauch, Berna. Poets Sing Of Visions. *Berkeley Barb,* vol. 20, no. 1 [issue 466] (July 19-25, 1974) p. 11.
Note: AG quoted briefly.

J1984   Sealing, Keith. Ginsberg Joins DiPrima And Waldman In Chanting And Poetry Reading In Macky. *Colorado Daily* (July 31, 1974) p. 1.

J1985   Como, William. The Golden Gait: The People Who Set the Pace. *After Dark,* vol. 7, no. 4 (Aug. 1974) pp. 58-59.

J1986   Goldman, Ivan. Gap-Bridger Ginsberg Pauses In Boulder To Reflect. *Denver Post* (Aug. 1, 1974) p. 66.
Note: AG quoted.

J1987   [review of *Allen Verbatim*]. *Kirkus Reviews,* vol. 42, no. 14 (Aug. 1, 1974) p. 818.

J1988   Cook, Stephen. Allen Ginsberg. *Maine Edition* (Aug. 1974) pp. 7-11.
Note: AG interview format.

J1989   Läutner, Alfred. The Nine Lives Of Poetry International. *New Review,* vol. 1, no. 5 (Aug. 1974) pp. 35-42.

J1990   Henry, Gerrit. [review of *The Fall Of America*]. *Poetry,* vol. 124, no. 5 (Aug. 1974) pp. 292-299.

J1991   [review of *Allen Verbatim*]. *Publishers Weekly,* vol. 206, no. 6 (Aug. 5, 1974) p. 57.

J1992   Knight, Arthur Winfield. [review of *Iron Horse*]. *New York Culture Review,* vol. 1, no. 8 (Aug. 9, 1974) pp. 4-5.

J1993 Weinraub, Bernard. India's Downtrodden Burst Into Literature. *New York Times* (Aug. 26, 1974) p. 2.

J1994 Blackbird. Speculations In a Labyrinth. *Berkeley Barb* (Sept. 1974)

J1995 Bowman, Jon. [review of *Iron Horse*]. *Kliatt Paperback Book Guide* (Sept. 1974) p. 103.

J1996 Lindborg, Henry J. [review of *Allen Verbatim*]. *Library Journal,* vol. 99, no. 15 (Sept. 1, 1974) pp. 2067-2068.

J1997 Plamondon, Pun. Ann Arbor Culture: Mecca Of the Midwest. *Ann Arbor Sun,* vol. 2, no. 17 (Sept. 6-20, 1974) Back To Ann Arbor supplement, pp. 4-5.

J1998 Razell, Robert. Son Has Acid Comments About Tim Leary. *New York Post* (Sept. 18, 1974) p. 4.

J1999 Fosburgh, Lacey. Leary Scored As 'Cop Informant' By His Son And 2 Close Friends. *New York Times* (Sept. 19, 1974) p. 84.
Note: AG quoted briefly, an earlier edition of this newspaper gives the title "Leary Denounced By Son And Friends" to the same article here on page 49.

J2000 Zane, Maitland. The Friends Of Tim Leary. *San Francisco Chronicle* (Sept. 19, 1974) p. 23.

J2001 Dooley, Nancy. Counterculture Event—Examination Into Timothy Leary's 'Lies'. *San Francisco Examiner* (Sept. 19, 1974) p. 3.
Note: AG quoted briefly.

J2002 Johnston, David. The Bitter Pill. *Berkeley Barb,* vol. 20, no. 10 [issue 475] (Sept. 20-26, 1974) pp. 3, 13.
Note: AG quoted briefly.

J2003 What's Behind the Testbook Dispute. *San Francisco Chronicle* (Sept. 20, 1974) p. 19.

J2004 Tallman, Warren. Wonder Merchants: Modernist Poetry In Vancouver During the 1960's. *Boundary 2,* vol. 3, no. 1 (Fall 1974) pp. 57-89.

J2005 Cargas, Harry J. An Interview With Allen Ginsberg. *Nimrod,* vol. 19, no. 1 (Fall-Winter 1974) pp. 24-29.
Note: AG interview format.

J2006 Is Leary Singing an Era's Swansong? *New York Times* (Sept. 22, 1974) section IV, p. 7.

J2007 Bell, Srilekha; Wallace, Brian; Finley, Robert; Prescott, N. Parker and Mathieu, Bertrand. Interview With Allen Ginsberg. *Noiseless Spider,* vol. 4, no. 1 [issue 7] (Fall 1974) pp. 2-15.
Note: AG interview format.

J2008 Allen Verbatim. *Paideuma,* vol. 3, no. 2 (Fall 1974) pp. 253-273.
Note: AG interview format.

J2009 Winslow, Pete. Beautiful Wreckage: An Essay On the Poetry Of Bob Kaufman. *St. Andrews Review,* vol. 3, no. 1 (Fall-Winter 1974) pp. 21-35.

J2010 McNally, Dennis. [review of *The Visions Of the Great Rememberer*]. *Below the Salt,* vol. 2, no. 3 (Sept. 26, 1974) pp. 1, 4.

J2011   Bacon, Leslie. Leary's Smiling Inquisitor. *Berkeley Barb,* vol. 20, no. 11 [issue 476] (Sept. 27-Oct. 3, 1974) p. 6.
Note: AG quoted briefly.

J2012   Newsmakers. *Newsweek,* vol. 84, no. 14 (Sept. 30, 1974) p. 49.

J2013   Johnston, David. The Bitter Pill. *Georgia Straight,* vol. 8, no. 364 (Oct. 3-10, 1974) pp. 1, 12.
Note: AG quoted briefly, reprinted from *Berkeley Barb* (Sept. 20, 1974).

J2014   Lomax, Michele. 'Monster Reading' By the Clock. *San Francisco Examiner* (Oct. 8, 1974) p. 23.

J2015   Newlove, Donald. [review of *The Visions Of the Great Rememberer*]. *Village Voice* (Oct. 10, 1974) p. 33.

J2016   Seelye, John. [review of *Allen Verbatim*]. *New Republic,* vol. 171, no. 15 [issue 3118] (Oct. 12, 1974) pp. 23-24.

J2017   [letter to the editor]. *Georgia Straight,* vol. 8, no. 366 (Oct. 17-24, 1974) p. 3.

J2018   Wilson, Robert Anton. Strongly Differing View On Tim. *San Francisco Phoenix,* vol. 2, no. 27 [issue no. 54] (Oct. 24, 1974) pp. 1, 7.

J2019   McArdle, Phil. [review of *Allen Verbatim*]. *Baltimore Sun* (Oct. 27, 1974)

J2020   Lewis, Barbara. Ginsberg Victimized In Greenwich Village. *Asbury Park Press* (Nov. 1974)
Note: AG quoted at length.

J2021   Tytell, John. From a Conversation With Allen Ginsberg. *Berkeley Barb,* vol. 20, no. 16 [issue 481] (Nov. 1-7, 1974) pp. 12-13.
Note: AG interview format, reprinted from *Partisan Review* (Summer 1974).

J2022   Grauerholz, James. The Fully-Clothed Lunch And Other Meals... *Changes,* no. 90 (Nov. 1974) pp. 10-11.

J2023   Young, Allen. Gay Sunshine Interview. *College English,* vol. 36, no. 3 (Nov. 1974) pp. 392-400.
Note: AG interview format, reprinted from *Gay Sunshine* (March 1973).

J2024   Spearman, Walter. [review of *Allen Verbatim*]. *Literary Lantern* (Nov. 3, 1974)

J2025   Farley, Paula Lillevand. [letter to the editor]. *Gazette,* vol. 1, no. 3 (Nov. 5, 1974) p. 4.

J2026   Venters, Travis. [review of *Allen Verbatim*]. *Salisbury Post* (Nov. 7, 1974)

J2027   [review of *Allen Verbatim*]. *Vector* (Nov. 8, 1974)

J2028   Jolliffe, David. Poet Allen Ginsberg Comments On Textbook Protest. *News-Register* (Nov. 10, 1974) p. 16.
Note: AG quoted at length.

J2029   Spearman, Walter. [review of *Allen Verbatim*]. *Greensboro Record* (Nov. 11, 1974)

J2030   Fields, Sidney. The Square And the Hip. *Daily News* (Nov. 12, 1974) p. 49.
Note: AG quoted briefly.

J2031   Goodwin, Michael; Hyatt, Richard and Ward, Ed. Q: How Does Allen Ginsberg Write Poetry? *City,* vol. 7, no. 52 (Nov. 13-26, 1974) pp. 30-34.
Note: AG interview format.

J2032   Fields, Sidney. Ginsberg Gains New Poem From Neighborhood Mugging. *Hartford Courant* (Nov. 13, 1974)
Note: AG quoted briefly.

J2033   Spearman, Walter. [review of *Allen Verbatim*]. *Southern Pines Pilot* (Nov. 13, 1974)

J2034   [review of *Allen Verbatim*]. *Chicago Tribune* (Nov. 17, 1974) Book World section, p. 8.

J2035   People. *Time,* vol. 104, no. 21 (Nov. 18, 1974) p. 52.
Note: AG quoted briefly.

J2036   Ginsberg's Little Bombshell. *San Francisco Chronicle* (Nov. 26, 1974) p. 4.

J2037   De Giere, Greg. Mysterious Leary May Materialize Here Again. *Vacaville Reporter* (Nov. 28, 1974) pp. 1, 8.
Note: AG quoted briefly.

J2038   Blicksilver, Edith. [review of *Allen Verbatim*]. *Atlanta Journal And Atlanta Constitution* (Dec. 1, 1974)

J2039   Staggs, Kenneth. [review of *Allen Verbatim*]. *Express And News* (Dec. 1, 1974)

J2040   Trotter, Bill. [review of *Allen Verbatim*]. *Greensboro Sun* (Dec. 1974) pp. 6-7.

J2041   Sachs, Sylvia. [review of *Allen Verbatim*]. *Pittsburgh Press* (Dec. 1, 1974)

J2042   Lewis, Barbara. Ginsberg Puts Mugging Into Marketable Verse. *Rocky Mountain News* (Dec. 1, 1974) Now section, pp. 16, 18.
Note: AG quoted.

J2043   Salzman, Jack. [review of *Allen Verbatim*]. *Washington Post* (Dec. 1, 1974) Book World section, p. 2.

J2044   Tucker, Carll. [review of *Allen Verbatim*]. *Village Voice* (Dec. 2, 1974) pp. 41-42.

J2045   Reynolds, Ric. Partying With the Poets. *Berkeley Barb,* vol. 20, no. 21 [issue 486] (Dec. 6-12, 1974) pp. 1, 5.

Silver, Sam. After Bucks To the Prisoners. *Berkeley Barb,* vol. 20, no. 21 [issue 486] (Dec. 6-12, 1974) p. 5.
Note: AG quoted briefly.

J2046   Shepard, Claudia. [review of *Allen Verbatim*]. *Winston-Salem Journal And Sentinel* (Dec. 8, 1974) p. C-4.

J2047   Donnelly, Kerry. Poet Scorns Political Slumber. *Rutgers Daily Targum* (Dec. 11, 1974) p. 6.
Note: AG quoted briefly.

J2048   Knight, Arthur Winfield. [review of *The Visions Of the Great Rememberer*]. *New York Culture Review,* vol. 1, no. 15-16 (Dec. 12, 1974) p. 16.

J2049 Ginsberg To Give Reading. *North Wind,* vol. 4, no. 12 (Dec. 12, 1974) p. 1.

J2050 Sylvester, Bruce. [review of *Allen Verbatim*]. *Patriot Ledger* (Dec. 14, 1974) p. 10.

J2051 Kameen, Paul J. [review of *Allen Verbatim*]. *Best Sellers,* vol. 34 (Dec. 15, 1974) p. 409.

J2052 Prescott, William. [review of *Allen Verbatim*]. *Charlotte Observer* (Dec. 15, 1974) p. 9B.

J2053 Weller, W. Robert. Disputed Texts Present Updated Issues, Roles. *News-Register* (Dec. 15, 1974)

J2054 Klinkowitz, Jerome. [review of *Allen Verbatim*]. *Richmond Times-Dispatch* (Dec. 15, 1974)

J2055 Feder, Lillian. Myth As Self-Revealing Instrument. *Books Abroad,* vol. 48, no. 1 (Winter 1974) pp. 7-14.

J2056 Tysell [sic: Tytell], John. Conversation Avec Allen Ginsberg. *Tel Quel,* no. 60 (Winter 1974) pp. 54-63.
Note: AG interview format in French only, translated by Harry Blake.

J2057 Offen, Ron. [review of *Allen Verbatim*]. *Chicago Daily News* (Dec. 28, 1974)

J2058 Goldman, Ivan. Jack Kerouac's Denver Friends Formed Theme For Novel. *Denver Post* (Dec. 29, 1974)

J2059 Kingswell, Henry A. and Martin, Thomas. The Brief Detroit Sojourn Of Jack Kerouac. *Detroit Free Press* (Dec. 29, 1974)

J2060 Goldman, Ivan. Bob Burford's Summer Of '47: A Different Story. *Denver Post* (Dec. 30, 1974)

J2061 Ball, Gordon and Tucker, Carll. The Battle Of Ginsberg. *Village Voice* (Dec. 30, 1974) pp. 31-32.

J2062 Goldman, Ivan. 'Doll Of the West' Recalls How It Was With Kerouac, Friends. *Denver Post* (Dec. 31, 1974)

J2063 Anderson, Don. 'Hebraic-Melvillian Bardic Breath': Whitman And Ginsberg. *New Poetry,* vol. 23, no. 1 (1974) pp. 5-17.

J2064 Shively, Charles. Notes On the Poem 'Please Master'. *Pro-Me-Thee-Us* (1974) pp. 17-32.
Note: Reprinted from *Gay Sunshine,* no. 17 (1973).

J2065 Young, Allen. Intervju Med Allen Ginsberg. *Vinduet,* vol. 28, no. 3 (1974) pp. 16-20.
Note: AG interview format in Norwegian only, translated by Olav Angell.

Books:

J2066 Aguilar, Mary Karen. *Allen Ginsberg And the Development Of Popular Poetry.* Unpublished Doctoral Dissertation. Temple University, 1974.

J2067   Andre, Kenneth Michael. *Levertov, Creeley, Wright, Auden, Ginsberg, Corso, Dickey: Essays And Interviews With Contemporary American Poets.* Unpublished Doctoral Dissertation. Columbia University, 1974.
Note: AG interview format.

J2068   Blair, Walter et al. *American Literature: A Brief History.* Glenview, IL: Scott, Foresman & Co., 1974, pp. 268, 306, 317. [revised edition]

J2069   Chassman, Neil A. (ed.). *Poets Of the Cities: New York And San Francisco 1950-1965.* New York, NY: Dutton, 1974.
Note: AG mentioned throughout.

J2070   Dorfman, Elsa. *Elsa's Housebook.* Boston, MA: David R. Godine, 1974, pp. 16-21.

J2071   Fleming, William. *Arts & Ideas.* New York, NY: Holt, Rinehart & Winston, 1974, pp. 399, 411.

J2072   Ginsberg, Allen. *Allen Verbatim: Lectures On Poetry, Politics, Consciousness.* New York, NY: McGraw-Hill, 1974.
Note: AG interview format.

J2073   Gunn, Drewey Wayne. *American And British Writers In Mexico, 1556-1973.* Austin, TX: University Of Texas Press, 1974, pp. 220-226.

J2074   Horowitz, Michael (ed.). *Apologia For Timothy Leary.* San Francisco, CA: Fitz Hugh Ludlow Memorial Library, 1974, pp. 21, 48.

J2075   Manchester, William. *The Glory And the Dream.* Boston, MA: Little, Brown & Co., 1974.
Note: AG mentioned throughout.

J2076   Mersmann, James F. *Out Of the Vietnam Vortex.* Lawrence, KS: University Press Of Kansas, 1974.
Note: AG mentioned throughout.

J2077   Norwood, Christopher. *About Paterson.* New York, NY: Saturday Review Press/E.P. Dutton, 1974, p. 90.

J2078   Packard, William (ed.). *The Craft Of Poetry: Interviews From the New York Quarterly.* Garden City, NY: Doubleday & Co., 1974.
Contents: Fortunato, Mary Jane; Medwick, Lucille and Rowe, Susan. Allen Ginsberg, pp. 53-78.
Note: AG interview format.

J2079   Rao, Vimala C. *Oriental Influence On the Writings Of Jack Kerouac, Allen Ginsberg And Gary Snyder.* Unpublished Doctoral Dissertation. Milwaukee, WI: University Of Wisconsin, 1974.

J2080   Riley, Carolyn and Harte, Barbara (eds.). *Contemporary Literary Criticism, vol. 2.* Detroit, MI: Gale Research Co., 1974, pp. 162-164.

J2081   Rodman, Selden. *Tongues Of Fallen Angels.* New York, NY: New Directions, 1974, pp. 183-199.
Note: AG quoted.

J2082   Rorem, Ned. *Pure Contraption.* New York, NY: Holt, Rinehart and Winston, 1974, p. 13.

J2083 Tysh, Christine. *Allen Ginsberg, Étude De Christine Tysh: Choix de Poèmes, Bibliographie, Illustrations.* Paris, France: Éditions Seghers, 1974.
Note: AG mentioned throughout.

J2084 Wosk, Julie Helen. *Prophecies For America: Social Criticism In the Recent Poetry Of Bly, Levertov, Corso, And Ginsberg.* Unpublished Doctoral Dissertation. University Of Wisconsin At Madison, 1974.

J2085 Young, Allen. *Allen Ginsberg: Gay Sunshine Interview.* Bolinas, CA: Grey Fox Press, 1974.
Note: AG interview format, reprinted from *Gay Sunshine* (Jan. 1973 and March 1973) issues.

1975

J2086 Miles. Eras Are Written Into Existence. *Bananas,* no. 1 (Jan.-Feb. 1975) p. 27.

J2087 Goldman, Ivan. Kerouac's Friend Helped Spark Style Of 'On the Road'. *Denver Post* (Jan. 1, 1975)

J2088 Kronsky, Betty. Allen Ginsberg In India: Therapy, Buddhism, And the Myth Of Happiness. *Humanist,* vol. 35, no. 1 (Jan.-Feb. 1975) pp. 32-35.

J2089 Sennett, John. The Lion And the Lamb. *Illinois Entertainer* (Jan.-Feb. 1975) p. 2.
Note: AG quoted, some in interview format.

J2090 Himes, Geoffrey. A Ginsberg Appreciation. *Sunrise,* vol. 3, no. 7 (Jan. 1975) pp. 16-17.

Zodiac. Leary Interrogated By Atty. Gen. Saxbe. *Sunrise,* vol. 3, no. 7 (Jan. 1975) p. 19.

J2091 Allen, Henry. The Poets' Poet. *Washington Post Potomac* (Jan. 5, 1975) pp. 10-11, 18-20.

J2092 Crosby, Kip. [review of *Allen Verbatim*]. *Boston Globe* (Jan. 9, 1975) p. 13.

J2093 Ginsberg's Search For Timothy Leary. *Vacaville Reporter* (Jan. 9, 1975) pp. 1, 14.
Note: AG quoted briefly.

J2094 Long, Steve. Saxbe Grilled Leary In Vain. *Georgia Straight,* vol. 9, no. 377 (Jan. 16-23, 1975) p. 4.

J2095 Metro, Jim. [review of *Allen Verbatim*]. *Advertiser And Alabama Journal* (Jan. 19, 1975)

J2096 Brinkmeyer, Robert. [review of *Allen Verbatim*]. *Durham Morning Herald* (Jan. 26, 1975) p. 3D.

J2097 Dandridge, Ned. [review of *Allen Verbatim*]. *News And Observer* (Jan. 26, 1975)

J2098 [review of *Allen Verbatim*]. *Booklist,* vol. 71, no. 11 (Feb. 1, 1975) p. 542.

J2099 Poet Ginsberg At TMC [Thomas More College]. *Kentucky Post* (Feb. 4, 1975)

J2100 Palmer, George. Mugging Bugging. *Cincinnati Enquirer* (Feb. 6, 1975) p. 16.
Note: AG quoted at length.

J2101 Sit Down, Shut Up. *Kentucky Post* (Feb. 6, 1975)
Note: AG quoted briefly.

J2102 Chat Before Lecture. *Huntsville News* (Feb. 8, 1975) p. 2.

J2103 Roop, Lee. 'Beat' Poet Allen Ginsberg Keeps Audience Laughing. *Huntsville Times* (Feb. 8, 1975) pp. 1, 3.
Note: AG quoted briefly.

J2104 Random Notes. *Rolling Stone* (Feb. 13, 1975) p. 20.

J2105 Kovarik, Lisa. Poet Chants Beatnik Lore. *Utopian,* vol. 7, no. 5 (Feb. 14, 1975) p. 1.

J2106 De Giere, Greg. The Timothy Leary Paradox: Paroled From One Prison To Another. *Vacaville Reporter* (Feb. 20, 1975) p. 3.

J2107 Kinkead, Linda. Allen Ginsberg Living Legend. *Queen's Jester* (Feb. 21, 1975) p. 21.
Note: AG quoted briefly.

J2108 McHarry, Charles. On the Town, Weekend Special. *Daily News* (Feb. 22, 1975) p. 24.

J2109 Long, Steve. Leary Clarifies His Stand. *Berkeley Barb* (Feb. 28, 1975)
Note: Reprinted from *Georgia Straight* (Jan. 16-23, 1975).

J2110 Ford, Michael C. [review of *Allen Verbatim*]. *Los Angeles Free Press* (Feb. 28, 1975)

J2111 Cutler, Hugh. Counter Culture Guru Ginsberg Sees Self As 'Beater Of Paranoia'. *Morning News* (Feb. 28, 1975) p. 37.
Note: AG quoted briefly.

J2112 McCullough, David. Eye On Books [review of *Allen Verbatim*]. *Book-Of-The-Month Club News* (March 1975) p. 6.
Note: AG quoted.

J2113 [review of *Allen Verbatim*]. *Choice,* vol. 12, no. 1 (March 1975) p. 72.

J2114 Brinnin, John Malcolm. [review of *Allen Verbatim*]. *New York Times Book Review* (March 2, 1975) pp. 4-5.

J2115 Caen, Herb. The Monday Hangup. *San Francisco Chronicle* (March 3, 1975) p. 17.

J2116 Carroll, Paul. Ginsberg & Burroughs...the Beat Goes On. *Chicago Daily News* (March 8-9, 1975) Panorama section, p. 6.

J2117 Kupcinet, Irv. Kup's Column. *Chicago Sun-Times* (March 10, 1975) p. 70.

J2118 Winer, Linda. It's a Homecoming For Beat Generation's Mellow Fellows. *Chicago Tribune* (March 12, 1975) section 4, p. 3.
Note: AG quoted briefly.

J2119 Ziomek, Jon. Pair Are Somewhat Offbeat, a Little Upbeat, But Still Beat. *Chicago Sun-Times* (March 17, 1975) p. 36.
Note: AG quoted at length.

J2120 The Ginsbergs, an Interesting Contrast. *Nightwatch* (March 17, 1975) p. 2.

J2121 Moberg, David. The Beats Go On...And On...And On... *Reader,* vol. 4, no. 24 (March 21, 1975) pp. 1, 4, 6, 10-12.
Note: AG interview format.

J2122 Williams, Richard. [review of *Allen Verbatim*]. *Carolina Quarterly,* vol. 27, no. 2 (Spring-Summer 1975) p. 113.

J2123 Leyland, Winston. John Giorno the Poet In New York. *Gay Sunshine,* no. 24 (Spring 1975) pp. 7-8.

J2124 Barb, Barbara. Allen Ginsberg & William Burroughs. *Out There,* no. 7 (Spring 1975) p. 18.
Note: AG interview format.

J2125 Sholem, Gershom. On Jews And Judaism In Crisis. *Shdemot,* no. 3 (Spring 1975) pp. 5-43.
Note: AG quoted briefly.

J2126 [review of *Allen Verbatim*]. *Times-Picayune* (March 23, 1975) section 3, p. 10.

J2127 Levy, Steven. Allen Ginsberg, Love Thy Mugger. *Drummer,* no. 341 (March 25, 1975) p. 8.
Note: AG quoted.

J2128 [review of *Allen Verbatim*]. *Press-Telegram* (March 25, 1975) p. B-3.

J2129 Guenther, John. The Spoken Poem Can Be a Kind Of Theater. *New York Times* (March 30, 1975) section 2, pp. 5-6.

J2130 Krassner, Paul. The Love Song Of Timothy Leary. *Arcade* (April 1975) pp. 16-18.

J2131 Brownstein, Michael. Three Generations Of American Tough-Guys Writers. *Changes* (April 1975) pp. 31-36.

J2132 Schoen, John E. [review of *Allen Verbatim*]. *Literary Tabloid,* vol. 1, no. 2 (April 1975) p. 27.

J2133 Glueck, Grace. Videotape Replaces Canvas For Artists Who Use TV Technology In New Way. *New York Times* (April 14, 1975) pp. 33, 63.

J2134 Levy, Steve. Long After Lunch, It's Almost Like Dessert. *Drummer,* no. 344 (April 15, 1975) p. 10.
Note: AG quoted briefly.

J2135 Schulke, Paul. In Your Own Back Yard. *New Look,* vol. 2, no. 9 (April 15, 1975) pp. 6-7, 9.

J2136 Morton, Carlos and Smith, Richard. Poetry Column. *Soho Weekly News* (April 17, 1975) p. 20.

J2137 Science, Poetry Linked In Focus On Energy Woes. *Independent Florida Alligator* (April 18, 1975) p. 13.

J2138 Grossberger, Lewis. Return Of the 'Beatnik Dope Fiends'. *New York Post* (April 18, 1975) p. 40.
Note: AG quoted briefly.

J2139 Stevens, John. Poet Ginsberg Here Tonight. *Florida Flambeau* (April 21, 1975) p. 1.

J2140 Ross, Cissy Steinfort. Poet And Scientists Discuss Man's Energy Consciousness. *Gainesville Sun* (April 21, 1975) p. 8B.
Note: AG quoted briefly.

J2141 [photo and caption]. *Independent Florida Alligator* (April 21, 1975) p. 3.

J2142 Ginsbergs Draw Attentive Crowd. *Nightwatch,* vol. 6, no. 7 (April 21, 1975) p. 1.

J2143 Miller, Cindy. Ginsberg: Poems, Chants. *Tallahassee Democrat* (April 22, 1975) p. 11.
Note: AG quoted briefly.

J2144 McCarthy, Colman. The Inner Ginsberg. *Washington Post* (April 22, 1975) p. A18.

J2145 Lee, Richard. Interview With Fuller, Assist From Ginsberg. *Florida Flambeau* (April 23, 1975) p. 3.
Note: AG interview format.

J2146 Buccino, Anthony. Poet Ginsberg: 'Keep On Breathing'. *Belleville Times-News* (April 24, 1975) p. 5.

J2147 Buccino, Anthony. Anthony Hears the Ginsbergs. *Independent Press* (April 24, 1975)

J2148 Haldane, David. Visions Of Neal Cassady. *Berkeley Barb* (April 25-May 1, 1975) pp. 14, 20.

J2149 Miller, Cindy. Beat Poet Is On-Again Off-Again Showman. *Tallahassee Democrat* (April 27, 1975) p. 4E.
Note: AG quoted briefly.

J2150 Thériault, Jacques. Un Bilan Positif Et Ouvert... *Le Devoir* (April 28, 1975) p. 12.

J2151 Barberis, Robert. Les Contre-Culturels. *Le Jour* (April 28, 1975) p. 11.

J2152 Leichtling, Jerry. The Broadway Book Of the Dead. *Village Voice* (April 28, 1975) p. 42.

J2153* Levinson, Ivy. Ginsberg To Appear At Awards. *Phoenix* (April 29, 1975) p. 2.

J2154 Del Villar, Arturo. Balance De La Literatura 'Beat'. *Arbor,* vol. 91, no. 353 (May 1975) pp. 110-113.

J2155 The Poets Ginsberg Debut A Deux. *Villager* (May 1, 1975) p. 5.

J2156 Cosimi, Edgar A. The Inner Ginsberg. *Washington Post* (May 2, 1975) p. A23.

J2157   Biographical Sketches Of Those Selected By Jurors For Pulitzer Prize For 1975. *New York Times* (May 6, 1975) p. 34.

Going Out Guide. *New York Times* (May 6, 1975) p. 46.

J2158   Kirsch, Robert. The Beat Movement's Brief Candle. *Los Angeles Times* (May 12, 1975) part 4, p. 18.

J2159   Notes On People. *New York Times* (May 23, 1975) p. 34.
Note: AG quoted briefly.

J2160   New Light On Leary. *Georgia Straight,* vol. 9, no. 396 (May 29-June 5, 1975) pp. 12-13.
Note: AG quoted briefly.

J2161   [article]. *Poetry Project Newsletter,* no. 26 (June 1, 1975) p. 7.

J2162   Ritchings, Gene. Ginsberg, Burroughs, Corso, Orlovsky: Alive In the Age Of the Nouveau Geek. *Aquarian,* vol. 10, no. 93 (June 4-18, 1975) pp. 8-9.

J2163   Hallock, Steve. Author Burroughs: Writing Is His Wealth. *Denver Post* (June 15, 1975) Roundup section, pp. 12-13.

J2164   Geneson, Paul. A Conversation With Allen Ginsberg. *Chicago Review,* vol. 27, no. 1 (Summer 1975) pp. 27-35.
Note: AG interview format.

J2165   Allen Ginsberg Joins Ranks Of the Pedagogues. *Rocky Mountain News* (June 22, 1975)
Note: AG quoted briefly.

J2166   Schorr, Burt. Opening Secret Files Of Government Yields Both Fiction And Fact. *Wall Street Journal* (June 27, 1975) pp. 1, 27.

J2167   P., C.A. Gallery Camera. *Vineyard Gazette* (July 1, 1975) p. 8.

J2168   Pomada, Elizabeth. The Bay Area's Best Sellers. *San Francisco Chronicle* (July 1, 1975) p. 43.

J2169   [article]. *Poetry Project Newsletter,* no. 27 (July 4, 1975) pp. 2, 5.

J2170   Lhamon, W.T., Jr. Ginsberg In Florida. *New Republic,* no. 173 (July 5 & 12, 1975) p. 29.

J2171   Hallock, Steve. Ginsberg Carries Spirit Of Kerouac, Cassady. *Denver Post* (July 20, 1975) Roundup section, pp. 3, 16.
Note: AG quoted.

J2172   Farnesworth, Clyde H. In Paris There's a Bookstore That Is a Story In Itself. *New York Times* (Aug. 7, 1975) p. 10.

J2173   Friedman, J.D. Disembodied Poetry. *Berkeley Barb,* no. 522 (Aug. 15-21, 1975) p. 11.
Note: AG quoted at length.

J2174   Teacher. *People Weekly,* vol. 4, no. 7 (Aug. 18, 1975) pp. 22-24.

J2175   Violence Erupts; 805 Arrested. *Wichita Eagle* (Aug. 24, 1975) pp. 1, 6.
Note: AG quoted briefly.

J2176 Friedman, J.D. Disembodied Tribute To Jack Kerouac. *Drummer,* no. 363 (Aug. 26, 1975) p. 4.
Note: AG quoted at length, first printed in *Berkeley Barb* (Aug. 15-21, 1971).

J2177 Burroughs, William S. Time Of the Assassins. *Crawdaddy* (Sept. 1975) pp. 12-13.

J2178 Vetter, Craig. Bring Me the Head Of Timothy Leary. *Playboy,* vol. 22, no. 9 (Sept. 1975) pp. 88-9, 96, 104, 204-6, 208-212.

J2179 Maud, Ralph. Charles Olson, On "History". *Olson,* no. 4 (Fall 1975) pp. 40-46.
Note: AG interview format.

J2180 Gertmenian, Donald. Remembering And Rereading 'Howl'. *Ploughshares,* vol. 2, no. 4 (Fall 1975) pp. 151-163.

J2181 Scoop. *Village Voice* (Sept. 29, 1975) p. 34.

J2182 Shechner, Mark. Down In the Mouth With Saul Bellow. *AR: American Review,* vol. 23, no. 23 (Oct. 1975) pp. 40-77.

J2183 Ouimet, P. Deux Bibites Dans Le System Ports. *Maclean's,* vol. 15, no. 46 (Oct. 1975) pp. 42-44.

J2184 Vendler, Helen. [review of *Kaddish And Other Poems*]. *Mademoiselle,* vol. 81, no. 10 (Oct. 1975) pp. 32, 100.

J2185 [review of *Allen Verbatim*]. *Publishers Weekly,* vol. 208, no. 15 (Oct. 13, 1975) p. 113.

J2186 Eder, Richard. 4 Shorts At Film Forum a Blend Of Charm And Naivete. *New York Times* (Oct. 17, 1975) p. 24.

J2187 Notes On People. *New York Times* (Oct. 25, 1975) p. 35.

J2188 Murray, Charles Shaar. Bob Dylan's On Fire. *New Musical Express* (Nov. 15, 1975) pp. 6-7.

J2189 Orth, Maureen. It's Me, Babe. *Newsweek,* vol. 86, no. 20 (Nov. 17, 1975) p. 94.
Note: AG quoted briefly.

J2190 The Masked Man. *Time,* vol. 106, no. 20 (Nov. 17, 1975) pp. 69-70.

A Sad, Solemn Sweetness. *Time,* vol. 106, no. 20 (Nov. 17, 1975) pp. 74, 76.
Note: AG quoted briefly.

J2191 Jones, Marta. Birthday Party In the Village. *Aquarian,* vol. 10, no. 103 (Nov. 19, 1975) p. 15.

Frick, Charles. Two Parties, Two Worlds. *Aquarian,* vol. 10, no. 103 (Nov. 19, 1975) pp. 20-21.

J2192 Chatter. *People Weekly,* vol. 4, no. 21 (Nov. 24, 1975) p. 80.

J2193 Young, Allen. Concert. *Win,* vol. 11, no. 40 (Nov. 27, 1975) pp. 19-20.

J2194 Rodriguez, Juan. Rolling Thunder Spirits In Peak Form. *Gazette* (Dec. 6, 1975) p. 49.

J2195 Moser, Norman. Ginsberg In Performance, 1959. *San Francisco Sunday Examiner And Chronicle* (Dec. 7, 1975) California Living magazine, pp. 9-10.

J2196 Hodenfield, Jan. Dylan And Friends: A Night For Hurricane. *New York Post* (Dec. 9, 1975) pp. 5, 22.

J2197 [review of *The Fall Of America*]. *Booklist,* vol. 72, no. 8 (Dec. 15, 1975) p. 562.

J2198 Ratner, Rochelle. [review of *First Blues*]. *Soho Weekly News,* vol. 3, no. 12 (Dec. 25, 1975) p. 20.

J2199 LePellec, Yves. La Nouvelle Conscience. *Entretiens,* vol. 34 (1975) pp. 41-58. *Note:* AG interview format, in French only.

Hochman, Sandra. Ginsberg Pere Et Fils. *Entretiens,* vol. 34 (1975) pp. 59-71. *Note:* AG interview format in French only.

J2200 Horovitz, Michael. To the Reader [editorial]. *New Departures,* no. 7-8 and 10-11 (1975) pp. vi-vii. *Note:* AG interview format with Eric Mottram.

J2201 Kerouac Interview. *Street Magazine,* vol. 1, no. 4 (1975) pp. 25-34.

J2202 [Andre, Michael]. Allen Ginsberg: Interview. *Unmuzzled Ox,* vol. 3, no. 2 [issue 10] (1975) pp. 14-25. *Note:* AG interview format.

Books:

J2203 Bloxham, Laura Jeanne. *William Blake And Visionary Poetry In the Twentieth Century.* Unpublished Doctoral Dissertation. Washington State University, 1975.

J2204 Christ, Carol T. *The Finer Optic.* New Haven, CT: Yale University Press, 1975, pp. 14-5, 22-4.

J2205 Cunliffe, Marcus (ed.). *American Literature Since 1900.* London, England: Barrie & Jenkins, 1975. *Contents:* Mottram, Eric. Sixties American Poetry, Poetics And Poetic Movements, pp. 271-311.

J2206 Falk, Richard A. *A Study Of Future Worlds.* New York, NY: Free Press, 1975, pp. 414-415.

J2207 Ginsberg, Allen. *Chicago Trial Testimony.* San Francisco, CA: City Lights Books, 1975. *Note:* AG transcript of his testimony in the Chicago conspiracy trial.

J2208 Kando, Thomas M. *Leisure And Popular Culture In Transition.* St. Louis, MO: C.V. Mosby Co., 1975, pp. 254-5, 257, 276, 281.

J2209 Kleps, Art. *Millbrook.* North Troy, VT: Neo-American Church, 1975, pp. 6, 25, 34.

J2210 Penglase, John Dolf. *Allen Ginsberg: The Flowering Vision Of the Heart.* Unpublished Doctoral Dissertation. University Of Wisconsin At Milwaukee, 1975.

J2211   Pivano, Fernanda. *Beat Hippie Yippie.* Madrid, Spain: Ediciones Jucar, 1975.
Note: Spanish translation by José Palao of this Italian original of the same title.

J2212   Winterowd, W. Ross. *The Contemporary Writer.* New York, NY: Harcourt
Brace Jovanovich, 1975, pp. 9-12.

1976

J2213   Sawazaki, Junnosuke. [The Influence Of Modernism On Contemporary Poets].
Eigo Seinen, vol. 121, no. 10 (Jan. 1, 1976) pp. 466-469.

J2214   Rockwell, John. The Pop Life: Bob Dylan And His 'Desire'. *New York Times*
(Jan. 9, 1976) p. 25.

J2215   Flippo, Chet. Hurricane's Night. *Rolling Stone,* no. 204 (Jan. 15, 1976) pp.
10-12.

Hentoff, Nat. The Pilgrims Have Landed On Kerouac's Grave. *Rolling Stone,*
no. 204 (Jan. 15, 1976) pp. 32-39.
Note: AG quoted at length.

J2216   Outrageous. *Advocate* (Jan. 28, 1976) p. 43.

J2217   Grodent, Michel. Le Poète Allen Ginsberg: De La Génération Sacrifieé À La
Révolution Paisible. *Le Soir* (Jan. 29, 1976) p. 9.
Note: AG interview format in French only.

J2218   Levine, Sharon. Puns, Poetry And, Sour Cream-Lunch With Allen And Louis
Ginsberg. *American Jewish Ledger,* vol. 32, no. 1 (Jan. 31, 1976) pp. 7-8.
Note: AG quoted briefly.

J2219   Jerome, Jim. Even Robert Zimmerman Sometimes Must Have To Stand Naked.
New Musical Express (Jan. 31, 1976) pp. 24-26.
Note: AG quoted at length.

J2220   Lanser, Hinda. Allen Ginsberg: Blowin' In the Breeze. *Six Thirteen,* no. 1 (Feb.
1976) pp. 64-67.
Note: AG interview format.

J2221   Pollak, Michael C. Love And Poetry. *Sunday Record* (Feb. 8, 1976) pp. B1,
B12, B17.
Note: AG quoted briefly.

J2222   Lally, Michael. [review of *First Blues*]. *Washington Post* (Feb. 8, 1976) Book
World section, p. G6.

J2223   Bockris, Victor. Burroughs & Death, pt. 2. *Drummer,* no. 387 (Feb. 10-17,
1976) pp. 5-18.
Note: AG quoted briefly.

J2224   Flander, Judy. Ginsberg's Poetry—Mafia And Meditation... *Washington Star*
(Feb. 10, 1976) p. D-2.
Note: AG quoted briefly.

J2225   Richard, Paul. Great, Gray Ghost, the Invisible Man. *Washington Post* (Feb.
11, 1976) pp. C1, C3.
Note: AG quoted briefly.

J2226   Sorensen, Tom. Ginsberg Captivating. *St. Cloud Daily Times* (Feb. 13, 1976)
p. 15.
Note: AG quoted briefly.

J2227   Rehert, Isaac. You Can't Do Anything About Anything, But Try—Ginsberg.
Baltimore Sun (Feb. 14, 1976) p. A8.
Note: AG quoted briefly.

J2228   Bockris, Victor. Dinner With Burroughs, pt. 3. *Drummer,* no. 388 (Feb. 17-24,
1976) p. 7.
Note: AG quoted briefly.

J2229   Cardwell, Nancy. For Arts Sake Nation's Small Presses Prefer Literary Values
To Commercial Success. *Wall Street Journal* (Feb. 24, 1976) pp. 1, 17.

J2230   Allen Ginsberg To Give Reading In Westchester. *Westchester Dish,* no. 2
(March 1976) p. 1.

J2231   Chowka, Peter. This Is Allen Ginsberg? *New Age Journal* (April [March 4]
1976) pp. 22-28.
Note: AG interview format.

J2232   Grimes, Paul. 80 Americans Appeal To India To Restore Fundamental Rights.
New York Times (March 5, 1976) p. 6.

J2233   Alvarenga, Teresa. Allen Ginsberg, El Llamado 'Pope' De La Poesia Beatnik
Llega A Los Cincuenta. *El Nacional* (March 6, 1976) p. 16.

J2234   Options. *Village Voice* (March 8, 1976) p. 56.

J2235   McLellan, Joseph. [review of *Allen Verbatim*]. *Washington Post* (March 21,
1976) Book World section, p. M4.

J2236   Lamantia, Philip. Poetic Matters. *Arsenal,* no. 3 (Spring 1976) pp. 6-10.

J2237   Faas, Ekbert. An Interview With Robert Bly. *Boundary,* vol. 2, no. 4 (Spring
1976) pp. 677-700.

J2238   Ashley, Franklin. James Dickey: The Art Of Poetry XX. *Paris Review,* vol. 17,
no. 65 (Spring 1976) pp. 53-88.

J2239   Starer, Jacqueline. 'Beatology' And Other Things. *Soft Need,* no. 9 (Spring
1976) pp. 7-9.

Miles. Interview With Claude Pelieu And Mary Beach. *Soft Need,* no. 9 (Spring
1976) pp. 19-23.

J2240   Thomas, Jack. Times Change, So Has Dylan. *Boston Globe* (March 24, 1976)
p. 33.
Note: AG quoted briefly.

J2241   [review of *Allen Verbatim*]. *American Jewish Archives,* vol. 28, no. 1 (April
1976) p. 88.

J2242   Burroughs, William, Jr. Just Because Allen Ginsberg Meditates Doesn't Make
Him Stupid. *Creem,* vol. 7, no. 11 (April 1976) pp. 54-56.
Note: AG quoted briefly.

J2243   On Tour With Bob Dylan. *Modern Screen,* vol. 70, no. 4 (April 1976) pp. 40, 42.

J2244   Campbell, Mark. Means And Meditation. *Colorado Daily* (April 14, 1976) pp. 9-10.

J2245   Latham, Aaron. The Columbia Murder That Gave Birth To the Beats. *New York,* vol. 9, no. 16 (April 19, 1976) pp. 41-53.
Note: AG quoted briefly.

J2246   Widder, Frank. Asian-American Festival: A Creative Union. *UCLA Daily Bruin* (April 19, 1976) p. 1.

J2247   Starr, Carol and Widder, Frank. Ginsberg Leads Buddhist Fest. *UCLA Daily Bruin* (April 21, 1976) pp. 2, 5.
Note: AG quoted.

J2248   Thériault, Jacques. Semaine De La Contre-Culture, Un Bilan Positif Et Ouvert. *Le Devoir* (April 28, 1976) p. 12.

J2249   [review of *To Eberhart From Ginsberg*]. *Booklist,* vol. 72, no. 17 (May 1, 1976) p. 1234.

J2250   Webb, Marilyn. Meditation And the Arts At Naropa. *East West Journal,* vol. 6, no. 5 (May 1976) pp. 18-21.

J2251   Felstiner, John. 'Psychologically, We Are Still In the Half-Life Of the War' Remembering the Poetry Of the Vietnam Years. *Stanford Observer* (May 1976) p. 3.

J2252   Williamson, Mitch. Ginsberg: Poet, Teacher, Learner. *Rutgers Daily Targum* (May 5, 1976) p. 18.
Note: AG quoted briefly.

J2253   Lask, Thomas. Publishing: What Makes Sheldon Run? *New York Times* (May 7, 1976) section 3, p. C16.

J2254   Narod, Susan. Ginsberg: Today's Youth More Aware. *Lerner Newspapers* (May 9, 1976)
Note: AG quoted.

J2255   Radcliffe, Rich. Not Ralph, Not Ralph! *Venue* (May 18, 1976) p. 9.

J2256   Beck, David L. Rock Artists Score Big In Salt Palace Show. *Salt Lake Tribune* (May 26, 1976) p. A13.

J2257   Palmer, Robert. The Pop Life. *New York Times* (May 28, 1976) p. C15.

J2258   Wilner, Paul. 'Flossie's' Death Ends an Era. *New York Times* (May 30, 1976) New Jersey Weekly section, section 11, pp. 10-12.

Palmer, Robert. Friends Perform In Ochs Concert. *New York Times* (May 30, 1976) p. 41.

J2259   [review of *First Blues*]. *Choice,* vol. 13, no. 4 (June 1976) p. 517.

J2260   Harrison, Pat. Who Really Gave Birth To the Beats? *New York,* vol. 9, no. 23 (June 7, 1976) pp. 12-13.

J2261 Vespa, Mary. The 1960's Come Alive On a New York Stage At a Memorial For the Tragic Phil Ochs. *People Weekly,* vol. 5, no. 23 (June 14, 1976) pp. 24-26.

J2262 Martin, Raymond. Der Fall Timothy Leary. *Päng,* vol. 6, no. 11 (Summer 1976) pp. 24-25.

J2263 Molesworth, Charles. 'We Have Come This Far': Audience And Form In Contemporary American Poetry. *Soundings: An Interdisciplinary Journal,* vol. 59, no. 2 (Summer 1976) pp. 204-225.

J2264 Weinstein, Raymond L. [review of *Sad Dust Glories*]. *Western American Literature,* vol. 11, no. 2 (Summer 1976) pp. 179-180.

J2265 Mamrak, Bob. Allen Ginsberg Recording His First Blues. *Happytimes* (June 23, 1976) p. 5.
Note: AG quoted.

J2266 Ziegler, Alan. Allen Ginsberg Sees His Father Through. *Village Voice* (July 5, 1976) pp. 120 [back page] & 79-80.
Note: AG quoted.

J2267 Louis Ginsberg, 80. [obituary]. *New York Times* (July 9, 1976) section 4, p. 11.

J2268 Louis Ginsberg Dies. *Village Voice* (July 19, 1976) p. 36.

J2269 Kramer, Sylvia. Poet's Inspiration, A Tribute To Louis Ginsberg. *Jewish News* (July 29, 1976) p. 19.

J2270 Throne, Geri. Beat Lit. *Sun Herald* (Aug. 5, 1976) p. 9.
Note: AG quoted briefly.

J2271 Saroyan, Aram. [review of *First Blues*]. *Village Voice* (Aug. 16, 1976) p. 30.

J2272 Billotte, Louise. "...Famous Some Day In Heaven." *Berkeley Barb,* vol. 24, no. 8 [issue 577] (Sept. 3-9, 1976) p. 11.
Note: AG quoted briefly.

J2273 Johnson, Bryan. Allen Ginsberg: Radical Crusader On Retreat. *Globe And Mail* (Sept. 4, 1976) p. 1.
Note: AG quoted.

J2274 LePellec, Yves. Ginsberg Temoigne. *Bretagnes,* no. 4 (Autumn 1976) pp. 24-29.
Note: AG interview format in French only first printed in *Entretiens* (1975).

J2275 I., C. Berg—Und Talfahrt. *Der Abend* (Sept. 23, 1976)

J2276 Lubowski, Bernd. Die Beat-Generation Erwies Sich Als Kritisches Gewissen Amerikas. *Berliner Morgenpost* (Sept. 23, 1976)

J2277 Rohde, Hedwig. Heiliger Und Maienkonig. *Der Tagesspiegel* (Sept. 24, 1976) p. 4.

J2278 S., C.I. Blumen Des Bosen. *Der Abend* (Sept. 25, 1976)

J2279 Bangs, Lester. Mother, Old Glory, Apple Pie, Bob Dylan. *New Musical Express* (Sept. 25, 1976) pp. 5-6.

J2280 Sinhuber, Bartel F. Die Polizei Soll Jeden Tag Meditieren. *Abendzeitung* (Oct. 1, 1976) p. 19.
Note: AG interview format in Germany only.

J2281 Hanck, Frauke. Ginsbergs Singsang Auf A. *Die Tageszeitung* (Oct. 2-3, 1976) p. 9.

J2282 B., E.G. Ginsberg Was Here. *Münchner Merkur* (Oct. 4, 1976) p. 7.

J2283 Formen Des Atems. *Süddeutsche Zeitung* (Oct. 4, 1976) p. 10.

J2284 Carruth, Hayden. [review of *To Eberhart From Ginsberg*]. *Bookletter* (Oct. 11, 1976) p. 7.

J2285 [review of *Allen Verbatim*]. *Journal Of Modern Literature,* vol. 5, no. 4 (Nov. 1976) p. 709.

J2286 Andre, Michael. Warhol Interviewed. *Small Press Review,* vol. 8, no. 11 [issue 46] (Nov. 1976) p. 6.

J2287 Jack Kerouac At the End. *Westchester Illustrated,* vol. 1, no. 6 (Nov. 1976) pp. 59-66.

J2288 Reid, Alfred S. Modern American Poetry Beyond Modernism. *Furman Studies,* vol. 24, no. 1 (Dec. 1976) pp. 1-12.

J2289 Gussow, Mel. 'Kerouac' By Duberman Limns One Side Of the Beat Generation. *New York Times* (Dec. 7, 1976) p. 56.

J2290 Raidy, William A. Very Strong Portrait. *Long Island Press* (Dec. 9, 1976) p. 12.

J2291 Sainer, Arthur. Kerouac Plays the Politics Of Ecstasy. *Village Voice* (Dec. 20, 1976) pp. 109-110.

Munk, Erika. Whose Visions? Kerouac's Or Duberman's? *Village Voice* (Dec. 20, 1976) p. 110.

J2292 Kikel, Rudy. [review of *First Blues*]. *Gay Sunshine,* no. 31 (Winter [Dec. 22, 1976] 1977) p. 27.

J2293 Tallman, Warren. Mad Song: Allen Ginsberg's San Francisco Poems. *Open Letter,* third series, no. 6 (Winter 1976-77) pp. 37-47. [issue called: Tallman, Warren. *Gadawful Streets Of Man*]

J2294 Cantor, Harold. Allen Ginsberg's 'Kaddish': A Poem Of Exorcism. *Studies In American Jewish Literature,* vol. 2, no. 2 (Winter 1976) pp. 10-26.

J2295 Courtney, Marian. Poet Operates Luncheonette. *Herald-News* (Dec. 28, 1976)

J2296 Zverev, Alexei. [review of *The Fall Of America* and *Allen Verbatim*]. *Contemporary Literature Abroad,* no. 5 (1976)

J2297 The Peoples Poems. *Mystery Gate* (1976) p. 2.

J2298 Notley, Alice. The Gorgeous Week. *Out There,* no. 9 (1976) pp. 78-80.

J2299 Belloli, Jay; Koshalek, Richard and Livet, Anne. Interview. *PA'Q [Performing Arts Quarterly]*, no. 1 (1976) unpaged.
Note: AG interview format.

J2300 Hahn, Stephen. The Prophetic Voice Of Allen Ginsberg. *Prospects: An Annual Of American Cultural Studies*, vol. 2 (1976) pp. 527-567.

J2301 Bockris-Wylie. Interviewettes. *Unmuzzled Ox*, vol. 4, no. 1 [issue 13] (1976) p. 140.
Note: AG brief interview format, first printed in *Drummer* (Feb. 12, 1974).

Books:

J2302 Cassady, Carolyn. *Heart Beat*. Berkeley, CA: Creative Arts Book Co., 1976.
Note: AG mentioned throughout.

J2303 Edmiston, Susan and Cirino, Linda D. *Literary New York*. Boston, MA: Houghton Mifflin, 1976.
Note: AG mentioned throughout.

J2304 Fields, Rick (ed.). *Loka 2*. Garden City, NY: Anchor Press, 1976, pp. 164-175.
Note: AG interview format.

J2305 Ginsberg, Allen. *To Eberhart From Ginsberg*. Lincoln, MA: Penmaen Press, 1976.
Contents: Eberhart, Richard. West Coast Rhythms, pp. 41-45.
Note: First printed in *New York Times Book Review* (Sept. 2, 1956).

J2306 Heymann, C. David. *Ezra Pound: The Last Rower*. New York, NY: Viking Press, 1976, pp. 297-298.
Note: AG quoted.

J2307 Kegan, Robert. *The Sweeter Welcome*. Needham Heights, MA: Humanitas Press, 1976, pp. 16, 28.

J2308 Lewis, Felice Flanery. *Literature, Obscenity & Law*. Carbondale, IL: Southern Illinois University Press, 1976, pp. 185, 197-200, 213-4.

J2309 Montgomery, John. *Kerouac West Coast*. Palo Alto, CA: Fels & Firn Press, 1976, p. 19
Note: AG quoted briefly.

J2310 Nin, Anaïs. *The Diary Of Anaïs Nin, 1956-1966*. New York, NY: Harcourt Brace Jovanovich, 1976, p. 344.
Note: AG quoted briefly.

J2311 Pinsky, R. *The Situation Of Poetry: Contemporary Poetry And Its Traditions*. Princeton, NJ: Princeton University Press, 1976.

J2312 Pivano, Fernanda. *C'Era Una Volta Un Beat*. Milan, Italy: Arcana Editrice, 1976.
Note: AG mentioned throughout.

J2313 Portuges, Paul Cornel. *The Visionary Poetics Of Allen Ginsberg, 1948-1963*. Unpublished Doctoral Dissertation. University Of California At Berkeley, 1976.

J2314 Schwartz, Marilyn Merritt. *From Beat To Beatific: Religious Ideas In the Writings Of Kerouac, Ginsberg, And Corso.* Unpublished Doctoral Dissertation. University Of California At Davis, 1976.

J2315 Srinivas, Krishna. *Great American World Poets.* Madras, India: Poet Press India, 1976, p. 113.

J2316 Tytell, John. *Naked Angels: The Lives And Literature Of the Beat Generation.* New York, NY: McGraw-Hill, 1976.
Note: AG mentioned throughout.

1977

J2317 Cooney, Seamus. [review of *To Eberhart From Ginsberg*]. *Library Journal,* vol. 102, no. 1 (Jan. 1, 1977) p. 109.

J2318 Literatur-Sendereihe "Lesung Und Gesprach". *Rias-Quartal,* vol. 4, no. 76 (Jan. 1977) pp. 22-23.
Note: AG interview format in German only.

J2319 Case, Brian. Sideswipe. *New Musical Express* (Jan. 8, 1977) pp. 22-23.

Parsons, Tony. Sideswipe. *New Musical Express* (Jan. 8, 1977) p. 23.

J2320 Thimmesch, Nick. Ehrlichman's In Prison. But First, This Word. *New York,* vol. 10, no. 4 (Jan. 24, 1977) pp. 31-38.

J2321 Kramer, Stanley. Ginsberg Recalls Dylan, LSD. *Daily Bruin,* vol. 100, no. 16 (Jan. 28, 1977) pp. 1, 3-4.
Note: AG quoted.

J2322 Grinberg, Miguel. El Destino De Un Poeta Visionario. *Revista "La Opinion"* (Feb. 1, 1977) p. 58.
Note: AG quoted briefly in Spanish only.

J2323 Victor, Thomas. Allen Ginsberg At the West End. *New York Times* (Feb. 4, 1977) p. C22.
Note: AG quoted briefly.

J2324 The Return Of the Yippie. *Newsletter On the State Of the Culture* (Feb. 6, 1977) pp. 1-2.
Note: AG quoted at length.

J2325 Shibazaki, Hiroma. [Allen Ginsberg]. *Puleiboi,* no. 8 (Feb. 8, 1977) pp. 44-49.
Note: AG interview format in Japanese only.

J2326 Yu Suwa. [Allen Ginsberg]. *Goru,* no. 4 (Feb. 24, 1977) pp. 46-51.
Note: AG interview format in Japanese only.

J2327 Allen Ginsberg Decries Arrests Of Russians. *New York Times* (Feb. 27, 1977) p. 42.

J2328 Belov, Miriam and Sobel, Elliot. Poet In Dharmaland: An Interview With Allen Ginsberg. *New Sun,* vol. 1, no. 4 (March 1977) pp. 12-15, 35.
Note: AG interview format.

J2329 Ince, Özdemir. Beat Generation Ve "Amerika" Üzerine. *Soyut,* no. 101 (March 1977) pp. 64-72.

J2330   Cooper, Claire. Court OKs Board's Right To Ban. *Rocky Mountain News* (March 5, 1977)

J2331   McTaggart, Lynne. Up From the Underground. *Daily News* (March 6, 1977) Leisure section, pp. 5, 10.
Note: AG quoted.

J2332   Landry, Donna. A Ginsberg Recitation: Barbs Tipped With Mirth. *Washington Post* (March 8, 1977) p. B2.

J2333   Kirb. [review of Allen Ginsberg's cabaret act]. *Variety* (March 9, 1977) p. 76.

J2334   Wortsman, Peter. Cosmic Imp Of Verse. *Villager,* vol. 45, no. 10 (March 10, 1977) p. 10.
Note: AG quoted briefly.

J2335   Bryan, John. Like a Visionary In the Sky, a Wild Prophet In the Night. *Berkeley Barb,* no. 604 (March 11-17, 1977) pp. 6-7.

J2336*   Cafe Confidential. *Soho Con/Fidential* (March 12, 1977) pp. 2-3.

J2337   Henneberry, Jay. Ginsberg Reads His Poetry At Passim's. *Tufts Observer,* vol. 2, no. 19 (March 25, 1977) p. 7.
Note: AG quoted briefly.

J2338   Duke, Elizabeth. [review of *Journals: Early Fifties Early Sixties*]. *Richmond Times-Dispatch* (March 27, 1977)

J2339   Chronology Of Soviet Dissident Activities. *Facts On File,* vol. 37, no. 1899 (April 2, 1977) p. 226.

J2340*   Hitler Eine Golden Shower Queen. *Him Applaus,* no. 4 (April 1977) pp. 8-12.
Note: AG quoted briefly.

J2341   Ginsberg Concentrates On Buddhism, Blues. *Rocky Mountain News* (April 1, 1977) Center section, pp. 6-7.
Note: AG quoted.

J2342   Shively, Charley. Ginsberg Triumphant. *Gay Community News,* vol. 4, no. 41 (April 9, 1977) pp. 10, 12.

J2343   Wilner, Paul. 'Courtier Poet' In the Classroom. *New York Times* (April 10, 1977) Connecticut section, p. CN3.

J2344   Kramer, Hilton. Trashing the Fifties. *New York Times Book Review* (April 10, 1977) pp. 3, 31.

J2345   Westerman, Keith F. Speaking With Ginsberg. *Mass Media,* vol. 11, no. 24 (April 12, 1977) p. 16.
Note: AG quoted briefly.

J2346   Poet Allen Ginsberg To Read At CWC Wednesday. *Riverton Ranger* (April 12, 1977) p. 1.

J2347   Bartley, Bruce M. World-Famous Poet To 'Howl' Tonight. *News-Record* (April 15, 1977) p. 1.

J2348   Stovall, Steve. Experience Decade Ending. *Star-Tribune* (April 15, 1977) p. 5.
Note: AG quoted.

J2349   Walbye, Phyllis. Ginsberg's Howl Changed To Mantra. *Loveland Reporter-Herald* (April 23-24, 1977) pp. 1, 3.

J2350   Bernard, Sidney. A Reading And a Mourning. *New York Times Book Review* (April 24, 1977) pp. 30, 32-33.

J2351   Della-Pietra, May. Center Hosts Events; Poet To Recite Works. *College Reporter* (May 1, 1977) p. 3.

J2352   Diser, Phil. Ginsberg Still Active, But No Longer Activist. *St. Paul Sunday Pioneer Press* (May 1, 1977) p. 4.
         Note: AG quoted briefly.

J2353   Allen, Henry. Allen Ginsberg: Burning For the Ancient Heavenly Connection To the Starry Dynamo Of Washington. *Washington Post* (May 1, 1977) Potomac section, pp. 10-11, 22, 26-28.
         Note: AG quoted.

J2354   Hessburg, L.J. Ginsberg's 'Buddha Blues' Howl Reaches U. *Minnesota Daily* (May 2, 1977) pp. 4, 9.
         Note: AG quoted briefly.

J2355   Poetry. *Metropolis,* vol. 1, no. 28 (May 3, 1977) p. 19.

J2356   Micheline, Jack. An Old Comrade Speaks Up For the Kerouac He Knew. *San Francisco Phoenix,* vol. 1, no. 17 (May 3, 1977) pp. 6-7.

J2357   Fleming, John. Allen Ginsberg In Minneapolis. *Metropolis,* vol. 1, no. 29 (May 10, 1977) p. 3.
         Note: AG quoted.

J2358   Kerr, Peter. Poet Allen Ginsberg Returns To Berkeley. *Daily Californian* (May 16, 1977) p. 3.
         Note: AG quoted briefly.

J2359   Caen, Herbert. That's Me All Over. *San Francisco Sunday Examiner And Chronicle* (May 19, 1977) p. 35.

J2360   Bryan, John. Ginsberg, McClure, Bly Bring Back the Muse. *Berkeley Barb,* vol. 25, no. 19 [issue 614] (May 20-26, 1977) p. 4.
         Note: AG quoted briefly.

J2361   Fox, Herb. Cosmic Comments From Greying Guru. *Santa Barbara News & Review,* vol. 6, no. 19 (May 20, 1977) pp. 28-30.
         Note: AG quoted at length.

J2362   Greenwald, Jeff. Ginsberg Gives SC His Heat. *Santa Cruz Independent,* vol. 1, no. 44 (May 20-26, 1977) p. 9.
         Note: AG quoted briefly.

J2363   Bryan, John. Ginsberg Wants Purified Politics. *Berkeley Barb,* vol. 25, no. 20 [issue 615] (May 27-June 2, 1977) p. 2.
         Note: AG quoted briefly.

J2364   Harris, Art. Allen Ginsberg: Nearly Out Of the Underground. *San Francisco Examiner* (May 27, 1977) p. 25.
         Note: AG quoted.

J2365 Chowka, Peter Barry. The Original Mind Of Gary Snyder, pt. 1. *East West Journal,* vol. 7, no. 6 (June 1977) pp. 24-38.

J2366 Ardinger, Rick; Ardinger, Rosemary P. and Morency, Judy. Interview With Carolyn Cassady. *Limberlost Review,* vol. 1, no. 3 (June 1977) pp. 43-51.

J2367 Bockris, Victor. The Egolessness Of Heroes: Conversations With Allen Ginsberg. *National Screw* (June 1977) pp. 6-10.
Note: AG quoted and first printed in *Drummer* (Feb. 12, 1974).

J2368 Elgherabli, [Eric]. Ginsberg's Blues. *Libération,* no. 1652 (June 2, 1977) p. 12.
Note: AG interview format in French only.

J2369 Mottram, Eric. Open Field Poetry. *Poetry Information,* no. 17 (Summer 1977) pp. 3-23.

J2370 Mottram, Eric. "Declaring a Behaviour": The Poetry Performance. *Rawz,* no. 1 (Summer 1977)

J2371 [review of *Journaux Indiens* (Christian Bourgois)]. *Cosmose,* no. 4 (July 1977) p. 49. [France]

J2372 Chowka, Peter Barry. The Original Mind Of Gary Snyder, pt. 2. *East West Journal,* vol. 7, no. 7 (July 1977) pp. 34-40, 42, 44.

J2373 Cantrell, Carol Helmstetter. Self And Tradition In Recent Poetry. *Midwest Quarterly,* vol. 18, no. 4 (July 1977) pp. 343-360.

J2374 Glass, Jesse, Jr. [review of *To Eberhart From Ginsberg*]. *Northeast Rising Sun* (July 1977) p. 19.

J2375 [review of *Journals: Early Fifties Early Sixties*]. *Publishers Weekly,* vol. 212, no. 2 (July 11, 1977) pp. 60-61.

J2376 Gray, Francine Du Plessix. Black Mountain, an American Place. *New York Times Book Review* (July 31, 1977) pp. 3, 25-26.

J2377 Chowka, Peter Barry. The Original Mind Of Gary Snyder, pt. 3. *East West Journal,* vol. 7, no. 8 (Aug. 1977) pp. 18-30.

J2378 [review of *Journals: Early Fifties Early Sixties*]. *Kirkus Reviews,* vol. 45, no. 15 (Aug. 1, 1977) part 2, p. 841.

J2379 Colorado Authors To Discuss Work. *Rocky Mountain News* (Aug. 2, 1977) p. 37.

J2380 Troelstrup, Glenn. 3 Writers Muse On Beginnings, Dreams. *Denver Post* (Aug. 8, 1977) p. 10.
Note: AG quoted briefly.

J2381 [Rosenthal, Irving]. Interrogation Of a Businessman By the Interior Police. *Kaliflower,* vol. 3, no. 17 (Aug. 26, 1977)
Note: AG interview format under pseud. "Crescent".

J2382 [review of *Journals: Early Fifties Early Sixties*]. *Arizona Republic* (Aug. 28, 1977)

J2383 Sims, Alfred. [review of *Journals: Early Fifties Early Sixties*]. *Nashville Tennessean* (Aug. 28, 1977)

J2384　Hall, Richard. [review of *Journals: Early Fifties Early Sixties*]. *Advocate* (Sept. 1977)

J2385　Molesworth, Charles. Republican Objects And Utopian Moments: The Poetries Of Robert Lowell And Allen Ginsberg. *American Poetry Review,* vol. 6, no. 5 (Sept.-Oct. 1977) pp. 35-39.

J2386　Portugés, Paul. An Interview With Allen Ginsberg. *Boston University Journal,* vol. 25, no. 1 ([Sept.] 1977) pp. 47-59.
　　　　Note: AG interview format.

J2387　Faas, Ekbert. From "Towards a New American Poetics". *Sparrow,* no. 60 (Sept. 1977) pp. 1-24.

J2388　Sipper, Ralph B. [review of *Journals: Early Fifties Early Sixties*]. *San Francisco Chronicle* (Sept. 4, 1977) This World section, p. 40.

J2389　Bender, Donald. [review of *Journals: Early Fifties Early Sixties*]. *Independent And Gazette* (Sept. 9, 1977) p. 13.

J2390　Guégan, Gérard. [review of *Howl And Other Poems* (Christian Bourgois)]. *Le Figaro* (Sept. 10, 1977)

J2391　Funsten, Kenneth. [review of *Journals: Early Fifties Early Sixties*]. *Library Journal,* vol. 102, no. 16 (Sept. 15, 1977) pp. 1852-3.

J2392　Bryan, John. An Ode To San Francisco's Beat Bard. *Berkeley Barb,* vol. 26, no. 9 [issue 631] (Sept. 16-22, 1977)

J2393　Davis, L.J. [review of *Journals: Early Fifties Early Sixties*]. *Chicago Tribune* (Sept. 18, 1977) Book World section, p. 6.

J2394　De Gregori, Thomas R. [review of *Journals: Early Fifties Early Sixties*]. *Houston Chronicle* (Sept. 18, 1977) p. 17.

J2395　Craig, Paul. [review of *Journals: Early Fifties Early Sixties*]. *Sacramento Bee* (Sept. 18, 1977)

J2396　Ehrlich, Rosanne; Kostar, Ron and Rogow, Zack. An Interview With Ted Berrigan. *City,* no. 6 (Fall 1977) pp. 78-92.

J2397　Krim, [Seymour]. [review of *Journals: Early Fifties Early Sixties*]. *Village Voice* (Sept. 26, 1977) p. 45.

J2398　Podhoretz, Norman. The Culture Of Appeasement. *Harper's,* vol. 255, no. 1529 (Oct. 1977) p. 31.

J2399　Around the Edges. *Poetry Project Newsletter,* no. 48 (Oct. 1, 1977) pp. 1-2.

　　　　Cassidy, Butch. The Naropa (Boulder) Report. *Poetry Project Newsletter,* no. 48 (Oct. 1, 1977) pp. 3-4.

J2400　Bageant, Joseph L. Allen Ginsberg. *Rocky Mountain Musical Express* (Oct. 1977) pp. 14-15.
　　　　Note: AG quoted briefly.

J2401　Messerli, Douglas. [review of *Journals: Early Fifties Early Sixties*]. *Washington Post* (Oct. 2, 1977) Book World section, p. E3.

J2402   Robb, Christina. [review of *Journals: Early Fifties Early Sixties*]. *Boston Globe* (Oct. 7, 1977) p. 16.

J2403   Simon, Jeff. [review of *Journals: Early Fifties Early Sixties*]. *Buffalo Evening News* (Oct. 8, 1977)

J2404   Messerli, Douglas. [review of *Journals: Early Fifties Early Sixties*]. *Rocky Mountain News* (Oct. 9, 1977)

J2405   Thompson, Francis J. [review of *Journals: Early Fifties Early Sixties*]. *Tampa Tribune* (Oct. 9, 1977) p. 5C.

J2406   Messerli, Douglas. [review of *Journals: Early Fifties Early Sixties*]. *New York Post* (Oct. 12, 1977)

J2407   Butazolidan, Alka. Witless In Naropa. *Newsart/New York Smith,* vol. 1, no. 4 (Oct. 15, 1977) pp. 1, 31, 50.
Note: AG quoted briefly.

J2408   Wallace, Kevin. An Old-Timers' Game For LSD All-Stars. *San Francisco Chronicle* (Oct. 15, 1977) p. 12.
Note: AG quoted briefly.

J2409   Barney, Walter. Grandfather Of LSD Meets the Acid Children. *San Francisco Sunday Examiner And Chronicle* (Oct. 16, 1977) section A, p. 8.

J2410   A Meeting Of Poets And Writers. *Honolulu Star-Bulletin* (Oct. 17, 1977) p. B4.

J2411   Black, Cobey. Ginsberg's Neck Is Still Out. *Honolulu Advertiser* (Oct. 19, 1977) p. D1.
Note: AG quoted.

J2412   Golden, Daniel. Allen Ginsberg—Politics Of Emptiness. *City On a Hill,* vol. 11, no. 4 (Oct. 20, 1977) special LSD supplement, p. 3.
Note: AG interview format.

Nelson, Erik. Outside, Looking In. *City On a Hill,* vol. 11, no. 4 (Oct. 20, 1977) special LSD supplement, p. 4.

J2413   Unterecker, John. The 1977 Allen Ginsberg. *Honolulu Star-Bulletin* (Oct. 20, 1977) section D, p. 1.
Note: AG quoted.

J2414   Lask, Thomas. Small-Press Book Fair Goes Tenting. *New York Times* (Oct. 21, 1977) p. C20.

J2415   Kostelanetz, Richard. [review of *Journals: Early Fifties Early Sixties*]. *New Republic,* vol. 177 (Oct. 22, 1977) pp. 33-35.

J2416   Murphy, Avon Jack. [review of *Journals: Early Fifties Early Sixties*]. *Grand Rapids Press* (Oct. 23, 1977) p. 2-F.

J2417   Simpson, Louis. [review of *Journals: Early Fifties Early Sixties*]. *New York Times Book Review* (Oct. 23, 1977) pp. 9, 46-47.

Koch, Kenneth. Allen Ginsberg Talks About Poetry. *New York Times Book Review* (Oct. 23, 1977) pp. 9, 44-46.
Note: AG interview format.

J2418   Trexler, Connie. [review of *Journals: Early Fifties Early Sixties*]. *Montgomery Advertiser And Alabama Journal* (Oct. 30, 1977)

J2419   [review of *Journals: Early Fifties Early Sixties*]. *Booklist,* vol. 74, no. 5 (Nov. 1, 1977) p. 451.

J2420   Spearman, Walter. [review of *Journals: Early Fifties Early Sixties*]. *Daily Tar Heel* (Nov. 2, 1977) p. 4.

J2421   Spearman, Walter. [review of *Journals: Early Fifties Early Sixties*]. *Southern Pines Pilot* (Nov. 2, 1977)

J2422   Goshorn, Gayle. [review of *Journals: Early Fifties Early Sixties*]. *Iowa City Iowan* (Nov. 3, 1977)

J2423   Random Notes. *Rolling Stone,* no. 251 (Nov. 3, 1977) pp. 56, 59.
Note: AG quoted briefly.

J2424   Herman, Jan. [review of *Journals: Early Fifties Early Sixties*]. *Burlington Free Press* (Nov. 4, 1977) pp. C1, C2.

J2425   Strachan, Don. [review of *Journals: Early Fifties Early Sixties*]. *Los Angeles Times* (Nov. 6, 1977) Book Review section, p. 10.

J2426   Carter, Ron. [review of *Journals: Early Fifties Early Sixties*]. *Richmond Times-Dispatch* (Nov. 6, 1977)

J2427   The 4:40 Ferry To S.I. Becomes Poetry Passage. *New York Times* (Nov. 11, 1977) p. B2.

J2428   Lore, Diane C. Russian Poet Captivates Ferry Commuters. *Staten Island Advance* (Nov. 11, 1977) p. A-12.

J2429   Elman, Richard. Beyond Self-Absorption [review of *Journals: Early Fifties Early Sixties*]. *Nation,* vol. 225, no. 16 (Nov. 12, 1977) pp. 500-501.

J2430   Strachan, Don. [review of *Journals: Early Fifties Early Sixties*]. *Huntsville Times* (Nov. 13, 1977)

J2431   Stuttaford, Genevieve. Allen Ginsberg. *Publishers Weekly,* vol. 212, no. 20 (Nov. 14, 1977) pp. 6-7.
Note: AG quoted.

J2432   Gengle, Dean. First Blues, Zen Music. *Advocate,* no. 228 (Nov. 16, 1977) pp. 25, 28.
Note: AG interview format.

Maves, Karl. [review of *Journals: Early Fifties Early Sixties*]. *Advocate,* no. 228 (Nov. 16, 1977) p. 28.

J2433   Strachan, Don. [review of *Journals: Early Fifties Early Sixties*]. *Binghamton Sunday* (Nov. 20, 1977)

J2434   Dachslager, E.L. [review of *Journals: Early Fifties Early Sixties*]. *Houston Post* (Nov. 20, 1977) pp. 18AA.

J2435   Strachan, Don. Ginsberg Potpourri Offers Heady Feast [review of *Journals: Early Fifties Early Sixties*]. *Indianapolis Star* (Nov. 20, 1977)
Note: AG quoted briefly.

J2436 O'Connor, John J. TV View. *New York Times* (Nov. 20, 1977) p. D33.
Note: AG quoted briefly.

J2437 Santi, Roberto. Allen Ginsberg: Un Poeta. *Il Rinnovamento,* vol. 7, no. 55-56 (Nov. 20-Dec. 20, 1977) pp. 48-57.

J2438 Miller, Steve. Ginsberg Remains Paradox. *Retriever Portfolio,* vol. 12, no. 12 (Nov. 21, 1977) pp. 1, 10.
Note: AG quoted briefly.

J2439 Giuliano, Mike. Ginsberg At 51. *City Squeeze* (Nov. 22, 1977) p. 7.
Note: AG quoted briefly.

J2440 Himes, Geoffrey. Allen Ginsberg: Custodian In a Museum. *Columbia Flier* (Nov. 24, 1977) p. 44.
Note: AG quoted briefly.

J2441 Strachan, Don. [review of *Journals: Early Fifties Early Sixties*]. *Lorain Journal* (Nov. 25, 1977)

J2442 Abhishaker, M.J. [review of *Journals: Early Fifties Early Sixties*]. *Minneapolis Tribune* (Nov. 27, 1977) p. 18D.

J2443 Berg, Paul. Portfolio. *St. Louis Post-Dispatch* (Nov. 27, 1977) Pictures section, p. 14.

J2444 Strachan, Don. [review of *Journals: Early Fifties Early Sixties*]. *Sandusky Register* (Nov. 28, 1977)

J2445 Tytell, John. Conversation Con Allen Ginsberg. *Eco,* vol. 32, no. 194 (Dec. 1977) pp. 186-197.
Note: AG interview format translated into Spanish by Bruno Mazzoldi.

J2446 Kyper, John. [review of *Journals: Early Fifties Early Sixties*]. *Gay Community News* (Dec. 1977) pp. 5-6.

J2447 Latour, Martine. [review of *Journals: Early Fifties Early Sixties*]. *Mademoiselle,* vol. 83, no. 12 (Dec. 1977) pp. 18, 20.

J2448 Powers, Francis Gary; Halberstam, David; Young, Andrew and Gravy, Wavy. The Sixties. *Rolling Stone,* no. 253 (Dec. 1, 1977) pp. 50-57.

J2449 Miller, Brown. [review of *Sad Dust Glories*]. *Small Press Review,* vol. 9, no. 12 [issue 59] (Dec. 1977) p. 5.

J2450 Himes, Geoffrey. Allen Ginsberg: Billie Holiday Meets the Book Of the Dead. *Unicorn Times* (Dec. 1977) p. 15.
Note: AG quoted.

J2451 Herman, Jan. [review of *Journals: Early Fifties Early Sixties*]. *Chicago Sun-Times* (Dec. 4, 1977)

J2452 Ginsberg And Traum In Concert. *Woodstock Times* (Dec. 8, 1977) p. 22.

J2453 Lawson, Carol. Reading For Children. *New York Times* (Dec. 9, 1977) p. C26.

J2454 Litterine, Lynn. Allen Ginsberg: Olde Garde Isn't So Avant Anymore. *Philadelphia Inquirer* (Dec. 10, 1977) pp. 7A, 8A.
Note: AG quoted briefly.

J2455   Quinn, James. The Beat Goes On. *Boston Phoenix* (Dec. 13, 1977) p. 2.
Note: AG quoted.

J2456   Ingram, Bob. Allen Ginsberg's University Of Awareness. *Drummer* (Dec. 13-20, 1977) p. 12.
Note: AG quoted briefly.

J2457   Maroney, Tom. Where Have You Gone, Allen Ginsberg? [supplement to *Acton Minute-Man, Bedford Minute-Man, Billerica Minute-Man, Burlington Times-Union, Concord Journal, The Hansconian,* and *Lexington Minute-Man*] (Dec. 15, 1977) p. 6.
Note: AG quoted.

J2458   [review of *Journals: Early Fifties Early Sixties*]. *Soho Weekly News* (Dec. 15, 1977)

J2459   Strachan, Don. [review of *Journals: Early Fifties Early Sixties*]. *Tuscaloosa News* (Dec. 16, 1977)

J2460   Strachan, Don. [review of *Journals: Early Fifties Early Sixties*]. *Springfield Republican* (Dec. 18, 1977)

J2461   Weaver, Helen. Nay, a Household Necessity. *Woodstock Times* (Dec. 22, 1977) p. 18.

Reed, Jim. A Divine Wind Blows Into Town. *Woodstock Times* (Dec. 22, 1977) pp. 18-19.

Blum, Peter. Two Events, Two Reactions. *Woodstock Times* (Dec. 22, 1977) p. 19.

J2462   Strachan, Don. [review of *Journals: Early Fifties Early Sixties*]. *Bergen Record* (Dec. 30, 1977) p. B5.

J2463   Burns, Glen. Indian Madness. *Sonderdruck Aus Amerikastudien,* vol. 22, no. 1 (ca. 1977) pp. 90-106.

J2464   Valaoritis, Nanos. La Poésie Américaine Aujourd'huc. *Surréalisme,* no. 2 (1977) pp. 48-53.

J2465   Justin, Henri and Chénetier, Marc. Allen Ginsberg's Howl: Fragments Of a Study. *Trema,* no. 2 (1977) pp. 81-96.

J2466   Goodman, Paul. The Politics Of Being Queer. *Unmuzzled Ox,* vol. 4, no. 3 (1977) pp. 48-57.

Boozer, Jack and Yaeger, Bob. An Interview With Gary Snyder. *Unmuzzled Ox,* vol. 4, no. 3 (1977) pp. 106-117.

Books:

J2467   Bernard, Sidney. *Witnessing: The Seventies.* New York, NY: Horizon Press, 1977.
Note: First printed in *New York Times Book Review* (April 24, 1977).

J2468   Bornstein, George (ed.). *Romantic And Modern.* Pittsburgh, PA: University Of Pittsburgh Press, 1977.
Contents: Heffernan, James A. Politics And Freedom: Refractions Of Blake In Joyce Cary And Allen Ginsberg, pp. 177-195.

J2469 Bungert, Hans (ed.). *Die Amerikanische Literatur Der Gegenwart.* Stuttgart, Germany: Philipp Reclam, 1977.
Note: AG mentioned throughout.

J2470 Callow, James T. and Reilly, Robert J. *Guide To American Literature From Emily Dickinson To the Present.* New York, NY: Barnes & Noble, 1977, pp. 107-109.

J2471 Carroll, Peter N. and Noble, David W. *The Free And the Unfree.* Harmondsworth, England: Penguin, 1977, pp. 369-370.

J2472 Cooney, Robert and Michalowski, Helen (eds.). *The Power Of the People.* Culver City, CA: Peace Press, 1977, pp. 186-7, 191.

J2473 Dickstein, Morris. *Gates Of Eden.* New York, NY: Basic Books, 1977.
Note: AG mentioned throughout.

J2474 *Enciclopedia Europea, vol. 5.* Italy: Garzanti, 1977, p. 490.

J2475 Fireman, Judy. *TV Book.* New York, NY: Workman, 1977, pp. 35-37.

J2476 Homberger, Eric. *The Art Of the Real: Poetry In England And America Since 1939.* London, England: Dent & Sons, 1977.
Note: AG mentioned throughout.

J2477 Kanaseki, Hisao. *America Gendaishi Noto.* Tokyo, Japan: Chuokoronsha, 1977.

J2478 *Life Cycle Planning.* Washington, DC: Center For Policy Process, 1977, p. 6.
Note: AG quoted briefly.

J2479 Malkoff, Karl. *Escape From the Self: A Study In Contemporary American Poetry And Poetics.* New York, NY: Columbia University Press, 1977.
Note: AG mentioned throughout.

J2480 Obst, Lynda Rosen (ed.). *The Sixties.* New York, NY: Random House/Rolling Stone Press, 1977, pp. 160-162.
Note: AG quoted briefly.

J2481 Pivano, Fernanda. *Beat Hippie Yippie.* Paris, France: Christian Bourgois Éditeur, 1977.
Note: AG mentioned throughout in this French translation by Jake Grassi.

J2482 Rather, Louis. *Bohemians To Hippies: Waves Of Rebellion.* Oakland, CA: Rather Press, 1977, pp. 99, 101-106, 135.

J2483 Sanders, Ed. *The Party: A Chronological Perspective On a Confrontation At a Buddhist Seminary.* Woodstock, NY: Poetry, Crime & Culture Press, 1977.
Note: AG quoted throughout.

J2484 Starer, Jacqueline. *Chronologie Des Écrivains Beats Jusqu'en 1969.* Paris, France: Didier, 1977.
Note: AG mentioned throughout.

J2485 Starer, Jacqueline. *Les Écrivains Beats Et Le Voyage.* Paris, France: Didier, 1977.
Note: AG mentioned throughout.

J2486 Tennant, Emma (ed.). *Bananas.* London, England: Quartet Books, 1977.
Contents: Miles. Eras Are Written Into Existence.
Note: First printed in *Bananas* (Jan.-Feb. 1975).

J2487 Thurley, Geoffrey. *The American Moment: American Poetry In Mid-Century.*
New York, NY: St. Martin's Press, 1977.
Note: AG mentioned throughout.

J2488 Wilhelm, James J. *The Later Cantos Of Ezra Pound.* New York, NY: Walker
and Co., 1977, pp. 7, 199.

J2489 Zavatsky, Bill and Padgett, Ron (eds.). *The Whole Word Catalogue 2.* New
York, NY: McGraw-Hill, 1977.
Contents: MacAdams, Lewis. A Talk About Teaching Poems To Kids, pp. 19,
21.

1978

J2490 [review of *As Ever*]. *Booklist,* vol. 74, no. 9 (Jan. 1, 1978) p. 726.

J2491 Hershman, Marcia. [review of *As Ever*]. *Boston Globe* (Jan. 1, 1978) p. A14.

J2492 [photograph]. *Culture Learning Institute Report* (Jan. 1978) p. 3.

J2493 Schwartz, William Carroll. Allen Ginsberg And Homoerotic Sensibility [review
of *Journals: Early Fifties Early Sixties*]. *Mandate,* vol. 3, no. 33 (Jan. 1978)
pp. 54-64, 66, 68-70.

J2494 Harris, David. [review of *Journals: Early Fifties Early Sixties*]. *New Age,* vol.
3, no. 8 (Jan. 1978) pp. 54-55.

J2495 Hayes, E. Nelson. [review of *Journals: Early Fifties Early Sixties*]. *Patriot
Ledger* (Jan. 5, 1978) p. 32.

Dawson, Ilona. Sees Hopelessness For the Country. *Patriot Ledger* (Jan. 5,
1978) p. 32.
Note: AG quoted briefly.

J2496 Strachan, Don. [review of *Journals: Early Fifties Early Sixties*]. *Santa Fe New
Mexican* (Jan. 7, 1978)

J2497 Patnaik, Deba P. [review of *Journals: Early Fifties Early Sixties*]. *Courier-
Journal* (Jan. 8, 1978) p. D5.

J2498 Ginsberg, Allen. A Poet Writes For the Stage. *New York Times* (Jan. 8, 1978)
section 2, pp. B1, B6.
Note: AG interviews Kenneth Koch.

J2499 Strachan, Don. [review of *Journals: Early Fifties Early Sixties*]. *Star-Ledger*
(Jan. 8, 1978) section 4, p. 9.

J2500 Long, Robert Emmet. [review of *Journals: Early Fifties Early Sixties*]. *New
Times,* vol. 10, no. 1 (Jan. 9, 1978) p. 6.

Merril, Sam. The Hollywood Laugh Track. *New Times,* vol. 10, no. 1 (Jan. 9,
1978) pp. 27-32, 36-7, 84-90.

J2501 Miles. Iggy Meets Poet For Loft Rub-Out. *New Musical Express* (Jan. 14,
1978)

J2502 Herman, Jan. [review of *Journals: Early Fifties Early Sixties*]. *Observer-Dispatch* (Jan. 15, 1978)

J2503 Herman, Jan. [review of *Journals: Early Fifties Early Sixties*]. *Poughkeepsie Journal* (Jan. 15, 1978)

J2504 Herman, Jan. [review of *Journals: Early Fifties Early Sixties*]. *Stockton Record* (Jan. 15, 1978)

J2505 Herman, Jan. [review of *Journals: Early Fifties Early Sixties*]. *Journal-News* (Jan. 22, 1978)

J2506 Desilets, E. Michael. [review of *Journals: Early Fifties Early Sixties*]. *New Haven Register* (Jan. 22, 1978) p. D5.

J2507 Smith, R.J. Beatnik Emeritus, Ginsberg Charms Crowd. *Michigan Daily* (Jan. 25, 1978) p. 1.
Note: AG quoted briefly.

J2508 Maslin, Janet. 'Renaldo And Clara', Film By Bob Dylan. *New York Times* (Jan. 26, 1978) p. C18.

J2509 Ginsberg To Appear In Tribute To Beats. *Argo,* vol. 18, no. 12 (Jan. 27, 1978) p. 3.

J2510 [review of *Journals: Early Fifties Early Sixties*]. *Choice,* vol. 14, no. 12 (Feb. 1978) p. 1644.

J2511 Chowka, Peter Barry. Poet At Mid-Century: An Interview With Allen Ginsberg. *East West [Journal],* vol. 8, no. 2 (Feb. 1978) pp. 52-55.
Note: AG interview format.

J2512 LSD Now: A Generation Later. *High Times,* no. 30 (Feb. 1978) pp. 42-6, 71, 79, 81.
Note: AG interview format.

J2513 Toohey, Francis. Notes On Ginsberg. *Nightfall,* vol. 4, no. 1 (Feb. 1978) pp. 20-21.
Note: AG quoted briefly.

J2514 Salzbrunn, Vern and Fox, Herb. Allen Ginsberg. *Playmen* (Feb. 1978) pp. 21-2, 24, 26.
Note: AG interview format in Italian only.

J2515 [photograph]. *X Motion Picture Magazine,* vol. 2, no. 2-3 (Feb. 1978) p. 47.

J2516 France, Peter. Where Have All the Flowers Gone? *Listener* (Feb. 2, 1978) pp. 135-136.
Note: AG quoted briefly.

J2517 Angelucci, Steve. Amram's "World Of Music". *Argo,* vol. 18, no. 13 (Feb. 3, 1978) p. 6.

J2518 DeMilo, David. Allen Ginsberg: Mindbreaths In the Night. *Harvard Crimson,* vol. 167, no. 4 (Feb. 4, 1978) p. 3.
Note: AG quoted.

J2519 Bronder, Howard. [review of *Journals: Early Fifties Early Sixties*]. *Tarentum Valley News Dispatch* (Feb. 8, 1978)

J2520 Garelik, Glenn. Ginsberg Howls Again. *Soho Weekly News,* vol. 5, no. 19 (Feb. 9-15, 1978) pp. 20, 42.
Note: AG quoted briefly.

J2521 Bookman, Alan. Poet: Ordinary Mind Is Supreme Reality. *Argo,* vol. 18, no. 14 (Feb. 10, 1978) pp. 1, 3.

J2522 K[atz], V[incent] and S[chneeman], P[aul]. Ginsberg Reveals the Origins Of "Punk". *Trinity Times,* vol. 46, no. 4 (Feb. 13, 1978) p. 3.
Note: AG interview format.

J2523 Connelly, David. Ginsberg Observes America. *Daily Texan* (Feb. 15, 1978) p. 12.

J2524 McQuay, David. Poet Allen Ginsberg Can't Sing, But His Music And Poems Ring. *News American* (Feb. 17, 1978) p. 3-A.
Note: AG quoted briefly.

J2525 McLellan, Joseph. [review of *Mind Breaths*]. *Washington Post* (Feb. 19, 1978) Book World section, p. E6.

J2526 Corliss, Richard. Rolling Thunder Re-Viewed. *New Times,* vol. 10, no. 4 (Feb. 20, 1978) pp. 70-71.

J2527 Lally, Michael. Hot Poets, Warm Scene. *Village Voice* (Feb. 20, 1978) pp. 89-90.

J2528 Hinckle, Warren. A Beat Prisoner Of Old North Beach. *San Francisco Chronicle* (Feb. 21, 1978) p. 2.

J2529 Whatmore, Levi. Interviewing the Man Who Invented Allen Ginsberg. *Austin Sun,* vol. 4, no. 7 (Feb. 24, 1978) pp. 3-4, 10.
Note: AG quoted.

J2530 Westerman, Keith F. Allen Ginsberg. *Boston Trader,* vol. 4, no. 6 (March-April 1978) p. 3.
Note: AG quoted briefly.

J2531 Harris, David. [review of *As Ever*]. *New Age* (March 1978) pp. 63-64.

J2532 Wallach, Glenn. Ginsberg Reads Work, Talks Of Past Activism. *Yale Daily News* (March 2, 1978) pp. 1, 3.
Note: AG quoted briefly.

J2533 Malzahn, Sue. The Ginsberg Impression. *Argo,* vol. 18, no. 17 (March 3, 1978)

J2534 Waller, G. Ik Zie Bob Dylan Naar Me Toe Komen. *NRC Handelsblad* (March 3, 1978) Cultureel Supplement.

J2535 Kuhn, Andy. The Poet Fences And Survives. *New Haven Advocate* (March 8, 1978) section 2, pp. 34-35.
Note: AG quoted briefly.

Kuhn, Andy. Flowing With the Breath. *New Haven Advocate* (March 8, 1978) section 2, p. 36.
Note: AG interview format.

J2536 Hall, John M. [review of *Mind Breaths*]. *Kansas City Star* (March 12, 1978) p. 12D.

J2537 Kirsch, Robert. Beats: Signed, Sealed, Delivered [review of *As Ever*]. *Los Angeles Times* (March 14, 1978) section 4, p. 6.

J2538 Curley, Arthur. [review of *As Ever*]. *Library Journal,* vol. 103, no. 6 (March 15, 1978) p. 664.

J2539 Sharp, Anne. [review of *Journals: Early Fifties Early Sixties* and *Mind Breaths*]. *Michigan Daily* (March 19, 1978) pp. 7-8.

J2540 Carruth, Hayden. Chants, Oracles, Body-Rhythms [review of *Mind Breaths*]. *New York Times Book Review* (March 19, 1978) pp. 15, 39.

J2541 Clanfield, D. The Picturesque To the Familiar. *Cinetract,* vol. 1, no. 4 (Spring 1978) p. 50.

J2542 Allen Ginsberg To Read At Poetry Festival In Park. *Great Falls Digest,* no. 16 (Spring 1978) pp. 1, 3.

J2543 C., C.L. [review of *Mind Breaths*]. *Kliatt Paperback Book Guide,* vol. 12, no. 3 (Spring 1978) p. 16.

J2544 Westerman, Keith F. Poet Allen Ginsberg On Drugs And CIA. *Mass Media,* vol. 12, no. 23 (March 22, 1978) p. 13.
Note: AG quoted briefly.

J2545 Boening, John. [review of *Journals: Early Fifties Early Sixties*]. *World Literature Today,* vol. 52, no. 2 (Spring 1978) pp. 293-294.

J2546 Henderson, Randi. Ginsberg Reads Poetry At City Jail. *Evening Sun* (March 28, 1978)
Note: AG quoted briefly.

J2547 Deutsch, Barbara. [review of *Journals: Early Fifties Early Sixties*]. *American Book Review,* vol. 1, no. 2 (April-May 1978) pp. 7-9.

J2548 Del Villar, Arturo. Ginsberg, Profeta 'Beat' Contra América. *Arbor,* vol. 99, no. 388 (April 1978) pp. 79-84.

J2549 Pearce, Paul F. [review of *Journals: Early Fifties Early Sixties*]. *Body Politic,* no. 42 (April 1978) p. 18.

J2550 Gardner, James. An Interview With Allen Ginsberg. *Lit,* vol. 1, no. 1 (April 1978) pp. 16-18.
Note: AG interview format.

J2551 Stokes, Daniel M.J. [review of *Mind Breaths*]. *Poets,* vol. 1, no. 3 (April 1978) pp. 7, 14.

J2552 Saunier-Ollier, Jacqueline. Whitman, Williams, Ginsberg: Histoire D'Une Filiation. *Revue Française D'Études Américaines,* vol. 3, no. 5 (April 1978) pp. 93-108.

J2553 Kuhn, Andy. The Coming Of Allen Ginsberg. *Hartford Advocate* (April 19, 1978) p. 24.
Note: AG quoted briefly.

J2554   Tilove, Jonathan. Ginsberg Sees Freedom 'Through Hopelessness'. *Morning Union* (April 19, 1978) p. C27.
Note: AG quoted briefly.

J2555   Haggerty, Dan. Ginsberg Guides Audience Through Time Trip. *Westfield Evening News* (April 19, 1978) p. 1.

J2556   Fripp, Bill. Medley. *Boston Globe* (April 22, 1978) p. 8.
Note: AG quoted briefly.

J2557   Stepno, Robert B. Bucolic Blesses Blissful Boulders. *Hartford Courant* (April 22, 1978) p. 16.
Note: AG quoted briefly.

J2558   Davis, Bob. New Activism Coming, Ginsberg Tells Hartwick Crowd. *Binghamton Press* (April 25, 1978)
Note: AG quoted briefly.

J2559   Sousa, Diane. Ginsberg Hits FBI Repression. *Cornell Daily Sun,* vol. 94, no. 135 (April 26, 1978) pp. 1, 8-9.
Note: AG quoted briefly.

J2560   Russell, Margaret. Ginsberg Is Back; Message Is the Same. *Ithaca Journal* (April 26, 1978) p. 3.
Note: AG quoted briefly.

J2561   Pivano, Fernanda. Buddha, Poesia, Musica E Cibo Zen. *Corriere Della Sera* (April 27, 1978) p. 3.

J2562   Young, Ian. [review of *As Ever* and *Mind Breaths*]. *Body Politic,* no. 43 (May 1978) p. 21.

J2563   [review of *As Ever*]. *Choice,* vol. 15, no. 3 (May 1978) p. 397.

J2564   [correction to *As Ever* review]. *Library Journal,* vol. 103, no. 9 (May 1, 1978) p. 973.

Cooney, Seamus. [review of *Mind Breaths*]. *Library Journal,* vol. 103, no. 9 (May 1, 1978) p. 978.

J2565   Peters, Charles. Tilting At Windmills.. *Washington Monthly,* vol. 10, no. 3 (May 1978) pp. 8, 18-19.

J2566   Hoover On Poetry. *San Francisco Chronicle* (May 3, 1978) p. 5.

J2567   Vierschilling, Pat. Literati Honor Williams. *Montclarion* (May 4, 1978)

J2568   Vitale, Tony. Ginsberg: Poet Or Guru? *Gay Community News,* vol. 5, no. 42 (May 6, 1978) pp. 10, 12.

J2569   Graham, Jim. Poet Ginsberg On Blake, Helms, LSD And FBI. *Washington Square News,* vol. 5, no. 50 (May 10, 1978) p. 11.
Note: AG interview format.

J2570   Groenfeldt, Tom. A Touch Of the Poet. *Bergen Record* (May 11, 1978) p. C-8.
Note: AG quoted briefly.

J2571   Herr, Pamela. [review of *As Ever*]. *San Francisco Bay Guardian* (May 11, 1978)

J2572   MacFarlane, Alison. Some Poetic Compassion For a 'Big Sad Poppa'. *Paterson Evening News* (May 12, 1978) pp. 11, 13.
Note: AG quoted briefly.

J2573   Pollak, Michael C. A Poet's Paterson. *Bergen Record* (May 12, 1978) pp. B1, B8.

J2574   Walsh, Taylor. On a Gray Day, the City 'Echo-ed' With Paterson's Poet. *Paterson Evening News* (May 19, 1978)

J2575   Post, Jonathan V. Allen Ginsberg At Big Shore Concert. *Sound Options* (June 1978) pp. 10-11.
Note: AG quoted briefly.

J2576   [review of *Mind Breaths*]. *New York Times Book Review* (June 4, 1978) p. 32.

J2577   Foehr, Stephen. Rocky Flats Is National Focus For the Anti-Nuclear Movement. *Colorado Daily* (June 12, 1978) pp. 1, 7.

J2578   Ruby, Robert. 4 Still Jailed After Recent Flats Arrest. *Daily Camera* (June 15, 1978) p. 3.
Note: AG quoted briefly.

J2579   Demonstrators Are Arrested. *Daily Sentinel* (June 15, 1978)

J2580   Poet Ginsberg Arrested In Flats Protest. *Denver Post* (June 15, 1978) p. 20.

J2581   Poet Allen Ginsberg Is Among 15 Arrested Near Rocky Flats Plant. *Rocky Mountain News* (June 15, 1978) pp. 1, 12.

J2582   Poet Ginsberg Arrested At Protest. *San Francisco Chronicle* (June 15, 1978) p. 14.

J2583   Foehr, Stephen. Rocky Flats Protestors Vow To Re-Establish Trackside Vigil. *Colorado Daily* (June 16, 1978) pp. 1, 8-9.
Note: AG quoted briefly.

J2584   Ashton, John. Poet Ginsberg Muses On Deadly Plutonium. *Rocky Mountain News* (June 16, 1978)
Note: AG quoted briefly.

J2585   Webb, Marilyn. Ginsberg Puts Poetry Up Against Plutonium. *Daily Camera* (June 17, 1978) pp. 1, 6.
Note: AG quoted briefly.

J2586   Allen Ginsberg Describes His Artistic Growth. *Sunday Camera* (June 18, 1978) p. 49.
Note: AG quoted briefly.

J2587   Schuman, Abby J. Flats Protestors Surprise Officials, Stop Trains. *Auraria Times,* vol. 4, no. 21 (June 19, 1978) pp. 1, 6.

J2588   McNally, Dennis. [review of *As Ever*]. *Western American Literature,* vol. 13, no. 2 (Summer 1978) pp. 204-205.

J2589   Smith, Howard. Abbie: Unhappy Wanderer. *Village Voice* (June 26, 1978) p. 34.
Note: AG quoted briefly.

J2590   [review of *Mind Breaths*]. *Choice,* vol. 15, no. 5-6 (July-Aug. 1978) p. 690.

J2591 Mottram, Eric. The Wild Good And the Heart Ultimately: Ginsberg's Art Of Persuasion. *Spanner,* vol. 2, no. 5 [issue 15] (July 1978) pp. 70-118.

J2592 Reuteman, Rob. Poet Allen Ginsberg Holds Rocky Flats Service. *Daily Transcript,* vol. 112, no. 132 (July 3, 1978) pp. 1, 3.
Note: AG quoted briefly.

J2593 AG Keeps On Trackin' — Now He's Against Plutonium Waste. *People,* vol. 10, no. 1 (July 3, 1978) p. 37.

J2594 Beaver, Harold. [review of *As Ever, Journals: Early Fifties Early Sixties* and *Mind Breaths*]. *Times Literary Supplement,* no. 3979 (July 7, 1978) p. 754.

J2595 [review of *Mind Breaths*]. *Booklist,* vol. 74, no. 22 (July 15, 1978) p. 1715.

J2596 Poniewaz, Jeff. [review of *Mind Breaths*]. *Bugle* (July 21-Aug. 17, 1978) p. 12.

J2597 Polk, Anthony. Two Poets, Angry Still, Sing In City. *Rocky Mountain News* (July 24, 1978) p. 6.
Note: AG quoted briefly.

J2598 Cracraft, Jane. Accreditation Goal Closer For Naropa. *Denver Post* (Aug. 1978)

J2599 Hiroshima Rally Sunday Marks Rocky Flats Protest Milestone. *Colorado Daily* (Aug. 4, 1978) p. 1.

J2600 Cunningham, Alan. Survivor Relates Hiroshima's Hell At Rocky Flats. *Rocky Mountain News* (Aug. 7, 1978) p. 6.

J2601 Flats 'Die-In' Ends With 66 Arrests. *Daily Transcript* (Aug. 10, 1978) p. 1.

J2602 Doll, Marice. Flats Demonstrators Vow To Carry On. *Denver Post* (Aug. 10, 1978) p. 3.

J2603 Six Flats Protesters Still Jailed: Japanese Doubt Ellsberg Statement. *Colorado Daily* (Aug. 11, 1978) pp. 1, 7.

J2604 Flats Protesters Still Undaunted. *Rocky Mountain News* (Aug. 11, 1978) p. 22.

J2605 Falduto, Frank and Milkowski, Bill. The Amazing (But Elusive) Mr. Antler. *Cityside* (Aug. 14, 1978) section 2, p. 3.

J2606 Personalien. *Stern,* no. 34 (ca. Aug. 20, 1978) p. 10.

J2607 Ziegler, Alan. Allen Ginsberg: Interview. *Some,* no. 9 (Aug. 23, 1978) [issue also called *Poets On Stage: The Some Symposium On Poetry Readings*] pp. 52-57.
Note: AG interview format.

J2608 Green, Blake. Allen Ginsberg: Some Things Have Changed. *San Francisco Chronicle* (Aug. 31, 1978) p. 37.
Note: AG quoted.

J2609 Rodman, Selden. [review of *Journals: Early Fifties Early Sixties*]. *National Review,* vol. 30, no. 35 (Sept. 1, 1978) pp. 1094-1095.

J2610 [review of *Mind Breaths*]. *Poets,* vol. 1, no. 5 (Sept. 1978) pp. 1, 16.

Smith, Jared. We Can't All Be Allen Ginsberg. *Poets,* vol. 1, no. 5 (Sept. 1978) pp. 2, 18.

J2611 Sindolic, Vojo. Moja Poruka Je: Produbite Osjecanje Savjesti. *Vidici,* vol. 24, no. 5-6 (Sept.-Oct. 1978) p. 13.
Note: AG interview in Serbo-Croatian only.

J2612 Peck, Jim. Hiroshima And Rocky Flats. *WRL News,* no. 208 (Sept.-Oct. 1978) p. 3.

J2613 Watts, Michael. Improvisations On a Musical Theme. *Melody Maker* (Sept. 9, 1978) p. 14.

J2614 [article]. *Take Over,* vol. 8, no. 8 (Sept. 10-Oct. 10, 1978) p. 17.

J2615 Vendler, Helen. [review of *Journals: Early Fifties Early Sixties* and *Mind Breaths*]. *New Yorker,* vol. 54, no. 31 (Sept. 18, 1978) pp. 165-6, 168, 170, 173.

J2616 Baizer, Eric; Divad Reywas [David Sawyer] and Peabody, Richard, Jr. An Interview With Allen Ginsberg. *Gargoyle,* no. 10 ([Sept. 20] 1978) pp. 2-5.
Note: AG interview format.

J2617 Gifford, Barry. Hitting the Road For Jack. *San Francisco Bay Guardian,* vol. 12, no. 48 (Sept. 21-29, 1978) pp. 13-15.
Note: AG quoted briefly.

J2618 Borawski, Walta. [review of *Mind Breaths*]. *Boston Gay Review,* no. 4-5 (Fall 1978) pp. 12-13.

J2619 Holt, Patricia. San Francisco's City Lights Celebrates 25 Years. *Publishers Weekly,* vol. 214, no. 13 (Sept. 25, 1978) pp. 122-123.

J2620 Radical Leaders From 60s Consider Future This Week. *Daily Cardinal* (Oct. 16, 1978) p. 1.

J2621 Stewart, Barbara. Beats Back Home. *Soho Weekly News* (Oct. 19, 1978) p. 78.

J2622 Voorhees, Mark. Voices From the Past Speak Of the Future. *Daily Cardinal* (Oct. 23, 1978) pp. 1-2.
Note: AG quoted briefly.

J2623 La Brasca, Bob. Ginsberg Calms Yippies, Closes 1980s Symposium. *Press Connection* (Oct. 23, 1978) p. 4.

J2624 Clark, Roy Peter. Kerouac: Another Generation Picks Up the Beat. *St. Petersburg Times* (Oct. 29, 1978) section G, p. 1.

J2625 Bell, Arthur. In a New Kinsey Report, Arthur Bell Studies Gays—From Cruisers To 'Marrieds'. *People,* vol. 10, no. 18 (Oct. 30, 1978) pp. 109-110, 115.

J2626 Clark, Tom. Ken Kesey In Boulder: On Being a Writer. *Boulder Monthly* (Nov. 1978) pp. 50-55.
Note: AG quoted briefly.

J2627 Gosciak, Josh. An Interview With Jack Micheline. *Contact II,* vol. 2, no. 11 (Nov.-Dec. 1978) pp. 32-35

J2628 Pivano, Fernanda. Naropa: A Lezione Dal Lama. *Corrierre Della Sera* (Nov. 1, 1978) p. 3.

J2629 The Future Is Hard To Find. *Take Over,* vol. 8, no. 9 (Nov. 1978) pp. 16-18.
Note: AG quoted briefly.

J2630 Friedman, Liz. The Future Is Now. *Isthmus Of Madison,* vol. 3, no. 41 (Nov. 3-9, 1978) pp. 3, 9.
Note: AG quoted briefly.

J2631 Poet Ginsberg Here This Weekend. *Phoenix* (Nov. 3, 1978) p. 8.

J2632 Turan, Kenneth. Cassady And Kerouac, The Heart Of Beat. *Washington Post* (Nov. 5, 1978) Style section, pp. L1, L7-L8.
Note: AG quoted.

J2633 Angelastro, Angelo. Quando L'Intimismo Diventa Disimpegno. *La Città Futura,* no. 42 (Nov. 8, 1978) p. 8.

Buda, Massimo. Perché Il Fascino Sottile Dell' Oriente. *La Città Futura,* no. 42 (Nov. 8, 1978) p. 8.

Amoruso, Vito. Una Radicale Solitudine. *La Città Futura,* no. 42 (Nov. 8, 1978) p. 9.

J2634 De Milo, David A. Intelligence. *Harvard Crimson* (Nov. 9, 1978) p. 3.
Note: AG quoted briefly.

J2635 Cott, Jonathan. Bob Dylan. *Rolling Stone* (Nov. 16, 1978) pp. 56-62.

J2636 Turan, Kenneth. Three On the Road. *New West,* vol. 3, no. 24 (Nov. 20, 1978) pp. 43-49.
Note: AG quoted briefly.

J2637 Coe, Robert. Dharma Master. *Village Voice* (Nov. 20, 1978) pp. 35-38.

J2638 Twigg, Alan. Interview With Allen Ginsberg. *Georgia Straight,* vol. 12, no. 575 (Dec. 1-8, 1978) pp. 5-6, 10.
Note: AG interview format.

J2639 Mayo, Anna. Geiger Counter. *Village Voice* (Dec. 4, 1978) p. 39.
Note: AG quoted briefly.

J2640 De Milo, David A. A Soul Survivor. *Weekly What Is To Be Done?,* vol. 3, no. 10 (Dec. 7, 1978) pp. 1, 7.
Note: AG quoted at length in this supplement to the *Harvard Crimson..*

J2641 Fleischer, Leonore. [review of *Journals: Early Fifties Early Sixties*]. *Washington Post* (Dec. 10, 1978) Book World section, p. E8.

J2642 Hoffman, Abbie. Fugitive On the Town. *Village Voice* (Dec. 18, 1978) pp. 1, 11-12, 14.
Note: AG quoted briefly.

J2643 Barr, Michael and Tooker, Peter. A Conversation With Allen Ginsberg And Friends. *Grapevine,* vol. 10, no. 18 (Dec. 20, 1978) pp. 1, 4-5.
Note: AG interview format.

J2644 Brand, Stewart. Five Minute Speeches. *CoEvolution Quarterly,* no. 20 (Winter 1978) p. 98.

J2645 Dunning, Jennifer. Poets Read the New Year In At Entermedia Benefit. *New York Times* (Dec. 29, 1978) p. C13.
Note: AG quoted briefly.

J2646 Milroy, Bill. Allen Ginsberg Interviewed. *Midwest Gay Academic Journal,* vol. 1, no. 3 (1978) pp. 31-32.
Note: AG quoted briefly.

J2647 Engel, Dave. The Allen Ginsberg Chair Of Disembodied Poetics. *Portage* (1978) pp. 39-42.
Note: AG quoted briefly.

J2648 McKenzie, James. An Interview With Allen Ginsberg. *Unspeakable Visions Of the Individual,* vol. 8 [issue also called *The Beat Journey*] (1978) pp. 3-45.
Note: AG interview format.

Books:

J2649 De Fanti, Charles. *The Wages Of Expectation: A Biography Of Edward Dahlberg.* New York, NY: New York University Press, 1978, pp. 217-219.
Note: AG quoted briefly.

J2650 Dimic, Moma. *Pesnik I Zemljotres.* Yugoslavia: Gradina, 1978, pp. 92-4, 292.

J2651 Faas, Ekbert (ed.). *Towards a New American Poetics: Essays & Interviews.* Santa Barbara, CA: Black Sparrow Press, 1978, pp. 269-288.
Note: AG interview format.

J2652 Ford, Arthur L. *Robert Creeley.* Boston, MA: Twayne, 1978.
Note: AG mentioned throughout.

J2653 Gifford, Barry and Lee, Lawrence. *Jack's Book.* New York, NY: St. Martin's Press, 1978.
Note: AG quoted and mentioned throughout.

J2654 Hodgson, Godfrey. *America In Our Time.* New York, NY: Vintage Books, 1978, pp. 322-323.

J2655 Köllhofer, Jakob L. (ed.). *Einführung In Die Amerikanische Literaturgeschichte.* Heidelberg, Germany: Deutsch-Amerikanisches Institut, 1978-79.
Contents: Vietta, Susanne. Die "Beat Generation", pp. 178-210.

J2656 Leyland, Winston (ed.). *Gay Sunshine Interviews, vol. 1.* San Francisco, CA: Gay Sunshine Press, 1978.
Contents: Young, Allen. Allen Young Interviews Allen Ginsberg, pp. 95-128.
Note: AG interview format.

J2657 Martin, Robert Kessler. *The "Half-Hid Warp": Whitman, Crane, And the Tradition Of "Adhesiveness" In American Poetry.* Unpublished Doctoral Dissertation. Brown University, 1978.

J2658 Oberg, Arthur. *Modern American Lyric.* New Brunswick, NJ: Rutgers University Press, 1978.
Note: AG mentioned throughout.

J2659   Olson, Charles. *Muthologos: The Collected Lectures And Interviews, vol. 1.* Bolinas, CA: Four Seasons Foundation, 1978, pp. 1-19. *Note:* AG interview format.

J2660   Portuges, Paul. *The Visionary Poetics Of Allen Ginsberg.* Santa Barbara, CA: Ross-Erikson, 1978. *Note:* AG interview quotes throughout.

J2661   Simpson, Louis. *A Revolution In Taste.* New York, NY: Macmillan, 1978. *Note:* AG quoted throughout.

J2662   Sloman, Larry. *On the Road With Bob Dylan.* New York, NY: Bantam, 1978. *Note:* AG mentioned throughout.

J2663   Smits, Ronald Francis. *Self-Exploration And Ecological Consciousness In the Poetry Of Allen Ginsberg.* Unpublished Doctoral Dissertation. Ball State University, 1978.

J2664   Zolla, Emémire (ed.). *L'Esotismo Nella Litteratura Angloamericana.* Florence, Italy: La Nuova Italia, 1978. *Contents:* Camboni, Marina. Da Occidente A Oriente E Ritorno: Influssi Del Pensiero Orientale Nella Poetica Di Allen Ginsberg, pp. 111-148.

1979

J2665   Lemaire, Gérard-Georges. Un Entretien Avec Allen Ginsberg. *Le Matin* (Jan. 3, 1979) p. 21. *Note:* AG interview format in French only.

J2666   Shechner, Mark. [review of *Mind Breaths*]. *Partisan Review,* vol. 46, no. 1 (Jan. 10, 1979) pp. 105-112.

J2667   Akst, Daniel M. William Carlos Williams And the American Scene 1920-1940. *Passaic Herald-News* (Jan. 19, 1979) pp. 17, 22. *Note:* AG quoted briefly.

J2668   Mayo, Anna. Allen Ginsberg And the Mother Of Us All. *Village Voice* (Jan. 29, 1979) pp. 29, 31.

J2669   Marin, Peter. Spiritual Obedience. *Harper's,* vol. 258, no. 1545 (Feb. 1979) pp. 43-58.

J2670   R., Gabriele. Poesia E Movimento. *Rivista Anarchica,* vol. 9, no. 1 (Feb. 1979) pp. 27-29.

J2671   Kyper, John. [review of *Journals: Early Fifties Early Sixties*]. *Win,* vol. 15, no. 4 (Feb. 8, 1979) pp. 20-21.

J2672   Notes On People. *New York Times* (Feb. 16, 1979) p. C24. *Note:* AG quoted briefly.

J2673   Lask, Thomas. [column]. *New York Times Book Review* (Feb. 18, 1979) p. 47.

J2674   Ratner, Rochelle. Poetry And All That Jazz. *Soho Weekly News* (Feb. 22, 1979) p. 57. *Note:* AG quoted briefly.

J2675   Geldzhaler Declares He's Gay. *New York Post* (Feb. 23, 1979)

J2676   Myerson, Allen. A Vindicated Ginsberg Sings the Poetry Of Consciousness. *Globe-Times* (Feb. 24, 1979) p. 10.
Note: AG quoted briefly.

J2677   Allen Ginsberg Gets Arts Medal. *New York Times* (Feb. 24, 1979) p. 16.

J2678   Lemaire, Gérard-Georges. Entretien Avec Allen Ginsberg. *L'Actualité Littéraire*, no. 17 (March 1979) p. 13.
Note: AG interview format in French only.

J2679   Clark, Tom (with Ed Dorn and others). When the Party's Over. *Boulder Monthly*, vol. 1, no. 5 (March 1979) pp. 41-3, 49-51.
Note: AG interview format.

J2680   Funsten, Kenneth. [review of *Poems All Over the Place*]. *Library Journal*, vol. 104, no. 5 (March 1, 1979) pp. 633-634.

J2681   Celebrations In a Jazz Cellar. *Naropa Institute Bulletin* (March 1979) p. 6.

Levy, Andrew. Blake Via Ginsberg, Etc. *Naropa Institute Bulletin* (March 1979) p. 16.

Ginsberg Award, And European Tour. *Naropa Institute Bulletin* (March 1979) p. 16.

J2682   Gleason, Linda. Citizens Of Cerrillos To Hold Benefit. *New Mexico Daily Lobo*, vol. 83, no. 110 (March 2, 1979) p. 10.

J2683   Lavin, Aileen. Poet Allen Ginsberg Opens Sophomore Literary Festival. *Observer*, vol. 13, no. 96 (March 5, 1979) pp. 1, 4.
Note: AG quoted briefly.

J2684   People. *Time*, vol. 113, no. 10 (March 5, 1979) p. 81.
Note: AG quoted briefly.

J2685   Anti-WIPP Benefit Held. *New Mexico Daily Lobo*, vol. 83, no. 113 (March 7, 1979) pp. 1, 3.

J2686   Commissioner Says He's Gay. *Gaysweek*, vol. 3, no. 7 (March 12, 1979) p. 6.

J2687   Hoffman, Steven K. Lowell, Berryman, Roethke, And Ginsberg: Communal Function Of Confessional Poetry. *Literary Review*, vol. 22, no. 3 (Spring 1979) pp. 329-341.

J2688   Averill, Earl. Bring Back the Eighties. *Open Road*, no. 9 (Spring 1979) p. 3.

J2689   The Plainspeak Interview With Allen Ginsberg. *Plainspeak*, vol. 1, no. 2 (Spring 1979) pp. 23-25.
Note: AG interview format.

J2690   Segura, Chris. 'New Individualism' Final Direction '79 Topic. *Times-Picayune* (March 25, 1979) p. 14.
Note: AG quoted briefly.

J2691   Mesh, Dana. Beat Poet Here. *Kingsman* (March 30, 1979) p. 3.

J2692   Simonaitis, Alphonse. Bewitched, Bothered, Bewildered And Beat. *Los Angeles Times* (April 22, 1979) Calendar section, p. 118.
Note: Fiction in the form of a newspaper article.

J2693 Messing, Risa. Profile: Death, Sex, Drugs, Tenements & Poetry. *Kingsman* (April 27, 1979) p. 4.
Note: AG quoted.

J2694 Lemaire, Gérard-Georges. Talora La Poesia È Come Un Lampo Che Continua. *Spirali,* no. 6 (May 1979) pp. 40-41.
Note: AG interview format in Italian only.

J2695 [review of *Das Geheul Und Andere Gedichte* (Limes Verlag)]. *Neue Volksblatt* (May 3, 1979)

J2696 Lask, Thomas. Poetry Festival Hails Paterson's Laureate. *New York Times* (May 4, 1979) p. C7.
Note: AG quoted briefly.

J2697 Klaperman, Barbara Archer. Rhyme's the Reason For a City Festival. *Bergen Record* (May 4, 1979) pp. B1, B17.

J2698 Redmond, Michael. Ginsberg's New Image Doesn't Soften Anti-Nuclear 'Howl'. *Star-Ledger* (May 6, 1979) p. 6.
Note: AG quoted.

J2699 Sasson, Victor E. A Poet Returns To Paterson. *Sunday Record* (May 6, 1979) pp. A27-28.
Note: AG quoted briefly.

J2700 Rothenberg, Randall. A Fix On the Founding Fug. *New York,* vol. 12, no. 19 (May 7, 1979) p. 82.

J2701 De Wan, George. Visions Of Ginsberg. *Newsday* (May 8, 1979) pp. 4-6.
Note: AG quoted.

J2702 Cook, Malcolm. Close Encounters With the Merry Prankster. *Soho Weekly News* (May 10, 1979) p. 17.

Navero, Bud. Return Of the Poetry Reading. *Soho Weekly News* (May 10, 1979) p. 31-2.

Bringing Back the Beats. *Soho Weekly News* (May 10, 1979) p. 33.

J2703 Hunter, Jerry. Reading Denver Poets. *Westword,* vol. 2, no. 19 (May 11-25, 1979) p. 13.
Note: AG quoted briefly.

J2704 De Wan, George. Ginsberg Is Still a Freak To Some, a Poet To Many. *Minneapolis Star* (May 25, 1979) pp. 1-C, 5-C.
Note: AG quoted.

J2705 Pasti, Daniela. Chi E Senza Peccato Scagli La Prima Rima. *L'Espresso,* vol. 25, no. 21 (May 27, 1979) pp. 146-151, 153, 155.

J2706 Forti, Luisa and Bocci, Mauro C. Mettete Degli Alberi Nei Vostri Reattori. *Il Secolo XIX* (May 27, 1979) p. 3.
Note: AG quoted briefly in Italian only.

J2707 Arcuri, Camillo. La Poesia Di Ginsberg Trascina In Piazza Il Quartiere Dormitorio. *Il Giorno* (May 28, 1979) p. 5.

J2708 Allen Ginsberg A Paris. *Libération* (May 31, 1979) p. 12.

J2709 Romizi, Gianni. La Mia Generazione È Ancora Viva. *L'Unita* (May 31, 1979) p. 15.
Note: AG quoted briefly in Italian only.

J2710 Camboni, Marina. Wichita Vortex Sutra Tra Viaggio Rituale E Meditazione Tantrica. *L'Esotismo Nella Letteratura Angloamericana,* vol. 2 (June 1979) pp. 121-154.

J2711 Jones, Woodstock. Amsterdam News Flash. *International Times,* vol. 5, no. 4 (June-July 1979) p. 11.

J2712 *Knipselkrant* (June 1979)
Note: AG mentioned throughout, this periodical composed of photocopies of newspaper articles.

J2713 Jones, Woodstock. Literary Knock Out At Melkweg: Ginsberg And Burroughs. *Melkweg* (June 1979) pp. [3-5].

J2714 Lebel, Jean-Jacques. Allen Ginsberg À Paris. *Le Monde,* no. 10679 (June 1, 1979) pp. 1, 26.
Note: AG interview format in French only.

J2715 Pott, Gregor. [review of *Iron Horse* (Expanded Media)]. *Sphinx Magazin,* no. 5 (June 1979) pp. 44-45.

J2716 Cambridge Poetry Festival. *Wordrow,* no. 5 (June 1979) p. W1.

J2717 Vromen, Galina. On the Road With A. Ginsberg, 53. *International Herald Tribune* (June 6, 1979)
Note: AG quoted briefly.

J2718 Embodiment Of Disembodiment. *Express & News* (June 8, 1979) p. 50.
Note: AG quoted briefly.

J2719 Bourgeoisification Time. *Guardian* (June 9, 1979) p. 13.
Note: AG quoted.

J2720 Wylie, Charlotte. A Lesson In Metaphysics. *New Musical Express* (June 16, 1979) p. 15.
Note: AG quoted briefly.

J2721 Mordillat, Gerard. Ginsberg Debárque [reviews of *Om...* and *La Chute De L'Amerique*]. *Le Nouvel Observateur* (June 18, 1979) p. 72.

J2722 Lemaire, Gérard-Georges. L'Illumination De Blake. *Nuits Magnetiques De France-Culture* (June 21, 1979)
Note: AG interview format in French only.

J2723 Writers And Poets. *Present Tense,* vol. 6 (Summer 1979) p. 36.

J2724 Pivano, Fernanda. Urla, Happeing E Versi. *Il Messaggero* (June 30, 1979) p. 4.

J2725 Lilli, Laura. Ma Il Poeta, O Vulgo Sciocco, È Davvero Un Gran Pitocco? *La Repubblica* (June 30, 1979)
Note: AG quoted briefly in Italian only.

Malatesta, Stefano. Cioè Cioè Cioè. *La Republica* (June 30, 1979) p. 14.

J2726 Feedback On Boulder Buddhism. *Boulder Monthly,* vol. 1, no. 9 (July 1979) pp. 47-50.

J2727 Cany, Bruno. Allen Ginsberg: Le Poete Travaille Avec La Confusion. *Canal,* no. 29-31 (July-Sept. 1979) p. 20.
Note: AG interview format in French only.

Elgherabli, Eric. Chaussures Frites, Diamants Cuits. *Canal,* no. 29-31 (July-Sept. 1979) p. 21.
Note: AG quoted briefly in French only.

J2728 Pivano, Fernanda. Tutto Fa Spettacolo, Tranne La Poesia. *Corriere Della Sera* (July 1, 1979) p. 3.

J2729 *Other World Poetry Newsletter,* vol. 1, no. 1 (July 1979)

J2730 Sedgwick, Don. Allen Ginsberg: Now And Then a Prohpet [sic]. *Poetry Toronto,* no. 43-44 (July-Aug. 1979) pp. 22-23.
Note: AG quoted briefly.

J2731 1950-1980 Ancora Ginsberg. *ReNudo,* vol. 9, no. 78-79 (July-Aug. 1979) pp. 4-6.
Note: AG interview format in Italian only.

Pivano, Fernanda. Ginsberg Sul Set. *ReNudo,* vol. 9, no. 78-79 (July-Aug. 1979) pp. 7-9.
Note: AG transcript from the movie, *Fried Shoes, Cooked Diamonds* translated by Fernanda Pivano into Italian.

J2732 Poet Allen Ginzberg's [sic]. *Chicago Sun-Times* (July 2, 1979)

J2733 Crolla Il Palco Nel Gran Finale All'Americana. *Corriere Della Sera* (July 2, 1979) p. 6.

J2734 Maestosi, Danilo. Gran Finale Con I Poeti Beat A Subito Incomincia L'Esodo. *Paese Sera* (July 2, 1979) p. 6.

J2735 Pennacchi, Gianni. Ieri All'Alba Ha Vinto La Poesia. *La Stampa* (July 2, 1979) p. 7.

J2736 Checco, Beniamino and Paoletto, Gianluca. "I Poeti Non Ufficiali": Strane Creature? *Lotta Continua,* vol. 8, no. 143 (July 3, 1979) pp. 14-15.
Note: AG quoted briefly in Italian only.

J2737 Annunziata, Lucia. Hanno Scritto Poesia Sulla Sabbia. *Il Manifesto,* vol. 9, no. 153 (July 3, 1979) p. 2.

J2738 Checco, Beniamino and Paoletto, Gianluca (eds.). Il Primo Non Fu. E Allora, Chi Fu? *Lotta Continua,* vol. 8, no. 144 (July 4, 1979) pp. 14-15.
Note: AG quoted briefly in Italian only.

J2739 Vassalli, Sebastiano. L'Arena, Il Poeta, Il Minestrone. *L'Unita,* vol. 56, no. 151 (July 4, 1979) p. 3.

J2740 Tanner, Henry. Poets Of the World Tame Rowdy Romans. *New York Times* (July 5, 1979) p. 2.

J2741 Lemaire, Gérard-Georges. Le Premier Festival De Poesie De Rome. *Le Matin* (July 9, 1979)

J2742 T., L.O. Intervista A Ginsberg. *Il Male,* vol. 2, no. 26 (July 11, 1979) p. 7.
Note: AG interview format in Italian only.

J2743 Costa, Corrado. Nudi Alla Rima. *L'Europeo,* vol. 35, no. 28 (July 12, 1979) pp. 6-7.

J2744 Manacorda, Giorgio. Poesia. *Il Manifesto* (July 14, 1979)

J2745 Gandus, Valeria. A Rime Abbracciate. *Panorama,* vol. 17, no. 691 (July 16, 1979) pp. 78-81.
Note: AG quoted briefly in Italian only.

Orengo, Nico. Ma La Poesia Sa "Stare Insieme"? *Panorama,* vol. 17, no. 691 (July 16, 1979) p. 81.

J2746 Pivano, Fernanda. Viaggiatore Solitario Oltre La Vita. *Corriere Della Sera* (July 23, 1979)

J2747 Bardin, Desdemone. Des Beatniks Aux Psychedeliks. *Maintenant,* no. 18 (July 28-Aug. 31, 1979) p. 43.
Note: AG quoted briefly in French only.

J2748 Buckley, Tom. At the Movies. *New York Times* (Aug. 3, 1979) p. C14.

J2749 Lehndorff, John M. Benefit Evening Features No-Nukes Poetry And Song. *Colorado Daily* (Aug. 4, 1979) pp. 1, 3.

J2750 S., E. La Maison De Shakespeare. *L'Express,* no. 1465 (Aug. 4-10, 1979) p. 64.

J2751 Freed, David. Proud Poets Gather To Orate And Entertain. *Rocky Mountain News* (Aug. 5, 1979) p. 4.

J2752 Ashton, John. The 'Orderly' Life Of William S. Burroughs. *Rocky Mountain News* (Aug. 8, 1979) pp. 58, 65.

J2753 Becker, Drew. Cassady Was 'Light Of Mind' To Ginsberg. *Denver Post* (Aug. 12, 1979) Roundup section, p. 28.
Note: AG quoted briefly.

J2754 Crewdson, John M. Poetry Fest Aids Efforts To Revive Arizona Mining Town. *New York Times* (Aug. 29, 1979) p. A14.

J2755 [review of *Poems All Over the Place*]. *Choice,* vol. 16, no. 7 (Sept. 1979) p. 832.

J2756 David, Christian. [article]. *Ecritures,* no. 4 (Sept. 1979) pp. 4-6.

J2757 Andrae, Irmgard. [review of *Das Geheul Und Andere Gedichte* (Limes Verlag)]. *EKZ-Informationsdienst* (Sept. 1979)

J2758 Woods, Eddie. Loose Change. *International Times,* vol. 5, no. 4 (Sept. 1979) pp. 6-7.
Note: AG quoted briefly.

J2759 Crowley, Kieran. Have Chair, Need Poet. *New York Post* (Sept. 1, 1979) p. 17.
Note: AG quoted briefly.

J2760 Ginsberg Comes To Present Tense, 1979. *Off the Strip,* vol. 1, no. 4 (Sept. 1979) p. 1.

J2761 Poezia Si Publicul. *Ramuri,* vol. 17, no. 9 (Sept. 1979) pp. 3, 12.
Note: AG quoted in Romanian only.

J2762 McMahon, Erik S. [review of *The Visionary Poetics Of Allen Ginsberg* by Paul Portuges]. *San Francisco Review Of Books,* vol. 5, no. 4 (Sept. 1979) pp. 10-11.

Miller, Brown. [review of *Poems All Over the Place*]. *San Francisco Review Of Books,* vol. 5, no. 4 (Sept. 1979) pp. 11-12.

J2763 [review of *Das Geheul Und Andere Gedichte* (Limes Verlag)]. *Der Kleine Bund,* no. 216 (Sept. 15, 1979) p. 4.

J2764 Butler, Katy. Ginsberg Is Back To Howl. *San Francisco Chronicle* (Sept. 18, 1979) p. 3.
Note: AG quoted.

J2765 Mosler, Peter. [review of *Das Geheul Und Andere Gedichte* (Limes Verlag)]. *Frankfurter Allgemeine Zeitung,* no. 220 (Sept. 21, 1979) p. 26.

J2766 Köhler, Michael. Poesie & Meditation: Das Naropa-Experiment. *Die Horen,* vol. 24, no. 3 [issue no. 115] (Fall 1979) pp. 161-171.
Note: AG interview format in German only.

J2767 Berman, Paul L. Intimations Of Mortality [review of *Journals: Early Fifties Early Sixties* and *Mind Breaths*]. *Parnassus,* vol. 8, no. 1 (Fall-Winter 1979) pp. 283-293.

J2768 Goldstein, Richard. An Interview With William Burroughs. *Rolling Stone College Papers,* no. 1 (Fall 1979) pp. 37-8, 41-2.

J2769 [transcript of panel discussion which includes AG]. *Soundings/East,* vol. 2, no. 2 [issue also called *Kerouac Issue*] (Fall-Winter 1979) pp. 1-89.
Note: AG interview format.

J2770 Kastelic, James. Sagebrush Drive Wins Support In Poetry Of Allen Ginsberg. *Las Vegas Review-Journal* (Sept. 23, 1979) p. 15A.
Note: AG quoted briefly.

J2771 Lyon, Laura Hinton. Allen Ginsberg: Sensing the Vanishing Daydream. *Las Vegas Sun* (Sept. 24, 1979) p. 13.
Note: AG quoted.

J2772 Gorski, Hedwig. Interview With: Andy Clausen. *Rumors, Gossip, Lies & Dreams,* vol. 3, no. 25 (Sept. 24, 1979) p. 3.

J2773 Jolidon, Larry. Poet Ginsberg Seeks 'Playful' Activism. *Austin American-Statesman* (Sept. 27, 1979) p. B1.
Note: AG quoted briefly.

J2774 Dameron, Chip. Standing Room Only Crowd Greets 'Beat' Poets. *Daily Texan* (ca. Sept. 27, 1979)

J2775* [review of *Journals: Early Fifties Early Sixties*]. *Books West Magazine,* vol. 1 (Oct. 1979) p. 41.

J2776 Rostagno, Aldo. Progetto Per Una Rivoluzione A New York. *Playmen* (Oct. 1979) pp. 48-57.
Note: AG quoted briefly in Italian only.

J2777 Peters, Charles. [column]. *Washington Monthly,* vol. 11, no. 8 (Oct. 1979) pp. 61-62.

J2778 [review of *Das Geheul Und Andere Gedichte* (Limes Verlag)]. *Tagblatt F. Oesterreich* (Oct. 13, 1979)

J2779 Holloway, Diane. Ginsberg, Poets Discuss the World On ACTV. *Austin American-Statesman* (Oct. 17, 1979) p. C9.

J2780 Pierce, Robert J. Listen America. *Soho Weekly News* (Oct. 18, 1979) pp. 8-9.

J2781 Smiljanich, Dorothy. St. Petersburg Hasn't Changed Much, Jack. *St. Petersburg Times* (Oct. 21, 1979) p. 2E.

J2782 Bell, Arthur. Bell Tells. *Village Voice* (Oct. 22, 1979) p. 40.
Note: AG quoted briefly.

J2783 Berman, Paul L. [review of *The Visionary Poetics Of Allen Ginsberg* by Paul Portuges]. *Village Voice* (Oct. 29, 1979) p. 40.

J2784 London, Jack. Thrills In Poetry Mag Review Shock! *New Musical Express* (Nov. 24, 1979) p. 12.

J2785 Small, Steve and Leon, Sara. Advocate Interviews Ginsberg. *Advocate* (Dec. 1979)
Note: AG quoted briefly.

J2786 Greenberg, J. Interview With Allen Ginsberg. *Other Voice* (Dec. 1979) pp. 7, 10.
Note: AG interview format.

J2787 Bauer, Jerry. Playmen Intervista: William Burroughs. *Playmen,* vol. 13, no. 12 (Dec. 1979) pp. 27-8, 30, 32-34.

J2788 De Goeroe Knipoogt Naar U. *De Vooruit-De Morgan* (Dec. 1, 1979)

J2789 [review of *Das Geheul Und Andere Gedichte* (Limes Verlag)]. *Handelsblatt* (Dec. 7, 1979)

J2790 Dullinger, Angie. Mit Dem Gefühl Und Der Phantasie Leben. *Abendzeitung* (Dec. 10, 1979)
Note: AG interview format in German only.

J2791 Pivano, Fernanda. Ginsberg, Poesia, Chiacchiere E Cinque Giorni In "Pullmino". *Corriere Della Sera* (Dec. 10, 1979) p. 3.

J2792 Köhler, Michael. Nur Ein Alternder Beatnik? *Süddeutsche Zeitung* (Dec. 11, 1979)

J2793 [review of *Das Geheul Und Andere Gedichte* (Limes Verlag)]. *Hanauer Anzeiger* (Dec. 20, 1979)

J2794 Pfeil, Ulrike. Von Wegen Alternder Hippie. *Südwest Presse* (Dec. 21, 1979)
Note: AG interview format in German only.

J2795 NYQ Tribute To Allen Ginsberg. *New York Quarterly,* no. 24 (Winter 1979) pp. 69-78.

Packard, William. [letter]. *New York Quarterly,* no. 24 (Winter 1979) p. 71.

Koch, Ed. [letter]. *New York Quarterly,* no. 24 (Winter 1979) p. 73.

J2796 Gruber, Ruth. An Interview/Conversation With Ted Berrigan, George Oppen, And Marvin Cohen. *Poetry Information,* no. 20-21 (Winter 1979-1980) *Note:* First printed in *Chicago* (Oct. 1973).

J2797 The Poets & Writers Party: Fun And More. *Poets & Writers News,* no. 1 (Winter 1979) p. 1.

J2798 Pfeil, Ulrike. Von Wegen Alternder Hippie. *Südwest Presse/Schwäbisches Tagblatt* (Dec. 22, 1979) *Note:* AG interview format in German only.

J2799 Johnstone, Paul. Discerning Poetry. *Artscribe,* no. 17 (1979) pp. 16-21.

J2800 Liefland, Wilhelm. [review of *Das Geheul Und Andere Gedichte* (Limes Verlag)]. *Jazz Podium,* no. 8 (1979)

J2801 Heliczer, Piero. Who Are We? *Little Caesar,* no. 9 (1979) pp. 381-392.

J2802 Shechner, Mark. [review of *As Ever* and *Journals: Early Fifties Early Sixties*]. *Partisan Review,* vol. 46, no. 1 (1979) pp. 105-112.

J2803 Konstantinovic, Radomir. The October Meeting Of Writers. *Relations,* no. 9-10 (1979) pp. 249-250.

Books:

J2804 Berthoff, Warner. *A Literature Without Qualities: American Writing Since 1945.* Berkeley, CA: University Of California Press, 1979. *Note:* AG mentioned throughout.

J2805 Bockris, Victor. *The Burroughs File.* Privately printed, 1979. *Note:* AG quoted throughout.

J2806 Bockris, Victor. *Con Burroughs.* Rome, Italy: Arcana Editrice, 1979. *Note:* AG quoted throughout in Italian translated by Alessandro Gebbia and Sergio Duichin.

J2807 Burroughs, William S. and Gysin, Brion. *Colloque De Tanger II.* Paris, France: Christian Bourgois, 1979. *Contents:* Lemaire, Gérard-Georges. La Deposition D'Allen Ginsberg Au Proces De Boston, pp. 125-137. *Note:* AG interview format in French only.

J2808 Cherkovski, Neeli. *Ferlinghetti: A Biography.* New York, NY: Doubleday, 1979. *Note:* AG mentioned throughout.

J2809 Christadler, Martin (ed.). *Amerikanische Literatur Der Gegenwart.* Stuttgart, W. Germany: Alfred Kröner Verlag, 1979. *Contents:* Vietta, Susanne. Allen Ginsberg, pp. 581-601.

J2810   Clauss, Anne R. (ed.). *America In the Fifties.* Copenhagen, Denmark: University Of Copenhagen, 1979.
Contents: Clunies, Bruce. Hip-Bop-Beat.

J2811   *Enciclopedia Italiana 1961-1978, appendice iv.* Rome, Italy: Enciclopedia Italiana, 1979.
Contents: Lalli, Biancamaria Tedeschini. Allen Ginsberg, p. 74.

J2812   Grinspoon, Lester and Bakalar, James B. *Psychedelic Drugs Reconsidered.* New York, NY: Basic Books, 1979.
Note: AG mentioned throughout.

J2813   Jaubert, Alain and Sacks, Susan (eds.). *Allen Ginsberg: Om..., Entretiens Et Témoignages (1963-1978).* Paris, France: Éditions Du Seuil, 1979.
Contents:
Guillot, Claude. Entretien Avec Thomas Clark (1965), pp. 19-62.
Note: AG interview format in French only.
Jaubert, Alain and Sacks, Susan. Entretien Avec Allen Young Pour Gay Sunshine (1972), pp. 149-208.
Note: AG interview format in French only.
Jaubert, Alain and Sacks, Susan. Le LSD Aujord'Hui: Une Génération Après (1977), pp. 209-210.
Note: AG interview format in French only.
Lemaire, Gérard-Georges. Du Bouddhism Aux Punks, Entretien Avec Gérard-Georges Lemaire (1978), pp. 211-221.
Note: AG interview format in French only.
Patenaude, Michel. Témoignage au Procès Des "Sept de Chicago" (1969), pp. 87-148.
Note: AG interview format in French only.
Portail, Claude. Conversation Avec Ernie Barry (1963), pp. 11-18.
Note: AG interview format in French only.
Portail, Claude and Gaines, Joseph. Rencontres Avec Ezra Pound, Notes De Journal (1967) [Encounters With Ezra Pound, Journal Notes], pp. 63-84.
Note: AG interview format in French only.

J2814   Jones, Peter. *An Introduction To Fifty American Poets.* London, England: Pan Books, 1979, pp. 316-322.

J2815   Lane, Gary (ed.). *Sylvia Plath: New Views On the Poetry.* Baltimore, MD: Johns Hopkins University Press, 1979.
Contents:
Perloff, Marjorie. Sylvia Plath's "Sivvy" Poems, p. 161.
Shapiro, David. Sylvia Plath: Drama And Melodrama, pp. 48-49, 51.

J2816   Martin, Robert K. *Homosexual Tradition In American Poetry.* Austin, TX: University Of Texas Press, 1979, pp. 16, 165-170.

J2817   Miller, James E., Jr. *The American Quest For a Supreme Fiction: Whitman's Legacy In the Personal Epic.* Chicago, IL: University Of Chicago Press, 1979.
Note: AG mentioned throughout.

J2818   Molesworth, Charles. *The Fierce Embrace.* Columbia, MO: University Of Missouri Press, 1979.
Note: AG mentioned throughout.

J2819   Praunheim, Rosa Von. *Armee Der Liebenden Oder Aufstand Der Perversen.* Munich, W. Germany: C Trikont Verlag, 1979, pp. 66-69.

J2820   Richards, Janet. *Common Soldiers.* San Francisco, CA: Archer Press, 1979.
Note: AG mentioned throughout.

J2821   Sloman, Larry. *Reefer Madness.* Indianapolis, IN: Bobbs-Merrill, 1979.
Note: AG quoted throughout.

J2822   Snyder, Don. *Aquarian Odyssey.* New York, NY: Liveright, 1979, p. 33.

J2823   Van Son, Jacques. *The Beat Generation/Bob Dylan.* Utrecht, The Netherlands:
Spektakel/Walhalla, 1979.
Contents: Chowka, Peter. Interview with Allen Ginsberg, p. 55.
Note: AG interview format translated into Dutch only.

J2824   Vinson, James (ed.). *Great Writers Of the English Language: Poets.* New York,
NY: St. Martin's Press, 1979.
Contents: Quartermain, Peter. Allen Ginsberg, pp. 413-416.

J2825   Waldman, Anne and Webb, Marilyn (eds.). *Talking Poetics From Naropa
Institute, vol. 2.* Boulder, CO: Shambhala, 1979.
Contents: Portugés, Paul. Visions Of Ordinary Mind: (1948-1955): Discourse
W/Questions & Answers, June 9, 1976, pp. 381-414.
Note: AG interview format.

1980

J2826   Seidman, Hugh; Ginsberg, Allen; Creeley, Robert and Zukofsky, Celia. A
Commemorative Evening For Louis Zukofsky. *American Poetry Review,* vol.
9, no. 1 (Jan.-Feb. 1980) pp. 21-27.
Note: AG interview format.

J2827   [review of *Das Geheul Und Andere Gedichte* (Limes Verlag)]. *Darmstädter Echo*
(Jan. 12, 1980)

J2828   Ploog, Jürgen. Der Poet Als Sekretär Des Gehirns. *Tip,* vol. 9, no. 2 (Jan. 18-
31, 1980) pp. [172-178].
Note: AG interview format in German only.

J2829   Herman, Jan. Allen Ginsberg: In Pursuit Of Gentleness. *Democrat And
Chronicle* (Jan. 26, 1980) p. C1.
Note: AG quoted.

J2830   Friedman, Richard. Kerouac And the Beats Live On In Film. *Toronto Star* (Jan.
26, 1980) Entertainment section, pp. F1, F3.
Note: AG quoted at length.

J2831   Pivano, Fernanda. Anche Le "Pantere Nere" Diventano Mistiche. *Corriere Della
Sera* (Jan. 31, 1980) p. 3.

J2832   Pacheco, Patrick. Heart Beat. *After Dark,* vol. 12, no. 10 (Feb. 1980) pp. 50-
56.

J2833   Attanasio, Paul A. William Burroughs. *Harvard Crimson* (Feb. 1, 1980) What
Is To Be Done? supplement, pp. 2, 10.

J2834   Lemaire, Gérard-Georges. L'Illumination De Blake. *Le Magazine Littéraire,* no.
157 (Feb. 1980) pp. 23-24.
Note: AG interview format in French only.

Sarner, Eric. Parler La Poesie... *Le Magazine Littéraire,* no. 157 (Feb. 1980) pp. 24-25.
Note: AG interview format in French only.

J2835 Herman, Jan. In the Gentle Way Of the Poet. *Philadelphia Inquirer* (Feb. 1, 1980) pp. 4B, 6B.
Note: AG quoted.

J2836 A., D.P. [review of *Das Geheul Und Andere Gedichte* (Limes Verlag)]. *Südhessische Post* (Feb. 2, 1980)

J2837 Herman, Jan. Poet Allen Ginsberg Still Keeps Faith In Gentleness. *Burlington Free Press* (Feb. 3, 1980) pp. D1, D6.
Note: AG quoted.

J2838 Herman, Jan. Heart-to-Heart With Ginsberg. *Chicago Sun-Times* (Feb. 3, 1980) section 3, p. 14.
Note: AG quoted.

J2839 Pivano, Fernanda. Ma Io Credo In Molti Dei. *Corriere Della Sera* (Feb. 3, 1980)

J2840 Herman, Jan. Poetic Justice, That's Still the Goal Of Allen Ginsberg. *Cleveland Plain Dealer* (Feb. 3, 1980) section C, pp. 1, 9.
Note: AG quoted.

J2841 Herman, Jan. The Ode Man Of the Mountains. *Toronto Star* (Feb. 4, 1980) p. C4.
Note: AG quoted.

J2842 Locke, Asia. Philadelphia Dreamin'. *Aquarian,* no. 301 (Feb. 13-20, 1980) p. 45.
Note: AG quoted briefly.

J2843 Martin, Jefferson K. Little Giant Of a Poet. *Climax,* vol. 4, no. 1 (Feb. 18, 1980) p. 5.
Note: AG quoted briefly.

J2844 Herman, Jan. Can Allen Ginsberg STILL Be a Beatnik? *Detroit Free Press* (Feb. 24, 1980) pp. 1D, 7D.
Note: AG quoted.

J2845 Herman, Jan. Allen Is Alive, Well And Speaking Out... *Houston Chronicle* (Feb. 24, 1980) Zest magazine section, p. 7.
Note: AG quoted.

J2846 Herman, Jan. Ginsberg's Poetics: From Illusion To Enlightenment. *Los Angeles Times* (Feb. 24, 1980) Calendar section, p. 5.
Note: AG quoted.

J2847 Herman, Jan. Countdown To Enlightenment. *Seattle Post-Intelligencer* (Feb. 24, 1980) section G, pp. 1, 5.
Note: AG quoted.

J2848 De Geest, Johan. Behoed De Wereld Voor De Katastrofe: Plant Een Notelaar. *Humo,* no. 2060 (Feb. 28, 1980) pp. 38-39, 42, 44, 47-48.
Note: AG interview format in Belgian only.

J2849 Sindolic, Vojo. Obo Je Ginsberg. *Halo,* no. 3 (March 1980) pp. 22-23.
Note: AG quoted in Serbo-Croatian only.

J2850   Cox, Brian. Stimulator Harley Flanagan. *Interview,* vol. 10, no. 3 (March 1980) pp. 50-51.

J2851   [article]. *Minnesota Zen Meditation Center,* vol. 4, no. 1 (March 1980) p. 3.

J2852   And the Beats Go On... *Real Paper* (March 1, 1980) p. 11.
Note: AG interview format.

J2853   Pivano, Fernanda. Una "Virginia" Riuscita Soltanto Come Femminista. *Corriere Della Sera* (March 2, 1980) p. 3.
Note: AG quoted in Italian only.

J2854   Pivano, Fernanda. Giovani USA: Violenza, Ti Ripudio In Nome Di Buddha. *Corriere Della Sera* (March 11, 1980) p. 3.

J2855   [review of *Das Geheul Und Andere Gedichte* (Limes Verlag)]. *Harzburger Nachrichten* (March 12, 1980)

J2856   Anti-Draft Rally Set. *Colorado Daily* (March 18, 1980) p. 1.

J2857   Olsen, Donald. Poet Ginsberg, Other Speakers Condemn Draft At Tuesday Rally. *Colorado Daily* (March 19, 1980) p. 1.
Note: AG quoted briefly.

J2858   Castrone, Linda. Draft Protest. *Daily Camera* (March 19, 1980) p. 3.
Note: AG quoted briefly.

J2859   [photograph with caption]. *Rocky Mountain News* (March 19, 1980) p. 6.

J2860   De Bruyn, André. Profeet Van Het Gnostisch Bewustzijn: Poezie In Pop-Formaat. *Audio-Visueel,* no. 1 ([Spring] 1980) pp. 67-70.

Van Son, Jacques. Interview Met Allen Ginsberg. *Audio-Visueel,* no. 1 ([Spring] 1980) pp. 70-75.
Note: AG interview format in Flemish only.

J2861   Raffel, Burton. Robert Lowell's *Life Studies. Literary Review,* vol. 23, no. 3 (Spring 1980) pp. 293-325.

J2862   Challis, Chris. The Guru Comes To Cambridge. *Over Here,* no. 1 (Spring 1980) pp. 16-25.
Note: AG quoted briefly.

J2863   Otto, Erwin. Allen Ginsbergs "Wichita Vortex Sutra" Als Gegenstand Der Amerikanstudien. *Anglistik Und Englischunterricht,* vol. 10 (April 1980) pp. 88-100.

J2864   Jerrom, Rick and Croft, Giles. Ginsberg Interview. *Bananas,* no. 20 (April 1980) pp. 23-25.
Note: AG interview format.

J2865   Rhodes, Joe. 'A More Interesting Time' Discovers a More Respectable Allen Ginsberg. *Minneapolis Tribune* (April 8, 1980) p. 7B.
Note: AG quoted.

J2866   Sorescu, Marin. Singuratatea Si Singuratatea Publica. *Ramuri,* vol. 17, no. 4 (April 15, 1980) p. 15.
Note: AG quoted briefly in Romanian only.

J2867 Weinberger, Eliot. Dharma Demogogy. *Nation,* vol. 230, no. 15 (April 19, 1980)

J2868 Brandenburg, John. Poet Delivers Recitation On Good Of Meditation. *Daily Oklahoman* (April 23, 1980) p. 4.
Note: AG quoted briefly.

J2869 Canby, Vincent. The Screen: At Home With Kerouac. *New York Times* (April 25, 1980) p. C8.

J2870 Bacharach, J.D. Beats At the Fox. *Free Venice Beachhead,* no. 125 (May 1980)

J2871 Hubbard, Jim. Reflections On Allan [sic] Ginsberg Visit: Does the Beat Go On? *Gay Lib Voice Twin Cities,* vol. 1, no. 14 (May 1980) p. 6.

J2872 Pons, Michael. 'Eliminate Confusion' For Peace Of Mind, Says Ginsberg. *Norman Transcript* (May 1, 1980) p. 11A.
Note: AG quoted briefly.

J2873 Priewe, Jens. [review of *Notizbücher 1952-1962* (Carl Hanser)]. *Zeit Magazin,* no. 19 (May 2, 1980) pp. 38, 40.

J2874 Hepher, Paul. Time Muffles Ginsberg's Howl. *Calgary Albertan* (May 5, 1980) p. 25.
Note: AG quoted briefly.

J2875 Denby, David. Faint 'Heart'. *New York,* vol. 13, no. 19 (May 12, 1980) pp. 62, 64.

J2876 Derschau, Christoph. Rebell Mit Schlips. *Stern,* no. 21 (May 14, 1980) pp. 170-173.
Note: AG quoted briefly in German only.

J2877 Brennan, Barry. Film Poem To Venice Artists. *Evening Outlook* (May 23, 1980) p. 9D.

J2878 Reed, Ishmael. American Poetry: Looking For a Center. *San Francisco Review Of Books,* vol. 6, no. 1 (June 1980) p. 20.

J2879 Singender Dichter. *Stern,* no. 26 (June 19, 1980) p. 140.

J2880 Portugés, Paul. Allen Ginsberg's Paul Cezanne And the Pater Omnipotens Aeterna Deus. *Contemporary Literature,* vol. 21, no. 3 (Summer 1980) pp. 435-449.

J2881 Andrei Voznesensky And Allen Ginsberg: A Conversation. *Paris Review,* vol. 22, no. 78 (Summer 1980) pp. 149-177.
Note: AG interview format.

J2882 Lester, Dave. Ginsberg Laments Social Trends. *Tribune-Review* (June 22, 1980) p. A12.
Note: AG quoted briefly.

J2883 Rockland, Michael A. True Grit. *New Jersey Monthly,* vol. 4, no. 9 (July 1980) pp. 52-57.
Note: AG quoted briefly.

J2884   Thomas, J.N. and Rumsey, Spencer. 'Tygers' Burn Bright At Keystone Korner. *Berkeley Barb,* vol. 30, no. 24 [issue 735] (July 3, 1980) p. 7. *Note:* AG quoted.

Thomas, J.N. New Book Is a Unique Testament To Love [review of *Straight Heart's Delight*]. *Berkeley Barb,* vol. 30, no. 24 [issue 735] (July 3, 1980) p. 7.

J2885   [review of *Straight Heart's Delight*]. *Publishers Weekly,* vol. 218, no. 1 (July 4, 1980) p. 86.

J2886   Gaeddert, Beth. Tibetan Buddhism Alive, Well In Boulder. *Rocky Mountain News* (July 14, 1980) pp. 4, 27. *Note:* AG quoted briefly.

J2887   Eichstaedt, Peter. Writers, Performers Gather For Festival Opening. *New Mexican* (July 16, 1980) pp. A-1, A-8.

J2888   Mazur, Carol. D.H. Lawrence Festival Attracts Literary Elite. *Albuquerque Journal* (July 17, 1980) p. A-3. *Note:* AG quoted briefly.

J2889   Eichstaedt, Peter. Readings By Contemporary Authors Open D.H. Lawrence Festival. *New Mexican* (July 17, 1980) p. A1.

J2890   Krolow, Karl. Ginsbergs Erleiden Und Antun [review of *Notizbücher 1952-1962* (Carl Hanser)]. *Basel Zeitung* (July 18, 1980)

J2891   Pile, Stephen. A Pilgrimage To D.H. Lawrence — Warts And All. *Sunday Times* (July 20, 1980) p. 32. *Note:* AG quoted briefly.

J2892   Berman, Paul L. Buddahgate: The Trashing Of Allen Ginsberg. *Village Voice* (July 23-29, 1980) pp. 37-40.

J2893   Lennon, Nigey. Only the Beats Know Venice. *Los Angeles Herald Examiner* (July 27, 1980) California Living section, pp. 9, 11, 14, 16.

J2894   Pivano, Fernanda. Nelle Notti Romane Qualcuno Ama I Poeti. *Corriere Della Sera* (July 29, 1980) p. 3.

J2895   La Poesia Saluta, Con Amore. *Il Messaggero* (July 30, 1980) p. 6.

J2896   Jyoti. The Bisbee Poetry Festival. *Bisbee Mountain Journal* (Aug. 1980) pp. 6-7.

J2897   Bowering, George. [review of *Straight Heart's Delight*]. *Vancouver Free Press,* vol. 2, no. 61 (Aug. 1-8, 1980)

J2898   Hoover, Eleanor. It Wasn't Just Idle 'Chatterley' When the Stars Came Out In Taos To Honor D.H. Lawrence. *People,* vol. 14, no. 5 (Aug. 4, 1980) pp. 20-21.

J2899   Abbott, Steve. [review of *Straight Heart's Delight*]. *Sentinel* (ca. Aug. 4, 1980)

J2900   De Milo, David A. When Police Took Poems, They Took His Heart, Too. *Miami Herald* (Aug. 16, 1980) section D, pp. 1, 2. *Note:* AG quoted briefly.

J2901   Johnston, Laurie. St. Mark's Bell Signals Church's Rise From Ashes. *New York Times* (Aug. 19, 1980) pp. B1, B5.

J2902   Voas, Jeremy. Mingling Minds. *Bisbee Daily Review,* vol. 83, no. 392 (Aug. 21, 1980) p. 1.

J2903   Fischer, Howard. Bisbee's 'Concerned' Say: Disgusting Poets, Away! *Arizona Daily Star* (Aug. 24, 1980) p. 11B.
Note: AG quoted briefly.

J2904   La Fave, Kenneth. Poets Do Their Thing, Whatever That Is. *Arizona Daily Star* (Aug. 25, 1980) section C, p. 3.

J2905   Dean, Susan Lyons. Howling In Bisbee. *Tucson Citizen* (Aug. 25, 1980) section B.
Note: AG quoted briefly.

J2906   Hallock, Steve. Ginsburg [sic] Inspires Poetry Passions At Bisbee Festival. *Arizona Republic* (Aug. 26, 1980)

Residents Have Nasty Words For the Nature Of 'Fine Arts'. *Arizona Republic* (Aug. 26, 1980)

J2907   Fischer, Howard. Bisbee 'Y' Chief Vows To Fight Tax Funding Of Poet 'Pornography'. *Bisbee Daily Review* (Aug. 27, 1980)

J2908   Johnstone, Bryan. Glimpses Of Ginsberg. *Arizona Daily Wildcat* (Aug. 28, 1980) pp. 8-9.

J2909   Schatzdorfer, Gunther. [review of *Das Geheul Und Andere Gedichte* (Limes Verlag)]. *Salzburger Nadviditeu* (Aug. 30-31, 1980)

J2910   Hallock, Steve. Poet Comfortable With Death, Doom, Destruction. *Arizona Republic* (Aug. 31, 1980)
Note: AG quoted briefly.

J2911   Carter, Jefferson. Bisbee Poetry Festival #2 '80. *Newsreal* (Sept. 1980) p. 6.

J2912   S., H. Poets Captivate. *Taos News* (Sept. 4, 1980)

J2913   Kooi, Cynthia. A Remote Festive Moment With the Poets. *San Francisco Chronicle* (Sept. 7, 1980) World section, p. 37.

J2914   [review of *Kaddisch* (Limes Verlag)]. *Arbeiter Zeitung* (Sept. 12, 1980)

J2915   Kobel, Peter and Kooi, Cynthia. Poetic Souls Towed To Bisbee. *Arizona Living* (Sept. 12, 1980)

J2916   [review of *Composed On the Tongue*]. *Booklist,* vol. 77, no. 2 (Sept. 15, 1980) p. 94.

J2917   Cawley, Janet. Ah! Ginsberg Still Chanting 12 Years Later. *Chicago Tribune* (Sept. 16, 1980) pp. 1, 4.
Note: AG quoted.

J2918   Leader Of 50s Beat Generation Allen Ginsberg To Be In Abilene. *Abilene Reflector-Chronicle* (Sept. 18, 1980)

J2919 Schwartz, Harry. Allen Ginsberg: Poet & Visitor Noon, Monday, Sept. 22, RGC. *Grackle,* vol. 5, no. 2 (Sept. 19, 1980)

J2920 Pivano, Fernanda. Ora Contestano Col Guru E Il Poeta. *Corriere Della Sera* (Sept. 21, 1980) p. 3.

J2921 Goldstein, Laurence. The American Poet At the Movies: A Life And Times. *Centennial Review,* vol. 24, no. 4 (Fall 1980) pp. 432-452.

J2922 Betsky-Zweig, S. An Uncommon Language: Crossing With Whitman. *Dutch Quarterly Review Of Anglo-American Letters,* vol. 10, no. 4 ([Fall] 1980) pp. 258-271.

J2923 Shively, Charles. [review of *Straight Heart's Delight*]. *Gay Sunshine,* no. 44-45 (Autumn-Winter 1980) pp. 22-23.

J2924 Lev, Donald. [review of *Composed On the Tongue*]. *Home Planet News,* vol. 2, no. 2 [issue 8] (Fall 1980) pp. 9, 23.

J2925 Wabol, Amy. Poet's Work Echoes Past Three Decades. *Slate* (Sept. 23, 1980) pp. 5, 8.
Note: AG quoted briefly.

J2926 Gunn, Steve. Ginsberg: Giant Insects Dictate Foreign Policy. *Dallas Times Herald* (Sept. 24, 1980) pp. C1, C6.
Note: AG quoted.

J2927 Berryhill, Michael. 'Ginsberg' Tells Who Allen Is. *Fort Worth Star-Telegram* (Sept. 24, 1980)
Note: AG quoted briefly.

J2928 Bowman, Harry. Poet Allen Ginsberg Is Still Singing Radical Stanzas. *Dallas Morning News* (Sept. 25, 1980) pp. 1C, 10C.
Note: AG quoted.

J2929 Kline, Betsy. And the Beat Goes On. *Kansas City Star* (Sept. 26, 1980) p. 1C.
Note: AG quoted briefly.

J2930 Broddle, Karen. Schizophrenic Fifties, Almost Now. *Abilene Reflector-Chronicle* (Sept. 27, 1980) p. 1.
Note: AG quoted briefly.

J2931 Brecheisen, Ray. Themes, Values Of '60s Alive For Ginsberg. *University Daily Kansan* (Sept. 29, 1980) pp. 1, 5.
Note: AG quoted.

J2932 Weems, Patricia. Poet Captivates Audience With Singing, Poetry. *University Daily Kansan* (Sept. 30, 1980) pp. 1, 5.

J2933 Phillips, Paul. Poet Brings Beat To Williams. *Williams Record* (Sept. 30, 1980) p. 4.

J2934 Nunley, Richard. Allen Ginsberg And Hayden Carruth. *Berkshire Eagle* (Oct. 1, 1980)

J2935 D., B. I Missed the Beat. *Esquire,* vol. 94, no. 4 (Oct. 1980) p. 123.

J2936 Peters, Robert. [review of *Straight Heart's Delight*]. *Library Journal,* vol. 105, no. 17 (Oct. 1, 1980) p. 2075.

J2937   Ginsberg To Read Works At Williams. *Transcript* (Oct. 1, 1980) p. 15.

J2938   Mannuzza, Vivi. Poet Ginsberg At Williams. *Berkshire Eagle* (Oct. 2, 1980)

J2939   Bailey, Elizabeth. Gregory Corso And the Whole Mess. *International Herald Tribune* (Oct. 3, 1980)

J2940   Chandler, Julie. Ginsberg Reads Poetry For Richland. *Richland Chronicle,* vol. 3, no. 5 (Oct. 3, 1980) p. 1.

J2941   Hartman, Donna. Ginsberg: World Is Headed To Doom. *Transcript* (Oct. 3, 1980) pp. 11, 20.
          Note: AG quoted.

J2942   Ginsberg Reads, Sings; Predicts Nuclear Doom. *Williams Record* (Oct. 7, 1980) pp. 1, 3.
          Note: AG quoted briefly.

J2943   McGraw, Tim. For Poets, Times Were Hard. *University News* (Oct. 9, 1980) p. 8.

J2944   The Beat Goes On For Allen Ginsberg. *El Paso Times* (Oct. 19, 1980) p. 14-E.
          Note: AG quoted briefly.

J2945   Ferris, Haviland. [review of *Straight Heart's Delight*]. *Washington Blade,* vol. 11, no. 21 (Oct. 24, 1980) pp. B1, B9.

J2946   Glusadz, Radomir. Zhvot I Snovi. *Nin* (Oct. 26, 1980) pp. 31-32.

J2947   Zivancevic, Nina and Biskupovic, Dragan. Pesnik Koji Pazi Na Disanje. *Mladost,* vol. 61, no. 1210 (Oct. 31, 1980) p. 9.
          Note: AG quoted briefly in Serbo-Croatian only.

J2948   N., R. Western Spy. *San Francisco Review Of Books,* vol. 6, no. 3 (Nov.-Dec. 1980) pp. 4-5.

          Reed, Ishmael. American Poetry Looking For a Center. *San Francisco Review Of Books,* vol. 6, no. 3 (Nov.-Dec. 1980) pp. 18-19.

J2949   Challis, Chris. The Most Celebrated American Poet Alive Today. *Southwest Review,* no. 9 (Nov. 1980) pp. 45-49.

J2950   Schwada, Jim and Schindling, Eric. Interview: Burroughs And Ginsberg. *Talk Talk,* vol. 2, no. 12 (Nov. 1980) pp. 19-23.
          Note: AG interview format.

J2951   Nisbet, Jim. Chasing the Last Fuckateer. *Wet,* vol. 5, no. 3 (Nov. 1980) pp. 50-53.
          Note: AG quoted briefly.

J2952   [review of *Kaddisch* (Limes Verlag)]. *2002 [Zweitausendundzwei],* no. 11 (Nov. 1980)

J2953   Velickovic, Dusan. Sllu A Bit-Generachi E. *Nin,* vol. 30, no. 1557 (Nov. 2, 1980) pp. 40-41.
          Note: AG quoted briefly in Serbo-Croatian only.

J2954 Bajats, Vladislav and Sindolic, Vojo. Svakog Jutra Se Budim Skhva Tajuhi Da Ne Postoji Pobeda. *Omladinske Novine,* no. 266 (Nov. 2, 1980) pp. 12-13.
Note: AG interview format in Serbo-Croatian only.

Brnih, Momir. Svest Pesnika Je Silovana. *Omladinske Novine,* no. 266 (Nov. 2, 1980) p. 13.
Note: AG interview format in Serbo-Croatian only.

J2955 Pivano, Fernanda. Nel Mondo Febbrile Degli Elettori Gay. *Corriere Della Sera* (Nov. 3, 1980)

J2956 Géza, Biskó. Allen Ginsberg. *Estillirlap,* vol. 25, no. 259 (Nov. 3, 1980) p. 2.
Note: AG quoted briefly in Hungarian only.

J2957 Borbevib, Nikola. Nadzhivekch Empajer Stejt Bilding. *Ilustrovana Polika,* no. 1148 (Nov. 4, 1980) pp. 52-54.
Note: AG interview format in Serbo-Croatian only.

J2958 Pivano, Fernanda. Poeti E "Punk" Al Posto Degli Hippies. *Corriere Della Sera* (Nov. 9, 1980) p. 3.

J2959 Sindolic, Vojo. U Pozadini Stvarnosti. *Zdravo!,* no. 118 (Nov. 10, 1980) pp. 49-51.
Note: AG quoted in Serbo-Croatian only.

J2960 Kirchner, Gerhard. [review of *Kaddisch* (Limes Verlag)]. *Frankfurter Allgemeine Zeitung* (Nov. 11, 1980) p. 26.

J2961 Angerer, P. Waffenbruder Des Wortes Im Kulturzentrum. *Tiroler Tageszeitung* (Nov. 15, 1980) p. 14.

J2962 Funsten, Kenneth. [review of *Composed On the Tongue*]. *Los Angeles Times* (Nov. 16, 1980) Book Review section, p. 10.

J2963 Janjatovic, Petar. Disati Svoj Dah! *Dzuboks,* no. 102 (Nov. 21, 1980) pp. 70-71.
Note: AG interview format in Serbo-Croatian only.

J2964 Proskauer, Paul F. [review of *Kaddisch* (Limes Verlag)]. *Aufbau* (Nov. 28, 1980) p. 20.

J2965 Burnes, Brian. Just Around the Corner. *Kansas City Star* (Nov. 30, 1980) Star supplement, pp. 9-10, 12, 14-18.
Note: AG quoted.

Burnes, Brian. Back In the Vortex. *Kansas City Star* (Nov. 30, 1980) Star supplement, pp. 18-19.
Note: AG quoted.

J2966 Breger, Udo. Auch Polizisten Müssten Meditieren. *Basler Zeitung,* no. 282 (Dec. 1, 1980) p. 39.
Note: AG interview format in German only.

J2967 Baran, Bogdan. Allen Ginsberg — Swiadomosc Niezroznicowana. *Nowy Wyraz,* vol. 9, no. 12 (Dec. 1980) pp. 22-25.

J2968 Ploog, Jürgen. Interview Mit Allen Ginsberg. *Sphinx Magazin,* no. 11 (Dec. 1980) pp. 23-27.
Note: AG interview format in German only.

J2969   Schwada, Jim. Interview: William S. Burroughs And Allen Ginsberg. *Talk Talk,* vol. 2, no. 13 (Dec. 1980) pp. 24-27.
Note: AG interview format, continued from Nov. 1980 issue.

J2970   S., A. Allen Ginsbergs Auftritt In Basel. *Basler Zeitung,* no. 285 (Dec. 4, 1980) p. 45.
Note: AG quoted briefly in German only.

J2971   Truninger, Curt. Mehr Meditieren, Weniger Prügeln! *Sonntags Blick* (Dec. 7, 1980) p. 15.
Note: AG interview format in German only.

J2972   Mantra Und Jodel. *Neue Zürcher Zeitung* (Dec. 9, 1980) p. 50.

J2973   Schelbert, Corinne. Der Grosse Gegenkultur-Eintopf. *Tages-Anzeiger Magazin* (Dec. 9, 1980) p. 25.

J2974   Young, Ian. [review of *Straight Heart's Delight*]. *Advocate,* no. 307 (Dec. 11, 1980) p. 47.

J2975   Longacre, Sarah. [centerfold photographs]. *Soho News* (Dec. 12-23, 1980) pp. 40-41.

J2976   Eine Kultfigur Und Freiheits-Statue Der "Anderen USA". *Neue Rhein Zeitung* (Dec. 13, 1980)

J2977   Behr, Axel. Und Eine Hymne Fur John Lennon. *Wuppertaler Zeitung* (Dec. 13, 1980) p. 13.

J2978   Shafarzek, Susan. [review of *Straight Heart's Delight*]. *Library Journal,* vol. 105, no. 22 (Dec. 15, 1980) p. 2546.

J2979   Baraka, Amiri. Confessions Of a Former Anti-Semite. *Village Voice* (Dec. 17-23, 1980) pp. 1, 19-20, 22-23.

J2980   Claire, William. Contemporary American Poetry At the Crossroads. *American Studies International,* vol. 18, no. 2 (Winter 1980) pp. 5-18.

J2981   Die...When You Die. *Die Tageszeitung* (Dec. 24, 1980) Magazin section, p. 9.
Note: AG quoted briefly in German only.

J2982   [anonymous]. A Season In Hell. *Home Grown International,* vol. 1, no. 8 (1980) pp. 7-10.

J2983   Krüll, Karl and Pieper, Werner. Allen Ginsberg. *Humus,* no. 4 (1980) pp. 52-53, 56.
Note: AG quoted briefly in German only.

J2984   [Rosenthal, Irving]. Interrogation Of a Business Man By the Interior Police. *Kaliflower,* vol. 5 (1980) pp. 90-100.
Note: AG interview format, AG identified by the pseudonym "Star".

J2985   Dorset, Gerald. [review of *Poems All Over the Place*]. *Literary Monitor,* vol. 3, no. 3-4 (1980) pp. 71-72.

J2986   The Little Poetry Pimp. *Northeast Rising Sun,* vol. 4, no. 18 (1980)

Books:

J2987 Anthony, Gene. *The Summer Of Love.* Berkeley, CA: Celestial Arts, 1980, pp. 154, 162-163.
Note: AG quoted briefly.

J2988 Ball, Gordon. *Journals Early Fifties, Early Sixties By Allen Ginsberg.* Unpublished Doctoral Dissertation. University Of North Carolina At Chapel Hill, 1980.

J2989 Bryan, John. *Whatever Happened To Timothy Leary?* San Francisco, CA: Renaissance Press, 1980.
Note: AG quoted throughout.

J2990 Burroughs, William S. *The Soft Machine, Nova Express, The Wild Boys: Three Novels.* New York, NY: Grove Press Outrider Book, 1980.
Contents: Ginsberg, Allen. Epilogue, pp. 185-190.
Note: AG interview format.

J2991 Clark, Tom. *The Great Naropa Poetry Wars.* Santa Barbara, CA: Cadmus Editions, 1980, pp. 52-67.
Note: AG interview format.

J2992 Ginsberg, Allen. *Composed On the Tongue.* Bolinas, CA: Grey Fox Press, 1980.
Note: AG interview format.

J2993 Greiner, Donald J. (ed.). *American Poets Since World War II, Part 1: A-K.* Detroit, MI: Gale Research Co., 1980. [Dictionary Of Literary Biography, vol. 5]
Contents: Ower, John. Allen Ginsberg, pp. 269-286.

J2994 Hofmann, Albert. *LSD: My Problem Child.* New York, NY: McGraw-Hill, 1980, p. 74.

J2995 Jones, Peter. *A Reader's Guide To Fifty American Poets.* Totowa, NJ: Barnes And Noble, 1980, pp. 316-322.
Note: A review of *Howl And Other Poems* and *Kaddish And Other Poems.*

J2996 Kraus, Michelle P. *Allen Ginsberg: An Annotated Bibliography, 1969-1977.* Metuchen, NJ: Scarecrow Press, 1980.
Note: AG mentioned throughout.

J2997 Leyland, Winston (ed.). *Sexualidade & Criação Literária.* Rio De Janeiro, Brazil: Editora Civilização Brasileira, 1980, pp. 73-124.
Note: Translation by Raul De Sá Barbosa of Allen Young's interview with AG in Portuguese only.

J2998 McCullough, David W. *McCullough's Brief Lives: Selected 'Eye On Books' Interviews.* New York, NY: Book-of-the-Month Club, 1980, pp. 65-67.
Note: AG quoted.

J2999 McGuinn, Rex Alexander. *Discourtesy Of Death: The Elegy In the Twentieth Century.* Unpublished Doctoral Dissertation. University Of North Carolina At Chapel Hill, 1980.

J3000 Novak, William. *High Culture.* New York, NY: Knopf, 1980.

J3001   Patterson, Tom (ed.). *Red Hand Book II.* Atlanta, GA: Pynyon Press, 1980, pp. 82-85.

J3002   Perez, Jose-Nicolas Valencia. *El Heroe Beat En El Poema De Allen Ginsberg 'Aullido'.* Unpublished Dissertation. Universidad Nacional Autonoma De Mexico, 1980.

J3003   Sargent, Mark. *Allen Ginsberg Comes To Olympia 1969-1980.* Portland, OR: Impossibilists, 1980. [Impossibilist Broadside 3]

J3004   Satsvarupa Dasa Goswami. *Planting the Seed, Srila Prabhupada-Lilamrta, vol. 2.* Los Angeles, CA: Bhaktivedanta Book Trust, 1980.
Note: AG quoted throughout.

J3005   Selerie, Gavin (ed.). *The Riverside Interviews: 1, Allen Ginsberg.* London, England: Binnacle Press, 1980.
Note: AG interview format.

J3006   Vendler, Helen. *Part Of Nature, Part Of Us: Modern American Poets.* Cambridge, MA: Harvard University Press, 1980.
Contents: Vendler, Helen. [review of *The Fall Of America*], pp. 197-203.

J3007   Vinson, James (ed.). *Contemporary Poets.* New York, NY: St. Martin's Press, 1980. [Third edition]
Contents: Byrd, Don. Allen Ginsberg, pp. 553-557.

J3008   Zweig, Ellen Marcia. *Performance Poetry: Critical Approaches To Contemporary Intermedia.* Unpublished Doctoral Dissertation. University Of Michigan, 1980.

1981

J3009   Dubler, Linda. Profile: Gordon Ball. *Art Papers,* vol. 5, no. 1 (Jan.-Feb. 1981) pp. 8-9.

J3010   Bettarini, Mariella. Shakespeare O Dante Sarebbero Serviti... *Salvo Imprevisti,* vol. 8, no. 1-2 [issue 22-23] (Jan.-Aug. 1981) pp. 8-9.
Note: AG interview format translated into Italian by Alida Vatta.

J3011   Plymell, Charles. The Big World Of the Coca Cola Guru. *San Francisco Review Of Books,* vol. 6, no. 4 (Jan.-Feb. 1981) p. 14.

Reed, Ishmael. American Poetry Looking For a Center. *San Francisco Review Of Books,* vol. 6, no. 4 (Jan.-Feb. 1981) pp. 17-18.

J3012   Inoue, Teruo. [review of *Indian Journals*]. *Will,* no. 1 (Winter [Jan.] 1981) p. 37.

J3013   Lake, Steve. Ginsberg: Keeping a Steady Beat... *Melody Maker* (Jan. 3, 1981) pp. 22, 28.
Note: AG quoted at length.

J3014   Mitgang, Herbert. Schlesinger Elected Head Of Arts And Letters Group. *New York Times* (Jan. 28, 1981) p. C22.

J3015   Harriott, Esther. Has Allen Ginsberg Been Certified As 'Safe'? *Buffalo Evening News* (Feb. 1, 1981) p. F-5.
Note: AG quoted.

J3016 Simon, Jeff. Commentary. *Buffalo Evening News/Gusto* (Feb. 6, 1981) p. 5.

J3017 Descamps, Christian. Beat Is Beautiful. *Libération,* no. 2173 (Feb. 10, 1981) p. 18.
Note: AG interview format.

J3018 Groves, Bob. Ginsberg Ever Grand. *Buffalo Courier-Express* (Feb. 12, 1981)

J3019 Hassinger, Andy. Ginsberg Reading: Poem Within a Poem. *Syracuse Post-Standard* (Feb. 13, 1981) p. C-6.
Note: AG quoted briefly.

J3020 Green, David. ECC Students Entertained By Allen Ginsberg. *Element,* no. 14 (Feb. 24, 1981) p. 1.

J3021 Romano, Carlin. 15 Years On the Firing Line. *Daily News* (Feb. 25, 1981) p. M8.
Note: AG quoted briefly.

J3022 Keisch, Ze've. Taped Conversation For Niagara-Erie Writers *NEWsletter:* Penelope Creeley, Robert Creeley, Allen De Loach, Allen Ginsberg And Peter Orlovsky. *NEWsletter: Niagara-Erie Writers,* vol. 3, no. 7 (March 1981) p. [7].
Note: AG interview format.

J3023 Herrmann, C.J. Ginsberg Introduces Poets To Overflow Audience At St. Mark's. *Aquarian Weekly,* vol. 18, no. 356 (March 4, 1981) p. 18.
Note: AG quoted briefly.

J3024 'Beat' Poet, Guru Allen Ginsberg To Give Reading. *Coloradoan* (March 13, 1981)

J3025 Echoes Of Vietnam: Celebrities Want U.S. Out Of El Salvador. *Los Angeles Times* (March 15, 1981) section 1, p. 4.

J3026 Journey To the End Of the Night. *Home Grown,* vol. 1, no. 9 ([Spring] 1981) pp. 27-29.

J3027 Aiken, William. Denise Levertov, Robert Duncan And Allen Ginsberg: Modes Of the Self In Projective Poetry. *Modern Poetry Studies,* vol. 10, no. 2-3 ([Spring] 1981) pp. 200-204.

J3028 Beat Poet Guru At Lincoln Center. *Collegian* (March 25, 1981) p. 9.

J3029 Allen Ginsberg In the Fort. *Fort Collins Review* (March 25, 1981) p. 8A.

J3030 Updike, Robin. Ginsberg May Sing a New Rock 'n' Roll Poem. *Coloradoan* (March 27, 1981) p. B4.
Note: AG quoted briefly.

J3031 Rankin, Chuck. Reflective Ginsberg Offers Experience. *Coloradoan* (March 30, 1981)

J3032 Mayer, Debby. Is There a Poetry Mafia? *Coda: Poets & Writers Newsletter,* vol. 8, no. 4 (April-May 1981) pp. 10-14.

J3033 Berman, Hedy. Ginsberg Continues As a Man Of His Times. *Ft. Collins Review* (April 1, 1981) p. 13.

J3034 [Cartwright, Louis]. A Triumvirate Of Sorts: Burroughs, Ginsberg, Huncke. *Newave*, vol. 1, no. 5 (April 1981) pp. 7-8.
Note: AG quoted in this transcript of the film *Nuclear Scorpions.*

J3035 Keisch, Ze'ev. Tape Conversation For Niagara-Erie Writers NEWsletter: Penelope Creeley, Robert Creeley, Allen De Loach, Allen Ginsberg And Peter Orlovsky (continued from March). *NEWsletter: Niagara-Erie Writers,* vol. 3, no. 8 (April 1981) pp. [7-8].
Note: AG interview format.

J3036 Bunge, Charles. [review of *Allen Ginsberg: An Annotated Bibliography, 1969-1977* by Michelle P. Kraus]. *Wilson Library Bulletin,* vol. 55, no. 8 (April 1981) p. 621.

J3037 Stephens, Julie. Allen Ginsburg's [sic] World Of Disembodied Poetics. *Collegian* (April 3, 1981) p. 15.

J3038 Newsman, Poet, Novelist Due At College. *County Shopper & Entertainment Guide* (April 14, 1981) p. 8.

J3039 McLaughlin, Jeff. Bob Donlin Loves the Folk At Passim. *Boston Globe* (April 15, 1981) p. 30.

J3040 [review of *Kaddisch* (Limes Verlag)]. *Offenbach Post* (April 21, 1981)

J3041 Hackett, Regina. Poetry Is Just a Party. *Seattle Post-Intelligencer* (April 23, 1981) p. D8.
Note: AG quoted briefly.

J3042 Taylor, Chick. Ginsberg Melds Old Ideas With New Wave. *Tri-City Herald* (April 24, 1981) p. 29.
Note: AG quoted briefly.

J3043 Case, Frederick. Ginsberg Hasn't Lost His Ability To Shock. *Seattle Times* (April 25, 1981) p. B4.
Note: AG quoted briefly.

J3044 Johnson, Eve. Ginsberg Goes 'Out Of His Depth'. *Vancouver Sun* (April 27, 1981) p. C6.
Note: AG quoted briefly.

J3045 [review of *Kaddisch* (Limes Verlag)]. *Wetzlarer Neue Zeitung* (April 28, 1981)

J3046 McFarland, Georgia. Ginsberg: A Steady Mind... *ArtSeattle* (April 29, 1981) pp. 8, 16.
Note: AG quoted.

J3047 Stone, Arlene. [review of *Straight Heart's Delight*]. *American Book Review,* vol. 3, no. 4 (May-June 1981) p. 10.

Knight, Arthur Winfield. [review of *Composed On the Tongue*]. *American Book Review,* vol. 3, no. 4 (May-June 1981) p. 11.

J3048 Auer, Tom and Vinay, J. Allen Ginsberg, Anne Waldman, Pat Donegan. *Bloomsbury Review,* vol. 1, no. 4 (May-June 1981) pp. 23-24.
Note: AG interview format.

J3049 Varty, Alex. Ginsberg's Single: Rock Stardom At Age 54? *Georgia Straight,* vol. 15, no. 699 (May 1-8, 1981) pp. 1-2, 5-6.
Note: AG interview format.

J3050 Swartz, Tom. Steve Allen, Allen Ginsberg On Kerouac. *New Blood,* no. 3 ([May] 1981) pp. 39-52, 70.
Note: AG interview format.

J3051 Ryan, William. Blake-Light Tragedy Among the Scholars Of War. *Poudre Magazine,* vol. 1, no. 5 (May 1981) pp. 6-9.
Note: AG interview format.

J3052 Picano, Felice. [review of *Straight Heart's Delight*]. *New York Native,* no. 11 (May 4-17, 1981) p. 24.

J3053 Kleiman, Dena. Parents' Groups Purging Schools Of 'Humanist' Books And Classes. *New York Times* (May 17, 1981) pp. 1, 16.

J3054 De Milo, David A. It Could Be Worse, You Could Be In Miami. *Real Paper* (May 21, 1981) pp. 11-14.
Note: AG quoted briefly.

J3055 Smith, Jeff. Ginsberg Invented 'Flower Power'. *Bellevue Community College* (May 22, 1981) p. 6.
Note: AG quoted.

J3056 Becher, Anne. Boulder Poet Reflects On Life: Past And Future. *Owl,* vol. 68, no. 28 (May 22, 1981) p. 3.
Note: AG quoted.

J3057 Infante, G. Cabrera. Bites From the Bearded Crocodile. *London Review Of Books,* vol. 3, no. 10 (June 4-17, 1981) pp. 3-8.

J3058 Coleman, Jane. Extraordinary Week Of Poetry. *Pittsburgh New Sun* (June 4, 1981) p. 17.

J3059 Brinkley-Rogers, Paul. Storm Brewing In Bisbee As Art Group Plans Third Poetry Festival. *Arizona Daily Star* (June 17, 1981) p. 3G.

J3060 Swartz, Tom. Steve Allen/Allen Ginsberg, Kerouac & On. *New Blood,* no. 4 ([Summer] 1981) pp. 74-77.
Note: AG interview format continued from *New Blood* (May 1981).

J3061 Michelson, Peter. The Blinding Lights Of Contrariety. *Rolling Stock,* vol. 1, no. 1 (Summer 1981) pp. 11-15.

J3062 Tanaka, Akiko. [review of *Composed On the Tongue*]. *Will,* no. 2 (Summer 1981) pp. 55-56.

J3063 Edmondson, Brad. Those Scenes Keep Changing... *Ithaca Times,* vol. 3, no. 50 (June 25, 1981) pp. 1, 5.
Note: AG quoted at length.

J3064 Allers, Chuck. Allen Ginsberg. *Out,* no. 52 (July 1981) pp. A16, A20.
Note: AG interview format.

J3065 Van Der Zee, John. The Man With the Golden Pen. *San Francisco Sunday Examiner & Chronicle* (July 12, 1981) California Living Magazine section, pp. 7-8.

J3066   Sanderson, Vicky. Four Tries, Four Successes In Marathon Theatre Evening. *Globe And Mail* (July 13, 1981) p. 16.

J3067   Crew, Bob. 2 Plays Well Worth Your While. *Toronto Star* (July 13, 1981) p. D4.

J3068   Jackson, David. Tales Of Ed Sanders; The Superbeat Moves On. *Village Voice* (July 22-28, 1981) p. 32.

J3069   Stern, Beverley. Sympathetic Views Offered On Human Relationships. *Canadian Jewish News* (July 30, 1981) p.11.

J3070   Charters, Ann. [review of *As Ever* and *Poems All Over the Place*]. *Stony Hills,* vol. 4, no. 1 [issue 10] (Aug.-Sept. 1981) p. 5.

J3071   Beat Buddha Joins Punksters. *Westword,* vol. 4, no. 24 (Aug. 6-20, 1981) p. 5. *Note:* AG quoted briefly.

J3072   Schwartzkopf, Emerson. Truckload Of Poets, Beer Fails To Draw Big Crowd In Commerce City Event. *Denver Post* (Aug. 10, 1981) p. 13.

J3073   En El Encuentro Internacional De Poetas En Morelia. *Excelsior* (Aug. 10, 1981) p. 2.

J3074   Logra Dona Carmen Romano Otro Recital De Los Mas Grandes Poetas. *Novedades Mexico* (Aug. 25, 1981)

J3075   Anaya, Marta. Un Insolito Y Extraordinario Concierto De Ocho Poetas Con Un Publico Maravilloso, En Su Mayoria De Jovenes. *Excelsior* (Aug. 26, 1981) p. 2.

Mendoza, Maria Luisa. Poesia En Uso. *Excelsior* (Aug. 26, 1981)

J3076   De Ita, Fernando. Se Congregaron Dos Mil Personas Para Estar Presentes En La Noche De Poesia. *Uno Mas Uno* (Aug. 26, 1981) p. 17.

J3077   Ibargoyen, Saul. La Actitud De Ginsberg. *Excelsior* (Aug. 28, 1981) p. 1.

J3078   Corbeil, Carole. Ginsberg a Man For All Decades. *Globe And Mail* (Sept. 5, 1981) p. E1. *Note:* AG quoted at length.

J3079   Adachi, Ken. Allen Ginsberg: Still Coming On Strong. *Toronto Sunday Star* (Sept. 6, 1981) p. F11. *Note:* AG quoted.

J3080   Mott, Gordon D. Poet Ginsberg Changes Tune To Rock 'n' Roll. *San Jose Mercury News* (Sept. 7, 1981) p. 6A. *Note:* AG quoted at length.

J3081   Mott, Gordon D. Ginsberg Still Ginsberg Behind Tie. *Hartford Courant* (Sept. 13, 1981) p. A16. *Note:* AG quoted at length.

J3082   Mott, Gordon D. Poet Ginsberg's Worried Song Is Apocalyptic Rock. *Chicago Tribune* (Sept. 14, 1981) Tempo section, pp. 1-2. *Note:* AG quoted at length.

J3083 Muscatello, Carlo. Ancora Un Urlo, Ma Sottovoce. *Il Piccolo* (Sept. 16, 1981)
Note: AG quoted briefly in Italian only.

J3084 Rose, Ben. Ginsberg Says He Likes Adaptation Of "Kaddish". *Canadian Jewish News,* vol. 22, no. 22 [issue 2070] (Sept. 17, 1981) p. 19.
Note: AG quoted.

J3085 Taverna, Salvatore. Poeti Nell'Aula Magna: Ed É Subito Polemica. *Il Messaggero* (Sept. 17, 1981)

J3086 Allen Ginsberg Al Maschio Angioino. *Paese Sera* (Sept. 17, 1981)

J3087 Layton, Tony. Allen Ginsberg Brings Out Birdbrain. *International Daily News* (Sept. 19, 1981) p. 17.
Note: AG quoted briefly.

J3088 Rosati, Ottavio. Ma Che Napoleone Quel Gance. *La Nuova Sardepie* (Sept. 19, 1981)

J3089 D'Orrico, Antonio. Poeti In Piazza: A Firenze Vince Il Fair-Play. *L'Unita* (Sept. 20, 1981)

I., I. Il Festival Dei Poeti Quest' Anno Com'e? "Perverso E Controverso". *L'Unita* (Sept. 20, 1981)

J3090 Stasera Il 'Via' Con Ginsberg E Le Roi Jones. *Paese Sera* (Sept. 21, 1981)

J3091 Santini, Roberto. Il Verso Usurato. *La Città* (Sept. 22, 1981)
Note: AG quoted briefly.

J3092 Johnson, Mark. Discovery As Technique: Allen Ginsberg's 'These States'. *Contemporary Poetry,* vol. 4, no. 2 ([Fall] 1981) pp. 23-45.

J3093 Roark, Randy. The Object Is To See Clearly. *Naropa Institute Bulletin* (Fall 1981-Winter 1982) pp. 9-10.
Note: AG quoted briefly.

J3094 Fiore, Antonio. L'America Urlata Di Ginzberg. *Il Mattino* (Sept. 23, 1981)
Note: AG interview format in Italian only.

J3095 Turchi, Roberto. Allen Ginsberg In Piazza E Al Bar. *La Nazione* (Sept. 23, 1981)
Note: AG interview format in Italian only.

J3096 Seneca, Lucio. Omero, Saffo E Il Beat. *Paese Sera* (Sept. 23, 1981)
Note: AG interview format in Italian only.

J3097 Pivano, Fernanda. E Ginsberg Cantò I Versi. *Corriere Della Sera* (Sept. 24, 1981)

J3098 Mott, Gordon D. A New Beat For Ginsberg. *Chicago GayLife,* vol. 7, no. 15 (Sept. 25, 1981) p. 2.
Note: AG quoted briefly.

J3099 Doni, Elena. Non Si Vive Di Solo Ginsberg. *Il Messagero* (Sept. 26, 1981)
Note: AG interview format in Italian only.

J3100 Rosati, Ottavio. Napoli Si Tinge Di Blues Cantando Con Ginsberg E Con Leroy Jones. *La Nuova* (Sept. 26, 1981) p. 19.

J3101   Taverna, Salvatore. Nell '82 Giro D'Italia Dei Poeti Con Fans Al Seguito? *Il Messaggero* (Sept. 27, 1981)

J3102   Friedman, Mickey. Book Scene: Out From Behind the Beard. *San Francisco Examiner* (Sept. 28, 1981) p. E3.
Note: AG quoted briefly.

J3103   Caen, Herb. Much Ado About Something. *San Francisco Chronicle* (Sept. 29, 1981) p. 21.

J3104   Hardy, Robin. Hero Of the Fever. *Body Politic,* no. 77 (Oct. 1981) pp. 28-31.

J3105   Rudensky, Alice. Allen Ginsberg Set For Local Reading. *Journal-Gazette* (Oct. 1, 1981) pp. D1, D4.

J3106   Petrone, Sandro. Musica E Versi Sciolti Nel Ginsberg Show. *Quotidiano D'Lecce* (Oct. 1, 1981)
Note: AG interview format in Italian only.

J3107   Robertson, Michael. Allen Ginsberg & the Light At the End Of the Time Tunnel: The Vietnam Of Our Decade? *San Francisco Chronicle* (Oct. 1, 1981) p. 46.
Note: AG quoted briefly.

J3108   Wilson, Paul. Allen Ginsberg: Helping Enlighten Woe Mankind. *Shades,* no. 19-20 (Oct.-Nov. 1981) pp. 16-17.
Note: AG quoted at length.

J3109   Birolini, Paolo. Il Grande Fesso. *Il Quotidiano Dei Lavoratori* (Oct. 2, 1981) p. 21.

Gargia, Giulio. Dopo Il Terremoto, La "Grande Bouffe". *Il Quotidiano Dei Lavoratori* (Oct. 2, 1981) p. 21.

J3110   O'Brien, Mike. And the Beat(nik) Goes On... *News-Leader* (Oct. 4, 1981) pp. 1E, 6E.
Note: AG quoted at length.

J3111   Broder, Peter. Ginsberg Is (Still) Outrageous. *Newspaper* (Oct. 7, 1981) p. 5.
Note: AG quoted at length.

J3112   Jung, Daryl. Ginsberg On Light, Life. *Toronto Now* (Oct. 8, 1981) pp. 6, 8.
Note: AG quoted at length.

J3113   Hershkovites, David. The Life & Times Of Al Aronowitz. *Soho News,* vol. 9, no. 3 (Oct. 21-27, 1981) pp. 11-14.

J3114   Rosen, Bruce. Dylan: Once More Born-Again. *Bergen Record* (Oct. 27, 1981) pp. A1, A8.

J3115   Lichtman, Irv. Hammond's Imprint Seeking Pop Action. *Billboard* (Oct. 31, 1981) pp. 10, 107.

J3116   Fabo. Fab Blabs. *Body Politic,* no. 78 (Nov. 1981) p. 36.
Note: AG quoted briefly.

J3117   Miller, Brown. Allen Ginsberg, Missing Poet. *San Francisco Review Of Books,* vol. 6, no. 9 (Nov.-Dec. 1981) p. 25.

J3118 Ginsberg Provokes Thought At WWC. *Daily Rocket-Miner* (Nov. 7, 1981) p. 1.
Note: AG quoted briefly.

J3119 Krza, Paul. Ginsberg Draws Large Rocks [sic] Springs Crowd. *Casper Star-Tribune* (Nov. 10, 1981) p. B1.
Note: AG quoted briefly.

J3120 Ginsberg To Read 'Howl'. *New York Times* (Nov. 11, 1981)

J3121 Urschel, Joe. Is Alexander Haig a Poet? *Detroit Free Press* (Nov. 12, 1981) p. 1.
Note: AG interview format.

J3122 Ginsberg To Read For 25th Of 'Howl'. *Star-Ledger* (Nov. 12, 1981) p. 63.

J3123 Adler, Bill. Poet Allen Ginsberg Comes Full Circle. *Daily News* (Nov. 13, 1981) pp. 1, 3.
Note: AG quoted at length.

J3124 McWhirter, Nickie. Rocket's Glare Outflashes a Spaced-Out Philosophy. *Detroit Free Press* (Nov. 13, 1981) p. 1D.

J3125 Tytell, John. Allen Ginsberg Howls Again. *Soho News* (Nov. 24, 1981) p. 6.

J3126 Haas, Scott. A Few Words With the Poet... *MetroTimes,* vol. 2, no. 4 (Nov. 26-Dec. 10, 1981) p. 21.
Note: AG interview format.

Tysh, Chris. The Poet Has a New Beat. *MetroTimes,* vol. 2, no. 4 (Nov. 26-Dec. 10, 1981) pp. 1, 21.
Note: AG quoted briefly.

J3127 Stickney, John. The Beatnik Goes On: Poet Allen Ginsberg Throws a 25th Birthday Party For "Howl". *People Weekly,* vol. 16, no. 22 (Nov. 30, 1981) pp. 44-45.
Note: AG quoted briefly.

J3128 István Eörsi. *New Blood,* no. 5 (Dec. 1981) pp. 20-37.
Note: AG interview format.

J3129 Barbarisi, Gaetano and Grattacaso, Giuseppe. Bird-Brain Runs the World. *Percorsi,* vol. 2, no. 5-6 (Dec. 1981) pp. 11-16.
Note: AG quoted briefly.

J3130 Britt, Alan. The Gurus Come To Read. *Columbia Flier* (Dec. 3, 1981) p. 74.

J3131 Nixon, Eli. The Beats: Many Will Gather In Boulder Next Year To Fete Author Who Began Revolution. *Daily Camera* (Dec. 6, 1981) pp. 1, 5.

J3132 Gunther, Catherine D. Allen Ginsberg Says Times Haven't Changed. *Baltimore Sun* (Dec. 7, 1981) p. D2.
Note: AG quoted briefly.

J3133 Lebar, Scott. Allen Ginsberg Keeps Swimming Against Tide. *News American* (Dec. 7, 1981) section B, p. B1.
Note: AG quoted briefly.

J3134 Henry, William A. In New York: Howl Becomes a Hoot. *Time,* vol. 118, no. 23 (Dec. 7, 1981) p. 8.

J3135 Ryan, William F. On the Road Again. *Washington Tribune,* vol. 5, no. 24 (Dec. 18, 1981-Jan. 14, 1982) pp. 1, 12-13.
Note: AG quoted at length.

J3136 Warren, Kenneth. [review of *Straight Heart's Delight*]. *Contact II,* vol. 5, no. 24-25 (Winter [Dec. 22, 1981]-Spring 1982) pp. 52-53.

J3137 The Decline Of the West, the Beat Generation, part 3. *Home Grown,* vol. 1, no. 10 (Winter 1981)

J3138 Beyle, Bill. Gregory Corso: Introductory Shot. *Unmuzzled Ox,* vol. 6, no. 2 (Winter 1981) pp. 73-78.

Andre, Michael. An Interview With Gregory Corso. *Unmuzzled Ox,* vol. 6, no. 2 (Winter 1981) pp. 123-158.

J3139 Satsvarupa Dasa Goswami Srila. Breaking the American Silence. *Back To Godhead,* vol. 16, no. 1-2 (1981) pp. 13-14, 30.
Note: AG quoted briefly.

J3140 Sharma, R.S. [review of *Indian Journals*]. *Literary Criterion,* vol. 16, no. 3 (1981) pp. 23-31.

Books:

J3141 Amirthanayagam, Guy and Harrex, Syd C. (eds.). *Only Connect: Literary Perspectives East And West.* Honolulu, HI: East-West Center, 1981.
Contents: Denney, Reuel. Breathing the Sublime: Respiration And Inspiration In the Poetics Of Allen Ginsberg, pp. 64-78.

J3142 Bacigalupo, Massimo and De Mari, Carola (eds.). *Poesia In Pubblico/Parole Per Musica: Atti Degli Incontri Internazionali Di Poesia 1979-1980.* Genova, Italy: Liguria Libri, 1981.
Note: AG interview format throughout.

J3143 Bartlett, Lee (ed.). *The Beats: Essays In Criticism.* Jefferson, NC: McFarland, 1981.
Contents: Breslin, James. Allen Ginsberg: The Origins Of *Howl* and *Kaddish*, pp. 66-89.
Note: AG quoted briefly.
Merrill, Thomas S. Allen Ginsberg's Reality Sandwiches, pp. 90-106.
Note: AG quoted briefly.

J3144 Bockris, Victor. *With William Burroughs: A Report From the Bunker.* New York, NY: Seaver Books, 1981.
Note: AG quoted throughout.

J3145 Christgau, Robert. *Christgau's Record Guide.* New Haven, CT: Ticknor And Fields, 1981, p. 153.
Note: Review of AG's recording of William Blake's poetry in *Songs Of Innocence And Experience.*

J3146 *Enciclopedia, vol. 12.* Torino, Italy: Einaudi, 1981.
Contents: Allen Ginsberg, p. 202.

J3147 Evory, Ann (ed.). *Contemporary Authors, vol. 2.* [New revision series]. Detroit, MI: Gale Research Co., 1981, pp. 247-251.
Note: AG quoted briefly.

J3148   Fossum, Robert H. and Roth, John K. *The American Dream.* Durham, England: British Association For American Studies, 1981, p. 31. [Series: BAAS Pamphlets In American Studies #6].

J3149   Ginsberg, Allen. *La Caduta Dell'America.* Milan, Italy: Arnoldo Mondadori, 1981.
         Contents: Portugés, Paul. Intervista Di Paul Portugés A Allen Ginsberg, pp. 345-364.
         Note: AG interview format in Italian only translated by Fernanda Pivano.

J3150   Hunt, Tim. *Kerouac's Crooked Road.* Hamden, CT: Archon Books, 1981.
         Note: AG quoted and mentioned throughout.

J3151   Litz, A. Walton (ed.). *American Writers: A Collection Of Literary Biographies, Supplement II, Part 1.* New York, NY: Scribner's, 1981.
         Contents: Mersmann, James. Allen Ginsberg, pp. 307-333.

J3152   McCullough, David W. *People, Books & Book People.* New York, NY: Harmony Books, 1981, pp. 64-66.
         Note: AG quoted.

J3153   *Pros In Poetry.* San Francisco, CA: Free Print Shop, 1981.
         Note: AG mentioned throughout.

J3154   Young, Allen. *Gays Under the Cuban Revolution.* San Francisco, CA: Grey Fox Press, 1981, pp. 20-21, 29.

1982

J3155   Baker, Paul. A Look At the Real Neal. *Commercial Appeal* (Jan. 3, 1982)

J3156   Codrescu, Andrei. That's No Legend, It's Just Poetry. *Baltimore Sun* (Jan. 10, 1982) Magazine section.
         Note: AG quoted briefly.

J3157   Hinerman, Stephen. [review of *Birdbrain* (recording)]. *Westword* (Jan. 14-28, 1982) pp. 18, 25.

J3158   Palmer, Robert. Beat Generation Lives In a Night Of Rock And Poetry. *New York Times* (Jan. 15, 1982) p. C6.

J3159   Zedek, Dan. Reviews. *Win,* vol. 18, no. 2 (Jan. 15, 1982) p. 30.

J3160   Dougherty, Steve. Allen Ginsberg, 55, Is Still Howling After All These Years. *Atlanta Journal And Atlanta Constitution* (Jan. 17, 1982) section F, pp. 1, 6.
         Note: AG quoted at length.

J3161   Gingsberg [sic] Asustó A Algunos En Recital. *La Prensa* (Jan. 23, 1982) pp. 1, 12.

J3162   El Dolor Del Pueblo Gringo En La Voz De Allen Ginsberg. *Barricada* (Jan. 27, 1982) p. 9.

J3163   Ryan, William F. A Meeting Of the Minds: Stone And Ginsberg Chat At Doctorow's Party. *Washington Tribune,* vol. 6, no. 2 (Jan. 29-Feb. 11, 1982) p. 20.

J3164   Lomax, Pearl Cleage. The Unforgettable Night That Allen Ginsberg Finally Visited Atlanta. *Atlanta Journal And Atlanta Constitution* (Jan. 31, 1982) p. 7F.

J3165   Miller, Jim. [review of *First Blues* (Folkways recording)]. *Beaumont Enterprise & Journal* (Jan. 31, 1982) p. 9D.

J3166   Nordland, Rod. East Meets West Over a Bottle Of Rum In Nicaragua. *San Francisco Examiner* (Feb. 3, 1982) p. A3.
Note: AG quoted briefly.

J3167   Intentionally omitted.

J3168   Cockburn, Alexander and Ridgeway, James. The Poles, the Left, And the Tumbrils Of '84. *Village Voice* (Feb. 10-16, 1982) pp. 10, 28-29, 95.

J3169   Filipini, David J. Words And Lyrics. *Albrightian* (Feb. 12, 1982) p. 4.

J3170   Courage, Ewan. A Moveable Fiesta. *Soho News* (Feb. 16, 1982) pp. 11-12.
Note: AG quoted.

J3171   Moran, Tom. Allen Ginsberg On Ronald Reagan And Rock 'n' Roll. *Los Angeles Herald Examiner* (Feb. 18, 1982) pp. 1, 8.
Note: AG interview format.

J3172   Clash Link Up With Ginsberg. *Rolling Stone* (Feb. 18, 1982) p. 33.
Note: AG quoted briefly.

J3173   Whitten, Patricia. Ginsberg Reads Ginsberg, Norse Reads Norse. *L.A. Weekly* (Feb. 19-25, 1982) p. 40.

Varney, Ginger. [review of *The Beats: An Existential Comedy*]. *L.A. Weekly* (Feb. 19-25, 1982) p. 42.

J3174   Barich, Bill. The Sporting Scene, Jumpers At Kempton Park. *New Yorker,* vol. 58, no. 1 (Feb. 22, 1982) pp. 74, 79-82, 84-91.

J3175   Williams, Albert. Ginsberg, Orlovsky To Read Here March 2. *Gay Life,* vol. 7, no. 37 (Feb. 26, 1982) pp. 1, 8.

J3176   Ross, Dave. The Return Of Allen Ginsberg. *Independent Press Telegram* (Feb. 26, 1982) Weekend section, p. 6.

J3177   Tillinghast, Richard. [review of *Plutonian Ode*]. *Boston Review,* vol. 7, no. 2 (March-April 1982) pp. 27-28.

J3178   Allen Ginsberg. *Heat,* no. 7 (ca. March 1982) l. 23.
Note: AG quoted briefly.

J3179   Ratner, Rochelle. [review of *Plutonian Ode*]. *Library Journal,* vol. 107, no. 5 (March 1, 1982) p. 552.

J3180   Janz, William. Ginsberg Howl Echos From the '50s. *Milwaukee Sentinel* (March 1, 1982)

J3181   Suzuki, Dean. [review of *First Blues* (Folkways recording)]. *OP Magazine* (March-April 1982) p. 10.

J3182 Littmann, William. Sharing Of Visions. *Daily Forty-Niner,* vol. 33, no. 98 (March 2, 1982) pp. 3-4.
Note: AG quoted briefly.

J3183 Stevens, Alison. Poets Bring 'Visions Of Peace' To Conference. *Union Daily* (March 2, 1982) pp. 1, 8.

J3184 Murray, Walt. Beat Lyricists Share the Stage Together. *Press-Telegram* (March 3, 1982) pp. C9-10.
Note: AG quoted briefly.

J3185 Powell, Tony. An Interview With Allen Ginsberg. *Union Daily* (March 3, 1982) p. 1.
Note: AG quoted briefly.

Tonkovich, Andrew. The Big Poet Comes To Campus. *Union Daily* (March 3, 1982) p. 1.
Note: AG quoted briefly.

J3186 Doherty, Will. Link Interview: Allen Ginsberg. *Link,* vol. 3, no. 3 (March 8-28, 1982) pp. 1, 12-13.
Note: AG interview format.

J3187 McNally, Joel. With Rhyme And Reason, Poet Looks At His Struggle. *Milwaukee Journal* (March 11, 1982) pp. 1-2.
Note: AG quoted.

J3188 Carroll, Charles Francis. Never To Be Beaten. *Other Voice,* vol. 3, no. 2 (March 11, 1982) p. 7.
Note: AG quoted briefly.

J3189 MacAdams, Lewis. Catching Up With Allen Ginsberg. *L.A. Weekly,* vol. 4, no. 15 (March 12-18, 1982) pp. 8-9.
Note: AG interview format.

J3190 Polak, Maralyn Lois. Allen Ginsberg: Still Howling After All These Years. *Philadelphia Inquirer* (March 14, 1982) Today Magazine section, pp. 10-11.
Note: AG quoted.

J3191 Estridge, Larry. Poets Of the Revolution. *New Haven Advocate* (March 17, 1982) pp. 1, 6, 8-10.
Note: AG interview format.

Houlding, Andrew. Grunge And Ginsberg. *New Haven Advocate* (March 17, 1982) pp. 2, 12.

J3192 Moore, Dave. A Beat Conversation, 1949. *Moody Street Irregulars,* no. 11 (Spring-Summer 1982) pp. 22-23.
Note: AG quoted.

J3193 Bartlett, Jeffrey. Howl In High School. *North Dakota Quarterly,* vol. 50, no. 2 (Spring 1982) pp. 68-75.

Bartlett, Jeffrey. Allen Ginsberg Today. *North Dakota Quarterly,* vol. 50, no. 2 (Spring 1982) pp. 76-80.

J3194 Pinckney, Darryl. [review of *Composed On the Tongue* and *Straight Heart's Delight*]. *Parnassus,* vol. 10, no. 1 (Spring-Summer 1982) pp. 99-116.

J3195 D'Souza, Dinesh. National Endowment For Pornography. *Policy Review,* no. 20 (Spring 1982) pp. 147-155.

J3196 Mind Breaths. *Ten Directions* (Spring 1982) p. 11.

J3197 Berman, Paul. [review of *Plutonian Ode*]. *Village Voice* (March 23, 1982) p. 42.

J3198 Kiesling, Bob. Alan [sic] Ginsberg Is Out To Play a Joke On the Nation. *Ranger,* vol. 10, no. 23 (March 25, 1982) p. 10.
Note: AG quoted briefly.

Kiesling, Bob and Rogers, Tony. Ranger Interviews Ginsberg. *Ranger,* vol. 10, no. 23 (March 25, 1982) p. 10.
Note: AG interview format.

J3199 Ryan, William F. The Good Fight Of Izzy Stone. *Washington Tribune* (March 26-April 8, 1982) p. 15.
Note: AG quoted briefly.

J3200 Estridge, Larry. A Breakthrough Of Bohemian Culture. *Valley Advocate,* vol. 9, no. 33 (March 31, 1982) pp. 1, 6A-8A.
Note: AG interview format.

J3201 Thurley, Geoffrey. The Beat Poets: Twenty Years On. *Akros,* vol. 17, no. 49 (April 1982) pp. 87-98.

J3202 Norman Mailer. *New Boston Review,* vol. 7, no. 2 (April 1982)

J3203 Rubin, Howard Jay. Ordinary Mind. *Sun,* no. 76 (April 1982) pp. 2-11.
Note: AG interview format, this issue's cover incorrectly states "no. 77".

J3204 Klein, Leif Owen. Speaking With Allen Ginsberg. *Talking Head,* vol. 1, no. 2 (Spring [April 6] 1982) pp. 3, 6.
Note: AG interview format.

J3205 Newmark, Judy J. Poet Allen Ginsberg: The '60s Guru At 55. *St. Louis Post-Dispatch* (April 11, 1982) section I, pp. 3, 9.
Note: AG quoted at length.

J3206 Allen Ginsberg: Kerval Y Yo. *Cambio,* no. 541 (April 12, 1982) pp. 173-174.
Note: AG interview format in Spanish only.

J3207 Ginsberg Conducts Class On 'Beats'. *Daily Camera Review,* vol. 3, no. 5 (April 15, 1982) p. 10.

J3208 O'Connor, Bill. 'Beatnik' Poet Ginsberg Still Writing, Teaching. *Toledo Blade* (April 25, 1982) section D, p. 2.
Note: AG quoted.

J3209 McDowell, Edwin. About Books And Authors. *New York Times Book Review* (April 25, 1982) p. 24.

J3210 Carroll, Charles Francis. [review of *Plutonian Ode*]. *Collegian* (April 28, 1982) p. 10.

J3211 Johnson, Ronna. [review of *First Blues* (Folkways recording)]. *Boston Globe* (April 29, 1982) Calendar Records section, p. 1.

J3212 Wilcox, Brent. [review of *Birdbrain* (recording)]. *OP Magazine* (May-June 1982)

J3213 Weigel, Tom. [review of *Plutonian Ode*]. *Poetry Project Newsletter,* no. 91 (May 1982) pp. [9-10].

J3214 Peel, Mark. [review of *First Blues* (Folkways recording)]. *Stereo Review,* vol. 47 (May 1982) p. 105.

J3215 Levin, S.K. Superpower Poet Sizes Up Nicaragua. *Colorado Daily* (May 7-8, 1982) pp. 1, 4-5, 8.
Note: AG quoted briefly.

Mason, M.S. Naropa's Aesthetic Draw: Investigations By an Alien. *Colorado Daily* (May 7-8, 1982) pp. 13, 16-17.
Note: AG quoted briefly.

J3216 Swanson, Jeffrey. [letter to the editor]. *Colorado Daily* (May 12, 1982) p. 5.

J3217 O'Connor, John J. 'Marco Polo', 'Paik On the Air'. *New York Times* (May 14, 1982) p. C30.

J3218 Jarvis, Elena. Ginsberg's Aura Packs a Punch. *Colorado Springs Gazette-Telegraph* (May 22, 1982) p. A12.
Note: AG quoted briefly.

J3219 Mills, Floyd and Marino, Richard. [letter to the editor]. *Colorado Daily* (May 26-27, 1982) p. 4.

J3220 Becher, Anne. Conference Examines Beatniks. *Owl* (May 28, 1982) pp. 1, 16.
Note: AG quoted briefly.

J3221 Marsh, Steve. Ginsberg On Ginsberg. *Up the Creek,* vol. 8, no. 26 (May 28, 1982) pp. 6-8.
Note: AG interview format.

J3222 Funsten, Kenneth. [review of *Plutonian Ode*]. *Los Angeles Times* (May 30, 1982) Book Review section, p. 13.

J3223 Schumacher, Mike. Ginsberg. *Oui,* vol. 11, no. 6 (June 1982) pp. 82-83, 113-115.
Note: AG interview format.

J3224 Jerome, Judson. American Bards. *Writer's Digest,* vol. 62, no. 6 (June 1982) p. 47.

J3225 Marsh, Steve. Ginsberg On Ginsberg [Continued]. *Up the Creek,* vol. 8, no. 27 (June 4, 1982) p. 7.
Note: AG interview format.

J3226 Palmer, Robert. Poets Put Their Stamp On Rock Lyrics. *New York Times* (June 20, 1982) p. H25.

J3227 Brand, Stewart. [article]. *CoEvolution Quarterly* (Summer 1982) p. 144.
Note: AG quoted briefly.

J3228 Wasserman, Martin. Madness As Religious Experience: The Case Of Allen Ginsberg. *Journal Of Religion And Health,* vol. 21, no. 2 (Summer 1982) pp. 145-151.

J3229   Gilbride, Michael. Catching-up With Allen Ginsberg. *New York City News* (June 23, 1982) p. 17.
Note: AG quoted briefly.

J3230   Poet Ginsberg Ready To 'Howl' At Creede Repertory Reading. *Mineral County Miner,* vol. 7, no. 45 (June 24, 1982) pp. 1A, 16A.

J3231   Young, Allen. Still Ginsberg After All These Years: At 55, the Beat Poet Is Not Afraid To Call Himself an 'Old Fairy'. *Gay News* (June 25-July 8, 1982) pp. 10-11, 17.
Note: AG interview format.

J3232   Ketcham, Diana. [review of *Scratching the Beat Surface* by Michael McClure]. *Oakland Tribune* (June 27, 1982)

J3233   Jack Kerouac To Be Probed. *Denver Post* (June 28, 1982) p. 5C.

J3234   Saltzgaver, H.M. Nothing Dull About the Movement's Poetic Edge. *Mineral County Miner,* vol. 7, no. 46 (July 1, 1982) pp. 1A, 3A.
Note: AG quoted.

Saltzgaver, H.M. Ginsberg's Looks Belie His Radical Perspective. *Mineral County Miner,* vol. 7, no. 46 (July 1, 1982) p. 3A.

J3235   Fields, Rick. On the Road With Jack Kerouac And the Dharma Poets. *New Age,* vol. 7, no. 12 (July 1982) pp. 50-56.
Note: AG quoted briefly.

J3236   Paradise, Sal. One Hour To Gentleness. *Poudre Magazine* (July 1982) p. 8.

J3237   Local Yokel. Allen Ginsberg/Still Life. *Rocky Mtn. Fuse,* no. 5 (ca. July 1982) p. 12.
Note: AG interview format.

J3238   Coleman, Wanda. Strange Susannah, Sweet Susannah. *L.A. Weekly* (July 9-15, 1982) pp. 10-13, 29.

J3239   Boulder Gatherers Will Relive 'Beat Generation'. *Wyoming Eagle* (July 14, 1982) p. 23.
Note: AG quoted briefly.

J3240   Chandler, Kurt. [review of *Birdbrain* (recording)]. *Colorado Daily* (July 16-17, 1982) pp. 9, 16.
Note: AG quoted briefly.

J3241   Beat Generation Gathers July 23. *Ogden Standard-Examiner* (July 17, 1982)
Note: AG quoted briefly.

J3242   Revolt's Over, But '60s Rebels Are Still Left. *Boston Herald American* (July 18, 1982)
Note: AG quoted briefly.

J3243   Sinisi, J. Sebastian. Kerouac Festival To Begin Friday. *Denver Post* (July 18, 1982) section R, p. 2.
Note: AG quoted at length.

J3244   Smith, Brad. Kerouac's 'On the Road'—25 Years Later. *Lowell Sun* (July 18, 1982) pp. C1, C5.
Note: AG quoted.

J3245   Ross, Michael. Conference Will Keep Kerouac's Ideas 'On the Road'. *Sunday Camera* (July 18, 1982) pp. 1, 8.

J3246   Slater, Wayne. 'Beat' Generation Pays Tribute To Author Kerouac. *Malvern Daily Record* (July [20] 1982)
Note: AG quoted briefly.

J3247   'Unprecedented Gathering' To Help Celebrate Anniversary. *Corbin Times-Tribune* (July 21, 1982)
Note: AG quoted briefly.

J3248   'On the Road' Fete Draws Beats To Boulder. *Longmont Daily Times-Call* (July 21, 1982)
Note: AG quoted briefly.

Parmelee, Jennifer. Even Punk Is a Medium For Poet Allen Ginsberg. *Longmont Daily Times-Call* (July 21, 1982)
Note: AG quoted briefly.

J3249   Slater, Wayne. Remembering 'On the Road'. *Santa Cruz Sentinel* (July 21, 1982)
Note: AG quoted briefly.

J3250   Toth, Carolyn. Getting There With Allen Ginsberg. *Audience* (July 22, 1982) p. 13.
Note: AG quoted at length.

J3251   Beat Generation Gathers To Study Kerouac Influence. *Brawley News* (July 22, 1982)
Note: AG quoted briefly.

J3252   Slater, Wayne. American Heart 'Beats' Anew In Boulder Tribute. *Colorado Springs Gazette-Telegraph* (July 22, 1982)
Note: AG quoted briefly.

J3253   Ross, Michael. Kerouac Festival Brings Literary Lights To Boulder. *Daily Camera* (July 22, 1982) Review section, p. 5.

J3254   Keasler, John. Up In Boulder And On the Road, the Beat Goes On. *Miami News* (July 22, 1982)

J3255   Slater, Wayne. The Beat Generation Remembers Kerouac. *Morning News* (July 22, 1982) p. D8.
Note: AG quoted briefly.

J3256   'Beat Generation's' Artists Plan Tribute To Jack Kerouac. *Providence Journal* (July 22, 1982)
Note: AG quoted briefly.

J3257   Slater, Wayne. They're Keeping 'Beat'. *State News* (July 22, 1982) p. 27.
Note: AG quoted briefly.

J3258   Kerouac King Of the Beats. *Boston Herald American* (July 23, 1982)
Note: AG quoted.

J3259   Nixon, Eli. Kerouac Conference Proves 'Beat' Goes On. *Daily Camera* (July 23, 1982) p. 1.

J3260   Blonston, Gary. Ginsberg Savoring a Reunion Of the Beat. *Detroit Free Press* (July 23, 1982) pp. 1A, 15A.
Note: AG quoted at length.

J3261   Bernheimer, Kathryn. Follower Celebrates Kerouac's Literary Prowess. *Daily Camera* (July 26, 1982)

J3262   Wheelan, Joe. '50s Activists Discuss the Beat Generation. *Fresno Bee* (July 26, 1982)
Note: AG quoted briefly.

J3263   The '50s Beat Generation Celebrates Leap To '80s. *Los Angeles Herald Examiner* (July 26, 1982)
Note: AG quoted briefly.

J3264   The Beats Go On At 10-Day Gathering Of Dingledodies. *Los Angeles Times* (July 26, 1982)
Note: AG quoted briefly.

J3265   Then And Now: Picking Up the Beat Of an Earlier Generation. *Newsday* (July 26, 1982)
Note: AG quoted briefly.

J3266   Wheelan, Joe. The Beat Generation Is Alive And Well In Boulder, Colo. *Oakland Tribune* (July 26, 1982)
Note: AG quoted briefly.

J3267   Beats Of the '50s Seek To Define Their Influence On '80s America. *Providence Journal* (July 26, 1982)

J3268   Take Power, Leary Urges Hippies, Beats. *Riverside Enterprise* (July 26, 1982)
Note: AG quoted briefly.

J3269   Beat Generation Stirs New Echo. *San Francisco Chronicle* (July 26, 1982) p. 2.
Note: AG quoted briefly.

J3270   Turn On, Tune In And Please Take Over. *San Jose Mercury News* (July 26, 1982)
Note: AG quoted briefly.

J3271   Salute Given To Beat Generation. *Santa Ana Register* (July 26, 1982)
Note: AG quoted briefly.

J3272   New Leary Tune. *Santa Rosa Press Democrat* (July 26, 1982)
Note: AG quoted briefly.

J3273   'The Beats Are Alive Today,' Hoffman Says Of '50 Cultists. *Syracuse Post-Standard* (July 26, 1982)
Note: AG quoted briefly.

J3274   Allen, Henry. Back On the Beat Path. *Washington Post* (July 26, 1982)
Note: AG quoted briefly.

J3275   Beat Generation Remnants Meet. *Worcester Telegram* (July 26, 1982) p. 14B.
Note: AG quoted briefly.

J3276   Kessner, Richard. The Beatniks. *Baltimore Sun* (July 27, 1982)

J3277 Smith, Brad. 'On the Road' Again. *Detroit News* (July 27, 1982) section B, pp. 1B, 3B.
Note: AG quoted briefly.

J3278 [article]. *Hartford Courant* (July 27, 1982)
Note: AG quoted briefly.

J3279 Tuesday's People. *Washington Times* (July 27, 1982)
Note: AG quoted briefly.

J3280 Bernheimer, Kathryn. Kerouac And Women. *Daily Camera* (July 28, 1982) pp. 23, 26.

J3281 Ashton, John. Kerouac Panel Recalls 'Old Days' In Denver. *Rocky Mountain News* (July 28, 1982) p. 52.
Note: AG quoted.

J3282 Ashton, John. Conversation With Ginsberg, Holmes. *Rocky Mountain News* (July 29, 1982) pp. 18-19.
Note: AG interview format.

J3283 Mason, M.S. Kerouac: Hearing the Poet's Own Voice. *Colorado Daily* (July 30-31, 1982) pp. 8-9, 19.

J3284 Schmidt, William E. Beat Generation Elders Meet To Praise Kerouac. *New York Times* (July 30, 1982) p. A8.
Note: AG quoted briefly.

J3285 Clurman, Irene. Many Visual Impressions Pay Tribute To Kerouac. *Rocky Mountain News* (July 30, 1982)

J3286 Kimelman, Donald. Kerouac In the '80s. *Seattle Times* (July 30, 1982) section C.
Note: AG quoted briefly.

J3287 Schmidt, William E. Beats Go On the Road To Celebrate Kerouac. *Baltimore Sun* (July 31, 1982) p. A8.
Note: AG quoted briefly.

J3288 Schmidt, William E. Beat Generation's Veterans, Fans Meet To Celebrate Kerouac. *Santa Ana Register* (July 31, 1982)
Note: AG quoted briefly.

J3289 Schmidt, William E. Aging 'Beat Generation' Honors 'The King'. *Bremerton Sun* (Aug. 1, 1982)
Note: AG quoted briefly.

J3290 Schmidt, William E. Friends, Admirers Honor King Of the Beats. *Contra Costa Independent* (Aug. 1, 1982)
Note: AG quoted briefly.

J3291 Intervju Med Allen Ginsberg. *Gateavisa,* no. 8 (Aug. 1982) pp. 12-15, 39.
Note: AG interview format in Norwegian only.

J3292 [review of *First Blues* (Folkways recording)]. *Goldmine* (Aug. 1982)

J3293 Kherman-Sekulin, Maja. Za "Knizheviu Rech" Govori Alen Ginzberg. *Knizhevna Rech* (Aug. 1982)
Note: AG interview format in Serbo-Croatian only.

J3294   Milankov, Ivana. Pesma Kao Dijagram Mikli. *Knizhevnost,* no. 9 ([Aug.] 1982) pp. 1354-1361.
Note: AG interview format in Serbo-Croatian.

J3295   Bernard, Sidney. Permanent Floating 24-Hour Poetry Readings. *Newsart* (Aug. 1982) p. 31.

Dorn, Ed. The Politics Of Poetics. *Newsart* (Aug. 1982) pp. 77-78, 27-29.

J3296   Mohrhenn, Wolfgang. Über Die Abschaffung Der Nationen. *Schreibheft, Zeitschrift Für Literatur,* no. 19 (Aug. 1982) pp. 31-32.

J3297   Nixon, Eli. Kerouac Conferees Divided On Future. *Daily Camera* (Aug. 2, 1982) pp. 1, 6.

J3298   Allen, Henry. 'On the Road' Again And Mad To Remember. *Washington Post* (Aug. 2, 1982) pp. C1-C3.
Note: AG quoted briefly.

J3299   Dortmund, Erhard. Beat Writer Kerouac Misunderstood. *Longview News* (Aug. 7, 1982)

J3300   Ashton, John. Gentle-Heart Beats. *Rocky Mountain News* (Aug. 8, 1982) pp. 2-N, 5-N.
Note: AG quoted briefly.

J3301   Zorn, Eric. Jack Kerouac's Beat Goes On, But Not Without Question. *Chicago Tribune* (Aug. 9, 1982) section 2, pp. 1, 4.
Note: AG quoted briefly.

J3302   Tucker, Ernest. The Clash's Slide Show Is Chattering Sideshow. *Rocky Mountain News* (Aug. 10, 1982) p. 53.

J3303   Johnson, Ronna. Celebrating Jack Kerouac And the Beats. *Boston Globe* (Aug. 12, 1982) pp. 57-58.
Note: AG quoted briefly.

J3304   Chandler, Kurt. British Clash Take Red Rocks By Force. *Daily Camera* (Aug. 13-14, 1982) pp. 8-9.

J3305   Becker, Bart. Howling With Allen Ginsberg. *Lincoln Journal* (Aug. 15, 1982)

J3306   [photo and caption]. *New Mexican* (Aug. 16, 1982) p. A2.

J3307   Zorn, Eric. Kerouac. *St. Louis Globe-Democrat* (Aug. 16, 1982) section B, p. 1.
Note: AG quoted briefly.

J3308   Graybill, Robert. Class Reunion For Woodstock Nation. *Santa Fe Reporter* (Aug. 18, 1982) pp. 24, 18.
Note: AG quoted briefly.

J3309   Doherty, Will. Certain Bohemian Truths: Talking With Allen Ginsberg. *Gay Community News,* vol. 10, no. 6 (Aug. 21, 1982) pp. 8-12.
Note: AG interview format.

J3310   Moramarco, Fred. Moloch's Poet: A Retrospective Look At Allen Ginsberg's Poetry. *American Poetry Review,* vol. 11, no. 5 (Sept.-Oct. 1982) pp. 10-14, 16-18.

J3311   Davis, Stephen. S-Punk Rock [review of *Blakes' Greatest Hits* and *Birdbrain* (recording)]. *New Age* (Sept. 1982) pp. 68, 70.

J3312   Slattery, Bob. Summer Freeze. *New Life News,* vol. 3, no. 8 (Sept. 1982) pp. 8-9.

J3313   Abbott, Steve. Camp Kerouac. *Poetry Flash,* no. 114 (Sept. 1982) pp. 1-2. *Note:* AG quoted briefly.

J3314   Lally, Michael. How To Publish Friends And Influence People [review of *First Blues* (Hammond recording)]. *Voice Literary Supplement* (Sept. 1982) pp. 21-22.

J3315   Pivano, Fernanda. Quello Che Rimane Della "Beat Generation". *Corriere Della Sera* (Sept. 7, 1982)

J3316   Pett, Sukey. Magic Revisited. *Aquarian* (Sept. 8-15, 1982) p. 5A.

J3317   Carroll, Charles Francis. Mariani Presents a New View Of an American Poet. *Campus Connection,* vol. 2, no. 2 (Sept. 8, 1982) pp. 3-4.

J3318   Todd, Paula. Voice Music On Film. *Excalibur* (Sept. 9, 1982) p. 8.

J3319   Brouillette, Paul. Visions Of Kerouac. *Gay Community News,* vol. 10, no. 8 (Sept. 11, 1982) pp. 12, 15.

J3320   Tucker, Ernest. Shrill Message Garbled. *Rocky Mountain News* (Sept. 12, 1982) p. 33N.

J3321   Scott, Jay. Poetry Movie a Delightful Surprise. *Globe And Mail* (Sept. 17, 1982)

J3322   Peters, Robert. Gifted Letters With a Weird Grandeur. *Los Angeles Times* (Sept. 19, 1982) p. 15.

J3323   Pincus, Robert. The Open Road Of Risk: George Herms, Wallace Berman, the Beats And West Coast Visionary Poetics. *Journal Of the Los Angeles Institute Of Contemporary Art* (Fall 1982) pp. 50-55.

J3324   Gall, Sally M. Domestic Monologues: The Problem Of Voice In Contemporary American Poetry. *Massachusetts Review,* vol. 23, no. 3 (Autumn 1982) pp. 489-503.

J3325   Ryan, William. Blake—Light Tragedy Among the Scholars Of War. *Moody Street Irregulars,* no. 12 (Fall 1982) pp. 18-21. *Note:* AG interview format.

J3326   [Transcript Of Discussion With Questions And Statements By AG]. *Naropa Institute Bulletin* (Fall 1982-Winter 1983) p. 4. *Note:* AG interview format.

J3327   Castro, Jan Garden: Castro, Michael and Mondello, John. Interview With Allen Ginsberg April 5, 1982, St. Louis. *River Styx,* no. 12 ([Fall] 1982) pp. 42-59. *Note:* AG interview format.

J3328   Stimpson, Catharine R. The Beat Generation And the Trials Of Homosexual Liberation. *Salmagundi,* no. 58-59 (Fall 1982-Winter 1983) pp. 373-392.

J3329   Owens, Christopher D. Kerouac Fans Gather — And the Beat Goes On. *Kansas City Star* (Sept. 26, 1982)

J3330   Mehren, Elizabeth. Writers Turn Their Talents To Diplomacy. *Los Angeles Times* (Sept. 29, 1982) View section, pp. 1, 8-9.
Note: AG quoted briefly.

J3331   Sloman, Larry and Barkin, George. Interview. *High Times,* no. 86 (Oct. 1982) pp. 32-37, 84-85.
Note: AG quoted.

J3332   Pivano, Fernanda. Che Fine Ha Fatto La "Beat Generation". *Leader* (Oct. 1982) pp. 24-27.

J3333   Stark, Andy. The Beat Convention. *New Criterion,* vol. 1, no. 2 (Oct. 1982) pp. 84-88.
Note: AG quoted briefly.

J3334   Shropshire, Neil. Beat Riffs Beat Raps: The Jack Kerouac Conference. *Poudre Magazine,* vol. 2, no. 8 (Oct. 1982) pp. 12-15.

J3335   Beats Challenge '80s With New Tunes. *State Of the Unions* (Oct. 1982) pp. 1, 6.

J3336   Hunter, Bob. On the Road Again. *Vancouver Sun* (Oct. 1982) pp. 106-112.
Note: AG quoted briefly.

J3337   Rubin, Daniel. Ginsberg, Radical Poet Still Writing To Own Beat...Opinions-Appearances At Annual Literary Festival, Old Dominion University. *Virginia Pilot* (Oct. 1, 1982) section B, pp. 1, B9.
Note: AG quoted.

J3338   Eichinger, Mariellen. Ginsberg Intoxicates School With His Poetry. *Mace And Crown* (Oct. 7, 1982)
Note: AG interview format.

J3339   Ranard, Andrew. Three Beats To the Measure. *City Lights,* vol. 3, no. 4 (Oct. 8-21, 1982) p. 4.

J3340   Davis, Nancy. Allen Ginsberg: Still Howling. *Times-Herald* (Oct. 9, 1982) Leisure section, pp. L3-4.
Note: AG quoted.

J3341   Moffet, Penelope. [review of *Plutonian Ode*]. *Los Angeles Times* (Oct. 17, 1982) Book Review section, p. 2.

J3342   Davis, Phil. 'Beat' Artists Delight, Fascinate. *Capital Times* (Oct. 19, 1982) p. 16.

J3343   Beat Writers Have Reunion. *Wisconsin State Journal* (Oct. 19, 1982) section 3, p. 1.
Note: AG quoted briefly.

J3344   Kart, Larry. Trio Keeps Up the Beat. *Chicago Tribune* (Oct. 20, 1982) section 4, p. 6.

J3345   Kurtz, Josh and St. Germaine, Anne. An Old Beat a New Tune? Three Legends In Madison. *Daily Cardinal* (Oct. 22, 1982) pp. 7, 9-10.
Note: AG quoted briefly.

J3346 Butler, Patrick. Allen Ginsberg—The Beat Goes On. *Weekend Booster* (Oct. 23-24, 1982) pp. 1, 12.
Note: AG quoted briefly.

J3347 Parmelee, Jennifer. From Howl To Harmony With Ginsberg. *Bergen Record* (Oct. 24, 1982) pp. C1, C18.
Note: AG quoted.

J3348 Parmelee, Jennifer. From Beat To Punk. *Houston Post* (Oct. 24, 1982) section F, p. 18F.
Note: AG quoted briefly.

J3349 Ruas, Charles. Susan Sontag: Past, Present And Future. *New York Times Book Review* (Oct. 24, 1982) pp. 11, 39-40.

J3350 Parmelee, Jennifer. Allen Ginsberg Howling With a Punk Band Now. *San Francisco Sunday Examiner And Chronicle* (Oct. 24, 1982) p. A2.
Note: AG quoted briefly.

J3351 Clark, Rod. Beats Go On. *Isthmus Of Madison* (Oct. 29, 1982) p. 3.

J3352 Brown, Gordon. New Film Makes Poetry a Performing Art. *Inside* (Nov. 1982)

J3353 Goldman, Connie. Allen Ginsberg. *Nit & Wit,* vol. 4, no. 6 (Nov.-Dec. 1982) pp. 54-55.
Note: AG interview format.

J3354 Smith, Steven. Poetry: Out Of the Closet And Onto the Screen. *Toronto Arts* (Nov. 1982) p. 6.

J3355 Stewart, Judy L. Ginsberg Blends Poetry With Rock. *Colorado Springs Sun* (Nov. 5, 1982) Weekend section, pp. 2, 19.
Note: AG quoted.

J3356 Brumer, Andy. Penetrating Spirit & 'Moral Hermit' [review of *Plutonian Ode*]. *San Francisco Chronicle* (Nov. 7, 1982) Review section, p. 13.

J3357 Hillen, Steven. Mann's Film Fate. *Now* (Nov. 11-17, 1982) p. 7.

J3358 Schlesinger, Toni. The Beats Go On. *Reader* (Nov. 12, 1982) pp. 51-52.

J3359 Logan, William. [review of *Plutonian Ode*]. *Times Literary Supplement,* no. 4154 (Nov. 12, 1982) p. 1251.

J3360 Kirkland, Bruce. Filmmaker Is Hot Stuff. *Toronto Sun* (Nov. 17, 1982) p. 75.

J3361 Frieberg, Camelia. Poetry In Motion Refreshing. *Contrast* (Nov. 19, 1982)

J3362 Mietkiewicz, Henry. Poetic Probe Full Of Ironies. *Toronto Star* (Nov. 19, 1982) p. D3.

J3363 Robert Kirsch Award Goes To Novelist Ross Macdonald. *Los Angeles Times* (Nov. 20, 1982) p. 1.

J3364 [review of *Plutonian Ode*]. *Los Angeles Times* (Nov. 21, 1982) Book Review section, p. 1.

J3365 Kirkland, Bruce. Film Chronicles Modern Poets In Motion. *Sunday Sun* (Nov. 21, 1982) p. 74.

J3366   Bemrose, John. Public Displays Of an Ancient Art. *Maclean's* (Nov. 22, 1982)

J3367   Parmelee, Jennifer. Ginsberg Going Strong As Punk Rocker. *Los Angeles Times* (Nov. 26, 1982) section XI, p. 3.
Note: AG quoted.

J3368   Fulford, Robert. As Poets, They're Great Performers. *Toronto Star* (Nov. 27, 1982) p. F5.

J3369   Bernheimer, Kathryn. Ginsberg's Revolution Evolves Into Film. *Sunday Camera* (Dec. 1982) pp. 1C, 9C.

J3370   Cohn, Robert A. Allen Ginsberg 'Howls' His Poems; Discusses His Jewishness In Exclusive Interview. *St. Louis Jewish Light* (Dec. 1, 1982) p. 7.
Note: AG quoted.

J3371   Clarke, Cera. [letter to the editor]. *Now* (Dec. 2-8, 1982)

J3372   Brumer, Andy. [review of *Plutonian Ode*]. *San Francisco Chronicle* (Dec. 5, 1982) p. 19.

J3373   Salvatori, Olivier. Allen Ginsberg, Toujours À La Pointe. *Libération* (Dec. 10, 1982) p. 5.
Note: AG quoted briefly in French only.

J3374   Guicciardi, Elena. "Guerra Alla Guerra" Mille Poeti A Parigi Per Un Festival All'Insegna Della Pace. *La Repubblica* (Dec. 12-13, 1982)

Ravizza, Filippo. I Poeti Sbarcano A Milano. *La Repubblica* (Dec. 12-13, 1982) p. 33.

J3375   *Voix Des Poétes.* Créteil, France: Dec. 12, 1982. Produced by Polyphonix.
Note: Handout at reading contains AG quotes translated by Jean-Jacques Lebel in French only.

J3376   Kasam, Viviana. Poeti D'Ogni Parte Del Mondo Cantano A Brera Contro La Barbarie, La Violenza E La Guerra. *Corriere Della Sera* (Dec. 14, 1982)

J3377   Klad. Poetry In Motion. *Variety* (Dec. 15, 1982)

J3378   Pivano, Fernanda. Artisti Di Tutto Il Mondo A Milano Hanno Dichiarato "Guerra Alla Guerra". *Corriere Della Sera* (Dec. 16, 1982)

J3379   Gabutti, Diego. La Poesia Sul Bastimento Della Pace. *Il Giornale* (Dec. 16, 1982)

J3380   "No" Alla Guerra Con Ginsberg E Tanti Poeti. *Il Giorno* (Dec. 16, 1982)

J3381   Curtin, John. A Howl At War, By Allen Ginsberg. *International Herald Tribune* (Dec. 17, 1982) Weekend section, pp. 7W, 10W.
Note: AG quoted briefly.

J3382   Ravizza, Filippo. Questa Guerra Dei Poeti Has Coinvolto I Milanesi. *La Repubblica* (Dec. 17, 1982) Milano section, p. 1.

J3383   Rota, Ornella. Ginsberg, Vecchia Anima Beat Al Meeting Contro La Guerra. *La Stampa* (Dec. 18, 1982)

J3384   C., M. Intanto Con Ferlinghetti I Poeti Sfidano La Guerra. *L'Unita* (Dec. 18, 1982)

J3385   Pivano, Fernanda. A Milano Poeti Di Tutto Il Mondo Hanno Detto "Guerra Alla Guerra". *Corriere Della Sera* (Dec. 19, 1982)

J3386   Recontre Avec Rimbaud. *Le Ardennais* (Dec. 21, 1982)

J3387   Barron, Len. Introduction Overvue: An Interview With Allen Ginsberg. *Friction*, vol. 1, no. 2-3 (Winter 1982) pp. 7-19.
Note: AG interview format.

Another Round: A Play In Three Acts. *Friction*, vol. 1, no. 2-3 (Winter 1982) pp. 86-88.
Note: AG quoted briefly.

Act II: The Washington Post. *Friction*, vol. 1, no. 2-3 (Winter 1982) pp. 89-96.
Note: AG quoted briefly.

J3388   "Noël Sur La Terre": Rencontres Arthur Rimbaud À Charleville-Mézières. *L'Union* (Dec. 22, 1982) p. 12.
Note: AG quoted briefly.

Braun, Daniel. Alan Ginsberg, Le "Pape" De La Beat Génération: "La Poésie, Elle Aussi, Est Capable De Changer La Vie". *L'Union* (Dec. 22, 1982) p. 12.
Note: AG interview format in French only.

J3389   Kotterer, Frans. Veel Mediteren En Veel Klaarkomen. *Het Parool* (Dec. 27, 1982)
Note: AG interview format in Dutch only.

J3390   De Waard, Elly. Wereldmachten Spelen Gelijk In Poezie-Wedstrijd. *De Volkskrant* (Dec. 31, 1982) p. 9.

J3391   MacAdams, Lewis. Kerouac Is Alive! *High Performance*, vol. 5, no. 3 [issue 19] (1982) pp. 16-23.
Note: AG quoted briefly.

J3392   Ucenje O Svesnom U Meditaciji Je U Istom Duhu Kao I Stvaranje Poezije. *Lica*, vol. 10, no. 9-10 (1982) pp. 35-36.
Note: AG quoted in Serbo-Croatian only.

J3393*   Orbán, Ottó. Ginsberg In Budapest. *New Hungarian Quarterly*, vol. 23, no. 86 (1982) pp. 91-93.

J3394   [review of *Gaté* (recording)]. *Razzamatazza*, no. 6 [1982]

J3395   Dean, John. Expressions Of Protest In American Popular Culture In the Fifties. *Recherches Anglaises Et Américaines*, no. 15 (1982) pp. 171-192.

J3396   [review of *Birdbrain* (recording)]. *Rocky Mountain Fuse*, no. 2 (1982) p. 9.

Books:

J3397   Amirthanayagam, Guy (ed.). *Writers In East-West Encounter*. London, England: Macmillan Press, 1982.
Contents: Portugés, Paul and Amirthanayagam, Guy. Buddhist Mediation And Poetic Spontaneity, pp. 10-31.
Note: AG quoted.

J3398 Behr, Hans-Georg. *Von Hanf Ist Die Rede.* Basel, Switzerland: Sphinx Verlag, 1982, pp. 215, 220.
Note: AG quoted briefly in German only.

J3399 Berman, Marshall. *All That Is Solid Melts Into Air.* New York, NY: Simon & Schuster, 1982.
Note: AG mentioned throughout.

J3400 Burroughs, William S. *Letters To Allen Ginsberg: 1953-1957.* New York, NY: Full Court Press, 1982.
Note: AG mentioned throughout.

J3401 Faas, Ekbert (ed.). *La Nuova Poetica Americana.* Milan, Italy: Newton Compton Editori, 1982.
Note: AG interview format in Italian only.

J3402 Fo, Dario. *L'Opera Della Sghignazzo.* Milan, Italy: Edizioni F.R. La Comune, 1982.
Note: Play inspired by the lyrics of AG and others.

J3403 Gefin, Laszlo. *Ideogram: History Of a Poetic Method.* Austin, TX: University Of Texas Press, 1982.
Note: AG mentioned throughout.

J3404 Gysin, Brion. *Here To Go: Planet R-101.* London, England: Quartet Books, 1982.
Note: AG mentioned throughout.

J3405 Hall, Donald. *To Read Poetry.* New York, NY: Holt, Rinehart & Winston, 1982.
Note: AG mentioned throughout.

J3406 Hart, Jeffrey. *When the Going Was Good!* New York, NY: Crown, 1982.
Note: AG mentioned throughout.

J3407 Hornick, Lita. *Night Flight.* New York, NY: Kulchur Foundation, 1982.
Note: AG mentioned throughout and quoted.

J3408 Kopcewicz, Andrzej and Sienicka, Marta. *Historia Literatury Stanow Zjednoczonych W Zarysie.* Warsaw, Poland: Panstwowe Wydawnictwo Naukowe, 1982.
Note: AG mentioned throughout.

J3409 Kostelanetz, Richard (ed.). *American Writing Today, vol. 1.* Washington, DC: Book Programs Division, Educational And Cultural Affairs Directorate, United States International Communication Agency, 1982.
Contents: Kostelanetz, Richard. An Interview With Allen Ginsberg, pp. 218-234.
Note: AG interview format.

J3410 Leyland, Winston (ed.). *Consules De Sodoma, vol. 1.* Barcelona, Spain: Tusquets Editores, 1982, pp. 15-69. [Series: Cuadernos Infimos 102]
Note: AG interview with Allen Young translated by Eduardo Wards Simon into Spanish only.

J3411 McBride, Dick. *Cometh With Clouds (Memory: Allen Ginsberg).* Cherry Valley, NY: Cherry Valley Edition, 1982.
Note: AG mentioned throughout and quoted briefly.

J3412 McClure, Michael. *Scratching the Beat Surface.* San Francisco, CA: North Point Press, 1982.
Note: AG mentioned throughout.

J3413 Magill, Frank N. (ed.). *Critical Survey Of Poetry, vol. 3.* Englewood Cliffs, NJ: Salem Press, 1982.
Contents: Guereschi, Edward. Allen Ginsberg, pp. 1088-1096.

J3414 Milosz, Czeslaw. *Visions From San Francisco Bay.* New York, NY: Farrar Straus & Giroux, 1982.
Note: AG mentioned throughout.

J3415 Montgomery, John (ed.). *The Kerouac We Knew.* Kentfield, CA: Fels & Firn Press, 1982.
Note: AG mentioned throughout.

J3416 Patterson, Tom and Allgood, Steve (eds.). *Red Hand Book III.* Atlanta, GA: Pynyon Press, 1982.
Contents: Feldman, Mitchell. Words And Music, Music, Music, pp. 76-85.
Note: AG interview format.

J3417 Peters, Robert. *The Great American Poetry Bake-Off.* [Second Series]. Metuchen, NJ: Scarecrow Press, 1982, p. 222.
Note: Review of *Straight Heart's Delight.*

J3418 Smith, David. *Closer To Jesus.* Los Angeles, CA: Ouija Madness Press, 1982, p. 16.

J3419 Stein, Jean. *Edie: An American Biography.* New York, NY: Knopf, 1982.
Note: AG mentioned throughout and briefly quoted.

J3420 Vono, Augusta Maria S. *Allen Ginsberg: Through the Gates Into Freedom.* Unpublished Master's Thesis. Sao Paulo, Brazil: Universidade Federal De Minas Gerais, 1982.

1983

J3421 Into, Markku. U—Miehet Kohtasivat Kristallinen Sylki Valaisi Vanhan. *Aloha!* (Jan. 1983) pp. 44-47.

J3422 [review of *First Blues* (Hammond recording)]. *Christopher Street,* vol. 6, no. 11 (Jan. 1983) pp. 12-13.

J3423 Hartt, Laurinda. Poetry In Motion. *Cinema Canada* (Jan. 1983) p. 42.

J3424 Into, Markku. Ginsberg. *Folkjournalen* (Jan. 1983) pp. 8-9.

J3425 Olsen, Tore. Rebellen "Carlo Marx" Alias Allen Ginsberg, Was In Town. *Musikkavisen Puls,* no. 3/83 ([Jan.-Feb.] 1983) pp. 21, 34.
Note: AG interview format in Norwegian only.

Olsen, Tore. The Beat Goes On. *Musikkavisen Puls,* no. 3/83 ([Jan.-Feb.] 1983) pp. 22-23.

J3426 Johansen, Ib. Allen Ginsberg I Danmark. *Information* (Jan. 3, 1983)

J3427 Van Son, J. D. Een Blijzieke Partij Op Nieuwjaarsdag. *Provinciale Zeeuwse Courant* (Jan. 3, 1983) p. 13.

J3428   Blom, Peter. Allen Ginsberg In Groningen: 'Beat-Dichter' Als Zanger. *Nieuwsblad Van Het Noorden* (Jan. 7, 1983) p. 23.

J3429   Bille, Torben. Den Moderne Lyriks Afskyelige Snemand. *Politiken* (Jan. 7, 1983) p. 4.

J3430   Thygesen, Erik. Allen Ginsberg. *Information* (Jan. 8, 1983)

J3431   Jørgensen, Birger. Skriget, Der Gav Genlyd. *Aarhuus Stiftstidende* (Jan. 9, 1983)

J3432   B., L. 60'ernes Hyl Er Nået Hertil. *Frederiksborg Amts Avis* (Jan. 9, 1983)

J3433   Ginsberg Blokeret. *Information,* vol. 39, no. 7 (Jan. 10, 1983) p. 1.

J3434   Hellmann, Helle. En Rejsende I Vibrationer. *Politiken,* vol. 99, no. 99 (Jan. 10, 1983) section 2, p. 1.
Note: AG quoted briefly in Danish only.

J3435   Hvidt, Erik. Digteren Som Samfundsrevser. *Berlingske Tidende* (Jan. 11, 1983)

J3436   Jensen, Anders Rou. Galskabens Grovkornede Sarkasme. *Aarhuus Stiftstidende* (Jan. 12, 1983)

J3437   B., L. Giraffen Var Her. *Frederiksborg Amts Avis* (Jan. 12, 1983)
Note: AG quoted briefly in Danish only.

J3438   Bille, Torben. Gaest Fra En Anden Tid. *Politiken* (Jan. 12, 1983)

J3439   Kis. Ginsbergs Folkelige Avantgarde. *Herning Folkeblad* (Jan. 14, 1983) p. 4.

J3440   Terp, Knud. Det Begyndte Med Et Hyl... *Fyens Stiftstidende* (Jan. 15, 1983)
Note: AG quoted briefly in Danish only.

J3441   Jensen, Kirsten. Verdens Aeldste Hippie. *Herning Folkeblad* (Jan. 19, 1983)
Note: AG interview format in Danish only.

J3442   Terp, Knud. Ginsbergs Jazz-Slang Er Moderne Folkemusik. *Frederiksborg Amts Avis* (Jan. 20, 1983)
Note: AG quoted briefly in Danish only.

J3443   Beat—Ginsberg. *Ylioppilaslehti* (Jan. 20, 1983)

J3444   Mortensen, Per. En Anspråkslös Poet Och Lärare. *Dagens Nyheter* (Jan. 24, 1983) p. 20.
Note: AG quoted briefly in Swedish only.

J3445   Strömdahl, Ingrid. Humor Och Distans. *Svenska Dagbladet* (Jan. 24, 1983)
Note: AG quoted briefly in Swedish only.

J3446   Von Malmborg, Ingvar. Häxmästare Poet, Guru. *Stockholms Tidningen* (Jan. 26, 1983)
Note: AG interview format in Swedish only.

J3447   Jónsson, Jón Sveinbjørn. "Hyl"—Pappa Kommer Til Byen. *Klassekampen,* no. 22 (Jan. 27, 1983) p. 5.

J3448   Angell, Olav. Ginsberg Til Norga. *Arbeiderbladet* (Jan. 28, 1983) p. 14.

J3449 Wandrup, Fredrik. Opprørsguruen Som Vil Se "The Fjords". *Dagbladet* (Jan. 28, 1983) p. 5.

J3450 Allen Ginsberg Suomeen. *Helsingin Sanomat* (Jan. 28, 1983)

J3451 Kokko, Karri. Vauhtia Runouteen. *Ilta-Sanomat* (Jan. 28, 1983)

J3452 Albret, Poul. Digte Kan Kommunikere På Et Meget Dybt Plan. *Information,* vol. 39, no. 24 (Jan. 29-30, 1983) p. 8.
Note: AG interview format in Danish only.

J3453 Forsblom, Harry. Allen Ginsberg Ei Anna Periksi. *Helsingin Sanomat* (Jan. 30, 1983) p. 14.
Note: AG quoted briefly in Finnish only.

J3454 Kresh, Paul. With Poets At the Microphone, the Words Are Often Music. *New York Times* (Jan. 30, 1983) p. 23H.

J3455 Niiniluoto, Maarit. Tulee Mieleen, Että Minä Olen Amerikka. *Uusi Suomi* (Jan. 30, 1983) p. 14.

J3456 Wandrup, Fredrik and Martinsen, Tom. Sirkus Ginsberg For Broket Forsamling. *Dagbladet* (Jan. 31, 1983)

J3457 Kokko, Karri. Yksi On Huuto Ylitse Muiden. *Ilta-Sanomat* (Jan. 31, 1983) p. 11.

J3458 Renberg, Ulf. Ginsberg—En Fest For Livet. *Arbeiderbladet* (Feb. 1, 1983) p. 15.

J3459 Christian. Ginsberg I Oslo. *Gateavisa,* no. 2 (Feb. 1983) p. 40.

J3460 Kover, Jonas. Utica Is Home To One Of the Last Beatnik Poets. *Observer Dispatch* (Feb.-March 1983)

J3461 Fuller, Mark and Daruvalla, Abi. And the Beat Goes On... *Other Paper,* no. 8 (Feb. 1983) pp. 1, 11.
Note: AG quoted.

J3462 Von Rosen, Wilhelm. Farvel Maskine. *Pan,* vol. 29, no. 1 (Feb.-March 1983) pp. 24-25.
Note: AG interview format in Danish only.

J3463 Keschke, Uwe. Allen Ginsberg. *Pavillon Notizen* (Feb. 1983) p. 9.

J3464 Daley, John. On the Road: A Beat Convention. *Poetry Project Newsletter,* no. 96 (Feb. 1983) pp. 10-11.

J3465 [flyer]. *Pumpwerk* (Feb. 1983)
Note: AG quoted briefly in German only.

J3466 Lystad, Magne and Skau, Jan Erik. Optimistisk Hippie-Poet. *Rampelys* (Feb. 1, 1983) p. 37.

J3467 Allen Ginsberg. *Ruhrgebeit* (Feb. 1983) p. 79.

J3468 Pietikainen, Seppo. Päivä Legendan Seurassa. *Soundi* (Feb. 1983) pp. 22-23.
Note: AG quoted briefly in Finnish only.

J3469   Ginsberg. *Stene* (Feb. 1983)

J3470   Mohrhenn, Wolfgang. Allen Ginsberg In Wuppertal. *Überblick* (Feb. 1983) p. 94.

J3471   L., G. Mit "Akustischer Literatur" Neue Wege Für Die "Pumpwerk"—Besucher Eröffnen. *Wilhelmshavener Zeitung* (Feb. 1, 1983) p. 4.

J3472   Wandrup, Fredrik and Martinsen, Tom. Lutefisk Og LSD. *Dagbladet* (Feb. 2, 1983) p. 4.

J3473   Mannheimer, Otto. Jag Talar Med Tre Röster. *Dagens Nyheter* (Feb. 3, 1983) p. 4.
    Note: AG interview format in Swedish only.

J3474   Lubowski, Bernd. Amerikas Literarisches Gewissen. *Hamburg Abendzeitung* (Feb. 3, 1983)
    Note: AG quoted briefly in German only.

J3475   Pajukallio, Arto. Beatrunoilijan Kantrivalssit. *Kansan Uutiset* (Feb. 3, 1983)

J3476   "Pumpwerk" Will Den Zugang Zur Literatur Erleichtern. *Neue Wilhelmshavener Zeitung* (Feb. 4, 1983)

J3477   Helliesen, Morten and Johansen, Terje. Fretex Og Sild For Ginsberg. *Rogalands Avis,* vol. 85, no. 29 (Feb. 4, 1983) pp. 1, 5.

J3478   Mallander, J.O. Allen Ginsberg: "Ilman Pysyvää Viitekehystä". *Suomi,* no. 1/1983 (Feb. 4, 1983) pp. 5-7.
    Note: AG quoted in Finnish only.

J3479   Allen Ginsberg. *Taz Hamburg* (Feb. 4, 1983) p. 18.

J3480   Henriksen, Joan. Samme Budskap—Ny Puls. *Stavanger Aftenblad* (Feb. 5, 1983) p. 5.
    Note: AG quoted in Norwegian only.

    Lode, Asgeir and Friestad, Jonas. Atomtrusselen En Bløff! *Stavanger Aftenblad* (Feb. 5, 1983) p. 5.

J3481   Toijonen, Vesa. Hae Se Passilauma Tanne. *Kansan Uutiset* (Feb. 6, 1983) Viikkolehtl supplement, pp. 16-17.

J3482   Luckow, Alexander. A. Ginsberg, Rebell Der Angepassten. *Hamburg Abendzeitung* (Feb. 7, 1983)

J3483   Henriksen, Joan. Ginsberg's "Beat" Today Spoken With New Rhythm. *Stavanger Aftenblad* (Feb. 8, 1983) p. 22.
    Note: AG quoted briefly.

J3484   Allan [sic] Ginsberg im "Pumpwerk". *Wilhelmshavener Zeitung* (Feb. 9, 1983)

J3485   Ginsberg Eroffnet Reihe "Akustische Literatur". *Neue Wilhelmshavener Zeitung* (Feb. 10, 1983)
    Note: AG quoted briefly in German only.

J3486   MCK. Wenn Eine Legende Schatten Boxt... *Berliner Morgenpost* (Feb. 11, 1983)

J3487 Rohde, Hedwig. Plutonium Und William Blake. *Der Tagesspiegel* (Feb. 11, 1983)

J3488 La Bardonnie, Mathilde. Nam June Paik's Tricolour Video. *Le Monde* (Feb. 13, 1983)

J3489 Groll, Ulrich. Züchter Poetischer Realitat. *Wilhelmshavener Zeitung* (Feb. 14, 1983)
Note: AG quoted briefly in German only.

J3490 S. Er Denkt Immer Weiter. *Wuppertaler Feuilleton* (Feb. 16, 1983) p. 13.

J3491 Ryan, William F. Displaced Poets. *Washington Tribune* (Feb. 17, 1983) p. 3.

J3492 Green, Robert M. The Beats Go On... *Evening Sun* (Feb. 18, 1983) section B, pp. 1, 4.

J3493 Himes, Geoffrey. Ginsberg: Best Of Bohemia [review of *First Blues* (Hammond recording)]. *Washington Post* (Feb. 18, 1983) Weekend section, p. 37.

J3494 Poets In the Spotlight. *New York Times* (Feb. 20, 1983) p. 19.

J3495 Reynolds, Stanley. On the Bowery. *Guardian* (Feb. 23, 1983)

J3496 Tucker, Ken. The Poet Of the Beat Era Takes His Turn At Recording [review of *First Blues* (Hammond recording)]. *Philadelphia Inquirer* (Feb. 27, 1983) p. 14-I.

J3497 Quaeso, Helene. Ginsburg [sic] Shows His Stuff. *Broadside,* vol. 32, no. 6 (Feb. 28, 1983) p. 4.

J3498 Sibley, Gay. Documents Of Presumption: The Satiric Use Of the Ginsberg Letters In William Carlos Williams' *'Paterson'. American Literature,* vol. 55, no. 1 (March 1983) pp. 1-23.

J3499 Shurilla, Mark. [review of *First Blues* (Hammond recording)]. *Express* (March 1983) p. 24.

J3500 Kaylin, Jennifer. Ginsberg Changes Image, But Not Beat. *New Haven Register* (March 1, 1983)
Note: AG quoted at length.

J3501 Davis, Joyce. 'Beat' Poets Read, Sing At Pierson. *Yale Daily News* (March 2, 1983) pp. 1, 3.
Note: AG quoted briefly.

J3502 Tucker, Ken. Ginsberg a Howl (But Aborigine Song Sticks?) [review of *First Blues* (Hammond recording)]. *Daily News* (March 3, 1983) p. 69.

J3503 Perry, Linda. [letter to the editor]. *Village Voice* (March 6, 1983)

J3504 Malitz, Nancy. Ginsberg Records To a Beat. *USA Today* (March 8, 1983) section D, p. 5.
Note: AG quoted briefly.

J3505 Cohen, Joseph. Reflections On Allen Ginsberg. *Jewish Times* (March 11, 1983)

J3506 Beat Kusagi. *Somut,* vol. 3, no. 32 (March 11, 1983) p. 7.

J3507 Magida, Arthur. Making Our Own Miracles. *Baltimore Jewish Times,* vol. 146, no. 11 (March 18, 1983) pp. 52-55.
Note: AG interview format.

J3508 Tucker, Ken. [review of *First Blues* (Hammond recording)]. *Atlanta Constitution* (March 20, 1983) section H, p. 10.

J3509 Salholz, Eloise. Newsmakers. *Newsweek,* vol. 101, no. 12 (March 21, 1983) p. 55.

J3510 Sayre, Henry M. The Object Of Performance: Aesthetics In the Seventies. *Georgia Review,* vol. 37, no. 1 (Spring 1983) pp. 169-188.

J3511 Gioia, Dana. Business And Poetry. *Hudson Review,* vol. 36, no. 1 (Spring 1983) pp. 147-171.

J3512 The Circle Of Sabotage. *New Pages,* vol. 2, no. 2 [issue no. 6] (Spring 1983) pp. 13, 15.
Note: AG interview format.

J3513 Kerouac, Jack. [letter]. *Passion Press,* no. 4 (Spring 1983) pp. 24-25.

J3514 Angell, Bob. Allen Ginsberg: Writing, Reading, Playing the Blues. *New Paper,* vol. 6, no. 251 (March 23-30, 1983) New section, p. 1.
Note: AG quoted.

J3515 J. Louis Gabin: Un Toy Rimbaldien. *Le Cobochard,* no. 78 (March 25-April 1, 1983) p. 15.

J3516 Erickson, Steve. Ginsberg's First Blues: An Off the Road Vehicle [review of *First Blues* (Hammond recording)]. *Los Angelas [sic] Reader* (March 25, 1983) pp. 17+.

J3517 Cohen, Joseph. Reflections On Allen Ginsberg. *Southern Israelite* (March 25, 1983) p. 14A.

J3518 Gussow, Mel. Theater: 'Jazz Poets At the Grotto'. *New York Times* (March 26, 1983) p. 21.

J3519 Network. *New Yorker,* vol. 59, no. 1 (March 28, 1983) pp. 29-30.

J3520 Cohen, Joseph. Reflections On Allen Ginsberg. *Jewish World* (March 31, 1983) p. 7.

J3521 Award Winning Poet To Perform At NEC. *New Englander,* vol. 40, no. 14 (March 31, 1983) p. 6.

J3522 Carroll, Charles Francis. Allen Ginsberg Finally Comes Out [review of *First Blues* (Hammond recording)]. *Other Voice* (March 31, 1983) p. 8.

J3523 Baskin, Fran. The Making Of a President. *Villager* (March 31, 1983) p. 29.

J3524 Robb, Christina. Gifts Given And Received. *Boston Globe* (April 1, 1983) p. 14.

J3525 Poettype, A. Nother. Allen Ginsberg Finally Admits He's Old. *Colorado Daisy* (April 1, 1983) pp. 15+.
Note: This is an April Fool's Day issue which spoofs an interview with AG.

J3526 Tamarkin, Jeff. [review of *First Blues* (Hammond recording)]. *Goldmine* (April 1983) p. 193.

J3527 Ehrenreich, Barbara. The Male Revolt. *Mother Jones,* vol. 8, no. 3 (April 1983) pp. 25-33, 41-42.

J3528 Alia, Valerie. Carolyn Cassady. *Quadrille,* vol. 15, no. 4 (April 1983) pp. 4-7, 22.

J3529 Krogsgaard, Michael. Allen Ginsberg. *Telegraph,* no. 11 (April 1983) pp. 34-37.
Note: AG interview format.

J3530 Allen Ginsberg: Framtiden Skapasnu. *299,* no. 2 (April 1983) pp. 26-32.

J3531 Judge, Paul. Allen Ginsberg Still an Event. *Valley News* (April 1, 1983) pp. 1, 12.
Note: AG quoted briefly.

J3532 Vinkenoog, Simon. De Lijn Van Rimbaud Tot Groen Haar. *Vinyl,* vol. 3, no. 24 (April 1983) pp. 24-25.
Note: AG interview format.

J3533 Pollock, Bruce. [review of *First Blues* (Hammond recording)]. *Wilson Library Bulletin,* vol. 57, no. 8 (April 1983) pp. 699, 719.

J3534 Kresh, Paul. An Art Between Speech And Music. *New York Times* (April 3, 1983) pp. 6, 20.

J3535 Green, Susan. Beat Poet Allen Ginsberg's Creativity Is Keeping Time With Pulse Of the Universe. *Burlington Free Press* (April 5, 1983) pp. 1D, 6D.
Note: AG quoted briefly.

J3536 Heilprin, Jean. Ginsberg, Poet Of the Beat Generation, Comes To Henniker. *Concord Monitor* (April 5, 1983) p. 3.
Note: AG quoted briefly.

J3537 Gambon, Jill. Ginsberg's Poetry In Motion. *Daily Free Press* (April 7, 1983)
Note: AG quoted briefly.

J3538 Poetry In Motion. *Daily News* (April 8, 1983) p. 10.

J3539 Flukinger, Scott. Ginsberg Brings Taste Of Counterculture With Readings. *Rice Thresher* (April 8, 1983) p. 11.

J3540 Goodman, Fred. Allen Ginsberg: A Poet's Career Marked By Music. *Cashbox,* vol. 44, no. 45 (April 9, 1983) pp. 9, 30.
Note: AG quoted briefly.

J3541 McCormack, Dick. Portrait Of the Artist As an Old Beatnik. *Vermont Vanguard Press,* vol. 6, no. 12 (April 10-17, 1983) pp. 16-17.
Note: AG quoted briefly.

J3542 Intentionally omitted.

J3543 Pierce, Naomi L. Keeping the Beat In the '80s. *Harvard Crimson* (April 14-20, 1983) *What Is To Be Done?* section, vol. 8, no. 9, pp. 1, 7-8.
Note: AG quoted.

J3544 Ratti, André. LSD—Polemische Würdigung. *Basel Zeitung* (April 15, 1983) p. 42.

J3545 Allen Ginsberg Concert To Be Free. *Press-Enterprise* (April 15, 1983)

J3546 Costa, Peter. Allen Ginsberg Fuses New Music With His Poetry. *Rocky Mountain News* (April 15, 1983) pp. 35-W, 48-W.
Note: AG quoted briefly.

J3547 Özlü, Demir. Beat Yazini. *Sanat Dergisi,* vol. 70, no. 430 (April 15, 1983) pp. 18-20.
Note: AG quoted briefly in Turkish only.

Baydar, Yavuz. Allen Ginsberg'le Söylesi. *Sanat Dergisi,* vol. 70, no. 430 (April 15, 1983) pp. 20-21.
Note: AG interview format in Turkish only.

J3548 Robins, Wayne. Record Howl From Allen Ginsberg. *Newsday* (April 17, 1983) part II, pp. 31-32.
Note: AG quoted briefly.

J3549 Foreman, T.E. Poet Ginsberg: Looks Different But Message Is Still the Same. *Press-Enterprise* (April 17, 1983) pp. B-4+.
Note: AG quoted briefly.

J3550 Ginsberg, the Poet, Moves To New Beat. *Milwaukee Sentinel* (April 18, 1983) p. 8.
Note: AG quoted briefly.

J3551 McNamee, Marian and Friedlander, Gus. Ginsberg Speaks On Life And Love. *Claremont Collage* (April 19, 1983) pp. 5, 12-13.
Note: AG quoted at length.

J3552 Smith, Mark C. Poet Ginsberg Delights Claremont College Crowd. *San Gabriel Valley Tribune* (April 19, 1983) pp. B1, B8.
Note: AG quoted.

J3553 Costa, Peter. Ginsberg Goes New Wave. *San Juan Star* (April 19, 1983) pp. 19, 22.
Note: AG quoted.

J3554 Humphrey, Mark. Ginsberg Resurfaces. *Evening Outlook* (April 21, 1983) p. B-1.
Note: AG quoted briefly.

J3555 Brayton, Colin. Ginsberg Grooves With Claremont. *Student Life* (April 22, 1983) p. 8.
Note: AG quoted briefly.

J3556 Inspirational Performance By Ginsberg. *Highlander* (April 25, 1983) pp. 1, 15.

J3557 Polito, Robert. The Beat Goes On. *Boston Phoenix* (April 26, 1983) section 3, pp. 7, 15-16.

J3558 Kaldon, Steve and Lebloas, Chris. Ginsberg Enlightens. *Ticker* (April 26, 1983) pp. 11, 13.
Note: AG quoted briefly.

J3559 De Bruyn, André. [review of *First Blues* (Hammond recording)]. *Audio-Visueel* (May 1983) pp. 25-27.

J3560 Charters, Ann. Faces Of the Beats And Others. *Columbia Library Columns,* vol. 32, no. 3 (May 1983) pp. 23-33.

J3561 Javer, Leonora. Dharma & Poetics. *Earth Star Press,* vol. 1, no. 7 (May 1983) p. 12.
Note: AG quoted briefly.

J3562 [review of *First Blues* (Hammond recording)]. *Musician,* no. 55 (May 1983)

J3563 Scholnick, Michael. [review of *First Blues* (Hammond recording)]. *Poetry Project Newsletter,* no. 99 (May 1983) p. 5.

J3564 Schumacher, Michael. An Interview With Allen Ginsberg. *Still Night Writings,* vol. 1, no. 1 (May [1], 1983) pp. 15-25.
Note: AG interview format.

J3565 Cromelin, Richard. Ginsberg Finds Poetry In Punk. *Los Angeles Times* (May 2, 1983) section VI, p. 5.
Note: AG quoted.

J3566 Costa, Peter. Beat Generation Poet Turns To New Wave. *Manchester Herald* (May 9, 1983) p. 12.
Note: AG quoted.

J3567 Holmes, John Clellon. The Philosophy Of the Beats. *Esquire,* vol. 99, no. 6 (June 1983) pp. 158-167.

J3568 Lounela, Pekka. Huutolainen. *Katso* (June 1983)

J3569 Weyler, Rex. Inside. *New Age,* vol. 8, no. 11 (June 1983) p. 5.

Fields, Rick. Allen In Wonderland. *New Age,* vol. 8, no. 11 (June 1983) pp. 30-39.
Note: AG quoted briefly.

Davis, Stephen. Allen Ginsberg's Bag Of Blues [review of *First Blues* (Hammond recording)]. *New Age,* vol. 8, no. 11 (June 1983) pp. 72-73.

MacDonald, Sandy. Elsa Dorfman, Magician Of the Moment. *New Age,* vol. 8, no. 11 (June 1983) p. 88.

J3570 Tallmer, Jerry. Sing Along With Ginsberg. *New York Post* (June 4, 1983) p. 11.
Note: AG quoted.

J3571 Ball, Gordon. Kerplunk! Beat Generation Meets Japan. *Japan Times* (June 5, 1983) p. 12.

J3572 Berg, Martin. Use Your Life Images, Ginsberg Tells Writers. *Sunday Gazette-Mail* (June 12, 1983) p. B1.
Note: AG quoted.

J3573 Groninger, Vicki. They Call Her 'Baby Driver'. *Daily Camera* (June 15, 1983) pp. 1, 5.

J3574 McBride, Stewart. Arion Press: Stretching the Notion Of What a Book Can Be. *Christian Science Monitor* (June 16, 1983) pp. 10-12.

J3575 Burtman, Bob. The Bard Sings the Blues [review of *First Blues* (Hammond recording)]. *Spectator*, vol. 5, no. 32 (June 16-23, 1983) pp. 26-27.

J3576 Carlin, Margaret. Kerouac's 'Mad' Daughter Has Settled Down. *Rocky Mountain News* (June 19, 1983) p. 28-N.

J3577 Petersen, Clarence. On the Road With Another Kerouac. *Chicago Tribune* (June 20, 1983) Tempo section, pp. 1, 4.

J3578 [article]. *Moody Street Irregulars,* no. 13 (Summer 1983)

J3579 Thiel, Greg. [review of *Allen Ginsberg With Still Life* (recording)]. *New Blood*, no. 10 (July 1983) pp. 72-73.

J3580 D'Orso, Mike. On the Road Again With Jack Kerouac. *William And Mary,* vol. 51, no. 1 (July-Aug. 1983) pp. 7-9.

J3581 Robertson, Michael. Timothy Leary Drops In And Turns On. *San Francisco Chronicle* (July 2, 1983) p. 9.

J3582 Greco, Stephen. Allen Ginsberg Sings His 'First Blues'. *Advocate,* no. 372 (July 21, 1983) pp. 53, 55.
Note: AG quoted at length.

J3583 Caldwell, Larry. 'Camp Kerouac' Expands Beyond Initial Horizon. *Daily Camera* (July 28, 1983) pp. 1, 5.

J3584 Camacho, Eduardo. Poetas Extranjeros Y Nacionales Rechazan El Festival De Morelia Por El "Desdén" Mostrado Por Los Organizadores Al Evento De 1982. *Excelsior* (July 28, 1983) p. 7.

J3585 Mexican And Foreign Poets Protest the Morelia Festival. *News* (July 28, 1983) p. 11.

J3586 Poetas Mexicanos Y Extranjeros Se Pronuncian En Contra Del Festival De Morelia. *Novedades Mexico* (July 28, 1983) p. 7.

J3587 Finholm, Valerie. Protesters Decry Military Aid. *Daily Camera* (July 31, 1983)

J3588 Beuys, Barbara. Die Gewaltlosen. *Stern,* vol. 32 (Aug. 1983) pp. 90-93H.

J3589 Lange, Timothy. Marchers Challenge Reagan Policies. *Colorado Daily* (Aug. 1-2, 1983) pp. 1-2.

J3590 Coakley, Tom. Boulder: Image Vs. Fact. *Denver Post* (Aug. 7, 1983) pp. 1-A, 10-A.
Note: AG quoted briefly.

J3591 Sohl, Norm. [review of *Allen Ginsberg: With Still Life* (recording)]. *OP Magazine* (Sept.-Oct. 1983) p. 77.

J3592 Phillips, Michael Joseph. [review of *Plutonian Ode*]. *Small Press Review,* vol. 15 (Sept. 1983) p. 12.

J3593 Farlekas, Chris. The Beat Goes On With Ginsberg Visit. *Times Herald Record* (Sept. 2, 1983) p. 5G.

J3594   De Palma, Rachelle. Program On Williams Will Begin Today. *New York Times* (Sept. 18, 1983) p. 24K.
Note: AG quoted briefly.

J3595   Poet Allen Ginsberg Is On the Road To Tampa. *Tampa Tribune* (Sept. 19, 1983) p. 2D.

J3596   Roy, Beckey. Ginsberg, Renowned 'Beatnik' Poet, To Appear On Campus. *Oracle,* vol. 18, no. 112 (Sept. 20, 1983) p. 1.

J3597   Thompson, Sandra. The Allen Ginsberg That Isn't. *St. Petersburg Times* (Sept. 20, 1983) section D, pp. 1-2.
Note: AG quoted at length.

J3598   Ginsberg To Appear At USF. *Intercom* (Sept. 21, 1983) p. 1.

J3599   Keller, Karl. Walt Whitman And the Queening Of America. *American Poetry,* vol. 1, no. 1 (Fall 1983) pp. 4-26.

J3600   An Evening With Allen Ginsberg. *Garuda,* no. 1 (Autumn 1983) p. 6.

J3601   Bowering, George. [review of *Plutonian Ode*]. *Line,* no. 2 (Fall 1983)

J3602   Thompson, Sandra. The Beat Goes On. *St. Petersburg Times* (Sept. 22, 1983) p. 10B.

J3603   Lindstrom, Andy. Allen Ginsberg, Beatnik Poet Brings His Perspective To Florida State Today. *Tallahassee Democrat* (Sept. 22, 1983) pp. 1B, 9B.
Note: AG quoted.

J3604   Hinson, Mark. Ginsberg: The Spirit Is Alive. *Florida Flambeau,* vol. 71, no. 20 (Sept. 23, 1983) pp. 1, 22.
Note: AG quoted.

Murphy, Jay. [review of *First Blues* (Hammond recording)]. *Florida Flambeau* (Sept. 23, 1983) pp. 9, 11.

J3605   Tozian, Greg. On the Road With Allen Ginsberg. *Tampa Tribune* (Sept. 23, 1983) pp. 1D, 8D.
Note: AG quoted.

J3606   Drennen, Eileen M. Ginsberg Displayed Charm, Vigor In Coping With Tallahassee. *Florida Flambeau,* vol. 71, no. 21 (Sept. 26, 1983) pp. 1, 11, 12.
Note: AG quoted briefly.

J3607   Vila, Hector. Beat Poet Howls At Student. *Oracle* (Sept. 27, 1983) pp. 6-7.
Note: AG interview format.

J3608   Echazabal, Margarita. Ginsberg: An Outspoken Survivor. *Neighbor,* vol. 11, no. 39 (Sept. 29-Oct. 5, 1983) pp. 1A, 7A.
Note: AG quoted.

J3609   Clark, Chris. Requiem For Heavyweights. *Colorado Daily* (Sept. 30-Oct. 1, 1983) Means And Media section, pp. 25-27.

J3610   Colby, Joy Hakanson. Papa Paik. *Detroit News* (Sept. 30, 1983) section D, p. 11D.

J3611   Cagle, Charles Harmon. Adonis Of Denver. *Blueboy* (Oct. 1983) pp. 23-26.

J3612   A Country Of Poets. *Detroit News* (Oct. 13, 1983) section A, p. 12A.

J3613   Burroughs. *Variety* (Oct. 19, 1983) p. 20.

J3614   [review of *First Blues* (Hammond recording)]. *Christopher Street,* vol. 6, no. 11 (Nov. 1983) pp. 12-13.

J3615   Pintarich, Paul. Ginsberg & Friends: The Beat Goes On. *Oregonian* (Nov. 11, 1983) p. F1.
Note: AG quoted.

J3616   Booe, Martin. Ginsberg's On the Move. *Daily Camera* (Nov. 20, 1983) Sunday Camera Magazine, pp. 16-23.
Note: AG quoted.

J3617   Uris, Joe. The Last Howl. *Willamette Week* (Nov. 22-28, 1983) p. 4.
Note: AG interview format.

J3618   Schaffnit, Michael. The Life And Times Of Allen Ginsberg. *Out Front,* vol. 8, no. 18 (Nov. 23, 1983) p. 9.

J3619   Compton, K.C. New Wave Music, Journeys Propel Ginsberg Into Future. *Albuquerque Journal* (Nov. 25, 1983) section C, p. 1.
Note: AG quoted at length.

J3620   Raether, Keith. America Hears Ginsberg Singing. *Albuquerque Tribune* (Nov. 25, 1983) section B, p. 1.
Note: AG quoted.

J3621   Kesey, Ken. Is There Any End To Kerouac Highway? *Esquire,* vol. 100, no. 6 (Dec. 1983) pp. 60-63.
Note: AG quoted briefly.

J3622   Richey, Joe. Dharma Poetics: A Memoir. *New Age Journal* (Dec. 1983) pp. 59-60.
Note: AG quoted briefly.

J3623   Sinisi, J. Sebastian. Allen Ginsberg. *Denver Post* (Dec. 4, 1983) Contemporary section, pp. 10-12, 14-16.
Note: AG quoted briefly.

J3624   Betterton, J.S. Allen Ginsberg, Poet, To Appear. *Citadel* (Dec. 9, 1983) pp. 1, 4.

J3625   Lepkowski, Frank J. Saving Poetry. *Library Journal,* vol. 108, no. 22 (Dec. 15, 1983) pp. 2304-2306.

J3626   Brown, Chip. Politics And Poetic Injustice. *Washington Post* (Dec. 19, 1983) Style section, pp. C1, C8.
Note: AG quoted.

J3627*   Sabatini, R. A Poet Prophet Seer; Allen Ginsberg. *RFD,* no. 37 (Winter 1983) p. 13.

J3628   Hochswender, Woody. Unpoetic Justice—No Bards In L.A. Olympics. *Los Angeles Herald Examiner* (Dec. 28, 1983) pp. A1, A4.
Note: AG quoted briefly.

J3629   Adams, Cindy. Paging Big Brother. *New York Post* (Dec. 28, 1983) p. 30.
Note: AG quoted briefly.

J3630   Masovic, Dragana R. Interpretativni Pristup Pesmi 'Amerike' Alena Ginsberga.
Gradina, vol. 18 (1983) pp. 117-121.

J3631   Olsen, Tore. The Beat Goes On. *Musikkavisen Puls,* no. 3/83 (1983) pp. 22-23.

J3632   Jónsson, Jón Sveinbjørn. Samtaler Med Allen Ginsberg 1983. *Poesi,* no. 1
(1983) pp. 158-163.
Note: AG interview format in Norwegian only.

J3633   Clark, Tom. Writer: A Life Of Jack Kerouac. *Rolling Stock,* no. 4 (1983) pp.
11-14.
Note: AG quoted briefly.

Dias, Juan. On the Road Again. *Rolling Stock,* no. 4 (1983) p. 14.

J3634   Carlsen, Erik Meier. At Føle Vaegten Af Sin Krop I Sine Sko. *Stupa,* no. 6
(1983) pp. 61-65.
Note: AG quoted briefly in Danish only.

J3635   Graham, Chuck. [review of *First Blues* (Hammond recording)]. *Tucson Citizen*
(1983) p. 16.

Books:

J3636   Bockris, Victor and Malanga, Gerard. *Up-Tight: The Velvet Underground Story.*
London, England: Omnibus Press, 1983, p. 37.
Note: AG quoted briefly.

J3637   Brown, Peter and Gaines, Steven. *The Love You Make: An Insider's Story Of
the Beatles.* New York, NY: McGraw-Hill, 1983, pp. 225, 356, 412.
Note: AG quoted briefly.

J3638   Bruccoli, Mary (ed.). *Dictionary Of Literary Biography, Documentary Series,
vol. 3.* Detroit, MI: Gale Research, 1983, p. 79.

J3639   Burns, Glen. *Great Poets Howl: A Study Of Allen Ginsberg's Poetry, 1943-
1955.* Frankfurt am Main, Germany: Peter Lang, 1983.

J3640   Charters, Ann (ed.). *The Beats: Literary Bohemians In Postwar America, Part 2:
M-Z.* Detroit, MI: Gale Research, 1983.
Contents: Charters, Ann. Peter Orlovsky, pp. 433-439. [Series: *Dictionary
Of Literary Biography, vol. 16*]
Christensen, Paul. Allen Ginsberg, pp. 214-241.

J3641   El-Sharif, Nabil Mahmoud. *Ecological Themes In the Poetry Of A.R. Ammons,
Allen Ginsberg, And Gary Snyder.* Unpublished Doctoral Dissertation.
Indiana University, 1983.

J3642   Goswami, Satsvarupa Dasa. *Prabhupada.* Los Angeles, CA: Bhaktivedanta
Book Trust, 1983, pp. 94, 97-99.

J3643   Hoberman, J. and Rosenbaum, Jonathan. *Midnight Movies.* New York, NY:
Harper & Row, 1983, pp. 39-41.

J3644   Hyde, Lewis. *The Gift.* New York, NY: Random House, 1983.
Note: AG mentioned throughout.

J3645   Johnson, Joyce. *Minor Characters.* Boston, MA: Houghton Mifflin, 1983.
Note: AG mentioned and quoted throughout.

J3646   Karl, Frederick R. *American Fictions 1940-1980.* New York, NY: Harper &
Row, 1983.
Note: AG mentioned throughout.

J3647   Leary, Timothy. *Flashbacks.* Los Angeles, CA: J.P. Tarcher, 1983.
Note: AG quoted and mentioned throughout.

J3648   Rosenthal, M.L. and Gall, Sally M. *The Modern Poetic Sequence: The Genius
Of Modern Poetry.* New York, NY: Oxford University Press, 1983.
Note: AG mentioned throughout.

J3649   Sarwar, Selim. *Apocalyptic Imagery In Four Twentieth-Century Poets: W.B.
Yeats, T.S. Eliot, Robert Lowell And Allen Ginsberg.* Unpublished Doctoral
Dissertation. Montreal, Canada: McGill University, 1983.

J3650   Snyder, Gary. *Passage Through India.* San Francisco, CA: Grey Fox Press,
1983.
Note: AG quoted and mentioned throughout.

J3651   Stokkink, Theo. *Walhalla.* Amsterdam, The Netherlands: KRO Radio, 1983.

J3652   Terrell, Carroll F.(ed.). *William Carlos Williams: Man and Poet.* Orono, ME:
National Poetry Foundation, 1983.
Note: AG mentioned throughout.

J3653   Warhol, Andy and Hackett, Pat. *Popism: The Warhol '60s.* New York, NY:
Harper & Row, 1983.
Note: AG quoted briefly and mentioned throughout.

1984

J3654   Krassner, Paul and Southern, Terry. The Hard-Nosed '60s Radicals, Where Are
They Today? *Hustler,* vol. 10, no. 7 (Jan. 1984) pp. 106-109, 112.

J3655   Nellis, Barbara. Fast Tracks. *Playboy,* vol. 31, no. 1 (Jan. 1984) p. 42.

J3656   Kitman, Marvin. Public TV's '1984' Disaster. *Newsday* (Jan. 4, 1984) part II,
p. 56.

J3657   Bishop, Gordon. Gems Of New Jersey Authors. *Star-Ledger* (Jan. 8, 1984)
Accent section, pp. 1, 6.

J3658   Bordsen, John F. Burroughs' Home On the Plains. *Newsday* (Jan. 23, 1984)
part II, p. 3.

J3659   Crichton, Jennifer. William Burroughs At 70. *Publishers Weekly,* vol. 225, no.
4 (Jan. 27, 1984) pp. 61-63.

J3660   Ball, Gordon. Allen Ginsberg And the Progress Of Poetry. *English Literature
And Language* (Feb. 1984) pp. 43-54.

J3661   The History Of the Communal Spiritual Movement, Kerista/Judaism. *Kaliflower*
(Feb. 1984) pp. 6, 13, 18-9, 46.

J3662   Rome, David. Dharma Poetics. *Naropa Magazine,* vol. 1, no. 1 (Feb. 1984) p. 42.
Note: AG interview format.

Roark, Randy. Poets. *Naropa Magazine,* vol. 1, no. 1 (Feb. 1984) p. 44.
Note: AG quoted briefly.

Richey, Joe. Noted. *Naropa Magazine,* vol. 1, no. 1 (Feb. 1984) p. 44.
Note: AG quoted briefly.

Richey, Joe. Why Write. *Naropa Magazine,* vol. 1, no. 1 (Feb. 1984) p. 45.
Note: AG quoted briefly.

J3663   Kramer, Hilton. The MLA Centennial Follies. *New Criterion,* vol. 2, no. 6 (Feb. 1984) pp. 1-8.

J3664   Allen, Henry. The Brutal Beat. *Washington Post* (Feb. 3, 1984) pp. E1, E6.

J3665   Russo, Vito. Burroughs. *Advocate,* no. 387 (Feb. 7, 1984) pp. 33-35.

J3666   Malarkey, Christopher. See, Hear, Experience the Man, Poet, Phenomenon. *Cooper Point Journal,* vol. 12, no. 13 (Feb. 9, 1984) p. 14.

J3667   Kingsley, D. Mark. Allen Ginsberg, Attention Paid. *Reporter Magazine,* vol. 60, no. 16 (Feb. 10, 1984) pp. 20-23.
Note: AG interview format.

J3668   Marks, Jim. Ginsberg On Drugs, AIDS, the Bomb. *Washington Blade,* vol. 15, no. 6 (Feb. 10, 1984) pp. 1, 18.
Note: AG interview format.

J3669   Zemek, Susan. Ginsberg: From Beat To Neat. *Olympian* (Feb. 12, 1984)

J3670   Lane, Dakota. Beat Poet Ginsberg Reflects On His Jewish Roots. *Northern California Jewish Bulletin* (Feb. 17, 1984) p. 11.
Note: AG quoted.

J3671   Allen Ginsberg Signs Contract With H&R. *Publishers Weekly,* vol. 225, no. 7 (Feb. 17, 1984) p. 51.

J3672   Burroughs, William S. My Purpose Is To Write For the Space Age. *New York Times Book Review* (Feb. 19, 1984) pp. 9-10.

J3673   Yoshida, Sachiko. From Particular To General And From General To Particular—The Social And Private Visions Of Allen Ginsberg And John Ashbery. *Amerika Kenkyu: American Review,* no. 18 (March 1984) pp. 106-133, 229-230.

J3674   Rumley, Larry. Ginsberg Visits. *Seattle Times-Seattle Post-Intelligencer* (March 4, 1984)
Note: AG quoted briefly.

J3675   Fain, Nathan. Health. *Advocate,* no. 390 (March 20, 1984) p. 20.
Note: AG quoted briefly.

J3676   Kanter, Ann. Allen Ginsberg. *NTID* [National Technical Institute For the Deaf] *Focus* (Spring-Summer 1984) pp. 22-25.
Note: AG interview format.

J3677   Lesh, Phil. [interview]. *Golden Road* (Spring 1984) p. 24.

J3678   [article]. *Moody Street Irregulars,* no. 14 (Spring 1984)

J3679   Seid, Steve. What a Start! *Send,* no. 9 (Spring 1984) p. 49.

J3680   Crowner, Mike. Ginsberg Speaks And Sings. *Eagle* (March 30, 1984)
Note: AG quoted briefly.

J3681   Thomas, Patrick. Allen Ginsberg Speaks On the Clash, King Crimson, Kerouac,
the Grateful Dead. *Notebook,* no. 3 (April 1984) pp. 5-7.
Note: AG interview format.

Metzger, Thomas. Allen Ginsberg Seeing Angels. *Notebook,* no. 3 (April 1984)
p. 12.

J3682   Rosenthal, M.L. Is There a Pound-Williams Tradition? *Southern Review,* vol.
20, no. 2 (April 1984) pp. 279-285.

J3683   Le Pellec, Yves and Pey, Serge. Allen Ginsberg Entretien. *Tribu,* no. 6 ([April-
June] 1984) pp. 25-34.
Note: AG interview format in French only.

J3684   Wild Bill Hiccup. *Vanity Fair,* vol. 47, no. 4 (April 1984) p. 16.

J3685   D'Souza, Dinesh. 60's Beat Poet Allen Ginsberg Still Battling Against
Conventions. *Dartmouth Review,* vol. 4, no. 20 (April 8, 1984) pp. 6-7.
Note: AG interview format.

J3686   Blundy, David. Return Of the Guru Of Beat. *Sunday Times* (April 15, 1984) p.
11.
Note: AG quoted briefly.

J3687   Miles. The Beats Go On. *Time Out* (April 19-25, 1984) p. 11.
Note: AG quoted briefly.

J3688   U.C. Plans Ginsberg Lectures. *Charleston Gazette-Mail* (April 22, 1984)

J3689   Horovitz, Michael. Wearing Apocalipstick At the Albert Hall. *Guardian* (April
23, 1984) p. 11.

J3690   Fox, Edward. Ginsberg, Best-Known U.S. Poet, Lectures, Performs Poetry At
U.C. *Charleston Gazette-Mail* (April 27, 1984) p. 14A.
Note: AG quoted.

J3691   Horner, Tom. World Renowned Poet Rises From 'Beat' Path. *Connecticut Daily
Campus* (April 27, 1984) pp. 1, 10, 11.
Note: AG quoted.

J3692   Kemp, Peter. The Old Cool. *Sunday Times* (April 29, 1984)

J3693   Horner, Tom. Ashcans And Unobtainable Dollars. *Connecticut Daily Campus*
(April 30, 1984) pp. 4, 6.
Note: AG quoted.

J3694   Tant, Ed. Allen Ginsberg. *Athens Night Life* (May 1984) pp. 8-9.

J3695   Schumacher, Michael. The Echoing Howl. *Writer's Digest,* vol. 64, no. 5 (May 1984) pp. 32-36.
Note: AG quoted at length.

J3696   Raether, Keith. For Ginsberg, Poetry Is a Song From the Heart. *Dallas Morning News* (May 4, 1984)
Note: AG quoted briefly.

J3697   Puckett, Daniel. Counterculture Poet Calls For Open Drug Market. *Bryan-College Station Eagle* (May 5, 1984) p. 2A.
Note: AG quoted briefly.

J3698   Winn, Jasper. Poetry International. *New Musical Express* (May 5, 1984) p. 39.

J3699   Chilton, W.E. and Haught, James A. FBI Used Drug Raids To Stifle Radicals, Poet Says. *Sunday Gazette-Mail* (May 6, 1984) p. 4D.
Note: AG quoted.

J3700   Free Speech. *Bryan-College Station Eagle* (May 8, 1984) p. 14A.

J3701   Fisk, Suzy. Poet Sings, Lectures. *Battalion* (May 9, 1984) p. 4.
Note: AG quoted briefly.

J3702   Meyers, Robert. Poet And Visionary. *Athens Observer* (May 17, 1984) pp. 1B, 7B.
Note: AG quoted briefly.

J3703   Small, Bob. Making Poetry And Conversation. *South Street Star,* vol. 4, no. 20 (May 17, 1984) pp. 4, 10.
Note: AG interview format.

J3704   Hebbelinck, André. Orakel En Hofnar. *De Morgen* (May 19, 1984) p. 23.
Note: AG interview format in Flemish only.

J3705   Buttgen, Bob. Not Your Average Poets. *News & Observer* (May 20, 1984) Volusia section C, pp. 8-9.

J3706   Hayes, Ed. Poet Allen Ginsberg To Speak At Rollins. *Orlando Sentinel* (May 20, 1984) p. C-3.

J3707   Van Hove, Jan. Nacht Van De Poëzie Trekt Minder Publiek. *De Standaard* (May 21, 1984) p. 1.

J3708   Beatkoning Allen Ginsberg Gooit Publiek Los. *Het Laatste Nieuws* (May 21, 1984) p. 7.

J3709   Buttgen, Bob. Three Talented Residents. *News & Observer* (May 27, 1984) Volusia section C, pp. 8-9.
Note: AG quoted briefly.

J3710   De Wilde, Marijke and De Schepper, Ronny. Er Kleeft Bloed Aan De Handen Van De New Left. *De Rode Vaan,* vol. 63, no. 23 (May 28-June 1, 1984) pp. 21-23.
Note: AG interview format in Flemish only.

J3711   Chotzinoff, Robin. Poetic Justice. *Westword,* vol. 7, no. 39 (May 30-June 5, 1984) pp. 16-17, 41.

J3712   Hayes, Ron. Allen Ginsberg: The 'Beat' Goes On. *Daytona Beach Sunday News-Journal* (June 3, 1984) pp. 1D, 2D.
Note: AG quoted.

J3713   Triplett, William. Allen Ginsberg Q & A. *City Paper,* [Washington, DC edition] vol. 4, no. 24 (June 15-21, 1984) pp. 10-12.
Note: AG interview format.

J3714   Horovitz, Michael. Allen Ginsberg's Jewishness. *Jewish Chronicle* (June 15, 1984) Literary supplement, pp. i-ii.
Note: AG quoted.

J3715   Loder, Kurt. Bob Dylan. *Rolling Stone* (June 21, 1984) pp. 14-5, 17-8, 23-5, 78.

J3716   Granger, Lenny. Literature Department Offers Visiting Writers Series. *American* (Summer 1984) p. 4.

J3717   Triplett, William. Allen Ginsberg Q & A. *City Paper,* [Baltimore, MD edition] vol. 8, no. 25 (June 22-28, 1984) pp. 16-17.
Note: AG interview format.

J3718   Jones, Peter. Naropa To Host Authors. *CU Campus Press* (June 28, 1984) p. 2.

J3719   Schmidt, Jürgen. Allen Ginsberg, Live On Video Und Weitergehende Betrachtungen. *Hiero Itzo* (July 1984) pp. 16-18.

J3720   Ryan, William F. Lawrence Ferlinghetti. *Hill Rag* (July 6, 1984) pp. 6-9.

J3721   Ruibal, Sal. Intellectual Discussion Lacks Soul. *Daily Camera* (July 9, 1984) pp. 1, 7.

J3722   Jones, Peter. Ginsberg 'Howls'. *CU Campus Press* (July 12, 1984) p. 8.
Note: AG quoted briefly.

J3723   Marks, Ron. Ginsberg To Speak On Campus. *Daily Texan* (July 20, 1984) p. 15.

J3724   Marks, Ron. Ginsberg Sings the Blues. *Daily Texan* (July 23, 1984) Images section, pp. 12-13.
Note: AG quoted.

J3725   Snyder, George. Bohemian Grove Arrests. *San Francisco Chronicle* (July 23, 1984) pp. 1, 16.

J3726   Petric, Mirko. Urlik Preko Oceana. *Danas,* no. 127 (July 24, 1984) pp. 55-56.

J3727   Lipton, Judith Eve. Howl. *New England Journal Of Medicine,* vol. 311, no. 4 (July 26, 1984) pp. 266-267.

J3728   Bunge, Nancy. How Can You Teach Poetry If You Don't Sing the Blues? *Washington Post* (July 29, 1984) p. C3.
Note: AG interview format.

J3729   Ellison, Helen S. Final Echoes [letter to the editor]. *Writer's Digest,* vol. 64, no. 8 (Aug. 1984) p. 5.

J3730 Allen Ginsberg At the *Observer*. *Texas Observer,* vol. 76, no. 16 (Aug. 17, 1984) p. 30.
Note: AG quoted briefly.

J3731 Collias, Karen. Teachers Who Harass Students Are Outlaws. *USA Today* (Aug. 28, 1984) p. 11A.
Note: AG quoted briefly.

J3732 Fenster, Robert and Kennan, Larry. At the End Of the Road. *On Campus* (Sept. 1984) pp. 27-30.

J3733 Henry, Patrick. Ginsberg Speaks At Trinity. *Trinity Tripod,* vol. 83, no. 2 (Sept. 18, 1984) p. 11.

J3734 Raphael Soyer's New York: People & Places. *At Cooper Union,* vol. 18, no. 3 (Fall 1984) pp. 5 and cover.

J3735 Greenwald, Elissa. "The Insistence Of Place": The Role Of New Jersey In the Poetry Of William Carlos Williams And Allen Ginsberg. *Journal Of Regional Cultures,* vol. 4, no. 2-vol. 5, no. 1 (Fall-Winter 1984—Spring-Summer 1985) pp. 131-151.

J3736 Heary, Deborah. Ginsberg Speaks Anti-War Anti-Nuke Message. *Hill News,* vol. 74, no. 1 (Sept. 27, 1984) p. 1.

J3737 Ison, John. Allan [sic] Ginsberg: A Guru Of the '60s Speaks To the '80s. *UCLA Daily Bruin* (Oct. 9, 1984) p. 24.

J3738 Hill, Brian. Poet Ginsberg 'Yacketayakks' At Zellerbach. *Daily Californian,* vol. 16, no. 36 (Oct. 11, 1984) pp. 1, 9.
Note: AG quoted briefly.

J3739 Wilson, Susan. The Folks Behind the Folk. *Boston Globe Calendar,* vol. 10, no. 2 (Oct. 18, 1984) pp. 10-11.

J3740 [photograph]. *Los Angeles Herald Examiner* (Oct. 18, 1984) p. B3.

J3741 Mehren, Elizabeth. Nine Writers On the Eve Of a China Adventure. *Los Angeles Times* (Oct. 24, 1984) section 5, pp. 1-3.
Note: AG quoted briefly.

J3742 Doyle, Michael. From a Howl To an Om. *Palo Alto Weekly* (Oct. 24, 1984) p. 33.
Note: AG quoted briefly.

J3743 Tripoli, Dana. Hearing a Poetic Voice. *Horizon,* vol. 27, no. 9 (Nov. 1984) p. 4.
Note: AG quoted briefly.

J3744 Clines, Francis X. Intimations Of Mortality. *New York Times Magazine* (Nov. 11, 1984) pp. 68-71, 88, 90, 92, 94, 96, 98.
Note: AG quoted briefly.

J3745 Nachman-Hunt, Nancy. The New Left's Last Stand. *Sunday Camera Magazine* (Nov. 11, 1984) pp. 6-13.

J3746 Snyder, Michael. These Folk Singers Are No Relics From the '50s. *San Francisco Sunday Examiner & Chronicle* (Nov. 11, 1984)

J3747   [review of *Collected Poems*]. *Teche News* (Nov. 14, 1984) section 2, p. 12.

J3748   [review of *Collected Poems*]. *Publishers Weekly,* vol. 226, no. 20 (Nov. 16, 1984) p. 59.

J3749   Abbott, Steve. The Collected Allen Ginsberg: On Paper, In Person, En Route To China. *Advocate,* no. 408 (Nov. 27, 1984) pp. 40-41.
Note: AG quoted at length.

J3750   Atlas, James. [review of *Collected Poems*]. *Atlantic,* vol. 254, no. 6 (Dec. 1984) pp. 132-134, 136.

J3751   [review of *Collected Poems*]. *Booklist,* vol. 81, no. 7 (Dec. 1, 1984) pp. 477-478.

J3752   Howard, Richard. [review of *Collected Poems*]. *Boston Review,* vol. 9, no. 6 (Dec. 1984) p. 33.

J3753   Lipari, Joseph A. [review of *Collected Poems*]. *Library Journal,* vol. 109, no. 20 (Dec. 1984) p. 2284.

J3754   Abbott, Steve. Talking To the Flowers: An Interview With Allen Ginsberg. *Poetry Flash,* no. 141 (Dec. 1984)
Note: AG interview format.

J3755   Ketcham, Diana. [review of *Collected Poems*]. *Oakland Tribune* (Dec. 2, 1984)

J3756   Clark, Tom. [review of *Collected Poems*]. *San Francisco Chronicle* (Dec. 2, 1984) Review section, p. 10.

J3757   Pettingell, Phoebe. [review of *Collected Poems*]. *New Leader,* vol. 67, no. 22 (Dec. 10, 1984) pp. 17-18.

J3758   Shapiro, Harvey. [review of *Collected Poems*]. *New York Times* (Dec. 15, 1984) p. 15.

J3759   Palmer, Robert. Rockers With Literary Aspirations Make Their Mark. *New York Times* (Dec. 16, 1984) section H, pp. 27, 30.

J3760   Axelrod, Steven Gould. [review of *Plutonian Ode*]. *World Literature Today,* vol. 58 (Winter 1984) p. 104.

J3761   Clark, Tom. [review of *Collected Poems*]. *San Francisco Sunday Examiner And Chronicle* (Dec. 23, 1984) Book Review section, pp. 1, 10.

Melnick, David. With History On His Mind. *San Francisco Sunday Examiner And Chronicle* (Dec. 23, 1984) Book Review section, pp. 1, 10-11.
Note: AG quoted at length.

J3762   Hyde, Lewis. [review of *Collected Poems*]. *New York Times Book Review* (Dec. 30, 1984) pp. 5-6.

J3763   Alyakrinsky, Oleg. Allen Ginsberg: The Fall Of L'Homme Revolté. *Contemporary Literature Abroad,* no. 2 (1984)

J3764   Weiss, Jason. Lawrence Ferlinghetti: Cellar Sessions. *Jazz Forum,* no. 89 (1984) pp. 44-47.

J3765   From the Egolessness Of Heroes: Conversations With Allen Ginsberg: Ginsberg On Rimbaud. *Radar,* no. 4 (1984) p. 69.
Note: AG quoted briefly.

J3766   Murphy, Jay and Ryals, Mary Jane. Red Bass Interview. *Red Bass,* no. 7 (1984) pp. 28-30.
Note: AG interview format.

J3767   Krassner, Paul. High Noon At Camp Kerouac. *Unspeakable Visions Of the Individual,* vol. 14 (1984) [issue called *The Beat Road*] pp. 9-15.
Note: AG quoted briefly.

Books:

J3768   Bellow, Saul. *Him With His Foot In His Mouth And Other Stories.* New York, NY: Harper & Row, 1984, pp. 12-15, 22-23.

J3769   Bosworth, Patricia. *Diane Arbus: A Biography.* New York, NY: Knopf, 1984.
Note: AG mentioned throughout.

J3770   Breslin, James E.B. *From Modern To Contemporary.* Chicago, IL: University Of Chicago Press, 1984.
Note: AG mentioned throughout.

J3771   Challis, Chris. *Quest For Kerouac.* London, England: Faber And Faber, 1984, pp. 178-179.
Note: AG quoted briefly.

J3772   Clark, Tom. *Jack Kerouac.* San Diego, CA: Harcourt Brace Jovanovich, 1984.
Note: AG mentioned and quoted throughout.

J3773   De Loach, Allen. *Literary Assays.* Buffalo, NY: White Pine Press, 1984. [set of 12 postcards]

J3774   Dillard, Annie. *Encounters With Chinese Writers.* Middletown, CT: Wesleyan University Press, 1984.
Note: AG quoted and mentioned throughout.

J3775   Goldman, Harold Raymond. *In the American Grain: A Definition Of the Beat Sensibility.* Unpublished Doctoral Dissertation. State University Of New York At Stony Brook, 1984.

J3776   Green, Jonathan. *American Photography.* New York, NY: Harry N. Abrams, 1984.
Note: AG mentioned throughout.

J3777   Hindus, Milton (ed.). *Charles Reznikoff: Man And Poet.* Orono, ME: National Poetry Foundation, 1984.
Contents: Ginsberg, Allen. Reznikoff's Poetics, pp. 139-150.
Note: AG quoted at length from lecture.

J3778   Hyde, Lewis (ed.). *On the Poetry Of Allen Ginsberg.* Ann Arbor, MI: University Of Michigan Press, 1984.
Note: AG mentioned and quoted throughout.

J3779   Joseph, Elsie Mary. *Black And White Literature In America: A Course Design In Rhetorical Interpretation Of Five Genres.* Unpublished Doctoral Dissertation. Catholic University Of America, 1984.

J3780 Kodama, Sanehide. *American Poetry And Japanese Culture.* Hamden, CT: Archon Books, 1984, pp. 132, 170-3.

J3781 Levey, Judith S. and Greenhall, Agnes (eds.). *The Concise Columbia Encyclopedia In Large Print, vol. 3.* New York, NY: Columbia University Press, 1984.

J3782 Malina, Judith. *The Diaries Of Judith Malina.* New York, NY: Grove Press, 1984.
Note: AG mentioned throughout.

J3783 Mallon, Thomas. *A Book Of One's Own.* New York, NY: Ticknor & Fields, 1984, pp. 133-135.

J3784 Matusow, Allen J. *The Unraveling Of America.* New York, NY: Harper & Row, 1984.
Note: AG mentioned throughout.

J3785 Perry, Charles. *The Haight-Ashbury.* New York, NY: Random House, 1984.
Note: AG mentioned throughout.

J3786 Skvorecky, Josef. *The Engineer Of Human Souls.* Toronto, Canada: Lester & Orpen Dennys, 1984, pp. 289-90, 292-4.

J3787 Sommerkamp, Sabine. *Der Einfluss Des Haiku Auf Imagismus Und Jungere Moderne.* Unpublished Doctoral Dissertation. Hamburg, West Germany: Universitat Hamburg, 1984, pp. 178-216.
Note: AG quoted and mentioned.

J3788 Torrey, E. Fuller. *The Roots Of Reason.* San Diego, CA: Harvest/HBJ Book, 1984, pp. 270, 279.

J3789 Wiener, John. *Come Together: John Lennon In His Time.* New York, NY: Random House, 1984.
Note: AG quoted and mentioned throughout.

1985

J3790 Ryan, William F. Allen Ginsberg—Beat Redidivus: Nightmares Of Moloch When the World Won't Turn. *Virginia Country* (Jan.-Feb. 1985) pp. 84-90, 94.
Note: AG quoted at length.

J3791 Rose, Barbara. Sassy Eye Of Sottsass. *Vogue,* vol. 75, no. 1 (Jan. 1985) pp. 230-237, 280.

J3792 Cech, John. [review of *Collected Poems*]. *USA Today* (Jan. 4, 1985) p. 3D.

J3793 Clark, Tom. [review of *Collected Poems*]. *Los Angeles Herald Examiner* (Jan. 6, 1985) pp. F5-F6.

J3794 Hogrefe, Jeffrey. Pictures From a Poet. *Washington Post* (Jan. 8, 1985) p. C7.
Note: AG quoted briefly.

J3795 Ricks, Christopher. [review of *Collected Poems*]. *Boston Globe* (Jan. 13, 1985) section B, pp. 10, 12.

J3796 Ketcham, Diana. 'The Shape Of the Mind' Intrigues Allen Ginsberg. *Oakland Tribune* (Jan. 13, 1985) Calendar section, pp. 3-6.
Note: AG interview format.

Nicosia, Gerald. [review of *Collected Poems*]. *Oakland Tribune* (Jan. 13, 1985) Calendar section, p. 6.

J3797 Cook, Bruce. Allen Ginsberg: The Beat Goes On [review of *Collected Poems*]. *Washington Post* (Jan. 13, 1985) Book World section, pp. 1-2.

J3798 Hart, Jeffrey. [review of *Collected Poems*]. *Washington Times Magazine* (Jan. 14, 1985) pp. 6M-7M.

J3799 Prado, Holly. [review of *Collected Poems*]. *Los Angeles Times* (Jan. 20, 1985) Book Review section, p. 3.

J3800 Salisbury, Harrison E. On the Literary Road: American Writers In China. *New York Times Book Review* (Jan. 20, 1985) pp. 3, 25.

J3801 A Hip Poet Revisits Home. *Paterson Morning Call* (Jan. 20, 1985)
Note: AG quoted briefly.

Students Put Gag On Poet. *Paterson Morning Call* (Jan. 20, 1985)
Note: AG quoted briefly.

J3802 Trebay, Guy. [review of AG's photograph exhibit at Holly Solomon Gallery]. *Village Voice* (Jan. 22, 1985) p. 89.

J3803 Ryan, William F. Allen Ginsberg Beat Of a Different Drummer. *Hill Rag* (Jan. 25, 1985)
Note: AG quoted briefly.

J3804 Weaver, Michael S. [review of *Collected Poems*]. *Baltimore Sun* (Jan. 27, 1985)

J3805 Sukenick, Ronald. Up From the Garret: Success Then And Now. *New York Times Book Review* (Jan. 27, 1985) p. 1.

J3806 Tucker, Ken. [review of *Collected Poems*]. *Village Voice* (Jan. 29, 1985) pp. 42-43.

J3807 Remnick, David. Podhoretz, Lion Of the Neos. *Washington Post* (Jan. 30, 1985) pp. C1-C9.

J3808 *Beat And Blues Survivors.* Berlin, W. Germany: Amerika Hause, Feb.-March 1985 seminar reports.
Note: AG mentioned throughout.

J3809 Bawer, Bruce. [review of *Collected Poems*]. *New Criterion*, vol. 3, no. 6 (Feb. 1985) pp. 1-14.

J3810 Walljasper, Jay. The Beats Go On. *Utne Reader* (Feb.-March 1985) p. 21.

J3811 Root, William Pitt. [review of *Collected Poems*]. *Denver Post* (Feb. 3, 1985) pp. 24, 27.

J3812 Cory, James M. [review of *Collected Poems*]. *Fort Worth Star-Telegram* (Feb. 3, 1985) p. 6D.

J3813 Miller, Brown. [review of *Collected Poems*]. *San Jose Mercury News* (Feb. 3, 1985) pp. 21, 25.

J3814 Sheppard, R.Z. [review of *Collected Poems*]. *Time,* vol. 125, no. 5 (Feb. 4, 1985) p. 72.
Note: AG quoted briefly.

J3815 Robinson, John. Dressing For the Opera. *Boston Globe* (Feb. 5, 1985) pp. 20-21.
Note: AG quoted briefly.

J3816 Matthews, Charles C. Ginsberg On the Beat [review of *Collected Poems*]. *Harvard Crimson* (Feb. 7, 1985) p. 2.
Note: AG quoted briefly.

J3817 [review of *Collected Poems*]. *Bookseller* (Feb. 9, 1985)

J3818 Gervais, Marty. Ginsberg Puts On Outside What People Think Inside. *Windsor Star* (Feb. 9, 1985) p. C8.
Note: AG quoted.

J3819 Mitchell, Harmen. Allen Ginsberg Brings His Passion And Scope To the DIA This Week. *Ann Arbor News* (Feb. 10, 1985) pp. G1-G2.
Note: AG quoted.

J3820 Wright, Sarah. [review of *Collected Poems*]. *Boston Herald* (Feb. 10, 1985)

J3821 Nicosia, Gerald. [review of *Collected Poems*]. *Chicago Tribune* (Feb. 10, 1985) section 14, pp. 36-37.

J3822 Milazzo, Lee. [review of *Collected Poems*]. *Dallas Morning News* (Feb. 10, 1985) p. 10C.

J3823 Krieger, Elliot. 'Serious' Poet Allen Ginsberg Doesn't Howl Anymore. *Providence Journal* (Feb. 10, 1985) pp. H-11, H-12.
Note: AG quoted briefly.

J3824 [review of *Collected Poems*]. *Tallahassee Democrat* (Feb. 10, 1985)

J3825 Jones, Stephen. [review of *Collected Poems*]. *Detroit Free Press* (Feb. 13, 1985)

McKelvey, Bob. Poet Allen Ginsberg Changes With the Times. *Detroit Free Press* (Feb. 13, 1985) p. 8C.
Note: AG quoted.

J3826 Gladysz, Thomas. Beat Generation Poet Talks About His Work [review of *Collected Poems*]. *State News* (Feb. 14, 1985)
Note: AG quoted briefly.

J3827 McLarin, Jennifer R. "Beat" Poet Ginsberg To Give Reading. *Muhlenberg Weekly,* vol. 105, no. 16 (Feb. 15, 1985) p. 1.

J3828 Shamy, Ed. Poet Of 'Beat Generation' Still At Home In the '80s. *Allentown Express* (Feb. 17, 1985) pp. A-1, A-2.
Note: AG quoted briefly.

J3829 Reinhard, Katherine. Muhlenberg Embraces Respectable Ginsberg. *Allentown Sunday Call* (Feb. 17, 1985) pp. B1, B13.
Note: AG quoted briefly.

J3830 Schenk, Charles and Rubenstein, H.G. Ginsburg [sic] Charms Crowd In LV Visit. *Globe-Times* (Feb. 17, 1985) pp. B1, B2.

J3831 Milazzo, Lee. [review of *Collected Poems*]. *News/Sun-Sentinel* (Feb. 17, 1985)

J3832 Guenther, Charles. [review of *Collected Poems*]. *St. Louis Post-Dispatch* (Feb. 17, 1985) p. 4B.

J3833 Redmond, Michael. Allen Ginsberg. *Sunday Star-Ledger* (Feb. 17, 1985) section 4, pp. 1, 23.
Note: AG quoted.

J3834 Graham, Elinor. Students Of the 1980s Meet Radical Of the '60s. *Canton Observer* (Feb. 18, 1985) p. 5B.
Note: AG quoted.

J3835 Lysaght, Brian. Schools Showed Backbone Having Ginsberg Speak. *Community Crier* (Feb. 20, 1985) p. 9.
Note: AG quoted briefly.

J3836 Calendar, Carl. Ginsberg Gains Literary Respect. *Asbury Park Press* (Feb. 21, 1985) p. D9.
Note: AG quoted briefly.

J3837 Stefaniak, Mike. Ginsberg: A Visit To Remember. *Setonian* (Feb. 21, 1985) p. 12.
Note: AG quoted briefly.

J3838 Edwards, Susan. [review of *Collected Poems*]. *Colorado Daily* (Feb. 22-23, 1985) pp. 15-16, 18.

J3839 Molesworth, Charles. [review of *Collected Poems*]. *Nation,* vol. 240, no. 7 (Feb. 23, 1985) pp. 213-215.

J3840 Low, Denise. [review of *Collected Poems*]. *Kansas City Star* (Feb. 24, 1985)

J3841 Hazo, Samuel. [review of *Collected Poems*]. *Pittsburgh Press* (Feb. 24, 1985)

J3842 De Santis, Tullio Francesco. Ginsberg Live! *Reading Eagle* (Feb. 24, 1985)

Thomas, Heather. A Beat Poet Finds New Beatitude. *Reading Eagle* (Feb. 24, 1985) pp. A14, A21.
Note: AG quoted.

J3843 Milazzo, Lee. [review of *Collected Poems*]. *Hartford Courant* (Feb. 27, 1985) p. B3.

J3844 It Don't Pay To Be an Honest Citizen. *Variety* (Feb. 27, 1985) p. 15.

J3845 Perloff, Marjorie. [review of *Collected Poems*]. *American Poetry Review,* vol. 14, no. 2 (March-April 1985) pp. 35-45.

J3846 Abrams, Alan. Still Making Poetic Waves. *Detroit Jewish News* (March 1, 1985) pp. 14-20.
Note: AG quoted at length.

J3847 [quotation]. *Libération,* special supplement to no. 1195 (March 1985) p. 53.
Note: AG quoted briefly in French only.

J3848 Leong, Evelyn. Ginsberg: Spirituality Needed In Teaching Poetry. *Pace Press* (March 1, 1985) p. 5.
Note: AG quoted.

J3849 Stuewe, Paul. [review of *Collected Poems*]. *Quill And Quire,* vol. 51, no. 3 (March 1985) p. 77.

J3850 Young, Luther. In the Eighties, the Beat Poet Goes On. *Baltimore Sun* (March 3, 1985) section G, pp. 1G, 10G.
Note: AG quoted at length.

J3851 Morin, Edward. [review of *Collected Poems*]. *Detroit News* (March 3, 1985) p. 2H.

J3852 Donovan, Laurence. [review of *Collected Poems*]. *Miami Herald* (March 3, 1985) p. 7E.

J3853 Burkhammer, Vic. [review of *Collected Poems*]. *Sunday Gazette-Mail* (March 3, 1985) p. 4A.

J3854 Schumacher, Michael. [review of *Collected Poems*]. *Milwaukee Journal* (March 4, 1985) p. 10.

J3855 Rosenblatt, Roger. [review of *Collected Poems*]. *New Republic,* vol. 192, no. 9 [issue 3659] (March 4, 1985) pp. 33-35.

J3856 Anderson, Susan Heller and Dunlap, David W. Day By Day. *New York Times* (March 4, 1985) p. B2.
Note: AG quoted briefly.

J3857 Caen, Herb. And So To Press. *San Francisco Chronicle* (March 7, 1985) p. 35.

J3858 Lofton, John. [review of *Collected Poems*]. *Washington Times* (March 8, 1985) p. 2D.

J3859 Christy, Jim. [review of *Collected Poems*]. *Vancouver Sun* (March 9, 1985) p. D13.

J3860 Berthoff, Robert. [review of *Collected Poems*]. *Buffalo News* (March 10, 1985) p. F8.

J3861 Marquand, Robert. [review of *Collected Poems*]. *Christian Science Monitor* (March 13, 1985) pp. 23-24.

J3862 Shobe, Alice. Learn To Meditate... *C.E.P. Perspective,* vol. 5, no. 7 (March 14, 1985) pp. 1, 5.
Note: AG quoted.

J3863 Salisbury, Stephan. A Guru Of the '60s Still Dissents—and Poetically. *Philadelphia Inquirer* (March 15, 1985) section C, pp. 1C, 4C.
Note: AG quoted at length.

J3864 Sinisi, J. Sebastian. East Meets West. *Denver Post* (March 16, 1985) section B, pp. 1, 3.
Note: AG quoted briefly.

J3865 [review of *Collected Poems*]. *Reporter* (March 16, 1985)

J3866 Milazzo, Lee. [review of *Collected Poems*]. *Peninsula Times Tribune* (March 17, 1985) p. E6.

J3867 Ayres, Jane. 'Ambassador From Bohemia': Gracious One Night, Tedious Next. *Times Tribune* (March 17, 1985) p. E-6.

J3868 Remnick, David. The World & Allen Ginsberg. *Washington Post* (March 17, 1985) Style section, pp. K1, K4, K5.
Note: AG quoted at length.

J3869 Miller, Don. Allen Ginsberg/The Beat Goes On. *Santa Cruz Sentinel* (March 20, 1985) p. A-12.
Note: AG quoted briefly.

J3870 Walsh, Susan Marie. An Interview With Allen Ginsberg. *Cassandra,* no. 6 (Spring 1985) pp. 4-5.
Note: AG interview format.

J3871 Bliss, Shepherd. Men, Poetry And the Military. *Changing Men,* no. 14 (Spring 1985) p. 30.

J3872 William Burroughs, Norman Mailer, Allen Ginsberg. *Naropa Magazine,* vol. 2 ([Spring] 1985) pp. 16-19.
Note: AG interview format.

Rosenthal, Bob. Faculty News. *Naropa Magazine,* vol. 2 ([Spring] 1985) p. 53.

J3873 Gladysz, Thomas. Catching Up a "Bitter Buddhist". *Red Cedar Review,* vol. 17, no. 1 & 2 (Spring 1985) pp. 82-89.
Note: AG interview format.

J3874 Denison, D.C. Allen Ginsberg. *Boston Globe* (March 24, 1985) Magazine section, pp. 2, 66-67.
Note: AG interview format.

J3875 Dobyns, Stephen. [review of *Collected Poems*]. *Philadelphia Inquirer* (March 24, 1985) Books & Leisure section, pp. P1, P8.

J3876 Salisbury, Stephan. 'Wild-Eye Poet' Beginning To Mellow. *Sunday Star* (March 24, 1985) pp. D1-D2.
Note: AG quoted briefly.

J3877 Priano, Giovanna; Bruzzone, Pierluigi and Pivano, Fernanda. Che Cosa Fanno Ginsberg & Company. *Epoca* (March 29, 1985) pp. 11-12.

J3878 Sinisi, J. Sebastian. Allen Ginsberg. *Denver Post* (March 30, 1985) section C, pp. 1C, 5C.

J3879 Warren, Ron. 57th Between A And D/Allen Ginsberg. *Arts Magazine,* vol. 59, no. 8 (April 1985) p. 38.

J3880 Berk, L. [review of *Collected Poems*]. *Choice,* vol. 22, no. 8 (April 1985) pp. 1157-1158.

J3881 Dowden, George. [review of *Collected Poems*]. *Kerouac Connection,* no. 6 (April 1985) pp. 13-15.

J3882 Stace, Wes. The Wanted Man Interview Allen Ginsberg. *Telegraph,* no. 20 (Spring [April] 1985) pp. 84-89.
Note: AG interview format.

J3883 Harding, William Harry. [review of *Collected Poems*]. *Westways,* vol. 77, no. 4 (April 1985) p. 69.

J3884 Robbins, Jonathan. Perfected Poet. *Brown Daily Herald* (April 4, 1985) pp. 1, 5.

J3885 Robbins, Jonathan. Visionary Poet. *Brown Daily Herald* (April 5, 1985) pp. 3, 9.

J3886 McCann, Janet. [review of *Collected Poems*]. *Bryan-College Station Eagle* (April 6, 1985) Book Week section, pp. 19-22.

J3887 Remnick, David. Ginsberg: The Beatific Beatitudes Of an Original Beat. *Fremont Argus* (April 7, 1985)
Note: AG quoted.

J3888 Somerville, Jane. [review of *Collected Poems*]. *Cleveland Plain Dealer* (April 7, 1985) p. 38-P.

J3889 Moss, Vicki. Poet Ginsberg Warms To Crowd At Local Store. *Fort Collins Coloradoan* (April 10, 1985) pp. 1, A6.
Note: AG quoted.

J3890 Kelley, Kevin J. Only Doing His Poetly Duty [review of *Collected Poems*]. *Guardian,* vol. 37, no. 27 (April 10, 1985) p. 20.
Note: AG interview format.

J3891 Bache-Snyder, Kaye. Beat Generation Poet Hyped On Teaching Craft. *Longmont Daily Times-Call* (April 10, 1985) p. 13.
Note: AG quoted.

J3892 Albrecht, Thomas and Gilman, Susan. Exposing Allen Ginsberg. *Banner Weekly,* vol. 1, no. 25 (April 11-18, 1985) pp. 4-5.
Note: AG interview format.

J3893 [review of *Collected Poems*]. *Time Out* (April 11, 1985)

J3894 Millard, Steve. Anti-CIA Protests Continue. *Daily Camera* (April 12, 1985) pp. 1B, 2B.

J3895 Kruger, Pamela. CU Protesters May Not Be Prosecuted. *Denver Post* (April 12, 1985) pp. 1, 3A.

J3896 Intentionally omitted.

J3897 Remnick, David. One Man's Pain Made Poetry. *Bergen Record* (April 12, 1985) pp. A20, A21.
Note: AG quoted.

J3898 Brennan, Charlie. 164 More Arrested In CIA Protest At CU. *Rocky Mountain News* (April 12, 1985) p. 10.
Note: AG quoted briefly.

J3899 Meinke, Peter. [review of *Collected Poems*]. *St. Petersburg Times* (April 14, 1985) p. 6D.

J3900   Maddox, Sam. Portrait Of a Popular Poet. *Sunday Camera* (April 14, 1985) pp. 1B, 2B.
Note: AG quoted.

J3901   Levin, Reva. [review of *Collected Poems*]. *Whole Life Times,* no. 42 (mid-April 1985) pp. 38-39.

J3902   Bache-Snyder, Kaye. Ginsberg, Beat Generation Poet Hypes Book. *County Newspaper* (April 18, 1985) p. 3.
Note: AG quoted.

J3903   Valeo, Tom. Ginsberg. *Daily Herald* (April 18, 1985) section 3, pp. 1, 3.
Note: AG quoted.

J3904   Abrams, Garry. Allen Ginsberg: Still Controversial [review of *Collected Poems*]. *Los Angeles Times* (April 18, 1985) section 5, p. 3.
Note: AG quoted briefly.

J3905   Spencer, Duncan. Ginsberg's Photo Album. *Washington Weekly* (April 19, 1985) p. 25.

J3906   Ferrell, Bonny. [review of *Collected Poems*]. *Post-Bulletin* (April 20, 1985)

J3907   Kunen, James S. Poet Allen Ginsberg Publishes His Collected Works And Grows Older, Wiser And Beat-er. *People Weekly,* vol. 23, no. 16 (April 22, 1985) pp. 106-108.
Note: AG quoted.

J3908   De Jongh, Nicholas. And the Beat Goes On. *Guardian* (April 24, 1985) p. 11.
Note: AG quoted briefly.

J3909   Ewart, Gavin. [review of *Collected Poems*]. *Listener,* vol. 113 (April 25, 1985) p. 25.

J3910   Walsh, Patrick. [review of *Collected Poems*]. *Rutgers Targum* (April 25, 1985)

J3911   Schneider, Roy. [review of *Collected Poems*]. *Tribune* (April 26, 1985) p. C-3.

J3912   Clines, Francis X. Allen Ginsberg—Andeutungen Von Sterblichkeit. *Tages-Anzeiger Magazin* (April 27, 1985) pp. 40-50.
Note: AG quoted briefly in German only.

J3913   Hollahan, Eugene. [review of *Collected Poems*]. *Atlanta Journal And Atlanta Constitution* (April 28, 1985)

J3914   Hillmore, Peter. If the Cap Fits...Wear It. *Observer* (April 28, 1985) p. 18.

J3915   Nevin, Charles. Glad To Be Ginsberg. *Sunday Telegraph* (April 28, 1985) p. 6.
Note: AG quoted briefly.

J3916   Porter, Henry. Still Howling, But Quietly. *Sunday Times* (April 28, 1985) p. 11.
Note: AG quoted briefly.

J3917   Robinson, Eugene. Allen Ginsberg. *Birth Of Tragedy,* no. 3 (May-July 1985) pp. [9-11].
Note: AG interview format.

J3918   Sante, Luc. Corporate Culture. *Manhattan, Inc.* (May 1985)

J3919   Scholnick, Michael. [review of *Collected Poems*]. *Poetry Project Newsletter,* no. 114 (May 1985) pp. [6-8].

J3920   Cantor, Judy. Old Beat Poets Never Die. *Vancouver Sun* (May 2, 1985) p. C4.
Note: AG quoted briefly.

J3921   Ryan, William F. Ginsberg's Angels. *Hill Rag* (May 3, 1985) p. 12.
Note: AG quoted briefly.

J3922   Read, Jeani. Guru Helps the Beat Go On. *Province* (May 3, 1985) p. 42.

Wyman, Max. In Sanity Lies the Truth. *Province* (May 3, 1985) p. 42.
Note: AG quoted.

J3923   Rush, Diane Samms. [review of *Collected Poems*]. *Eagle And Beacon* (May 5, 1985)

J3924   Morrison, Blake. [review of *Collected Poems*]. *Observer* (May 5, 1985) p. 25.

J3925   Hamilton, Ian. [review of *Collected Poems*]. *Sunday Times* (May 5, 1985) p. 44.

J3926   Weaver, Helen. [review of *Collected Poems*]. *Woodstock Times* (May 9, 1985) pp. 12-13.

J3927   Widgery, David. [review of *Collected Poems*]. *New Society* (May 9, 1985) pp. 197-198.

J3928   Dalton, Kevin. Oldest Swinger. *Cherwell* (May 10, 1985)
Note: AG quoted briefly.

J3929   Case, Brian. Cool Beat. *Melody Maker* (May 11, 1985)
Note: AG quoted briefly.

J3930   Hart, Jeffrey. [review of *Collected Poems*]. *St. Louis Post-Dispatch* (May 11, 1985) section B, p. 3B.

J3931   Intentionally omitted.

J3932   Cantor, Judy. Beat Goes On, In New Tempo, For Poet Ginsberg. *Journal Inquirer* (May 14, 1985) p. 27.
Note: AG quoted briefly.

J3933   Collins, Daniel. Allen Ginsberg's Traveling Circus. *Monday Magazine,* vol. 11, no. 21 (May 16-22, 1985) pp. 13-14.
Note: AG quoted.

J3934   Hart, Jeffrey. [review of *Collected Poems*]. *National Review,* vol. 37 (May 17, 1985) pp. 46-47.

J3935   McCormack, Ed. A Real Howl. *Daily News* (May 19, 1985) Magazine section, pp. 6-10, 22, 24, 26.
Note: AG quoted briefly.

J3936   Shapiro, Harvey. [review of *Collected Poems*]. *Press Democrat* (May 19, 1985) p. 14C.

J3937 Boasberg, Leonard W. 6 Poets Look To Their Jewish Roots. *Philadelphia Inquirer* (May 22, 1985)
Note: AG quoted briefly.

J3938 Selerie, Gavin. Bye, Bye, Romance. *City Limits* (May 24-30, 1985) p. 18.
Note: AG quoted at length.

J3939 Mackinnon, Lachlan. [review of *Collected Poems*]. *Times Literary Supplement,* no. 4286 (May 24, 1985) p. 574.

J3940 Weaver, Helen. [review of *Collected Poems*]. *Litchfield County Times* (May 31, 1985) p. 28.

J3941 Issue, Marc. The Howling. *Blitz,* no. 32 (June 1985) pp. 34-36.
Note: AG quoted at length.

J3942 Tremblay, Bill. [review of *Collected Poems*]. *Bloomsbury Review,* vol. 5, no. 9 (June 1985) pp. 3, 10.

J3943 Poetry Videos: "A Global Cafe Of Sorts." *Coda: Poets & Writers Newsletter,* vol. 12, no. 5 (June-July 1985) pp. 1, 8-9.
Note: AG quoted briefly.

J3944 M., G. L'Occhio Del Poeta: Fotografie Di Allen Ginsberg. *Fotografare* (June 1985) p. 117.

J3945 Bratkowski, Piotr. [review of *Utwory Poetyckie*]. *Literatura,* vol. 4, no. 33 (June 1985) pp. 52-53.

J3946 Ginsberg: Home Again. *Naropa Institute Update* (June 1985) p. 1.

J3947 Pickard, Tom. [review of *Collected Poems*]. *New Musical Express* (June 1, 1985) p. 46.

J3948 Waldman, Anne. Passage To More Than India. *Vajradhatu Sun,* vol. 6, no. 5 (June-July 1985) p. 14.

Heath, Jennifer. Ernesto Cardenal Speaks In Boulder. *Vajradhatu Sun,* vol. 6, no. 5 (June-July 1985) p. 14.

J3949 Richey, Joe. Poetry, Ginsberg's Benefits. *Maine Times* (June 15, 1985)
Note: AG quoted briefly.

J3950 Grier, Tom. 'Lines' Series a Cultural Oasis. *West Oakland* (June 19, 1985) pp. 1, 3.
Note: AG quoted briefly.

J3951 Jarman, Mark. [review of *Collected Poems*]. *Hudson Review,* vol. 38, no. 2 (Summer 1985) pp. 330-331.

J3952 Nisker, Wes. Road News. *Inquiring Mind,* vol. 2, no. 1 (Summer 1985) pp. 1, 15.
Note: AG interview format.

J3953 Monte, Bryan R. [review of *Collected Poems*]. *No Apologies,* no. 5 ([Summer] 1985) pp. 4-5.

J3954 [review of *Collected Poems*]. *Virginia Quarterly Review,* vol. 61, no. 3 (Summer 1985) p. 97.

J3955   Myers, George, Jr. The '60s Revisited. *Columbus Dispatch* (June 26, 1985) p. B1.
Note: AG quoted.

J3956   Buckley, Kirk McG. [review of *Collected Poems*]. *Ohio State Lantern* (June 27, 1985) p. 10.

Daniels, Robert. Beat Poet Concerned With Conservative Wave. *Ohio State Lantern* (June 27, 1985) p. 10.
Note: AG quoted.

J3957   Nye, Robert. [review of *Collected Poems*]. *Times* (June 27, 1985) p. 11.

J3958   Blum, Peter. Building For Buddha. *Woodstock Times,* vol. 14, no. 26 (June 27, 1985) pp. 7, 1.

J3959   Plagenz, George R. Ginsburg [sic] Calls America 'Evil', Himself 'Insane'. *Columbus Citizen-Journal* (June 28, 1985) p. 7.
Note: AG quoted.

J3960   Myers, George, Jr. Ginsberg's Music, Words Captivate Park Crowd. *Columbus Dispatch* (June 28, 1985) p. 7C.
Note: AG quoted briefly.

J3961   D'Souza, Dinesh. A Small Circle Of Friends. *American Spectator,* vol. 18, no. 7 (July 1985) pp. 17-19.
Note: AG quoted briefly.

J3962   Richman, Robert. [review of *Collected Poems*]. *Commentary,* vol. 80, no. 1 (July 1, 1985) pp. 50-55.

J3963   Anderson, Thomas. [review of *Collected Poems*]. *Creem* (July 1985) p. 44.

J3964   Pitchford, Kenneth. [review of *Collected Poems*]. *New York Native* (July 1-14, 1985) pp. 62-64.

J3965   McKibben, Robert. Ezra Pound Conference. *Maine Times* (July 5, 1985) pp. 16-17.
Note: AG quoted briefly.

J3966   Horovitz, Michael. [letter to the editor]. *Times Literary Supplement,* no. 4292 (July 5, 1985) p. 749.

J3967   Orth, Kevin. Poetry Infiltrates High Places: The Governor's Mansion. *Dublin Suburbia News* (July 10, 1985) p. 11.

J3968   Smalldon, Jeffrey L. [letter to the editor]. *Booster* (July 17, 1985) p. 5.

J3969   Chandler, Kurt. Burroughs Returns To Boulder's Acclaim. *Sunday Camera* (July 21, 1985) pp. 1E, 3E.

J3970   Shea, Gary. William S. Burroughs. *Colorado Daily* (July 22-23, 1985) pp. 1, 4.

J3971   Sinisi, J. Sebastian. Biographer Finds a New Image Of Burroughs. *Sunday Denver Post* (July 28, 1985) p. 22.

J3972   Zivancevic, Nina and Poe, Richard. Ginsberg Speaks. *East Village Eye,* vol. 7, no. 57 (Aug. 1985) pp. 24-25, 32.
Note: AG interview format.

J3973   Marvel, Bill. Allen Ginsberg, the Guru Of Beat. *Dallas Times Herald* (Aug. 16, 1985) Weekend section, pp. 1, 18-19.
         Note: AG quoted briefly.

J3974   Seipp, Catherine. Looks Like Another Eisenhower Era To Allen Ginsberg. *Los Angeles Herald Examiner* (Aug. 16, 1985) p. 35.
         Note: AG quoted.

J3975   Hyndman, Robert. Allen Ginsberg: Leaving a Literary Legacy. *Daily Pilot Datebook,* vol. 1, no. 34 (Aug. 23, 1985) pp. 3, 10.
         Note: AG quoted.

J3976   Diggory, Terence. [review of *Collected Poems*]. *American Book Review,* vol. 7, no 6 (Sept.-Oct. 1985) pp. 13, 23.

J3977   Alexander, Michael and Sullivan, A.D. Here's...Ginsberg. *Scrap Paper Review,* no. 19 (Sept. 1985) pp. 1-2.
         Note: AG quoted briefly.

J3978   McInerney, Jay. Paul Bowles In Exile. *Vanity Fair,* vol. 48, no. 9 (Sept. 1985) pp. 68-76, 131.
         Note: AG quoted briefly.

J3979   Bezner, Kevin. Ginsberg: The Beat Goes On. *Washington Book Review,* vol. 1, no. 1 (Sept. 1985) pp. 1, 6-7.
         Note: AG interview format.

         Bezner, Kevin. Charles Plymell: Wichita Maverick. *Washington Book Review,* vol. 1, no. 1 (Sept. 1985) pp. 18-19.

J3980   Cunningham, Peter. Allen Ginsberg Captures Audience At Ashawagh Hall. *Southampton Press* (Sept. 14, 1985)

J3981   Lane, Jane F. Bearing the Indian Message. *Woman's Wear Daily* (Sept. 18, 1985) p. 6.
         Note: AG quoted briefly.

J3982   Kimmel, Daniel M. On the Road Did Not Lead To Uforia. *Boston Ledger* (Sept. 19, 1985) This Week supplement, p. 4A.

J3983   Smith, Jeff. Allen Ginsberg Interview. *Feminist Baseball,* no. 2 (Autumn 1985) pp. 11-16.
         Note: AG interview format.

         Smith, Jeff. [review of *Collected Poems*]. *Feminist Baseball,* no. 2 (Autumn 1985) p. 28.

J3984   Rights Of a Writer. *Hartford Courant* (Sept. 23, 1985)
         Note: AG quoted briefly.

J3985   Alday, Roxanna. Life On the Ranch. *Westword* (Sept. 25-Oct. 1, 1985) p. 36.
         Note: AG quoted briefly.

J3986   Martin, Robert K. [review of *Collected Poems*]. *Body Politic,* no. 119 (Oct. 1985) p. 35.

J3987   Perloff, Marjorie. [letter to the editor]. *Commentary,* vol. 80, no. 4 (Oct. 1985) pp. 6, 8.

Breslin, James E.B. [letter to the editor]. *Commentary,* vol. 80, no. 4 (Oct. 1985) p. 8.

Richman, Robert. [letter to the editor]. *Commentary,* vol. 80, no. 4 (Oct. 1985) p. 8.

J3988 *Maine Writers And Publishers Alliance* (Oct.-Nov. 1985)
Note: AG mentioned throughout.

J3989 The Right Howls At a Beat Poet. *Mother Jones,* vol. 10, no. 8 (Oct. 1985) p. 13.

J3990 Saner, Reg. [review of *Collected Poems*]. *Muse,* no. 38 (Oct.-Nov. 1985) pp. 1, 13.

J3991 Pinsky, Robert. T.S. Eliot: A Memoir. *Southern Review,* vol. 21, no. 4 (Oct. 1985) pp. 1155-1159.

J3992 McDowell, Edwin. Writers Assail F.B.I. Seizures In Puerto Rico. *New York Times* (Oct. 2, 1985) section 2, p. B9.

J3993 Kikel, Rudy. Night Out With the Boys. *Bay Windows* (Oct. 3, 1985) pp. 21-22.

J3994 Curtin, Edward J. [review of *Collected Poems*]. *America,* vol. 153, no. 8 [issue 3869] (Oct. 5, 1985) pp. 206-207.

J3995 Ginsberg To Speak At UVa. *Piedmont* (Oct. 5, 1985) p. 3.

J3996 Mitchell, Harmen. [review of *Collected Poems*]. *Ann Arbor News* (Oct. 13, 1985) p. F2.

J3997 Becker, Robert. High Priest Of Protest Not Angry Now. *Daily Progress* (Oct. 13, 1985) p. D1.
Note: AG quoted.

Kerr, Tim. [review of *Collected Poems*]. *Daily Progress* (Oct. 13, 1985) pp. D1, D4.

J3998 Paul, Alan. Ginsberg: 'Every Thing Is Upside Down'. *Michigan Daily* (Oct. 16, 1985) p. 7.
Note: AG quoted at length.

J3999 Paul, Alan. Ginsberg Entertains Full House. *Michigan Daily* (Oct. 17, 1985) p. 1.
Note: AG quoted briefly.

J4000 Shiraishi, Kazuko. Zenshishu Da Shita Ginzubagu. *Namkai Nichinichi Shibun* (Oct. 19, 1985) p. 3.

J4001 [column]. *Hartford Courant* (Oct. 30, 1985)
Note: AG quoted briefly.

J4002 Kurtz, Josh. Beat Generation Poet Charms Westchester Audience. *Gannett Westchester* (Nov. 1, 1985) p. 3.
Note: AG quoted briefly.

J4003 Atlas, James. The Literary Life In San Francisco. *Vanity Fair,* vol. 48, no. 11 (Nov. 1985) pp. 42, 45.

J4004 Poe, Richard and Zivancevic, Nina. The Prophet Looks Inward. *Fairfield County Advocate* (Nov. 6, 1985) p. 20.
Note: AG interview format.

J4005 Poe, Richard and Zivancevic, Nina. The Prophet Looks Inward. *Hartford Advocate* (Nov. 6, 1985) p. 19.
Note: AG interview format.

J4006 Poe, Richard and Zivancevic, Nina. The Prophet Looks Inward. *New Haven Advocate* (Nov. 6, 1985) p. 16.
Note: AG interview format.

J4007 Allen Ginsberg Coming. *Santa Monica College Corsair* (Nov. 6, 1985) pp. 1, 11.

J4008 Poe, Richard and Zivancevic, Nina. The Prophet Looks Inward. *Valley Advocate* (Nov. 6, 1985) p. 19.
Note: AG interview format.

J4009 Van Cleave, Susanne. Shrouded In Truth. *Daily Nexus* (Nov. 7, 1985) Arts & Entertainment section, pp. 4A, 7A.
Note: AG interview format.

J4010 Wolf, Donna. Ginsberg's Vision. *Focus On Union County* [supplement to the following newspapers: *Union Leader, Springfield Leader, Mountainside Echo, Linden Leader, The Spectator, Kenilworth Leader*] (Nov. 7, 1985) pp. 1-2.
Note: AG quoted.

J4011 Donoghue, Denis. [review of *Collected Poems*]. *London Review Of Books,* vol. 7 (Nov. 7, 1985) pp. 20-22.

J4012 Elster, C.H. The Beat Mind. *Reader,* vol. 14, no. 44 (Nov. 7, 1985) pp. 1, 11.

J4013 Woodard, Josef. After the Howl. *Weekly,* vol. 7, no. 61 (Nov. 7, 1985)
Note: AG interview format.

J4014 Poet Ginsberg To Speak Nov. 12. *Insider,* vol. 6, no. 4 (Nov. 8, 1985) pp. 1, 3.

J4015 May, Patrick. Beatnik Poet Charms a New Generation. *Miami Herald* (Nov. 8, 1985) section C, pp. 1C, 2C.

J4016 Leavitt, Linda. Allen Ginsberg Reveals Mellow Side At Reading. *Scarsdale Inquirer* (Nov. 8, 1985) pp. 6, 19.
Note: AG quoted briefly.

J4017 Green, Frank. No Way Is He Conforming, Alan [sic] Ginsberg Claims. *San Diego Union* (Nov. 9, 1985) p. D-8.
Note: AG quoted at length.

J4018 Scobie, W.I. [review of *Collected Poems*]. *Advocate,* no. 433 (Nov. 12, 1985) pp. 46-47.

J4019 Brantingham, Barney. Ginsberg Makes Show a Toe-Tapper. *Santa Barbara News-Press* (Nov. 12, 1985) pp. B1, B2.

J4020 Rathbone, R. Andrew. Poet Ginsberg's Beat Surprises. *Daily Aztec/Stampa* (Nov. 13, 1985) pp. 7, 12.

J4021 Poet Allen Ginsberg Recites To Standing-Room Crowd. *Santa Monica College Corsair,* vol. 56, no. 10 (Nov. 13, 1985) pp. 1, 8.
Note: AG quoted briefly.

J4022 Van Cleave, Susanne. The Angelheaded Hipster Speaks. *Daily Nexus* (Nov. 14, 1985) pp. 4A, 7A.
Note: AG interview format, continued from the Nov. 7, 1985 issue.

J4023 Nolan, Jack. Ginsberg: Still Goin' Down. *Daily Nexus* (Nov. 15, 1985)

J4024 Dowd, Maureen. A Different Bohemia. *New York Times Magazine* (Nov. 17, 1985) pp. 26-33.

J4025 People, Etc. *Sunday Camera Magazine* (Nov. 17, 1985) p. 29.
Note: AG quoted briefly.

J4026 Pivano, Fernanda. Ginsberg: 'Sogno La Mamma E Scrivo Una Poesia'. *Corriere Della Sera* (Nov. 19, 1985) p. 3.
Note: AG interview format.

J4027 Sadler, Martha. Allen Ginsberg Apologizes To the *News And Review. Santa Barbara News & Review* (Nov. 21, 1985) Feature section.
Note: AG interview format.

J4028 Carr, C. The Needle And the Damage Done. *Village Voice* (Nov. 26, 1985) p.72.
Note: AG quoted briefly.

J4029 Moore, Geoffrey. [review of *Collected Poems*]. *Financial Times* (Nov. 30, 1985)

J4030 American, Soviet Writers Don't Go By Book In Talks. *Times-Picayune* (Nov. 30, 1985) section A, p. 21.
Note: AG quoted briefly.

J4031 Sahihi, Arman. ...Concept—Action—Music—Words. *Englisch Amerikanische Studien,* vol. 7, no. 4 (Dec. 1985) pp. 671-673.
Note: AG interview format.

Wimmer, Adi. Zwischen "Revelation" Und "Revolution". *Englisch Amerikansiche Studien,* vol. 7, no. 4 (Dec. 1985) pp. 674-684.

J4032 Regier, W.G. [review of *Collected Poems*]. *Prairie Schooner,* vol. 59, no. 4 (Winter [Dec.] 1985) pp. 105-109.

J4033 Pisanje Je Atletika. *Intervju,* no. 118 (Dec. 6, 1985) pp. 30-32.
Note: AG interview format in Serbo-Croatian only.

J4034 Ginsberg Gets Visa. *New York Times* (Dec. 6, 1985) section 3, p. C14.

J4035 Wright, David. [review of *Collected Poems*]. *Sunday Telegraph* (Dec. 15, 1985)

J4036 Brandmark, Wendy. [review of *Collected Poems*]. *City Limits* (Dec. 20, 1985)

J4037 Holborn, Mark. Allen Ginsberg's Sacramental Snapshots. *Aperture,* no. 101 (Winter 1985) pp. 8-15.
Note: AG interview format.

J4038 Igoe, Michael. Lines On Ginsberg—A Retrospective. *Earthwise News* (Winter-Spring 1986) pp. 5-6.
Note: AG quoted briefly.

J4039 K., R. Poets [The Best Of New York Issue]. *New York,* vol. 18, no. 50 (Dec. 23-30, 1985) p. 91.

J4040 Kerouac Memorial May Tell City's 'Human Story'. *Lowell Sun* (Dec. 23, 1985) p. 9.

J4041 Carroll, Charles Francis. [review of *Collected Poems*]. *Bibliofile* (ca. 1985) pp. 10-11, 13-14.

J4042 Newlove, Donald. [review of *Collected Poems*]. *Gallery* (ca. 1985) p. 24.

J4043 Hirschman, Jack. [review of *Collected Poems*]. *Left Curve,* no. 10 (1985) pp. 29-32.

J4044 Mitchell, Sharon A. Allen Ginsberg: A Profile. *Metrosphere,* no. 3 (1985-86) pp. 50-52.
Note: AG quoted at length.

J4045 *Poetry San Francisco,* no. 1 (1985)
Note: AG mentioned throughout.

J4046 Williamson, Alan. [review of *Collected Poems*]. *Sulfur,* vol. 5, no. 2 [issue 14] (1985) pp. 159-166.

Books:

J4047 Ahrends, Günther and Seeber, Hans Ulrich (eds.). *Englische Und Amerikanische Naturdichtung Im 20. Jahrhundret.* Tübingen, W. Germany: Gunter Narr, 1985.
Contents: Ahrends, Günter. Wandlungen Der Naturkozeption In Der Amerikanischen Lyrik Des 20. Jahrhunderts, pp. 215-234.
Geraths, Armin. Natur Und Spontaineität. Zur Ästhetik Der Kunstlosigkeit In Der Amerikanischen Lyrik Des 19. Und 20. Jahrhunderts, pp. 370-395.
Kreutzer, Eberhard. Zur Aktualität Zeitgenössicher Naturdichtung: Gary Snyder Und Der Ökologische Imperative, pp. 335-352.
Schiffer, Reinhold. Ist Adam Ein Löwe?, pp. 353-369.

J4048 Beaver, Harold Lowther. *The Great American Masquerade.* Totowa, NJ: Barnes & Noble, 1985, pp. 154, 199-205, 207-8.

J4049 Bornstein, George (ed.). *Ezra Pound Among the Poets.* Chicago, IL: University Of Chicago Press, 1985.
Note: AG mentioned throughout.

J4050 Bowering, George. *Craft Slices.* Ottawa, Canada: Oberon Books, 1985.
Note: Review of *Indian Journals.*

J4051 Bowles, Jane. *Out In the World.* Santa Barbara, CA: Black Sparrow Press, 1985, pp. 197-198.
Note: AG quoted briefly.

J4052 Breslin, James E.B.(ed.). *Something To Say: William Carlos Williams On Younger Poets.* New York, NY: New Directions Book, 1985.
Note: AG mentioned throughout.

J4053 Bunge, Nancy L. *Finding the Words.* Athens, OH: Swallow Press/Ohio University Press, 1985, pp. 41-52.
Note: AG interview format.

J4054   Butler, Evelyn Anne. *The Suspended Soul In Anglo-Saxon And Modern American Poetry: "Howl," "The Waste Land," "Wanderer And Seafarer;" Ginsberg, Eliot.* Unpublished Doctoral Dissertation. University Of California, San Diego, 1985.

J4055   Crumb, R. *Meet the Beats.* Sudbury, MA: Water Row Press, 1985.

J4056   *The Fifties.* New York, NY: Pantheon Books, 1985, p. 90.

J4057   Gwynne, James B. (ed.). *Amiri Baraka: The Kaleidoscopic Torch.* Harlem, NY: Steppingstones Press, 1985.
Contents: Bourne, St. Clair. An Interview With Allen Ginsberg, pp. 76-83.
Note: AG interview format.

J4058   Hayagriva Dasa. *The Hare Krishna Explosion.* n.p.: Palace Press, 1985.
Note: AG quoted and mentioned throughout.

J4059   Higginson, William J. *The Haiku Hand Book.* New York, NY: McGraw-Hill, 1985, pp. 58-59, 78, 248.

J4060   Horemans, Rudi (ed.). *Beat Indeed!* Antwerp, Belgium: EXA, 1985 [also called *Restant,* vol. 13, no. 1 (1985)]
Note: AG mentioned throughout.

J4061   Lee, Martin A. and Shlain, Bruce. *Acid Dreams.* New York, NY: Grove Press, 1985.
Note: AG quoted and mentioned throughout.

J4062   McDarrah, Fred W. *Kerouac & Friends.* New York, NY: William Morrow, 1985.
Note: AG mentioned throughout.

J4063   Plymell, Charles. *The Harder They Come...* Santa Barbara, CA: Am Here Books, 1985, pp. 4-8.

J4064   Sorescu, Martin. *Tratat De Inspiratie.* Craiova, Romania: Scrisul Romanesc, 1985, pp. 60-62.
Note: AG interview format in Romanian only.

1986

J4065   Hart, Jeffrey. [review of *Collected Poems*]. *Dialogue,* no. 71 (Jan. 1986) pp. 72-73.
Note: French translation of the review first published in *National Review* (May 17, 1985).

J4066   Darlington, Andy. [review of *Collected Poems*]. *Kerouac Connection,* no. 9 (Jan. 1986) pp. 19-20.

J4067   Johnson, Janis. Personalities. *Philadelphia Inquirer* (Jan. 5, 1986) Magazine section, p. 3.
Note: AG quoted briefly.

J4068   Vendler, Helen. [review of *Collected Poems*]. *New Yorker,* vol. 61, no. 47 (Jan. 13, 1986) pp. 77-84.

J4069   McDowell, Edwin. Grass Vs. Bellow Over U.S. At PEN. *New York Times* (Jan. 15, 1986) section 3, p. C15.
Note: AG quoted briefly.

J4070   No Se Puede Escribir Después De Muerto. *Barricada* (Jan. 16, 1986) p. 8.

J4071   Pivano, Fernanda. Dov'è La Libertà? Zuffa Tra Scrittori. *Corriere Della Sera* (Jan. 18, 1986)

J4072   "Aqui Los Poetas Están En El Poder". *Barricada* (Jan. 23, 1986) p. 8.

J4073   Ginsberg Lee En Nicaragua Documento Censurado En EU. *El Nuevo Diario* (Jan. 26, 1986) p. 8.
         Note: AG quoted briefly in Spanish only.

J4074   Hirschman, Jack. [letter]. *Rolling Stock,* no. 12 ([Jan. 27] 1986) p. 2.

         Warner, Patrick. Talking Politics At the Sandinista Writer's Union. *Rolling Stock,* no. 12 ([Jan. 27] 1986) pp. 8, 11.
         Note: AG interview format.

         Warner, Patrick. Discussion With Salvadoran Writers. *Rolling Stock,* no. 12 ([Jan. 27] 1986) pp. 9-10.
         Note: AG interview format.

J4075   La Prensa: Luchamos Por Los Ideales Democráticos. *La Prensa* (Jan. 28, 1986) pp. 1, 10. [Managua, Nicaragua]
         Note: AG quoted briefly.

J4076   Guevara, Onofre L. Los Sofismas De Don Pablo. *Barricada* (Jan. 30, 1986) p. 3.

J4077   Ivri, Benjamin. [review of *Collected Poems*]. *Jewish News* (Jan. 30, 1986) section B, pp. 12, 27.

J4078   Gass, William H. East Vs. West In Lithuania: Rising Tempers At Writers' Meeting. *New York Times Book Review* (Feb. 2, 1986) pp. 3, 29.

J4079   Elvin, John. For Who Cannot But Love Kerouac? *Washington Times Magazine* (Feb. 10, 1986) p. 2M.

J4080   Seavor, Jim. AIDS Aid. *Providence Journal* (Feb. 14, 1986)

J4081   Ivri, Benjamin. [review of *Collected Poems*]. *Rhode Island Herald* (Feb. 14, 1986)

J4082   Crusader Takes On AIDS. *USA Today* (Feb. 17, 1986)

J4083   McIntyre, James. Controversial Poet To Lecture At UC. *Charleston Daily Mail* (Feb. 21, 1986)

J4084   Krause, Peter C. Ginsberg Signs For AIDS Benefit. *Harvard Crimson* (Feb. 21, 1986) pp. 1, 4.
         Note: AG quoted briefly.

J4085   McIntyre, James. Beat Bard Reaching For New Generation. *Charleston Daily Mail* (Feb. 26, 1986) p. 8A.
         Note: AG quoted briefly.

J4086   Oder, Norman. Poet Ginsberg Offers Evening Of Verse, Song. *Charleston Gazette* (Feb. 26, 1986)
         Note: AG quoted briefly.

J4087   Fox, Edward. Ginsberg, Best-Known U.S. Poet, Lectures, Performs At U.C. *Charleston Gazette* (Feb. 27, 1986) p. 14A.
Note: AG quoted briefly.

J4088   Smith, Robert. An Evening Of Poets Warms Crowd, pt. 1. *Vermont Cynic* (Feb. 27, 1986) pp. 14, 18.
Note: AG interview format.

J4089   Steelhammer, Rick. Ginsberg Likens Soviet Political Bureaucracy To Moral Majority. *Charleston Gazette* (Feb. 28, 1986) pp. 1C, 5C.
Note: AG quoted briefly.

J4090   [photographs]. *Shig's Review,* no. 35 (March 1986)
Note: AG mentioned throughout.

J4091   Ginsberg Levitates! *Vajradhatu Sun* (March-April 1986)
Note: AG quoted briefly.

J4092   Glueck, Grace. Alex Katz, Painting In the High Style. *New York Times Magazine* (March 2, 1986) pp. 36-8, 84-6.

J4093   Ginsberg At Saint Rose. *Albany Eagle* (March 3, 1986)

J4094   Smith, Robert. The Musings Of a Poet Ginsburg's [sic] Dialogue On Society, pt. 2. *Vermont Cynic* (March 5, 1986)
Note: AG interview format.

J4095   Barnard, Elissa. Rebellious Beat Poet Settles Down To Teach. *Mail-Star* (March 7, 1986) p. 1-E (30).
Note: AG quoted briefly.

J4096   Chilton, W.E., III. Poet Allen Ginsberg Talks Of World Drug Scene. *Sunday Gazette-Mail* (March 9, 1986) pp. 4B-5B.
Note: AG interview format.

J4097   Syinide, Kenny. Allen Ginsberg Remembers a Lost Generation. *Daily News* (March 11, 1986) p. 9.
Note: AG quoted briefly.

J4098   Berton, Lee. Allen Ginsberg: No Longer Howling In the Wilderness. *Wall Street Journal* (March 11, 1986) [Eastern edition] p. 28; [Western edition] p. 30.
Note: AG quoted briefly.

J4099   Shively, Charley. Ginsberg Meditates On Death And Eternity. *Gay Community News,* vol. 13, no. 34 (March 15, 1986) pp. 7, 10, 12.
Note: AG quoted briefly.

J4100   Schubarth, Cromwell. Beat Survivor Coming To Kerouac's Home. *Lowell Sun* (March 16, 1986) p. B1.
Note: AG quoted briefly.

J4101   Konner, Melvin. [letter to the editor]. *New York Times Book Review* (March 16, 1986) p. 38.

J4102   Heath, Jennifer. The Sword And the Pen. *Sunday Camera Magazine* (March 16, 1986) pp. 6-15.
Note: AG quoted briefly.

J4103 Grondahl, Paul. At 59, Allen Ginsberg Hasn't Lost the Beat. *Albany Times-Union* (March 20, 1986) p. B-2.
Note: AG quoted briefly.

J4104 Smith, Helen. Ginsberg Revisits. *Daily Hampshire Gazette* (March 21, 1986) pp. 1, 7.
Note: AG quoted briefly.

J4105 Allen Ginsberg To Teach At Brooklyn College. *New York Times* (March 21, 1986) p. C17.

J4106 Petriano, Michael. Hail (To the Tune Of 'Howl'). *Georgetown Journal* (Spring 1986) p. 2.

J4107 Hamalian, Linda. Allen Ginsberg In the Eighties. *Literary Review,* vol. 29, no. 3 (Spring 1986) pp. 293-300.
Note: AG interview format.

Hamalian, Linda. [review of *Collected Poems*]. *Literary Review,* vol. 29, no. 3 (Spring 1986) pp. 376-378.

J4108 Tillinghast, R. [review of *Collected Poems*]. *Parnassus,* vol. 13, no. 2 (Spring-Summer 1986) p. 193.

J4109 Christensen, Paul. Postmodern Bildungsromans: The Drama Of Recent Autobiography. *Sagetrieb,* vol. 5, no. 1 (Spring 1986) pp. 29-40.

J4110 Poetry, Politics & Pragmatics. *Westwind,* vol. 29, no. 2 (Spring 1986) pp. 24-30.
Note: AG interview format.

J4111 Zlatni Venats Alenu Ginsbergu. *Dnevnik* (March 29, 1986)

J4112 Tsvetkoski, B. Krupna Figura Na Modernata Sretska Poezija. *Nova Makedonija* (March 29, 1986) p. 6.

J4113 Bakevski, Petre. Na Sinoto Ezero Na Poezijata. *Vecher* (March 29, 1986) p. 10.
Note: AG quoted briefly in Serbo Croatian only.

J4114 Lalin, M. and Bogutovin, D. Buntovnik S Razlogom. *Becherne Novosti* (April 1, 1986)
Note: AG interview format in Serbo-Croatian only.

J4115 Raddatz, Fritz J. A Pound-Per. *Nagyvilág,* vol. 31, no. 4 (April 1986) pp. 560-561.
Note: AG interview format in Hungarian only.

J4116 Sindolic, Vojo. Urlik Pred Praznim Ogledal Om. *Reporter,* no. 964 (April 1986) pp. 22-23.
Note: AG interview format in Serbo-Croatian only.

J4117 Atlas, James. A PEN Scrapbook. *Vanity Fair,* vol. 49, no. 4 (April 1986) p. 32.

J4118 Velickovin, Dusan. Chaplin Kosmichkog Dobo. *Nin,* vol. 37, no. 1840 (April 6, 1986) pp. 32-33.
Note: AG quoted briefly in Serbo-Croatian only.

J4119   Boynton, Suzanne. Write For Yourself, Ginsberg Tells Poets. *Santa Rosa Press Democrat* (April 6, 1986)
   Note: AG quoted briefly.

J4120   Bibb, Scott. Ginsberg's Haunted 'Howl'. *Diamondback* (April 8, 1986) p. 10.

J4121   A., V. Mudrosta Na Revoltot. *Studentski Zbor* (April 8, 1986)
   Note: AG quoted briefly in Serbo-Croatian only.

J4122   Poetry Ginsberg To Speak At Wes. *Wesleyan Argus* (April 8, 1986) p. 3.

J4123   Singer, Ron. Singing Ginsberg Moves Crowd. *Sonoma State Star* (April 14-20, 1986) pp. 9-10.
   Note: AG quoted briefly.

J4124   Power, Edward. Ginsberg Rages Against a Different Kind Of 'Madness'. *Philadelphia Inquirer* (April 16, 1986)
   Note: AG quoted briefly.

J4125   De Angelis, Martin. Generation Later, Beat Goes On. *Press* (April 16, 1986) p. 28.
   Note: AG quoted briefly.

J4126   Zablotsky, Susan. Allen Ginsberg At IC: Poet, Political Satirist, Entertainer. *Ithacan* (April 17, 1986) pp. 10-11.
   Note: AG quoted briefly.

J4127   Eberhart And Ginsberg Win Frost Poetry Medal. *New York Times* (April 17, 1986) section 3, p. C29.

J4128   Friedman, Sally. Beat Poet Longs For 'Traditional Values'. *Camden Times* (April 18, 1986)
   Note: AG quoted briefly.

J4129   Halijan, Doug. Literary Arts Festival Hosts Alan [sic] Ginsberg. *Sou'wester,* vol. 72, no. 17 (April 24, 1986) p. 1.

J4130   Conner, Robert. Poet Ginsberg Still Iconoclast. *Post-Star* (April 25, 1986) pp. B1, B12.
   Note: AG quoted briefly.

J4131   Johnson, Jill. Beat Generation Guru Tempers Social Temper. *Commercial Appeal* (April 30, 1986) p. C-3.
   Note: AG quoted briefly.

J4132   Wakoski, Diane. Picketing the Zeitgeist. *American Book Review* (May-June 1986) p. 3.

J4133   Karasick, Adeena. Excerpts From a Journal On Allen Ginsberg's 'Howl, part 1'. *Anerca,* vol. 1, no. 1 (May 1986) p. [11].

J4134   Cutler, Evan Ross and Kunz, Scott Michael. Allen Ginsberg. *Leading Edge,* vol. 2 (May 1986) pp. 6-7.
   Note: AG interview format.

J4135   Tematika — Aktivnost Uma. *Polja,* vol. 32, no. 327 (May 1986) p. 236.
   Note: AG quoted in Serbo-Croatian only translated by Zoran Petkovic.

J4136 Discovering Joy. *Windhorse Review,* vol. 2, no. 2 ([May] 1986) [Special supplement] pp. [2-3].
Note: AG interview format.

J4137 Thomas, William. Ginsberg Traveling In Blazer, Striped Tie. *Commercial Appeal* (May 4, 1986)
Note: AG quoted briefly.

J4138 [letters to the editor]. *Pioneer,* vol. 3, no. 9 (May 6, 1986) pp. 2-3.

J4139 Dunne, Mike. Does Allen Ginsberg Matter Anymore? *Sacramento Bee* (May 6, 1986) pp. AA7, AA10.
Note: AG quoted briefly.

J4140 Cleaveland, Carol L. Allen Ginsberg: 'Emotions Intact' And the Beat Goes On. *Post-Standard* (May 8, 1986) p. B-3.
Note: AG quoted briefly.

J4141 Bourke, Brian G. Ginsberg Protests From 'Safe' Classrooms. *Syracuse Herald-Journal* (May 8, 1986) p. D5.
Note: AG quoted briefly.

J4142 Poetry And Music Of India In the Park. *New York Times* (May 9, 1986)

J4143 What Happened To Kerouac? *New York Times* (May 23, 1986) p. 16.

J4144 Ginsberg Thanks Peace Marchers. *Daily Camera* (May 25, 1986)
Note: AG quoted briefly.

J4145 Bouchillon, Kim. 'Beat' Poet Sings Generation Blues. *Jackson Clarion-Ledger* (May 31, 1986) pp. 1B-2B.
Note: AG quoted briefly.

J4146 McQuay, David. Mr. Magic And the Cosmos. *Denver Post* (June 1, 1986) Empire supplement, pp. 14-20.
Note: AG quoted briefly.

J4147 Clines, Francis X. Ginsberg, Treinta Años Después. *Diario De Poesía,* no. 1 (June 1986) pp. 3, 5.
Note: AG quoted briefly in Spanish only.

J4148 Vidyadhara In Esquire. *Vajradhatu Sun,* vol. 8, no. 5 (June-July 1986) p. 7.

J4149 Väth-Hinz, Henriette. [review of *White Shroud* illustrated by Francesco Clemente]. *Wolkenkratzer Art Journal,* vol. 3, no. 13 (June-Aug. 1986) pp. 70-73.
Note: Translated into English by Clara Seneca.

J4150 Jones, Kevin. A Generation Or Two Later, Ginsberg Is Still Misunderstood. *Jackson Daily News* (June 2, 1986) p. 3C.
Note: AG quoted briefly.

J4151 Boyd, Brian. The Poetry Project. *New Manhattan Review,* vol. 2, no. 6 (June 11, 1986) pp. 20-23.
Note: AG quoted briefly.

J4152 Seitz, Fred. Ginsberg Shows Mature Side. *Pocono Record* (June 12, 1986) p. 13.
Note: AG quoted briefly.

J4153   Compton, Robert. A Man Of Rhyme And Reasons. *Dallas Morning News* (June 16, 1986) pp. 1E, 6E.
Note: AG quoted briefly.

J4154   Mikhajlova, Dijana. Zhivotot E Se Vo Mojot Zhivot. *Nova Makedonija*, vol. 42, no. 14156 (June 21, 1986) p. 6.
Note: AG interview format in Macedonian only.

J4155   Talking About Words. *Beef,* vol. 6, no. 19 (Summer 1986) p. 25.

J4156   Skerl, Jennie. Ginsberg On Burroughs: An Interview. *Modern Language Studies,* vol. 16, no. 3 (Summer 1986) pp. 271-278.
Note: AG interview format.

J4157   Volpendesta, David. The Rebel Bookshop Doesn't Look Back. *North Beach Magazine,* vol. 2, no. 2 (Summer 1986) pp. 8-14, 36-41.

J4158   Sax, Robert. Refusing To Be Burned Out! *Solid!,* vol. 1, no. 1 (Summer 1986) pp. 22-27.
Note: AG interview format.

J4159   Changing Society Through Art? *Guardian,* vol. 38, no. 38 (June 25, 1986) p. 1.

J4160   Pound's Influence. *American Poetry Review,* vol. 15, no. 4 (July-Aug. 1986) pp. 7-8.
Note: AG transcript of speech.

J4161   I Love Old Whitman So. *Atlantic Report* (July 1986) l. [9].
Note: AG quoted briefly.

J4162   Touch Whom You Touch...Die When You Die. *Rutgers Alumni Monthly* (July 1986) p. 1.

J4163   Social Action Beyond Hope And Fear. *Vajradhatu Sun,* vol. 8, no. 6 (Aug.-Sept. 1986) pp. 3, 10-11, 16.
Note: AG interview format.

   Allen Ginsberg's 60th Birthday Celebration. *Vajradhatu Sun,* vol. 8, no. 6 (Aug.-Sept. 1986) p. 17.
Note: AG quoted briefly.

J4164   Palmer, Robert. The Pop Life. *New York Times* (Aug. 13, 1986) p. C20.

J4165   Hobo Blues Band. *P.M.,* vol. 35, no. 33 (Aug. 13-20, 1986) pp. 42-3.

J4166   Konformisti, Odete Si Doma. *Nova Makedonija* (Aug. 16, 1986)
Note: AG quoted briefly in Macedonian only.

J4167   Vicanovic, Vican. Allen Ginsberg. *Panorama Subotom,* no. 430 (Aug. 16, 1986) p. 20.

J4168   Chandler, Kurt. Naropa's New Age. *Sunday Camera Magazine* (Aug. 17, 1986) pp. 6+.
Note: AG quoted.

J4169   Rusi, Iso. Allen Ginsberg: Svatko Ima Svoju Viziju. *Danas,* no. 235 (Aug. 19, 1986) pp. 28-32.
Note: AG interview format in Serbo-Croatian only.

J4170 Mazova, Ljiljana. Petindvajsetic Skupaj Odposlanci Lepega In Dobrega. *Delo* (Aug. 21, 1986)

J4171 Jaukoviy, M. and Laliy, M. „Septembar" Na Drimu. *Novosti* (Aug. 21, 1986)
Note: AG interview format in Serbo-Croatian only.

J4172 Mrvosh, Bogdan. Alen Ginsberg: Govorimo Istinu. *Borba* (Aug. 22, 1986)

J4173 Pisane Kao Zhivot. *Dnevnik* (Aug. 22, 1986)

J4174 An., T. Luchoshu Za Kou Se Zdoruva. *Ekran* (Aug. 22, 1986)

J4175 Poetot Im Pomaga Na Lugeto. *Nova Makedonija* (Aug. 22, 1986)

J4176 Simic, Goran. Svijest O Nashem Smrtnom Prisustvu. *Oslobodenji* (Aug. 22, 1986)
Note: AG quoted briefly in Serbo-Croatian only.

J4177 Mrvosh, Bogdan. U Potrazi Za Nezhnoshbu. *Borba* (Aug. 23, 1986)

J4178 Covjek Nebrojenih Suprotnosti. *Glas* (Aug. 23, 1986)
Note: AG quoted briefly in Serbo-Croatian only.

J4179 Kuzmanovic, Jasmina. Allen Ginsberg, Pjesnik Proslosti. *Panorama Subotom,* no. 431 (Aug. 23, 1986) p. 4.
Note: AG quoted briefly in Serbo-Croatian only.

J4180 Pishi Kao Shtozhivish. *Pobjeda* (Aug. 23, 1986)
Note: AG quoted briefly in Serbo-Croatian only.

J4181 Stigao Ginsberg, Upaljena Vatra. *Slobodna Dalmacija* (Aug. 23, 1986)

J4182 Plakalo, Safet. Ziv Medu Zivim Mrtvacima. *Vecerje Novin* (Aug. 23, 1986)

J4183 Bakevski, Petre. Se Chuvstvuvam Kako Star Pes. *Vecher* (Aug. 23, 1986)
Note: AG interview format in Serbo-Croatian only.

Protokol. *Vecher* (Aug. 23, 1986)

Takovski, E. Poteche Poet-Skiot Zbor. *Vecher* (Aug. 23, 1986)

J4184 Pjesnicki Mostovi Nade. *Vjesnik* (Aug. 23, 1986)

J4185 Kostin, D. Poetski Portret Alena Ginsberga. *Jedinstvo* (Aug. 24-25, 1986)
Note: AG quoted briefly in Serbo-Croatian only.

J4186 Velickovic, Dusan. Misljenja Kralja Maja. *Nin*, vol. 37, no. 1860 (Aug. 24, 1986) pp. 26-28.
Note: AG quoted briefly in Serbo-Croatian only.

J4187 Sartalicc, Rada. Um Je Velik Kao Nedo. *Politika*, vol. 83, no. 26181 (Aug. 24, 1986) p. 12.
Note: AG interview format in Serbo-Croatian only.

J4188 Predstavljen Portret Allena Ginsberga. *Novi List* (Aug. 25, 1986)

J4189 Laureat U „Svetoj Sofiji". *Pobjeda* (Aug. 25, 1986)
Note: AG quoted briefly in Serbo-Croatian only.

J4190   Takovski, E. Doslednost Kon Poezijata. *Vecher* (Aug. 25, 1986)

J4191   Poezija U Ohridskoj Katedrali. *Vjesnik* (Aug. 25, 1986)

J4192   Pesmi V Katedrali. *Dnevnik* (Aug. 26, 1986)

J4193   Uruchena Priznana. *Pobjeda* (Aug. 26, 1986)

J4194   Pisi, Kot Zivis, Zivi, Kot Pises. *Vecher* (Aug. 26, 1986)
          Note: AG quoted briefly in Serbo-Croatian only.

          Gogovski Go Primi Ginsberg. *Vecher* (Aug. 26, 1986)

          Zlati Venec Ginsbergu. *Vecher* (Aug. 26, 1986)

J4195   Zavrsene Struske Veceri Poezije. *Vjesnik* (Aug. 26, 1986)

J4196   Mrvosh, Bogdan. Zavodliva Mon Pesme. *Borba* (Aug. 27, 1986)

J4197   S.G. — B. Ts. Novi Odushevuvana Od Majstorite Na Poezijata. *Nova Makedonija* (Aug. 27, 1986)

J4198   Kostin, Dragan. Ginsberg Se Klana Desanki. *Ivdinstvo* (Aug. 28, 1986)

J4199   [photographs and captions of AG]. *Nova Makedonija* (Aug. 28, 1986)

J4200   Veres, Sasa. Struga I Allen. *Oko,* vol. 13, no. 377 (Aug. 28, 1986)

J4201   Strushki Vecherina Poezijata '86. *Ekran* (Aug. 29, 1986)

J4202   Kitanovski, Misho. Dostojanstvo Nasheg Vremena. *Komunist* (Aug. 29, 1986)

J4203   R., K. Ginsberg U Beogradu. *Politika Ekspres* (Aug. 29, 1986)

J4204   Kamenski, B. Vitalnost Sezdesetih. *Vecernji List* (Aug. 29, 1986)

J4205   Obrenovic, J. Bastina Beat-Pjesnistva. *Vjesnik* (Aug. 29, 1986)

J4206   S., D.D. Portret Alena Ginsberga. *Vecherye Novosti,* vol. 34, no. 2 (Aug. 30, 1986) p. 11.

J4207   Otrov Za Buducnost. *Dnevnik* (Aug. 31, 1986)
          Note: AG quoted briefly in Serbo-Croation only.

J4208   Georgievski, S.; Tsvetkovski, B. and Bajo, N. Besmrtnite Misli Na Poetskiot Um. *Nova Makedonija* (Aug. 31, 1986) pp. 1, 10.
          Note: AG quoted briefly in Serbo-Croatian only.

          Literaturna Vecher Na Alen Ginsberg. *Nova Makedonija* (Aug. 31, 1986)

J4209   Tallman, Warren. [letter to the editor]. *Anerca,* vol. 1, no. 3 (Sept. 1986) pp. 24-26.

J4210   Gray, Francine Du Plessix. Inside the New China: A State Of Perpetual Surprise. *Vogue,* vol. 176, no. 9 (Sept. 1986) pp. 476, 479, 481, 483, 485-7.
          Note: AG quoted briefly.

J4211   Struske Veceri Poezije. *Odien* (Sept. 1, 1986)

J4212 Stancic, Mladen. Sa Pesnickog Mosta U Nezaborav. *4 Jul* (Sept. 2, 1986)

J4213 Potocnik, Peter. Na Moc Urejeni Pesniski Oce "Tepene Generacije". *Delo* (Sept. 4, 1986)
Note: AG quoted briefly in Serbo-Croatian only.

J4214 Glisic, M. Struga Naseg Zadovoljstva. *Dzepni,* vol. 7, no. 8 [issue 336] (Sept. 4, 1986) p. 33.
Note: AG quoted briefly in Serbo-Croatian only.

J4215 Bajt, Drago. Poezija: Prava V Pravem Svetu. *Dnevnik* (Sept. 5, 1986)

J4216 Plakalo, Safet. Urlik (Do) Bitnika. *Svijet* (Sept. 5, 1986)

J4217 Susret Sa Ginzbergom. *Tu Novostn* (Sept. 5, 1986) p. 11.

J4218 Brdaric, D. Prosjeda Brada Bitnickoga Barda. *Vecernji List* (Sept. 5, 1986)

J4219 Perovin, Sreten. Praznik Pjesnichke Rijechi. *Pobjeda* (Sept. 6, 1986)

J4220 Ivackovic, Ivan. Susrets Velikanima Poezijai Biografske Pikanterije. *Nasi Dani* (Sept. 12, 1986)

J4221 Platt, Adam. Chinese Students: The Long Visit. *Insight* (Sept. 15, 1986) pp. 22-24.

J4222 Berry, Steve. He Leaves Them Howling. *Columbus Dispatch* (Sept. 16, 1986)
Note: AG quoted briefly.

J4223 Carneci, Radu. Laureatul De La Struga '86. *Contemporanul,* no. 38 (Sept. 19, 1986) p. 15.
Note: AG quoted in Romanian only.

J4224 Stoilkovin, Petar and Stojanovin, Krasimirka. Monolog Struge. *Vranske Novine* (Sept. 19, 1986)

J4225 Ritkes, Daniel. Interview: Allen Ginsberg. *Blue Window,* vol. 1, no. 1 (Fall-Winter 1986) pp. 20-23.
Note: AG interview format.

J4226 Kostelanetz, Richard. The Present State Of American Poetry, v. *New York Quarterly,* no. 31 (Fall 1986) pp. 115-119.

J4227 [photographs]. *Shig's Review,* no. 43 ([Fall] 1986)
Notes: AG mentioned throughout.

J4228 Cohn, Jim. The New Deaf Poetics: Visible Poetry. *Sign Language Studies* (Fall 1986) pp. 263-277.
Note: AG quoted.

J4229 [review of *White Shroud Poems*]. *Publishers Weekly,* vol. 230, no. 13 (Sept. 26, 1986) p. 63.

J4230 Craig, Jane T. and Ide, Chris. Ginsberg. *End Times,* no. 9 ([Sept. 29] 1986) pp. [7-10].
Note: AG interview format.

J4231 Rau, Aurel. Struga 1986 Prin Allen Ginsberg. *Steaua,* vol. 37, no. 10 (Oct. 1986) pp. 18-20.

Deaconescu, Ion. Cu Allen Ginsberg Despre Sine Si Poezie. *Steaua,* vol. 37, no 10 (Oct. 1986) p. 21.
Note: AG interview format in Romanian only.

J4232 Wyckoff, P.L. Poets Bring Words To Life. *Daily Record* (Oct. 12, 1986) pp. B1, B16.
Note: AG quoted briefly.

J4233 Miklaszewski, Krzysztof. Z Allenem Ginsbergiem Spotkanie Wtore. *Zycie Literackie,* vol. 36, no. 41 (Oct. 12, 1986) p. 7.
Note: AG interview format in Polish only.

J4234 Bajraj, Fadil. Fragmente Nga Biseda Me Alen Ginzbergun. *Fjala,* vol. 19, no. 18 (Oct. 15, 1986) p. 9.
Note: AG quoted briefly.

J4235 McDonald, Lavern. Ginsberg Named Distinguished Professor. *Kingsman,* vol. 73, no. 7 (Oct. 24, 1986) p. 1.
Note: AG quoted briefly.

J4236 Henderson, Jess C. Songs Of Innocence And Experience. *Spectrum,* no. 36 (Oct. 29-Nov. 11, 1986) p. 14.

J4237 Ficara, Ken. Allen Ginsberg Eases Pain At BC. *Kingsman,* vol. 73, no. 8 (Oct. 31, 1986) pp. 5-6.
Note: AG quoted.

J4238 [letter to the editor]. *American Book Review,* vol. 8, no. 6 (Nov.-Dec. 1986) pp. 3, 23.

J4239 [review of *White Shroud Poems*]. *Booklist,* vol. 83, no. 5 (Nov. 1, 1986) p. 382.

J4240 Silverman, Herschel. High And Nostalgic On the Beats. *Kerouac Connection,* no. 12 (Nov. 1986) pp. 5-7.

J4241 Silberman, Steve. Ginsberg At 60: Freeing the Spirit [review of *White Shroud Poems*]. *San Francisco Sentinel* (Nov. 1986)

J4242 Muro, Mark. Boston Globe Book Festival. *Boston Globe* (Nov. 2, 1986) p. C22.

J4243 In a Reflective Mood. *Boston Globe* (Nov. 7, 1986) p. 23.

J4244 Grundberg, Andy. Affirming And Dissident Visions Of America. *New York Times* (Nov. 9, 1986) pp. H31, 35.

J4245 Clark, Tom. [review of *Howl* (Facsimile edition) and *White Shroud Poems*]. *San Francisco Chronicle* (Nov. 9, 1986) Review section, pp. 1, 11.

J4246 Cunha, Robert F., Jr. Politics, Pederasty And Consciousness [review of *White Shroud Poems*]. *Harvard Crimson* (Nov. 20, 1986) p. 2.
Note: AG interview format.

J4247 Robb, Christina. [review of *White Shroud Poems*]. *Boston Globe* (Nov. 28, 1986) p. 87.

J4248 Grossman, Ron. The Beat Goes On. *Chicago Tribune* (Nov. 30, 1986) Books section, pp. 1, 4.
Note: AG quoted briefly.

J4249 Krieger, Elliot. Ginsberg, Snyder: Beating the Odds [review of *White Shroud Poems*]. *Providence Journal* (Nov. 30, 1986) pp. I-1, I-3.

J4250 Moskowitz, Barry. A Peripatetic Poet Settles Down At Brooklyn. *Brooklyn College Magazine,* vol. 3, no. 1 (Dec. 1986) pp. 15-16.
Note: AG quoted briefly.

J4251 De Mers, Tom. Censorship Exposed At the DPL. *Muse* (Dec. 1986-Jan. 1987) pp. 8-9.
Note: AG quoted briefly.

J4252 Levine, Daniele. Stuy Welcomes Allen Ginsberg, Revolutionary Poet. *Spectator,* vol. 132, no. 3 (Dec. 1986) pp. 1, 7.
Note: AG quoted briefly.

J4253 Wimmer, Adi. Die Transzendierung Blosser Referentialität Als Akt Der Leserbeteiligung. *Zeitschrift Für Anglistik Und Amerikanistik,* vol. 34, no. 4 (Dec. 1986) pp. 325-342.

J4254 Czaplinski, Czeslaw. Rzady Sie Zmieniaja Kultura Zostaje. *Nowy Dziennik,* vol. 15, no. 4013 (Dec. 4, 1986) p. 5.

J4255 Bamber, Linda. Writers Can Be Friends. *New York Times Book Review* (Dec. 14, 1986) pp. 1, 40-41.
Note: AG quoted briefly.

J4256 Berman, Paul. The Dream Apartment. *Village Voice* (Dec. 16, 1986) p. 40.
Note: AG quoted briefly.

J4257 Smith, Helen. Some Personal Favorites And Views On Sharing...[review of *White Shroud Poems*] *Daily Hampshire Gazette* (Dec. 17, 1986)

J4258 Jennings, Karla. Allen Ginsberg Remembers Viietnam [sic] At SUSB. *Three Village Herald* (Dec. 17, 1986)
Note: AG quoted briefly.

J4259 Hass, Robert. The Howl Heard Round the World. *San Francisco Chronicle* (Dec. 21, 1986) Image section, pp. 26-29, 39.

J4260 Boruch, Marianne. Dickinson Descending. *Georgia Review,* vol. 40, no. 4 (Winter 1986) pp. 863-877.

J4261 Butscher, Edward. [review of *Collected Poems*]. *Poet Lore,* vol. 80, no. 4 (Winter 1986) pp. 234-238.

J4262 Martone, John. [review of *Collected Poems*]. *World Literature Today,* vol. 60, no. 1 (Winter 1986) p. 113.

J4263 Rosenberg, Liz. [review of *White Shroud Poems*]. *Chicago Tribune* (Dec. 26, 1986) section 5, p. 3.

J4264 Clark, Tom. The Wandering Minstrel. *Denver Post* (Dec. 28, 1986) pp. 15, 18.
Note: AG quoted briefly.

J4265 [letter to AG]. *Fessenden Review,* vol. 11, no. 2 (1986) p. 3.

J4266 [quotation]. *Irregular Quarterly,* vol. 3, no. 2 (1986) pp. 107-108.
Note: AG quoted briefly.

J4267 Alyakrinsky, Oleg. Three Versions Of Protest: Beat Poets Since Then, Allen Ginsberg, Lawrence Ferlinghetti And Gary Snyder. *Literaturnaya Uchoba,* no. 6 (1986)

Books:

J4268 Balakian, Anna. *Surrealism: The Road To the Absolute.* Chicago, IL: University Of Chicago Press, 1986, pp. 8-9, 20.

J4269 Charters, Ann. *Beats And Company.* Garden City, NY: Doubleday, 1986.
Note: AG mentioned throughout.

J4270 Gilbert, James. *Another Chance: Postwar America, 1945-1985.* Chicago, IL: Dorsey Press, 1986, p. 253.

J4271 Köbányai, János. *Ká! Ká! Ká!: Fotó Ginsberg Koponyájáról.* Budapest, Hungary: Magvetö Könyvkiadó, 1986, pp. 48-52.
Note: AG quoted briefly in Hungarian only.

J4272 Montgomery, John (ed.). *Kerouac At the "Wild Boar".* San Anselmo, CA: Fels & Firn Press, 1986.
Note: AG mentioned throughout.

J4273 Morgan, Bill and Rosenthal, Bob (eds.). *Best Minds: A Tribute To Allen Ginsberg.* New York, NY: Lospecchio Press, 1986.
Note: AG mentioned and quoted throughout.

J4274 Morgan, Bill. *Kanreki: A Tribute To Allen Ginsberg, Part 2.* New York, NY: Lospecchio Press, 1986.
Note: AG mentioned throughout.

J4275 Shelton, Robert. *No Direction Home.* New York, NY: Beech Tree Books/William Morrow, 1986.
Note: AG quoted and mentioned throughout.

J4276 Weinberg, Jeffrey H. (ed.). *Writers Outside the Margin.* Sudbury, MA: Water Row Press, 1986.
Note: AG quoted and mentioned throughout.

J4277 Weinberger, Eliot. *Works On Paper, 1980-1986.* New York, NY: New Directions, 1986.
Note: AG mentioned throughout.

1987

J4278 Torgersen, Eric. Will the Rock-and-Roll Generation Of Poets Ever Grow Up? *American Book Review,* vol. 9, no. 1 (Jan.-Feb. 1987) pp. 3-4.

J4279 Terkel, Studs. Studs Terkel Interviews Allen Ginsberg, Gregory Corso & Peter Orlovsky, 1959. *And,* vol. 1, no. 2 (Jan.-Feb. 1987) pp. 1, 13-18.
Note: AG interview format.

J4280 Severi, Rita. I "Beats", Il Viaggio, L'Italia. *Bollettino Del C.I.R.V.I.,* vol. 8, no. 1-2 [issue 15-16] (Jan.-Dec. 1987) pp. 95-116.

J4281 Kowalczyk, Dariusz. «Ciezar Na Mej Melacholijnij Glowie...» *Poezja,* vol. 22, no. 1 [issue 251] (Jan. 1987) pp. 102-104.

J4282 Quotable Quotes. *Underground Forest,* vol. 4, no. 1 (Jan. 1987) p. 4.
Note: AG quoted briefly.

J4283 Podhoretz, Norman. Strange Honor For a False Prophet. *New York Post* (Jan. 6, 1987) p. 19.

J4284 Podhoretz, Norman. A Monument To Jack Kerouac? *Washington Post* (Jan. 8, 1987) p. A21.

J4285 Milazzo, Lee. Allen Ginsberg: Metamorphosis Of a Radical [review of *Howl* (Facsimile edition) and *White Shroud Poems*]. *Dallas Morning News* (Jan. 11, 1987) p. 10C.

J4286 Kohler, Vince. 'King Of the Beats' And His Recurring Howl [review of *Howl* (Facsimile edition) and *White Shroud Poems*]. *Oregonian* (Jan. 11, 1987) Books section, p. 22.

J4287 West, Diana. Beat Poet Still 'Howls'. *Washington Times* (Jan. 14, 1987)
Note: AG quoted briefly.

J4288 Wolfe, Jane. Ginsberg Bitten By Photo Bug. *Dallas Morning News* (Jan. 17, 1987) p. 1C.

Compton, Robert. A Poet's Record Of His Time. *Dallas Morning News* (Jan. 17, 1987) pp. 1F, 2F.
Note: AG quoted briefly.

J4289 Gaydos, Jeff. [review of *Howl* (Facsimile edition) and *White Shroud Poems*]. *Detroit News* (Jan. 18, 1987) section B, p. 9B.

J4290 Anderson, Roger. Chains Of Flashing Images. *Daily Californian* (Jan. 30, 1987) pp. 9, 13-14.
Note: AG interview format.

J4291 Silberman, Robert. Outside Report: Robert Frank. *Art In America,* vol. 75, no. 2 (Feb. 1987) pp. 130-139.

J4292 Gargan, William. [review of *White Shroud Poems*]. *Library Journal,* vol. 112, no. 3 (Feb. 1, 1987) p. 81.

Kniffel, Leonard. American Literature—Who's Publishing It? *Library Journal,* vol. 112, no. 3 (Feb. 1, 1987) pp. 103-109.

J4293 Buchsbaum, Herbert. The Beat Family Album Comes To Life. *Miami Herald* (Feb. 1, 1987) Neighbors section, p. 34.

J4294 Abrams, Sam. Ginsberg Now: A Potent Dose Of Medicine [review of *White Shroud Poems*]. *Rochester Democrat And Chronicle* (Feb. 1, 1987) pp. 8D, 12D.

J4295 Buchsbaum, Herbert. Ginsberg Pictures His Past. *Miami Herald* (Feb. 2, 1987) p. 5D.
Note: AG quoted briefly.

J4296 Gaarder, Harold. The Droll Master Of the Throwaway Line. *Christian Science Monitor* (Feb. 9, 1987)

J4297   Silberman, Steve. Allen Ginsberg, Elder Statesman Of Bohemia, Still Howling At 60. *San Francisco Sentinel* (Feb. 13, 1987) pp. 18-19, 28-29.
Note: AG interview format.

J4298   Charters, Ann. [review of *Howl* (Facsimile edition) and *White Shroud Poems*]. *Los Angeles Times* (Feb. 15, 1987) Book Review section, p. 2.

J4299   Schumacher, Michael. Ginsberg Still Turning the Spotlight Inward. *Milwaukee Journal* (Feb. 15, 1987) pp. 1E-2E.
Note: AG quoted briefly.

J4300   Schogol, Marc. The Kerouac Mystique. *Newsday* (Feb. 15, 1987) Magazine section, pp. 30-34, 36.
Note: AG quoted.

J4301   Sanoff, A.P. The Poet's Pursuit: Capturing Dreams. *U.S. News & World Report,* vol. 102, no. 6 (Feb. 16, 1987) p. 74.
Note: AG quoted at length.

J4302   Sagan, Miriam. [review of *White Shroud Poems*]. *Albuquerque Journal* (Feb. 17, 1987)

J4303   Krieger, Elliot. [review of *White Shroud Poems*]. *Enterprise* (Feb. 22, 1987)

Landsberg, Mitchell. Literary Ghosts Haunt Shelves Of Gotham Book Mart. *Enterprise* (Feb. 22, 1987)
Note: AG quoted briefly.

J4304   Landsberg, Mitchell. Final Chapter In Store For Famous Bookshop. *Roseburg News-Review* (Feb. 22, 1987)
Note: AG quoted briefly.

J4305   Chollet, Laurence. Allen Ginsberg's Beatific Beat Goes On. *Sunday Record* (Feb. 22, 1987) section F, pp. 1, 8-9.
Note: AG quoted.

J4306   Berk, L. [review of *Howl* (Facsimile edition) and *White Shroud Poems*]. *Choice,* vol. 24, no. 7 (March 1987) p. 1058.

J4307   Schaeneman, Taryn. Allen Ginsberg's Academic Beat Poetry Series. *Cover,* vol. 1, no. 3 (March 1987) p. 35.

J4308   Schwartz, John. Searching For Wisdom. *Newsweek On Campus* (March 1987) pp. 33-34.
Note: AG quoted briefly.

J4309   Gold, Herbert. [review of *White Shroud Poems*]. *San Francisco Focus,* vol. 34, no. 3 (March 1987) p. 40.

J4310   Allen Ginsberg. *Examiner Centennial* [special edition of *San Francisco Examiner*] (March 3, 1987) pp. 31-32.

J4311   Dodsworth, Martin. [review of *Howl* (Facsimile edition) and *White Shroud Poems*]. *Guardian* (March 6, 1987)

J4312   Pettingell, Phoebe. [review of *Howl* (Facsimile edition) and *White Shroud Poems*]. *New Leader,* vol. 70, no. 3 (March 9, 1987) pp. 15-16.

J4313 Jones, Stephen. [review of *White Shroud Poems*]. *Detroit Free Press* (March 15, 1987)

J4314 Thwaite, Anthony. [review of *Howl* (Facsimile edition) and *White Shroud Poems*]. *Observer* (March 15, 1987) p. 26.

J4315 Vigliarolo, Peter F. Shopping For Images Of Allen Ginsberg. *English Majors' Newsletter,* vol. 5, no. 2 (Spring 1987) pp. 13-15.
Note: AG interview format.

J4316 Gefin, Laszlo K. Through Images Juxtaposed: Two Hungarian Poetic Responses To Allen Ginsberg's Howl. *Hungarian Studies Review,* vol. 14, no. 1 (Spring 1987) pp. 49-60.

J4317 Dougherty, Jay. [review of *Mind Breaths*]. *Sagetrieb,* vol. 6, no. 1 (Spring 1987) pp. 81-92.

J4318 Guenther, Charles. [review of *Howl* (Facsimile edition) and *White Shroud Poems*]. *St. Louis Post-Dispatch* (March 22, 1987) section C, p. 5C.

J4319 [review of *Howl* (Facsimile edition) and *White Shroud Poems*]. *Virginia Quarterly Review,* vol. 63, no. 2 (Spring 1987) pp. 66-68.

J4320 Gray, Francine Du Plessix. Charles Olson And an American Place. *Yale Review,* vol. 76, no. 3 (Spring 1987) pp. 341-352.

J4321 Allen Ginsberg. *Current Biography,* vol. 48, no. 4 (April 1987) pp. 26-30.

J4322 Aarons, Victoria. The Ethical Fiction Of Delmore Schwartz, Identity, Generation, And Culture. *Jewish Quarterly Review,* vol. 77, no. 4 (April 1987) pp. 255-282.

J4323 Lewis, Joel. [review of *Howl* (Facsimile edition)]. *Poetry Project Newsletter,* no. 126 (April-May 1987) p. 4.

J4324 Schumacher, Michael. [review of *Howl* (Facsimile edition)]. *Writer's Digest* (April 1987) pp. 39-40.

J4325 Basler, George. Inner Vision Leads Artist, Poet Says. *Press & Sun Bulletin* (April 5, 1987) pp. 1B, 2B.
Note: AG quoted briefly.

J4326 Mr. Peepers: PEN Goes the Way Of All Flesh. *New York,* vol. 20, no. 15 (April 13, 1987) pp. 29-30.

J4327 Ginsberg To Visit Ole Miss This Week. *Oxford Eagle* (April 13, 1987) p. 12.

J4328 Poet To Speak At Ole Miss Today. *Northeast Mississippi Daily Journal* (April 15, 1987)

J4329 Mikell, Ray. Beat Poet To Share Works With Oxford. *Daily Mississippian* (April 15, 1987) p. 1.

J4330 Hathorn, Clay. The Song Of Liberation Is Gaining Momentum, Says 'Beat' Pioneer. *Commercial Appeal* (April 17, 1987)
Note: AG quoted briefly.

J4331 Sumrall, Bill. 'Gentle Guru' Talks Of the World And Its Concerns. *Northeast Mississippi Daily Journal* (April 17, 1987) pp. 1A, 14A.
Note: AG quoted briefly.

J4332 Friggieri, Oliver. The Modern Writer And Social Commitment. *Sunday Times* (April 19, 1987) p. 40.
Note: AG quoted briefly.

J4333 Mikell, Ray. American Countercultural Figure And Poet Talks. *Daily Mississippian* (April 22, 1987) p. 6.
Note: AG quoted briefly.

J4334 Ford, Mark. [review of *Howl* (Facsimile edition) and *White Shroud Poems*]. *London Review Of Books,* vol. 9, no. 8 (April 23, 1987) pp. 22-23.

J4335 Helms, Dave. 100 Attend Poet's Performance In Mobile. *Mobile Press Register* (April 25, 1987) p. 10A.
Note: AG quoted briefly.

J4336 Powell, Clark. Column. *Harbinger,* vol. 5, no. 13 (April 28-May 12, 1987) p. 2.
Note: AG quoted briefly.

Adams, S. Allen Ginsbeg [sic]. *Harbinger,* vol. 5, no. 13 (April 28-May 12, 1987) p. 7.

J4337 [transcript]. *1987 Summer Writing Program Newsletter* (April 28, 1987) pp. [4-6].
Note: Transcript of AG speech.

J4338 Link, David and Ramphrey, Juliette. Controversial Poet Voices Radical Opinions. *Vanguard* (April 29, 1987) p. 8.
Note: AG quoted briefly.

J4339 Nye, Robert. [review of *White Shroud Poems*]. *Times* (April 30, 1987) p. 14.

J4340 Ivry [sic: Ivri], Benjamin. [review of *Howl* (Facsimile edition) and *Collected Poems*]. *Congress Monthly,* vol. 54, no. 4 (May-June 1987) pp. 19-20.

J4341 Pérémarti, Thierry. Les Amis D'Allen Ginsberg. *Jazz Hot,* no. 441 (May 1987) pp. 34-35.
Note: AG interview format in French only.

J4342 Golden Poets Find Silver Lining. *Pulse,* vol. 1, no. 8 (May 1987) pp. [1-2].

J4343 Hirschman, Jack. [letter to the editor]. *Rolling Stock,* no. 12 ([May 3] 1987) p. 2.

J4344 Local Residents Laugh, Wonder About the Hart Affair. *Town And Country* (May 7, 1987) p. 7.

J4345 Connell, Joan. No Ordinary Buddhist. *San Jose Mercury News* (May 9, 1987) section C, pp. 1C, 12C.
Note: AG quoted briefly.

J4346 Hutchinson, Mike. All But the Laundry Bills [review of *Howl* (Facsimile edition)]. *Hampstead And Highgate Express* (May 22, 1987)

J4347 Gershuny, Grace. Rainbow Seen At Ceremony. *Caledonian-Record* (May 27, 1987) pp. 1, 14.
Note: AG quoted briefly.

J4348 Cornett, Linda. 3,000 Say Goodbye To Trungpa. *Daily Camera* (May 27, 1987) pp. 1A, 6A.
Note: AG quoted briefly.

J4349 Stork, Gretchen. 'Common Karma' At Buddhist Rite. *Weekly News,* vol. 15, no. 20 (May 27, 1987) pp. 1, 6-7.
Note: AG quoted briefly.

J4350 Goldman, Ari L. 2,000 Attend Buddhist Cremation Rite In Vermont. *New York Times* (May 27, 1987) p. A16.
Note: AG quoted briefly.

J4351 Kita. Ginzbuga No Arubamu. *Gyarari,* vol. 23 (June 1987) pp. 55-56.

J4352 Poetry... Of Family And Friends. *Mill Street Forward,* vol. 1, no. 1 (June 1987) pp. 8, 10.
Note: AG quoted briefly.

J4353 Christy, Dave. Neal Cassady. *N'Importe Quelle Route,* vol. 1, no. 2 (June 1987) pp. 18-19.

J4354 Quan, Liang Shan. Ginsberg In the Mountain City. *North American Review,* vol. 272, no. 2 (June 1987) pp. 4-5.
Note: AG quoted briefly.

J4355 Musician, Poet, Singer On Stage. *Charleston Gazette* (June 5, 1987) pp. 1D-2D.

J4356 Cunningham, John. Off the Beaten Track. *Guardian* (June 5, 1987) p. 17.

J4357 Friggieri, Oliver. Tahdita Ma' Allen Ginsberg. *Lehen Is-Sewwa* (June 6, 1987) pp. 8, 10.
Note: AG quoted briefly in Maltese only.

J4358 Carr, C. Burning Questions. *Village Voice* (June 9, 1987) pp. 29-30.
Note: AG quoted briefly.

J4359 Goodwin, David. Drama, And Then Some, At Poetry Project's Gala Benefit. *Villager,* vol. 57, no. 19 (June 11, 1987) p. 5.

J4360 Cochran, Tracy. The New Beat Generation. *New York,* vol. 20, no. 24 (June 15, 1987) p. 24.
Note: AG quoted briefly.

J4361 Rinpoche. *Facts On File,* vol. 46, no. 2430 (June 19, 1987) p. 456.

J4362 Moore, Geoffrey. Poet Power [review of *White Shroud Poems*]. *Financial Times* (June 20, 1987)

J4363 McQuay, David. When Father Knows Best. *Denver Post* (June 21, 1987) Contemporary section, p. 24.
Note: AG quoted briefly.

J4364 French, Warren. The Beat Goes On. *Calapooya Collage II* (Summer 1987) p. 7.

J4365   Lerner, Laurence. What Is Confessional Poetry? *Critical Quarterly,* vol. 29, no. 2 (Summer 1987) pp. 46-66.

J4366   Moore, Steven. [review of *Howl* (Facsimile edition)]. *Kerouac Connection,* no. 14 (Summer 1987) p. 20.

J4367   Wolmuth, Roger. Flower Power Revisited. *People Weekly,* vol. 27, no. 25 (June 22, 1987) pp. 92-102.
Note: AG quoted briefly.

J4368   Mikell, Ray. American Counterculture Poet Allen Ginsberg Talks. *Southern Register* (Summer 1987) p. 13.
Note: AG quoted briefly.

J4369   Keefer, Michael H. History And the Canon: The Case Of Doctor Faustus. *University Of Toronto Quarterly,* vol. 56, no. 4 (Summer 1987) pp. 498-522.

J4370   Pivano, Fernanda. Ginsberg & Poeti Orfani Del Loro "Buddha". *Corriere Della Sera* (June 25, 1987) p. 3.
Note: AG quoted briefly in Italian only.

J4371   Solotaroff, Ted. The Literary Campus And the Person-of-Letters. *American Poetry Review,* vol. 16, no. 4 (July-Aug. 1987) pp. 7-11.

J4372   McMaster, Carolyn. Artists Plan Reunion Visit To 'River City'. *Lawrence Daily Journal-World* (July 1, 1987)

J4373   Lagayette, Pierre. Robinson Jeffers: La Redécouverte. *Revue Française D'Études Américaines,* vol. 12, no. 33 (July 1987) pp. 437-446.
Note: AG quoted briefly.

J4374   Hamilton, Tim. Authors Invited For Reunion. *University Daily Kansan* (July 1, 1987)

J4375   Borak, Jeffrey. Poetry Is the Medium In New Message Play. *Berkshire Eagle* (July 7, 1987) p. B4.

J4376   Borak, Jeffrey. 'Plutonian Ode': Gallows Humor And Hope. *Berkshire Eagle* (July 9, 1987) p. C4.

J4377   Sinisi, J. Sebastian. Allen Ginsberg Talks In Photos, Old And New. *Denver Post* (July 9, 1987) pp. 5D, 14D.
Note: AG quoted briefly.

J4378   Paul, Steve. Beat Generation To Return To KU Campus In September. *Kansas City Star* (July 12, 1987) p. 9D.

J4379   McMaster, Carolyn. Artists Set River City Reunion. *Lawrence Daily Journal-World* (July 12, 1987) pp. 1D, 2D.

J4380   Menconi, David. Ginsberg Redux. *Sunday Camera Magazine* (July 12, 1987) pp. 6-10.
Note: AG quoted at length.

J4381   Shreener, Karen. Play Review 'Plutonian Ode'. *Berkshire Courier* (July 16, 1987) p. 11.

J4382 Sandrock, Michael. Allen Ginsberg At 61: On Life, Fame, Nicaragua And the Blues. *Boulder Courier* (July 16, 1987) pp. 19-20, 22.
Note: AG quoted at length.

J4383 'Reunion' Will Bring Together Beats, Hippies. *Wichita Eagle-Beacon* (July 19, 1987)

J4384 Hirschorn, Michael W. Buddhist College Steers Path From '60's Energy' To Accreditation. *Chronicle Of Higher Education,* vol. 33, no. 46 (July 29, 1987)
Note: AG quoted briefly.

J4385 Lawrence Plans the Big Reunion. *Topeka Capital-Journal* (July 29, 1987)

J4386 Holden, Stephen. The Fugs Look Back To 1967's 'Summer Of Love'. *New York Times* (Aug. 21, 1987) p. C20.

J4387 Rowland, Jennifer. Beat Poets, Writers Coming To Lawrence. *University Daily Kansan* (Aug. 24, 1987) p. 3.

J4388 Goldberg, Michael. John Hammond, 1910-1987. *Rolling Stone* (Aug. 27, 1987) pp. 23, 26-27.
Note: AG quoted briefly.

J4389 Brown, Tony. Beats, Hippies And Punks Are Coming Home. *Wichita Eagle-Beacon* (Aug. 30, 1987) pp. 1F, 2F.
Note: AG quoted briefly.

J4390 Paul, Steve. Poet-Musician Ed Sanders To Be Part Of Reunion. *Kansas City Star* (Aug. 31, 1987)

J4391 Fernandez, Lluis. Sexo Y Homosexualidad En La Era Del Sida. *Cuadernos Del Norte,* vol. 8, no. 44 (Sept.-Oct. 1987) pp. 24-31.

J4392 Douglass, Fred. Beat Nouveau. *KC Pitch,* no. 81 (Sept. 1987) p. 10.

J4393 Sullivan, Mark. [review of *Üvöltés with the Hobo Blues Band* (recording)]. *Option Magazine* (Sept.-Oct. 1987)

J4394 Silberman, Steve. No More Bagels. *Whole Earth Review,* no. 56 (Fall [Sept. 1] 1987) pp. 20-25.
Note: AG interview format.

J4395 Gibbs, Stephen. Reunion Brings 'Beat' Artists Together. *Topeka Capital-Journal* (Sept. 4, 1987)

J4396 Paul, Steve. Beats And Offbeats Return To River City. *Kansas City Star* (Sept. 6, 1987) section D, pp. 1D, 11D.

J4397 McMaster, Carolyn. Two Decades Of Avant Garde. *Lawrence Daily Journal-World* (Sept. 6, 1987) section D, pp. 1D, 2D.

J4398 McMaster, Carolyn. Party Kicks Off a Week's Worth Of River City Reunion Activities. *Lawrence Daily Journal-World* (Sept. 8, 1987) p. 3A.

J4399 Brown, Tony. Beat Goes On. *Chicago Tribune* (Sept. 9, 1987) section 7, p. 31.
Note: AG quoted briefly.

J4400 Paul, Steve. The Poet As Visionary Social Critic. *Kansas City Star* (Sept. 10, 1987) pp. 1C, 4C.
Note: AG quoted briefly.

J4401 McMaster, Carolyn. A Life In Poetry And Protest. *Lawrence Daily Journal-World* (Sept. 10, 1987) pp. 1A, 7A.
Note: AG quoted briefly.

J4402 McMahon, Julie. Ginsberg Reads Old New Work. *University Daily Kansan* (Sept. 10, 1987) pp. 1, 6.
Note: AG quoted briefly.

Baresch, Brian. Beat Poet Still 'Howl'-ing. *University Daily Kansan* (Sept. 10, 1987) p. 7.
Note: AG quoted briefly.

Baresch, Brian. A Week For Memories. *University Daily Kansan* (Sept. 10, 1987) p. 7.

J4403 McMaster, Carolyn. Songs, Readings Flow From Hard Times. *Lawrence Journal-World* (Sept. 11, 1987)

J4404 McMahon, Julie. River City Reunion Gets Enthusiastic Responses. *University Daily Kansan* (Sept. 11, 1987)
Note: AG quoted briefly.

J4405 Simons, Dolph C., Jr. Saturday Column. *Lawrence Journal-World* (Sept. 12, 1987)
Note: AG quoted briefly.

J4406 Toplikar, David. Lawrence's Reunion Of Writers: A Brief, Bright Invasion. *Lawrence Journal-World* (Sept. 13, 1987)

J4407 Gibbs, Stephen. Rubbing Elbows With the Beats. *Topeka Capital-Journal* (Sept. 13, 1987) pp. 33-34.

J4408 McMaster, Carolyn. Sunflowers And Rock Music Mark Conclusion Of River City Reunion. *Lawrence Journal-World* (Sept. 14, 1987) pp. 3A, 9A.

J4409 McMahon, Julie. Performers Merge Generations. *University Daily Kansan* (Sept. 14, 1987) p. 6.

Peterson, Debra A. Reunion Ends With a Flourish. *University Daily Kansan* (Sept. 14, 1987) p. 6.
Note: AG quoted briefly.

J4410 Hanson, Blake. Hello, Mr. Ginsberg Sir? *Southampton Press* (Sept. 17, 1987) p. 21.
Note: AG quoted briefly.

J4411 Garcia, Guy D. People. *Time,* vol. 130, no. 12 (Sept. 21, 1987) p. 79.
Note: AG quoted briefly.

J4412 Stewart, Robert and Presson, Rebekah. Sacred Speech: A Conversation With Allen Ginsberg. *New Letters,* vol. 54, no. 1 (Fall 1987) pp. 72-86.
Note: AG interview format.

J4413 Eshleman, Clayton. [review of *Collected Poems*]. *Ohio Review,* no. 40 (Autumn 1987) pp. 102-126.

J4414 Dunn, Jeffrey Scott. A Conversation: Ginsberg On Burroughs. *Pennsylvania Review,* vol. 3, no. 2 (Fall-Winter 1987) pp. 39-51.
Note: AG interview format.

J4415 Horovitz, Michael. [review of *Howl* (Facsimile edition) and *White Shroud Poems*]. *Poetry Review,* vol. 77, no. 3 (Autumn 1987) pp. 22-24.

J4416 Allen Ginsberg Grapples With Age Old Grievances. *Riverstone,* vol. 12, no. 3 (Fall 1987) p. 5.
Note: AG quoted briefly.

J4417 Schmidt, Lawrence K. When the Text Speaks the Truth: The Preconception Of Completion. *Southern Journal Of Philosophy,* vol. 25, no. 3 (Fall 1987) pp. 395-405.

J4418 Perloff, Marjorie. 'Howl' And Its Enemies: The Genteel Reaction. *Sulfur,* vol. 7, no. 20 (Fall 1987) pp. 132-141.

J4419 Leddy, Michael. [review of *Howl* (Facsimile edition)]. *World Literature Today,* vol. 61, no. 4 (Autumn 1987) pp. 630-631.

J4420 Different Views. *San Francisco Chronicle* (Sept. 30, 1987) p. A13.
Note: AG quoted briefly.

J4421 Baresch, Brian. Kansas Zen Center Residents Seek Path To Enlightenment. *University Daily Kansan* (Sept. 30, 1987)

J4422 Harmonic Convergence. *Kansas Alumni Magazine,* vol. 86, no. 2 (Oct. 1987) p. 6.
Note: AG quoted briefly.

J4423 Keida, Yusuke. Jack Kerouac In Japan. *N'Importe Quelle Route,* vol. 1, no. 3 (Oct. 1987) pp. 30-31.

Choudhuri, Pradip. Le Faux Nom Qu'Était Jack Kérouac. *N'Importe Quelle Route,* vol. 1, no. 3 (Oct. 1987) pp. 32-33.

J4424 Bradley, Jeff. Scholars And Fans Explore the Roots Of Author Kerouac. *Lawrence Journal-World* (Oct. 2, 1987)
Note: AG quoted briefly.

J4425 Voisard, Anne-Marie. Deux Amis Intimes De L'Écrivain Racontent D'Émouvants Souvenirs. *Le Soleil* (Oct. 3, 1987) p. C-3.

J4426 Voisard, Anne-Marie. Un Destin Différent Pour Un Kérouac Québécois. *Le Soleil* (Oct. 4, 1987) p. C-1.

J4427 Ginsberg Shines. *Calgary Herald* (Oct. 10, 1987) section F, p. 1.
Note: AG quoted briefly.

J4428 Berger, Josephe. Thirst For Verse: Poetry Readings Multiply. *New York Times* (Oct. 24, 1987) pp. 33, 36.
Note: AG quoted briefly.

J4429 Fury, Rutger. On the Road. *Harvard Crimson* (Nov. 10, 1987)

J4430 Brown, Peggy. Allen Ginsberg: Only the Office Is Academic. *Newsday* (Nov. 11, 1987)
Note: AG quoted briefly.

J4431   Smith, Peter. Ginsberg Espouses a Familiar Refrain. *St. Petersburg Times* (Nov. 18, 1987) section D, pp. 1, 4.
Note: AG quoted briefly.

J4432   Take One. *People,* vol. 28, no. 21 (Nov. 23, 1987) p. 43.

J4433   Lehmann-Haupt, Christopher. Books Of the Times [review of *Howl* (Facsimile edition)]. *New York Times* (Nov. 30, 1987) p. C17.

J4434   Fortin, Andrée. Vision De Jack. *Nuit Blanche,* no. 30 (Dec. 1987-Jan. 1988) pp. 32-36.
Note: AG quoted in French only.

   Tardif, Richard. Un Écrivain Sous Influence. *Nuit Blanche,* no. 30 (Dec. 1987-Jan. 1988) pp. 37-39.

J4435   Levine, Herbert J. The Hyphenated Life Of American-Jewish Poetry. *Reconstructionist,* vol. 53, no. 3 (Dec. 1987) pp. 23-27.
Note: AG quoted briefly.

J4436   Mintz, Penny. Ginsberg Takes Them On. *WBAI Folio* (Dec. 1987) p. 7.
Note: AG quoted briefly.

J4437   Roark, Randy. [review of *Collected Poems*]. *American Poetry,* vol. 4, no. 2 (Winter 1987) pp. 93-96.

J4438   Ashley, Paul. [review of *White Shroud Poems*]. *Another Chicago Magazine,* vol. 17 (1987) pp. 191-197.

J4439   Bernstein, Charles. A Conversation With Allen Ginsberg. *Cops Hate Poetry,* vol. 1, no. 2 (1987) pp. 3-4.
Note: AG interview format.

J4440   Eörsi, István. On the Road To Debrecen With Ginsberg And Company. *Cross Currents,* no. 6 (1987) pp. 89-99.
Note: AG quoted briefly.

J4441   Allworthy, A.W. [review of *Howl* (Facsimile edition) and *White Shroud Poems*]. *Fessenden Review,* vol. 11, no. 4 (1987) pp. 73-78.

J4442   Stepanchev, Stephen. The Present State Of American Poetry, viii. *New York Quarterly,* no. 34 (1987) pp. 105-121.

J4443   Rato, Mariano Antolin. En El Peor De Los Mundos Posibles. *Quimera,* no. 70-71 (1987) pp. 6-13.

Books:

J4444   Breslin, Paul. *The Psycho-Political Muse: American Poetry Since the Fifties.* Chicago, IL: University Of Chicago Press, 1987.
Note: AG mentioned throughout.

J4445   Carroll, Jim. *Forced Entries.* New York, NY: Penguin, 1987, pp. 24-29.
Note: AG quoted briefly.

J4446   *Chronicle Of the 20th Century.* Mount Kisco, NY: Chronicle Publications, 1987, pp. 808, 974.

J4447   Clark, C.E. Frazer, Jr. *Concise Dictionary Of American Literary Biography: The New Consciousness, 1941-1968.* Detroit, MI: Gale, 1987, pp. 214-243.

J4448   Coroniti, Joseph A. *Rich Relations: The Theory And Practice Of Setting Poetry To Modern Music (Including Nine Original Settings).* Unpublished Doctoral Dissertation. Brandeis University, 1987.

J4449   Dalgard, Per and Lauridsen, Inger Thorup. *The Prose Of the Beat Generation And the Russian New Wave: A Comparison.* Unpublished Doctoral Dissertation. University Of Alberta, 1987.

J4450   Darras, Jacques (ed.). *Arpentage De La Poésie Contemporaine.* Amiens, France: Trois Cailloux, 1987, pp. 121-123.
Note: AG interview format in French only.

J4451   Evers, Alf. *Woodstock: History Of an American Town.* Woodstock, NY: Overlook Press, 1987, p. 653.

J4452   *Grande Dizionairio Enciclopedico UTET, vol. 9.* Torino, Italy: UTET, 1987, pp. 497-8.

J4453   Gray, Michael and Bauldie, John (eds.). *All Across the Telegraph.* London, England: Sidgwick & Jackson, 1987.
Note: AG quoted and mentioned throughout.

J4454   Henderson, Bill (ed.). *Rotten Reviews II.* Wainscott, NY: Pushcart Press, 1987, pp. 39-40, 85.

J4455   Hendrick, George. *The Selected Letters Of Mark Van Doren.* Baton, Rouge, LA: Louisiana State University Press, 1987.

J4456   Hirooka, Minoru. *America Gendai-Shi Ni-Okeru Witman-Zo.* Tokyo, Japan: Yamaguchi, 1987.

J4457   Honan, Park (ed.). *The Beats: An Anthology Of 'Beat' Writing.* London, England: M. Dent & Sons, 1987.

J4458   *KM 80: A Birthday Album For Kenneth Muir.* Liverpool, England: Liverpool University Press, 1987.
Contents: Schoenbaum, S. Carl Solomon, Allen Ginsberg And *Howl.*

J4459   Knight, Arthur and Knight, Kit (eds.). *The Beat Vision: A Primary Sourcebook.* New York, NY: Paragon House, 1987.
Note: AG quoted and mentioned throughout.

J4460   Konig, Hans. *Nineteen Sixty-Eight.* New York, NY: Norton, 1987, p. 46.

J4461   Lauridsen, Inger Thorup. *The Poetry Of the Beat Generation And the Russian New Wave: A Comparison.* Unpublished Doctoral Dissertation. University Of Alberta, 1987.

J4462   Law, Lisa. *Flashing On the Sixties.* San Francisco, CA: Chronicle Books, 1987.
Note: AG mentioned.

J4463   Meyers, Jeffrey (ed.). *The Legacy Of D.H. Lawrence.* New York, NY: St. Martin's Press, 1987, pp. 10, 59, 118.

J4464   Moritz, Charles (ed.). *Current Biography Yearbook 1987.* New York, NY: H.W. Wilson, 1987, pp. 204-208.

J4465   Packard, William (ed.). *The Poet's Craft.* New York, NY: Paragon House, 1987, pp. 30-51.
Note: AG interview format reprinted from *The Craft Of Poetry (1974).*

J4466   Parkinson, Thomas. *Poets, Poems, Movements.* Ann Arbor, MI: UMI Research Press, 1987, pp. 309-311.
Note: A reprint of a review of *Planet News* first appearing in *Concerning Poetry* (Spring 1969).

J4467   Perkins, David. *A History Of Modern Poetry: Modernism And After.* Cambridge, MA: Harvard University Press, 1987.
Note: AG mentioned throughout.

J4468   Perreault, Robert B. *Au-Dela De La Route.* Quebec: Le Secretariat Permanent Des Peuples Francophones, 1987.

J4469   Poland, Timothy Craig. *"Exuberance Is Beauty": Method And Meaning In Beat Literature And Beyond.* Unpublished Doctoral Dissertation. Georgia State University, College Of Arts And Sciences, 1987.

J4470   Poteet, Maurice. *The Image Of Quebec In Kerouac's Fiction.* Quebec: Le Secretariat Permanent Des Peuples Francophones, 1987.

J4471   Rorem, Ned. *The Nantucket Diary.* San Francisco, CA: North Point Press, 1987.
Note: AG quoted and mentioned throughout.

J4472   Schmit, John Stephen. *Walt Whitman And the Development Of American Free-Verse Poetics.* Unpublished Doctoral Dissertation. University Of Texas At Austin, 1987.

J4473   Shechner, Mark. *After the Revolution: Studies In the Contemporary Jewish-American Imagination.* Bloomington, IN: Indiana University Press, 1987.
Note: AG mentioned throughout.

J4474   Snow, Craig Robert. *Folksinger And Beat Poet: The Prophetic Vision Of Bob Dylan.* Unpublished Doctoral Dissertation. Purdue University, 1987.

J4475   Stephenson, Gregory. *Friendly And Flowing Savage.* Clarence Center, NY: Textile Bridge Press, 1987.
Note: AG mentioned throughout.

J4476   Sukenick, Ronald. *Down And In.* New York, NY: Beech Tree Books/William Morrow, 1987.
Note: AG quoted and mentioned throughout.

J4477   Taylor, Derek. *It Was Twenty Years Ago Today.* New York, NY: Bantam Books, 1987.
Note: AG quoted and mentioned throughout.

J4478   Tytell, John. *Ezra Pound: The Solitary Volcano.* New York, NY: Anchor/Doubleday, 1987, pp. 312, 336-337.

J4479   Vernoff, Edward and Shore, Rima. *The International Dictionary Of 20th Century Biography.* New York, NY: New American Library, 1987, p. 256.

J4480   Weinreich, Regina. *The Spontaneous Poetics Of Jack Kerouac.* Carbondale, IL: Southern Illinois University Press, 1987, pp. 57, 120.

J4481 Whitmer, Peter O. *Aquarius Revisited.* New York, NY: Macmillan, 1987.
Note: AG quoted and mentioned throughout.

1988

J4482 Emerson, Bo. Ginsberg Poem 'Howl' To Be Rebroadcast. *Atlanta Constitution* (Jan. 1, 1988) section C, p. 2C.

J4483 Literary Vision. *Cover* (Jan. 1, 1988) pp. 10-11.

J4484 Yarrow, Andrew L. Allen Ginsberg's 'Howl' In a New Controversy. *New York Times* (Jan. 6, 1988) section C, p. 22.
Note: AG quoted briefly.

J4485 McDougal, Dennis. FCC Firm On Decency Code; 'Howl' Muffled. *Los Angeles Times* (Jan. 8, 1988) section 6, pp. 1, 26.

J4486 Toppman, Lawrence. People. *Charlotte Observer* (Jan. 9, 1988) p. 10B.
Note: AG quoted briefly.

J4487 McDougal, Dennis. Stations Ask If 'Howl' Beats Censors' Rules. *Daily Camera* (Jan. 9, 1988)

J4488 Navrozov, Andrei. [review of *Collected Poems*]. *Times* (Jan. 9, 1988) p. 19.

J4489 Guilliatt, Richard. Censors Get Their Way And Ginsberg Is Silenced After 30 Years. *Times On Sunday* (Jan. 10, 1988) p. 9.
Note: AG quoted briefly.

J4490 Ameryka Allena Ginsberga. *Echo Krakowa,* vol. 42, no. 7 (Jan. 12, 1988)

J4491 Emerson, Bo. Was Ginsberg's 'Howl' Cut Off Or Put On Ice? *Atlanta Constitution* (Jan. 14, 1988) section D, p. 1.

J4492 Holden, Stephen. Glass And Ginsberg. *New York Times* (Jan. 20, 1988) section 3, p. C20.

J4493 Noveck, Jocelyn. 60,000 Protest Treatment Of Palestinians. *San Francisco Examiner* (Jan. 24, 1988) p. A-8.
Note: AG quoted briefly.

J4494 Berman, Paul. Putsch Comes To Shove. *Village Voice* (Jan. 28, 1988) pp. 25, 27.

J4495 Mee, Suzi. Allen Ginsberg And the Beat Poets. *Literary Cavalcade,* vol. 40, no. 5 (Feb. 1988) pp. 34-35.

J4496 Rothenberg, Jerome. The History/Pre-History Of the Poetry Project. *Poetry Project [Newsletter],* no. 127 (Feb.-March 1988) pp. [19-20].

J4497 Poniewaz, Jeff. Ginsberg Returns. *Surplus Cheaper Hands,* vol. 3, no. 1 (Feb. 1988) pp. 4-6.

J4498 Meimaris, Spyros. Sto Rythmo Ton "Beat". *Το Τεταρτο [To Tetarto],* no. 34 (Feb. 1988) pp. 26-31. [Athens, Greece]

J4499 Kramer, Adam. Ginsberg At NYU. *Undergraduate English And Drama Organization Newsletter,* vol. 1, no. 1 (Feb. 1988) pp. 1-2.
Note: AG quoted briefly.

J4500   Casey, Kathleen. Student Activists Gather At Rutgers To Forge National 'Radical' Network. *Sunday Star-Ledger* (Feb. 7, 1988) p. 78.
Note: AG quoted briefly.

J4501   Vinzant, Carol. Poet Ginsberg Slated To Speak At U. *Daily Pennsylvanian* (Feb. 24, 1988) p. 5.

J4502   Bergen, Jay and Sussman, Edward. Allen Ginsberg. *Daily Pennsylvanian* (Feb. 26, 1988) p. 3.
Note: AG interview format.

J4503   Higgins, Jim. Beat Goes On the Road, Thrives. *Milwaukee Sentinel* (Feb. 26, 1988) p. 6.

J4504   Unterberger, Richie. Radio Activity. *Option Magazine* (March-April 1988) p. 127.

J4505   Musial, Grzegorz. Zelazne Regimenty Mody. *Twórczosc,* vol. 44, no. 3 [issue 508] (March 1988) pp. 93-99.

J4506   Beat Poet Reads Tuesday, Lectures Today. *All State* (March 2, 1988) p. 4.

J4507   McNally, Joel. Different Beats. *Milwaukee Journal* (March 4, 1988) p. 78.

J4508   [review of *Hairspray* (film)]. *Downtown,* no. 87 (March 9, 1988) cover, p. 25.

J4509   Cardinale, Anthony. Ginsberg's Poetry Lecture At UB Is a Bit Whitmanesque. *Buffalo News* (March 11, 1988) p. C-5.
Note: AG quoted briefly; another edition of this newspaper has the title "Poet Lecturing At UB Sees Rhyme And Reason In Sanctity Of Speech."

J4510   Continelli, Louise. Allentown Stroll With the Beat Bard. *Buffalo News* (March 15, 1988) pp. C4-C5.
Note: AG quoted briefly; another edition of this newspaper has the title "Politics Still Stokes Fires Inside a Roaming Allen Ginsberg."

J4511   Poet Allen Ginsberg Discusses Photography. *Harvard Crimson* (March 16, 1988) p. 6.
Note: AG quoted briefly.

J4512   Wozniak, Mary. Allen Ginsberg: Pure Poetry. *Niagara Gazette* (March 16, 1988) pp. 11A-12A.
Note: AG quoted briefly.

J4513   R., J. "Sakraine Migawki" Allena Ginsberga. *Echo Krakowa,* vol. 42, no. 55 (March 18-20, 1988) pp. 1, 3.

J4514   Hart, Jeffrey. [review of *White Shroud Poems*]. *National Review,* vol. 40, no. 5 (March 18, 1988) p. 52.

J4515   De Dostoïevski A Lhassa. *Filigrane* [new series] no. 1 (Spring-Summer 1988) pp. 45-55.
Note: AG interview format.

J4516   Montagne, Michael. The Influence Of Literary And Philosophical Accounts On Drug Taking. *Journal Of Drug Issues,* vol. 18, no. 2 (Spring 1988) pp. 229-244.

J4517   Sail, Lawrence. [review of *White Shroud Poems*]. *Stand,* vol. 29, no. 2 (Spring 1988) pp. 73-80.

J4518   O'Shea, Clare.   Ginsberg Notes a 'Bewilderment' In American Society. *Reporter,* vol. 19, no. 22 (March 24, 1988) p. 4.
Note: AG quoted at length.

J4519   Zor. Nowe Oblicze Allena Ginsberga. *Express Wieczorny,* vol. 42, no. 81 (March 26, 1988) p. 1.

J4520   Why Ginsberg Can't Broadcast 'Howl'. *Index On Censorship,* vol. 17, no. 4 (April 1988) p. 6.

J4521   Breault, Richard.   On the Face Of It. *N'Importe Quelle Route,* vol. 2, no. 1 (April 1988) pp. 10-11.

J4522   Beat Poet Allen Ginsberg Has a Message Still. *Pennsylvania Gazette,* vol. 86, no. 6 (April 1988) pp. 15-17.
Note: AG quoted briefly.

J4523   Best Minds: A Tribute To Allen Ginsberg. *Tempus Fugit,* no. 4 (April 1988) pp. 179-180.

J4524   Richards, Robert. [letter to the editor]. *Times Literary Supplement,* no. 4437 (April 15-21, 1988) p. 423.

J4525   Rinehart, Steve. Poet Terms Nukes 'Planetary Bummer'. *Colorado Daily* (April 22-24, 1988) pp. 13, 16.
Note: AG quoted briefly.

J4526   McAllister, Margie.   Reunion For Flats Protesters. *Daily Camera* (April 23, 1988) pp. 1D-2D.
Note: AG quoted briefly.

J4527   Fabrikant, Geraldine. Glamour And Writers At Fund-Raiser. *New York Times* (April 28, 1988) section 2, p. B3.

J4528   Istel, John. The Faces Of Paranoia. *American Theatre,* vol. 5, no. 2 (May 1988) pp. 4-5.
Note: AG quoted briefly.

J4529   Weschler, Lawrence. The Art Of Fischl. *Interview,* vol. 18, no. 5 (May 1988) pp. 62-65, 68, 70.

J4530   Holden, Stephen.   A Second Festival Of Serious Iconoclasm. *New York Times* (May 4, 1988) p. C17.

J4531   Giles, Jeff.   Allen Ginsberg. *New York Woman,* vol. 2, no. 9 ([May 5, 1988] June-July 1989) p. 75.
Note: AG quoted briefly.

J4532   Weiss, Philip. The Literary Gild. *Seven Days* (May 11, 1988) pp. 7-8.
Note: AG quoted briefly.

J4533   Aiello, John. Another Kerouac On the Road. *San Francisco Chronicle* (May 15, 1988) This World section, pp. 10-11.

J4534   Young, Carter. Ginsberg's Rhyme And Reason. *San Jose Metro* (May 19-25, 1988) p. 13.
Note: AG quoted briefly.

J4535   Snider, Burr. Ginsburg [sic] Still Howling. *San Francisco Examiner* (May 21, 1988) section B, pp. B1, B3.
Note: AG quoted briefly; the title appears in another edition of this newspaper as "The Good Gray Bear Finds His Way Back, Goes For the Jugular".

J4536   Belik, Helio. "Hoje Sou Apenas Um Poeta", Diz Ginsberg. *Folha De S. Paulo* (May 22, 1988) p. A47.
Note: AG quoted briefly in Portuguese only.

J4537   Hill, Richard. Kerouac At the End Of the Road. *New York Times Book Review* (May 29, 1988) pp. 1, 11.

J4538   Müller, Wolfram. Kosmopolitische Grüsse. *Hamburger Musikleben,* no. 34-11 (June-July 1988) p. 9.

J4539   Von Ziegesar, Peter. *Kansas City Magazine & The Town Squire,* vol. 13, no. 6 (June 1988) pp. 28, 30.
Note: AG quoted briefly.

J4540   Rexroth, Larissa. Cosmopolitan Greetings. *Kultur Für Alle* (June 1988) pp. 4-5.

J4541   Powers, John J. and Nash, Paul. An Open Mind: An Interview With Allen Ginsberg. *Poetry Flash,* no. 183 (June 1988) pp. 1, 5-8.
Note: AG interview format.

J4542   Müller-Schöll, Nikolaus. Der Letzte Traum Des Intendanten. *Stern,* no. 23 (June 1988)

J4543   Zabka, Thomas. Das Genie Geht. *Szene-Hamburg* (June 1988) pp. 30-31.

J4544   Peters, Charles. I Was a New York Snob. *Washington Monthly,* vol. 20, no. 5 (June 1988) pp. 41-46, 48-49.
Note: AG quoted briefly.

J4545   Borchardt, Georg. "Cosmopolitan Greetings": Der Tänzer Is Kein Einzelkämpfer. *Die Welt* (June 8, 1988)

J4546   Laages, Michael. Die Suche Nach Der Richtigen Schuhgrösse. *Die Welt* (June 9, 1988)

J4547   Fabry, Monika. Ein Leben Ohne Roten Faden. *Hamburger Abendblatt* (June 10, 1988)

J4548   Ein Freier Geist, Der Alles Probiert. *Hamburger Morgenpost* (June 11, 1988)
Note: AG quoted briefly in German only.

J4549   Laages, Michael. Man Darf Doch Deine Planeten Wegwerfen! *Die Welt* (June 11, 1988) p. 23.
Note: AG quoted briefly in German only.

J4550   Glossner, Herbert. Ein Weltmann Grüsst. *Deutsches Allgemeines Sonntagablatt* (June 12, 1988)

J4551 Silberman, Steve. On Tour With Allen Ginsberg. *San Francisco Chronicle* (June 12, 1988) This World section, pp. 1, 12-14. *Note:* AG quoted briefly.

J4552 Haas, Peter. Der Letzte Liebermann... *Welt Am Sonntag* (June 12, 1988) p. 72.

J4553 Schröder, Walter. 3 Millionen Mark Für Die Teuerste Premiere. *Bild-Hamburg* (June 13, 1988) p. 6.

J4554 Lesch, Helmut. Kult-Räume Der Phantasie. *Hamburger Abendzeitung* (June 13, 1988) p. 9.

J4555 Schirrmacher, Renate. Abschied Ohne Wehmut Mit "Cosmopolitan Greetings". *Hamburger Abendblatt* (June 13, 1988) p. 5.

Söring, Helmut. Gruntz' Swingende Jazz-Show. *Hamburger Abendblatt* (June 13, 1988) p. 11.

J4556 Burmester, Kalle. Ein Amerikanischer Traum Mit Open-End. *Hamburger Morgenpost* (June 13, 1988)

J4557 Laages, Michael. Wunderwelt Aus Wort Und Jazz. *Neue Rhein Zeitung* (June 13, 1988)

J4558 Rockwell, John. Jazz Opera In Hamburg: A Look At Bessie Smith. *New York Times* (June 13, 1988) section C, p. C15.

J4559 Gillen, Harald. Freiräume Für Jazz Vom Feinsten. *Stader Tageblatt* (June 13, 1988)

J4560 Warnecke, Kläre. Eine Blues-Kaiserin Auf Den Spuren Madame Butterflys. *Die Welt* (June 13, 1988)

J4561 Koch, Gerhard R. Liebermanns Geschenk. *Frankfurter Allgemeine Zeitung* (June 14, 1988)

J4562 B., W. Rolf Liebermanns Flotter Abschied Mit Jazz. *Die Neue Ärztliche* (June 14, 1988)

J4563 Faszinierendes Nebeneinander—Wenig Synergie. *Neue Zürcher Zeitung* (June 14, 1988)

J4564 Asche, Gerhart. Eine Flut Polierter Bilder. *Die Rheinpfalz* (June 14, 1988)

J4565 Eine Perfekte Schau. *Neue Rhein Zeitung* (June 14, 1988)

J4566 Burkhardt, Werner. In Schönheit Stirbt Die Blues-Frau Bessie Smith. *Süddeutsche Zeitung* (June 14, 1988) p. 10.

J4567 Singldinger, Josef. Stationen, Wege, Bewegungen. *Hamburger Neuendian* (June 15, 1988)

J4568 Berndt, Hans. Rolf Liebermanns Abschiedsgrüsse. *Mannheimer Morgen* (June 15, 1988)

J4569 Auerswald, Horst. Oper Als Jazz-Jazz Als Oper. *Passauer Neue Presse Niederbayerische Zeitung* (June 15, 1988)

J4570 Lesle, Lutz. Zum Abschied Ein Musenfest. *Stuttgartler Zeitung* (June 15, 1988)

J4571 Hablützel, Niklaus. Zum Abschied Stehende Bilder. *Die Tageszeitung* (June 15, 1988)

J4572 Berndt, Hans. Weltbürgerliche Grüsse Im Grauen Experimentierschuppen. *Weisbadener Kurier* (June 15, 1988)

J4573 Berndt, Hans. Abschied Mit Pfiff. *Handelsblatt* (June 16, 1988)

J4574 Volkhardt-Ferrer, Sabine. Operntraum Von Robert Wilson. *Neue Westfaliche* (June 16, 1988)

J4575 Preuss, Evelyn. Europa Lässt Grüssen. *Südkurier* (June 16, 1988)

J4576 Michaelis, Rolf. Totentanz Für Amerika In Europa. *Die Zeit* (June 17, 1988) p. 39.

J4577 Dériaz, Philippe. Le Jazz Rend Allegre Meme Bob Wilson! *Journal De Geneve* (June 18, 1988)

J4578 Glossner, Herbert. Black And White. *Deutsches Allgemeines Sonntagsblatt* (June 19, 1988)

J4579 Berndt, Hans. Der Traum Des Weltbürgers. *Saarbruecker Zeitung* (June 21, 1988)

J4580 Objectivism & Emotion. *Bombay Gin,* new series, vol. 1, no. 3 (Summer 1988) pp. 20-22.
Note: AG interview format.

Steve Allen & Allen Ginsberg On Kerouac. *Bombay Gin,* new series, vol. 1, no. 3 (Summer 1988) pp. 48-57.
Note: AG interview format.

Meditation And Poetics. *Bombay Gin,* new series, vol. 1, no. 3 (Summer 1988) pp. 83-86.
Note: AG interview format.

J4581 Sampson, Dennis. [review of *White Shroud Poems*]. *Hudson Review,* vol. 41, no. 2 (Summer 1988) pp. 389-391.

J4582 Evanoff, Richard. Haiku Goes West. *Kyoto Journal* (Summer 1988) pp. 22-28.

J4583 Weber, Bruce. Cases Of Literary Censorship In the United States And Europe. *Reverse,* vol. 1, no. 1 (Summer-Fall 1988) pp. 1-3.

J4584 Morita, James R. In Search Of Epic: Gozo Yoshimasu's "Osiris, the God Of Stone." *World Literature Today,* vol. 62, no. 3 (Summer 1988) pp. 396-403.

J4585 L., M. Sie Sucht Neue Wege. *Die Welt* (June 23, 1988)

J4586 S., D.R. Musik Zum Hören, Sehen, Leben. *Frankfurter Rundschau* (June 25, 1988)

J4587 Kerouac's Road Leads To a Memorial. *Hartford Courant* (June 26, 1988) p. A3.
Note: AG quoted briefly.

J4588 Pizzi, Doug. Jack Kerouac Finds Peace And Honor At Last In Lowell. *Lowell Sun* (June 26, 1988) pp. 1, 4.

Pizzi, Doug. Photographs Record Offbeat Generation. *Lowell Sun* (June 26, 1988) p. 4.

J4589   Fath, Rolf. Rolf Liebermanns Abschied. *Wiener Zeitung* (June 26, 1988)

J4590   Freese, Uwe. Eine Musikalische Sensation. *Holsteinischer Courier* (June 29, 1988) p. 5.

J4591   Torrez, Juliette. Ginsberg Sees Prophesies Of Ecology. *New Mexico Daily Lobo* (June 30, 1988) pp. 9-10.
Note: AG quoted briefly.

J4592   Stewart, Robert and Presson, Rebekah. I Sing Of Norman P. *Harper's,* vol. 277, no. 1658 (July 1988) p. 28.
Note: AG interview format, first printed in *New Letters* (Fall 1987).

J4593   Back Home. *Village Voice* (July 5, 1988) p. 18.

J4594   Santino, S.J. The Beats Go On. *Boston Phoenix* (July 15, 1988) section 2, pp. 1, 4-5, 12-13.
Note: AG quoted briefly.

J4595   The Talk Of the Town: Kerouac. *New Yorker,* vol. 64, no. 22 (July 18, 1988) pp. 18-19.

J4596   Swed, Mark. Ginsberg And Glass. *Connoisseur,* vol. 218, no. 919 (Aug. 1988) p. 18.

J4597   Chase, Stacey. Redefining Kerouac In Granite. *Pearl Street,* vol. 1, no. 16 (Aug. 1, 1988) pp. 8-10.

J4598   Kaliszewski, Wojciech. Antysielanka Czyli Swiadectwa Anomii. *Tworczosc,* vol. 44, no. 8 [issue 513] (Aug. 1988) pp. 76-89.

J4599   Holden, Stephen. Talk And Action By Cultural Provocateurs. *New York Times* (Aug. 7, 1988) p. 52.

J4600   N.Y. Cops Attack Fierce Mob. *San Francisco Chronicle* (Aug. 8, 1988) p. A2.
Note: AG quoted briefly.

J4601   Ginsberg's Poetic Heart Still Beats. *Daily Freeman* (Aug. 14, 1988)
Note: AG quoted briefly.

J4602   Little, Carl. 'Kaddish' At the Eye And Ear Theatre. *Art In America,* vol. 76, no. 9 (Sept. 1988) pp. 183-184.

J4603   A Bum Rap. *Cover,* vol. 2, no. 8 (Sept. 1988) p. 5.
Note: AG quoted briefly.

J4604   [Ney, William]. A Talk With Allen Ginsberg. *New Common Good* (Sept. 1988) pp. 1, 7, 9, 11, 13, 15.
Note: AG interview format.

J4605   Commune Flourishes, As Does Neighborliness. *New York Times* (Sept. 1, 1988) p. A18.

J4606   Open Membership Meeting Held On the Question Of Israel. *PEN American Center Newsletter,* no. 66 (Sept. 1988) pp. 8-9.

J4607   Nathan, Jean Elson. The Paris Review At 35. *New York Observer* (Sept. 5, 1988) p. 9.
Note: AG quoted briefly.

J4608   Hoffert, Barbara. [review of *Allen Ginsberg: Photographs*]. *Library Journal,* vol. 113, no. 15 (Sept. 15, 1988) p. 43.

J4609   Daurer, Gregory. School Of Disembodied Poetics. *Advocate* (Sept. 20, 1988) p. 10.
Note: AG quoted briefly.

J4610   Ney, William. A Talk With Allen Ginsberg. *Shig's Review,* no. 85 (ca. Fall 1988) pp. 1-4.
Note: AG interview format reprinted from *New Common Good* (Sept. 1988).

J4611   McGee, Lynn. Allen Ginsberg Interview. *Columbia: A Magazine Of Poetry And Prose,* no. 13 ([Oct.] 1988) pp. 49-61.
Note: AG interview format.

J4612   Kwan, Shirley. Interview With Allen Ginsberg. *Cross And Talk,* no. 10 (Oct. 1988) pp. 4-9.
Note: AG interview in Japanese only translated by Michie Yamakawa.

J4613   Sogyo, Fukumura. [Why Allen Ginsberg Now?] *Nigen Kazoku,* no. 178 (Oct. 1, 1988) pp. 26-29.
Note: AG quoted in Japanese only.

J4614   Eberly, David. [review of *White Shroud Poems*]. *Bay Windows,* vol. 6, no. 40 (Oct. 6, 1988) p. 22.

Grabosky, Tom. Remembering When. *Bay Windows,* vol. 6, no. 40 (Oct. 6, 1988) p. 22.

J4615   James, George. Mayor Sees City's (And His) Renewal. *New York Times* (Oct. 11, 1988) p. B2.

J4616   Wise, Kelly. Portraits Document Moments Of Beat Life. *Boston Globe* (Oct. 22, 1988) p. 13.

J4617   Keeping Faith On the Lower East Side. *Newsday* (Oct. 24, 1988) pp. 49-50.
Note: AG interview format.

J4618   Bonetti, David. Undress For Success. *Boston Phoenix* (Nov. 11, 1988) section 3, p. 7.

J4619   Giuliano, Charles. Perspective. *Art New England* (Dec. 1988-Jan. 1989) p. 4.
Note: AG quoted briefly.

J4620   Krassner, Paul. The Birth Of the Yippies. *Bill Of Rights Journal,* vol. 21 (Dec. 1988) p. 20.
Note: AG quoted briefly.

J4621   Pivano, Fernanda. Formidabili Quei Beat. *Caravel America,* vol. 2, no. 3 [issue 6] (Dec. 1988) pp. 84-87.
Note: AG quoted in Italian only.

J4622   Anderson, Jon and Swanson, Stevenson. Chicago Hears 2 Poets From Different Corners. *Chicago Tribune* (Dec. 1, 1988) section 1, p. 24.
Note: AG quoted briefly.

J4623 Milward, John. The Beat Goes On And On. *Boston Globe* (Dec. 4, 1988) Magazine section, pp. 26-28, 32, 34, 36, 38-40.
Note: AG quoted.

J4624 Spontaneität. *Südwest Presse-Schwäbisches Tagblatt* (Dec. 5, 1988)

J4625 Silberman, Steve. Interview. *Inquiring Mind,* vol. 4, no. 2 (Winter 1988) p. 26.
Note: AG interview format, reprinted from *Whole Earth Review* (Fall 1987).

J4626 Golden, Mike. D.A. Levy: The Life, Death & Legacy Of a Poet. *New York Writer,* vol. 1, no. 1 (Winter [Dec. 22, 1988] 1989) pp. 57-71.

J4627 O'Kane, John. Satirical Realism, Political Cabaret, Consciousness Expansion: Interview With Paul Krassner. *Enclitic,* vol. 11, no. 1 [issue 21] (1988) pp. 9-30.

J4627x Allan, Blaine. The Making (And Unmaking) Of Pull My Daisy. *Film History,* vol. 2 (1988) pp. 185-205.

J4628 Eman, Ennio Jimenez. Entrevista Con Allen Ginsberg. *Poesia,* vol. 12, no. 4-5 [issue 69-70] (1988) pp. 1-6.
Note: AG interview format in Spanish only.

J4629 [photographs]. *Shig's Review,* no. 62 (1988)

Books:

J4630 Carpenter, Humphrey. *A Serious Character.* Boston, MA: Hougton Mifflin, 1988, pp. 897-899.
Note: AG quoted briefly.

J4631 Caute, David. *The Year Of the Barricades.* New York, NY: Harper & Row, 1988.
Note: AG mentioned throughout.

J4632 Cherkovski, Neeli. *Whitman's Wild Children.* Venice, CA: Lapis Press, 1988.
Note: AG quoted throughout.

J4633 Farber, David. *Chicago '68.* Chicago, IL: University Of Chicago Press, 1988.
Note: AG mentioned throughout.

J4634 Fogel, Jean-Francois and Rondeau, Daniel (eds.). *Pourquoi Écrivez-Vous?* Paris, France: Liberation, 1988, pp. 148-149.
Note: AG quoted in French only.

J4635 Ginsberg, Allen. *Improvisation Und Poetik.* Hannover, Germany: Apartment Edition, 1988. [Series: Überlegungen Zur Poesie 1]
Note: AG interview format by Jürgen Schmidt in German only.

J4636 Ginsberg, Allen. *Riverside Interview.* Hannover, Germany: Apartment Edition, 1988. [Series: Überlegungen Zur Poesie 2]
Note: AG interview format by Jürgen Schmidt in German only.

J4637 Ginsberg, Allen. *Die Poesie Des Dharma.* Hannover, Germany: Apartment Edition, 1988. [Series: Überlegungen Zur Poesie 3]
Note: AG lecture transcript translated by Jürgen Schmidt in German only.

J4638 Hindus, Milton. *Essays: Personal And Impersonal.* Santa Rosa, CA: Black Sparrow Press, 1988, pp. 77, 86.

J4639   Holmes, John Clellon. *Representative Men.* Fayetteville, AR: University Of Arkansas Press, 1988.
Note: AG quoted and mentioned throughout.

J4640   Leonard, Thomas; Crippen, Cynthia and Aronson, Marc. *Day By Day: The Seventies.* New York, NY: Facts On File Publications, 1988, vol. 1, p. 467; vol. 2, p. 827.

J4641   Levy, Steven. *The Unicorn's Secret.* New York, NY: Prentice Hall, 1988, p. 310.
Note: AG quoted briefly.

J4642   McGuire, William. *Poetry's Catbird Seat.* Washington, DC: Library Of Congress, 1988.
Note: AG mentioned throughout.

J4643   Mitgang, Herbert. *Dangerous Dossiers.* New York, NY: Donald I. Fine, 1988, pp. 266-269.
Note: AG quoted.

J4644   Morgan, Ted. *Literary Outlaw: The Life And Times Of William S. Burroughs.* New York, NY: Holt, 1988.
Note: AG quoted and mentioned throughout.

J4645   Peters, Charles. *Tilting At Windmills.* Reading, MA: Addison-Wesley Pub., 1988.
Note: AG quoted and mentioned throughout.

J4646   *Who's Who In the World, 9th edition.* Wilmette, IL: Marquis Who's Who, 1988, p. 387.

J4647   Woods, Gregory. *Articulate Flesh: Male Homo-Eroticism And Modern Poetry.* New Haven, CT: Yale University Press, 1988.

J4648   Zinsser, William and Campbell, Colin G. *Thoughts On Leaving Wesleyan.* Middletown, CT: Wesleyan University, 1988, p. 3.
Note: AG quoted briefly.

1989

J4649   Johnson, Joyce. Cashing In On Kerouac. *Fame,* vol. 2, no. 1 (Jan. 1989) pp. 80-91.
Note: AG quoted briefly.

J4650   Mitzel. Common Sense. *The Guide* (Jan. 1989) p. 16.
Note: AG quoted briefly.

J4651   Jarab, Josef. [review of *Collected Poems*]. *Svetova Literatura,* vol. 34 (Jan. 1989) pp. 241-244.

J4652   Sharbutt, Jay. Ginsberg the Multimedia Man. *Los Angeles Times* (Jan. 28, 1989) section V, pp. 1, 10.
Note: AG quoted briefly.

J4653   Giuliano, Charles. Indecent Exposure? *ARTnews,* vol. 88, no. 2 (Feb. 1989) p. 31.
Note: AG quoted briefly.

J4654   Glassgold, Peter. The Beats At Thirty. *Columbia,* vol. 14, no. 4 (Feb.-March 1989) pp. 25-29.
Note: AG interview format.

J4655   Tokunaga, Shozo. [Allen Ginsberg No Shi Rodokukai]. *Eigo Seinen,* vol. 134, no. 11 (Feb. 1, 1989) pp. 582-583.

J4656   Ginsberg, Allen. Watashi Ni Totte Togo Towa [Lecture]. *Gendaishi Techo,* vol. 32, no. 2 (Feb. 1989) pp. 1-15.
Note: AG lecture transcript translated by Yuzuru Katagiri in Japanese only.

Katagiri, Yuzuru. [Comment On Allen Ginsberg's Lecture In Kyoto]. *Gendaishi Techo,* vol. 32, no. 2 (Feb. 1989) pp. 16-17.

Poetry Reading Na Megutte. *Gendaishi Techo,* vol. 32, no. 2 (Feb. 1989) pp. 64-79.
Note: AG interview format in Japanese only.

Shimizu, Tetsuo. [He Was Fine]. *Gendaishi Techo,* vol. 32, no. 2 (Feb. 1989) pp. 86-87.

Ono, Kazuo. [Ginsberg's Wagon]. *Gendaishi Techo,* vol. 32, no. 2 (Feb. 1989) pp. 88-89.

Iida, Toshiaki. [Ginsberg Is Moderate And Burroughs Is Crazy]. *Gendaishi Techo,* vol. 32, no. 2 (Feb. 1989) pp. 90-93.

Nikura, Shunichi. [Pound And Ginsberg]. *Gendaishi Techo,* vol. 32, no. 2 (Feb. 1989) pp. 94-96.

Suwa, Yu. [Let's Sing the Blues To the Sky]. *Gendaishi Techo,* vol. 32, no. 2 (Feb. 1989) pp. 97-99.

Tomiyama, H. [Allen Ginsberg's Kaddish]. *Gendaishi Techo,* vol. 32, no. 2 (Feb. 1989) pp. 100-105.

Hara, Saikichi. [Singing Ginsberg]. *Gendaishi Techo,* vol. 32, no. 2 (Feb. 1989) pp. 106-111.

Sasaki, Mikio. [Only Yesterday]. *Gendaishi Techo,* vol. 32, no. 2 (Feb. 1989) pp. 112-114.

J4657   Dateline New York City — 12/4/88. *Poetry Project Newsletter,* no. 132 (Feb.-March 1989) p. 2.
Note: AG quoted briefly.

J4658   Le Pellec, Yves. A Collage Of Voices. *Revue Française D'Études Américanes,* vol. 14, no. 39 (Feb. 1989) pp. 91-110.
Note: AG interview format.

J4659   Cry For Freedom. *Newsday* (Feb. 3, 1989) p. 7.

J4660   Sharbutt, Jay. For Poet And Teacher Allen Ginsberg, the Sounds Of the Beats Still Go On. *Hartford Courant* (Feb. 4, 1989)
Note: AG quoted briefly.

J4661   Sharbutt, Jay. From a Howl To a Whisper. *San Francisco Chronicle* (Feb. 16, 1989) p. B5.
Note: AG quoted briefly.

J4662   Gross, Esther. If the Beat Still Goes On, Thank Poet Allen Ginsberg. *Syracuse Herald-Journal* (Feb. 16, 1989) pp. C1, C6.

J4663   Patrick, Robert. Close Encounters With My Own Kind. *New York Native* (Feb. 20, 1989) pp. 18-20.
Note: AG quoted briefly.

J4664   Beat In Syracuse. *New Times,* no. 934 (Feb. 22-March 1, 1989) p. 3.
Note: AG quoted briefly.

J4665   Stewart, Isaiah. Poet Ginsberg Shows His Stuff. *Chronicle* (Feb. 23, 1989) p. 5.
Note: AG quoted briefly.

J4666   Ceniceros, Roberto. Counterculture Writer To Perform Work In Pub. *Daily Titan* (Feb. 23, 1989) pp. 1-2.
Note: AG quoted briefly.

J4667   Jorgensen, Chris. Beat Poet Ginsberg 'Howls' At U. Of U. — At 63, He Hasn't Lost Irreverent Touch. *Salt Lake Tribune* (Feb. 23, 1989) pp. B1-B2.
Note: AG quoted briefly.

J4668   The Beat Goes On. *Maine Sunday Telegram* (Feb. 26, 1989)
Note: AG quoted briefly.

J4669   Sharon, Keith. Poet Allen Ginsberg Howls His Thoughts To a New Generation. *Orange County Register* (Feb. 27, 1989)
Note: AG quoted briefly.

J4670   Interview With Allen Ginsberg. *Alternative Orange,* vol. 1, no. 5 (March 2-23, 1989) pp. 6-7.
Note: AG interview format.

J4671   Ginsberg, Allen. What the East Means To Me. *Kyoto Review,* no. 22 (Spring [March 20] 1989) pp. 1-15.
Note: AG lecture transcription.

Gibson, Morgan. Allen Ginsberg In Kyoto. *Kyoto Review,* no. 22 (Spring [March 20] 1989) pp. 16-19.
Note: AG interview format.

J4672   Cherkovski, Neeli. Ginsberg, Whitman And America. *Another Chicago Magazine,* no. 18 ([Spring 1989] 1988) pp. 211-221.
Note: AG quoted.

J4673   Silberman, Steve. Who Was Cowboy Neal? *Golden Road,* no. 19 (Spring 1989) pp. 28-40.

J4674   Gratton, Claude and Blais, Sylvie. Allen Ginsberg. *N'Importe Quelle Route,* vol. 3, no. 1 (Spring 1989) pp. 20-21.

J4675   Interview With Allen Ginsberg Part II. *Alternative Orange,* vol. 1, no. 6 (March 23-April 6, 1989) pp. 5, 9.
Note: AG interview format.

J4676   Alaton, Salem. The Road From Marginal Prophetic Wisdom To Mainstream Insight. *Globe And Mail* (March 31, 1989) p. A2.
Note: AG quoted.

J4677   Swanson, John. Beat Poet To 'Howl' Tonight. *University Of Massachusetts Collegian* (April 11, 1989)

J4678   Schoemer, Karen. At 62, Allen Ginsberg Continues To Reinvent Himself. *7 Days* (April 12, 1989) p. 47.
Note: AG quoted.

J4679   Swanson, John. Beat Poet Ginsberg 'Howls' In Ballroom. *University Of Massachusetts Collegian* (April 12, 1989) pp. 1, 6.
Note: AG quoted briefly.

J4680   Crowley, Kieran. Abbie: Tears Of a Clown. *New York Post* (April 14, 1989) p. 14.
Note: AG quoted briefly.

J4681   Arvoy, Morris. Ginsberg Closes Poetry Series. *Pleiad,* vol. 105 (April 14, 1989) p. 1.

J4682   Macklin, William R. Cope Carries Poetic Lineage. *Grand Rapids Press* (April 16, 1989) pp. B1, B3.

Sharbutt, Jay. Ginsberg: His World Is Still One Of Music And Poetry. *Grand Rapids Press* (April 16, 1989) pp. B1, B5.
Note: AG quoted.

J4683   Good, Philip. Camden Links Its Future To Its Whitman Legacy. *New York Times* [New Jersey edition] (April 16, 1989) p. 8.
Note: AG quoted briefly.

J4684   Giordano, Al. Rapmaster Ginsberg. *Valley Advocate* (April 17, 1989)

J4685   Stenos, Marina. Ginsberg, Goodman Gig Goes Great. *Hunter Envoy* (April 18, 1989)

J4686   Macklin, William R. If No One Else, You Can Trust Poets, Ginsberg Says. *Grand Rapids Press* (April 21, 1989) pp. C-1, C-2.
Note: AG quoted briefly.

J4687   Fleming, Michael and Freifeld, Karen. Inside New York. *Newsday* (May 1, 1989) p. 11.

J4688   Köhler, Michael. Der "Beat" Geht Weiter [review of *Reality Sandwiches* (photographs)]. *Photographie,* vol. 13, no. 5 (May 1989) pp. 89-90.

J4689   Protests At CUNY Spread. *Newsday* (May 2, 1989) pp. 5, 27.

J4690   Fotografie. *Taz Hamburg* (May 19, 1989)

J4691   Bratfisch, Rainer. [review of *Reality Sandwiches* (photographs)]. *Börsenblatt,* no. 29 (May 26, 1989) pp. 529-530.

J4692   Dokumentarist Der Beat-Generation. *Taz Hamburg* (May 26, 1989) p. 27.

J4693   Durchblick. *Bremer Anzeiger* (May 27, 1989) p. 4.

J4694   Ausstellung: Fotos Eines Beat-Gurus. *Piste* (May 28, 1989) p. 8.

J4695   S., B. Ginsberg War Da! *Taz Hamburg* (May 29, 1989) p. 19.

J4696   Feins, John. From an Interview With Allen Ginsberg. *Once And For Almanack* (Spring [June] 1989) pp. 80-89.
Note: AG interview format.

J4697   T., J.O. [review of *Reality Sandwiches* (photographs)]. *Profifoto Bücher* (June 1989) pp. 66, 68.

J4698   L., R.K. [review of *Reality Sandwiches* (photographs)]. *Rosa Flieder,* no. 65 (June-July 1989)

J4699   Fukumura, Sogyu. [Here Comes Allen Ginsberg, Ho! Ho! Ho!]. *Sekai,* no. 528 (June 1989) pp. 218-221.
Note: AG quoted in Japanese only.

J4700   Shulman, Alix Kates. The Beat Queens. *Voice Literary Supplement* (June 1989) pp. 18-23.

J4701   Skotnicki, Irene. [review of *Howl* (Facsimile edition) and *White Shroud Poems*]. *Zeitschrift Für Anglistik Und Amerikanistik,* vol. 37, no. 2 (June 1989) pp. 188-190.

J4702   W., D. Erinnerungen An Die Beatniks. *Feuilleton,* no. 121 (June 2, 1989) p. 28.

J4703   [review of *Reality Sandwiches* (photographs)]. *Der Spiegel,* vol. 43, no. 23 (June 5, 1989) p. 246.

J4704   [review of *Reality Sandwiches* (photographs)]. *Berliner Morgenpost* (June 11, 1989)

J4705   Requiem For a Yippie. *Bergen Record* (June 12, 1989) p. A6.

J4706   Smith, Howard. Full Moon Over the Stonewall. *Village Voice* (June 13, 1989) pp. 31-32.
Note: AG quoted briefly.

J4707   [review of *Reality Sandwiches* (photographs)]. *Stern* (June 15, 1989) p. 23.

J4708   Foerstner, Abigail. Provocative Portraits From Allen Ginsberg, Annie Liebovitz. *Chicago Tribune* (June 16, 1989) section 7, pp. 91, 96.
Note: AG quoted briefly.

J4709   Talking With Allen Ginsberg. *No More Censorship,* no. 3 (Summer 1989) pp. 8-9.
Note: AG interview format.

J4710   White, Michael. Interviews With William S. Burroughs And Allen Ginsberg. *Psychedelic Monographs And Essays,* vol. 4 (Summer 1989) pp. 225-247.
Note: AG interview format.

J4711   B., S. [review of *Reality Sandwiches* (photographs)]. *Wedel-Schulauer Tageblatt* (June 26, 1989)

J4712   Feins, John. The Alchemy Of the Word. *Naropa Weekly* (Summer [June 28] 1989) pp. 1, 4, 6, 8, 10.
Note: AG interview format with another version of the same interview printed in *Once And For Almanack* (Spring [June] 1989).

J4713　Civil Liberties And Porpoise Power. *Brooklyn College Magazine,* vol. 5, no. 3 (July 1989) pp. 20-21.
Note: AG quoted briefly.

J4714　Pine, Evelyn. A Life At Odds. *Poetry Flash* (July 1989) pp. 1, 15.

J4715　Bonik, Manuel. [review of *Reality Sandwiches* (photographs)]. *Wiener* (July 1989) p. 111.

J4716　Bendrix, Freddie. Punkrock Your My Big Crybaby. *X-Poseur Magazine,* vol. 2, no. 2 ([July] 1989) pp. 10-11.

J4717　S., A. [review of *Reality Sandwiches* (photographs)]. *Basler Magazin,* no. 27 (July 8, 1989)

J4718　Z., A.-T. [review of *Reality Sandwiches* (photographs)]. *Die Welt,* no. 156 (July 8, 1989)

J4719　[article]. *San Diego Union* (July 16, 1989) p. D-3.
Note: AG quoted briefly.

J4720　[review of *Reality Sandwiches* (photographs)]. *Neue Presse* (July 25, 1989)

J4721　[review of *Ginsberg: A Biography* by Barry Miles]. *Publishers Weekly,* vol. 236, no. 4 (July 28, 1989) p. 209.

J4722　Devereux, Maura. Allen Ginsberg: 'Were We Responsible For the Lack Of Genius In the Women We Knew?'. *Sunday Camera Magazine* (July 30, 1989) p. 7.
Note: AG quoted.

J4723　L., F. [review of *Reality Sandwiches* (photographs)]. *Die Neue Ärztliche* (July 31, 1989)

J4724　Colville, Georgiana. Deux Phares Du XXe Siecle: *Les Pâques À New York De* Blaise Cendrars Et *Howl* D'Allen Ginsberg. *La Revue Des Lettres Modernes,* no. 892-897 (Aug. 1989) pp. 75-95.

J4725　Bob Dylan Interviewed By Allen Ginsberg (and Pierre Cotrell). *Telegraph,* no. 33 (Summer [Aug.] 1989) pp. 9-33.
Note: AG interview format.

J4726　Mandl, Erich. [review of *Reality Sandwiches* (photographs)]. *Vernissage* (Aug. 1989) pp. 17-19.

J4727　[review of *Reality Sandwiches* (photographs)]. *Mannheimer Morgen* (Aug. 7, 1989)

J4728　Langer, Freddy. [review of *Reality Sandwiches* (photographs)]. *Taz Hamburg* (Aug. 10, 1989)

J4729　[review of *Ginsberg: A Biography*]. *Dallas Morning News* (Aug. 19, 1989)

J4730　Simon, Linda. [review of *Ginsberg: A Biography* by Barry Miles]. *Boston Herald* (Aug. 20, 1989)

J4731　Aiello, John. The Beat Goes On [review of *Ginsberg: A Biography*]. *San Francisco Chronicle* (Aug. 20, 1989) Review section, pp. 1, 11.

J4732   Milazzo, Lee. The Beat Goes On [review of *Ginsberg: A Biography*]. *Dallas Morning News* (Aug. 27, 1989) pp. 10C, 11C.

J4733   Gunn, Thom. Allen Ginsberg—A Record [review of *Collected Poems*]. *European Gay Review,* vol. 5 ([Sept.] 1989) pp. 16-28.

J4734   Cockburn, Alexander. [review of *Ginsberg: A Biography* by Barry Miles]. *Interview,* vol. 19, no. 9 (Sept. 1989) pp. 136, 150.

J4735   Veil, Helmut. [review of *Reality Sandwiches* (photographs)]. *Kommune* (Sept. 1989) pp. 47, 49.

J4736   Hörmann, Egbert. [review of *Reality Sandwiches* (photographs)]. *Männer Aktuell* (Sept. 1989) pp. 46-47.

J4737   Acker, Kathy. [review of *Reality Sandwiches* (photographs)]. *Männer Vogue* (Sept. 1989) pp. 168-171.

J4738   C[hase], S[tacey]. A Talk With Allen Ginsberg. *Poets & Writers Magazine* (Sept.-Oct. 1989) p. 19.
Note: AG quoted.

J4739   LuLu. [review of *Reality Sandwiches* (photographs)]. *Station To Station* (Sept. 1, 1989) p. 121.

J4740   Silesky, Barry. [review of *Ginsberg: A Biography* by Barry Miles]. *Chicago Tribune* (Sept. 3, 1989) section 14, p. 4.

J4741   Wallach, Amei. The Funding Fight. *Newsday* (Sept. 5, 1989) part 2, pp. 8-10.
Note: AG quoted briefly.

J4742   Jones, Peter. Allen Ginsberg, the Bard Of the Beats On Record. *Goldmine* (Sept. 8, 1989) pp. 36, 38, 40-41, 103, 114.
Note: AG interview format.

J4743   McCormick, Marion. [review of *Ginsberg: A Biography* by Barry Miles]. *Montreal Gazette* (Sept. 9, 1989) p. K10.

J4744   Murray, G.E. Literary Lives [review of *Ginsberg: A Biography* by Barry Miles]. *Chicago Sun-Times* (Sept. 10, 1989) Book Week section, p. B1.

J4745   Kimball, Karen. [review of *The Beat Generation: An American Dream* (film)]. *Suttertown News* (Sept. 14-21, 1989) p. 9.

J4746   Davis, Alan. [review of *Ginsberg: A Biography* by Barry Miles]. *Cleveland Plain Dealer* (Sept. 17, 1989)

J4747   Gibson, Morgan. The Buddhist Poetry Of Allen Ginsberg. *Butsumon* (Fall 1989) p. 4.

J4748   [photograph]. *Folk Art Messenger,* vol. 3, no. 1 (Fall 1989) p. 3.

J4749   Perrizo, Jim. [review of *Ginsberg: A Biography* by Barry Miles]. *Kerouac Connection,* no. 18 (Autumn 1989) pp. 32-34.

J4750   Interview With Billy Burroughs. *Moment,* no. 11 (Fall 1989) pp. 20-22.

J4751 Freifeld, Elazar. Conversation With Allen Ginsberg. *Tel Aviv Review,* vol. 2 (Fall 1989-Winter 1990) pp. 307-314.
Note: AG interview format.

J4752 M. Chronik Wider Willen. *Volksstimme* (Sept. 22, 1989)

J4753 Anaya, José Vicente. Los Poetas Que Cayearon Del Cielo. *Semanal,* no. 15 [new series] (Sept. 24, 1989) pp. 21-24.

J4754 Abbott, Steve. [review of *Ginsberg: A Biography* by Barry Miles]. *Advocate,* no. 534 (Sept. 26, 1989) p. 60.

J4755 Bild-Legenden. *Wochenpresse* (Sept. 29, 1989)

J4756 Truscott, Brian. [review of *Ginsberg: A Biography* by Barry Miles]. *Vancouver Sun* (Sept. 30, 1989) p. H4.

J4757 Beam, J. [review of *Ginsberg: A Biography* by Barry Miles]. *Lambda Book Report,* vol. 2, no. 1 (Oct. 1989) p. 9.

J4758 Hazard, James. [review of *Ginsberg: A Biography* by Barry Miles]. *Milwaukee Journal* (Oct. 1, 1989)

J4759 Farrell, Chris. NAMBLA Conference Will Feature Poet Ginsberg. *NAMBLA Bulletin,* vol. 10, no. 8 (Oct. 1989) pp. 14-15.

J4760 Berman, Paul. [review of *Ginsberg: A Biography* by Barry Miles]. *New York Times Book Review* (Oct. 1, 1989) pp. 3, 39.

J4761 Goldstein, Avi. Free Speech Has Its Limits. *Night Call, vol. 39, no.1 (Oct. 1989) p. 6.*

J4762 Licciardello, Nicola. Conversazione Con Allen Ginsberg. *Paramita,* vol. 8, no. 32 (Oct.-Dec. 1989) pp. 51-54.
Note: AG interview format.

J4763 Silberman, Steve. [review of *Ginsberg: A Biography* by Barry Miles]. *Poetry Flash,* no. 199 (Oct. 1989) pp. 1, 6-7.

J4764 Mand, Andreas. [review of *Reality Sandwiches* (photographs)]. *Stadtblati Osnabrück* (Oct. 1989) p. 7.

J4765 S., G.E. [review of *Reality Sandwiches* (photographs)]. *Stuttgart Live* (Oct. 1989)

J4766 WW Word Choice. *Willamette Week* (Oct. 5-11, 1989) p. 33.

J4767 Shahan, Richard. [review of *Ginsberg: A Biography* by Barry Miles]. *Denver Post* (Oct. 8, 1989)

J4768 Hughes, Samuel. [review of *Ginsberg: A Biography* by Barry Miles]. *Philadelphia Inquirer* (Oct. 8, 1989)

J4769 Pintarich, Paul. Ginsberg Entertains Irreverently. *Oregonian* (Oct. 8, 1989) p. E2.

J4770 Dixon, Eric. Ginsberg & NAMBLA. *Kingsman* (Oct. 9, 1989) pp. 1, 5.
Note: AG quoted briefly.

J4771   [editorial]. *Brooklyn College Excelsior* (Oct. 10, 1989) p. 10.

J4772   Spears, Larry.   For Bay Area Poetry Lovers, Festival Is a Dream Come True. *Oakland Tribune* (Oct. 11, 1989) section C, pp. 1-2.

J4773   Lattin, Don.   Dalai Lama's Bay Area Pilgrimage. *San Francisco Chronicle* (Oct. 11, 1989) pp. A1, A2.
Note: A G quoted briefly.

J4774   Pivano, Fernanda.   Sulle Strade Di Kerouac. *Corriere Della Sera* (Oct. 15, 1989) pp. 1-2.

J4775   Schwarz, K. Robert.   [letter to the editor]. *Kingsman* (Oct. 16, 1989) p. 11.

J4776   Doblhofer, Hannes.   [review of *Reality Sandwiches* (photographs)]. *Wiener Zeitung* (Oct. 20, 1989) Beilage Extra section, p. 3.

Doblhofer, Hannes.   Erster Gedanke-Bester Gedanke. *Wiener Zeitung* (Oct. 20, 1989) Beilage Extra section, p. 4.

J4777   Werner, Hans.   [review of *Ginsberg: A Biography* by Barry Miles]. *Toronto Star* (Oct. 21, 1989) Magazine section, p. M7.

J4778   Sanyal, Nripendra.   Madman Allen Finally Made It. *Sunday Statesman* (Oct. 29, 1989) p. 11.

J4779   Schreiber, Bob.   The Ginsberg Connection: Foolishness Defined. *Kingsman* (Oct. 30, 1989) p. 9.

J4780   Eckhoff, Sally S.   [review of *Your Reason & Blake's System*]. *Village Voice* (Oct. 31, 1989) p. 67.

J4781   Koenig, Thilo.   [review of *Reality Sandwiches* (photographs)]. *Kunstforum*, no. 104 (Nov.-Dec. 1989) p. 361.

J4782   S., K.   [review of *Reality Sandwiches* (photographs)]. *Löwen* (Nov. 1989)

J4783   Never Proscribe Free Speech. *Night Call*, vol. 39, no. 2 (Nov. 1989) p. 5.

Repetti, Rick.   On Goldstein, NAMBLA, And Ginsberg: Tu Quoque, Excelsior. *Night Call*, vol. 39, no. 2 (Nov. 1989) pp. 7, 18.

J4784   The Beat Goes On. *Stuttgart Live* (Nov. 1989) p. 30.

J4785   Farber, Jim.   Hal Wilner. *Taxi* (Nov. 1989) p. 19.

J4786   Klawans, Stuart.   [review of *Collected Poems* and *Ginsberg: A Biography* by Barry Miles]. *Voice Literary Supplement*, no. 80 (Nov. 1989) pp. 21-23.

J4787   [review of *Reality Sandwiches* (photographs)]. *Wolkenkratzer Art Journal* (Nov.-Dec. 1989)

J4788   Donohue, Marlena.   The Galleries. *Los Angeles Times* (Nov. 3, 1989) pp. F26-27.

J4789   I., S.T.   [review of *Reality Sandwiches* (photographs)]. *Westfälischer Auseiger* (Nov. 4-5, 1989)

J4790   Thorpe, Peter. [review of *Ginsberg: A Biography* by Barry Miles]. *Rocky Mountain News* (Nov. 5, 1989)

J4791   Klawans, Stuart. The Beat Goes On. *Voice Literary Supplement* (Nov. 7, 1989) pp. 21-23.

J4792   Mayers, Todd. Ginsberg Shows He Hasn't Lost '60s Flair. *Public Opinion* (Nov. 11-12, 1989) p. 1.
Note: AG quoted briefly.

J4793   Mitchell, Harmen. The Odd Couple. *Ann Arbor News* (Nov. 12, 1989) pp. F1-F2.
Note: AG quoted briefly.

J4794   Marks, Ben. Allen Ginsberg, Photographs. *Artweek,* vol. 20 (Nov. 16, 1989) p. 15+.

J4795   E., K. [review of *Reality Sandwiches* (photographs)]. *LB Wochenblatt* (Nov. 16, 1989)

J4796   Saul, Murray. Allen Ginsberg: A Conversation With a Literary Giant. *Scene* (Nov. 16-21, 1989)
Note: AG interview format.

J4797   Waddington, Miriam. [review of *Ginsberg: A Biography* by Barry Miles]. *Globe & Mail* (Nov. 18, 1989) p. E5.

J4798   Gensco, Goggo. Sex, Drogen Und Musik. *St. Nachrichten* (Nov. 18, 1989)

J4799   Guinn, John. Artistic Sentiments From Ginsberg And Glass. *Detroit Free Press* (Nov. 19, 1989) p. 7H.

J4800   Ruriani, Christine. Sapphic Measures In Modern English Poetry. *Brooklyn College Excelsior,* vol. 3, no. 11 (Nov. 20, 1989) p. 8.
Note: AG quoted briefly.

J4801   Blick Ins Familienalbum Eines Bürgerschrecks. *Ludwigsberg Kreiszeitung* (Nov. 25, 1989)

J4802   Skir, Leo. [review of *Ginsberg: A Biography* by Barry Miles]. *St. Paul Pioneer Press-Dispatch* (Nov. 26, 1989)

J4803   Gitlin, Todd. [review of *Ginsberg: A Biography* by Barry Miles]. *Sunday Camera Magazine* (Nov. 26, 1989) p. 9.

J4804   Pederson, Stephen. Great Glass, Ginsberg. *Chronicle-Herald & Mail-Star* (Nov. 27, 1989) p. A14.

J4805   Pettingell, Phoebe. [review of *Ginsberg: A Biography* by Barry Miles]. *New Leader,* vol. 72, no. 18 (Nov. 27, 1989) pp. 15-16.

J4806   Curran, Ann. The Ginsberg Beat Goes On. *Providence Journal-Bulletin* (Nov. 27, 1989) section D, pp. D1-D2.
Note: AG quoted briefly.

J4807   Rüger, Wolfgang. [review of *Reality Sandwiches* (photographs)]. *Auftritt* (Dec. 1989) pp. 40-41.

J4808   Lofton, John. The Puritan And the Profligate. *Chronicles: A Magazine Of American Culture* (Dec. 1989) pp. 44-54.
Note: AG interview format.

J4809   Censors Among Us. *The Guide,* vol. 9, no. 12 (Dec. 1989) p. 6.

NY Community Center Nixes Ginsberg Poetry Reading. *The Guide,* vol. 9, no. 12 (Dec. 1989) pp. 9-10.

J4810   Corso, Gregory. Beat Rap. *Interview,* vol. 19, no. 12 (Dec. 1989) pp. 64-67, 126.
Note: AG interview format.

J4811   Andriette, Bill. Ginsberg's Poetry Thrills Up-Beat Conference. *NAMBLA Bulletin,* vol. 10, no. 10 (Dec. 1989) pp. 8-9.
Note: AG quoted.

J4812   [Andre], Michael. Pre-Anti-Post-Modern. *Small Press Review* (Dec. 1989) p. 8.

J4813   Lloyd, Robert. [review of *The Lion For Real* (recording)]. *Spin,* vol. 5, no. 9 (Dec. 1989) pp. 94-95.

J4814   [review of *Reality Sandwiches* (photographs)]. *Zitty* (Dec. 1989) p. 40.

J4815   A Real Howler. *New York Press* (Dec. 8, 1989) p. 11.
Note: AG quoted.

J4816   [review of *The Lion For Real* (recording)]. *CMJ New Music Report,* no. 185 (Dec. 15, 1989) p. 2.

J4817   [review of *The Lion For Real* (recording)]. *Beach Beat* (Dec. 17, 1989)

J4818   Caffrey, Ken, Jr. A View From the Cushion. *Vanguard Press,* vol. 12, no. 47 (Dec. 21-28, 1989) p. 18.
Note: AG quoted briefly.

J4819   Not Quite the End Of the West End. *Columbia College Today* (Winter 1989) pp. 9-10.
Note: AG quoted briefly.

J4820   Ritkes, Daniel. William S. Burroughs And Allen Ginsberg. *Onthebus,* vol. 1, no. 4 (Winter 1989) pp. 163-171.
Note: AG interview format.

J4821   Silverman, David. Setting the Scene. *Chicago Tribune* (Dec. 24, 1989) section 13, p. 8.
Note: AG quoted briefly.

J4822   Baraka, Amiri. [review of *Ginsberg: A Biography* by Barry Miles]. *Washington Post* (Dec. 24, 1989) Book World section, p. 9.

J4823   Codrescu, Andrei. [review of *Ginsberg: A Biography* by Barry Miles]. *Nation,* vol. 249, no. 22 (Dec. 25, 1989) pp. 798-800.

J4824   Gerbaud, Colette. L'Un Et Le Multiple. *Americana,* no. 3 (1989) pp. 107-122.

Wolf, Michele. Kaddish: A Socio-Religious Enquiry. *Americana,* no. 3 (1989) pp. 123-134.

J4825   Cooper, Colin. [review of *Ginsberg: A Biography* by Barry Miles]. *Beat Scene,* no. 8 (1989) p. 1.

J4826   Gibson, Morgan. The Buddhist Poetry Of Allen Ginsberg. *Chukyo University, Faculty Journal* (1989) pp. 23-52.

J4827   Schöny, Roland. Photographische Poetik. *Falter,* no. 40 (1989)

Books:

J4828   Abramson, Glenda. *The Blackwell Companion To Jewish Culture.* Cambridge, MA: Blackwell Reference, 1989.
        Contents: Sorkin, Adam J. Allen Ginsberg, pp. 364-365.

J4829   Davidson, Michael. *The San Francisco Renaissance.* Cambridge, England: Cambridge University Press, 1989.

J4830   Eshleman, Clayton. *Antiphonal Swing: Selected Prose, 1962-1987.* Kingston, NY: McPherson & Co., 1989.
        Contents: Eshleman, Clayton. [review of *Collected Poems*], pp. 101-122.

J4831   Gardner, Ralph D. *Writers Talk To Ralph D. Gardner.* Metuchen, NJ: Scarecrow Press, 1989, pp. 147-160.
        Note: AG interview format.

J4832   Hetmann, Frederik. *Bis Ans Ende Aller Strassen.* Weinheim, Germany: Beltz Verlag, 1989.

J4833   Hornick, Lita. *The Green Fuse.* New York, NY: Giorno Poetry Systems, 1989.
        Note: AG quoted and mentioned throughout.

J4834   Kerkhoff, Ingrid. *Poetiken Und Lyrischer Diskurs Im Kontext Gesellschaftlicher Dynamik-USA: The Sixties.* Frankfurt, Germany: Peter Lang, 1989.
        Note: AG mentioned throughout.

J4835   Michel, Albin. *Allen Ginsberg & La Beat Génération 89.* Paris, France: Question De Littérature, 1989. [Series: Filigrane 3]
        Contents: Le Pellec, Yves and Farcet, Gilles. Lower East Side Meditation, pp. 20-41.
        Note: AG interview format in French only.

J4836   Miles, Barry. *Ginsberg: A Biography.* New York, NY: Simon & Schuster, 1989.
        Note: AG mentioned and quoted throughout.

J4837   Parker, Brad. *Jack Kerouac: An Introduction.* Lowell, MA: Lowell Corp. For the Humanities, 1989.
        Note: AG mentioned throughout.

J4838   Ricard, Serge (ed.). *Les Etats-Unis: Images Du Travail Et Des Loisirs.* Aix-En-Provence, France: University De Provence, 1989.
        Contents: Kerblat-Houghton, Jeanne. Work And Leisure: To Revise Or Not: Ginsberg His Method Or 'First Thought, Best Thought', pp. 181-204.

J4839   Rorem, Ned. *Settling the Score.* New York, NY: Anchor Books/Doubleday, 1989, pp. 226, 311, 327.

J4840   Sawyer-Lauçanno, Christopher. *An Invisible Spectator: A Biography Of Paul Bowles.* New York, NY: Weidenfeld And Nicolson, 1989.
Note: AG mentioned throughout.

J4841   Solomon, Barbara Probst. *Horse-Trading And Ecstasy.* San Francisco, CA: North Point Press, 1989.
Contents: Solomon, Barbara Probst. The University: Everyone's Gold Mine (Diana Trilling And Allen Ginsberg At Columbia), pp. 49-55.

J4842   Solomon, Carl. *Emergency Messages.* New York, NY: Paragon House, 1989.
Note: AG quoted and mentioned throughout.

J4843   Spiegelman, Willard. *The Didactic Muse.* Princeton, NJ: Princeton University Press, 1989.

J4844   Stephenson, Gregory. *Exiled Angel: A Study Of the Work Of Gregory Corso.* London, England: Hearing Eye, 1989.
Note: AG mentioned throughout.

J4845   Watari, Shizuko. *Ai Rabu Ato.* Tokyo, Japan: Nihon/Japan Broadcast Publishing, 1989, pp. 203-236.
Note: AG interview format in Japanese only.

1990

J4846   Lofton, John. When Worlds Collide. *Harper's,* vol. 280, no. 1676 (Jan. 1990) pp. 13-16, 18, 20.
Note: AG interview format first printed in *Chronicles* (Dec. 1989).

J4847   Farrell, Chris. Conference Celebrated Milestones In NAMBLA History. *NAMBLA Bulletin,* vol. 11, no. 1 (Jan.-Feb. 1990) pp. 10-11, 13.

J4848   [review of *Ginsberg: A Biography* by Barry Miles]. *Tempus Fugit,* no. 10 (Jan. 1990) p. 183.

J4849   Carpenter, Dan. Ginsberg Sees Aversion To Indiana As Poetic Justice. *Indianapolis Star* (Jan. 4, 1990) section B.
Note: AG quoted briefly.

J4850   McManus, Manus. Poet Allen Ginsberg Sees a Future For Glasnost—in U.S. *Morning Call* (Jan. 7, 1990) pp. F1, F2.
Note: AG quoted briefly.

J4851   Pierre's Party. *Woman's Wear Daily* (Jan. 9, 1990) p. 24.

J4852   Townsend, Bob. [review of *The Lion For Real* (recording)]. *Atlanta Journal* (Jan. 14, 1990) section N, p. 3.

J4853   A Gala With Cardin And a Party For Art. *New York Times* (Jan. 14, 1990) p. 37.

J4854   Silverberg, Ira. Howling For the Masses? [review of *The Lion For Real* (recording)]. *Out Week,* no. 29 (Jan. 14, 1990) pp. 60-61.
Note: AG quoted briefly.

J4855   Horovitz, Michael. [review of *Ginsberg: A Biography* by Barry Miles]. *Sunday Times* (Jan. 14, 1990) section H, p. 1.

J4856   George, Lynell. [review of *The Lion For Real* (recording)]. *L.A. Weekly* (Jan. 19, 1990)

J4857   Bradfield, Scott. Hymns From The Heart Of The Beat [review of *Ginsberg: A Biography*]. *Independent* (Jan. 20, 1990) p. 30.

J4858   McGonigle, Tom. The Poet And the Unblinking Eye. *Manchester Guardian* (Jan. 20-21, 1990) Weekend Guardian section, pp. 14-15.
        Note: AG quoted briefly.

J4859   Kiernan, Fran. The Great Publishing Crash Of 1989. *7 Days,* vol. 3, no. 3 (Jan. 24, 1990) pp. 12-19.

J4860   Dannatt, Adrian. Hippie Hero Of Beat Generation [review of *Ginsberg: A Biography*]. *Times* (Jan. 25, 1990) p. 16.

J4861   Mitchell, Adrian. Escape From Cloud Cliche Land [review of *Ginsberg: A Biography* by Barry Miles]. *New Statesman & Society,* vol. 3, no. 85 (Jan. 26, 1990) pp. 32-33.

J4862   Pivano, Fernanda. Io, Allen, Ultimo Dei Vagabondi. *Corriere Cultura* (Jan. 28, 1990) p. 6.

J4863   Matthews, Peter. A Prophet Born Of Affluence [review of *Ginsberg: A Biography*]. *Observer* (Jan. 28, 1990)

J4864   Frampton, Saul. [review of *Ginsberg: A Biography* by Barry Miles]. *Time Out* (Jan. 31, 1990)

J4865   [review of *Ginsberg: A Biography* by Barry Miles]. *City Limits* (Feb. 1, 1990)

J4866   March, Peter. Allen Ginsberg. *Crossroads,* vol. 1, no. 4 (Feb.-May 1990) pp. 6-10.
        Note: AG interview format.

J4867   Reynolds, Stanley. Saint Allen [review of *Ginsberg: A Biography* by Barry Miles]. *Guardian* (Feb. 1, 1990) p. 23.

J4868   Johnson, Maria Miro. Ginsberg Delights Crowd At RISD. *Journal-Bulletin* (Feb. 1, 1990)
        Note: AG quoted briefly.

J4869   [review of *Reality Sandwiches* (photographs)]. *Leica Fotografie International* (Feb. 1990) p. 36.

J4870   Laird, Inge. A Voice Of America [review of *Ginsberg: A Biography* by Miles]. *Sunday Times* (Feb. 1990) p. 8.

J4871   Kavanagh, P.J. Life & Letters: Saying It How It Is [review of *Ginsberg: A Biography* by Miles]. *Spectator,* vol. 264, no. 8430 (Feb. 3, 1990) p. 34.
        Note: AG quoted briefly.

J4872   Pierre's Party. *W* (Feb. 5-12, 1990) pp. 12-13.

J4873   Fallowell, Duncan. Not a Passionate Pansy, More a Dopey Daffodil [review of *Ginsberg: A Biography* by Barry Miles]. *Spectator,* vol. 264, no. 8432 (Feb. 17, 1990) pp. 29-30.

J4874   Sandrock, Mike. Ginsberg Fears 'Chilling Effect'. *Colorado Daily* (Feb. 23-25, 1990) pp. 17, 23-24.
Note: AG quoted briefly.

J4875   Menconi, David. [review of *The Lion For Real* (recording)]. *Daily Camera* (Feb. 23, 1990) Friday Magazine section, p. 3D.

J4876   Small, Michael. Picks & Pans-Song [review of *The Lion For Real* (recording)]. *People Weekly,* vol. 33, no. 8 (Feb. 26, 1990) pp. 18-21.

J4877   Abbott, Steve. Poetry Capital Of the World. *S.F. Weekly,* vol. 8, no. 59 (Feb. 28, 1990) pp. 1, 11, 20.

J4878   Shanker, Todd Avery. [review of *The Lion For Real* (recording)]. *Alternative Press,* no. 27 (March 1990)

J4879   [review of *Reality Sandwiches* (photographs)]. *Jazzthetik* (March 1990)

J4880   O'Connor, Brian. Space Sounds. *Long Island Monthly,* vol. 3, no. 3 (March 1990) p. 101.

J4881   Shirley, David. [review of *The Lion For Real* (recording)]. *Option Magazine* (March-April 1990) pp. 103-104.

J4882   Foye, Raymond. John Wieners: A Day In the Life. *Poetry Flash,* no. 204 (March 1990) pp. 1, 6-7.
Note: AG quoted briefly.

J4883   Webster, Duncan. [review of *Ginsberg: A Biography* by Barry Miles]. *Q* (March 1990)

J4884   George, Lynell. Allen Ginsberg. *L.A. Weekly* (March 2-8, 1990)

J4885   Ginsberg's 'Innocence'. *New York Times* (March 3, 1990) p. C22.

J4886   Wennergren, Mike. Under Influence Of Ginsberg. *Santa Barbara News-Press* (March 4, 1990) pp. G1, G3.
Note: AG quoted briefly.

J4887   Bustin, Martha. [review of *The Lion For Real* (recording)]. *Rolling Stone,* no. 573 (March 8, 1990) p. 106.

J4888   Redmond, Michael. Well-Versed. *Star-Ledger* (March 8, 1990) pp. 69, 73.

J4889   Hitchens, Christopher. Spared the Pits [review of *Ginsberg: A Biography* by Barry Miles]. *Times Literary Supplement,* no. 4536 (March 9, 1990) p. 255.

J4890   Nevis, Ben. Books: Beat Roots-Ginsberg [review of *Ginsberg: A Biography* by Barry Miles]. *Punch,* vol. 298, no. 7781 (March 16, 1990) p. 40.

J4891   Codrescu, Andrei. Poetic Laughter. *Baltimore Sun* (March 18, 1990)
Note: AG quoted briefly.

J4892   Poet, Author Protest Law Banning Radio 'Indecency'. *Los Angeles Times* (March 20, 1990) Calendar section, p. 8.
Note: AG quoted briefly.

J4893 Tallmer, Jerry. His Howl Turns Into a Song. *New York Post* (March 21, 1990) p. 21.
Note: AG quoted briefly.

Brooke, Jill. Ginsberg Howls Over Plans To Ban On-Air 'Indecency'. *New York Post* (March 21, 1990) p. 57.
Note: AG quoted briefly.

J4894 Grauerholz, James W. [review of *Ginsberg: A Biography* by Barry Miles]. *New Letters* (Spring 1990) pp. 1, 14.

J4895 Craft Interview With Anne Waldman. *New York Quarterly,* no. 41 (Spring 1990) pp. 24-43.

J4896 Ratzan, Richard M. A Note On How Dr. Williams Probably Did Not Deliver Allen Ginsberg In 1926. *William Carlos Williams Review,* vol. 16, no. 1 (Spring 1990) pp. 36-37.

J4897 Galloway, Paul. A New Journal Asserts: Free Verse Is a Curse, Meter Is Sweeter, It's High Time For Rhyme. *Chicago Tribune* (March 23, 1990) section 5, pp. 1, 9.

J4898 Paul, Alan. [review of *The Lion For Real* (recording)]. *St. Petersburg Times* (March 23, 1990)

J4899 Li, Guohua. Driving Mr. Ginsberg. *Vagabond,* vol. 2, no. 3 (March 24—April 24, 1990) p. 3.
Note: AG quoted.

J4900 Hirsh, David. A New 'Howl' Over Censorship Repression. *Au Courant,* vol. 8, no. 19 (March 26, 1990) pp. 1, 7, 16.
Note: AG quoted at length.

J4901 [photograph with legend]. *New York Observer* (March 26, 1990) p. 4.

J4902 Dougherty, Sean Thomas. [review of *The Lion For Real* (recording)]. *Beat Scene,* no. 9 (April 1990)

Ring, Kevin. [review of *Ginsberg: A Biography* by Barry Miles]. *Beat Scene,* no. 9 (April 1990)

J4903 Rosen, Brenda. Philip Glass And Allen Ginsberg In Concert. *Monthly Aspectarian,* vol. 11, no. 8 (April 1990) pp. 40-42.

A Conversation With Allen Ginsberg. *Monthly Aspectarian,* vol. 11, no. 8 (April 1990) pp. 43, 45-49.
Note: AG interview format.

J4904 Silberman, Steve. Live Energy. *Poetry Flash,* no. 205 (April 1990) pp. 1, 4-5.

J4905 Pearlman, Ellen. Biography, Mythology And Interpretation. *Vajradhatu Sun* (April-May 1990) pp. 16-17, 19-20.
Note: AG interview format.

J4906 Ilic, David. [review of *The Lion For Real* (recording)]. *City Limits* (April 12, 1990)

J4907 Sorgue, Pierre. Allen Ginsberg: L'Objectif Amateur. *Libération* (April 12, 1990)

J4908   Simon, Ellen. Ginsberg Speaks Softly, In Prose. *Daily Northwestern,* vol. 111, no. 104 (April 13, 1990) p. 1.
Note: AG interview format.

J4909   Voedisch, Lynn. Glass Puts Musical Spin On Ginsberg's Poetry. *Chicago Sun-Times* (April 15, 1990)

J4910   Kozinn, Allan. Undefeated By Storm, Spoleto To Open In May. *New York Times* (April 15, 1990) section 1, p. 42.

J4911   Valeo, Tom. Performance Weds Ginsburg's [sic] Poetry To Philip Glass' Music. *Daily Herald* (April 16, 1990)

J4912   Voedisch, Lynn. Glass, Ginsberg Offer an Evening Of Adventure. *Chicago Sun-Times* (April 18, 1990)

J4913   Voedisch, Lynn. Glass And Ginsberg Present 'Jukebox' Preview In Skokie. *Chicago Sun-Times* (April 19, 1990)

J4914   Not Salem Witch-Hunt. *Communications Daily,* vol. 10, no. 77 (April 20, 1990) p. 6.

J4915   Wright, Michael. [review of *The Lion For Real* (recording)]. *Goldmine* (April 20, 1990)

J4916   Zeidenberg, Leonard. Allen Ginsberg, Morality In Media Square Off Over Indecency. *Broadcasting,* vol. 118, no. 17 (April 23, 1990) pp. 59-60.
Note: AG quoted briefly.

J4917   Elon, Amos. Letter From Jerusalem. *New Yorker,* vol. 66, no. 10 (April 23, 1990) pp. 97-98.

J4918   Bornstein, Lisa. Ginsberg And Glass Mix Poetry And Music. *Hyde Park Herald* (April 25, 1990)
Note: AG quoted briefly.

J4919   Jones, Robert. 'Hydrogen Jukebox' Given Enthusiastic Reception. *News And Courier* (April 30, 1990) p. 3B.

J4920   Nelson, Nels. 'Hydrogen' At Plays And Players. *Philadelphia Daily News* (April 30, 1990)

J4921   Webster, Daniel. 'Hydrogen Jukebox' At Plays And Players Theater. *Philadelphia Inquirer* (April 30, 1990) p. 4E.

J4922   Baxter, Robert. 'Hydrogen Jukebox' Stunning Music Piece. *Courier-Post* (May 1, 1990) p. 4C.

J4923   [review of *The Lion For Real* (recording)]. *Los Angeles Magazine* (May 1990)

J4924   McDonnell, Evelyn. Blood Of a Poet. *Village Voice* (May 1, 1990) pp. 43, 46.
Note: AG quoted briefly.

J4925   Roca, Octavio. 'Hydrogen' Won't Slow For Anything (It's a Gas). *Washington Times* (May 1, 1990) pp. E1, E3.

J4926   Fletcher, Tony. [review of *The Lion For Real* (recording)]. *Which CD* (May 1990) p. 41.

J4927 Davis, Derek S.B. The Entertainer. *Welcomat* (May 2, 1990) After Dark section, p. 31.

J4928 Groome, Clark. Poetry, Music, Drama Linkage Doesn't Work In 'Jukebox'. *Chestnut Hill Local* (May 3, 1990) p. 64.

J4929 McLellan, Joseph. 'Jukebox': A Fuller Glass. *Washington Post* (May 3, 1990) p. D4.

J4930 Picnic In Budapest. *Facts On File,* vol. 50, no. 2580 (May 4, 1990) p. 327.

J4931 [review of *The Lion For Real* (recording)]. *Independent* (May 4, 1990)

J4932 Burbank, Carol. Theater Shorts. *Philadelphia City Paper* (May 4-11, 1990) p. 14.

J4933 Rotenberk, Lori. As '90s Dawn, Poet Ginsberg Isn't Beat. *Chicago Sun-Times* (May 6, 1990)
Note: AG quoted briefly.

J4934 [review of *The Lion For Real* (recording)]. *Sunday Correspondent* (May 6, 1990)

J4935 [review of *The Lion For Real* (recording)]. *Zip Code* (May 6, 1990)

J4936 Rauvolf, Josef. Labyrint Kultury. *Reflex,* no. 6-90 (May 10, 1990)
Note: AG quoted briefly in Czechoslovakian only.

J4937 Franch, Pere. Allen Ginsberg. *Avui Cultura* (May 12, 1990) Semanal supplement, pp. 1-3.
Note: AG interview format in Spanish only.

J4938 Böhne, Kai Fritz. Burroughs-, Beat- Und Biermann-Bilder [review of *Reality Sandwiches* (photographs)]. *Göttinger Tageblatt* (May 18, 1990) Woche section, p. 9.

J4939 Cariaga, Daniel. A 'Hydrogen Jukebox' Draws Together a Pair Of Neighbors. *Los Angeles Times* (May 20, 1990) Calendar section, pp. 9, 54.
Note: AG quoted briefly.

J4940 Tucker, Mark. Waking Up To the 80's In the 90's. *New York Times* (May 20, 1990) pp. H25, H30.
Note: AG quoted briefly.

J4941 Blomster, Wes. Prague Welcomes Allen Ginsberg Back 25 Years Later. *Sunday Camera* (May 20, 1990) pp. 1C, 8C.
Note: AG quoted briefly.

J4942 Cariaga, Daniel. Allen Ginsberg's Anti-War Poem Adapted To Make Beautiful Music. *Denver Post* (May 27, 1990) p. 4D.
Note: AG quoted briefly.

J4943 Henry, Derrick. Glass Interpretation Of Ginsberg Poetry Gripping In 'Jukebox'. *Atlanta Journal* (May 28, 1990) section C, p. 1.

J4944 [article]. *Brooklyn College Notes,* vol. 7, no. 15 (May 29, 1990)

J4945 22 Win Book Awards. *New York Times* (May 31, 1990) section B, p. B7.

J4946   Poland, Tim. [review of *Ginsberg: A Biography* by Barry Miles]. *American Literature,* vol. 62, no. 2 (June 1990) pp. 351-352.

J4947   Heimgartner, S. Der Duft Der Grossen Weiten Welt. *Du: Die Zeitschrift Der Kulture,* no. 6 [issue 592] (June 1990) pp. 86-87.

J4948   Katz, Vincent. Ginsberg: Beat With a Beat. *Interview,* vol. 20, no. 6 (June 1990) p. 74.
Note: AG interview format.

J4949   Silberman, Steve. A Son Of Enlightenment. *Poetry Flash,* no. 207 (June 1990) pp. 1, 4-6.
Note: AG quoted briefly.

J4950   Thayil, Jeet. [review of *Indian Journals*]. *Times Of India* (June 3, 1990)

J4951   Henahan, Donal. A Spoleto Premiere: Glass And Ginsberg. *New York Times* (June 4, 1990) section C, p. 13.

J4952   Names In the News. *Vancouver Sun* (June 6, 1990) p. A2.
Note: AG quoted briefly.

J4953   Johnson, Reed. On the Ginsberg Beat. *Times-Union* (June 7, 1990) section C, pp. 1C, 4C.
Note: AG quoted.

J4954   Grooms, John. Allen Ginsberg: The CL Interview. *Creative Loafing,* vol. 4, no. 11 (June 9, 1990) pp. 1, 13-14.
Note: AG interview format.

[review of Philip Glass' *Hydrogen Jukebox*]. *Creative Loafing,* vol. 4, no. 11 (June 9, 1990) p. 9.

J4955   Giù Le Mani Da Venezia. *L'Espresso* (June 10, 1990) p. 57.
Note: AG quoted in Italian only.

J4956   Huff, Steven. At 64, Ginsberg Is Still Lively And Outrageous As Ever. *Brighton-Pittsford Post* (June 11, 1990)
Note: AG quoted.

J4957   Graham, Bill. [review of *The Lion For Real* (recording)]. *Hot Press* (June 14, 1990)

J4958   Cheek, Cris. The Threat To Our Freedom Gets Verse. *Times* (June 14, 1990) p. 20.
Note: AG quoted briefly.

J4959   Glanvill, Rick. [review of *The Lion For Real* (recording)]. *Guardian* (June 15, 1990)

Morgan, Alex. Beat And Dub And Us And Dem. *Guardian* (June 15, 1990) p. 37.

J4960   Harris, Martyn. The Beat Goes On And On And On. *Sun Telegraph* (June 17, 1990) p. 20.
Note: AG quoted briefly.

J4961   Nadelson, Reggie. Forty Years On And Still Allen Ginsberg. *Independent* (June 18, 1990) p. 14.
Note: AG quoted briefly.

J4962   'Beat' Sairi Ginsberg Türkiye'de. *Cumhuriyet* (June 20, 1990) pp. 1, 16.

J4963   Duru, Sezer. Bir Kusagi Siiriyle Etkiledi. *Cumhuriyet* (June 21, 1990) p. 8.
Note: AG quoted in Turkish only.

J4964   Duru, Orhan. Muzir Sair (!) Aramizda. *Hürriyet* (June 21, 1990) p. 17.
Note: AG quoted in Turkish only.

J4965   Craft Interview With James Broughton. *New York Quarterly,* no. 42 (Summer 1990) p. 24.

J4966   Nosálek, Petr. Ginsberg V Olomouci. *Rock & Pop* (June 22, 1990) pp. 6-7.
Note: AG interview format in Czech only.

J4967   Snodgrass, W.D. Against Your Beliefs. *Southern Review,* vol. 26, no. 3 (Summer 1990) pp. 479-495.

J4968   Allen Ginsberg In Istanbul. *Dateline,* no. 19 (June 23, 1990)
Note: AG quoted.

J4969   Minore, Renato. Il Ragazzo Del Juke-Box. *Il Messaggero* (June 27, 1990) Piu supplement, p. 10.
Note: AG quoted in Italian only.

Sala, Rita. Due, Anzi Mille Mondi. *Il Messaggero* (June 27, 1990)

J4970   Bentivoglio, Leonetta. Philip Glass: "Canto Il Declino Dell' Impero Usa". *La Repubblica* (June 27, 1990)

J4971   Mattei, Luciana. Ginsberg, Scialoja E Tanto Cinema. *Il Tempo* (June 27, 1990)

J4972   Valente, Erasmo. Per Amore Di Spoleto. *L'Unita* (June 27, 1990)

J4973   Minore, Renato. Ventitré Anni Fa Quel Poetico Incontro. *Il Messaggero* (June 28, 1990)

Sala, Rita. Il Gran Ritorno Dei "Maledetti". *Il Messaggero* (June 28, 1990)

J4974   Baldo, Ernesto. Uno Spoleto All'Idrogeno. *La Stampa* (June 28, 1990)

J4975   Gaudio, Silvana. E Allen Ginsberg Lancia Ancora Urla All'Idrogeno. *Il Tempo* (June 28, 1990)
Note: AG quoted in Italian only.

J4976   Passa, Matilde. Impegno Civile E Buddismo Zen. *L'Unita* (June 28, 1990)
Note: AG quoted in Italian only.

J4977   Neri, Carmela. Ginsberg: Vecchie Proteste Per Una Poesia Sempre Giovane. *Corriere Dell' Umbria* (June 29, 1990)
Note: AG quoted in Italian only.

J4978   Sala, Rita. Ginsberg, Poeta Con Rabbia. *Il Messaggero* (June 30, 1990)
Note: AG quoted in Italian only.

J4979 Lucchesini, Paolo. Il Professor Ginsberg Non Tradisce La Poesia. *La Nazione* (June 30, 1990)

J4980 Mead, Helen. Live. *New Musical Express* (June 30, 1990)

J4981 Bratfisch, Rainer. [review of *Reality Sandwiches* (photographs)]. *Art & Action* (July 1990) p. 13.

J4982 Crowe, Thomas Rain. Hydrogen Jukebox. *Arts Journal,* vol. 15, no. 10 (July 1990) pp. 8-12.
Note: AG quoted.

J4983 Raboni, Giovanni. Ginsberg Sedato Intona Blues Con L'Organetto. *Corriere Della Sera* (July 1, 1990) p. 17.

J4984 Darlington, Andy. On And Off the Road. *Hot Press* (July 1990) pp. 20-22.

J4985 Kindra, Jaspreet. [review of *Indian Journals*]. *National Mail* (July 1, 1990)

J4986 Trull, P.J. [review of *The Lion For Real* (recording)]. *Reflex* (July 1990)

J4987 [review of *The Lion For Real* (recording)]. *Straight No Chaser* (July 1990)

J4988 Scanlon, Bill. Our Wasteful Habits May Cost the Planet. *Daily Camera* (July 8, 1990) pp. 1, 2D.

J4989 Hemmadi, Usha. [review of *Indian Journals*]. *[Indian] Express Magazine,* vol. 4 (July 8, 1990) p. 4.

J4990 Suvanjieff, Ivan. The Beats Go On In Boulder. *Rocky Mountain News* (July 10, 1990)

J4991 Ellis, Simone. And the Beats Go On. *New Mexican* (July 18, 1990) pp. 22-23, 34.
Note: AG quoted briefly.

J4992 Gillespie, Elgy. Wave After Wave Of Words. *Sunday Independent* (July 22, 1990)
Note: AG quoted briefly.

J4993 Jenkins, Mark. [review of *The Lion For Real* (recording)]. *Washington Post* (July 22, 1990) section G, pp. 1, 7.

J4994 Burns, Jim. Talking With Ginsberg. *Beat Scene,* no. 10 (ca. Aug. 1990) pp. 25-29.
Note: AG quoted.

J4995 Esser, Greg. Exclusive: Interview With Allen Ginsberg. *Quest: For a Positive Lifestyle!* (Aug. 1990)
Note: AG interview format.

J4996 Rosen, Steve. The Beat Goes On. *Denver Post* (Aug. 5, 1990) Contemporary section, pp. 13-16.
Note: AG quoted.

J4997 Watrous, Peter. America's Poetry: Mississippi Blues And the Beat. *New York Times* (Aug. 5, 1990) section 2, p. 25.

J4998 Radov, Egor. Zaiavka Na Talant. *Kntszhnoe Obozrentse,* no. 32 (Aug. 10, 1990) p. 5.
Note: AG quoted in Russian only.

J4999 [review of *Reality Sandwiches* (photographs)]. *Nürnberger Nachrichten* (Aug. 17, 1990) p. 15.

J5000 Watrous, Peter. Old Poetry Remains Alive On New CD [review of *The Lion For Real* (recording)]. *Milwaukee Journal* (Aug. 21, 1990) pp. 1-2.

J5001 Over 700 Participate In World Congress Of Poets. *Korea Herald* (Aug. 23, 1990) p. 3.

J5002 Young-Gull, Kim. Allen Ginsberg: Poetry—An Ideal Medium For Liberty Of Expression. *Korea Times* (Aug. 23, 1990) p. 7.
Note: AG quoted.

J5003 700 Versifiers On Hand At 12th World Congress Of Poets. *Newsreview* (Aug. 25, 1990) p. 26.

J5004 Jung-Tae, Song. 'First Thought Is the Best', Says Ginsberg. *Korea Herald* (Aug. 26, 1990)
Note: AG quoted.

J5005 Young-Gull, Kim. Poet Voznesensky: Politics Departs From Soviet Literature. *Korea Times* (Aug. 26, 1990) p. 7.

J5006 Ko, Ginsberg Recite Poems. *Korea Times* (Aug. 30, 1990) p. 7.

J5007 Shiobara, Hideo. Loveletter From Prague. *Nigen Kazoku,* vol. 199 (Sept. 1, 1990) pp. 16-19.

J5008 Worden, Mark. Allen Ginsberg, the Voice Of a Generation. *Speak Up,* vol. 6, no. 66 (Sept. 1990) pp. 2-4.
Note: AG interview format.

J5009 Pohl, Robert. Ginsberg To Spearhead Attack On Censorship. *Buffalo News* (Sept. 2, 1990)

J5010 Farber, Jim. The Masters Go On the Record. *Daily News* (Sept. 2, 1990) p. 25.

J5011 Kimmelman, Michael. The Body As Provocateur And Victim. *New York Times* (Sept. 2, 1990) section H, p. 25.

J5012 Johnson, George. [review of *Ginsberg: A Biography* by Barry Miles]. *New York Times Book Review* (Sept. 2, 1990) p. 22.

J5013 Senne, Thomas. [review of *Reality Sandwiches* (photographs)]. *Rheinpfalz* (Sept. 3, 1990).

J5014 Schoemer, Karen. With Words And Music, a Union Is Forged. *New York Times* (Sept. 14, 1990) section C, p. 26.
Note: AG quoted.

J5015 Grondahl, Paul. Writers Institute Plans Ambitious Spring Conference. *Albany Times-Union* (Sept. 17, 1990) section C, pp. C1, C8.

J5016 Perkins, William. Poetry SLAM: Comes To San Francisco. *Howl, SF Poetry News,* vol. 1, no. 2 (Sept. 21, 1990) pp. 1, 7.

J5017   Meyer, Adam. "One Of the Great Early Counselors": The Influence Of Franz
Kafka On William S. Burroughs. *Comparative Literature Studies,* vol. 27, no.
3 ([Fall] 1990) pp. 211-229.

J5018   You Can't Always Get What You Want. *Inquiring Mind,* vol. 7, no. 1 (Fall
1990) p. 20.
Note: AG interview format.

J5019   Duckett, Ian. Allen Ginsberg—Royal Festival Hall. *Kerouac Connection,* no. 20
(Autumn 1990) p. 24.

J5020   Gontarski, S.E. An Interview With Michael McClure. *Review Of Contemporary
Fiction,* vol. 10, no. 3 (Fall 1990) pp. 116-123.

J5021   Byrd, Donald. The Shapely Mind. *Writers,* vol. 4, no. 2 (Fall 1990) p. 1.

J5022   Columbia Offers Laurels To a Band Of Poets. *New York Times* (Sept. 23, 1990)
p. 44.
Note: AG quoted.

J5023   Loidl, Christian. Pizza Im Gewitter. *Die Presse* (Sept. 29-30, 1990) pp. 1-2.

J5024   [review of *Reality Sandwiches* (photographs)]. *Tagesspiegel* (Sept. 30, 1990)

J5025   Bouchard, Fred. Beat Me, Daddy [review of *The Lion For Real* (recording)].
Down Beat, vol. 57, no. 10 (Oct. 1990) p. 36.

J5026   Bratfisch, Rainer. [review of *Reality Sandwiches* (photographs)]. *Greif-
Literatürmagazin* (Oct. 1990) p. 8.

J5027   Spinrad, Norman. SF/Beat. *Le Magazine Littéraire,* no. 281 (Oct. 1990) pp. 47-
51.
Note: Translated by Robert Louit.

Molesworth, Charles. Poésie: La Guerre De Trente Ans. *Le Magazine Littéraire,*
no. 281 (Oct. 1990) pp. 60-65.

J5028   Csaszar, Tom. Hydrogen Jukebox. *New Art Examiner,* vol. 18, no. 2 (Oct.
1990) p. 48.

J5029   Violanti, Anthony. The Poet Takes a Stand. *Buffalo News* (Oct. 3, 1990)
section B, pp. B7, B8.
Note: AG quoted.

J5030   Hartigan, Patti. Ginsberg Gives the Censors a Beating. *Boston Globe* (Oct. 4,
1990) pp. 61, 64.
Note: AG quoted.

J5031   Yuhas, Joseph. Howling Poet At the Birchmere. *Journal* (Oct. 5, 1990) p. B6.
Note: AG quoted briefly.

J5032   Himes, Geoffrey. [review of *The Lion For Real* (recording)]. *Washington Post*
(Oct. 5, 1990) section WW, p. 19.

J5033   Baumes, Amy. Ginsberg Dominates. *Generation Magazine* (Oct. 9, 1990) p. 27.

J5034   Taylor, Chuck. [article]. *Seattle Times* (Oct. 11, 1990)
Note: AG quoted briefly.

J5035 Beat Poets & Musicians Return In a Howl. *Revelations* (Oct. 12, 1990) section 2, p. 1.

J5036 Ceswick, Sue. Beat Goes On Through Ginsberg's Poems. *Oregonian* (Oct. 14, 1990)
Note: AG quoted briefly.

J5037 Keith, Harold. The Inner Environment. *Howl, SF Poetry News,* vol. 1, no. 3 (Oct. 18, 1990) p. 3.
Note: AG quoted briefly.

J5038 Neri, Luca. Il Golfo Del Poeta. *Il Manifesto* (Oct. 21, 1990) p. 31.
Note: AG interview format in Italian only.

J5039 Dollar, Steve. Echoes From the Beat Generation. *Atlanta Journal And Atlanta Constitution* (Oct. 30, 1990) section C, pp. C1, C3.
Note: AG quoted briefly.

J5040 Mesmer, Sharon. Clouds Of Sexless Hydrogen. *Cover,* vol. 4, no. 9 (Nov. 1990) pp. 30-31.
Note: AG interview format.

J5041 Nelms, Ben F. and Nelms, Elizabeth D. Choosing the Poet Laureate: Were They Listening? *English Journal,* vol. 79, no. 7 (Nov. 1990) pp. 84-87.

J5042 Allen Ginsberg. *Photo Reporter* (Nov. 1990)

J5043 Barone, Roger. Andrei Voznesensky And Allen Ginsberg Read Poetry At Penn. *South Philadelphia American* (Nov. 2, 1990)

J5044 Grondahl, Paul. Ginsberg Still Races Through Hectic Days. *Albany Times-Union* (Nov. 4, 1990) pp. G1, G4.
Note: AG quoted.

J5045 C., M. Ginsberg. *Libération* (Nov. 6, 1990) p. 40.

J5046 Leblé, Christian. Zender Entre Joyce Et Le Stylite. *Musique* (Nov. 6, 1990) p. 40.

J5047 Cressole, Michel. Ginsberg, Après-Midi Avec Un Faune. *Libération* (Nov. 12, 1990) pp. 42-43.
Note: AG quoted in French only.

J5048 Castle, Chris. The Allen Ginsberg Interview. *Howl, SF Poetry News,* vol. 1, no. 4 (Nov. 19, 1990) pp. 1, 6.
Note: AG interview format.

J5049 Dister, Alain. On the Road. *Le Nouvel Observateur* (Nov. 22, 1990)

J5050 Haymes, Greg. Ginsberg's Fires Of Poetic Rage Still Burn. *Sunday Gazette* (Nov. 25, 1990) pp. H1, H9.
Note: AG quoted.

J5051 Gogola, Tom. Go Ask Allen. *Metroland,* no. 580 (Nov. 29-Dec. 5, 1980) pp. 17, 21.
Note: AG quoted.

J5052   Nelis, Karen. Ginsberg Urges America To Resist Gulf War. *Albany Times-Union* (Nov. 30, 1990)
Note: AG quoted briefly.

J5053   Williams, Dina. Ginsberg Delivers Graphic Reading. *Albany Times-Union* (Dec. 1, 1990) p. D5.

J5054   Le Poete Comme Multitude, Allen Ginsberg. *L'Autre Journal,* no. 7 (Dec. 1990) pp. 81-88.

J5055   Couteau, Robert. Allen Ginsberg's 'Family' Album Exhibited. *Paris Free Voice,* vol. 12, no. 6 (Dec. 1990-Jan. 1991)

J5056   Kaminski, John. The Poet As Friendly Lion. *Leisure Weekly* (Dec. 5-11, 1990) pp. 1, 10.
Note: AG interview format.

J5057   Jambon, Jean-Charles. Le "Trou Du Cul" De Ginsberg. *Gai Pied* (Dec. 6, 1990) pp. 66-68.
Note: AG quoted in French only.

J5058   Murphy, Mary. Porche And Ginsberg Revitalize Tradition Of Contemporary Poetry. *Brattleboro Reformer* (Dec. 13, 1990) p. 9.
Note: AG quoted briefly.

J5059   Joseph, Jaiboy. [review of *Indian Journals*]. *New Delhi Financial Express* (Dec. 16, 1990) p. 9.

J5060   Chevrolet, Richard. [review of *The Lion For Real* (recording)]. *New York Review Of Records,* vol. 1, no. 5 (Winter 1990-91) p. 1.

J5061   McDonald, Arthur W. [review of *Hydrogen Jukebox* by Philip Glass]. *Southern Theatre,* vol. 32, no. 2 (Winter [1990] 1991) pp. 22-26.

J5062   Lives & Letters [review of *Ginsberg: a Biography* by Barry Miles]. *Virginia Quarterly Review,* vol. 66, no. 1 (Winter 1990) p. 19.

J5063   Silesky, Barry. Allen Ginsberg, a Conversation. *Another Chicago Magazine,* no. 21 (1990) pp. 158-172.
Note: AG interview format.

J5064   Salerno, Joe. Yowl. *Black Swan Review,* no. 3 (1990) pp. 19-23.

J5065   Middleton, Stephen C. Slants On Luminosity. *Ostinato,* no. 3 (1990) pp. 52-59.
Note: AG quoted briefly.

J5066   Thomas, Kenn and Gounis, Phil. Ed Sanders, Investigative Poet: An Interview. *River Styx,* no. 33 (1990) pp. 1-11.

Books:

J5067   Anctil, Pierre and others (eds.). *Un Homme Grand: Jack Kerouac At the Crossroads Of Many Cultures.* Ottawa, Canada: Carleton University Press, 1990.
Note: AG mentioned throughout.

J5068   Bauldie, John (ed.). *Wanted Man: In Search Of Bob Dylan.* London, England: Black Spring Press, 1990.
Note: AG quoted and mentioned throughout.

J5069 Cassady, Carolyn. *Off the Road.* New York, NY: William Morrow, 1990.
Note: AG quoted and mentioned throughout.

J5070 Clark, Tom. *The Poetry Beat.* Ann Arbor, MI: University Of Michigan Press, 1990, pp. 30-38.
Note: review of *Collected Poems* and *White Shroud Poems.*

J5071 Codrescu, Andrei. *The Disappearance Of the Outside.* Reading, MA: Addison-Wesley, 1990.
Note: AG mentioned throughout.

J5072 Demac, Donna A. *Liberty Denied.* New Brunswick, NJ: Rutgers University Press, 1990, p. 51.

J5073 Dowden, George. *Allen Ginsberg: The Man/The Poet On Entering Earth Decade His Seventh.* Montreal, Canada: Alpha Beat Press, 1990.
Note: review of *White Shroud Poems.*

J5074 Gray, Richard. *American Poetry Of the Twentieth Century.* London, England: Longman, 1990.
Note: AG mentioned throughout.

J5075 Hamalian, Linda. *A Life Of Kenneth Rexroth.* New York, NY: Norton, 1990.
Note: AG quoted and mentioned throughout.

J5076 Herron, Don. *The Literary World Of San Francisco And Its Environs.* San Francisco, CA: City Lights Books, 1990.
Note: AG mentioned throughout.

J5077 Hickey, Morgen. *The Bohemian Register: An Annotated Bibliography Of the Beat Literary Movement.* Metuchen, NJ: Scarecrow, 1990.

J5078 Honan, Park. *Author's Lives.* New York, NY: St. Martin's Press, 1990, pp. 231-246.

J5079 Huncke, Herbert. *Guilty Of Everything.* New York, NY: Paragon House, 1990.
Note: AG quoted and mentioned throughout.

J5080 Jones, Hettie. *How I Became Hettie Jones.* New York, NY: Dutton, 1990.
Note: AG quoted and mentioned throughout.

J5081 Kesey, Ken. *The Further Inquiry.* New York, NY: Viking, 1990.
Note: AG quoted and mentioned throughout.

J5082 Kessler, Lauren. *After All These Years.* New York, NY: Thunder's Mouth Press, 1990, pp. 175, 177.

J5083 Knabb, Ken. *The Relevance Of Rexroth.* Berkeley, CA: Bureau Of Public Secrets, 1990, pp. 7, 71.

J5084 Landesman, Jay. *Rebel Without Applause.* New York, NY: Paragon House, 1990.
Note: AG mentioned throughout.

J5085 Lauridsen, Inger Thorup and Dalgard, Per. *The Beat Generation And the Russian New Wave.* Ann Arbor, MI: Ardis, 1990, pp. 21-36.
Note: AG interview format.

J5086   Lee, Martin A. and Solomon, Norman. *Unreliable Sources: A Guide To Detecting Bias In News Media.* New York, NY: Lyle Stuart, 1990, p. 295.

J5087   Lhamon, W.T., Jr. *Deliberate Speed: The Origins Of a Cultural Style In the American 1950s.* Washington, DC: Smithsonian Institution Press, 1990.
Note: AG mentioned throughout.

J5088   *PEN Montblanc Literary Gala 1990: The Writer's Choice.* New York, NY: PEN Club, 1990, p. 23.

J5089   Perry, Paul and Babbs, Ken. *On the Bus.* New York, NY: Thunder's Mouth Press, 1990.
Note: AG quoted and mentioned throughout.

J5090   Roylance, Brian (ed.). *Blinds & Shutters: Michael Cooper.* Guildford, England: Genesis/Hedley, 1990.
Note: AG quoted and mentioned throughout.

J5091   Silesky, Barry. *Ferlinghetti: The Artist In His Time.* New York, NY: Warner Books, 1990.
Note: AG quoted and mentioned throughout.

J5092   Solnit, Rebecca. *Secret Exhibition: Six California Artists On the Cold War Era.* San Francisco, CA: City Lights, 1990.
Note: AG mentioned throughout.

J5093   *Spoleto Festival 90.* Charleston, SC: Spoleto Festival, 1990.
Contents: Howell, John. Hydrogen Jukebox, pp. 24-27.

J5094   Stephenson, Gregory. *The Daybreak Boys.* Carbondale, IL: Southern Illinois University Press, 1990.
Note: AG mentioned throughout.

J5095   Terrill, Richard. *Saturday Night In Baoding.* Fayetteville, AR: University Of Arkansas Press, 1990, pp. 87-90.

1991

J5096   Bell, Marvin. Homage To the Runner, Poetry A To Z. *American Poetry Review,* vol. 20, no. 1 (Jan.-Feb. 1991) pp. 15-20.

J5097   Viviant, Arnaud. Blind Taste. *Best,* no. 270 (Jan. 1991) pp. 76-77.
Note: AG interview format in French only.

J5098   Bratfisch, Rainer. [review of *Reality Sandwiches* (photographs)]. *Fotografie* (Jan. 1991) pp. 18-21.

J5099   Hase, Masaharu. Goodnotice. *Switch,* vol. 8, no. 6 (Jan. 1991) pp. 124-133.

J5100   Censor, Catherine. Poet Ginsberg Finds Enthusiastic Young Crowd At Downtown School. *Phoenix,* vol. 19, no. 31 (Jan. 17, 1991)
Note: AG quoted briefly.

J5101   McNally, Owen. Allen Ginsberg: The Beat Goes On. *Hartford Courant* (Jan. 24, 1991) Calendar section, pp. 1, 15.
Note: AG quoted.

J5102   Kazin, Alfred. When Bohemia Was In Bloom. *New York Times* (Jan. 25, 1991) pp. C1, C24.

J5103 Son, Noisy. Les Surdoues De La Revolte. *Blah Blah News* (Feb. 1991)
unpaged.
Note: AG quoted in French only.

J5104 Anderson, Dawne. Allen Ginsberg, Chinese Chef. *Nice Paper,* vol. 3, no. 5
(Feb. 6-12, 1991) p. 10.
Note: AG interview format.

J5105 Macnie, Jim. Eight Days a Week. *The Newspaper* (Feb. 7, 1991) section 2, p.
2.
Note: AG quoted briefly.

J5106 Ginsberg. *V.M.I. Cadet,* vol. 80, no. 16 (Feb. 15, 1991) p. 12.

J5107 Doctorow, E.L. and others. War Covers Crackdown On Palestinians. *New York
Times* (Feb. 18, 1991) section A, p. 22.

J5108 Laurant, Darrell. The Corps Meets Allen Ginsberg. *News & Daily Advance*
(Feb. 20, 1991)
Note: AG quoted briefly.

J5109 Beat Generation Poet's Visit To VMI Goes Over Well. *Richmond News Leader*
(Feb. 21, 1991) p. 4.
Note: AG quoted briefly.

J5110 Macy, Beth. Ultimate Beatnik Finds Common Ground Among VMI Cadets.
Roanoke Times & World News (Feb. 21, 1991) Extra section, pp. 1, 3.
Note: AG quoted briefly.

J5111 VMI Welcomes Ginsberg's Change of Pace. *Richmond Times-Dispatch* (Feb.
22, 1991) p. B4.
Note: AG quoted briefly.

J5112 Rodreguez, Tim and Williams, Dave. Ginsberg Plays VMI. *V.M.I. Cadet,* vol.
80, no. 17 (Feb. 22, 1991) p. 1.
Note: AG interview format.

Kendall, James R. [letter to the editor]. *V.M.I. Cadet,* vol. 80, no. 17 (Feb. 22,
1991) pp. 2, 7.

J5113 Harwood, Doug. Beat Poet Provides VMI With Provocative Lesson In Freedom.
Rockbridge Weekly (Feb. 27, 1991) pp. 1, 12.
Note: AG quoted briefly.

J5114 Pecka, Zdenek. Vodikovy Jukebox. *Rock & Pop* (Feb. 28, 1991) p. 13.
Note: AG quoted briefly in Czech only.

J5115 Barnwell, Randall. Consumer's Guide To World LPs [review of *The Lion For
Real* (recording)]. *Boston Rock* (March 1991)

J5116 Powers, Lisa S. The Official Dope On Ginsberg. *Current,* vol. 3, no. 5 (March
1991) p. 33.
Note: AG quoted.

J5117 Sasloglov, Izampela. Count Down Beat Generation. *Periodiko,* no. 49 (March
1991) pp. 70-79.
Note: AG interview format in Greek only.

J5118   Hinely, Patrick. First Thought, Best Thought. *News-Gazette* (March 6, 1991)
section B, p. 15.
Note: AG quoted briefly.

J5119   Prime, John Andrew. Ginsberg Fights Against War. *Shreveport Times* (March
6, 1991) p. 6C.
Note: AG quoted briefly.

J5120   Fogel, C.J. Ginsberg Keeps the Poet's View Alive. *Shreveport Times* (March 7,
1991) pp. 1A, 18A.
Note: AG quoted briefly.

J5121   Monfourny, Renaud. Je Remercie La Police. *Les Inrockuptibles,* no. 27 (March
8, 1991) pp. 52-57.
Note: AG interview format in French only.

J5122   Paglia, Camille. Junk Bonds And Corporate Raiders: Academe In the Hour Of
the Wolf. *Arion* (Spring 1991)

J5123   Loidl, Christian. Interview Mit Allen Ginsberg. *Bestände,* no. 19-20 (Spring
1991) pp. 38-29.
Note: AG interview format in German only.

J5124   Kröller, Eva-Marie. Notes [review of *Ginsberg: a Biography* by Barry Miles].
Canadian Literature, no. 128 (Spring 1991) p. 230.

J5125   Paglia, Camille. Milton Kessler: A Memoir. *Sulfur* (Spring 1991)

J5126   Block, Adam. Pictures Worth a Thousand Words [review of *Allen Ginsberg:
Photographs*]. *Advocate,* no. 573 (March 26, 1991) pp. 62-64.
Note: AG quoted briefly.

J5127   Harris, Lisa M. [letter to the editor]. *Central Michigan Life* (March 27, 1991) p.
5A.

Batkie, Anthony. Ginsberg Attack Issues With Poetry. *Central Michigan Life*
(March 27, 1991) p. 6A.
Note: AG quoted briefly.

J5128   Oracle Of the 60's: Alan Watts, Tim Leary, Allen Ginsberg, & Gary Snyder On
God, Revolution, Psychedelics, & Dropping Out... *Open Exchange* (April-
June 1991) pp. 10, 65.
Note: AG interview format reprinted from *City Of San Francisco Oracle* (Feb.
1967).

J5129   Whitworth, John. [review of *Ginsberg: a Biography* by Barry Miles]. *Poetry
Review,* vol. 81, no. 1 (Spring [April] 1991) pp. 48-50.

J5130   Aletti. Photo. *Village Voice* (April 9, 1991)

J5131   Meister, Marcus. Laute Stimme Der Beat-Generation. *Frankfurter Rhundschau*
(April 12, 1991) p. 65.

J5132   Sorgue, Pierre. Allen Ginsberg: L'Objectif Amateur. *Lyon Liberation* (April 12,
1991)

J5133   Lowe, Charlotte. At Age 65, Poet Allen Ginsberg Continues To Howl Against
Injustice. *Tucson Citizen* (April 15, 1991) Living section, pp. 1E, 3E.
Note: AG quoted.

J5134   Wheatcroft, Geoffrey. [article]. *Sunday Telegraph* (April 21, 1991)

J5135   Horovitz, Michael. [letter to the editor]. *Sunday Telegraph* (April 28, 1991)

J5136   Monfourny, Renaud. ...Doy Gracias A La Policia. *Ajoblanco,* no. 33 (May 1991) pp. 56-62.
        Note: AG interview format in Spanish only.

J5137   Page, Tim. 'Howl' Set To Music? *Connoisseur,* vol. 201, no. 5 (May 1991) p. 17.

J5138   Allen Ginsberg, Photographe. *Le Tout Lyon* (May 2, 1991)

J5139   Turan, Kenneth. [review of *Allen Ginsberg: Photographs*]. *Los Angeles Times Book Review* (May 5, 1991) p. 6.

J5140   Rockwell, John. The Wonderworld Of a Stage Designer Who Defies Reality. *New York Times* (May 5, 1991) p. 14H.

J5141   Paglia, Camille. Ninnies, Pedants, Tyrants And Other Academics. *New York Times Book Review* (May 5, 1991) pp. 1, 29, 33.

J5142   Zakariasen, Bill. 'Jukebox': Music's The Thing. *Daily News* (May 9, 1991) p. 44.

J5143   Goodman, Peter. A 'Jukebox' Selection Of Ginsberg. *New York Newsday* (May 9, 1991) pp. 78-79.

J5144   Fleming, Shirley. Glass' Catchy 'Jukebox'. *New York Post* (May 9, 1991) p. 35.

J5145   Rockwell, John. Glass And Ginsberg Cycle: 'Hydrogen Jukebox'. *New York Times* (May 9, 1991) section C, p. 17.

J5146   Rosen, Steven. The '50s Beat. *Denver Post* (May 22, 1991) section G, pp. 1G-2G.

J5147   Borawski, Walta. Poetry In Motion. *Gay Community News,* vol. 18, no. 43 (May 26-June 1, 1991) pp. 8, 12.
        Note: AG quoted briefly.

J5148   Delatiner, Barbara. For Brothers, Poetry Is In Their Genes. *New York Times* (May 26, 1991) Long Island section, p. 13.
        Note: AG quoted briefly.

J5149   Davis, Peter G. Hydrogen Bomb. *New York,* vol. 24, no. 21 (May 27, 1991) p. 69.

J5150   Grahnke, Lon. Powerful 'War' Attacks Bush And Desert Storm. *Chicago Sun-Times* (May 28, 1991) p. 34.

J5151   Kogan, Rick. Courting Controversy. *Chicago Tribune* (May 28, 1991) section 5, p. 7.

J5152   Kadzis, Peter. With Pen And Lens. *Boston Phoenix* (May 31, 1991) PLS section, pp. 6-7.
        Note: AG interview format.

J5153 Littlejohn, Maureen. Back To Beat. *Images,* vol. 8, no. 3 (June-July 1991) p. 20.

J5154 Silberman, Steve. [review of *Allen Ginsberg: Photographs*]. *Poetry Flash,* no. 219 (June 1991) pp. 4-5.

J5155 Gold, Herbert. When San Francisco Was Cool. *San Francisco Examiner* (June 2, 1991) Image section, pp. 6-15, 28.

J5156 Wallace, George. Walt Whitman House Hosts the Lion, For Real. *Long Islander,* vol. 153, no. 51 (June 6, 1991) pp. 17, 21.
Note: AG quoted briefly.

J5157 Rabago, Joaquin. Ginsberg. *El Independiente* (June 9, 1991) pp. 12-13.
Note: AG interview format in Spanish only.

J5158 Alberto Huerta, S.J. California: Beat And Beatitude. *Dialogue And Humanism,* vol. 1, no. 2 (Summer 1991) pp. 49-70.

J5159 Gunn, Thom. [review of *Collected Poems* and *White Shroud Poems*]. *James White Review,* vol. 8, no. 4 (Summer 1991) pp. 14-15.

J5160 Whitworth, John. [review of *Ginsberg: a Biography* by Barry Miles]. *Spectator,* vol. 266, no. 8503 (June 29, 1991) p. 30.

J5161 Lewis, Joel. [review of *The Lion For Real* (recording)]. *American Poetry Review,* vol. 20, no. 4 (July-Aug. 1991) pp. 29-32.

J5162 Lebel, Jean-Jacques. Allen Ginsberg "Photographe". *Gironde Magazine,* no. 25 (July-Sept. 1991)

J5163 Perry, Ginger. Benefit For Naropa. *Icon* (July 1991) p. 7.

J5164 Karr, John F. [review of *Allen Ginsberg: Photographs*]. *Bay Area Reporter,* vol. 21, no. 27 (July 4, 1991) p. 45.

J5165 McCabe, Bruce. Ginsberg Hasn't Missed a Beat. *Boston Globe* (July 6, 1991) pp. 16, 21.
Note: AG quoted.

J5166 Blomster, Wes. Cover: Glass, Ginsberg & Fenley. *Daily Camera* (July 19, 1991) Friday Magazine section, p. 21D.

J5167 Bradley, Jeff. Poet Ginsberg, Composer Blass Remain True To Maverick Visions. *Denver Post* (July 23, 1991) section E, pp. 1E, 4E.
Note: AG quoted briefly.

J5168 Shulgold, Marc. In the Company Of Collaborators. *Rocky Mountain News* (July 24, 1991) pp. 58-59.
Note: AG quoted briefly.

J5169 Sinisi, J. Sebastian. Benefit For Naropa Inspired Performance. *Denver Post* (July 25, 1991) p. 4B.

J5170 Shulgold, Marc. Artistic Trio Present Evening To Savor. *Rocky Mountain News* (July 25, 1991) p. 67.

J5171 Silberman, Steve. Cloud House. *City,* vol. 2, no. 7 (Aug. 1991) pp. 23-25.
Note: AG quoted briefly.

J5172   Gladysz, Thomas. Interview With Allen Ginsberg. *Photo Metro,* vol. 9, no. 91 (Aug. 1991) pp. 3-4.
Note: AG interview format.

J5173   Gladysz, Thomas. Poet/Photographer Allen Ginsberg. *WestArt* (Aug. 9, 1991) p. 10.

J5174   Bonetti, David. Shooting With a 35mm Chimera [review of *Allen Ginsberg: Photographs*]. *San Francisco Chronicle And Examiner* (Aug. 18, 1991) pp. C1, C4.

J5175   Alex, Patricia. When a Beat Poet Beat a Drug Charge. *Bergen Record* (Aug. 24, 1991) p. A2.

J5176   Monfourny, Renaud. ...Doy Gracias A La Policia. *Pagina/30,* vol. 2, no. 14 (Sept. 1991) pp. 60-66.
Note: AG interview format in Spanish only.

J5177   Anglesey, Zoe. [review of *The Lion For Real* (recording)]. *Rocket* (Sept. 1991) p. 40.

J5178   Friedman, Robert. Ginsberg, Behind the Camera And On the Page. *San Francisco Sentinel* (Sept. 5, 1991) p. 19.

J5179   St. George, Julia. Ginsberg To Read In E. Meredith. *Daily Star* (Sept. 20, 1991) pp. 1, 12.
Note: AG quoted briefly.

J5180   Macy, Beth. Different Beat. *Roanoke Times And World News* (Sept. 21, 1991) Extra section, pp. 1-2.
Note: AG quoted briefly.

J5181   Wallenstein, Barry. Poetry And Jazz—A 20th Century Wedding. *Black American Literature Forum,* vol. 25, no. 3 (Fall 1991) pp. 595-620.

J5182   Allen Ginsberg, American Dharma. *Journal Of the Print World* (Fall 1991) p. 43.

J5183   Hass, Robert. Families And Prisons. *Michigan Quarterly Review,* vol. 30, no. 4 (Fall 1991) pp. 553-572.

J5184   Boyle, Shane Patrick. Right To Read Too Precious To Give Away. *Daily Cougar* (Sept. 24, 1991) p. 3.

J5185   Ragland, Kelley. Films Provide Insight Into 'Beats'. *Kenyon Collegian* (Sept. 26, 1991) p. 3.

J5186   Galt And Glass Turn Out To Help Tibetan Museum. *Staten Island Advance* (Sept. 29, 1991)

J5187   Delson, Jennifer. Paterson 'Tunes Into' Beat Poet Years Later. *North Jersey Herald & News* (Sept. 30, 1991) pp. A1, A3.
Note: AG quoted briefly.

J5188   Feins, John. Howl Now [part 1]. *Emergency Horse,* no. 1 (Oct. 1991) pp. 11-14.
Note: AG interview format.

J5189   Beal, Eileen. Ginsberg's 'Beat' Goes On... *Cleveland Jewish News* (Oct. 4, 1991) p. 33.
Note: AG quoted briefly.

J5190   Toolen, Tom. Ginsberg Returns To City That Inspires His Poetry. *Bergen Record* (Oct. 6, 1991) p. 2.
Note: AG quoted briefly.

J5191   Ginsberg In the Flesh! *Nuvo* (Oct. 9-16, 1991) p. 3.

J5192   Harvey, Jay. Allen Ginsberg Recalls Hoosier 'Hospitality'. *Indianapolis Star* (Oct. 10, 1991) pp. 1, 5.
Note: AG quoted briefly.

J5193   Sutherland, Scott. 'Hydrogen Jukebox' Calls America To Redeem. *Burlington Free Press* (Oct. 14, 1991) section D, p. 1D.

J5194   Thomas, Dana. Limelight. *Washington Post* (Oct. 20, 1991)
Note: AG quoted briefly.

J5195   Ciuraru, Carmela. Ginsberg Comes To GMU For Washington Premiere Of 'Hydrogen Jukebox'. *Broadside* (Oct. 21, 1991) p. 17.
Note: AG quoted briefly.

J5196   Madlas, Mike. Glass Sets Ginsberg's Poetry To Music On Stage In New Way. *South End* (Oct. 21, 1991) p. 4.

J5197   Sparks, Amy. Dharma And Crosses. *Cleveland Edition,* vol. 7, no. 1 (Oct. 24-30, 1991) p. 24.

J5198   Ciuraru, Carmela. Ginsberg Turns On the "Hydrogen". *Broadside* (Oct. 28, 1991) p. 20.

Byl. Jukebox Talk. *Broadside* (Oct. 28, 1991) p. 20.

J5199   Smith, Arthur R. 'Hydrogen,' An Old-Fashioned Good Time. *Washington Post* (Oct. 31, 1991)

J5200   Feins, John. Double Exposure [part 2]. *Emergency Horse,* no. 2 (Nov. 1991) pp. 16-18.
Note: AG interview format.

J5201   Hübsch, Hadayatullah. Die Geschlagene, Die Verzückte, Die Glückselige, Die Literatur Der Beat-Generation. *Der Literat,* vol. 33, no. 11 (Nov. 1991) pp. 15-18.

J5202   Zinsser, John. [review of *Dharma Bums* (recording)]. *Publishers Weekly,* vol. 238, no. 48 (Nov. 1, 1991) p. 55.

J5203   Bonesteel, Michael. Ginsberg's Cosmic Beat Goes On. *Evanston Review* (Nov. 7, 1991) Diversions section, p. D2.
Note: AG quoted briefly.

J5204   Smith, Joan. Allen Ginsberg Growing Up—Slowly. *San Francisco Examiner* (Nov. 7, 1991) pp. D-1, D-10.
Note: AG quoted briefly.

J5205   Dante, Robert. American Distilled In a Hydrogen Jukebox. *Public News,* no. 497 (Nov. 13, 1991) p. 8.
Note: AG quoted briefly.

J5206   Sarvay, John F. 'Old Beat Poet' Back With Message. *Richmond Times-Dispatch* (Nov. 16, 1991) p. B3.
Note: AG quoted briefly.

J5207   Henken, John. 'Hydrogen Jukebox' Premieres At UCLA. *Los Angeles Times* (Nov. 25, 1991) p. F4.

J5208   Harney, Steve. Ethnos And the Beat Poets. *Journal Of American Studies,* vol. 25, no. 3 (Dec. 1991) pp. 363-380.

J5209   Loidl, Christian. Don't Do It, If It's Not Fun. *Lesezirkel,* no. 54 (Dec. 1991) pp. 15-17.
Note: AG quoted briefly.

J5210   Helmling, Steven. Twilight Of the Idols [review of *Ginsberg: a Biography* by Barry Miles]. *Kenyon Review,* vol. 13, no. 1 (Winter 1991) pp. 177-187.

J5211   Schwartz, Stephen. Allen Ginsberg Recovering After Mild Heart Failure. *San Francisco Chronicle* (Dec. 30, 1991) p. A15.

J5212   Poet Ginsberg Is Recovering. *Buffalo News* (Dec. 31, 1991) p. C-2.

J5213   Allen Ginsberg On the Mend. *Newark Star Ledger* (Dec. 31, 1991)

J5214   Ginsberg Recuperating. *Washington Post* (Dec. 31, 1991) p. C3.

J5215   Hebel, Udo J. Breaking Through the "Suburban Wasteland." *Arbeiten Aus Anglistik Und Amerikanistik [AAA],* vol. 16, no. 1 (1991) pp. 13-29.

J5216   Crowe, Thomas Rain. Philip Glass: An Interview. *Cold-Drill* (1991) pp. 142-146.

J5217   Blechman, Max. Anarchism And Revolution In Amerikkka, an Interview With Allen Ginsberg. *Drunken Boat,* no. 1 [1991] pp. 18-19, 32.
Note: AG interview format.

J5218   L'Aminot, Tanguy. Entretien Avec Gilles Farcet Sur J.-J. Rousseau, Henry David Thoreau Et Gary Snyder. *Etudes Jean-Jacques Rousseau,* no. 5 (1991) pp. 179-189.

J5219   An Interview With Allen Ginsberg. *Hika,* vol. 52, no. 1 (1991-1992) pp. 23-35.
Note: AG interview format.

J5220   Robbie, Andrew M. [review of *The Lion For Real* (recording)]. *Moody Street Irregulars,* no. 24-26 (1991) p. 34.

J5221   Lernout, Geert. De Amerikaanse Vinkenoog. *Nieuw Wereldtijdschrift,* no. 3 (1991) pp. 75-77.

J5222   Reilly, Evelyn. Naked Allen Ginsberg [review of *Ginsberg: a Biography* by Barry Miles]. *Parnassus,* vol. 16, no. 2 (1991) pp. 161-171.

J5223   Pohl, Volker. [review of *Reality Sandwiches* (photographs)]. *Photonews* (1991) p. 10.

J5224   [review of *Reality Sandwiches* (photographs)]. *Zeitschrift Für Literatur,* no. 23
(1991) p. 90.

Books:

J5225   Bartlett, Jeffrey. *One Vast Page.* Berkeley, CA: privately printed, 1991.
Note: AG mentioned throughout.

J5226   Campbell, James. *Talking At the Gates: A Life Of James Baldwin.* New York,
NY: Penguin, 1991, pp. 128, 138-9.

J5227   Cherkovski, Neeli. *Hank: The Life Of Charles Bukowski.* New York, NY:
Random House, 1991, pp. 118, 122, 167, 195.

J5228   Crafton, John Michael (ed.). *International Conference On Representing
Revolution: Selected Essays.* Carrollton, GA: West Georgia College, 1991.
Contents: Ball, Gordon. Ginsberg And Revolution, pp. 137-149.

J5229   Drexel, John (ed.). *The Facts On File Encyclopedia Of the 20th Century.* New
York, NY: Facts On File, 1991, p. 374.

J5230   French, Warren. *The San Francisco Poetry Renaissance, 1955-1960.* Boston,
MA: Twayne Publishers, 1991.
Note: AG mentioned throughout.

J5231   Green, Michelle. *The Dream At the End Of the World.* New York, NY:
HarperCollins, 1991.
Note: AG quoted and mentioned throughout.

J5232   Halper, Jon (ed.). *Gary Snyder: Dimensions Of a Life.* San Francisco, CA:
Sierra Club Books, 1991.
Note: AG mentioned throughout.

J5233   Heylin, Clinton. *Dylan: Behind the Shades.* New York, NY: Viking, 1991, pp.
303-304.
Note: AG quoted briefly and mentioned throughout.

J5234   Kostelanetz, Richard (ed.). *American Writing Today.* Troy, NY: Whitston Pub.,
1991, pp. 176-190.
Note: AG interview format, reprinted from the *Voice Of America.*

J5235   Leyland, Winston (ed.). *Gay Roots.* San Francisco, CA: Gay Sunshine Press,
1991, pp. 323-325.

J5236   Maynard, John Arthur. *Venice West: The Beat Generation In Southern
California.* New Brunswick, NJ: Rutgers University Press, 1991.
Note: AG mentioned throughout.

J5237   Occhiogrosso, Peter. *Through the Labyrinth.* New York, NY: Viking, 1991, p.
160.
Note: AG quoted briefly.

J5238   Pacernick, Gary. *Sing a New Song.* Cincinnati, OH: American Jewish Archives,
1991, pp. 8, 27, 28.

J5239   Peck, Abe. *Uncovering the Sixties.* New York, NY: Citadel Press, 1991.
Note: AG mentioned throughout.

J5240 Rollyson, Carl. *The Lives Of Norman Mailer.* New York, NY: Paragon House, 1991, p. 135.

1992

J5241 Muratori, Fred. Poetry—The Before Columbus Foundation Poetry Anthology: Selections From the American Book Awards, 1980-1990. *Library Journal,* vol. 117, no. 1 (Jan. 1992) p. 132.

J5242 Chronicle. *New York Times* (Jan. 1, 1992) p. 38.

J5243 Mascitti, Al. Something To Howl About. *News Journal* (Jan. 1, 1992) p. D4.
Note: AG quoted briefly.

J5244 Harmens, Erik Jan. Allen Ginsberg In Nederland. *Poezie Nieuws,* no. 0 (Jan. 1992) p. 1.
Note: AG quoted briefly.

J5245 Corrias, Pino. Viaggi Acidi. *La Stampa* (Jan. 1992) Tutto Libri section, p. 1.

J5246 Ball, Gordon. Wide Open And Intimate. *Swissair Gazette* (Jan. 1, 1992) pp. 42-47.

J5247 Ferraris, Gabriele. Un Urlo Anni Sessanta: Allen Ginsberg E Philip Glass "Utopia Americana" Al Regio. *La Stampa* (Jan. 3, 1992) Torino Sette section, p. 5.

J5248 Steenberghe, Max. Schrijven Moet'n Desillusie Zijn. *Eindhovens Dagblad* (Jan. 14, 1992) p. 13.
Note: AG interview format in Dutch only.

J5249 Van Oppen, John. Hippie—Hogepriester In Lindenberg. *De Gelderlander* (Jan. 16, 1992)

J5250 O'Toole, Lawrence. Doing 'Naked Lunch': How Robocop Met William Burroughs. *Washington Post* (Jan. 19, 1992) section G, p. 1.

J5251 Pivano, Fernanda. Arriva Ginsberg, Carico D'Allori E Di Utopie. *Corriere Della Sera* (Jan. 21, 1992) p. 5.

J5252 Martinat, Giuliana. "Io, Poeta Dell'Utopia". *La Repubblica* (Jan. 24, 1992) pp. 1, 16.

Campo, Alberto. La Strana Coppia Di Profeti. *La Repubblica* (Jan. 24, 1992)

J5253 Neirotti, Marco. Il «Poeta Maledetto» Fa Rivivere Gli Anni Sessanta. *La Stampa* (Jan. 24, 1992)
Note: AG quoted briefly.

J5254 Buzzolan, Dario. Glass E Ginsberg: L'Utopia Americana. *Stampa Sera* (Jan. 24, 1992)

J5255 Ponte, Meo. L'Ultimo Americano. *La Repubblica* (Jan. 25, 1992) p. 12.

J5256 T., A. Utopia A Torino. *Corriere Della Sera* (Jan. 26, 1992) p. 15.

J5257 Castaldo, Gino. La Poesia E Il Suo Doppio. *La Repubblica* (Jan. 26-27, 1992) p. 26.

J5258   Orengo, Nico. Ginsberg, Finita La Rabbia. *La Stampa* (Jan. 26, 1992) p. 17.
Note: AG quoted briefly.

J5259   Paterno, Cristiana. "Restate Irresponsabili". Parola Del Re Di Maggio. *L'Unita* (Jan. 26, 1992) p. 17.
Note: AG quoted briefly.

J5260   Bergero, Silvia. Ginsberg A Torino: La Certezza Della Poesia, Il Dubbio Del Maestro. *L'Indipendente* (Jan. 27, 1992) p. 9.
Note: AG quoted briefly.

J5261   Radio Free Detroit. *MetroTimes* (Jan. 29-Feb. 4, 1992)

J5262   McGraw, Bill. Howl On the Air. *Free Press* (Jan. 30, 1992)

J5263   Daurer, Gregory. The High Times Interview, Allen Ginsberg. *High Times,* no. 198 (Feb. 1992) pp. 12-16.
Note: AG interview format.

J5264   Pivano, Fernanda. Papa Walt, Che Sei Nei Nostri Cuori. *Il Tema* (Feb. 2, 1992) pp. 1-2.
Note: AG quoted briefly in Italian only.

J5265   Smith, Joan. The Beats. *San Francisco Examiner* (Feb. 9, 1992) pp. D1, D5-D6.

J5266   Williams, Jennifer. Ginsberg Reads His Unpublished Works. *Washington Square News,* vol. 19, no. 82 (Feb. 24, 1992) pp. 1, 5.
Note: AG quoted.

J5267   Gray, Kevin. Ginsberg Song, Poetry Wow Campus Throng. *Daily Item* (Feb. 28, 1992)
Note: AG quoted briefly.

J5268   Fraser, Vernon. The Poetry-Jazz Fusion. *Poets & Writers Magazine,* vol. 20, no. 2 (March-April 1992) pp. 26-28, 30.
Note: AG quoted briefly.

J5269   Sion, Michael. Keeping the Beat. *Reno Gazette-Journal* (March 2, 1992)
Note: AG quoted briefly.

J5270   Gener, Randy. Beat-ing His Way To Reno. *Sagebrush* (March 3, 1992) p. 6.
Note: AG quoted briefly.

J5271   Gener, Randy. A Late Night With Poet Allen Ginsberg. *Sagebrush* (March 10, 1992) pp. 1, 7.
Note: AG quoted briefly.

J5272   Page, Jeffrey. Poets To Celebrate the City. *Bergen Record* (March 11, 1992) pp. PS-1, PS-5.

J5273   Sion, Mike. Notes From the Jungle. *Reno Gazette-Journal* (March 13, 1992)

J5274   Italie, Hillel. Allen Ginsberg Walks Through Leaves Of Grass. *Sunday Freeman* (March 22, 1992) p. 25.
Note: AG quoted briefly.

J5275 Micek, John L. An Afternoon With Alan [sic] Ginsberg. *Touchstone* (March 25, 1992)
Note: AG quoted briefly.

J5276 Italie, Hillel. Allen Ginsberg Salutes Whitman. *Recorder* (March 26, 1992) pp. 19, 28.
Note: AG quoted briefly.

J5277 Prothero, Stephen. On the Holy Road: The Beat Movement As Spiritual Protest. *Harvard Theological Review,* vol. 84, no. 2 (April 1992) pp. 205-222.

J5278 [letter to the editor]. *Pique,* vol. 4, no. 4 (April 1992) pp. 8-9.

J5279 Crager, Jack. Song Of a Favorite Son. *Bay Ridge Paper* (April 3-9, 1992) p. B1.
Note: AG quoted briefly.

J5280 Maraniss, David and Dionne, E.J., Jr. The Race For President: A Daily Digest. *Washington Post* (April 3, 1992) section A, p. 16.

J5281 Balz, Dan. Campaign Journal: Democrats Give Boomers Deja Vu. *Washington Post* (April 4, 1992) section A, p. 1.

J5282 Marsico, Ron. Ginsberg Lauds Paterson With Williams' Poem. *Star-Ledger* (April 5, 1992) p. 3.
Note: AG quoted briefly.

J5283 The Poets Of Paterson. *News Journal* (April 5, 1992) p. B4.

J5284 Cascade Of Poetry Falls On City. *Asbury Park Press* (April 6, 1992) p. A3.
Note: AG quoted briefly.

J5285 The Talk Of the Town: Walt. *New Yorker,* vol. 68, no. 8 (April 13, 1992) pp. 28-30.

J5286 McPhail, Rebecca. Beat-Poet Ginsberg To Recite On Campus. *Daily Cougar* (April 21, 1992) pp. 1, 12.
Note: AG quoted briefly.

J5287 Hamilton, Kendra. A Hoot And a 'Howl'. *Houston Chronicle* (April 24, 1992) pp. 1F, 3F.
Note: AG quoted briefly.

J5288 Ginsberg, Allen. Exorcising Burroughs. *Observer* (April 26, 1992) Magazine section, pp. 26-27, 29-30.
Note: AG interview format.

J5289 Holt, Jim. Jerry's Kids. *New Republic,* vol. 206, no. 17 (April 27, 1992) p. 19.

J5290 Gann, Kyle. Square Rhythms. *Village Voice* (April 28, 1992)
Note: AG quoted briefly.

J5291 Hackensberger, Alfred. Das Paradies Den Schreibenden Wilden. *Süddeutsche Zeitung* (May 16-17, 1992) p. 203.

J5292 Winders, Jim. Allen Ginsberg: Poet, Citizen, "Courage-Teacher". *Flagpole Magazine,* vol. 6, no. 19 (May 20, 1992) p. 12.

J5293   Burroughs And Ginsberg, Naked Burroughs. *San Francisco Review Of Books,*
vol. 17, no. 1 (Summer [May 20] 1992) pp. 33-35.
Note: AG interview format.

J5294   Mislow, Brad. Beat Poet To Rap All About America Today. *Red And Black*
(May 21, 1992) p. 3.
Note: AG quoted briefly.

J5295   Roberts, Michael. Back Beat. *Westword* (May 27-June 2, 1992) p. 58.

J5296   Howe, Barton G. Remembering a Day Of Violence, Fear. *Sunday Camera* (May
31, 1992) pp. 1B, 4B.

J5297   [article]. *Film Culture,* no. 76 (June 1992) pp. 29-30.
Note: AG quoted briefly.

J5298   Bishop, Gordon. Word Star. *Star-Ledger* (June 2, 1992) pp. 37, 44.
Note: AG quoted briefly.

J5299   Boudreau, John. The Beat Goes On. *Los Angeles Times* (June 3, 1992) pp. E1,
E10.
Note: AG quoted briefly.

Wilson, William. Wally Berman, Semina Figure. *Los Angeles Times* (June 3,
1992) pp. F1, F18-19.

J5300   Burns, John. Adventures With Allen Ginsberg. *Inside* (June 10, 1992) pp. 18,
19.
Note: AG quoted briefly.

J5301   Reichard, Dennis. The Morning With Ferlinghetti. *Guidelines,* vol. 14, no. 3
(Summer 1992) pp. 8-9.

J5302   Money, Peter. An Interview With Allen Ginsberg. *Provincetown Arts,* vol. 8
([July 1] 1992) pp. 92-96.
Note: AG interview format.

J5303   Ginsberg, Allen. Interview With William S. Burroughs. *Switch,* vol. 10, no. 3
(July 1992) pp. 13-47.
Note: AG interview format translated by Akiko Sakagami in Japanese only.

J5304   Black, Stephanie. Poets Ginsberg, Waldman To Speak, Read At AIDS Benefit.
Aspen Times (July 11-12, 1992) p. 13B.
Note: AG quoted briefly.

J5305   Dumas, Alan. The Beat Goes On... *Rocky Mountain News* (July 26, 1992)
Sunday magazine, pp. 10M-12M.
Note: AG quoted.

J5306   [review of *Dharma Lion* by Michael Schumacher]. *Kirkus Reviews,* vol. 60
(Aug. 1, 1992) p. 977.

J5307   Bonder, Nilton. Allen Ginsberg. *Shalom,* vol. 27, no. 296 (Aug. 1992) pp. 70-
72.

Willer, Claudio. Poeta E Herói Da Geracão Beat. *Shalom,* vol. 27, no. 296
(Aug. 1992) p. 73.

J5308 Gillespie, Elgy. The Beat Is On the Road Again. *Melbourne Age* (Aug. 19, 1992) p. 5.

J5309 Stuttaford, Genevieve. [review of *Dharma Lion* by Michael Schumacher]. *Publishers Weekly,* vol. 239, no. 38 (Aug. 24, 1992) pp. 68-69.

J5310 Jones, Jamey. Poet Heroes And Hovering Angels. *Legend* (Sept. 1992) pp. 4-5.

J5311 Gargan, William. [review of *Dharma Lion* by Michael Schumacher]. *Library Journal,* vol. 117, no. 14 (Sept. 1, 1992) p. 176.

J5312 [review of *Dharma Lion* by Michael Schumacher]. *New York,* vol. 25, no. 36 (Sept. 14, 1992) p. 111.

J5313 Schumacher, Michael. In Back Of the Real. *Metro,* vol. 8, no. 29 (Sept. 17-23, 1992) pp. 20-22, 24, 26.

J5314 Plymell, Charles. Autobiography. *Atom Mind,* vol. 3, no. 9 (Fall 1992) pp. 40-62.
Note: AG quoted briefly.

J5315 Dander, Nicholas. A Conversation With the Barded One: Allen Ginsberg. *Lullabye Jesus* (Fall 1992) pp. 8-9.
Note: AG interview format.

J5316 Long, Philomene Gyokuho. The Flow Of the Mind In Time: An Interview With Allen Ginsberg. *Ten Directions,* vol. 13, no. 2 (Fall-Winter 1992) pp. 35-38.
Note: AG interview format.

J5317 Mariani, Alisa. The 1992 Civil Liberties Awards. *Civil Liberties Reporter,* vol. 26, no. 4 (Oct.-Dec. 1992)
Note: AG quoted briefly.

J5318 Goldsmith, Jeffrey. Allen Ginsberg: America's Beat Laureate Repackages His Past And Foresees Our Future. *Details,* vol. 11, no. 5 (Oct. 1992) pp. 140-142.
Note: AG quoted.

J5319 Foley, Jack. Poet And Film. *Poetry USA,* no. 24 ([Oct.] 1992) pp. 2-5.
Note: AG interview format, transcript of *Getting It Together (film).*

J5320 Ginsberg, Allen. Drogas Bombas Y Libros Y Sexo. *Culturas,* vol. 16, no. 364 (Oct. 3, 1992) pp. 1-2, 6.
Note: AG interview format translated by Julio Ramón Ribeyro and J.A. Millán in Spanish only.

J5321 Perry, David. Ginsberg Celebrates the Life Of Poet, Friend Jack Kerouac. *Sun* (Oct. 4, 1992) pp. 1, 4.
Note: AG quoted briefly.

J5322 Allee, Rod. Louis Ginsberg, Celebrated. *Bergen Record* (Oct. 9, 1992) pp. E1, E4.

J5323 Money, Peter. Word From Ginsberg. *Lame Duck,* no. 5 ([Oct. 11] 1992) p. 33.
Note: AG interview format, reprinted from *Provincetown Arts* (July 1, 1992).

J5324 Gates, David. [review of *Dharma Lion* by Michael Schumacher]. *Newsweek,* vol. 120, no. 15 (Oct. 12, 1992) p. 80.

J5325 Olson, Ray. [review of *Dharma Lion* by Michael Schumacher]. *Booklist,* vol. 89 (Oct. 15, 1992) p. 393.

J5326 Keiser, Ellen. Allen Ginsberg At Guild Hall. *Dan's Papers* (Oct. 16, 1992) p. 7.

J5327 Koenig, Rhoda. [review of *Dharma Lion* by Michael Schumacher]. *New York,* vol. 25, no. 42 (Oct. 26, 1992) p. 95-96.

J5328 Brozan, Nadine. Allen Ginsberg Shares Details Of His Morning Routine With the World. *New York Times* (Nov. 5, 1992) p. A33.
Note: AG quoted briefly.

J5329 [photograph]. *Columbia Daily Spectator,* vol. 116, no. 119 (Nov. 16, 1992) p. 1.

J5330 [review of *I Hjertet Av Malstrommen*]. *Stavanger Aftenblad* (Nov. 24, 1992)

J5331 Silesky, Barry. [review of *Dharma Lion* by Michael Schumacher]. *Chicago Tribune* (Nov. 29, 1992) section 14, p. 1+.

J5332 Nicosia, Gerald. [review of *Dharma Lion* by Michael Schumacher]. *Los Angeles Times* (Nov. 29, 1992) Book Review section, pp. 4, 13.

J5333 Morgan, Bill. A Brief Guide For Collectors And Dealers. *AB Bookman's Weekly,* vol. 90, no. 22 (Nov. 30, 1992) pp. 2052, 2054-9.

J5334 St. John, Peter K.B. Ginsbergology 101/102. *Ecco,* vol. 24, no. 9 (Dec. 1992) pp. 1, 3, 5.
Note: AG quoted briefly.

J5335 Bø, Tore. Beat-Generasjonens Gudfar. *Norske Argus* (Dec. 8, 1992)

J5336 Budman, Matthew. [review of *Dharma Lion* by Michael Schumacher]. *Jewish Bulletin* (Dec. 11, 1992)

J5337 Nicosia, Gerald. [review of *Dharma Lion* by Michael Schumacher]. *Daily Camera* (Dec. 13, 1992) p. 5F.

J5338 Sullivan, Kevin. Well-Versed In Politics? Lyrical Advice For Clinton From Some Of America's Premier Poets. *Washington Post* (Dec. 13, 1992) section F, p. 1.

Streitfeld, David. Book Report: Life After Nobel. *Washington Post* (Dec. 13, 1992) Book World section, p. 15.

J5339 Sortland, Bjørn. Ein Godbeat [review of *I Hjertat Av Malstrommen*]. *Vart Land* (Dec. 15, 1992) Bok Forum section.

J5340 Cosper, Doug. Naropa To Bless Site Of Ginsberg Library. *Daily Camera* (Dec. 17, 1992) p. 6B.

J5341 Dunn, Geoffrey. A Couple For the Road. *Metro,* vol. 8, no. 42 (Dec. 17-23, 1992) pp. 20-25.
Note: AG quoted briefly.

J5342 Price, Michael H. CD Captures Beat Mystique. *Sunday Camera* (Dec. 20, 1992) p. 6B.

J5343   Hamill, Pete. The Brilliance Of New York. *New York,* vol. 25, no. 50 (Dec. 21-28, 1992) pp. 60-63.

J5344   Nicosia, Gerald. [review of *Dharma Lion* by Michael Schumacher]. *Kansas City Star* (Dec. 27, 1992) p. J-10.

J5345   Sinisi, J. Sebastian. Naropa Institute Changing With the Times. *Denver Post* (Dec. 29, 1992)

J5346   Anarkisme Og Revolusjon I Amerikkka. *Basta!,* vol. 3, no. 5 (1992) p. 12.
        Note: AG interview format translated by Oisten Holen in Norwegian only, first published in *Drunken Boat* (1991).

J5347   [article]. *Corrige Du Devoir,* no. 1-2, series 11-12 (1992)
        Note: AG mentioned throughout.

J5348   Medovoi, L. Mapping the Rebel Image—Postmodernism And the Masculinist Politics Of Rock In the USA. *Cultural Critique,* no. 20 (1992) pp. 153-188.

J5349   Rauvolf, Josef. Nejlip To Spalit-Cenzura v USA? *Svetova Literatura,* vol. 37, no. 1 (1992) pp. 157-161.

J5350   Chwin, Krystyna. Spotkanie Z Allenem Ginsbergiem. *Tytulu,* vol. 5, no. 1 (1992) pp. 44-46.

Books:

J5351   Ambrose, Joe and others. *Man From Nowhere.* Dublin, Ireland: The Gap And Subliminal Books, 1992, unpaged.

J5352   Bockris, Victor. *Keith Richards: The Biography.* New York, NY: Poseidon Press, 1992.
        Note: AG mentioned throughout.

J5353   Clemente, Francesco. *Evening Raga & Paradiso.* New York, NY: Gagosian Gallery/Rizzoli, 1992, pp. 7-14.
        Note: AG interview format.

J5354   Finlayson, Iain. *Tangier: City Of the Dream.* New York, NY: HarperCollins, 1992.
        Note: AG mentioned throughout.

J5355   Fischel, Jack and Pinsker, Sanford (eds.). *Jewish-American History And Culture: An Encyclopedia.* New York, NY: Garland, 1992.
        Contents: Stern, Gerald. Poetry, pp. 485-496.

J5356   Gibinska, Marta and Mazur, Zygmunt (eds.). *Proceedings Of the Fifth International Conference: New Trends In American Studies.* Krakow, Poland: Jagiellonian University, 1992.
        Contents: Ball, Gordon. Allen Ginsberg And Charles Reznikoff, pp. 261-275.

J5357   Hoffman, Michael J. and Murphy, Patrick D. (ed.). *Critical Essays On American Modernism.* New York, NY: G.K. Hall, 1992, pp. 142, 170, 192.

J5358   Jayakar, Pupul. *Indira Gandhi: An Intimate Biography.* New York, NY: Pantheon Books, 1992, p. 124.

J5359   Jezer, Marty. *Abbie Hoffman: American Rebel.* New Brunswick, NJ: Rutgers University Press, 1992.
Note: AG mentioned.

J5360   Kurtz, Michael. *Stockhausen: A Biography.* Boston, MA: Faber and Faber, 1992.
Note: AG mentioned.

J5361   LePellec, Yves (ed.). *Direction De Travail, Anglais, no. 1-3, A. Ginsberg.* France: Centre De Vanves, 1992. [correspondence course publication].
Note: AG mentioned throughout.

J5362   Loidl, Christian; Hintze, Christina Ide and Gindl, Winfried (eds.). *Die Jack Kerouac School Of Disembodied Poetics.* Klagenfurt, Germany: Sisyphus, 1992.
Contents: Loidl, Christian. Lade Gedanken Nicht Zum Tee Ein, pp. 33-37.
Hintze, Christian Ide. Von Mann Zu Mann, pp. 75-84.
   Note: AG interview format in German only.
Loidl, Christian. Kann Sein, Du Lebst, Kann Sein, Du Stirbst, pp. 89-94.
   Note: AG interview format in German only.

J5363   Mekas, Jonas. *Every Minute As We Are Talking Films Are Falling To Dust.* New York, NY: Film Makers' Cooperative, 1992.
Note: AG mentioned throughout.

J5364   Miles, Barry. *Two Lectures On the Work Of Allen Ginsberg.* London, England: Turret, 1992.
Note: AG mentioned throughout.

J5365   Miles, Barry. *William Burroughs: El Hombre Invisible.* London, England: Virgin Books, 1992.
Note: AG quoted briefly throughout.

J5366   Paglia, Camille. *Sex, Art, And American Culture.* New York, NY: Vintage Books, 1992, pp. ix, 126, 219, 229.

J5367   Parisi, Joseph. *Poets In Person: A Listener's Guide.* Chicago, IL: Modern Poetry Association/American Library Association, 1992, pp. 13-29.
Note: AG quoted.

J5368   Robins, Natalie. *Alien Ink.* New York, NY: William Morrow, 1992.
Note: AG quoted and mentioned throughout.

J5369   Ruland, Richard and Bradbury, Malcolm. *From Puritanism To Postmodernism.* New York, NY: Viking, 1992, pp. 395-397.

J5370   Sawyer-Lauçanno, Christopher. *The Continual Pilgrimage.* New York, NY: Grove Press, 1992.
Note: AG quoted and mentioned throughout.

J5371   Schumacher, Michael. *Dharma Lion: A Critical Biography Of Allen Ginsberg.* New York, NY: St. Martin's Press, 1992.
Note: AG mentioned and quoted throughout.

J5372   Silverman, Herschel. *High On the Beats.* Brooklyn, NY: Pinched Nerves Press, 1992.
Note: AG mentioned throughout.

J5373 Stanley, Linda C.; Shimkin, David and Lanner, Allen H. (eds.). *Ways To Writing.* New York, NY: Macmillan, 1992.
Contents: Fenton, Patrick. A Second Look At Allen Ginsberg, pp. 205-210.
Note: AG quoted.

J5374 Wakefield, Dan. *New York In the Fifties.* Boston, MA: Houghton Mifflin/Seymour Lawrence, 1992.
Note: AG quoted and mentioned throughout.

J5375 Williams, Paul. *Bob Dylan: Performing Artist, the Middle Years: 1974-1986.* Novato, CA: Underwood-Miller, 1992.
Note: AG mentioned throughout.

J5376 Young, Robyn V. (ed.). *Poetry Criticism, vol. 4.* Detroit, MI: Gale Research, 1992, pp. 42-96.

1993

J5377 Trungpa/Ginsberg/Rome. *Shambhala Sun,* vol. 1, no. 5 (Jan.-Feb. 1993) pp. 56-58.
Note: AG interview format.

J5378 McDonough, John. Leisure & Arts: Jazz: Very Cool, Very Hot. *Wall Street Journal* (Jan. 11, 1993) section A, p. 12.

J5379 Lewis, Joel. [review of *Dharma Lion* by Michael Schumacher]. *Forward* (Jan. 22, 1993) pp. 9-10.

J5380 Hart, Hugh. Beat Goes On. *Chicago Tribune* (Jan. 25, 1993) section 5, pp. 1-2.

J5381 Valentine, Sara. Needles Exchange Gets a Shot In the Arm. *New York Planet,* vol. 1, no. 5 (Feb. 3, 1993) p. 1.

J5382 On the Air. *New York Press* (Feb. 3-9, 1993) p. 8.

J5383 Konyndyk, Michele. A Man Of History, Allen Ginsberg To Visit GRCC. *Collegiate,* vol. 37, no. 7 (Feb. 10, 1993) p. 5.

J5384 Frisch, Don. [review of *Dharma Lion* by Michael Schumacher]. *Grand Rapids Press* (Feb. 14, 1993) p. K7.

J5385 Vann, Sonya. Ginsberg: People Are Better Served By Poetry Than By Politics. *Grand Rapids Press* (Feb. 17, 1993) Flair section, p. C-1.
Note: AG quoted.

J5386 Vann, Sonya. Poetry Lives! *Grand Rapids Press* (Feb. 20, 1993) p. A3.

J5387 Rothstein, Edward. New Ways Of Honoring Tibetans' Old Ways. *New York Times* (Feb. 25, 1993) section C, p. 10. [NY City edition only]

J5388 [review of *Dharma Lion* by Michael Schumacher]. *Progressive,* vol. 57, no. 3 (March 1993) p. 42.

J5389 Hitchens, Christopher. Angels Over Broadway. *Vanity Fair,* vol. 56, no. 3 (March 1993) pp. 72, 74, 76.

J5390 Activist Ginsberg Sets Lecture At OU Thursday. *Norman Transcript* (March 2, 1993) p. 7.

J5391   Medley, Robert. Beat Generation Poet Howling At Generation X. *Daily Oklahoman/Oklahoma City Times* (March 3, 1993) section 6, pp. 1-2.

J5392   Ruiz, Debbie. Ginsberg Speaks At OU Tonight. *Oklahoma Daily* (March 4, 1993) p. 1.

J5393   Thursday. *Oklahoma Gazette* (March 4, 1993) p. 23.

J5394   Minner, Jenni. Beat This. *Arbiter* (March 9, 1993) pp. 10, 13.

J5395   Scharf, Lee. Allen Ginsberg, Agent Of Change. *Boise Weekly,* vol. 1, no. 34 (March 9-15, 1993) pp. 11, 24.

J5396   Crump, Steve. 30 Years Later, Ginsberg's Job Continues To Raise Consciousness. *Times-News* (March 9, 1993)
Note: AG quoted.

J5397   Ginsberg: Poet, Visionary Reads At Liberty Theater. *Idaho Mountain Express* (March 10-16, 1993) p. 25.

J5398   First Amendment: Trampled By Telephone. *Mountain Express,* vol. 20, no. 10 (March 10, 1993)

J5399   The Beat Goes On. *Wood River Valley Tempo* (March 10, 1993) section B, pp. 1, 3.

Preston, Scott. Ginsberg: Poet's Soul, Activist's Heart. *Wood River Valley Tempo* (March 10, 1993) section B, p. 3.

J5400   Prichard, Ron. The Beat Goes On. *Idaho Statesman* (March 12, 1993) section D, pp. 1, 6.
Note: AG quoted.

J5401   Crump, Steve. Poet Allen Ginsberg, Who Helped Chronicle a Generation, Hits the Road. *Times-News* (March 12, 1993) pp. B5-B6.

J5402   Celuzza, Elinor. The Beat Goes On. *Valley Optimist* (March 15-28, 1993) pp. 1, 36.
Note: AG quoted.

J5403   McAlpin, R.D. Ginsberg Says Meditation Makes Poetry, Not Drugs. *Mountain Express* (March 17, 1993)
Note: AG quoted.

J5404   Karamargin, C.J. Ginsberg Honors Ezra Pound. *Wood River Journal* (March 17, 1993) pp. 1, 4, 8.
Note: AG quoted.

Ridler, Keith. One Man's Vision. *Wood River Journal* (March 17, 1993) section B, pp. 1, 4, 8.
Note: AG quoted.

J5405   Albright, Alex. Before He Went West, He Had To Go South: Kerouac's Southern Aesthetics. *North Carolina Humanities* (Spring 1993) pp. 53-70.
Note: AG quoted.

J5406   Daurer, Gregory. Wywiad Z Allanem Ginsbergiem: Nie Lubie Kokainy. *Piatek Wieczorem,* no. 10 (Spring-Summer 1993) pp. 18-19.
Note: AG interview format first published in *High Times* (Feb. 1992).

J5407   Schmaltz, Ken. The Unbeatable Beatniks Of Life. *Streets,* vol. 6 (Spring 1993) pp. 65-67.

J5408   Hooks, Liz. Green Card Writers. *Brooklyn College Excelsior* (March 29, 1993) p. 8.
Note: AG quoted.

J5409   Brown, David and McClen, Rebecca. Allen Ginsberg: The Sacred Howl. *Magical Blend,* no. 38 (April 1993) pp. 14-16, 18, 20, 72, 74.
Note: AG interview format.

J5410   Kinsler, Robert. Ginsberg's Beat Powerful, Political. *Orange County Register* (April 2, 1993)

J5411   Intentionally omitted.

J5412   Sulkis, Karen. The Beat Goes On. *Oakland Tribune* (April 8, 1993) section D, pp. D1, D4.
Note: AG quoted.

J5413   Creech, Steve. Caustic Poet Ginsberg Retains Beat. *Orange City News Weekly* (April 8, 1993)

Schulz, Lawrence. Ginsberg's Works Haven't Dimmed. *Orange City News Weekly* (April 8, 1993)

J5414   Buddhist Holy Man To Speak In Lincoln. *Lincoln Journal-Star* (April 10, 1993) p. 9.

J5415   Wolgamott, L. Kent. Famous Poem Written On '66 Trip Here. *Lincoln Journal-Star* (April 11, 1993) p. 5H.
Note: AG quoted.

J5416   Barnes, Harper. Beat Generation Poet Allen Ginsberg To Appear Here. *St. Louis Post-Dispatch* (April 11, 1993)
Note: AG quoted.

J5417   Baldridge, Mark. Man And Myth: Counterculture Poet To Give UNL Reading. *Daily Nebraskan* (April 16, 1993)

J5418   Wade, Gerald. Poet Ginsberg's Lincoln Visit To Help Monks. *World-Herald* (April 17, 1993) pp. 25, 31.

J5419   Wolgamott, L. Kent. Poem From '66 Visit Still Strong. *Lincoln Journal-Star* (April 18, 1993) section E, p. 1.
Note: AG quoted.

J5420   Grant, Matthew. The Beat Goes On: Ginsberg's Experiences, Interests Commonly Linked By Poetry. *Daily Nebraskan* (April 19, 1993) pp. 10-11.
Note: AG quoted

J5421   Kemp, Al. People. *News Journal* (April 20, 1993) p. D3.
Note: AG quoted briefly.

J5422   Poet Doodles For Cash. *News Tribune* (April 20, 1993) p. A2.
Note: AG quoted briefly.

J5423   People. *St. Louis Post-Dispatch* (April 20, 1993)
Note: AG quoted briefly.

J5424   Levy, Emanuel. Reviews. *Variety,* vol. 350, no. 13 (April 26, 1993) p. 70.

J5425   Fuss, Troy. Allen Ginsberg: The Poet For Real. *State Press Magazine,* vol. 6, no. 16 (April 29, 1993) p. 6.
Note: AG interview format.

J5426   Meyers, Christene C. Gentle Rebel Nurtures Hope For a Troubled Planet. *Billings Gazette* (May 1, 1993) p. 4C.
Note: AG quoted briefly.

J5427   AJ. The *From the Ashes* Interview With Allen Ginsberg. *From the Ashes,* no. 2 (May 1993) pp. 6-7.
Note: AG interview format.

J5428   Gorman, Peter. Allen Ginsberg. *High Times,* no. 213 (May 1993) pp. 47-48.
Note: AG quoted.

J5429   Anderson, Jack. A Role For Allen Ginsberg. *New York Times* (May 1, 1993) section A, p. 18.

J5430   Mr. Ginsberg Comes To Town. *Rocket* (May 1993) p. 6.
Note: AG quoted briefly.

J5431   Thielen, Greg. Inside the Real. *University Planet,* vol. 1, no. 3 (May 1993) pp. 18-19, 21-22.
Note: AG interview format.

J5432   Mead, Rebecca. The Beats Are Back. *New York,* vol. 26, no. 18 (May 3, 1993) pp. 30-37.

J5433   Anderson, Marcella. Ginsberg Comes To EC. *Earlham Word* (May 7, 1993) pp. 1, 3.
Note: AG quoted briefly.

J5434   Nance, Kevin. They Dig That Beat. *Lexington Herald-Leader* (May 15, 1993) pp. B1, B5.

J5435   Grünberg, Serge. La Révolte Beatnik. *Globe Hebdo,* no. 17 (June 2-8, 1993) pp. 57-66.

J5436   Romano, Lois. [article]. *Washington Post* (June 3, 1993) Style section, p. 3.

J5437   O'Connor, Patrick Joseph. Moody's Skidrow Beanery. *Atom Mind,* vol. 3, no. 11 (Summer 1993) pp. 47-50.

J5438   Perlotto, Franco. West Coast, Poesia Off Limits. *Avvenire* (June 22, 1993)

J5439   Crawford, Martin. The Allen Ginsberg Interview. *Gown Literary Supplement,* new series, no. 2 (Summer 1993) pp. 9-12.
Note: AG quoted.

J5440   Katz, Vincent. Hal Willner: The Master Of Mix 'n' Match. *Creem* (July 1993) pp. 92-95.

J5441   Stack, Peter. Documentary About Allen Ginsberg Is Pure Beauty. *San Francisco Chronicle* (July 9, 1993) p. C7.

J5442   Pongpaiboon, Naowarat. Going To See Allen Ginsberg Read Poems. *Matichon Weekly* (July 16, 1993) p. 65.

J5443 Steinberg, David. Poet Ginsberg Draws A Crowd In The City Different. *Albuquerque Journal* (July 25, 1993)
Notes: AG quoted briefly.

J5444 Beatnik Ginsberg's '90s Niche. *Denver Post* (July 23-25, 1993) USA Weekend Magazine section, p. 18.
Note: AG quoted.

J5445 Honan, William H. Ferlinghetti Reflects On Glow Of City Lights. *New York Times* (July 29, 1993) section C, p. 14.

J5446 Calic, Zoran. Kosmopolitski Pozdravi. *Bagdala,* vol. 35, no. 404-405 (Aug.-Oct. 1993) pp. 12-13.
Note: AG interview format in Serbian only.

J5447 Krisanda, Joel. The Angelheaded Hipster Raps With *Ergo. Ergo Magazine,* vol. 2, no. 6 (Aug. 1993) pp. 15-17.
Note: AG interview format.

J5448 Giovannini, Marco. Quarant'anni On the Road. *Panorama* (Aug. 1, 1993) pp. 111, 113.

J5449 Streitfeld, David. Wild Bill. *Details,* vol. 12, no. 4 (Sept. 1993) pp. 109-193.

J5450 Bennett, Philip. North Beach. *Boston Globe* (Sept. 5, 1993) pp. A73, A76.

J5451 Praschl, Bernhard. Wie Wird Man Ein Bohemien? *Kurier* (Sept. 10, 1993) p. 12.
Note: AG quoted in German only.

J5452 Pohl, Ronald. Der Alltag Als Lehrstoff Der Kunst. *Der Standard* (Sept. 10, 1993) p. 9.
Note: AG interview format in German only.

J5453 Murray, Joe. Ghost, Square Dancers Make Up For Alan [sic] Ginsberg's Absence In Boulder. *Atlanta Journal* (Sept. 15, 1993) section A, p. 11.

J5454 Nüchtern, Klaus. Everybody Fucks. *Falter,* no. 37-93 (Sept. 17-23, 1993) pp. 48-49.
Note: AG quoted at length in German only.

J5455 Yamazaki, Jiro. Drop Into The New York Poet's River. *Bar-F-Out,* vol. 2 (Autumn 1993) pp. [10-19].
Note: AG quoted in Japanese only.

J5456 Lowe, Ron. Satori In St. Petersburg. *Dharma Beat,* vol. 1, no. 1 (Fall 1993) pp. [5-6].

J5457 Jarraway, David R. Standing By His Word: The Politics Of Allen Ginsberg's Vietnam 'Vortex'. *Journal Of American Culture,* vol. 16, no. 3 (Fall 1993) pp. 81-88.

J5458 Ball, Gordon. Talking Continuously. *San Jose Studies,* vol. 19, no. 3 (Fall 1993) pp. 24-59.
Note: AG interview format.

J5459 Himes, Geoffrey. Manzarek Meets McClure, Melodrama. *Washington Post* (Sept. 24, 1993) Weekend section, p. 17.

J5460   Despotov, Vojislav. Hvatajte Svoj Bes. *Borba* (Sept. 29, 1993) p. 17.
Note: AG interview format in Serbian only.

J5461   Távolodó, Marton László and Tamás, Szönyei. Ami Eleven. *Magyar Narancs,*
vol. 5, no. 39 (Sept. 30, 1993) pp. 40-41.
Note: AG interview format in Hungarian only.

J5462   Zsuzsa, Láng. Nyüszítés. *Népszabadság* (Sept. 25, 1993) p. 33.
Note: AG interview format in Hungarian only.

J5463   Ganguly, Suranjan. Allen Ginsberg In India: An Interview. *Ariel: A Review Of
International English Literature,* vol. 24, no. 4 (Oct. 1993) pp. 21-32.
Note: AG interview format.

J5464   Musial, Grzegorz. Allen Ginsberg W Bydgoszczy. *Gazeta Regionalna* (Oct. 1,
1993) pp. 1, 6.
Note: Article includes a reproduction of AG's holographic inscription to this
author on the title page of a book.

J5465   Grady, John. Kerouac's Quest For Sex. *Penthouse Forum* (Oct. 1993) pp. 40-
47.

J5466   Engel, Matthew. Author! Author! Author! *Guardian* (Oct. 15, 1993) pp. 2-3.

J5467   Dillon, Cathy. Tweed Suit Lures Allen Ginsberg To Dublin. *Irish Press* (Oct.
15, 1993) p. 17.
Note: AG quoted briefly.

J5468   McFadden, Hugh. Beat Poet To Howl Tonight. *Irish Press* (Oct. 17, 1993) p.
41.
Note: AG quoted briefly.

J5469   McFadden, Hugh. Ginsberg On the Irish Beat. *Irish Press* (Oct. 18, 1993) p.
13.
Note: AG quoted briefly.

J5470   Rauvolf, Josef. Ràd Bych Se Podíval Smrti Do Ocí. *Magazin Dnes + TV,* vol.
4, no. 1 (Oct. 21, 1993) pp. 30-32.
Note: AG interview format in Czechoslovakian only.

J5471   Wandrup, Fredrik. Ginsberg-Feber I Oslo. *Dagbladet* (Oct. 24, 1993) p. 5.
Note: AG interview format in Norwegian only.

J5472   Haarstad, Bente. Ginsberg Den Siste Hippie? *Arbeider-Avisa* (Oct. 26, 1993) p.
30.

J5473   Lundemo, Trygve. Ginsberg Sprer Godhet. *Adresseavisen* (Oct. 26, 1993) p.
28.
Note: AG interview format in Norwegian only.

J5474   Reilly, David. Ginsberg Reads To an Irish Beat. *Irish Times* (Oct. 26, 1993)
Note: AG quoted briefly.

J5475   Opprorer I Hulen. *Bergen BA* (Oct. 27, 1993)

J5476   Sorensen, Britt. Guruen Ginsberg I Hulen. *Bergens Tidende* (Oct. 27, 1993) p.
43.

J5477   Grindaker, Siw. Ginsberg Klar Igjen. *Dagbladet* (Oct. 27, 1993) p. 41.

J5478   Lundemo, Trygve. Ginsberg I Toppform. *Adresseavisen* (Oct. 28, 1993)

J5479   Sorensen, Britt. Skriv Sannheten! *Bergens Tidende* (Oct. 28, 1993) p. 47.
        Note: AG quoted briefly in Norwegian only.

J5480   Olsen, Magne and Christensen, Paul. —Mer Sild Og Kultur Til Folket.
        Stavanger Aftenblad (Oct. 29, 1993) p. 13.
        Note: AG quoted briefly in Norwegian only. [Stavanger, Norway]

J5481   Mahoney, Maura. Back In Black On the Beaten Path. *Baffler,* no. 5 (Nov. 1993)
        pp. 149-151.

J5482   Thompson, Toby. The Happy Buddha Of Kitkitdizze. *Outside*, vol. 18, no. 11
        (Nov. 1993) pp. 58-64, 162-167.

J5483   Gábor, Szántó T. A Leples Bitang Kozmopolita Üdvözlete. *Szombat,* vol. 5, no.
        9 (Nov. 1993) p. 34.

        Ákos, Gózon and Tunde, Poor. Fedezd Fel, Ami Eleven. *Szombat,* vol. 5, no. 9
        (Nov. 1993) pp. 35-36.
        Note: AG interview format in Hungarian only.

J5484   Dajbor, Agnieszka. Ginsberg Wstrzymany. *Gazeta Wyborcza* (Nov. 3, 1993)

J5485   Hintermeier, Hannes. Aufrichtigkeit Statt Gehirnwäsche. *Munich Abendzeitung*
        (Nov. 3, 1993) p. 10.
        Note: AG interview format in German only.

J5486   Sawicka, Rozmawiaka Elzbieta. Allen, Dobry Czlowieku. *Rzeczpospolita,* no.
        257 (Nov. 3, 1993)

J5487   Bruckmaier, Karl. Einladung Zum Om-Gebrumpfel. *Süddeutsche Zeitung,* no.
        254 (Nov. 3, 1993) p. 18.

J5488   Michalzik, Peter. Leben Ist Ein Traum, Deer Schon Zu Ende Ist. *Süddeutsche
        Zeitung* (Nov. 5, 1993) p. 19.
        Note: AG interview format in German only.

J5489   T., G.Ö. Mimicking [review of *Reality Sandwiches* (photographs)].
        Süddeutsche Zeitung, no. 257 (Nov. 6-7, 1993) p. 4.

J5490   Ensslin, John. Rhyme & Reason: Naropa's Anne Waldman. *Rocky Mountain
        News* (Nov. 7, 1993) Colorado People section, pp. 8M-11M.
        Note: AG quoted briefly.

J5491   Leitfigur Der "Beat Generation": Allen Ginsberg Kommt Nach Berlin. *Berliner
        Zeitung* (Nov. 9, 1993)

J5492   Kuhlbrodt, Detlef. Schöne Männer—Harte Frauen. *Die Tageszeitung* (Nov. 11,
        1993)

J5493   A Knightly Ginsberg, Just As Feisty As Ever. *International Herald Tribune*
        (Nov. 12, 1993) p. 24.
        Note: AG quoted briefly.

J5494   Kemp, Al. People. *News Journal* (Nov. 12-14, 1993) 55 Hours section, p. 2.

J5495   France Honors Allen Ginsberg. *Recorder* (Nov. 12, 1993) p. 16.

J5496   Waxman, Leanne. The Beats Are Back. *Sunday Camera* (Nov. 14, 1993) section B, pp. 1B, 2B.
Note: AG quoted briefly.

J5497   Waxman, Leanne. And the Beat Goes On... *Florida Times Union* (Nov. 15, 1993) pp. B3, B5.
Note: AG quoted briefly.

J5498   Lamy, Jean-Claude. La Sagesse Biologique Sauvera La Planète. *L'Actualité* (Nov. 17, 1993) p. 28.
Note: AG quoted briefly in French only.

J5499   Skre, Ragnar. Bevissthet For Fred. *Klassekampen* (Nov. 18, 1993) pp. 18-19.
Note: AG interview format in Norwegian only.

J5500   Lubowski, Bernd. Jeder Könnte Ein Dichter Sein. *Berliner Morgenpost* (Nov. 21, 1993)
Note: AG interview format in German only.

J5501   Bernard, April. [review of *Snapshot Poetics*]. *New York Newsday* (Nov. 21, 1993) Fan Fare section, p. 44.

J5502   Heine, Matthias. Ich Bin Jude, Homo, Poet, Buddhist. *Berliner Zeitung* (Nov. 22, 1993)
Note: AG quoted briefly in German only.

J5503   Bratfisch, Rainer. Weise Narren An Die Macht? *Berliner Zeitung* (Nov. 23, 1993)
Note: AG quoted briefly in German only.

J5504   Kirstaedter, Margitta. Leben In Grotesken Bildern Aufgezeigt. *Rhein Zeitung* (Nov. 23, 1993)

J5505   Lackmann, Thomas. Eine Party Im Lebensraum. *Der Tagesspiegel* (Nov. 23, 1993)

J5506   Ginsberg Fasziniert Noch Immer. *Westfalische Nachrichten* (Nov. 23, 1993)

J5507   B., C. Allen Ginsberg. *Zitty* (Nov. 23, 1993)

J5508   Staudacher, Cornelia. Wenn Nichtraucher Zuviel Singen. *Die Tagesspiegel* (Nov. 24, 1993)

J5509   Work In Progress. *Zurnál UP* (Nov. 24, 1993) p. 1.

J5510   Sonnenburg, Gisela. Der Ewige Rebell. *Neues Deutschland* (Nov. 25, 1993)

J5511   Waxman, Leanne. Still Beat, Still Howling. *Staten Island Advance* (Nov. 28, 1993) p. C5.
Note: AG quoted briefly.

J5512   A., D.P. Politisch Umweltvert. *Süddeutsche Zeitung,* no. 276 (Nov. 30, 1993) p. 14.

J5513   Fasano, Steve. Allen Ginsberg: An Annotated Bibliography, 1977-1990. *Bulletin Of Bibliography,* vol. 50, no. 4 (Dec. 1993) pp. 279-293.

J5514   O Alen Ginsberg Ston Athena. Ελλαδα *[Ellada]* (Dec. 1, 1993)

J5515 Best Of Interview. *State Press Magazine,* vol. 7, no. 14 (Dec. 2, 1993) p. 3.
Note: AG quoted briefly.

J5516 Lebel, Jean-Jacques. El Pensamiento Desnudo Es El Mas Claro. *Babelia* (Dec. 4, 1993)
Note: AG interview format in Spanish only.

J5517 Paglia, Camille. I, The Jury. *Washington Post* (Dec. 5, 1993) Book World section, p. 4.

J5518 Teixidor, Emili. Crits, Udols, Planys. *Avui* (Dec. 6, 1993)
Note: AG quoted in Spanish only.

J5519 Massot, Dolors. Ginsberg: "Ya Pertenezco Al Sistema, Pero Siguen Censurando Mi Poesia". *ABC* (Dec. 8, 1993) p. 66.
Note: AG quoted in Spanish only.

J5520 Massot, Dolors. Ginsberg: "He Envejecido, Tengo Diabetes, Insuficiencia Cardiaca Y Soy Impotente". *ABC Catalunya* (Dec. 8, 1993)
Note: AG quoted in Spanish only.

J5521 G., C. Allen Ginsberg: "Vull Descriure En Els Meus Poemes La Textura De La Meva Consciencia". *Avui* (Dec. 8, 1993) p. 35.
Note: AG quoted in Spanish only.

J5522 Gafarot, Xavier. Allen Ginsberg: "Nadie Cree Que En Estados Unidos Haya Censura". *Diario 16* (Dec. 8, 1993)
Note: AG quoted in Spanish only.

J5523 Ranteboy Me Ton Alen Ginsberg. *Η Καθημερινη [E Kathemerine]* (Dec. 8, 1993)

J5524 Allen Ginsberg: "Als EUA No Hi Ha Lliure Mercat D'idees". *Nou Diari* (Dec. 8, 1993)
Note: AG quoted briefly in Spanish only.

J5525 Moret, Xavier. Ginsberg Se Define Como "Homosexual 'Beatnik', Intelectual De Cafe Y Judio". *El Pais* (Dec. 8, 1993) p. 20.
Note: AG quoted in Spanish only.

J5526 Massot, Josep. Allen Ginsberg Asegura Que En Estados Unidos No Existe El Libre Mercado De Ideas. *La Vanguardia* (Dec. 8, 1993) p. 36.
Note: AG quoted at length in Spanish only.

J5527 P., S. Erchetai O Ginsberg. *Αυγη [Auge]* (Dec. 9, 1993)

J5528 Pons, Agusti. Ginsberg, Allen. *Avui* (Dec. 9, 1993)
Note: AG quoted in Spanish only.

J5529 Erchetai O Alen Ginsberg. *Εθνοσ [ethnos]* (Dec. 9, 1993)

J5530 Geli, Carles. Allen Ginsberg Pasea Por BCN El Espiritu 'Beat'. *El Periodico: Cosas De La Vida* (Dec. 9, 1993) p. 32.
Note: AG quoted at length in Spanish only.

J5531 Canalis, Xavier. Allen Ginsberg, El Poeta Maleit De La Generacio 'Beat' Parla A Barcelona. *Nou Diari* (Dec. 9, 1993)
Note: AG quoted in Spanish only.

Canalis, Xavier. Censurat Fins A Les Vuit Del Vespre. *Nou Diari* (Dec. 9, 1993)
Note: AG quoted in Spanish only.

J5532 Siotes, Ntinos. Papas Me Eisiterio. Πανοραμα *[Panorama]* (Dec. 9, 1993) p. 9.

J5533 Ginsberg Rech. Αεηνοραμα *[Aeenorama]* (Dec. 10-16, 1993)

J5534 M., X. Ginsberg Recita, Canta Y Provoca En El Instituto Norteamericano. *El Pais* (Dec. 10, 1993)

J5535 Allison, John. Comes Thrice the King Of May. *Prognosis,* vol. 3, no. 25 (Dec. 10-23, 1993) p. 3B.
Note: AG quoted briefly.

J5536 C., M.F. Allen Ginsberg I Antoni Tapies Collaboren Junts En Un Llibre D'Artista. *Avui* (Dec. 11, 1993)

J5537 Gironell, Marti. Ginsberg I Tapies Reprenen El Projecte D'Editar Junts Un "Llibre-Objecte" De Poemes. *Diari De Girona* (Dec. 11, 1993)

J5538 Schina, Katerinas. Alen Ginsberg: Apo To "Oyliachto" Sten Parasemophoria. *Η Καθημερινη [E Kathemerine]* (Dec. 12, 1993) p. 30.

J5539 Papaspurou, Stauroula. Eisiterio Gia Ena "Oyrliachto". Κυριακατικη Αυγη *[Kuriakatike Auvi]* (Dec. 12, 1993) p. 31.
Note: AG quoted in Greek only.

J5540 Lala, Thanase. Alen Ginsberg: E Poieoe Einai Diaphemioe Tes Psyches. Τοαλλοβημα *[Toallobema]* (Dec. 12, 1993) pp. 8, 13.
Notes: AG interview format in Greek only.

J5541 Molina, Maria Angela. Libros Para No Leer. *ABC Cataluna* (Dec. 13, 1993)
Note: AG quoted in Spanish only.

Calderon, Manuel. Ginsberg Y Tapies: Tras El Espiritu De Papel. *ABC Cataluna* (Dec. 13, 1993)

J5542 Recital De Allen Ginsberg En El Circulo De Bellas Artes. *Diario 16* (Dec. 13, 1993)

J5543 Ginsberg, Un Trozo De La "Generacion Beat" En Madrid. *Guia Del Ocio* (Dec. 13, 1993)

J5544 Castellano, A. Allen Ginsberg, Loco Por La Musica. *ABC* (Dec. 14, 1993)

J5545 Polentas, Manolis. The Howl Of a Generation. *Athens News* (Dec. 14, 1993)

J5546 Uriarte, Marian. Allen Ginsberg: "Sigo Siendo Un Escritor Homosexual, Beatnik Y Judio". *Diario 16* (Dec. 14, 1993) p. 39.
Note: AG quoted in Spanish only.

J5547 Rato, Mariano Antolin. Los Gobiernos Se Confunden Al Prohibir El LSD. *El Mundo* (Dec. 14, 1993) pp. 68-69.
Note: AG interview format in Spanish only.

J5548 Palacios, Luis Costa. Allen Ginsberg: La Poesia Como Articulacion Ritmica. *Cuadernos Del Sur* (Dec. 16, 1993) p. 34.
Note: AG quoted in Spanish only.

J5549 Alas, Leopoldo. Madrid Se Pone Estupenda. *El Mundo* (Dec. 16, 1993)

J5550 Drogas, Poemas, Conciencia. *La Veidad* (Dec. 16, 1993)

J5551 Dibole, Christiana. Epayaotates Kai Sta 67 Toy O Ginsberg. *Απογευματινη [Apogeumatine]* (Dec. 18, 1993)

J5552 Michalopoyloy, A. O Ginsberg Sten Athena. *Η Καθημερινη [E Kathemerine]* (Dec. 18, 1993) p. 15.
Note: AG quoted briefly in Greek only.

J5553 Kalamara, Basile. Kalos Erthes, Alen. *Κυριακατικη [Kyriakatike]* (Dec. 19, 1993)
Note: AG interview format in Greek only.

J5554 Babasakes, Ikaros. Allen Ginsberg, Aps Ten Arnese Sten Kataphase. *Πριν [Prin]* (Dec. 19, 1993) p. 21.

J5555 E Gripe Ton Sternse Ten Akropole. *Απογευματινη [Apogeumatine]* (Dec. 20, 1993)
Note: AG quoted in Greek only.

J5556 Tolmeres... Apaggelies Kai Sbneyse Apo Kabaphe. *Εθνοσ [Ethnos]* (Dec. 20, 1993) p. 42.
Note: AG quoted in Greek only.

J5557 Sinteta, Agky. E Pleiopsephia Ton "Mpitnik". *Μεσημβρινε [Mesembrine]* (Dec. 20, 1993) p. 15.
Note: AG quoted in Greek only.

J5558 Gerase O Amphisvetias! *Ελλαδα [Ellada]* (Dec. 20, 1993)
Note: AG quoted briefly in Greek only.

J5559 Kabaphns, Sappho Kai Ayakreoy. *Νικη [Nike]* (Dec. 20, 1993)

J5560 Charhtoylarhe, Michela. To Sooy Toy Poiete. *Πανοραμα [Panorama]* (Dec. 20, 1993) p. 3.
Note: AG quoted at length in Greek only.

J5561 Kalamara, Basile K. To Mellon Tes Poieoes Einai E Eilikrineia. *Τεχνεσ Γραμματα [Technes Grammata]* (Dec. 20, 1993) p. 55.
Note: AG quoted at length in Greek only.

J5562 Boykala, Pantele. O Alen Ginsberg, E Poiese Kai To Theana. *Η Καθημερινη [E Kathemerine]* (Dec. 21, 1993) p. 14.

J5563 Papaspurou, Stauroula. Henas Zontanos Mythos. *Ηαυγη [Eayge]* (Dec. 21, 1993) p. 13.
Note: AG interview format in Greek only.

J5564 Moysikos Ginsberg Sto "Rex". *Εθνοσ [Ethnos]* (Dec. 21, 1993) p. 33.
Note: AG quoted briefly.

J5565 Symbainoyn. *Μεσημβρινε [Mesembrine]* (Dec. 21, 1993) p. 15.

J5566 Chartoylare, Michela. "Tigre" Kai Armonio. *Πανοραμα [Panorama]* (Dec. 21, 1993) p. 12.

J5567 Kalamara, Basile K. Parata To Toigaro Soy To Okoypidi, Men Kapvizeis...
Τεχνεσ Γραμματα [Technes Grammata] (Dec. 21, 1993)
Note: AG quoted in Greek only.

J5568 Polentas, Manolis. Best Mind Of a Generation. *Athens News* (Dec. 22, 1993) p. 7.
Note: AG quoted.

J5569 Tsatsoy, Marias. Me Piyk-Poyk Sten Abysso. *Η Καθημερινη [E Kathemerine]* (Dec. 22, 1993) p. 15.

J5570 Apodechtheite Tis Akrotetes Sos. *Μεσημβρινε [Mesembrine]* (Dec. 22, 1993) p. 9.
Note: AG quoted in Greek only.

J5571 Papaspurou, Stauroula. An Eicha Ena Noy Thabotheke Ap Ton Erota: Alen Ginsberg. *Ελευθεροτυπια [Eleutherotupia]* (Dec. 24, 1993)
Note: AG quoted in Greek only.

J5572 Lorenci, Miguel. Ginsberg, Un Guru De Corbata En Semestre Sabatico. *Hoy* (Dec. 24, 1993)
Note: AG quoted in Spanish only.

J5573 Angel Del Arco, Miguel. Los Escritores Homosexuales Espanoles Se Des'Apan. *Tiempo* (Dec. 27, 1993) pp. 138-139.

J5574 Demoy, Nikos. Grammata Anagnoston. *Η Καθημερινη [E Kathemerine]* (Dec. 28, 1993) p. 12.

J5575 Ring, Kevin. [review of *Allen Ginsberg: Photographs*]. *Beat Scene,* no. 15 (1993) p. 43.

J5576 Evans, Thomas. Beat Ambassador. *Beat Scene,* no. 17 (1993) pp. 9-15.

Books:

J5577 Beard, Rick and Berlowitz, Leslie Cohen (eds.). *Greenwich Village: Culture And Counterculture.* New Brunswick, NJ: Rutgers University Press, 1993.
Note: AG mentioned throughout.

J5578 Bowles, Paul. *In Touch.* New York, NY: Farrar, Straus And Giroux, 1993.

J5579 Brown, David Jay and Novick, Rebecca McClen. *Mavericks Of the Mind.* Freedom, CA: Crossing Press, 1993, pp. 261-278.
Note: AG interview format.

J5580 Cage, John. *Writer: Previously Uncollected Pieces.* New York, NY: Limelight, 1993.

J5581   Dellinger, David. *From Yale To Jail.* New York, NY: Pantheon Books, 1993.
Note: AG mentioned throughout.

J5582   Dorfner, John J. *Kerouac: Visions Of Lowell.* Lowell, MA: Cooper Street Publications, 1993.
Note: AG mentioned throughout.

J5583   Gooch, Brad. *City Poet: The Life And Times Of Frank O'Hara.* New York, NY: Knopf, 1993.
Note: AG quoted and mentioned throughout.

J5584   Halberstam, David. *The Fifties.* New York, NY: Villard Books, 1993.
Note: AG quoted briefly.

J5585   Krassner, Paul. *Confessions Of a Raving, Unconfined Nut.* New York, NY: Simon & Schuster, 1993, pp. 136, 318-9, 329.
Note: AG quoted briefly.

J5586   Sangharakshita. *The Priceless Jewel.* Glasgow, Scotland: Windhorse Pubs., 1993, pp. 215-218.

J5587   White, Edmund. *Genet: A Biography.* New York, NY: Knopf, 1993.
Note: AG quoted briefly and mentioned throughout.

1994

J5588   Nottle, Diane. For Ireland's Book Of Kells, History Repeats. *New York Times* (Jan. 1, 1994) p. 13, 23.

J5589   Solomon, Charles. Paperbacks [review of *Snapshot Poetics*]. *Los Angeles Times* (Jan. 2, 1994) Book Review section, p. 12.

J5590   Jenkins, Mark. Pop Recordings: Waits's 'The Black Rider': Burroughs To a New Beat. *Washington Post* (Jan. 9, 1994) Show section, p. 10.

McLellan, Joseph. Classical Recordings: There's No Escaping John Cage And His Postmodern Influence. *Washington Post* (Jan. 9, 1994) Show section, p. 11.

J5591   Wetzel, Maria. Der Freie Markt Der Ideen Ist Noch Nicht Verwirklicht. *Querschnitt* (Jan. 15, 1994) p. 50.
Note: AG quoted in German only.

J5592   Jelloun, Tahar Ben. Allen Ginsberg Vuelve A Tánger. *El Pais* (Jan. 18, 1994) p. 28. [Madrid, Spain]
Note: AG quoted in Spanish only.

J5593   Goodman, Peter. Playing Carnegie Hall With a 'Howl'. *New York Newsday* (Jan. 22, 1994) p. 21.

J5594   Rothstein, Edward. Quartet Offers Light, Poetry, Motion, Even Ideology. *New York Times* (Jan. 22, 1994) section A, p. 11, 13.

J5595   Tommasini, Anthony. Kronos Players Take a Beat From Ginsberg. *Boston Globe* (Jan. 24, 1994) pp. 30, 32.

J5596   Edmonds, Ben. The Lion Of Dharma Still Roars. *MetroTimes* (Jan. 26-Feb. 1, 1994) pp. 20-21.
Note: AG quoted.

J5597   The Beat Goes On: An Interview With Allen Ginsberg. *Between the Lines,* no. 11 (Feb. 1994) pp. 20, 18.
Note: AG interview format.

J5598   Monder, Eric. Childless Father To Man. *Cover,* vol. 8, no. 2 (Feb. 1994) p. 34.

J5599   Goodman, David. Saddle Up For Some Stand-Up Cinema. *Interview,* vol. 24, no. 2 (Feb. 1994) p. 72.

J5600   Harrison, Laird. Café Culture: San Francisco Is Still the City Of Poets. *Modern Maturity* (Feb.-March 1994)
Note: AG quoted briefly.

J5601   Golembiewski, Chris. Still On the Edge. *Lansing State Journal* (Feb. 2, 1994) pp. 1C, 3C.
Note: AG quoted.

J5602   Kohn, Martin F. The Long, Strong 'Howl'. *Detroit Free Press* (Feb. 4, 1994) section D, pp. 1D, 8D.
Note: AG quoted.

J5603   Kobell, Rona. Ginsberg Looks Ahead To the '90s. *Michigan Daily* (Feb. 4, 1994) p. 9.
Note: AG quoted.

J5604   Simich, Mark Killian. Ginsberg Howls. *South End,* vol. 30, no. 21 (Feb. 8, 1994) ppl. 4, 7.
Note: AG quoted.

J5605   Cheshire, Godfrey. You're Next: Abel Is Able, Allen Is...Ginsberg. *New York Press* (Feb. 9-15, 1994) p. 25.

J5606   Brown, Georgia. Howlers. *Village Voice* (Feb. 15, 1994) p. 56.

J5607   McKenna, Kristine. Our Goal Was To Save the Planet. *Los Angeles Times* (Feb. 16, 1994) section F, pp. 1, 9.
Note: AG interview format.

J5608   Rainer, Peter. A Warm Look At a Counterculture Guru. *Los Angeles Times* (Feb. 17, 1994) section F, p. 3.

J5609   People. *Province* (Feb. 17, 1994) p. A26.

J5610   Pincus, Robert L. The Beat Goes On For Allen Ginsberg. *San Diego Union-Tribune* (Feb. 17, 1994) pp. E1, E4.
Note: AG quoted at length.

J5611   Sterritt, David. Freeze Frames. *Christian Science Monitor* (Feb. 18, 1994) p. 12.

J5612   Turin, David. The Life And Art Of Allen Ginsberg. *L.A. Village View,* vol. 8, no. 29 (Feb. 18-24, 1994) pp. 26-27.
Note: AG interview format.

J5613   Maslin, Janet. Trying To Turn a Poet Into Cinematic Prose. *New York Times* (Feb. 18, 1994) section C, p. 10.

J5614   Campbell, Bob. 'Allen Ginsberg' Offers Lively Portrait Of Surprising Jersey Poet. *Jersey Journal* (Feb. 19, 1994) p. 20.

J5615   Loud, Lance. Beat Poet Still Keeps the Beat. *Advocate,* no. 649 (Feb. 22, 1994) p. 65.
Note: AG quoted briefly.

Frascella, Lawrence. Beat Boy. *Advocate,* no. 649 (Feb. 22, 1994) p. 76.

J5616   Casey, Kim. Profile Of a Legend: Allen Ginsberg Speaks. *Barnard Bulletin ,* vol. 101, no. 12 (Feb. 22, 1994) pp. 16, 11.
Note: AG quoted.

J5617   Hinson, Hal. More Halo Than Howl. *Washington Post* (Feb. 25, 1994) Style section, p. 6.

Howe, Desson and Brown, Joe. Film Capsules. *Washington Post* (Feb. 25, 1994) Weekend section, p. 38.

J5618   Dangerfield, Achim. Interview: Allen Ginsberg On Tap. *City Times,* vol. 50, no. 2 (Feb. 28, 1994) pp. 6-7.
Note: AG quoted.

J5619   Sandrock, Mike. Ginsberg Says Penny Lane Shouldn't Die. *Colorado Daily* (March 1, 1994) pp. 1, 4.
Note: AG quoted briefly.

J5620   Fox, Susan K. Beat And 1960s Literature. *Firsts,* vol. 4, no. 3 (March 1994) pp. 22-26.

J5621   Scovell, Nell. Allen Ginsberg. *Vanity Fair,* vol. 57, no. 3 (March 1994) p. 186.
Note: AG interview format.

J5622   Evans, Clay. Penny Lane Is Sent Packing By Landlord. *Daily Camera* (March 2, 1994) p. 1.

J5623   Gilbert, Matthew. An Affectionate Paean To Allen Ginsberg. *Boston Globe* (March 4, 1994) p. 51.

J5624   Waxman, Leanne. On the Road Again. *Reporter-Herald* (March 5-6, 1994) Weekend section, p. 6.
Note: AG quoted briefly.

J5625   Allison, John. Letter From Prague: Hanging Out In Wenceslas Square. *Washington Post* (March 6, 1994) Book World section, p. 15.
Note: AG quoted briefly.

J5626   Cosper, Doug. Naropa Still Growing At Age 20. *Daily Camera* (March 10, 1994) p. 9A.

J5627   Travers, Peter. Now Playing. *Rolling Stone,* no. 677 (March 10, 1994) p. 60.

J5628   Waxman, Leanne. Beats Still an Inspiration For Disillusioned. *Chicago Tribune* (March 16, 1994) Evening section, p. 8.

J5629   [review of *Snapshot Poetics*]. *Washington Post* (March 20, 1994) Book World section, p. 12.

J5630   Haye, Christian. Paul Beatty. *Bomb* (Spring 1994) pp. 22-24.

J5631   Ganguly, Suranjan. On Baul Poetry: An Interview And Six Poems. *Michigan Quarterly Review,* vol. 33, no. 2 (Spring 1994) pp. 350-359.
Note: AG interview format.

J5632   Wissolik, Richard David. Bob Dylan's "Training" And Reading. *On the Tracks,* no. 3 (Spring 1994) pp. 37-39.

J5633   Solomon, Deborah. The Gallery: A Career Behind the Camera. *Wall Street Journal* (March 25, 1994) section A, p. 7.

J5634   [review of *Cosmopolitan Greetings*]. *Publishers Weekly,* vol. 241, no. 13 (March 28, 1994) p. 87.

J5635   Amburn, Ellis. The Death Of Neal Cassady. *Island Life,* vol. 8, no. 12 (March 31, 1994) p. 11.
Note: AG quoted briefly.

J5636   Hoover, Bob. The Beat Goes On. *Pittsburgh Post-Gazette* (April 8, 1994)
Note: AG quoted.

J5637   Rosenberg, Scott. 'Ginsberg' Is a First-Rate Effort Despite Falling Short On Organization. *Star-Tribune* (April 8, 1994)

J5638   Jenkins, Mark. 'Changing Parts' Of Glass's Art. *Washington Post* (April 8, 1994) Weekend section, p. 21.

J5639   Kasselman, Barbara Claire. Where Beat Movement First Pulsated. *Philadelphia Inquirer* (April 10, 1994) pp. T1, T11.

J5640   Dumas, Alan. A Disembodied Tribute To Allen Ginsberg At Boulder's Naropa Institute. *Rocky Mountain News* (April 10, 1994)

J5641   Hoover, Bob. 50 Years Later, Ginsberg Is Still Beat. *News Journal* (April 17, 1994) p. K5.
Note: AG quoted briefly.

J5642   Smart, Paul. Naked Mirror. *Woodstock Times* (April 21, 1994) Times II section, pp. 1, 6.

J5643   Alexander, Gary. Poet Headlines Literary Weekend: College's Regional Book Fair Follows. *Daily Freeman* (April 22, 1994) p. 25.
Note: AG quoted.

J5644   Muratori, Fred. [review of *Cosmopolitan Greetings*]. *Library Journal,* vol. 119, no. 8 (May 1, 1994) p. 107.

J5645   Rothschild, Matthew. [review of *Cosmopolitan Greetings*]. *Progressive* (May 1994) pp. 50, 52.

J5646   Vitale, Anthony. And the Beat Goes On [review of *Cosmopolitan Greetings*]. *Brooklyn College Excelsior* (May 2, 1994) p. 19.
Note: AG quoted briefly.

J5647   Zucconi, Vittorio. Beat Generation, La Strada Dei Ribelli. *La Stampa* (May 12, 1994) p. 19.

Gorlier, Claudio. Un "Urlo" Arrabbiato Contro I Miti Del Progresso. *La Stampa* (May 12, 1994) p. 20.

Serri, Mirella. Allen Nudo E Fumato Nel Prato Di Inge. *La Stampa* (May 12, 1994) p. 21.

J5648 Beats Return To Washington Square. *New York Times* (May 15, 1994) p. CY-15.

J5649 Hoover, Bob. Allen Ginsberg Still Beat After All These Years. *San Juan Star* (May 15, 1994)
Note: AG quoted.

J5650 Bruning, Fred. Allen Ginsberg's Quiet Howl. *New York Newsday* (May 18, 1994) pp. B4-5.
Note: AG quoted briefly.

J5651 Pareles, Jon. Original Beatniks Trip Back To the Past. *New York Times* (May 21, 1994) section A, p. 13.

J5652 White, Julie H. Ginsberg's Poetry Is Still Angry, Powerful [review of *Cosmopolitan Greetings*]. *South Bend Tribune* (May 22, 1994)

J5653 Randolph, Eleanor. Still Cool: The Beat Goes On. *Washington Post* (May 23, 1994) Style section, p. 2.

J5654 Redmond, Michael. Hip Audience Celebrates the Literature And Music Of the Beat Generation. *Star-Ledger* (May 24, 1994) p. 47.

J5655 Applebranch, John Peter. The Most Famous Jewish Buddhist Homosexual Whitmanesque Spiritual Erotic Visceral Beat Poet Still Alive At the Age Of Almost 68. *San Diego Reader* (May 26, 1994) p. 45.

J5656 Wilmington, Michael. [review of *The Life And Times of Allen Ginsberg* (film)]. *Chicago Tribune* (May 27, 1994) section 7, p. F.

J5657 McGrory, Brian. Penniless Kerouac Focus Of Costly Court Fight. *Boston Globe* (May 29, 1994) pp. 1, 22.
Note: AG quoted briefly.

J5658 Lippincott, Robin. And the Beats Go On [review of *Snapshot Poetics*]. *New York Times Book Review* (May 29, 1994) p. 14.

J5659 Lambert, Stephen, Jr. Ginsberg Still Howls [review of *Cosmopolitan Greetings*]. *Tampa Tribune-Times* (May 29, 1994) p. 7.

J5660 Hayden, Niki. Ginsberg: Portraits Show History Of Life, Friends. *Daily Camera* (June 1994) p. 28D.

J5661 Scalese, Stephen. 50 Years Of Beatness: An Overview. *Ergo Magazine* (June 1994) p. 8.

J5662 Ginsberg, Allen and Depp, Johnny. Phone Call. *Interview* (June 1994) pp. 16, 110.
Note: AG interview format.

J5663 Cline, Kurt. Who's Wearing the Pants? *Poetry Flash*, no. 253 (June-July 1994) pp. 1, 12, 14, 32.

J5664 Garchik, Leah. Allen Ginsberg Pitches a Poem. *San Francisco Chronicle* (June 3, 1994) p. C16.
Note: AG quoted briefly.

J5665   Bruning, Fred. For Poet Allen Ginsberg, Now a Professor, the Beats Go On. *Hartford Courant* (June 6, 1994)
   Note: AG quoted briefly.

J5666   Gehr, Richard. On the Road Again. *Village Voice* (June 7, 1994) pp. 17-18.

J5667   Stamets, Bill. The Beat Goes On: Ginsberg Hits Book Tour Circuit. *Chicago Sun-Times* (June 8, 1994) pp. 41, 44.
   Note: AG quoted briefly.

J5668   Litzky, Tsaurah. Eros And Existence: Scrotums. *Downtown,* no. 347 (June 8-29, 1994) pp. 30-31.

J5669   Fast Talk. *Oregonian* (June 8, 1994) p. F1.
   Note: AG quoted briefly.

J5670   Preston, Rohan B. Ginsberg Takes Stock Of His Life In Introspective Reading. *Chicago Tribune* (June 9, 1994) p. 32.
   Note: AG quoted briefly.

J5671   Preston, Rohan B. Ginsberg Sees In Himself a Life Worthy Of Poem. *Chicago Tribune* (June 10, 1994) p. 3.
   Note: AG quoted briefly.

J5672   Sommers, Pamela. Five Questions For...Two Brians: A Pair Ideally Weighted For 'Godot'. *Washington Post* (June 12, 1994) section G, p. 1.
   Note: AG quoted briefly.

J5673   Pintarich, Paul. Beat Ebbs, Buddhist Flows. *Oregonian* (June 21, 1994) p. C4.
   Note: AG quoted briefly.

J5674   Jackson, Kevin. Beatstock. *Arena* (Summer 1994) pp. 62-67.

J5675   Foehr, Stephen. Allen Ginsberg: Boulder Conference Pays Tribute To Beat Poet. *Boulder Magazine* (Summer 1994) pp. 22, 24.
   Note: AG quoted briefly.

J5676   Cohen, Rob. Good Head: The Allen Ginsberg Interview. *Caffeine,* no. 8 (Summer 1994) pp. 43-46.
   Note: AG interview format.

J5677   Morgan, Robert C. The Beat Generation At NYU—A 50 Year Celebration. *Cover,* vol. 8, no. 6 (Summer 1994) p. 42.

J5678   Moore, Jim. Public Heart: An Interview With Allen Ginsberg. *Hungry Mind Review,* no. 30 (Summer 1994) pp. 42-43.
   Note: AG interview format.

J5679   Hicks, Robert. Allen Ginsberg Looks Back, And Around. *Villager* (June 22, 1994) p. 7.
   Note: AG quoted.

J5680   Sandrock, Michael. The Beat Goes On For Allen Ginsberg. *Colorado Daily* (June 24-26, 1994) Weekend section, pp. 17, 20.
   Note: AG quoted briefly.

J5681   Dumas, Alan. Ginsberg: Still Avant-Garde After All These Years. *Rocky Mountain News* (June 26, 1994)
   Note: AG quoted.

J5682 Mikelbank, Peter. Paris' 'Beat Hotel'. *Times-Picayune* (June 26, 1994) section
E, pp. E1, E4.
Note: AG quoted briefly.

J5683 Rees, Brennan. Glorious Indecency: An Interview With Allen Ginsberg. *New
City* (June 27-July 3, 1994) pp. 6-7.
Note: AG interview format.

J5684 Pivano, Fernanda. Non Sparate Sui Beat. *Corriere Della Sera* (June 29, 1994) p.
1.

J5685 Sinisi, J. Sebastian. The Beat Goes On. *Denver Post* (June 30, 1994) section E,
pp. 1-2.
Note: AG quoted briefly.

J5686 Ginsberg, Allen. Lecture Transcript On William Blake's Auguries Of Innocence.
New Censorship, vol. 5, no. 4 (July 1994) pp. 1-21.
Note: AG lecture transcript.

J5687 Carolan, Trevor. Neobeats: On the Road Again. *Shambhala Sun,* vol. 2, no. 6
(July 1994) pp. 23-24.
Note: AG quoted briefly.

J5688 Misao, Mizuno. Allen Ginsberg: Poetry Shooting. *Switch,* vol. 12, no. 3 (July
1994) pp. 116-121.

J5689 Kurtz, Howard. Limbaugh, Under Fire And Shooting Back. *Washington Post*
(July 1, 1994) section D, p. 1.

J5690 Morris, Chris. Beat Goes On With Ginsberg's CD Set For Rhino. *Billboard,*
vol. 106, no. 27 (July 2, 1994) pp. 1, 115.
Note: AG quoted briefly.

J5691 Cosper, Doug. Institutional Version Of Open Mind. *Daily Camera* (July 2, 1994)
pp. 1A, 2A.

J5692 Moehringer, J.R. Beat Icons Have Words For the Wild—Go Easy. *Rocky
Mountain News* (July 2, 1994) p. 4A.

J5693 Lopez, Greg. When Ginsberg Speaks About Fun, It's Serious. *Rocky Mountain
News* (July 3, 1994) pp. 4A, 16A.
Note: AG quoted.

J5694 Thies, Kirsten. Howling For Ginsberg: Beats Gather In Boulder To Celebrate
Poet Allen Ginsberg. *Sunday Camera* (July 3, 1994) pp. 1B-2B.

Knopper, Steve. Icon Influenced Music From Jazz To Dylan. *Sunday Camera*
(July 3, 1994) pp. 1B, 3B.

Bernheimer, Kathryn. Tribute Offers Chance To See Beat-Era Films. *Sunday
Camera* (July 3, 1994) pp. 1B, 3B.

Blomster, Wes. Beauty Of the Beats Was Their Love Of the Spontaneous
Moment. *Sunday Camera* (July 3, 1994) pp. 1B, 4B.

Blomster, Wes. 'Swapping Ideas' Inspired Philip Glass, Allen Ginsberg
Collaboration. *Sunday Camera* (July 3, 1994) p. 5B.
Note: AG quoted briefly.

Cosper, Doug. Naropa Reunites Beat Generation Writers This Week. *Sunday Camera* (July 3, 1994) p. 5C.

Allen, Gary. Allen Ginsberg: Honesty Combined With Technique. *Sunday Camera* (July 3, 1994) p. 5E.
Note: AG interview format.

J5695   Ginsberg And Supporters. *Daily Camera* (July 4, 1994) pp. 1A, 2A.

J5696   Hernandez, Romel. Ginsberg Gets His Day—And His Library. *Rocky Mountain News* (July 4, 1994) p. 6A.
Note: AG quoted briefly.

Hernandez, Romel. Sometimes a Great Commotion: Kesey Rolls Through Naropa. *Rocky Mountain News* (July 4, 1994) p. 10A.

J5697   People. *Bergen Record* (July 5, 1994) p. A-2.

J5698   Sinisi, J. Sebastian. Kesey: 'Beat' Goes On. *Denver Post* (July 5, 1994) p. 2B.

J5699   One For the Books. *News Journal* (July 5, 1994) p. D3.

J5700   Ensslin, John C. Naropa Turns 20, Protected And Pure. *Rocky Mountain News* (July 5, 1994) p. 10A.

Moehringer, J.R. Even the Rebels Take Up the Patriotic Cause. *Rocky Mountain News* (July 5, 1994) p. 10A.

J5701   Sinisi, J. Sebastian. Kesey, Finally, Wows Ginsberg Event. *Denver Post* (July 6, 1994) p. 4B.

J5702   Moehringer, J.R. Writing Cures Blues, Keeps the Beauty. *Rocky Mountain News* (July 6, 1994) pp. 4A, 6A.

Campbell, Jackie. Kesey's 'Twister' a Dreadful Hodgepodge Of Images. *Rocky Mountain News* (July 6, 1994) p. 16A.

Dumas, Alan. '60s Rebel Sees Things More Pragmatically. *Rocky Mountain News* (July 6, 1994) p. 16A.

J5703   Cosper, Doug. And the Beat Goes On. *Daily Camera* (July 7, 1994) pp. 1A, 7A.
Note: AG quoted briefly.

J5704   Sinisi, J. Sebastian. Sparks Fly At Ginsberg Panel. *Denver Post* (July 7, 1994) p. 3B.
Note: AG quoted briefly.

Rosen, Steven. Offbeat Ginsberg CD Boasts Taste Of Denver. *Denver Post* (July 7, 1994) pp. 8E, 5E.

J5705   Cosper, Doug. Early Beats Replanted the Seeds Of Rebellion. *Daily Camera* (July 8, 1994) pp. 1A, 8A.
Note: AG quoted.

J5706   Bonelli, Winnie. The Beat Goes On: Rhino Releasing Ginsberg CD. *North Jersey Herald & News* (July 10, 1994)

J5707   Moehringer, J.R. Offended Kesey Leaves Festival Early. *Rocky Mountain News* (July 10, 1994) p. 15A.

Moehringer, J.R. Beats And Other Rebel Angels Fly Low During Their Self-Love Fest In Boulder. *Rocky Mountain News* (July 10, 1994) Spotlight section, p. 47A.

May, Clifford D. The Beat Goes On. *Rocky Mountain News* (July 10, 1994) p. 72A.
Note: AG interview format.

J5708   Maestosi, Danilo. E Noi Vi Sfideremo A Colpi Di Versi. *Il Messaggero* (July 11, 1994) p. 13.

J5709   Koh, Barbara. Beat Poet May Sell His Stuff To Stanford. *San Jose Mercury News* (July 14, 1994) pp. 1A, 16A.

J5710   Perry, Ginger. A Look Back At Naropa Tribute To Ginsberg. *Colorado Daily* (July 18-19, 1994) p. 8.
Note: AG quoted briefly.

J5711   Wernick, Joan Leonard. [letter to the editor]. *Daily Camera* (July 20, 1994) p. 2C.

J5712   Barry, Dave. Book Tour Includes Denver And Ginsberg. *Sunday Camera* (July 24, 1994)

J5713   Barry, Dave. Being an Author Isn't Nearly As Easy As You Might Think. *Press Of Atlantic City* (July 25, 1994) pp. B1, B4.

J5714   De Luca, Dan. The Latest Word. *Philadelphia Inquirer* (July 28, 1994) pp. E1-E2.
Note: AG quoted briefly.

J5715   Rothschild, Matthew. Allen Ginsberg. *Progressive,* vol. 58, no. 8 (Aug. 1994) pp. 34-39.
Note: AG interview format.

J5716   People. *Bergen Record* (Aug. 2, 1994)

J5717   Yurkovsky, Alexandra. [review of *Cosmopolitan Greetings*]. *Express* (Aug. 2, 1994)

J5718   Perry, Tony. The Beats Are Cool—And Hot. *Los Angeles Times* (Aug. 2, 1994) pp. A1, A21-22.
Note: AG quoted briefly.

J5719   Perry, Tony. Flashback To the '50s: The Beats Are Back, Man. *Hartford Courant* (Aug. 3, 1994) pp. A1, A4.
Note: AG quoted briefly.

J5720   Hovdenakk, Sindre. Gi Ginsberg Nobelprisen. *Dagbladet* (Aug. 4, 1994) p. 5.

J5721   Chase, Alfonso. Para Recordar A Los Beatniks. *Ancora* (Aug. 7, 1994) section D, pp. 1-3.

J5722   Lacayo, Richard. If Everyone Is Hip, Is Anyone Hip? *Time,* vol. 144, no. 6 (Aug. 8, 1994) pp. 48-55.
Note: AG quoted briefly.

J5723 Hall, Molly. Sparks Fly As Naropa Brings East To West. *Minneapolis Star Tribune* (Aug. 9, 1994) pp. 1E, 3E.
Note: AG quoted briefly.

J5724 Scott, Janny. Back To Woodstock, For Better Or Worse. *New York Times* (Aug. 11, 1994) pp. A1, B6.
Note: AG quoted briefly.

J5725 Hall, Molly. A School Where East Meets West. *Los Angeles Times* (Aug. 13, 1994)
Note: AG quoted briefly.

J5726 Landrigan, Dan. Jack Kerouac's Renaissance. *Lowell Sun* (Aug. 14, 1994) pp. 1, 4.
Note: AG quoted briefly.

J5727 Mead, Rebecca. The Next Big Lit-Crit Snit. *New York,* vol. 27, no. 32 (Aug. 15, 1994) pp. 40-42.
Note: AG quoted briefly.

J5728 Swed, Mark. On Disc: Philip Glass In a New Light. *Wall Street Journal* (Aug. 15, 1994) Section A, p. 9.

J5729 Hall, Molly. Eastern And Western Traditions Blend At Naropa. *Capper's* (Aug. 16, 1994)
Note: AG quoted briefly.

J5730 Lawrence, Larry. Poetry: New Volumes Have Wide Range [review of *Cosmopolitan Greetings*]. *Abilene Reporter* (Aug. 28, 1994)

J5731 Kubernik, Harvey R. [review of *Holy Soul Jelly Roll* (recording)]. *Huh* (Sept. 1994)

J5732 Beat Box [review of *Holy Soul Jelly Roll* (recording)]. *Ice* (Sept. 1994) p. 14.

J5733 [review of *Holy Soul Jelly Roll* (recording)]. *Out* (Sept. 1994)

J5734 Petros, George. Allen Ginsberg: Groovin' Guru. *Seconds,* no. 28 ([Sept.] 1994) pp. 70-82.
Note: AG interview format.

J5735 Birnbaum, Robert. Talking With Allen Ginsberg. *Stuff Magazine* (Sept. 1994) pp. 50-53.
Note: AG interview format.

J5736 Levine, Eleanor. Beat Boy-Lover. *10 Percent,* vol. 2, no. 010 (Sept.-Oct. 1994) p. 47.
Note: AG quoted briefly.

J5737 Edgers, Geoff. [review of *Holy Soul Jelly Roll* (recording)]. *Middlesex News* (Septl. 4, 1994)

J5738 Perry, David. For Ginsberg, The Beat Goes On [review of *Holy Soul Jelly Roll* (recording)]. *Lowell Sun* (Sept. 4, 1994) pp. 51, 54.

J5739 Galvin, Peter. [review of *Holy Soul Jelly Roll* (recording)]. *Advocate,* no. 663 (Sept. 6, 1994)

J5740   Rapalus, Peter. Ginsberg's Archive Added To Collections Of 20th Century Lit. *Campus Report* (Sept. 7, 1994) pp. 1, 16.
Note: AG quoted briefly.

J5741   Chen, David W. The Beat Generation Goes On. *San Jose Mercury News* (Sept. 7, 1994) pp. 1, back page.

J5742   Stanford Keeps Mum On Ginsberg Collection Cost. *Ann Arbor News* (Sept. 8, 1994) p. A2.

J5743   People. *Bergen Record* (Sept. 8, 1994) p. A-2.

J5744   Garofoli, Joe. Ginsberg Unplugged. *Contra Costa Times* (Sept. 8, 1994) pp. 1F, 2F.
Note: AG quoted.

J5745   Beat Poet Allen Ginsberg Brings "Howl" To City. *Grunion Gazette* Sept. 8, 1994)

J5746   Stanford Buys Ginsberg Archives. *News Journal* (Sept. 8, 1994) p. A13.

J5747   Workman, Bill. Stanford Buys Ginsberg Items. *San Francisco Chronicle* (Sept. 8, 1994) pp. A15-A16.

J5748   Willis, Scott. Allen Ginsberg As a Child [political cartoon]. *San Jose Mercury News* (Sept. 8, 1994)

J5749   Beat It. *USA Today* (Sept. 8, 1994)

J5750   Stanford Buys Poet's Archives. *Detroit News* (Sept. 9, 1994)

J5751   Krout-Hasegawa, Ellen. Reading Pick Of the Week: Allen Ginsberg. *L.A. Weekly* (Sept. 9-15, 1994) p. 122.

J5752   Beatnik Of Time. *News Journal* (Sept. 9-11, 1994) p. 2.

J5753   Howling At Stanford. *San Francisco Chronicle* (Sept. 9, 1994) p. A22.

J5754   Price, Michael H. [review of *Holy Soul Jelly Roll* (recording)]. *Fort Worth Star-Telegram* (Sept. 10, 1994)

J5755   Whiting, Sam. Solo Mio Festival Plays On the Past. *San Francisco Chronicle* (Sept. 11, 1994) pp. 29, 31, 47.
Note: AG quoted briefly.

J5756   Reinhard, Pam. USS Grants Funding For Prominent Poet, Writer. *Daily Kent Stater* (Sept. 13, 1994) pp. 1, 8.

J5757   Anastis, Cait. Poet's Appearance At KSU Questioned. *Record Courier* (Sept. 14, 1994) pp. 1, 10.

J5758   Something To Howl About. *Library Journal,* vol. 119, no. 15 (Sept. 15, 1994) p. 13.

J5759   Surrence, Matthew. Allen Ginsberg Returns To San Francisco Roots. *Fremont Argus* (Sept. 17, 1994) pp. C-1, C-10.
Note: AG quoted.

J5760   Chen, David W. Why Poet Chose Stanford. *San Jose Mercury News* (Sept. 17, 1994) pp. 1B, 4B.
Note: AG quoted.

J5761   Surrence, Matthew. Allen Ginsberg Returns To San Francisco Roots. *Tri-Valley Herald* (Sept. 17, 1994) section B, pp. B1, B10.
Note: AG quoted briefly.

J5762   Mikelbank, Peter. Off The Beat Path. *San Diego Union-Tribune* (Sept. 18, 1994) pp. F2, F6.
Note: AG quoted.

J5763   Raisfeld, Robin. The 1994 Salary Survey. *New York,* vol. 27, no. 37 (Sept. 19, 1994) pp. cover, 48-57.

J5764   Green, Judith. Allen Ginsberg Live: Not With a Howl, But a Whimper. *San Jose Mercury News* (Sept. 19, 1994)

J5765   Margolick, David. An Unlikely Home For Ginsberg's Archive. *New York Times* (Sept. 20, 1994) pp. C15-16.
Note: AG quoted briefly.

J5766   Gieske, Tony. Ginsberg Takes To The Road For Rhino [review of *Holy Soul Jelly Roll* (recording)]. *Santa Barbara News-Press* (Sept. 21, 1994)

Margolick, David. An Unlikely Home For Ginsberg's Archive. *Santa Barbara News-Press* (Sept. 21, 1994) section D, p. 1.
Note: AG quoted briefly.

J5767   Ronan, Stephen. The Beats At 50. *Dharma Beat,* no. 3 (Fall 1994) pp. [6-7].

Christenson, Jon. Naropa. *Dharma Beat,* no. 3 (Fall 1994) p. [8].

J5768   Aburamoto, Tatsuo. Beat Conference. *North Beach Quarterly,* vol. 1, no. 2 ([Fall] 1994) pp. 1-12.

J5769   Shin, Laura. Stanford Acquires Collection Of Ginsberg Poetry, Personal Items. *Stanford Daily* (Sept. 22, 1994) p. 21A.
Note: AG quoted briefly.

J5770   Coe, Robert. Becoming Buddha: The Life And Times Of Poet John Giorno. *Tricycle,* vol. 4, no. 1 (Fall 1994) pp. 74-85.

J5771   Perry, David. Ginsberg Lights Up Kerouac Fest With Powerful Poetry. *Lowell Sun* (Sept. 24, 1994) p. 9.

J5772   Tucker, Ken. Ginsberg At Center Of Spoken-Word Trend [review of *Holy Soul Jelly Roll* (recording)]. *Mexico City News* (Sept. 25, 1994) p. 24.

J5773   Tucker, Ken. From Beat Poet To Pop Chic [review of *Holy Soul Jelly Roll* (recording)]. *New York Times* (Sept. 25, 1994) pp. 34, 39.

J5774   Dixon, Stephen; Pepper, Robert D. and Gusack, Nancy. [letters to the editor]. *New York Times* (Sept. 28, 1994) p. A20.

J5775   Gaar, Gillian G. The Original Dharma Bum [review of *Holy Soul Jelly Roll* (recording)]. *Seattle Rocket* (Sept. 28-Oct. 12, 1994) p. 9.
Note: AG quoted briefly.

J5776   Katchmer, George. The Making Of a Western Dharma. *USAsians,* vol. 2, no. 9 (Sept. 28, 1994) pp. 8, 10.

J5777   Barth, Dan. Ginsberg Knows It [review of *Holy Soul Jelly Roll* (recording)]. *Sacramento News And Review* (Sept. 29, 1994) Word section, pp. 1, 5.

J5778   DiMattio, Joe. [review of *Cosmopolitan Greetings*]. *Cover,* vol. 8, no. 8 (Oct. 1994) p. 36.

J5779   The Beat Goes On. *Esquire,* vol. 122, no. 4 (Oct. 1994) p. 38. *Note:* AG quoted briefly.

J5780   Kubernik, Harvey R. [review of *Holy Soul Jelly Roll* (recording)]. *Huh* (Oct. 1994)

J5781   McCaln, Gillian. Dirt. *Poetry Project Newsletter,* no. 154 (Oct.-Nov. 1994) p. 4.

J5782   Ginsberg Archive To Stanford Gets Beat Poet's Issue Research. *Library Hotline,* vol. 23, no. 39 (Oct. 3, 1994) pp. 1-2. *Note:* AG quoted briefly.

J5783   Levine, Harold. Acquiring Ginsberg Collection Was Not a Well-Thought Decision. *Stanford Daily* (Oct. 3, 1994) p. 4.

J5784   Abrams, Sam. [letter to the editor]. *New York Times* (Oct. 4, 1994) p. A20.

J5785   Sitton, Janice. Prominent Poet Will Make Appearance At UNCA. *Blue Banner,* vol. 23, no. 6 (Oct. 6, 1994) pp. 1, 8.

J5786   Petäjä, Jukka. Woodstockin Jalkeen Tuli Beatstock. *Helsingin Sanomat* (Oct. 8, 1994) p. C1.

J5787   Intentionally omitted.

J5788   Neal, Dale. Allen Ginsberg's 'Howl' Launched a New Generation. *Asheville Citizen-Times* (Oct. 9, 1994) p. 2D. *Note:* AG quoted briefly.

J5789   Patterson, Tom. 'Beat' Poet To Read At UNC-Asheville. *Winston-Salem Journal* (Oct. 9, 1994) pp. E1, E4. *Note:* AG quoted.

J5790   Love, B. [review of *Holy Soul Jelly Roll* (recording)]. *UR: University Reporter* (Oct. 13, 1994)

J5791   Brooks, Holden. Renowned Beat Poet To Share His Works Here. *Caledonian-Record* (Oct. 19, 1994) p. 16. *Note:* AG quoted.

J5792   Brown, Ben. Kerouac's Back. *USA Today* (Oct. 19, 1994) section D, pp. 1-2. *Note:* AG quoted briefly.

J5793   Lippman, Laura. Ginsberg 'Howls' Again As Lawyers Battle FCC Rule. *Baltimore Sun* (Oct. 20, 1994) pp. 1D, 10D. *Note:* AG quoted briefly.

J5794   Intentionally omitted.

J5795   Aversa, Jeannine. Court Reviews Rules Limiting Indecency On the Airwaves. *News Journal* (Oct. 20, 1994) p. A8.

J5796   Rinehart, Bettie. Mr. Howl. *Phoenix New Times* (Oct. 20-26, 1994) p. 100.
Note: AG interview format.

J5797   Schudel, Matt. End Of the Road. *Sunshine: The Magazine Of South Florida,* no. 577 (Oct. 23, 1994) pp. 8-12, 14, 22-23.

J5798   Petras, Michael and Verjee, Aman. Stanford Buys Ginsberg Collection. *Stanford Review,* vol. 13, no. 4 (Oct. 24, 1994) pp. 1, 11.

J5799   Katchmer, George. To Produce, One Must First Act. *USAsians,* vol. 2, no. 10 (Oct. 27, 1994) pp. 6, 15.

J5800   Blumenthal, Michael. Allen Ginsberg, Millionaire? *New York Times* (Oct. 29, 1994) p. 19.

J5801   [review of *Holy Soul Jelly Roll* (recording)]. *Boomer* (Nov. 1994) pp. 22-23.

J5802   Pro-Pedophile Poet Paid $1M By Stanford. *Campus Report,* vol. 9, no. 10 (Nov. 1994) p. 1.
Note: AG quoted briefly.

J5803   O'Donnell, Will. An Open Letter To Allen Ginsberg. *Durt Cheep,* vol. 2, no. 4 (Nov. 1, 1994) pp. 1, 4.
Note: AG quoted briefly.

J5804   Law, Victoria. The Best Minds Of Their Generation. *New Youth Connections* (Nov. 1994) p. 6.

J5805   Coley, Byron. Blue Light Special [review of *Holy Soul Jelly Roll* (recording)]. *Spin* (Nov. 1994)

J5806   Corbett, William. Allen's Song [review of *Holy Soul Jelly Roll*]. *Boston Phoenix* (Nov. 4, 1994) p. 13.

J5807   Daily, Victoria and Berman, Paul. [letters to the editor]. *New York Times* (Nov. 5, 1994) p. 22.

J5808   Mahapatra, Jayanta. On the Mountain With Allen G. *Sunday Review* (Nov. 6, 1994) pp. 6-7.
Note: AG quoted briefly.

J5809   Oguntoyinbo, Lekan. Few Protesters Show For Controversial Poet. *Cleveland Plain Dealer* (Nov. 8, 1994)

J5810   Milanowski, Ann. Poetry, Music And Politics. *Daily Kent Stater* (Nov. 8, 1994) pp. 1, back cover.
Note: AG quoted.

J5811   Pivano, Fernanda. Beat Generation '94: La Riscossa. *Corriere Della Sera* (Nov. 15, 1994)

J5812   Wright, Fred. An Interview With Allen Ginsberg, In Two Parts. *Tab Magazine,* vol. 3, no. 1 ([Dec.] 1994) pp. 16-19.
Note: AG interview format.

J5813   Cut Special Collections Budget In Half. *Stanford Review* (Dec. 5, 1994)

J5814   Lingaard, Jade. Ginsberg Presents New CD Collection. *Washington Square News* (Dec. 6, 1994)
Note: AG quoted.

J5815   Mullinax, Gary. Pair Of Slacks. *News Journal* (Dec. 11, 1994) pp. H1, H3.

J5816   Chalmers, Robert. The Beat Goes On...And On. *Observer* (Dec. 11, 1994) Life section, pp. 26-28, 30, 32.
Note: AG quoted at length.

J5817   Cowan, Guy. Still Beating The Drum. *Ham & High* (Dec. 16, 1994) p. 18.
Note: AG quoted.

J5818   Campbell, James. Mantra Man. *Scottsman Weekend* (Dec. 17, 1994) p. 12.
Note: AG quoted.

J5819   Davies, Andrew. [review of *Cosmopolitan Greetings*]. *Big Issue* (Dec. 19, 1994)
Note: AG quoted briefly.

J5820   Waintrop, Edouard. Ginsberg, Label Beat. *Le Cahier Livres De Liberation* (Dec. 22, 1994) p. iv.
Note: AG interview format in French only.

J5821   Williams, Paul. [review of *Holy Soul Jelly Roll* (recording)]. *Crawdaddy,* new series, no. 7 (Winter [Dec. 22, 1994] 1995) pp. 9-12.

J5822   Motoharu, Sano. Beat And Other Rebel Angels. *This,* vol. 1, no. 1 (Winter [Dec. 22, 1994] 1995) pp. 22-45.

J5823   O'Flaherty, Mark C.O. Beat Master. *Pink Paper* (Dec. 23, 1994)
Note: AG quoted briefly.

J5824   Gilbert, Matthew. The Beat Goes On [review of *Holy Soul Jelly Roll* (recording)]. *Boston Globe* (Dec. 25, 1994) p. B3.

J5825   Britt, Alan. Prodding the Dead. *Duckabush Journal* (1994-1995) pp. 77-83.
Note: AG quoted briefly.

J5826   Seven, Dean and Herbert, Justine. Ginsberg's Things. *Fad Megazine,* no. 33 (1994) pp. 38-41.
Note: AG interview format.

J5827   Kerouac, Jack. Letters From Jack Kerouac To Ed White, 1947-68. *Missouri Review,* vol. 17, no. 3 (1994) pp. 109-160.

J5828   Grady, John. Beat It On Down the Line. *Relix,* vol. 21, no. 5 (1994) pp. 52-53.

J5829   Bain, William. The Flatness Of Flat. *Snack,* no. 4 (1994) pp. 50-51.
Note: AG quoted briefly.

Books:

J5830   Fetherling, Douglas. *Travels By Night: A Memoir Of the Sixties.* Toronto, Canada: Lester Publishing, 1994.
Note: AG mentioned throughout.

J5831   Ginsberg, Allen. *Poem, Interview, Photographs.* Louisville, KY: White Fields
Press, 1994.
Contents: O'Bryan, Danny. An Interview With Allen Ginsberg.
Note: AG interview format.

J5832   Jayakar, Pupul. *The Children Of Barren Women.* New Delhi, India: Penguin
Books, 1994, pp. 162-176, 181, 185.
Note: AG quoted.

J5833   Licciardello, Nicola. *Il Ballo Immune.* Rome, Italy: Fermenti Editrice, 1994.
Contents: Dialogo Sulla Poesia (Da Un'Intervista Ad Allen Ginsberg), p. 20.
Note: AG interview format in Italian only.

J5834   Pincus, Robert L. *On a Scale That Competes With the World: The Art Of Edward
And Nancy Reddin Kienholz.* Berkeley, CA: University Of California Press,
1994.
Note: AG mentioned throughout.

J5835   Woolmer, J. Howard (ed.). *The Leonard L. Milberg Collection Of American
Poetry.* Princeton, NJ: Princeton University Library, 1994, pp. 101-108.

Titles and First Lines Index

General Index

American Literature [Durham, NC], J3498, 4946

American Literature [China], H46

American Literature: A Brief History, J2068

American Literature Since 1900, J2205

The American Moment, J2487

American PEN [New York, NY], J1082

American Photography, J3776

American Poetry [Albuquerque, NM], J3599, 4437

American Poetry And Japanese Culture, J3780

American Poetry In The Twentieth Century, J1565

American Poetry Of The Twentieth Century, J5074

American Poetry Review [Philadelphia, PA], J1755, 1819, 1853, 1955, 2385, 2826, 3310, 3845, 4160, 4371, 5096, 5161

American Poetry Since 1945, J517

American Poetry Since 1960, J1885

American Poets Since World War II, J2993

The American Quest For a Supreme Fiction, J2817

American Review [New York, NY], J2182

American Scholar [Washington, DC], J1767

American Spectator [Bloomington, IN], J3961

American Studies International [Washington, DC], J2980

American Theatre [New York, NY], J4528

American Writers, J3151

American Writing Today, J3409, 5234

Americana [New York, NY], J4824

Américas [Washington, DC], J212

Americka Knjizevnost [Yugoslavia], H631

Amerika, H764

Amerika Hansen Shishu, H395

Amerika Kenkyu [Japan], J3673

Amerika No Botsuraku, H388

Amerika No Sekai, H396

Amerikai Költök Antológiája, H300

Amerikanische Literatur Der Gegenwart, J1869, 2469, 2809

Amerikanische Literatur Im 20. Jahrhundert, J1568

Amerikanische Lyrik, H191

Amerikansk Undergroundpoesi, H741

Amerikanskaya Poeziya, H556

Amerikanski Poeti, H24

Amiri Baraka: The Kaleidoscopic Torch, J4057

Amirthanayagam, Guy, J3141, 3397

Amlong, William R., J1678

Ammons, A.R., J369

Amoruso, Vito, J2633

Amphetamin Cowboy, H192

Amram, David, J1244

Anarchia E Creativita, H350

Anastas, Peter, J1865

Anastis, Cait, J5757

Anaya, José Vicente, H655, 712, J4753

Anaya, Marta, J3075

Anchor [Providence, RI], J1935

Ancient Myth In Modern Poetry, J1550

Ancoechea, Nicanor, H32

Ancora [Heredia, Costa Rica], H733, J5721

Anctil, Pierre, J5067

And [Hendon, England], J234

And [Rochester, NY], J4279

Anders, Willi, H187

Anderson, Dawne, J5104

Anderson, Don, J1634, 2063

Anderson, Jack, J1438, 1541, 1916, 5429

Anderson, Jon, J4622

Anderson, Marcella, J5433

Anderson, Roger, J4290

Anderson, Susan Heller, J3856

Anderson, Thomas, J3963

Anderson, Tom, J1030

Andrae, Irmgard, J2757

Andre, Kenneth Michael, J2067

Andre, Michael, J1673, 2202, 2286, 3138, 4812

Andrews, George, J818

Andrews, Lyman, J94, 1786

Andriette, Bill, J4811

Andy Warhol, A Retrospective, H134, 203, 352, 398

Anerca [Vancouver, Canada], J4133, 4209

El Angel Del Altillo [Buenos Aires, Argentina], H699

Angel Del Arco, Miguel, J5573

Angelastro, Angelo, J2633

Angelini, Claudio, J794

Angelucci, Steve, J2517

Angell, Bob, J3514

Angell, Olav, H454-6, 458, 462, J3448

Angerer, P., J2961

Angiolillo, Gioia Zannino, H367

Anglesey, Zoe, J5177

Anglistik Und Englischunterricht [Trier, Germany], J2863

Angoff, Charles, J258

Ankor Wat [reviews], J987, 990, 992, 1073, 1076, 1096, 1218, 1277

Ann Arbor Argus [Ann Arbor, MI], J1043, 1240, 1440

Ann Arbor News [Ann Arbor, MI], J1527, 3819, 3996, 4793, 5742

Ann Arbor Sun [Ann Arbor, MI], J1532, 1927, 1936, 1965, 1997

Annunziata, Lucia, J2737

Another Chance, J4270

Another Chicago Magazine [Chicago, IL], J4438, 4672, 5063

Ansen, Alan, J161

Anspacher, Carolyn, J63, 65

An Anthology Of American Beat Poetry, H267

Anthony, Gene, J2987

Antin, David, J1693

Antioch College Record [Yellow Springs, OH], J590

Antiphonal Swing, J4830

Antiquarian Bookman [see...AB Bookman's Weekly]

Antología Bilingüe De Poesía Norteamericana Contemporánea: 1950-1980, H670

Antologia Da Novissima Poesia Norte-Americana, H515

Antología De La "Beat Generation", H663

Antologia De La Poesía Norteamericana, H660

Antología Del Primer Festival Internnacional De Poesía, H667

Antología Poética, H650

Aullido, Kaddish Y Otros Poemas, H655
Aullido, Seleccion De Poemas, H652
Aullido Y Otros Poemas, H651, 656, 658
Auraria Times [Denver, CO], J2587
Austin American-Statesman [Austin, TX],
    J2773, 2779
Austin Sun [Austin, TX], J2529
Australian [Adelaide, Australia], J1607, 1614,
    1625
Author's Lives, J5078
Autoren Im Haus, H199
L'Autre Journal [Paris, France], H163, J5054
Ave Maria [South Bend, IN], J1097
Averill, Earl, J2688
Aversa, Jeannine, J5795
Avidan, David, H273
Avui [Barcelona, Spain], J5518, 5521, 5528,
    5536
Avui Cultura [Spain], J4937
Avvenire [Italy], J5438
Axelrod, Steven Gould, J3760
Ayres, Jane, J3867

BLM [Stockholm, Sweden], H747
Babasakes, Ikaros, J5554
Babbs, Ken, J5089
Babcox, Deborah, J1225
Babcox, Peter, J1225
Babel To Byzantium, J21, 973
Babelia [Spain], J5516
Bacchielli, Rolando, H362
Bacharach, J.D., J2870
Bache-Snyder, Kaye, J3891, 3902
Bachmann, Marcy, J1642
Bacigalupo, Massimo, H348, J3142
Back To Godhead [New York, NY], J969, 3139
Background Papers On Student Drug
    Involvement, J825
Bacon, Leslie, J2011
Baffler [Chicago, IL], J5481
Bagdaia [Yugoslavia], H591
Bagdala [Belgrade, Serbia], H645, J5446
Bageant, Joseph L., J2400
Bahrenburg, Bruce, J835
Bailey, Elizabeth, J2939
Bailly, Catherine, H110
Bain, William, J5829
Baizer, Eric, J2616
Bajac, Vladislav, H571, 573
Bajats, Vladislav, J2954
Bajcom, Vladislavom, H631
Bajo, N., J4208
Bajraj, Fadil, H5, 7-14, J4234
Bajt, Drago, J4215
Bakalar, James B., J2812
Baker, A.T., J1474
Baker, George, J54
Baker, Kelley, J534
Baker, Paul, J3155
Baker, Russell, J384
Bakevski, Petre, J4113, 4183
Bakken, Dick, J1715
Balakian, Anna, J4268
Balázs, Attila, H311, 313
Balázs, Györe, H283, 296, 299

Baldacci, Luigi, J544
Baldo, Ernesto, J4974
Baldridge, Mark, J5417
La Balena Bianca E Altri Miti, J293
Ball, Gordon, J1955, 2061, 2988, 3571, 3660,
    5228, 5246, 5356, 5458
Il Ballo Immune, J5833
Baltimore Jewish Times [Baltimore, MD], J3507
Baltimore Sun [Baltimore, MD], J706, 718,
    1077, 1845, 2019, 2227, 2546, 3132, 3156,
    3276, 3287, 3492, 3804, 3850, 4891, 5793
Balz, Dan, J5281
Bamber, Linda, J4255
Bananas, J2486
Bananas [London, England], J2086, 2864
Bangs, Lester, J1155, 1326, 2279
Banner Weekly [Providence, RI], J3892
Bannon, Anthony, J1006
Baraka, Amiri, J2979, 4822
Baran, Bogdan, H466, 493-4, J2967
Barb, Barbara, J2124
Barbarisi, Gaetano, J3129
Barbeau, C.C., J819
Barber, James, J1803
Barberis, Robert, J2151
Bard College Community Magazine [Annandale-
    On-Hudson, NY], J1384
Bardin, Desdemone, J2747
Baresch, Brian, J4402, 4421
Bar-F-Out [Tokyo, Japan], J5455
Barich, Bill, J3174
Barkin, George, J3331
Barnard, Elissa, J4095
Barnard Bulletin [New York, NY], J5616
Barnatán, Marcos Ricardo, H663
Barnes, Clive, J1320, 1579, 1584, 1641
Barnes, Harper, J1718, 5416
Barney, Walter, J2409
Barnwell, Randall, J5115
Barone, Roger, J5043
Barr, Michael, J2643
Barricada [Managua, Nicaragua], J3162, 4070,
    4072, 4076
Barrilete [Buenos Aires, Argentina], H701
Barron, Len, J3387
Barry, Dave, J5712-3
Barry, Ernie, J367
Barry, Joseph, J175
Barth, Dan, J5777
Bartlett, Jeffrey, J3193, 5225
Bartlett, Lee, J3143
Bartley, Bruce M., J2347
Bartra, Agustí, H683
Bartz, Anne, J1944
Basel Zeitung [Basel, Switzerland], J2890, 3544
Baseler Nachrichten [Basel, Switzerland], J1657
Basile, Jean, H150
Baskin, Fran, J3523
Basler, George, J4325
Basler Magazin [Basel, Switzerland], J4717
Basler Zeitung [Basel, Switzerland], J2966, 2970
Bass, Liz, J1418
Basta! [Oslo, Norway], H462, J5346
Bastian, Hans, H176
Bastian, Heiner, H172, 176-7, 219, 244

Burns, Glen, J2463, 3639
Burns, Jim, J4994
Burns, John, J5300
Burroughs, William S., H59, 71, 120-1, 124-5,
    129, 190, 195, 257, 338, 393, 665, 745,
    J288, 314, 677, 2177, 2807, 2990, 3400,
    3672
Burroughs, William S. III, J2242
The Burroughs File, J2805
Burt, Douglas, J324
Burtman, Bob, J3575
Burton, Ken, J1053
Buss, William G., J42
Bustin, Martha, J4887
Butazolidan, Alka, J2407
Butler, Evelyn Anne, J4054
Butler, Katy, J2764
Butler, Patrick, J3346
Butscher, Edward, J4261
Butsumon [Japan], J4747
Buttenhuis, Peter, J1056
Butterick, George, J1300
Buttgen, Bob, J3705, 3709
Buzássy, Ján, H646
Buzzolan, Dario, J5254
Byrd, Don, J3007, 5021

CAL [Caracas, Venezuela], H690
CEA Critic [East Orange, NJ], J243
C.E.P. Perspective [New York, NY], J3862
CMJ New Music Report [Great Neck, NY],
    J4816
COSMEP Newsletter [San Francisco, CA],
    J1339
CU Campus Press [Boulder, CO], J3718, 3722
La Caduta Dell'America, H334, J3149
Caellian [New Brunswick, NJ], J1503
Caen, Herb, J336, 503, 1509, 2115, 2359, 3103,
    3857
Caffeine [Woodland Hills, CA], J5676
Caffery, Bethia, J1697
Caffrey, Ken, J4818
Cage, John, J5580
Cagle, Charles Harmon, J3611
Le Cahier Livres De Liberation [Paris, France],
    J5820
Le Cahiers De L'Herne: Henri Michaux, H118
Les Cahiers Noirs Du Soleil, H166
La Caida De America, H653
Caiet [Romania], H527
El Caimán Barbudo [Havana, Cuba], H727
Calamus, H198
Calapooya Collage II [Monmouth, OR], J4364
Calderon, Manuel, J5541
Caldwell, Larry, J3583
Caldwell, William A., J399
Caledonian-Record [St. Johnsbury, VT], J4347,
    5791
Calendar, Carl, J3836
Calgary Albertan [Calgary, Canada], J2874
Calgary Herald [Calgary, Canada], J4427
Calic, Zoran, J5446
California Aggie [Davis, CA], J1448-9
Callaghan, Barry, J946
Callahan, John P., J651

Calligarich, Gianfranco, J800
Callow, James T., J2470
Camacho, Eduardo, J3584
Cambio [Managua, Nicaragua], J3206
Cambon, Glauco, H353
Camboni, Marina, J2664, 2710
Cambridge News [Cambridge, MA], J1029
Cambridge Phoenix [Cambridge, MA], J1121
Camden Times [Camden, NJ], J4128
Le Camé, H129
Campbell, Bob, J5614
Campbell, Colin G., J4648
Campbell, Jackie, J5702
Campbell, James, J5226, 5818
Campbell, Mark, J2244
Campbell, Mary, J1608
Campe, Joachim, H205
Campo, Alberto, J5252
Campus Connection [Amherst, MA], J3317
Campus Report [Washington, DC], J5740, 5802
Campus-Times [Rochester, NY], J850
Canaday, John, J565
Canadian Forum [Canada], J947
Canadian Jewish News [Toronto, Canada], J3069,
    3084
Canadian Literature [Vancouver, Canada], J939,
    5124
Canal [Paris, France], H155, J2727
Canalis, Xavier, J5531
Canby, Vincent, J2869
Candito, Mimmo, J791
Il Canguro [Milan, Italy], J799
Canton Observer [Canton, MI], J3834
Cantor, Harold, J2294
Cantor, Judy, J3920, 3932
Cantrell, Carol Helmstetter, J2373
Cany, Bruno, J2727
Capital Times [Madison, WI], J737, 3342
Capp, Al, J363
Capper's [Topeka, KS], J5729
Capra, Umberto, H333
Caprariu, Al, H526
Caraion, Ion, H523
Caravel America [Italy], J4621
Cardenal, Ernesto, H97, 660, 678, 681, 715,
    717, 734-5
Cardinale, Anthony, J4509
Cardwell, Nancy, J2229
Cargas, Harry J., J1724-5, 2005
Cariaga, Daniel, J4939, 4942
Caric, Marin, H589
Carleton Miscellany [Northfield], J372
Carlin, Margaret, J3576
Carlsen, Erik Meier, J3634
Carlson, Barbara, J867
Carlson, Peter, J1893
Carmona, Dário, J191
Carneci, Magda, H550-1
Carneci, Radu, J4223
Carolan, Trevor, J5687
Carolina Israelite [Charlotte, NC], J418
Carolina Quarterly [Chapel Hill, NC], J2122
Carpenter, Dan, J4849
Carpenter, Humphrey, J4630
Carr, C., J4028, 4358

Cunningham, Alan, J2600
Cunningham, John, J4356
Cunningham, Peter, J3980
Cuore Di Beat, H349
Curley, Arthur, J2538
Curran, Ann, J4806
Current [Ann Arbor, MI], J5116
Current Biography [New York, NY], J1298, 4321
Current Biography Yearbook, J1557, 4464
Currier, Barbara, J391
Curtin, Edward J., J3994
Curtin, John, J3381
Curto, Bobby, H699
Cushman, Jerome, J1345
Cutler, Evan Ross, J4134
Cutler, Hugh, J2111
Czaplinski, Czeslaw, J4254
Czarnecki, John, J1849

Dachslager, E.L., J2434
Dagan, Diane, J38
Dagbladet [Oslo, Norway], J3449, 3456, 3472, 5471, 5477, 5720
Dagens Nyheter [Stockholm, Sweden], H757, J3444, 3473
Dagnino, Antonio Eduardo, J894
Daily, Victoria, J5807
Daily Aztec/Stampa [San Diego, CA], J4020
Daily Bruin [see...UCLA Daily Bruin]
Daily Californian [Berkeley, CA], J1928, 1963, 2358, 3738, 4290
Daily Californian Arts Magazine [Berkeley, CA], J1611
Daily Camera [Boulder, CO], J1660, 2578, 2585, 2858, 3131, 3253, 3259, 3261, 3280, 3297, 3304, 3573, 3583, 3587, 3616, 3721, 3894, 4144, 4348, 4487, 4526, 4875, 4988, 5166, 5337, 5340, 5622, 5626, 5660, 5691, 5695, 5703, 5705, 5711
Daily Camera Review [Boulder, CO], J3207
Daily Cardinal [Madison, WI], J2620, 2622, 3345
Daily Cougar [Houston, TX], J5184, 5286
Daily Democrat [Woodland, CA], J1450
Daily Express [London, England], J454, 459
Daily Forty-Niner [Long Beach, CA], J3182
Daily Free Press [Boston, MA], J3537
Daily Freeman [Kingston, NY], J4601, 5643
Daily Hampshire Gazette [Northampton, MA], J4104, 4257
Daily Herald [Chicago, IL], J3903, 4911
Daily Intelligencer [Doylestown, PA], J1756
Daily Item [White Plains, NY], J5267
Daily Journal [Union, NJ], J1120, 1124, 1126, 1132, 1136
Daily Kent Stater [Kent, OH], J1442, 5756, 5810
Daily Mail [London, England], J455, 482
Daily Mirror [New York, NY], J11
Daily Mirror [Sydney, Australia], J1628
Daily Mississippian [University, MS], J4329, 4333
Daily Nebraskan [Lincoln, NE], J534, 536, 5417, 5420

Daily News [New York, NY], J12, 139, 363, 594, 600, 620, 640, 809, 950, 1110, 1712, 1791, 2030, 2108, 2331, 3021, 3123, 3502, 3538, 3935, 5010, 5142
Daily News [Halifax, Canada], J4097
Daily Nexus [Santa Barbara, CA], J1792, 4009, 4022-3
Daily Northwestern [Evanston, IL], J4908
Daily Oklahoman [Oklahoma City, OK], J2868, 5391
Daily Orange [Syracuse, NY], J580, 1360
Daily Pennsylvanian [Philadelphia, PA], J4501-2
Daily Pilot Datebook [Costa Mesa, CA], J3975
Daily Planet [Miami, FL], J1243, 1273, 1516, 1525, 1670
Daily Press [Newport News, VA], J1431
Daily Princetonian [Princeton, NJ], J352
Daily Progress [Charlottesville, VA], J3997
Daily Record [Cedar Falls, IA], J859
Daily Record [NJ], J4232
Daily Rocket-Miner [Rock Springs, WY], J3118
Daily Sentinel [CO], J2579
Daily Sketch [London, England], J460
Daily Star [Oneonta, NY], J5179
Daily Sun Reporter [Miami, FL], J1677
Daily Tar Heel [Chapel Hill, NC], J2420
Daily Telegraph [Australia], J1626, 1629
Daily Telegraph [London, England], J765
Daily Telegraph And Daily News [Australia], J1630
Daily Texan [Austin, TX], J721, 723, 725, 2523, 2774, 3723-4
Daily Times-News [Mt. Pleasant, MI], J1856
Daily Titan [Fullerton, CA], J4666
Daily Transcript [Golden, CO], J2592, 2601
Daily Trojan [Los Angeles, CA], J717, 720
Daily World [New York, NY], J1811
Dajbor, Agnieszka, J5484
Daley, John, J3464
Dalgard, Per, J4449, 5085
Dallas Morning News [Dallas, TX], J2928, 3696, 3822, 4153, 4285, 4288, 4729, 4732
Dallas Times Herald [Dallas, TX], J2926, 3973
Dalton, Kevin, J3928
Damascus Free Press [Damascus, MD], J1084
Dameron, Chip, J2774
Danas [Zagreb, Yugoslavia], J3726, 4169
Dander, Nicholas, J5315
Dandridge, Ned, J2097
Dangerfield, Achim, J5618
Dangerous Dossiers, J4643
Daniel Berrigan And Contemporary Protest Poetry, J1724
Danielius, Antanas, H441
Daniels, Robert, J3956
Dannatt, Adrian, J4860
Dan's Papers [Long Island, NY], J5326
Dante, Robert, J5205
Darlington, Andy, J4066, 4984
Darmstädter Echo [Darmstädt, Germany], J2827
Darnton, John, J1655
Darras, Jacques, H133, J4450
Dartmouth [Hanover, NH], J637
Dartmouth Review [Hanover, NH], J3685
Daruvalla, Abi, J3461

Galloway, David, H82, 198
Galloway, Paul, J4897
Galvin, Peter, J5739
Gambon, Jill, J3537
Gandus, Valeria, J2745
Gangopadhya, Sunil, H21
Ganguly, Suranjan, H281, J5463, 5631
Gann, Kyle, J5290
Gannett Westchester [White Plains, NY], J4002
Gar [Austin, NY], J1705, 1897, 1972
Garchik, Leah, J5664
Garcia, Bob, J986
Garcia, Guy D., J4411
Gardner, James, J2550
Gardner, Ralph D., J4831
Gardut, Traian, H545
Garelik, Glenn, J2520
Gargan, William, J4292, 5311
Gargia, Giulio, J3109
Gargoyle [Bethesda, MD], J2616
Garofoli, Joe, J5744
Garrity, Can, J540
Gartenberg, Max, J128, 187, 240
Gärtender Erinnerung, H176
Garuda [Eugene, OR], J3600
Garun [USSR], H18
Gary Snyder: Dimensions Of A Life, J5232
Gasolin [Frankfurt, Germany], H220
Gass, William H., J4078
Gaté [reviews], J3394
Gateavisa [Oslo, Norway], J3291, 3459
Gates, David, J5324
Gates Of Eden, J2473
The Gates Of Wrath [reviews], J1800, 1820,
    1835, 1915
Gaudio, Silvana, J4975
Gay [New York, NY], J1523, 1593
Gay Community News [Boston, MA], J2342,
    2446, 2568, 3309, 3319, 4099, 5147
Gay Lib Voice Twin Cities [Minneapolis-St.
    Paul, MN], J2871
The Gay Liberation Book, J1884
Gay Life [Chicago, IL], J3175
Gay News [Philadelphia, PA], J3231
Gay News [London, England], J1790, 1825,
    1827
Gay Roots, J5235
Gay Sunshine [San Francisco, CA], J1740,
    1758, 1800, 1888, 1914, 2123, 2292, 2923
Gay Sunshine Interviews, J2656
Gay Sunshine Interviews [reviews], J1974
Gaydos, Jeff, J4289
Gays Under The Cuban Revolution, J3154
Gaysweek [New York, NY], J2686
Gazeta Regionalna [Bydgoszcz, Poland], J5464
Gazeta Wyborcza [Poland], J5484
Gazette [San Francisco, CA], J2025, 2194
Gazzetta Del Popolo [Italy], J524
Il Gazzettino [Italy], J568
Gdje [Yugoslavia], H588
Gebbia, Alessandro, J2806
Gefen, Pearl Sheffy, J1473
Gefin, Laszlo, J3403, 4316
Geher, István, J285
Das Geheul Für Carl Solomon, H184

Das Geheul Und Andere Gedichte, H170, 178
Das Geheul Und Andere Gedichte [reviews], J198,
    204-5, 210, 221, 225-6, 235, 2695, 2757,
    2763, 2765, 2778, 2789, 2793, 2800, 2827,
    2836, 2855, 2909
Gehr, Richard, J5666
Geist, Peter, H204
Geist Und Zeit [Dammstadt, W. Germany], J235
De Gelderlander [The Netherlands], J5249
Geli, Carles, J5530
Geller, Allen, J445
Geller, Andrew, J801
Gendai Shi Techo [Tokyo, Japan], H401, 409,
    412-4, 421, 424, J184, 4656
Gendaisin No Shiso, H394
Gener, Randy, J5270-1
La Generacion De La Paz, H668
Generation Magazine [Buffalo, NY], J5033
Geneson, Paul, J2164
Genet: A Biography, J5587
Gengle, Dean, J2432
Gensco, Goggo, J4798
Gent, George, J1421, 1788
George, Gerald, J583
George, Lynell, J4856, 4884
George, Stefan, H72
Georgetown Journal [Washington, DC], J4106
Georgia Review [Athens, GA], J3510, 4260
Georgia Straight [Vancouver, Canada], J1004,
    1013, 1021, 1024, 1037, 1191, 1206, 1461,
    1687, 1744, 1751, 1759, 1806, 1810, 1813,
    1957, 1974, 1982, 2013, 2017, 2094, 2160,
    2638, 3049
Georgievski, S., J4208
Gerald, Gregory Fitz, J1633
Geraths, Armin, J4047
Gerbaud, Colette, J4824
Gershuny, Grace, J4347
Gertmenian, Donald, J2180
Gervais, Marty, J3818
Gervis, Stephanie, J319
Géza, Biskó, J2956
Gibbs, Barbara, J163
Gibbs, Stephen, J4395, 4407
Gibinska, Marta, J5356
Gibson, Julie, J1512
Gibson, Morgan, J4671, 4747, 4826
Gieske, Tony, J5766
Gifford, Barry, J1872, 2617, 2653
The Gift, J3644
Gigli, Lorenzo, J524
Gilbert, Claude, H126
Gilbert, James, J4270
Gilbert, Matthew, J5623, 5824
Gilbert, Richard, J698
Gilbride, Michael, J3229
Gildea, William, J1953
Giles, Jeff, J4531
Gill, John J., J270
Gillen, Beth, J1310
Gillen, Harald, J4559
Gillespie, Elgy, J4992, 5308
Gilman, Susan, J3892
Gilroy, Harry, J562
Gindl, Winfried, J5362

Ginsberg, Louis, J162, 989, 1078, 1085, 1347
Ginsberg: A Biography, J4836
Ginsberg: A Biography [reviews], J4721, 4729-
   32, 4734, 4740, 4743-4, 4746, 4749, 4754,
   4756-8, 4760, 4763, 4767-8, 4777, 4786,
   4790, 4797, 4802-3, 4805, 4822-3, 4825,
   4848, 4855, 4857, 4860-1, 4863-5, 4867,
   4870-1, 4873, 4883, 4889-90, 4894, 4902,
   4946, 5012, 5062, 5124, 5129, 5160, 5210,
   5222
Gioia, Dana, J3511
Giordano, Al, J4684
Il Giornale [Italy], J3379
Il Giorno [Milan, Italy], J2707, 3380
Giovannini, Marco, J5448
Gironde Magazine [France], J5162
Gironell, Marti, J5537
Giroux, Roger, H140
Girri, Alberto, H661-2
Gitlin, Todd, J4803
Giudici, Giovanni, H354
Giuliano, Charles, J4619, 4653
Giuliano, Mike, J2439
Gjendiktninger, H457
Gladfelter, David D., J789, 862
Gladysz, Thomas, J3826, 3873, 5172-3
Glanvill, Rick, J4959
Glas [Sofia, Bulgaria], H30
Glas [Banja Luka, Yugoslavia], J4178
Glaser, Alice, J321
Glasgow Review [Glasgow, Scotland], J1829
Glass, Ian, J1252
Glass, Jesse, J2374
Glassgold, Peter, J4654
Glazer, Fred, J1302
Gleaner [Camden, NJ], J1929
Gleason, Linda, J2682
Gleason, Ralph J., J33, 39, 371, 506, 604, 607,
   908
Glinn, Burt, J52
Glisic, M., J4214
Globe And Mail [Toronto, Canada], J661, 878,
   895, 933, 2273, 3066, 3078, 3321, 4676,
   4797
Globe Hebdo [Paris, France], J5435
Globe-Times [Bethlehem, PA], J2676, 3830
Glooskap's Children, J1865
The Glory And The Dream, J2075
Glossner, Herbert, J4550, 4578
Gloucester Daily Times [Gloucester, MA],
   J1267, 1274
Glueck, Grace, J2133, 4092
Glusadz, Radomir, J2946
Glusman, Paul, J1195
Gogola, Tom, J5051
Gold, Barbara, J1077
Gold, Herbert, J93, 694, 4309, 5155
Gold, Michael, J296
Gold, Robert S., J1880
Goldberg, Art, J936
Goldberg, M.F., J1375
Goldberg, Michael, J4388
Golden, Daniel, J2412
Golden, Gerald A., J1314
Golden, Mike, J4626

Golden Gater [San Francisco, CA], J30
Golden Road, J3677, 4673
Goldhurst, Richard, J418
Goldman, Ari L., J4350
Goldman, Connie, J3353
Goldman, Harold Raymond, J3775
Goldman, Ivan, J1986, 2058, 2060, 2062, 2087
Goldmine [Iola, WI], J3292, 3526, 4742, 4915
Goldsmith, Jeffrey, J5318
Goldstein, Al, J145
Goldstein, Avi, J4761
Goldstein, Joel, J1327
Goldstein, Laurence, J2921
Goldstein, Richard, J1894, 2768
Golembiewski, Chris, J5601
Golffing, Francis, J163
Gömöri, Gy, H303
Gone Soft [Salem, MA], J1956
Gontarski, S.E., J5020
Gonzaga Bulletin [Spokane, WA], J1047
Gooch, Brad, J5583
Good, Philip, J4683
Good 5¢ Cigar [Kingston, RI], J1780
Good Times [San Francisco, CA], J1087, 1153,
   1469, 1480, 1487
Goodhue, Huntly, J708
Goodman, David, J5599
Goodman, Fred, J3540
Goodman, Mitchell, J1390
Goodman, Paul, J238, 2466
Goodman, Peter, J5143, 5593
Goodman, Richard, J1890
Goodman, Susan, J376
Goodwin, David, J4359
Goodwin, Michael, J2031
Goriika [Japan], H402-3
Gorlier, Claudio, H355, J5647
Gorman, Peter, J5428
Gornick, Vivian, J1123
Goro [see....Goru]
Gorov, Georgi, H28
Gorski, Hedwig, J2772
Goru [Tokyo, Japan], H416, J2326
Gorzelski, Roman, H475, 490
Gosciak, Joseph, J1754
Gosciak, Josh, J2627
Goshorn, Gayle, J2422
Goswami, Satsvarupa Dasa, J3642
Gothic Times [Jersey City, NJ], J634
Götter Dämmerung [Binningen, W. Germany],
   H227
Göttinger Tageblatt [Göttinger, Germany], J4938
Gould, Gordon, J138
Gould, Whitney, J737
Gounis, Phil, J5066
Gown Literary Supplement [Belfast, Northern,
   Ireland], J5439
Grabosky, Tom, J4614
Gracan, Giga, H572
Grackle [New York, NY], J2919
Gradina [Yugoslavia], H595, 613, 619, 630,
   J3630
Graduate Student Journal [Berkeley, CA], J355
Grady, John, J616, 5465, 5828
Graeff, Ron, J580

Higgins, Jim, J4503
Higginson, William J., J4059
High On The Beats, J5372
High Culture, J3000
High Performance [Los Angeles, CA], J3391
High Priest, J979
High Times [New York, NY], J2512, 3331, 5263, 5428
Highlander [Riverside, CA], J3556
Hika [Gambier, OH], J5219
Hiki, H387
Hill, Brian, J3738
Hill, Richard, J4537
Hill, Tracey, J1919
Hill News [Canton, NY], J3736
Hill Rag [Washington, DC], J3720, 3803, 3921
Hillen, Steven, J3357
Hillmore, Peter, J3914
Hillson, Jon, J1001
Him Applaus, J2340
Him With His Foot In His Mouth And Other Stories, J3768
Himes, Geoffrey, J2090, 2440, 2450, 3493, 5032, 5459
Hinckle, Warren, J2528
Hindus, Milton, J3777, 4638
Hinely, Patrick, J5118
Hinerman, Stephen, J3157
Hinson, Hal, J5617
Hinson, Mark, J3604
Hintermeier, Hannes, J5485
Hintze, Christian Ide, J5362
Hipp, Edward S., J1662
The Hippies, J820
Hippies, Drugs And Promiscuity, J1732
Hirooka, Minoru, J4456
Hirschman, Jack, J923, 4043, 4074, 4343
Hirschorn, Michael W., J4384
Hirsh, David, J4900
Historia Literatury Stanow Zjednoczonych W, Zarysie, J3408
A History Of Modern Poetry, J4467
Hitchens, Christopher, J4889, 5389
Hobbs, Lisa, J502
Hoberman, J., J3643
Hobo Blues Band, H327
Hochman, Sandra, J2199
Hochswender, Woody, J3628
Hodenfield, Jan, J2196
Hodgson, Godfrey, J2654
Hoehl, Egbert, J221, 226
Hoffert, Barbara, J4608
Hoffman, A.P., J48
Hoffman, Abbie, J1728, 2642
Hoffman, Frederick J., J827
Hoffman, Michael J., J5357
Hoffman, Steven K., J2687
Hofmann, Albert, J2994
Hogan, William, J36, 1946
Hogrefe, Jeffrey, J3794
Hoko, H377
Hol Van Vietnam?, H286
Holborn, Mark, J4037
Holden, Stephen, J4386, 4492, 4530, 4599
Holen, Oisten, J5346

Holiday [Philadelphia, PA], J545
Hollahan, Eugene, J3913
Hollander, Charles, J825
Hollander, John, J29
Höllerer, Walter, H199, 211
Hollo, Anselm, H91-5, 171, 188, 213, 215-6, 218, J304
Holloway, Diane, J2779
Holmes, John Clellon, J104, 826, 1746, 3567, 4639
Holmes, Richard, J991
Holsteinischer Courier [Holstein, Germany], J4590
Holt, Jim, J5289
Holt, John, J675
Holt, Patricia, J2619
The Holy Barbarians, J182
Holy Soul Jelly Roll [reviews], J5731-3, 5737-9, 5754, 5766, 5772-3, 5775, 5777, 5780, 5790, 5801, 5805-6, 5821, 5824
Homberger, Eric, J2476
Home Grown [London, England], J3026, 3137
Home Grown International [London, England], J2982
Home Planet News [New York, NY], J1504, 2924
Un Homme Grand, J5067
Homosexual Tradition In American Poetry, J2816
Honan, Park, J4457, 5078
Honan, William H., J5445
Honi Soit [Sydney, Australia], J1620
Honolulu Advertiser [Honolulu, HI], J2411
Honolulu Star-Bulletin [Honolulu, HI], J2410, 2413
Hooks, Liz, J5408
Hoover, Bob, J5636, 5641, 5649
Hoover, Eleanor, J2898
Horemans, Rudi, J4060
Die Horen [Hannover, W. Germany], J2766
Horizon [New York, NY and Montgomery, AL], J117, 272, 1200, 3743
Hörmann, Egbert, J4736
Horn, Clayton W., J101
Horner, Tom, J3691, 3693
Hornick, Lita, J275, 3407, 4833
Horoskop Orloje, H58
Horovitz, Michael, J481, 1232, 2200, 3689, 3714, 3966, 4415, 4855, 5135
Horowitz, Michael, J2074
Horse-Trading And Ecstasy, J4841
Horton, A.M., J1577
Hot Press, J4957, 4984
Hotcha! [Zurich, Switzerland], J1119, 1142, 1159
Hoto Ere [Albania], H4
Houlding, Andrew, J3191
Houltzén, Eva, H761
Houston Chronicle [Houston, TX], J2394, 2845, 5287
Houston Post [Houston, TX], J2434, 3348
Hovdenakk, Sindre, J5720
How I Became Hettie Jones, J5080
How I Hear Howl, J1227
How I Work As A Poet And Other Essays, J1887

Li, Yan, H48-9
Liberation [New York, NY], J311, 844
Libération [Paris, France], J2368, 2708, 3017, 3373, 3847, 4907, 5045, 5047
Liberation News Service [Washington, DC], J1533
Liberty Denied, J5072
Library Hotline [Newton, MA], J5782
Library Journal [New York, NY], J112, 919, 1345, 1801, 1996, 2317, 2391, 2538, 2564, 2680, 2936, 2978, 3179, 3625, 3753, 4292, 4608, 5241, 5311, 5644, 5758
Library Of Congress Information Bulletin [Washington, DC], J1937
Lica [Yugoslavia], H597, 611, J3392
Licciardello, Nicola, J4762, 5833
Lichtenstein, Arthur, J1108
Lichtman, Irv, J3115
Liefland, Wilhelm, J2800
Life [Chicago, IL], J71, 75, 177, 200, 588, 748, 771
Life Cycle Planning, J2478
Life Is A Lousy Drag, J129
A Life Of Kenneth Rexroth, J5075
Lilli, Laura, J2725
Lilly, Russ, J897
Limberlost Review [Boise, ID], J2366
Liming, Robert G., J1652
Lin, Maurice Y., J1879
Linceul Blanc, H114
Lincoln Journal [Lincoln, NE], J537, 3305
Lincoln Journal-Star [Lincoln, NE], J5414-5, 5419
Lindberg, John, J868
Lindborg, Henry J., J1996
Lindh, Howard, J1846
Lindstrom, Andy, J3603
Line [Canada], J3601
Lines Of Feeling, H236
Lingaard, Jade, J5814
Link, David, J4338
Link, Franz, H191
Link [Cambridge, MA], J3186
Linville, Jack, J713
The Lion For Real [reviews], J4813, 4816-7, 4852, 4854, 4856, 4875-6, 4878, 4881, 4887, 4898, 4902, 4906, 4915, 4923, 4926, 4931, 4934-5, 4957, 4959, 4986-7, 4993, 5000, 5025, 5032, 5060, 5115, 5161, 5177, 5220
Lionni, Paolo, H361
Lipari, Joseph A., J3753
Lippincott, Robin, J5658
Lippman, Laura, J5793
Lipscomb, Joe, J1058
Lipsky, Jon, J1857
Lipton, Judith Eve, J3727
Lipton, Lawrence, J20, 182, 513, 945, 966, 996, 1004, 1079, 1410
Lira [Borovo, Yugoslavia], H629
Listener [London, England], J115, 775, 796, 944, 2516, 3909
Liston, Carol, J627
Lit [New York, NY], J2550
Lit. Vestnik [Bulgaria], H29

Litchfield County Times [Litchfield, CT], J3940
Literarische Messe 1968, J981
Literary Assays, J3773
Literary Cavalcade [New York, NY], J4495
Literary Criterion [Mysore, India], J1466, 3140
Literary Lantern [Chapel Hill, NC], J2024
Literary Monitor [Sunnyvale, CA], J2985
Literary New York, J2303
Literary Noviny [Prague, Czechoslovakia], H60, J425
Literary Outlaw, J4644
Literary Review [Madison, NJ], J2687, 2861, 4107
Literary Tabloid [Bergenfield, NJ], J2132
Literary Times [Chicago, IL], J732
Literary Transcendentalism, J1867
The Literary World Of San Francisco And Its Environs, J5076
Der Literat [Germany], J5201
Literatura [Krakow, Poland], H503, J3945
Literatura Ir Menas [Vilnius, USSR], H442
Literatura Na Swiecie [Warsaw, Poland], H482, 485, 487, 499, 506
Literature, Art, Philosophy, H438
Literature Gazeta [USSR], J1524
Literature, Obscenity And Law, J2308
A Literature Without Qualities, J2804
Literaturnaya Gazeta [Moscow, USSR], H562
Literaturnaya Uchoba [Moscow, USSR], J4267
Litfass [Berlin, Germany], H248
Litteraria [Poland], H488
Litterine, Lynn, J2454
Little, Carl, J4602
Little, John, J1902
Little Caesar [Los Angeles, CA], J2801
Littlejohn, Maureen, J5153
Littmann, William, J3182
Litz, A. Walton, J3151
Litzky, Tsaurah, J5668
The Lives Of Norman Mailer, J5240
Livet, Anne, J2299
The Living Theatre, J1722
Lloyd, Robert, J4813
Load [Purchase, NY], J1906
Locke, Asia, J2842
Lode, Asgeir, J3480
Loder, Kurt, J3715
Löfström, Tomas, J1973
Lofton, John, J3858, 4808, 4846
Logan, William, J3359
Logos [Montreal, Canada], J1288
Logue, Christopher, J166
Loidl, Christian, H244-6, J5023, 5123, 5209, 5362
Loka 2, J2304
Lomax, Michele, J1960, 2014
Lomax, Pearl Cleage, J3164
London, Jack, J2784
London Daily Worker [London, England], J456
London Magazine [London, England], J477, 1574
London Review Of Books [London, England], J3057, 4011, 4334
London Tribune [London, England], J464
Long, Philomene Gyokuho, J5316
Long, Robert Emmet, J2500

Nola Express [New Orleans, LA], J1340, 1361, 1371
Nolan, Frank, J1646
Nolan, Jack, J4023
Non [Belgrad, Yugoslavia], H626, 639
Nordland, Rod, J3166
Norman Transcript [Norman, OK], J2872, 5390
Norris, Ruth, J1811
Norske Argus [Oslo, Norway], J5335
North American Review [Cedar Falls, IA], J4354
North Beach Magazine [San Francisco, CA], J4157
North Beach Quarterly [Yokahama, Japan], J5768
North Carolina Anvil [Durham, NC], J1270
North Carolina Humanities [ND], J5405
North Dakota Quarterly [Grand Forks, ND], J3193
North Jersey Herald And News [NJ], J5187, 5706
North Shore Seventy [Beverly, MA], J1274
North Wind [London, England], J2049
Northeast Mississippi Daily Journal [Tupelo, MS], J4328, 4331
Northeast Rising Sun [Baltimore, MD], J2374, 2986
Northern California Jewish Bulletin [San Francisco, CA], J3670
Northern Iowan [Cedar Falls, IA], J854, 870, 875
Northern Star [Demarest, NJ], J671
Northern Territory News [Darwin, Australia], J1636
Northwest Passage [Bellingham, WA], J1766, 1941
Norton, Edward C., J843, 1097
Norwood, Christopher, J2077
Nosálek, Petr, J4966
Nosferatu [Buenos Aires, Argentina], H705
Notebook [Rochester, NY], J3681
Notes From The Garage Door [Cincinnati, OH], J669
Notes From The New Underground, J978
Nothing More To Declare, J826
Notizbücher 1952-1962, H179
Notizbücher 1952-1962 [reviews], J2873, 2890
Notley, Alice, J2298
La Notte [Italy], J535
Nottle, Diane, J5588
Nou Diari [Spain], J5524, 5531
Le Nouvel Observateur [Paris, France], H164, J2721, 5049
La Nouvelle Chute De L'Amerique, H112
Nova Makedonija [Skopje, Yugoslavia], H448, 451-2, J4112, 4154, 4166, 4175, 4197, 4199, 4208
Novak, William, J3000
Noveck, Jocelyn, J4493
Novedades Mexico [Mexico], J3074, 3586
Novi Americti Basnici, H56
Novi List [Rijeka, Yugoslavia], J4188
Novick, Julius, J1592
Novick, Rebecca McClen, J5579
Novosti [Belgrad, Yugoslavia], J4171
Now [Toronto, Canada], J3357, 3371
Nowlan, Alden, J700-1
Nowy Dziennik [New York, NY], J4254
Nowy Swiat [Poland], J236

Nowy Wyraz [Warsaw, Poland], H481, 484, 494, J2967
Nüchtern, Klaus, J5454
Nuclear Scorpions, J3034
Nuestro Cine [Madrid, Spain], H693
Nueva Poesia U.S.A., H664
El Nuevo Diario [Managua, Nicaragua], H715, J4073
Nugget [New York, NY], J229, 303
Nuit Blanche [Quebec, Canada], J4434
Nuits Magnetiques De France-Culture [France], J2722
Nummi, Lassi, J1134
Nunley, Richard, J2934
La Nuova [Sardaque, Italy], J3100
Nuova Antologia [Rome, Italy], J622
La Nuova Poetica Americana, J3401
Nuova Presenza [Italy], H359
La Nuova Sardepie [Italy], J3088
Nürnberger Nachrichten [Nuremberg, Germany], J4999
Nuspeak [Glasgow, Scotland], J1836
Nuttal, Jeff, J983
Nuvo [Indianapolis, IN], J5191
Nye, Robert, J3957, 4339
Nyt Fra Jorden, H69

OP Magazine [Olympia, WA], J3181, 3212, 3591
O.S.U. Lantern [see...Ohio State Lantern]
Oakland Tribune [Oakland, CA], J82, 957, 3232, 3266, 3755, 3796, 4772, 5412
Obenzinger, Hilton, J1596
Oberg, Arthur, J2658
Obrenovic, J., J4205
O'Brien, Mike, J3110
O'Brien, William, J494
O'Bryan, Danny, J5831
Observation Post [New York, NY], J952
Observer [South Bend, IN], J995, 997, 2683
Observer [London, England], J102, 254, 990, 1649, 3914, 3924, 4314, 4863, 5288, 5816
Observer-Dispatch [Utica, NY], J2502, 3460
Observer Weekend Review [London, England], J451, 1280
Obst, Lynda Rosen, J2480
Occasional Drop, J970
Occhiogrosso, Peter, J5237
O'Connor, Bill, J3208
O'Connor, Brian, J4880
O'Connor, John, J1601, 2436, 3217
O'Connor, Patrick Joseph, J5437
Octopus [Ottawa, Canada], J1149, 1166
Oda Plutoniana Y Otros Poemas, H657
Oder, Norman, J4086
Odglosy [Poland], H475
Odien [Sarajevo, Yugoslavia], J4211
Odjek [Yugoslavia], H634
O'Donnell, Will, J5803
Odra [Poland], H507
Odradek [Liege, Belgium], H151
Odyssey [Chicago, IL], J181
Oeuf [Geneva, Switzerland], H147
Off The Road, J5069

Off The Strip [Las Vegas, NV], J2760
Offen, Ron, J2057
Offenbach Post [W. Germany], J3040
O'Flaherty, Mark, J5823
Ogar, Richard A., J1041
O'Gara, Francis B., J84
Ogden Standard-Examiner [Ogden, UT], J3241
Oguntoyinbo, Kekan, J5809
Ohio Review [Athens, OH], J4413
Ohio State Lantern [Columbus, OH], J1071, 3956
Ohio University Review [Athens, OH], J508
O'Kane, John, J4627
Oklahoma City Times [Oklahoma City, OK], J1948, 5391
Oklahoma Daily [Norman, OK], J1942, 1950, 5392
Oklahoma Gazette [Oklahoma City, OK], J5393
Oko [Zagreb, Yugoslavia], H620, 622, J4200
Okolice [Poland], H489
Olean Times Herald [Olean, NY], J1072
Oliver, Edith, J1590
Olsen, Donald, J2857
Olsen, Jack, J1661
Olsen, Magne, J5480
Olsen, Tore, J3425, 3631
Olson, Charles, J2659
Olson, Ray, J5325
Olson [Storrs, CT], J2179
Oly Sokáig Voltunk Lenn, H327
Olympian, J3669
Om..., Entretiens Et Témoignages, H130, J2813
Om..., Entretiens Et Témoignages [reviews], J2721
Omaha World Herald [Omaha, NE], J538
Omer, Dan, H267
Omladinska ISKRA [Split, Yugoslavia], H640
Omladinske Novine [Belgrad, Yugoslavia], J2954
Omladinski Tjednik [Yugoslavia], H587
On A Scale That Competes With The World, J5834
On Campus [Adelaide, Australia], J3732
On Paper Gallery, H399
On The Bus, J5089
On The Poetry Of Allen Ginsberg, J3778
On The Road With Bob Dylan, J2662
On The Tracks [Grand Junction, CO], J5632
Once And For Almanack [Boulder, CO], J4696
One Vast Page, J5225
O'Neil, Paul, J177, 292
Oneonta Star [Oneonta, NY], J941
Onley, Betty, J1047
Only Connect, J3141
Onnepaulu, Tonu, H90
Ono, Kazuo, J4656
Onthebus [Los Angeles, CA], J4820
Open City [Los Angeles, CA], J735, 851, 896, 923, 986
Open Exchange [Berkeley, CA], J5128
Open Head [reviews], J1613, 1615, 1634
Open Letter [Toronto, Canada], J2293
Open Road [Vancouver, Canada], J2688
Open Space [San Francisco, CA], J348
L'Opera Della Sghignazzo, J3402
Opiewam Nowoczesnego Czlowieka, H473

Opium [Buenos Aires, Argentina], H691
Oppen, George, J307
Option Magazine [Santa Monica, CA], J4393, 4504, 4881
Opus International [Paris, France], J943
Oracle [Tampa, FL], J1696, 3596, 3607
Orange City News Weekly, J5413
Orange County Register [Santa Ana, CA], J4669, 5410
Orbán, Ottó, H282-3, 285, 290-1, 300, 326, J3393
Ord & Bild [Stockholm, Sweden], H749, 751
Oregon Journal [Portland, OR], J1774, 1945, 1958
Oregon State Daily Barometer [Corvallis, OR], J740-1
Oregonian [Portland, OR], J744, 747, 3615, 4286, 4769, 5036, 5669, 5673
Orengo, Nico, J2745, 5258
Orfeo [Santiago, Chile], H698
Organ [Berkeley, CA], J1331
Origin [Kyoto, Japan], J262
Orizont [Timisoara, Romania], H544-5, 549
Orlando, Ruggero, J576
Orlando Sentinel [Orlando, FL], J3706
Orlovsky, Peter, J358
Ørnskov, Ib, H70
Orth, Kevin, J3967
Orth, Maureen, J2189
Ory, Carlos Edmundo De, H34, 724, 726, 729-30
O'Shea, Clare, J4518
Oslobodenji [Sarajevo, Yugoslavia], H616, J4176
Ossman, David, J345
Ostinato [London, England], J5065
Other Paper [Amsterdam, The Netherlands], J3461
Other Voice [Binghamton, NY], J2786, 3188, 3522
Other World Poetry Newsletter [Amsterdam, The Netherlands], J2729
O'Toole, Lawrence, J5250
Ottawa Citizen [Ottawa, Canada], J1146
Ottersberger Abreiss, H249
Otto, Erwin, J2863
Oui [New York, NY], J3223
Ouimet, P., J2183
Our Time, J1730
Ouroussoff, Alessandro, J1923, 1963
Out [Pittsburgh, PA], J3064, 5733
Out Front [Denver, CO], J3618
Out Of The Vietnam Vortex, J2076
Out In The World, J4051
Out There [Skokie, IL], J2124, 2298
Out Week [New York, NY], J4854
Outlaw [St. Louis, MO], J1445
Outside [Chicago, IL], J5482
Ovdje [Yugoslavia], H592-3
Over Here [Leicester, England], J2862
Overseas Weekly, J1541
Oviedo, José Miguel, H649, 675
Owens, Christopher D., J3329
Ower, John, J2993
Owl [Boulder, CO], J3056, 3220

J211, 293, 406, 498, 522, 546, 1223, 1362,
1560, 1726, 1736-7, 1873, 2211, 2312,
2481, 2561, 2628, 2724, 2728, 2731, 2746,
2791, 2831, 2839, 2853, 2894, 2920, 2955,
2958, 3097, 3149, 3315, 3332, 3378, 3385,
3877, 4026, 4071, 4370, 4621, 4774, 4862,
5251, 5264, 5684, 5811
Pizzi, Doug, J4588
Plagenz, George R., J3959
Plain Dealer [see...Cleveland Plain Dealer]
Plainspeak [Denver, CO], J2689
Plaintiff [Mankato, MN], J1026
Plakalo, Safet, J4182, 4216
Plamondon, Pun, J1997
Plamuk [Bulgaria], H28
Planet News [reviews], J987, 991, 996, 1004,
1016, 1025, 1027, 1031, 1041, 1055, 1073-
4, 1081, 1084, 1086, 1095, 1101, 1104,
1109, 1218, 1242, 1277, 4466
Planet News (Carl Hanser), H172
Planet News (Christian Bourgois), H99
Planet News [Christian Bourgois - reviews],
J1456
Planete, H703
Planète Plus, H148
Planhammar, Per, H760
Planting The Seed, J3004
Platt, Adam, J4221
Playboy [Chicago, IL], J306, 1008, 1034, 1085,
1324, 1746, 2178, 3655
Playmen [Italy], J773, 2514, 2776, 2787
Plays And Players [London, England], J1639
Pleasants, Ben, J1413
Pleiad [Albion, MI], J4681
Plimpton, George, J828
Ploog, Jürgen, J2828, 2968
Ploughshares [Boston, MA], J2180
Ploutonia Ode, H254
Plural [Mexico City, Mexico], H718, 723
Plutonian Ode, Poems 1977-1980 [reviews],
J3177, 3179, 3197, 3210, 3213, 3222, 3341,
3356, 3359, 3364, 3372, 3592, 3601, 3760
Plutonische Ode/Plutonian Ode, H77
Plymell, Charles, J3011, 4063, 5314
Pobjeda [Titograd, Yugoslavia], H624, J4180,
4189, 4193, 4219
Pocono Record [Stroudsburg, PA], J4152
Podhoretz, Norman, J74, 106, 126x, 292, 829,
2398, 4283-4
Podium [Austria], H221
Poe, Richard, J3972, 4004-6, 4008
The Poem In Its Skin, J972
Poem, Interview, Photographs, J5831
Poems All Over The Place, Mostly 'Seventies
[reviews], J2680, 2755, 2762, 2985, 3070
Poesi [Oslo, Norway], J3632
Poesi Fran USA, H742
Poesia [Montevideo, Uruguay], J4628
Poesia Americana Del '900, H335
Poesia Anglesa I Nord-Americana Contempor-
ània, H672
Poesia Beat, H666
Poesia Degli Ultimi Americani, H336
Poesia E Rabbia, H340
Poesia In Pubblico, H348

Poesia In Pubblico/Parole Per Musica, J3142
Poesia Libre [Managua, Nicaragua], H717
Poesia Norteamericana Contemporanea, H661
Poesie, H347
Poesie Allena Ginsberga, H68
La Poésie De La Beat Generation, H117
Poesie Der Welt Nordamerika, H200
Die Poesie Des Dharma, J4637
Poesiealbum 127, H177
Poesis [Bucharest, Romania], H552
Poet Lore [Washington, DC], J4261
Poetiken Und Lyrischer Diskurs Im Kontext
Gesellschaftlicher Dynamik-USA, J4834
Poetry [Chicago, IL], J68, 122, 307, 369, 1086,
1096, 1990
Poetry [Japan], H410
Poetry [Korea], H436
The Poetry Beat, J5070
Poetry Broadsides [New York, NY], J34, 99
Poetry Criticism, J5376
Poetry Flash [Berkeley, CA], J3313, 3754, 4541,
4714, 4763, 4882, 4904, 4949, 5154, 5663
Poetry Information [London, England], J2369,
2796
Poetry International 1979, H89
Poetry International Rotterdam, H88
Poetry/Poezija, H443
Poetry Project Newsletter [New York, NY],
J2161, 2169, 2399, 3213, 3464, 3563, 3919,
4323, 4496, 4657, 5781
Poetry Review [London, England], J911, 1381,
4415, 5129
Poetry San Francisco [San Francisco, CA],
J4045
Poetry Society Of America Bulletin [New York,
NY], J350, 564
Poetry Toronto [Toronto, Canada], J2730
Poetry USA [Oakland, CA], J5319
Poetry's Catbird Seat, J4642
Poets [New York, NY], J2551, 2610
Poets And Writers Magazine [Philadelphia, PA],
J4738, 5268
Poets And Writers News [New York, NY], J2797
Poet's Catbird, J4465
Poets In Person: A Listener's Guide, J5367
Poets Of The Cities, J2069
Poets On Stage: The Some Symposium On
Poetry Readings, J2607
Poets, Poems, Movements, J4466
Poettype, A. Nother, J3525
Poezie Nieuws [Amsterdam, The Netherlands],
J5244
Poezja [Warsaw, Poland], H480, 500, J4281
Pohjolan Sanomat [Helsinki, Finland], J1176
Pohl, Ronald, J5009, 5452
Pohl, Volker, J5223
Poiemata, H252-3
Pokress, Jack, J5
Polak, Maralyn Lois, J3190
Poland, Timothy, J4469, 4946
Polar Star [Fairbanks, AK], J1646
Polentas, Manolis, J5545, 5568
Polet [Yugoslavia], H584
Poliat, Frank, J1961
Policy Review [Washington, DC], J3195

The Politics Of Ecstasy, J980
Politika [Belgrad, Yugoslavia], H625, J4187
Politika Ekspres [Belgrad, Yugoslavia], J4203
Politiken [Copenhagen, Denmark], H74, J1222,
   3429, 3434, 3438
Polito, Robert, J3557
Polja [Yugoslavia], H581, 594, 617, J1009,
   4135
Polk, Anthony, J2597
Pollak, Michael C., J2221, 2573
Pollard, Gayle, J1678
Poller, Nidra, H128
Pollock, Bruce, J3533
Pomada, Elizabeth, J2168
Pongpaiboon, Naowarat, J5442
Poniewaz, Jeff, J2596, 4497
Pons, Agusti, J5528
Pons, Michael, J2872
Ponte, Meo, J5255
Pop-Cornis, Marcel, H530, 532, 543-4
Pope, Richard L., J99
Popescu, Horia, H546
Popism: The Warhol '60s, J3653
Popov, Nikolay, H24
Popovic, Srda, H582
Popper, George A., J73, 79
Porche, Verandah, J715
Portable Lower East Side [New York, NY], H726
Portage [Stevens Point, WI], J2647
Portail, Claude, H130, 154, J2813
Porter, G. Bruce, J569
Porter, Henry, J3916
Portland Press Herald [Portland, ME], J1125
Portland Review Magazine [Portland, OR], J1715
Portland Scribe [Portland, OR], J1961
Portugés, Paul, J2313, 2386, 2660, 2825, 2880,
   3149, 3397
Post, Jonathan V., J2575
Post-Bulletin [Rochester, MN], J3906
Post-Crescent [Milwaukee, WI], J849, 853, 858,
   860, 865, 876
Post-Standard [Syracuse, NY], J4140
Post-Star [Glens Falls, NY], J4130
Poteet, Maurice, J4470
Potocnik, Peter, J4213
Pott, Gregor, J2715
Potter, Tully, J911
Poudre Magazine [Fort Collins, CO], J3051,
   3236, 3334
Poughkeepsie Journal [Poughkeepsie, NY],
   J1355, 2503
Poulikakoz, Demetrez, H255, 259
Poulin, A., J1354, 1563
Pourquoi Écrivez-Vous?, J4634
Powell, Clark, J4336
Powell, Tony, J3185
Power, Edward, J4124
The Power Of The People, J2472
Powers, Francis Gary, J2448
Powers, John J., J4541
Powers, Lisa S., J5116
Pozziya Ssha, H555
Prabhupad [See...Bhaktivedanta Swami]
Prabhupada, J3642
Prabhupada-Lilamrta, Srila [See...Bhaktivedanta

Swami]
Prado, Holly, J3799
Prague News Letter [Prague, Czechoslovakia],
   J424
Prairie Schooner [Lincoln, NE], J162, 4032
Praschl, Bernhard, J5451
Pratsines, Nikos, H257
Praunheim, Rosa Von, J2819
Prendic, Dubravka, H617
La Prensa [Managua, Nicaragua], J3161, 4075
La Prensa [Lima, Peru], J217
Preradovic, Nikola, H579
Prescott, J. Oliver, J1698
Prescott, N. Parker, J2007
Prescott, William, J2052
Present Tense, J2723
Press [Atlantic City, NJ], J4125
Press [Cortland, NY], J1846
Press And Sun Bulletin [Binghamton, NY],
   J4325
Press Connection [Madison, WI], J2623
Press Democrat [Santa Rosa, CA], J3936
Press-Enterprise [Riverside, CA], J3545, 3549
Press Herald [Portland, ME], J1951
Press Of Atlantic City [Atlantic City, NJ], J5713
Press-Telegram [Long Beach, CA], J2128, 3184
La Presse [Montreal, Canada], J1140
Die Presse [Germany], J5023
Presson, Rebekah, J4412, 4592
Preston, Rohan B., J5670-1
Preston, Scott, J5399
Preuss, Evelyn, J4575
Prial, Frank, J377, 613
Priano, Giovanna, J3877
Price, Michael H., J5342, 5754
The Priceless Jewel, J5586
Prichard, Ron, J5400
Pridal, Antonin, H58
Priewe, Jens, J2873
Prime, John Andrew, J5119
Primi Blues, H332
Prin [Greece], J5554
Prince, Lourie, J45
Princeton Alumni Weekly [Princeton, NJ], J586
Prior, Tom, J1624
Pritchard, William H., J1840
Pritchett, V.S., J118
Pro-Me-Thee-Us [New York, NY], J2064
Proceedings Of The Fifth International
   Conference, J5356
Proef M'n Tong In Je Oor, H75, J685
Profifoto Bücher [Germany], J4697
Prognosis [Prague, Czechoslovakia], J5535
Progressive [Mount Morris, IL], J105, 5388,
   5645, 5715
Promethean Review [New York, NY], J194
Proraby Dukha, H557
Pros In Poetry, J3153
Prose Contribution To Cuban Revolution
   [reviews], J816
Proskauer, Paul F., J2964
Prospects: An Annual Of American Cultural
   Studies [New York, NY], J2300
Prospetti [Italy], H357
Protean Radish [Chapel Hill, NC], J1258

Söring, Helmut, J4555
Sorkin, Adam J., J4828
Sorrentino, Gilbert, J410
Sortland, Bjørn, J5339
Sosnory, Vukmora, H553
Sotera, Ntina, H257
Sotnick, Barton, J644, 646
Souffles D'Esprit, H115
Sound Options [Lincroft, NJ], J2575
Soundi [Helsinki, Finland], H3468
Soundings [Knoxville, TN], J2263
Soundings/East [Salem, MA], J2769
Sousa, Diane, J2559
South America Of The Poets, J1397
South Bend Tribune [South Bend, IN], J5652
South End [Detroit, MI], J1108, 5196, 5604
South Philadelphia American [Philadelphia, PA],
　J5043
South Street Star [Philadelphia, PA], J3703
Southampton Press [Southampton, NY], J3980,
　4410
Southern, Terry, J3654
Southern Israelite [Atlanta, GA], J3517
Southern Journal Of Philosophy [Memphis, TN],
　J4417
Southern Pines Pilot [Southern Pines, NC],
　J2033, 2421
Southern Register [University, MS], J4368
Southern Review [Baton Rouge, LA], J3682,
　3991, 4967
Southern Review [Adelaide, Australia], J1838
Southern Theatre [Greensboro, NC], J5061
Southwest Review [Dallas, TX], J1633, 2949
Southwick, Tom, J1144
Sou'wester, J4129
Sovetskaya Molodezh [Nalchik, USSR], H561
Sovremennaia Amerikanskaia Pozziia, H554
Soyut [Turkey], J2329
Space City [Houston, TX], J1489
Spanner [England], J2591
Spark [Chicago, IL], J1441
Sparks, Amy, J5197
Sparrow [Santa Rosa, CA], J2387
Speak Up [Milan, Italy], J5008
Speaking For Ourselves, J1230
Spearman, Walter, J2024, 2029, 2033, 2420-1
Spears, Larry, J4772
Spears, Monroe K., J1400
Spectator [Bloomington, IN], J551, 636, 1000,
　1022, 1028, 3575
Spectator [New York, NY], J4252
Spectator [Hamilton, Canada], J1349-50
Spectator [London, England], J328, 4871, 4873,
　5160
Spector, R.D., J351
Spectrum [Little Rock, AR], J4236
Spectrum [Buffalo, NY], J553-4, 884, 1315,
　1368
Speech Teacher [Milwaukee, WI], J1409
Spencer, Duncan, J3905
Spender, Stephen, J1239
Spengler, David, J1511, 1522, 1587
Sphinx Magazin [Basel, Switzerland], H156,
　233, J2715, 2968
Der Spiegel [Hamburg, W. Germany], J289,

4703
Spiegel Van De Engelse Pöezie Uit De Gehele
　Wereld, H83
Spiegelman, Willard, J4843
Spin [New York, NY], J4813, 5805
Spinrad, Norman, J5027
Spirali [Italy], J2694
Spitzer, John, J1387
Spokane Natural [Spokane, WA], J1064
Spoleto Festival 90, J5093
The Spontaneous Poetics Of Jack Kerouac, J4480
Sprache Im Technischen Zeitalter [Berlin, W.
　Germany], H230
Sprague, Bob, J1411
Springfield Herald [Springfield, MA], J1091
Springfield Republican [Springfield, MA], J2460
Square Journal [New York, NY], J361
Srinivas, Krishna, J2315
Sruaa [Helsinki, Finland], J1151, 1178
Stace, Wes, J3882
Stack, Peter, J5441
Stader Tageblatt [Germany], J4559
Stadtblati Osnabrück [Osnabrück, Germany],
　J4764
Staff [Los Angeles, CA], J1488
Stafford, Peter, J1328, 1333, 1738
Staggs, Kenneth, J2039
Stamets, Bill, J5667
La Stampa [Torino, Italy], 531, 754, 761, 2735,
　3383, 4974, 5245, 5247, 5253, 5258, 5647
Stampa Sera [Italy], J5254
Stancic, Mladen, J4212
Stanciu, Virgil, H541
Stand [Leeds, England], J4517
De Standaard [The Netherlands], J3707
Der Standard [Austria], J5452
Standish, Myles, J1707
Stanford Daily [Palo Alto, CA], J5769, 5783
Stanford Observer [Palo Alto, CA], J2251
Stanford Review [Palo Alto, CA], J5798, 5813
Stanley, David, J338
Stanley, Linda C., J5373
Star, Leanne, J697
Star, J958
Star-Bulletin [see...Honolulu Star-Bulletin]
Star-Ledger [Newark, NJ], J1583, 2499, 2698,
　3122, 3657, 4888, 5282, 5298, 5654
Star-Tribune [Casper, WY], J2348, 5637
Starbuck, Jeff, J1434
Starer, Jacqueline, H152, J2239, 2484-5
Stark, Andy, J3333
Starr, Carol, J2247
Starscrewer [Berguette, France], J1741
Start With The Sun, J239
Starting Over, J1388
State [Columbia, SC], J1652
State News [Dover, DE], J3257, 3826
State Of The Unions [Madison, WI], J3335
State Press Magazine [Tempe, AZ], J5425, 5515
Staten Island Advance [Staten Island, NY],
　J2428, 5186, 5511
States-Item [New Orleans, LA], J1359
Statesman [Stony Brook, NY], J879
Station To Station [Kiel, Germany], J4739
Staudacher, Cornelia, J5508

Tip [Berlin, W. Germany], J2828
Tiroler Tageszeitung [Austria], J2961
Tish [Vancouver, Canada], J329
To Bema [Greece], H262
To Eberhart From Ginsberg, J2305
To Eberhart From Ginsberg [reviews], J2249,
   2284, 2317, 2374
To Oyrliachto, H255
To Read Poetry, J3405
To Tetarto [Athens, Greece], J4498
Toallobema [Greece], J5540
Tobias, Allen, J832
Today's Spirit [Philadelphia, PA], J1754
Todd, Paula, J3318
Toijonen, Vesa, J3481
Tokunaga, Shozo, H410, J4655
Toledo Blade [Toledo, OH], J1529, 3208
Tomis [Romania], H531, 533
Tomiyama, Hidetoshi, H387-8, 421, 424, J4656
Tommasini, Anthony, J5595
Tongues Of Fallen Angels, J2081
Tonkovich, Andrew, J3185
Too Beat To Split, H577
Toohey, Francis, J2513
Tooker, Peter, J2643
Toolen, Tom, J5190
Topeka Capital-Journal [Topeka, KS], J4385,
   4395, 4407
Topeka Daily Capital [Topeka, KS], J528
Toplikar, David, J4406
Toppman, Lawrence, J4486
Torgersen, Eric, J4278
Toronto Arts [Toronto, Canada], J3354
Toronto Daily Star [Toronto, Canada], J691
Toronto Globe And Mail [See...Globe And Mail]
Toronto Life [Toronto, Canada], J921
Toronto Now [Toronto, Canada], J3112
Toronto Star [Toronto, Canada], J1352, 2830,
   2841, 3067, 3362, 3368, 4777
Toronto Sun [Toronto, Canada], J3360
Toronto Sunday Star [Toronto, Canada], J3079
Toronto Telegram [Toronto, Canada], J692, 946
Torrey, E. Fuller, J3788
Torrez, Juliette, J4591
Toth, Carolyn, J3250
Touchstone [Manhattanville, NY and Toronto,
   Canada], J473, 5275
Le Tout Lyon [Lyon, France], J5138
Towards A New American Poetics, J2651
Towerlight [Towson, MD], J1852
Town [London, England], J698
Town And Country [Boulder, CO], J4344
Townsend, Bob, J4852
Tozian, Greg, J3605
Trace [London, England], J395
Trag [Yugoslavia], H596
Tragica America, J984
Transcript [Williamstown, MA], J2937, 2941
Transition [Kampala, Uganda], J510
Tratat De Inspiratie, H525, J4064
Travels By Night, J5830
Travers, Peter, J5627
Trebay, Guy, J3802
Trema [Paris, France], J2465
Tremblay, Bill, J3942

Trente-Cinq Jeunes Poètes Américains, H116
Trenton Times Advertiser [Trenton, NJ], J886
Trescott, Jacqueline, J1954
Trexler, Connie, J2418
Tribble, Edwin, J1423
Tribu [Toulouse, France], H162, J3683
Tribuna [Romania], H526, 528-9
Tribune [San Diego, CA], J3911
Tribune-Review [PA], J2882
Tri-City Herald [Pasco, WA], J3042
Tricycle [New York, NY], J5770
Trilling, Diana, J154, 407
La Trinchera [Barcelona, Spain], H32
Trinitonian [San Antonio, TX], J1284
Trinity Times [New York, NY], J2522
Trinity Tripod [Hartford, CT], J3733
Trip, H573
Triplett, William, J3713, 3717
Tripoli, Dana, J3743
Tripper, T., J1533, 1571
Tri-Valley Herald [Pleasonton, CA], J5761
Troelstrup, Glenn, J2380
Trotter, Bill, J2040
Trull, P.J., J4986
Truninger, Curt, J2971
Truscott, Brian, J4756
Truszskowska, Teresa, H470, 479, 482-3, 495-7,
   502
Tsatsoy, Marias, J5569
Tsvetanovski, Savo, H443-4, 447-52
Tsvetkovski, B., J4112, 4208
Tu Novostn [Belgrad, Yugoslavia], J4217
Tucker, Arlene, J48
Tucker, Carll, J2044, 2061
Tucker, Dan, J103, 132
Tucker, Ernest, J3302, 3320
Tucker, Ken, J3496, 3502, 3508, 3806, 5772-3
Tucker, Mark, J4940
Tucson Citizen [Tucson, AZ], J1048, 2905,
   3635, 5133
Tufts Observer [Medford, MA], J2337
Tulane Hullabaloo [New Orleans, LA], J1358,
   1493
Tunde, Poor, J5483
Turan, Kenneth, J2632, 2636, 5139
Turchi, Roberto, J3095
Turell, Dan, H74
Turil, Dan [See...Turell, Dan]
Turin, David, J5612
Turner, David, J1066
Turner, Elizabeth Carey, J1944
Turner, Jean-Rae, J1120
Turner, Wallace, J1462
Turun Sanomat [Helsinki, Finland], J1164,
   1192, 1321
Tuscaloosa News [Tuscaloosa, AL], J2459
Tussen Hemel En Hema, H80
Tuttle, Peter, J1374
Twenty Three [23], H138
Twen [The Netherlands], J231
Twigg, Alan, J2638
299 [Two Hundred Ninety Nine] [Stockholm,
   Sweden], J3530
Two Lectures On The Work Of Allen Ginsberg,
   J5364

Wichita State Sunflower [Wichita, KS], J539-40
Wichita Sunday Eagle And The Wichita Beacon
    [See...Wichita Eagle-Beacon]
Widder, Frank, J2246-7
Widgery, David, J685, 3927
Widmer, Kingsley, J1389
Wiener, John, J3789
Wiener [Hamburg, Germany], J4715
Wiener Zeitung [Vienna, Austria], J4589, 4776
Wiersze, H467
Wigoder, Geoffrey, J1398
Wij Twee Jongens, H82
Wilcox, Brent, J3212
Wilentz, Joan, J1339
Wilhelm, James J., J2488
Wilhelmshavener Zeitung [Wilhelmshaven, W.
    Germany], J3471, 3484, 3489
Will [Tokyo, Japan], J3012, 3062
Willamette Bridge [Portland, OR], J915, 1198,
    1451
Willamette Week [Portland, OR], J3617, 4766
Willer, Cláudio, H513, J5307
William And Mary [Williamstown, VA], J3580
William Burroughs: El Hombre Invisible, J5365
William Burroughs: The Algebra Of Need, J1558
William Carlos Williams: Man And Poet, J3652
William Carlos Williams Review [Austin, TX],
    J4896
Williams, Albert, J3175
Williams, Chris, J1290
Williams, Dave, J5112
Williams, Dina, J5053
Williams, H.L., J804
Williams, Hugo, J477
Williams, Jennifer, J5266
Williams, Liza, J966
Williams, Paul, J5375, 5821
Williams, Richard, J2122
Williams, Shirley, J1052
Williams, William Carlos, H337, J76, 1051
Williams Record [Williamstown, MA], J2933,
    2942
Williamson, Alan, J4046
Williamson, Mitch, J2252
Willis, Ellen, J1378
Willis, Scott, J5748
Wilmington, Michael, J5656
Wilmink, William, H80
Wilner, Paul, J2258, 2343
Wilson, Paul, J3108
Wilson, Robert Anton, J224, 311, 2018
Wilson, Susan, J3739
Wilson, William, J5299
Wilson Library Bulletin [New York, NY], J3036,
    3533
Wimmer, Adi, J4031, 4253
Win [New York, NY], J806, 1289, 1347, 1969,
    2193, 2671, 3159
Winders, Jim, J5292
Windhorse Review [Boulder, CO], J4136
Windsor Star [Windsor, Canada], J3818
Winer, Linda, J2118
Winfrey, Lee, J1407, 1680
Winn, Jasper, J3698
Winslow, Pete, J2009

Winston-Salem Journal [Winston-Salem, NC],
    J5789
Winston-Salem Journal And Sentinel [Winston-
    Salem, NC], J2046
Winterowd, W. Ross, J2212
Wirick, Richard, J1084
Wisconsin Patriot [Madison, WI], J1656
Wisconsin State Journal [Madison, WI], J1648,
    3343
Wisconsin Studies In Contemporary Literature
    [Madison, WI], J396
Wise, Kelly, J4616
Wiseman, Thomas, J252
Wiskari, Werner, J305
Wissolik, Richard David, J5632
With William Burroughs, J3144
Without Stopping, J1723
Witnessing: The Seventies, J2467
Wittebols, Jim, J1855
Wittkopf, Rudolf, H170, 177, 189, 207, 210
Wizjonerzy I Buntownicy, H470
Wochenpresse [Germany], J4755
Wolf, Daniel, J317
Wolf, Donna, J4010
Wolf, Guy W., J45
Wolf, Michele, J4824
Wolf, Robert, J1285
Wolfe, Jane, J4288
Wolff, R., J1104
Wolgamott, L. Kent, J5415, 5419
Wolkenkratzer Art Journal [Frankfurt, W.
    Germany], J4149, 4787
Wolmuth, Roger, J4367
Woman's Wear Daily [New York, NY], J3981,
    4851
Wood River Journal [ID], J5404
Wood River Valley Tempo [Ketchum, ID], J5399
Woodard, Josef, J4013
Woods, Eddie, J2758
Woods, Gregory, J4647
Woodstock: History Of An American Town,
    J4451
Woodstock Times [Woodstock, NY], J2452,
    2461, 3926, 3958, 5642
Woolmer, J. Howard, J5835
Worcester Telegram [Worcester, MA], J3275
Word [Boston, MA], J1055
Worden, Mark, J5008
Wordrow [England], J2716
Worker [New York, NY], J278, 296
Workman, Bill, J5747
Works [New York, NY], J892
Works On Paper, 1980-1986, J4277
World [New York, NY], J1924
World-Herald [Lincoln, NE], J5418
World Journal Tribune, J635
World Literature [China], H44
World Literature Today [Norman, OK], J2545,
    3760, 4262, 4419, 4584
The World Of Translation, J1560
Das Wort [W. Germany], J934
Wortsman, Peter, J2334
Wosk, Julie Helen, J2084
Wozniak, Mary, J4512
Wozu?, H128

Recent Titles in
Bibliographies and Indexes in American Literature

Images of Poe's Works: A Comprehensive Descriptive Catalogue of Illustrations
Burton R. Pollin, compiler

Through the Pale Door: A Guide to and through the American Gothic
Frederick S. Frank

The Robert Lowell Papers at the Houghton Library, Harvard University
Patrick K. Miehe, compiler

Bernard Malamud: A Descriptive Bibliography
Rita N. Kosofsky

A Tale Type and Motif Index of Early U.S. Almanacs
J. Michael Stitt and Robert K. Dodge

Jerzy Kosinski: An Annotated Bibliography
Gloria L. Cronin and Blaine H. Hall

James Fenimore Cooper: An Annotated Bibliography of Criticism
Alan Frank Dyer, compiler

Ralph Waldo Emerson: An Annotated Bibliography of Criticism, 1980–1991
Robert E. Burkholder and Joel Myerson, compilers

John Updike: A Bibliography, 1967–1993
Jack De Bellis, compiler

The Works of Allen Ginsberg, 1941–1994: A Descriptive Bibliography
Bill Morgan

James A. Michener: A Checklist of His Works, with a Selected, Annotated
Bibliography
F. X. Roberts and C. D. Rhine, compilers

The Proverbial Eugene O'Neill: An Index to Proverbs in the Works of
Eugene Gladstone O'Neill
George B. Bryan and Wolfgang Mieder, compilers

About the Author

BILL MORGAN is a librarian and archival consultant in New York City. His previous publications include *The Works of Allen Ginsberg, 1941–1994: A Descriptive Bibliography* (Greenwood Press, 1995) and *Lawrence Ferlinghetti: A Comprehensive Bibliography* (1982).

ISBN 0-313-29536-0

9 780313 295362

HARDCOVER BAR CODE

EAN

90000>